The Vampire
IN SLAVIC CULTURES

REVISED EDITION

THOMAS J. GARZA

UNIVERSITY OF TEXAS–AUSTIN

cognella
San Diego, CA

First published in the United States of America in 2010 by Cognella, a division of University Readers, Inc.

14 13 12 11 10   1 2 3 4 5

Printed in the United States of America

ISBN: 978-1-934269-67-1

www.cognella.com 800.200.3908

Contents

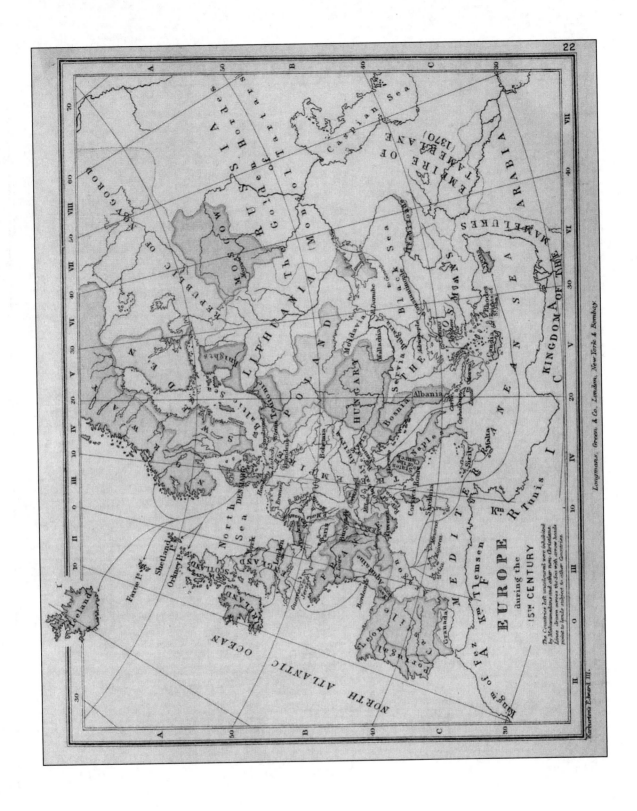

CENTRAL AND EASTERN EUROPE

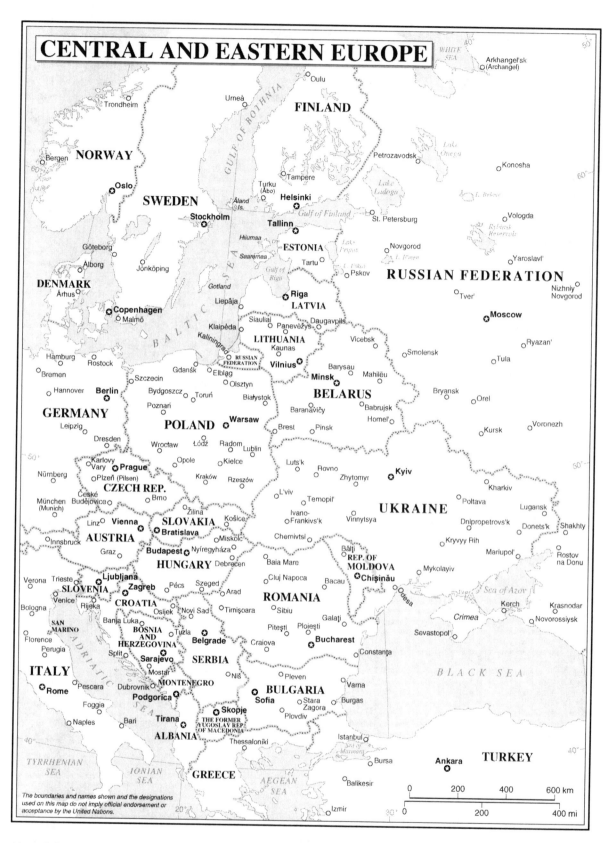

Map of Central and Eastern Europe. Reprinted with the permission of the UN Cartographic Section.

Map of Central Europe and Transylvania.

Introduction

By Thomas J. Garza

The vampire at once intrigues and horrifies, seduces and repels. It has become one of the most enduring figures of Western—and, in an even more ancient context, Eastern—literatures and cultures. For more than a thousand years, stories of reanimated creatures that sustain their own lives by taking away the "life force" of other living beings have filled our imaginations and the pages of world literature. These tales, which deal with the most essential questions of life and death, continue to resonate and fascinate around the globe in novels, film, and popular culture.

This volume draws together original historical texts, critical commentaries, and literary works to create a unique portrait of the vampire in the Western experience in general, and in the Slavic and Eastern European context in particular. It aims to provide a substantial sample of the historical, geographic, religious, folkloric, and cultural backgrounds on which literary and, more recently, filmic depictions of the vampire are based. This edition provides a broad, topical introduction to the creatures of the night that remain a fixed feature of Slavic cultures to the present day.

Beginning with the myriad of definitions of the word "vampire," the volume invites the reader to come to an understanding of the "universals" in meaning from varying suggestions. Next, religious, folkloric, and pagan sources for early vampire tales are presented as the basis for the development and expansion of the vampire story from Old World mythology to newfound religious practices. Early images and representations of the vampire as a female harpy set the stage for the development of a long line of vampiric successors, including the first male vampires and werewolves.

A substantial portion of the volume is devoted to history's "real life" vampires: Vlad Tepes Dracula of Transylvania and Elizabeth Bathory of Hungary, whose remarkable reigns accorded them infamous reputations. Though there is no documented evidence that either of these figures actually consumed human blood, their respective exploits were heinous and bizarre enough to give each the moniker of "vampire." Significantly, as Romanian and Hungarian historical figures, neither is linguistically nor ethnically "Slavic"; however, the geographic proximity of their dominions to the lands of the Slavs clearly had an effect on the development of the vampire myth in those neighboring countries and thus, both Dracula and Bathory figure prominently there.

With the place of the vampire in European history established, the volume continues with a survey of the development of vampire lore and myth throughout the Balkans,

Central and Eastern Europe, and Russia. These stories incorporate the diverse cultures and traditions of indigenous peoples, as well as of transient populations in the region such as the Roma. Through these various portraits, the reader becomes familiar with the major similarities among the regions and their stories, as well as with their inherent differences. Some of the earliest recorded stories from these regions are provided to highlight the most significant markers of each region's particular slant on the vampire tale.

The literary portraits of the vampire presented in this volume focus on those from Eastern European and Slavic writers, beginning with several examples from Russia's early literary tradition in the late eighteenth and early nineteenth centuries. Classic writers such as Nikolai Karamzin, Vasily Zhukovsky, and Aleksandr Pushkin, each famous for his prose and poetic works, tapped into themes of death and revenants and added a Gothic twist to the ages of Russian Sentimentalism and Romanticism. Russia's Golden Age of great literature began later in the nineteenth century, and the theme of the vampire developed in tandem. Writer Nikolay Gogol, known primarily for his humorous works of satire, invokes vampires, witches, and werewolves in his story "Viy." Other writers including dramatist Aleksey K. Tolstoy and novelist Ivan Turgenev (best remembered for his novels of the Russian gentry, such as *Fathers and Sons*), all contributed major works to the vampire genre.

Even writers of the Soviet period, such as the author Mikhail Bulgakov, incorporated vampires into their works. Bulgakov writes an early short story on revenants and includes vampires in his brilliant novel *The Master and Margarita*. The collapse of the Soviet Union in 1991 does not slow the production of Slavic literature featuring vampires, as evidenced by Viktor Pelevin's story about post-Soviet werewolves and Sergei Lukyanenko's popular *Watch* trilogy.

No edition dealing with the subject of vampires would be complete without a section on the dispatching of the creatures. Well before Buffy slew her first vampire and even before Dr. Van Helsing faced off with Dracula, an entire history of how to prevent, ward off, and ultimately destroy the vampire developed in the Slavic lands. From the uses of garlic to the efficacy of wooden stakes, the lore and practice of vampire slaying is discussed.

Finally, this volume includes the lyrics to some popular Russian songs of the 1990s and the 2000s, which also resonate with the vampire theme. Harking back to a wickedly satirical musing on his own funeral by Vladimir Vysotsky in 1973, these songs embrace not only the Russian fascination with the subject, but the wide range of meaning that has been ascribed to vampires and vampirism in contemporary Russian popular culture.

For some, it is the first reading of Bram Stoker's seminal novel, *Dracula*. For others, it is a youthful crush on Buffy or Angel; for others still, it is the lure of the gothic club scene and its New Romantics lifestyle. As for myself, it was a road trip into Transylvania and the uncanny experience of standing amid the ruins of Dracula's castle. We all find our particular initial way into the vampire myth and develop a unique understanding of the relevance of the story in our own lives and experience. But in every instance and for every person, there is no question that once the vampire's story takes hold in one's psyche, it does not easily let go.

TJG
Austin, Texas

Definitions of Vampire

A Definition of Vampire from
Funk and Wagnalls Standard Dictionary of Folklore, Mythology, and Legend

Edited by Maria Leach

VAMPIRE

One of the types of the undead; a living corpse or soulless body that comes from its burial place and drinks the blood of the living. Belief in vampires is found all over the world—in India, China, Malaya, Indonesia, etc.—but typically it is a Slavic concept; Russia, Poland, Bulgaria, Croatia, Slovenia and thence Greece, Rumania, Albania, Hungary, are the great vampire area. In Hungary in the 18th century, the uproar about vampires was as great as that during the witch hunts of colonial New England. The vampire cannot rest in the grave; it must spend the night searching for a victim, but at cockcrow, when the sun rises, or when the bells ring in the morning, it must return to the coffin. Anyone bitten by a vampire becomes a vampire upon death; vampires are also made if a cat or other baneful creature jumps or flies over the corpse before it is buried; suicides, witches, those under a curse become vampires. Light, bells, iron, garlic are all effective against vampires. If a corpse about to be buried has its mouth open, it will probably be a vampire; the mouth must be stuffed with clay before the coffin is closed. If it is suspected that a certain corpse already buried is a vampire, it must be dug up and examined; if it proves to be red-cheeked and fresh, not decomposed, with blood-stains around the mouth, it is a vampire. Such a body must be decapitated, burned, buried at a crossroads, or a wooden stake driven through its heart. It will twist in agony as the stake pierces it, but after that it will lie in peace.

A Definition of Vampire from
Brewer's Dictionary of Phrase and Fable

Edited by Ivor H. Evans

VAMPIRE

A fabulous being supposed to be the ghost of a heretic, criminal, etc., who returned from the grave in the guise of a monstrous bat to suck the blood of sleeping persons who usually became vampires themselves. The only way to destroy them was to drive a stake through their body. The superstition is essentially Slavonic.

> But first on earth, as vampire sent,
> Thy corse shall from its tomb be rent, Then ghastly haunt thy native place
> And suck the blood of all thy race.
>
> BYRON: *The Giaour*, 755.

The word is applied to one who preys upon his fellows—a "blood-sucker".

One of the classic horror stories, Bram Stoker's *Dracula* (1897), centres on vampirism. The Dracula of Transylvanian legend appears to originate from Vlad V of Wallachia (1456–1476), known as Vlad the Impaler, although he was not a vampire. It is suggested that Stoker's Count Dracula was a composite figure derived from Vlad the Impaler and the Countess Báthori, who was arrested in 1610 for murdering girls. It was her habit to wash in the blood of her several hundred girl victims in order to maintain her skin in a youthful condition. The name comes from Vlad's membership of the Order of the Dragon, although *dracul* in Rumanian also means *devil*.

A Definition of Vampire from
The Encyclopedia of Ghosts and Spirits

By Rosemary Guiley

VAMPIRE

In folklore, the undead. There are many types of vampires in beliefs found all over the world. A vampire is either the living dead—a resurrected corpse—or the spirit of a corpse that leaves its grave at night and walks the world of the living to feed off of them to survive. Some vampires, particularly in Eastern, Middle Eastern and tribal mythologies, are demons that attack at night, and are associated with night terrors.

The term "Vampire" came into English usage in 1732, handed down from German and French accounts of vampire superstitions discovered in Eastern Europe. The Slavic vampire cult contains many words for "vampire" with different shades of meaning that refer to werewolves, reverants, demons that eat the sun and moon, humans who can shape-shift, certain kinds of witches, and monstrous sucking animals, as well as living corpses.

In the Balkans, where a vampire cult flourished in the late Middle Ages, a vampire was suspected of infesting a graveyard when people reported seeing apparitions of the dead that pestered them and bit them, or sat on their chests and suffocated them at night. Such symptoms are similar to cases of biting poltergeists and to the old hag. Vampires also were blamed for plagues, invisible terrors that bothered people at night and wasting diseases that brought death. A search of graves was made, and if a body was found seemingly incorrupt with signs of fresh blood on it, it was decreed a vampire and was dispatched by being dismembered, burned or staked through the heart. Such measures are universally employed to keep ghosts of the dead from leaving their graves and wandering about.

Modern researchers have suggested premature burial as a natural explanation for the incorrupt corpse. It is more likely that normal decomposition conditions perhaps medically unknown in earlier times explain the vampire corpse. For example, it is normal for corpses to shift; this might give the appearance of life and movement when a coffin was opened, A corpse that is staked may emit noises interpreted as "shrieks" simply from air in the lungs being forced past the glottis. The "fresh blood" probably is the corpse's own blood, which often leaks from orifices. The shiny nailbeds that earlier peoples took to be fresh fingernail growth probably are the underfeeds that are exposed when the outer finger nails slough off.

Western fiction and film have popularized the vampire as an entirely different creature, a glamorous and seductive living dead person who bites people (usually on the neck) to drink their blood.

FURTHER READING

Barber, Paul. *Vampires, Burial and Death: Folklore and Reality.* New Haven: Conn.: Yale University Press, 1988. Guiley, Rosemary Ellen. *Vampires Among Us.* New York: Pocket Books, 1991.

Definitions of Upyr' and Vampire

By Thomas J. Garza

УПЫРЬ, в славянской мифологии мертвец, нападающий на людей и животных; образ У. заимствован народами Западной Европы у славян (см. *Вампир*). Согласно древнерусским поучениям против язычников, те клали требу (приношения) У. и берегиням до того, как стали поклоняться Перуну. По позднейшим поверьям, У. становится после смерти человек, рождённый от *нечистой силы* или испорченный ею (ребёнка-У. можно узнать по двойным рядам зубов), умерший, через гроб которого перескочила чёрная кошка (чёрт), чаще — нечистый («заложный») покойник, самоубийца, умерший неестественной смертью, особенно колдун. По ночам У. встаёт из могилы и в облике налитого кровью мертвеца или зооморфного существа убивает людей и животных, реже высасывает кровь, после чего жертва погибает и сама может стать У.; известны поверья о целых селениях У. В литературе, начиная с Пушкина, У. неточно отождествляли с вурдалаком, волком-оборотнем (см. *Волкодлак*). Ср. также тюрк. *Убыр*.

В. Я. Петрухин

UPYR', in Slavic mythology is a corpse which attacks people and animals; the peoples of Western Europe have borrowed the form of the *upyr'* (cf, "Vampire"). In accordance with ancient Russian preachings against paganism, they would give rites (offerings) to *upyr'* and other gods that they began to worship Perun [Slavic god of the underworld], According to recent beliefs, *upyr'* becomes a person after death, born of *evil* or touched by it (a child-*upyr'* can be recognized by its double rows of teeth), or having died in grave across which a black cat (a devil) has jumped, or more frequently—a dishonorable ("marked") deceased, a suicide who died by artificial means, especially in a well. By night the *upyr'* rises from the grave and in the form of a blood covered corpse or animal being kills people and animals—more rarely by sucking their blood, after which the attacked dies and itself becomes an *upyr'*; there are known beliefs of entire settlements of *upyr'*. In literature, beginning with Pushkin, the *upyr'* is inaccurately identified with the *vurdolak*, the werewolf (cf. *vurdolak*). See also the Turkish *ubyr'*.

V. J. Tsetrukhin

ВАМПИР, в низшей мифологии народов Европы мертвец, по ночам встающий из могилы или являющийся в облике летучей мыши, сосущий кровь у спящих людей, насылающий кошмары. В. становились «нечистые» покойники — преступники, самоубийцы, умершие преждевременной смертью и погибшие от укусов В. Считалось, что их тела не разлагались в могилах, и прекратить их злодеяния можно было, вбив в тело В. осиновый кол, обезглавив его и т. п. Оберегами против В. служили также чеснок, железо, колокольный звон и др. В славянской мифологии — *упырь*.

М. Ю.

VAMPIRE, in the lowest mythology of peoples of Europe, is a corpse that by night rises from the grave or takes the form of a bat, which sucks the blood of sleeping people, invoking nightmares. "Impure" deceased became vampires—criminals, suicides, premature deaths, and deaths by vampire bite. It was believed that their bodies did not decay in the grave, and that their evildoings could be stopped by driving an aspen stake into their body, or beheading them, etc. Protection against vampires also included garlic, iron, a bell chime, and others. In Slavic mythology—it is *upyr'*.

M.J.

What Is a Vampire?

By Dudley Wright

What is a vampire? The definition given in Webster's *International Dictionary* is: "A blood-sucking ghost or re-animated body of a dead person; a soul or re-animated body of a dead person believed to come from the grave and wander about by night sucking the blood of persons asleep, causing their death."

Whitney's *Century Dictionary* says that a vampire is: "A kind of spectral body which, according to a superstition existing among the Slavic and other races on the Lower Danube, leaves the grave during the night and maintains a semblance of life by sucking the warm blood of living men and women while they are asleep. Dead wizards, werwolves, heretics, and other outcasts become vampires, as do also the illegitimate offspring of parents themselves illegitimate, and anyone killed by a vampire."

According to the *Encyclopædia Britannica:* "The persons who turn vampires are generally wizards, suicides, and those who come to a violent end or have been cursed by their parents or by the Church. But anyone may become a vampire if an animal (especially a cat) leaps over the corpse or a bird flies over it."

Among the specialists, the writers upon vampire lore and legend, two definitions may be quoted:—Hurst, who says that: "A vampyr is a dead body which continues to live in the grave; which it leaves, however, by night, for the purpose of sucking the blood of the living, whereby it is nourished and preserved in good condition, instead of becoming decomposed like other dead bodies"; and Scoffern, who wrote: "The best definition I can give of a vampire is a living mischievous and murderous dead body. A living dead body! The words are idle, contradictory, incomprehensible, but so are vampires."

"Vampires," says the learned Zopfius, "come out of their graves in the night time, rush upon people sleeping in their beds, suck out all their blood and destroy them. They attack men, women, and children, sparing neither age nor sex. Those who are under the malignity of their influence complain of suffocation and a total deficiency of spirits, after which they soon expire. Some of them being asked at the point of death what is the matter with them, their answer is that such persons lately dead rise to torment them."

Not all vampires, however, are, or were, suckers of blood. Some, according to the records, despatched their victims by inflicting upon them contagious diseases, or strangling them without drawing blood, or causing their speedy or retarded death by various other means.

Messrs Skeat and Blagden, in *Pagan Races of the Malay Peninsula* (vol. i. p. 473), state that "a vampire, according to the view of Sakai of Perak, is not a demon—even though it is incidentally so-called—but a being of flesh and blood," and support this view by the statement that the vampire cannot pass through walls and hedges.

The word *vampire* (Dutch, *vampyr*; Polish, *wampior* or *upior*; Slownik, *upir*; Ukraine, *upeer*) is held by Skeat to be derived from the Servian *wampira*. The Russians, Morlacchians, inhabitants of Montenegro, Bohemians, Servians, Arnauts, both of Hydra and Albania, know the vampire under the name of *wukodalak, vurkulaka,* or *vrykolaka,* a word which means "wolf-fairy," and is thought by some to be derived from the Greek. In Crete, where Slavonic influence has not been felt, the vampire is known by the name of *katakhaná.* Vampire lore is, in general, confined to stories of re-suscitated corpses of male human beings, though amongst the Malays a *penangglan*, or vampire, is a living witch, who can be killed if she can be caught in the act of witchery. She is especially feared in houses where a birth has taken place, and it is the custom to hang up a bunch of thistle in order to catch her. She is said to keep vinegar at home to aid her in re-entering her own body. In the Malay Peninsula, parts of Polynesia and the neighbouring districts, the vampire is conceived as a head with entrails attached, which comes forth to suck the blood of living human beings. In Transylvania, the belief prevails that every person killed by a *nosferatu* (vampire) becomes in turn a vampire, and will continue to suck the blood of other innocent people until the evil spirit has been exorcised, either by opening the grave of the suspected person and driving a stake through the corpse, or firing a pistol-shot into the coffin. In very obstinate cases it is further recommended to cut off the head, fill the mouth with garlic, and then replace the head in its proper place in the coffin; or else to extract the heart and burn it, and strew the ashes over the grave.

The *murony* of the Wallachians not only sucks blood, but also possesses the power of assuming a variety of shapes, as, for instance, those of a cat, dog, flea, or spider; in consequence of which the ordinary evidence of death caused by the attack of a vampire, viz. the mark of a bite in the back of the neck, is not considered indispensable. The Wallachians have a very great fear of sudden death, greater perhaps than any other people, for they attribute sudden death to the attack of a vampire, and believe that anyone destroyed by a vampire must become a vampire, and that no power can save him from this fate. A similar belief obtains in Northern Albania, where it is also held that a wandering spirit has power to enter the body of any individual guilty of undetected crime, and that such obsession forms part of his punishment.

Some writers have ascribed the origin of the belief in vampires to Greek Christianity, but there are traces of the superstition and belief at a considerably earlier date than this. In the opinion of the anthropologist Tylor, "the shortest way of treating the belief is to refer it directly to the principles of savage animism. We shall see that most of its details fall into their places at once, and that vampires are not mere creations of groundless fancy, but causes conceived in spiritual form to account for specific facts of wasting disease." It is more than probable that the practice of offering up living animals as sacrifices to satisfy the thirst of departed human beings, combined with the ideas of the Platonist and the teachings of the learned Jew, Isaac Arbanel, who maintained that before the soul can be loosed from the fetters of the flesh it must lie some months with it in the grave, may have influenced the belief and assisted its development. Vampirism found a place in Babylonian belief and in the folk-lore and traditions of many countries of the Near East. The belief was quite common in Arabia, although there is no trace of it there in pre-Christian times. The earliest references to vampires are found in Chaldean and Assyrian tablets. Later, the pagan Romans gave their adherence to the belief that the dead bodies of certain people could be allured from their graves by sorcerers, unless the bodies had actually undergone decomposition, and that the only means of effectually preventing such "resurrections" was by cremating the remains. In Grecian lore there are many wonderful stories of the dead rising from their graves and feasting upon the blood of the young and beautiful. From Greece and Rome the superstition spread throughout Austria, Hungary, Lorraine, Poland, Roumania, Iceland, and even to the British Isles, reaching its height in the period from 1723 to 1735, when a vampire fever or epidemic broke out in the south-east of Europe, particularly in Hungary and Servia. The belief in vampires even spread to Africa, where the Kaffirs held that bad men alone live a second time and try to kill the living by night. According to a local superstition of the Lesbians, the unquiet ghost of the Virgin Gello used to haunt their island, and was supposed to cause the deaths of young children.

Various devices have been resorted to in different countries at the time of burial, in the belief that the dead could thus be prevented from returning to earth-life. In some instances, *e.g.* among the Wallachians, a long nail was driven through the skull of the corpse, and the thorny stem of a wild rose-bush laid upon the body, in order that its shroud might become entangled with it, should it attempt to rise. The Kroats and Slavonians burned the straw upon which the suspected body lay. They then locked up all the cats and dogs, for if these animals stepped over the corpse it would assuredly return as a vampire and suck the blood of the village folk. Many held that to drive a white thorn stake through the dead body rendered the vampire harmless, and the peasants of Bukowina still retain the practice of driving an ash stake through the breasts of suicides and supposed vampires—a practice common in England, so far as suicides were concerned, until 1823, when there was passed "An Act to alter and amend the law relating to the interment of the remains of any person found *felo de se*," in which it was enacted that the coroner or other officer "shall give directions for the private interment of the remains of such person *felo de se* without any stake being driven through the body of such person." It was also ordained that the burial was only to take place between nine and twelve o'clock at night.

The driving of a stake through the body does not seem to have had always the desired effect. De Schartz, in his *Magia Postuma*, published at Olmutz in 1706, tells of a shepherd in the village of Blow, near Kadam, in Bohemia, who made several appearances after his death and called certain persons, who never failed to die within eight days of such call. The peasants of Blow took up the body and fixed it to the ground by means of a stake driven through the corpse. The man, when in that condition, told them that they were very good to give him a stick with which he could defend himself against the dogs which worried him. Notwithstanding the stake, he got up again that same night, alarmed many people, and, presumably out of revenge, strangled more people in that one night than he had ever done on a single occasion before. It was decided to hand over his body to the public executioner, who was ordered to see that the remains were burned outside the village. When the executioner and his assistants attempted to move the corpse for that purpose, it howled like a madman, and moved its feet and hands as though it were alive. They then pierced the body through with stakes, but he again uttered loud cries and a great quantity of bright vermilion blood flowed from him. The cremation, however, put an end to the apparition and haunting of the spectre. De Schartz says that the only remedy for these apparitions is to cut off the heads and burn the bodies of those who come back to haunt their former abodes. It was, however, customary to hold a public inquiry and examination of witnesses before proceeding to the burning of a body, and if, upon examination of the body, it was found that the corpse had begun to decompose, that the limbs were not supple and mobile, and the blood not fluidic, then burning was not commanded. Even in the case of suspected persons an interval of six to seven weeks was always allowed to lapse before the grave was opened in order to ascertain whether the flesh had decayed and the limbs lost their suppleness and mobility. A Strigon or Indian vampire, who was transfixed with a sharp thorn cudgel, near Larbach, in 1672, pulled it out of his body and flung it back contemptuously.

Bartholin, in *de Causa contemptus mortis,* tells the story of a man, named Harpye, who ordered his wife to bury him exactly at the kitchen door, in order that he might see what went on in the house. The woman executed her commission, and soon after his death he appeared to several people in the neighbourhood, killed people while they were engaged in their occupations, and played so many mischievous pranks that the inhabitants began to move away from the village. At last a man named Olaus Pa took courage and ran at the spectre with a lance, which he drove into the apparition. The spectre instantly vanished, taking the spear with it. Next morning Olaus had the grave of Harpye opened, when he found the lance in the dead body, which had not become corrupted. The corpse was then taken from the grave, burned, and the ashes thrown into the sea, and the spectre did not afterwards trouble the inhabitants.

To cross the arms of the corpse, or to place a cross or crucifix upon the grave, or to bury a suspected corpse at the junction of four cross-roads, was, in some parts, regarded as an efficacious preventive of vampirism. It will be remembered that it was at one time the practice in England to bury suicides at the four cross-roads. If a vampire should make its appearance, it could be prevented from ever appearing again by forcing it to take the oath not to do so, if the words "by my winding-sheet" were incorporated in the oath.

One charm employed by the Wallachians to prevent a person becoming a vampire was to rub the body in certain parts with the lard of a pig killed on St Ignatius's Day.

In Poland and Russia, vampires make their appearance from noon to midnight instead of between nightfall and dawn, the rule that generally prevails. They come and suck the blood of living men and animals in such abundance that sometimes it flows from them at the nose and ears, and occasionally in such profusion that the corpse swims in the blood thus oozing from it as it lies in the coffin. One may become immune from the attacks of vampires by mixing this blood with flour and making bread from the mixture, a portion of which must be eaten; otherwise the charm will not work. The Californians held that the mere breaking of the spine of the corpse was sufficient to prevent its return as a vampire. Sometimes heavy stones were piled on the grave to keep the ghost within, a practice to which Frazer traces the origin of funeral cairns and tombstones. Two resolutions of the Sorbonne, passed between 1700 and 1710, prohibited the cutting off of the heads and the maiming of the bodies of persons supposed to be vampires.

In the German folk-tale known as *Faithful John*, the statue said to the king: "If you, with your own hand, cut off the heads of both your children and sprinkle me with their blood, I shall be brought to life again." According to primitive ideas, blood is life, and to receive blood is to receive life: the soul of the dead wants to live, and, consequently, loves blood. The shades in Hades are eager to drink the blood of Odysseus's sacrifice, that their life may be renewed for a time. It is of the greatest importance that the soul should get what it desires, as, if not satisfied, it might come and attack the living. It is possible that the bodily mutilations which to this day accompany funerals among some peoples have their origin in the belief that the departed spirit is refreshed by the blood thus spilt. The Samoans called it an "offering of blood" for the dead when the mourners beat their heads till the blood ran.

The Australian native sorcerers are said to acquire their magical influence by eating human flesh, but this is done once only in a lifetime. According to Nider's *Formicarius,* part of the ceremony of initiation into wizardry and witchcraft consisted in drinking in a church, before the commencement of Mass, from a flask filled with blood taken from the corpses of murdered infants.

The methods employed for the detection of vampires have varied according to the countries in which the belief in their existence was maintained. In some places it was held that, if there were discovered in a grave two or three or more holes about the size of a man's finger. It would almost certainly follow that a body with all the marks of vampirism would be discovered within the grave. The Wallachians employed a rather elaborate method of divination. They were in the habit of choosing a boy young enough to make it certain that he was innocent of any impurity. He was then placed on an absolutely black and unmutilated horse which had never stumbled. The horse was then made to ride about the cemetery and pass over all the graves. If the horse refused to pass over any grave, even in spite of repeated blows, that grave was believed to shelter a vampire. Their records state that when such a grave was opened it was generally found to contain a corpse as fat and handsome as that of a full-blooded man quietly sleeping. The finest vermilion blood would flow from the throat when out, and this was held to be the blood he had sucked from the veins of living people. It is said that the attacks of the vampire generally ceased on this being done.

In the town of Perlepe, between Monastru and Kiuprili, there existed the extraordinary phenomenon of a number of families who were regarded as being the offspring of *vrykolakas,* and as possessing the power of laying the wandering spirits to which they were related. They are said to have kept their art very dark and to have practised it in secret, but their fame was so widely spread that persons in need of such deliverance were accustomed to send for them from other cities. In ordinary life and intercourse they were avoided by all the inhabitants.

Although some writers have contended that no vampire has yet been caught in the act of vampirism, and that, as no museum of natural history has secured a specimen, the whole of the stories concerning vampires may be regarded as mythical, others have held firmly to a belief in their existence and inimical power. Dr Pierart, in *La Revue Spiritualists* (vol. iv. p. 104), wrote: "After a crowd of facts of vampirism so often proved, shall we say that there are no more to be had, and that these never had a foundation? Nothing comes of nothing. Every belief, every custom, springs from facts and causes which give it birth. If one had never seen appear in the bosom of their families, in various countries, beings clothed in the appearance of departed ones known to them, sucking the blood of one or more persons, and if the deaths of the victims had not followed after such apparitions, the disinterment of corpses would not have taken place, and there would never have been the attestation of the otherwise incredible fact of persons buried for several years being found with the body soft and flexible, the eyes wide open, the complexion rosy, the mouth and nose full of bloody and the blood flowing fully when the body was struck or wounded or the head cut off."

Bishop d'Avranches Huet wrote: "I will not examine whether the facts of vampirism, which are constantly being reported, are true, or the fruit of a popular error; but it is beyond doubt that they are testified to by so many able and trustworthy authors, and by so many *eye-witnesses,* that no one ought to decide the question without a good deal of caution."

Dr Pierart gave the following explanation of their existence: "Poor, dead cataleptics? buried as if really dead in cold and dry spots where morbid causes are incapable of effecting the destruction of their bodies, the astral spirits enveloping itself with a fluidic ethereal body, is prompted to quit the precincts of its tomb and to exercise on living bodies acts peculiar to physical life, especially that of nutrition, the result of which, by a mysterious link between soul and body which spiritualistic science will some day explain, is forwarded to the material body lying still within its tomb, and the latter is thus helped to perpetuate its vital existence."

Apart from the spectre vampire there is, of course, the vampire bat in the world of natural history, which is said to suck blood from a sleeping person, insinuating its tongue into a vein, but without inflicting pain. Captain Steadman, during his expedition to Surinam, awoke early one morning and was alarmed to find his hammock steeped almost through and himself weltering in bloody, although he was without pain. It was discovered that he had been bitten by a vampire bat. Pennant says that in some parts of America they destroyed all the cattle introduced by the missionaries.

Vampires

By Brad Steiger

On Monday, January 15, 1991, the day following the premiere of the new primetime *Dark Shadows* television series featuring actor Ben Cross as the vampire Barnabas Collins, a bearded man approached a 42-year-old woman in a library parking lot in Missoula, Montana, and demanded money. The woman complied and handed him two dollars. Then the man pulled her hair back, cut her neck with some kind of sharp object, and kissed the open wound. Police detectives launched an intense manhunt for the grisly vampire bandit.

In February 1991, a jury in Australia convicted Annette Hall of stalking and killing Charles Reilly so her vampire lover, Susi Hampton, could drink his blood. Hall described in detail how her girlfriend had gone into a "feeding frenzy" after she had stabbed Reilly over a dozen times. Ms. Hampton, a self-confessed vampire who lives on human blood, pleaded guilty and both women were sentenced to life in prison.

For Anne Rice, author of such bestselling novels as *Interview with the Vampire,* the vampire is a "romantic, enthralling" figure. She perceives the vampire's image to be that of a "person who never dies … takes a blood sacrifice in order to live, and exerts a charm over people." In the view of Rice and the millions of readers who enjoy her novels, the vampire is a "handsome, alluring, seductive person who captivates us, then drains the life out of us so that he or she can live. We long to be one of them, and the idea of being sacrificed to them becomes rather romantic."

The vampire legend, like that of the werewolf, is universal. The villagers of Uganda, Haiti, Indonesia, and the Upper Amazon all have their local variety of nocturnal blood sucker. The Native American tribes, the Arctic Eskimos, and many Arabian tribes know the vampire well and have as many elaborate precautions against the undead as do the inhabitants of Transylvanian villages.

In the eighteenth century, the highly respected French philosopher Jean Jacques Rousseau wrote: "If there ever was in the world a warranted and proven history, it is that of vampires; nothing is lacking, official reports, testimonials of persons of standing, of surgeons, of clergymen, of judges; the judicial evidence is all-embracing."

Theories to explain the universality of the vampire myth are many and varied. All cultures, regardless of how primitive, have come to understand the basic fact that blood is the vital fluid of life. To lose one's vital fluid is to lose one's mortality—the spark of life. Such knowledge would be a powerful stimulant to fear in the primitive mind and the creation of hideous monsters intent on draining one's life essence would not be long in coming.

In appearance, the traditional vampire is a grotesque, demonic presence, perhaps best captured cinematically in *Nosferatu* (1922). A newly rereleased Werner Herzog version of *Nosferatu the Vampyre* (1979), starring Klaus Kinski, was praised by Michael Sauter in the February 5, 1999, issue of *Entertainment Weekly:* "Like Max Schreck's original Nosferatu, Klaus Kinski's Transylvanian count is a far cry from the Bela Lugosi model. Sporting sunken eyes, devil ears, and talons, he lurks in Herzog's expressionistic shadows like some oversize vermin."

The classic vampire is also a shapeshifter, able to transform itself not only into the familiar form of the bat, but also into a wolf—and it was able to command the rat, the owl, the moth, the fox. The vampire of tradition is able to see in the dark and travel on moonbeams and mist. At times, the vampire could vanish in a puff of smoke. The hypnotic powers of the vampire are irresistible. And woe to anyone who boldly grabbed hold of the monster, for it has the strength of a dozen men.

After Bram Stoker's novel *Dracula* (1897) became a popular play and a classic motion picture version with Bela Lugosi as Count Dracula, the image of the vampire transmutated from hideous demon to a suave, sophisticated, handsome, well-dressed fellow who would fit right in at the very best parties. And his sisters and mistresses of the night are beautiful, sensuous, voluptuous creatures who fill out their evening dresses in the most delightful ways. With few exceptions, contemporary audiences know the vampire only as an attractive and seductive presence, an emissary of the dark side who presents a very compelling case for letting him or her bite your neck so that you may join the ranks of the undead. Of course days at the beach and power breakfasts are now out of the question.

On the other hand, the fact that the modern vampire is virtually undetectable from the rest of us—with the exception of the aversion to sunlight and the hunger for blood—preys upon another basic fear of humankind. The menace of a monster hidden among us can oftentimes be more horrifying than a grotesque, easily identified creature that lurks out there in the darkness. The ever-present thought that your congenial chess partner who always seems to arrive late at the club, or the attractive pale-complexioned man who kept trying to get you to dance with him out on the terrace, or the beautiful lady who will only meet you after dark might be a member of the society of vampires can be a very frightening thought. How can we fight vampires if we can't tell them from our friends?

Well, of course, there's wolfbane, the lotus flower, wild garlic, and sacred objects such as the crucifix and holy water. But do they really render a fanged fiend powerless?

Maybe it would best to be prepared like Buffy the Vampire Slayer and always carry a couple of wooden stakes in your purse or attache case. A stake in the heart just has to work. Of course that is best applied, according to tradition before and after *Dracula* and Hollywood, when the vampire lies at rest in his coffin during the daylight hours. Or if you're not quite up to the stake in the heart bit, you can destroy his coffin while he's on his nocturnal hunt and let the rays of the early morning sun scorch him to ashes.

Even at the dawn of the scientific age, scholars and members of the clergy were convinced of the vampire's existence. In the eighteenth century, a Benedictine monk, Dom Calmet, turned his attention to the subject of vampires and tried to offer a "scientific" explanation:

> Chemical substances of the soil may conserve corpses indefinitely. By the influence of warmth, the nitre and sulphur in the earth may render liquid co-agulated blood. The screams of the vampires [caused no doubt when vigilante vampire hunters went about driving stakes in the chests of suspect corpses] are produced when air passing through their throats is stirred by the pressure which the stake causes in the body. Often people are buried alive, and certain dead, such as the excommunicated, can rise from their tombs; but it is not possible to leave the grave bodily without digging up the soil, and none of the stories about vampires mention that their tombs were disturbed.

When we begin to examine the spark of truth behind the legend of the vampire, we soon discover that the myth disguises a very morbid reality. Today medical science recognizes a vampire psychosis wherein troubled individuals may become convinced that their life depends upon drawing fresh blood from human victims. The persons suffering from such a psychosis may, in extreme cases, actually believe themselves to be dead.

The sexual metaphors to be found in the many cinematic and literary portrayals of the vampire's seductive bite are many and are undeniably a large part of the appeal of the vampire in contemporary popular culture. And while the sexual symbolism may be sensually appealing when a sophisticated Count Dracula or a cultured and stylish Barnabas Collins emerges from the shadows and bites his beautiful victim's bare throat, the bloody accounts of real-life vampires reveal that they seldom act with such dignity and poetry.

A classic case of vampirism was that of Vincent Verzini, who terrorized an Italian village during 1867 to 1871. Verzini's method of attack was to seize a victim by the neck, bite her on the throat, then suck her blood. He murdered two women and victimized many others before he was apprehended.

Although Verzini's examiners found "no evidence of psychosis," there can be little doubt that his vampirism was the expression of deep derangement and sexual perver-sion. That such was the case is shown lucidly in Verzini's own words:

I had an unspeakable delight in strangling women, experiencing during the act erections and real sexual pleasure … I took great delight in drinking … blood … It never occurred to me to touch or to look at the [women's] genitals … It satisfied me to seize the women by the neck and suck their blood.

John George Haigh was a British vampire who, it is said, acquired a taste for blood when he accidentally tasted his own while sucking a scratch. Intoxicated by the act of drinking blood, he was soon "tapping" the jugular veins of his victims so that he might indulge both his perverse thirst and his fanaticism.

In keeping with the religious bent of his illness, Haigh evolved a ritual. First he would sever the jugular vein of his victim, then he would carefully draw off the blood, a glassful at a time. The actual drinking of the blood was observed with great ceremony. Haigh later became convinced that his faith could only be sustained by the sacrifice of others and by the drinking of their blood.

For nearly a week in February 1960, women in the town of Monteros in Argentina were terrorized by the nocturnal attacks of a vampire. At least 15 women were victimized by the midnight marauder, who crept into bedrooms through windows left open because of a heat wave. Hysterically, the women told police of savage teeth biting deeply into their throats and drawing blood.

When officers managed to track the vampire to his lair, they discovered a young man sleeping in a coffin which he had secreted in a cave on the outskirts of the city. He lay swathed in a black cloak, his eyes closed in deep sleep. On his lips was the dried blood of his most recent victim.

In police custody, the real-life Dracula identified himself as Florenico Fernandez, age 25, a stonemason. He was at a complete loss to present an intelligible explanation for his sadistic attacks.

On October 30, 1981, James P. Riva II, a self-proclaimed vampire, was convicted in Brockton, Massachusetts, of murdering his grandmother by shooting her with gold-tipped bullets, then attempting to drink her blood from the wounds. Riva's mother, Janet Jones of Middlebury, Vermont, testified that her son had believed himself to be a vampire for four years. According to Mrs. Jones, Riva had told her that voices informed him that he was a vampire and insisted that he must drink blood.

Defense psychiatrist Dr. Bruce Harry testified that Riva was insane at the time that he murdered his grandmother. According to the young vampire, the voices had told him that he could not become a good person until he killed someone and drank their blood.

John T. Spinale, defense attorney, explained to the court that Riva felt that he needed human and animal blood in order to survive. Riva truly believed that he was a vampire who must roam the countryside in search of his demonically prescribed "food." According to Spinale, Riva did not eat normal meals. He ate what he could find in the evening, then went in search of animal blood.

Superior Court judge Peter E Brady sentenced the 24-year-old James Riva II to a mandatory life sentence at Walpole State Prison on the charge of second-degree murder.

On February 12, 1998, a 12-member jury heard graphic testimony from self-professed teenage vampire Rod Ferrell to help them decide whether he should be sentenced to death or jailed for life without parole. The 17-year-old Ferrell, the leader of a coven of vampires, pled guilty to the murders of Richard and Naoma Ruth Wendorf on November 25, 1996. Ferrell said that he had initiated the Wendorfs' 15-year-old daughter into the cult with a blood-drinking ritual in a graveyard. Ferrell's mother, Sondra Gibson, was also a member of a vampire cult and had pleaded guilty in 1997 to attempting to seduce a 14-year-old boy as part of a vampire ritual.

The late parapsychologist Stephen Kaplan, director of the Vampire Research Center in Elmhurst, New York, stated c. 1982 that his research indicated that at that time there were at least 21 "real" vampires secretly living in the United States and Canada. Some of these vampires had admitted to Kaplan that, on occasion, they had even murdered humans to obtain blood. He also stated that some of the vampires may truly have been as old as 300 years, but still appeared amazingly youthful, due to the blood they ingested. Or at least the vampires believed that "there are some elements in the human blood that slow down the aging process," enabling them to live far longer than nonblood drinking humans.

At that time, Kaplan's survey found that the vampires were distributed throughout North America, but Massachusetts was in the lead with three self-proclaimed vampires, followed by Arizona, California, and New Jersey, with two each.

Kaplan told of one vampire who worked as a technician in a hospital. He simply took blood from the hospital's reserves whenever he needed it. Although the man was nearly 60, Kaplan said, he passed as a man in his early twenties.

The vampire researcher met a vampire in Arizona who looked like a teenager, but who was actually in his late thirties. He posed as a university student and lured people into the desert to drink their blood.

One attractive blonde vampire appeared to be in her vigorous twenties, but was really in her sixties. She exchanged sexual favors in return for blood from her dates. Kaplan said that he was present on one occasion when such a barter occurred: "I watched her drink blood from a willing victim. I watched her use a scalpel to make several incisions in the body and drink some blood."

Kaplan found that the blood needs of the vampires varied considerably. Some required two pints a week; others, half-gallon. Some vampires admitted that they would sometimes render a victim unconscious to take some blood, but that they always left their unwilling donors alive. Those who confessed to having killed humans for blood insisted that they preyed mostly on hitchhikers, the homeless, and people they assumed to be transients with few family associations.

Although it appeared that the vampires he interviewed were long-lived, Kaplan stated, they were not immortal. They slept in beds, rather than coffins. They possessed no preternatural ability to transform themselves into bats, wolves, or other animals. They could function equally well in daylight or in darkness, and they had absolutely no fear of a crucifix.

Kaplan came to believe that true vampirism is a genetic disorder, that people were born into it. "Their mothers and fathers were vampires," he said, "and it appears that their children are always vampires."

SOURCES

"Gruesome Evidence Heard in Florida 'Vampire' Case." Reuters, February 12, 1998.

Masters, R. E. L, and Eduard Lea. *Perverse Crimes in History*. New York: The Julian Press, 1963.

Melton, J. Gordon. *The Vampire Book: The Encyclopedia of the Undead*. Farmington Hills: Visible Ink Press, 1998.

Steiger, Brad. *Bizarre Crime*. New York: Signet, 1992.

Origins of the Vampire

Heretics as Vampires and Demons in Russia

By Felix Oinas

In English, *heretic* (Greek *hairetikos* "able to choose") means "a person who professes any heresy; especially, a church member who holds beliefs opposed to the official church doctrines."[1] The meaning of the word *eretik,* "heretic" in Russian is basically the same: "the follower of heresy, a person who deviates from the dogmas of the predominating church." The question regarding the Old Believers is not clear: some do and others do not include them as heretics.[2] Primarily in the Russian north, "heretics" have developed into a heterogeneous group of sorcerers, witches, and vampires called *eretik, eretnik, eretica, eretnica, erestun,* and others. Zelenin includes heretics (*eretnik*) among sorcerers (*Zauberer*), and remarks that they do not belong to evil forces and do not have tails.[3]

In northern Russia and Siberia heretics appear after death as evil, blood-thirsty vampires. Efimenko defines the meaning of the word *eretik* current in the Šenkursk district of Karelia as "a person who does not believe in God and who repudiates his laws, or who is not yet an Old Believer." He continues:

> There were such people, who roamed around at night in villages, captured people and ate them. The *eretiki* were not alive, but dead. Therefore, if they really got on the nerves of the people, the people gathered at the grave of the one who was known as a sorcerer during his lifetime, opened it up with stakes, took out the *eretik* who was lying with his face downwards, and burned him in a bonfire or pierced his back with an aspen stick. ... The person—magician (*kudesnik*), wizard (*znaxar*) or harmer (*porčelnik*)—who was called a "sorcerer" (*koldun*) in his lifetime, would become an *eretik* after his death, if he walks around at night and begins to eat people, as it has been going on for centuries. (186–87.)

This description shows that the *eretiki* appear as clear-cut vampires: sorcerers who become vampires after their deaths, devour human beings, and are destroyed by fire or stake.

According to the Academy Dictionary, the term *eretik* means "heretic"; "teacher of heresy, who does not believe in the true God and does not follow the church customs and rites"; "one who is associated with the evil spirit; wizard, sorcerer"; and "the spirit of the dead sorcerer." In Siberia, *eretik* also denotes "vampire." The ideas of the *eretik* as a vampire are similar to those held in Senkursk: "Eretik ... a dead person who comes out of the grave ... [He] walked around as *eretik*, but they drove an aspen stick into him, then he stopped." According to the same source, the term *eretik, eretnik* is used widely in Russia, especially in the north, as a word of abuse.[4] In the same function it has also become known in Ludic and Vepsian.[5]

Rybnikov presents a different type of heretic as a vampire (*erestun*) from Olonec:

> Evil sorcerers do not give peace to Christians even after their deaths and become *erestuny* (or *xloptuny, kloxtuny, šoptuny*); they seize the moment when a neighbor is near his death and, as soon as the soul has left the body, they enter the deceased. After that, unpleasant things happen to the family. There are *erestuny* who "transform themselves," i.e., acquire another person's face and endeavor to sneak into their own or into another family. Such an *erestun* lives, it seems, as is fitting for a good peasant, but soon people in the family or in the village begin to disappear one after another; the *erestun* devours them. In order to destroy the transformed sorcerer, it is necessary to take the whip used for a heavily loaded horse and give him a thorough thrashing. Then he will fall down and give up his ghost. In order to prevent him from coming to life in the grave, it is necessary to drive an aspen stake into his back between the shoulders.[6]

According to this report, an ordinary person may become a vampire (*erestun*) if an evil sorcerer enters his body while he is dying. Similar beliefs are held by the South Slavs. According to the Bulgarians, "evil spirits enter into the bodies of villains, robbers, and in general people with depraved inclinations, and they become vampires."[7] The Serbian vampire (*vukodlak*) is a person "who forty days after his death is entered by some kind of demonic spirit, who revives him."[8] This revival among the South Slavs refers to the temporary animation of a dead vampire. The Olonecian *erestun*, on the other hand, is a living vampire who, outwardly a good peasant, pursues his vampiristic activity among the village people like a wolf in a sheepcote.

The *eretica* (pi. *ereticy*), known in the Elatomsk district (east-central Russia), is a variegated figure. The following is part of a description given by Zvonkov:

It is difficult to tell definitely who the *eretic*y actually are. According to the majority of accounts, they are women who have sold their souls to the devil during their lifetimes and are now [after their deaths] roaming the earth, turning people away from their genuine faith. In daytime they walk around as ugly old women in rags, by the evening they gather in "heathen" (*poganyx*) ravines, but at night they enter sunken graves and sleep in the coffins of the impious dead. Sunken graves are often to be found in our churchyards, and each of them is considered definitely to be the dwelling of an *eretica*. If you fall into such a grave up to your belt, you will wither, and if you accidentally see an *eretica* there, you will cease to live in this world. … *Eretic*y walk around only in the spring and late fall. If they do not get into a grave, they go through the chimney to the bathhouse, loudly splash around, and jump and dance to the accompaniment of the devil. One such *eretica* will later give birth to the Antichrist.[9]

Using this description as our guide, we have to agree with Zvonkov that it is difficult to define the *eretic*y precisely. Their figure is very complex. That they are basically sectarians is seen not only in their name which means "(female) heretic," but also in the fact they they are said to turn people away from their faith. However, *eretic*y have also acquired numerous traits from witches, as is evidenced by the selling of their souls to the devil, dancing to the devil's accompaniment in the bathhouse, and giving birth to the Antichrist. Gatherings in ravines for the evening and in cemeteries at night are very similar to the witches Sabbat in the West.

Sleeping in sunken graves and in the coffins of the impious dead tends to link *eretic*y with a special type of the dead—vampires. The fatal consequences of falling into such a grave or seeing an *eretica* there (his withering or even dying) is clearly vampiristic. This vampirism appears graphically in an episode further related by Zvonkov:

I was told in Temirev that a peasant's daughter died; he [the peasant] invited his godfather to his house, treated him with food and drink, and asked him to dig the grave. Being drunk, the godfather, who had taken a spade along, strolled directly to the cemetery. He found a sunken grave, descended into it, and began to dig. The spade hit a coffin, and, all of a sudden, through a rotten branch he saw the eye of an *eretica*. The peasant jumped out quickly and ran home without looking back. When he arrived, he climbed onto the stove, but the *eretica* was lying there and looking at him with the same evil eye. The man ran to the yard and then to the manger, but the accursed *eretica* had anticipated him: she was lying in the manger, shaking with demonic laughter. From that time on the godfather began to wither and wither. They held services to Zosima and Savvatij, sprinkled him with holy water, but whatever they did. nothing helped, and the godfather died. (78.)

In this description, special attention should be given to the detail concerning the eye of the *eretica*. In Russia and Germany there is a belief that the open eyes of a corpse can draw someone into the grave (Afanas'ev, 162–63). For this reason, the eyes of the deceased are closed at the time of death. The Kashubs believe that when a vampire (*vieszcy*) dies, his left eye remains open (Afanas'ev, 162–63). Zvonkov's story is an indication that the Russians, like the Kashubs, were familiar with the tradition of the vampire's open eye. According to the Gypsies of Yugoslavia, some parts of the human body, such as the eye, can become vampires.[10] The godfather is constantly followed by the eye of the *eretica* in the story recorded by Zvonkov. Here the eye seems to function as a full-fledged vampire which draws out the godfather's life substance and causes him to wither away.

While the eye of this *eretica* is clearly vampiristic, other traits, such as her anticipation of the godfather's movements day and night and her demonic laughter, are not. Laughter is typical of numerous spirits, for instance, water and forest spirits, but we have not come across laughter as typical of vampires.

To summarize: the examples given here of "heretics" (*eretik, eretnik, erestun, eretica*) show that the basic meaning of the terms as "the follower of heresy, one who deviates from the dogmas of the Orthodox church" has generally been retained. The term "heretic" has acquired a strongly negative connotation as "a person engaged in black magic, witch, sorcerer, wizard," and is used as a word of abuse. The same term with its different variants has also come to denote various types of vampires: *eretik*—the deceased who comes out of the grave and eats people; *erestun*—a living vampire, revived by a sorcerer who has penetrated a person's body at the moment of his death; and *eretica*—whose eye functions as a full-fledged vampire. The means for destroying heretic-vampires are burning and staking, and, in the case of the *erestum*, flogging. The heretic as a vampire appears primarily in the Russian north, in Siberia, and in some parts of central Russia.

The heretic (*eretik*) denoting "vampire" and a word of abuse appears in Russian literature as well. In Čulkov's *The Mocker or Slavic Tales* (*Peresmešnik ili slavenskie skazki*, 1766–68), a rich peasant, a practitioner of black magic, immediately after his death picks a fight with a dog next to his coffin. The priest at first refuses to bury him and to read the burial service "over such an heretic (*eretik*), who has the devil within him." After he is finally buried, the corpse does not stay in the grave at night, but strolls about the village, seizes people by the back of their heads, throws them out of windows, and drags them by their beards along the street. People leave the village. They dare to return only after a hunter has killed the corpse with a hatchet.[11]

The corpse's behavior in this story is not strictly that of a vampire. Like a vampire, he comes out of the grave at night, roams about the village, and catches people. However, he does not eat them, as the Russian heretic-vampire does, but abuses and harms them. It is obvious that this modified figure of the vampire is the fruit of Čulkov's own fantasy.

Zelenin suggests that "the idea of the bloodthirsty vampire has penetrated only to the Ukraine and Belorussia (Ukr. *upýr*, BR *vúpor*) from Western Europe; it is not known to the Great Russians. This idea quickly became familiar here, since it has much in common with the indigenous cult of the unclean dead." (393.) Zelenin's position is not tenable. The vampire has deep roots in Eastern Europe, especially in the Balkans (Bulgaria, Yugoslavia, Romania), Poland, and among the Kashubs. In the European south the image of the vampire has become almost completely mixed with that of the werewolf, which indicates the great age of this tradition.[12] Among the East Slavs, in addition to the Ukrainians and Belorussians, beliefs in the vampire are well-documented among the early Russians. The term "vampire" appears as the name of a Novgorodain prince (*Upir' Lixyj*) as early as 1047, and resurfaces as a peasant's name (*Makarenko Upir'*) in Novgorod in 1495. This term has also been recorded in western Russia as both personal and place names (*Klim' Upir', Upiry, Upirów*). The previous existence in Russia of a vampire cult is also illustrated by the fight clerics waged in encyclicals against sacrifices to vampires.[13] We have to agree with Tokarev, who states that "the very belief in 'a living dead,' who brings harm to people, existed among all the East Slavs as well as among other peoples."[14]

The term *upyr'* "vampire," has been unknown among the Great Russians during the past few centuries (Tokarev, 41). How are we to explain the curious fact of the existence of the notion of "vampire" among them, and the lack of a special term for it? Our position is that the beliefs pertaining to vampires were transferred to heretics and the term "heretic" was extended to also include vampire. As a result, the term *upyr'* faded away in the sixteenth-seventeenth centuries.

The transfer of the notion of vampires to heretics is connected with the extreme cruelty with which the heretics were persecuted in Russia. Hösch writes:

> Russland lebt in der Erinnerung der Nachwelt als Hort einer unbeugsamen und unnachglebigen Orthodoxie fort, die Quirinus Kuhlmann, den Protopopen Avvakum und eine grosse Zahl Ungenannter auf die Scheiterhaufen schickte und jede Regung von Heterodoxie mit brutalen Verfolgungsmassnahmen, zu denen der Staat durch die Jahrhunderte seinen starken Arm lien, unnachsichtig ausrotten liess.[15]

Since the "heresy theology" (*Ketzertheologie*) was discussed and disputed in the inner circles of the churchy the common people were not aware of the theoretical basis of the struggle of Orthodoxy against heresy. They could only witness the hysterical campaign waged against the heretics, their brutal imprisonments and executions. The joining of the ecclesiastical and worldly powers, including the grand princes (later czars), into this drive and the fanfare with which it was done, must have led the people to believe in the extreme danger constituted by the heretics. This danger could have been no less than the greatest sins imaginable—killing of Christians, drinking their blood and eating their flesh—just as the vampires were believed to do.

In the confusion between the vampires and the heretics, an additional fact should also be considered: the possibility of the incorruptibility of the bodies of both. Some scholars argue that the views of the Roman and Byzantine churches concerning the religious relics were different. If the flesh of relics was found intact, this, in Rome's view, was a sign of sanctity. But, these scholars claim, Byzantium believed the opposite: "the refusal of the flesh to rot was a certain sign of heresy. ..."[16] Following this trend of thought, the heretics shared with vampires the quality of undecomposed flesh, which could have facilitated the transfer of other vampiristic qualities to them as well. In the heretics' garb and under their name, the vampire has continued to live vigorously in the Russian north.

A parallel can be found on the Greek island of Crete, where the Saracens became demons. Clad in iron, these demons ride wild and ironclad horses and drag heavy chains behind them, frightening people. During the summer and at noon they are seen exhibiting their immense wealth in the sunshine. The demonization of the Saracens in Crete has its origin in the period 826–961, when the island was under the domination of the Saracens, whose religion differed from the Greeks' and who oppressed the Cretans terribly. The demonization process was reinforced by the pirates (also called "Saracens"), who for centuries afterwards raided Crete and neighboring areas. Imellos suggests that the term "Saracen" as the name of demons was substituted in Crete for an original Greek name—a development that parallels the substitution in Russia of such terms as *eretik* and *erestun* for the original *upyr'*.[17]

The term *inovercy* ("adherents of different faith, creed") has been used in Russia rather loosely. It denotes those who profess some faith other than Russian Orthodoxy, and such sectarians as Old Believers and Flagellants. Both of these groups were strongly discriminated against and, especially the sectarians, were persecuted by the government. When the *inovercy* died, they were identified with the "unclean" dead (*založnye pokojniki*). As such, they were not buried in cemeteries, but were left or thrown into the so-called *ubogie doma*—special shacks with a large hole in them, or just plain holes made for collecting the "unclean" dead. Their funeral took place only after *Semik*—the seventh Thursday after Easter. Discarding the corpses in the *ubogie doma* was forbidden in 1771, but people continued the practice for a long time.

This method of disposing of the *inovercy* has left its traces in the beliefs connected with them. Zelenin states that in popular beliefs the *inovercy* are similar to the "unclean" dead. They died without confession, that is, in sin. Since they did not believe in the true God (in the Orthodox view), it is possible that they had served the Devil and were, consequently, sorcerers. It was felt that there was something uncanny about the *inovercy,* and this sentiment was extended to the places where they were buried. In Nižgorod province, there was an old cemetery called *Mordovskaja gora* (Mordvin Hill or Mountain), which had a very bad reputation: "God help you not to be late here or stay overnight. Surely some evil spirit will frighten you, will turn you away from the road, will lead you into a ravine, break your carriage, or something similar. All this was obviously ascribed to the heathen Mordvins who were buried there."[18]

Occasionally the deceased *inovercy* were considered to have caused prolonged droughts, as the "unclean" dead did. In order to bring rain, their graves were opened and the corpses were abused. A leader of the sect of Flagellants, Šamborov, was buried with his adherents on Sionsk Mountain (in the Saratov province) in the seventeenth century. During a drought it was decided to exhume his body and throw it into the Volga River. They found, however, only a deep hole where the grave had been—so deep that even the longest rope could not reach the bottom. There was no trace of Šamborov—he had vanished into the inferno. It was said that at night black dogs ran barking out of Šamborov's grave. In the Taraščansk district, the grave of an Old Believer was opened in 1868, since he also was considered to be the cause of a drought. The people beat the skull of the corpse while repeating "Give rain!" and poured water on it from a sieve. Afterwards they laid the corpse back into the grave. (Zelenin, *Očerki russkoj mifologii*, I, 70, 80.)

In Olonec it was believed that *poluviricy* (*poluvericy*), literally "half-believers," lived in the forest. The Brothers Sokolov reported that they were evil beings who professed both the Orthodox and, at the same time, the Devil's creed. A *poluvirica* was naked. She had a long face, long hanging breasts and three braids of hair on her back; she walked with a child in her arms. It was said that a *poluvirica* had been killed by an old woman who was very bold—she was not even afraid of rapacious beasts or devils. According to a fabulate (*byvai'ščina*), a *poluvirica,* referred to as a she-devil (*čertovka*), had the habit of coming to a peasant's hut in the wilderness at dinner time, after the men had gone to bed. Once when she came—naked, with loosened hair, and a child in her arms—she sat upon the range that the men had heated. She burned her buttocks, and never came again.[19] Zelenin lists *poluvéricy* as "petty forest spirits" (*kleine Waldgeister*) (*Russische (ostslavische) Volkskunde*, 389).

The term *poluviricy, poluvericy,* denoting a kind of female forest spirit. is no doubt identical with *poluvericy,* used in Pskov and Vitebsk provinces for denoting half-Russified Estonians and Latvians.[20] Similar terms, *poluvertsiki* or *poluverniki* (Estonian *poluvertsikud, poluvernikud*), are also used for the Russians in East Estonia—in Räpina, Mustvee, and Alutaguse (northeast Estonia). The majority of these Russians fled to Estonia from Russia in the seventeenth century to escape persecution by the czarist government; some of them had gone there earlier. The faith of the *poluvertsiki* is a combination of Greek Orthodoxy, beliefs of the sectarians (especially the Old Believers), and Evangelical Lutheranism.[21] The term "half-believer" shows that only a part of their creed (the Orthodox) is recognized as the real creed, whereas the other ingredients are considered heretical.

The religious ideas and practices of the heretics-sectarians differed from those of the majority of the people. This, coupled with the most vigorous persecution by the church and government and the tremendous zeal with which the sectarians themselves pursued their cause, made them highly suspicious in the eyes of the Orthodox and led to their identification with vampires and evil spirits.

NOTES

1. *Webster's New World Dictionary of the American Language* (Cleveland and New York: The World Publ. Co. 1964), 679.

2. *Bol'šaja sovetskaja ėntsiklopedija*, 2nd. ed. (51 Vols.; n.p.: Gos. naučnoe izd., 1949–58), XV, 528. The term "heretic" has also been used in Russia by certain religious groups, primarily the Old Believers, to designate all those who do not belong to them. See P. S. Efimenko, *Materialy po ėtnografii russkogo naselenija Arxangel'skoj gubernii* (2 vols.; M., 1877), I, 106, 186.

3. Dmitrij Zelenin, *Russische (ostslavische) Volkskunde* (Berlin and Leipzing: Walter de Gruyter, 1927), 395.

4. *Slovar' russkogo jazyka* (9 vols.; SPb.: Imp. Ak. nauk, 18914930), II/l, 123, 126.

5. Lauri Posti, "Kerettiläinen," in *Kielenja kulttuurin kentältä: Professori Igor Vahrokselle hanen täyttaessään 60 vuotta, vuotta*, ed. Lauri Posti *et ai* (Neuvostoliittoinstituutin Vuosikirja, 25; Helsinki, 1977), 137.

6. *Pesni, sobrannye P. N. Rybnikovym* (3 vols.; M.: Sotrudnik škol, 1910), III, 189-90.

7. A. N. Afanas 'ev, "Poetic Views of the Slavs Regarding Nature," in *Vampires of the Slavs*, ed. Jan L. Perkowski (Cambridge, Mass.: Slavica, 1976), 161.

8. Vuk Stef. Karadjić, *Srpski rječnik* (Belgrade: Štamparija Kraljevine Jugoslavije, 1935), 82.

9. A. Zvonkov, "Očerk verovanij krest'jan Elatomskogo uezda," *Etnografičeskoe obozrenie*, 1889, kn. 2, 77–78.

10. T. P. Vukanović, "The Vampire," in *Vampires of the Slavs*, 207.

11. A. V. Zapadov and G. P. Makogonenko, eds., *Russkajaproza XVIII veka* (M.-L.: GIXL, 1950), 99–100.

12. See for example Montague Summers, *The Werewolf* (London: K. Paul, Trench, Trubner, 1933), 15.

13. Kazimierz Moszyński, "Slavic Folk Culture," in *Vampires of the Slavs*, 185.

14. S. A. Tokarev, *Religioznye verovanija vostocnoslavjanskix narodov* (M.-L.: AN SSSR, 1957), 42.

15. Edgar Hösch, *Orthodoxie und Häresie im alten Russland* (Schriften zur Geistesgeschichte des östlichen Europa, 7; Wiesbaden: Otto Harrassowitz, 1975), 12.

16. Paul Johnson, *A History of Christianity* (New York: Atheneum, 1976), 165. And Ernest Jones, *On the Nightmare* (New York: Liveright, 1971), 103—4, writes: "… the Greek Orthodox Church—it is said in a spirit of opposition to the Roman Catholic pronouncement that the bodies of saints do not decompose—supported the dogma (sic) that it is the bodies of wicked, unholy, and especially excommunicated persons which do not decompose. Just as the Roman Catholic Church taught that heretics could be turned into Werewolves, the Greek Orthodox Church taught that heretics became Vampires after death." Some scholars, on the contrary, claim that the non-corruption of the flesh is, according to the teachings of the Eastern Church, a sign of the process of Deification.

See Vladimir Lossky, *The Mystical Theology of the Eastern Church* (London: J. Clarke, 1957), 222–25, 104, and Arthur Stanley, *Lectures on the History of the Eastern Church* (New York: Charles Scribner, 1862), 382. Professor Georges Florovsky informs me that the views of the scholars concerning the incorruptibility of the corpse are contradictory and that in this question there are "no unified practices and no common interpretation" (personal communication on 4 March 1978).

17. Steph. D. Imellos, "E demonopoiēsis ton sarakēnōn en Krētē," Anatypon ek tēs Epetēridos tou Kentrou Ereynēs Ellēnikēs Laographias, Vol. K' -Ká (Athens, 1969).

18. Dmitrij Zelenin, *Očerki russkoj mifologii*, I: *Umeršie neeste'stvennoj smert 'ju i rusalki* (Petrograd: A. V. Orlov, 1916), 76, 293. A forced conversion of the Mordvins began only in the sixteenth century.

19. Boris and Jurij Sokolov, *Skazki i pesni Beiozerskogo kraja* (M.: Imp. ak. nauk, 1915), xiii, 72.

20. Vladmir Dal', *Tolkovyj slovar' živogo velikorusskogo jazyka* (4 vols.; SPb.-M.: M. O. Vol'f, 1903–09), 677.

21. Ju. Trusman, "Poluvericy," *Živaja starina*, I (1890), 35 *ff.;* Otu Liiv, *Vene asustusest Alutagusel kuni XVIII sajandi esimese veerandini* (Tartu: Loodus, 1928), 35–36, 68–69.

Wie facht sich an gar ein grauſſem

lidhe erſchröckenliche Hyſtorien. von dem wilden wütrich Dracole weyde Wie er die leüt geſpiſt hat vnd
gep:aten vñ mit den Haßtern yn einē keſſel geſotten

Vampirism: Old World Folklore

By Raymond MacNally and Radu Floreşçu

The notion behind vampirism traces far back in time—to man the hunter, who discovered that when blood flowed out of a wounded beast or a fellow human, life, too, drained away. Blood was the source of vitality. Thus men smeared themselves with blood and sometimes drank it. The idea of drinking blood to renew vitality thereupon entered history. To the vampire, indeed, "The blood is the life," as Dracula, quoting from Deuteronomy 12:33, tells us in Stoker's novel, though the actual biblical passage is a warning *against* drinking human blood.

Vampire belief is universal; it has been documented in ancient Babylon, Egypt, Rome, Greece, and China. Vampire accounts exist in completely separate civilizations, where any direct borrowing would not have been possible. The vampire is known by various names—*vrykolakes, brykilakas, barbarlakos, borborlakos,* or *bourdoulakos* in modern Greek; *katakhanoso* or *baital* in the ancient Sanskrit; *upiry* in Russian; *upiory* in Polish; *blutsäuger* in German, etc. Early Chinese were afraid of the *giang shi,* a demon who drinks blood. In China, it was reported that vampires existed there in 600 B.C. Depictions of vampires are found on ancient Babylonian and Assyrian pottery going back thousands of years before Christ. The belief flourished in the New World as in the Old. Ancient Peruvians believed in a class of devil worshippers called *canchus* or *pumapmicuc,* who sucked blood from the sleeping young in order to partake of their life. Aztecs sacrificed the hearts of prisoners to the sun in the belief that their blood fed the sun's continuing energy.

In ancient Greece there were *empusa* or *lamia* akin to the vampire—horrible winged demon-women who lured handsome youths to their death in order to drink their blood and eat their flesh. Lamia was once the beloved of Zeus who was driven insane by Zeus's jealous wife, Hera. Lamia killed her own children and goes about at night killing human children for revenge.

The first woman on earth was Lilith, or Lilitu, according to ancient Semitic belief. In the Talmud, the book of Jewish laws, customs, and tradition, Adam had a wife before Eve named Lilith. But she was disobedient to Adam and challenged his authority. In a state of anger she left Adam, though three angels, Sanvi, Sansanvi, and Semangelaf, tried to convince her to stay. Because of her disobedience, her children were killed and she was transformed into a night-roaming monster. Eve then came into the picture and bore Adam children. Extremely jealous, Lilith went about taking her revenge by killing the sons and daughters of Adam and Eve. Since humans are all descended from Adam and Eve, everyone must defend himself against Lilith's attacks. The medieval Jews had special amulets to guard against the attacks of Lilith, one made for male children and another for female. Traditionally, these depicted the three angels who attempted to persuade Lilith not to leave Adam.

Early in the Christian era the learned Bhavabhūti wrote classic Indian tales, including twenty-five stories of a vampire who animates dead bodies and is seen hanging upside down from a tree like a bat. The female Hindu god Shiva shares many similarities with the vampire, such as being creator and destroyer at the same time. Behind the vampire is the Oriental concept of eternal return, in which nothing is ever really destroyed but comes back in endless recreations and reincarnations. The vampire takes blood from the living, but should she mix her blood with that of her victim, that person in turn becomes an undead, having survived mortal death.

Proof that vampires were considered to be essentially female, without male organs, comes from Saint Augustine and the early church fathers. For example, Augustine writes that demons have "bodily immortality and passions like human beings" but cannot produce semen. Instead they gather semen from the bodies of real men and inject it into sleeping women to cause pregnancy. Saint Clement testifies that the demons have human passions but "no organs, so they turn to humans to make use of their organs. Once in control of suitable organs, they can get whatever they want."

During the eighteenth century, a vampire of renown named Peter Poglojowitz emerged from a small village in Hungary. Following his death in 1725 his body was disinterred. They found fresh blood flowing from his mouth and his body appeared to be without any signs of *rigor mortis* or decay. So the local peasants thought he was a vampire and burned his body.

In 1732 the case of the Serbian vampire Arnold Paole from Medvegia stimulated eighteenth-century scientific research into vampires. At the height of rationalism in 1751 a Dominican scholar, Augustin Calmet, wrote a treatise about vampires in Hungary and Moravia.

Vampire beliefs are particularly strong today throughout southeastern Europe, especially among the modern Greeks. The southerly Cyclades island of Santorini is infamous for its vampires. Many authors noted this fact as early as the seventeenth century. In fact, if a suspected vampire were uncovered on mainland Greece, the body was customarily shipped off to Santorini because the people there had a long history and vast experience in dealing with vampires. An old Greek saying is "bringing vampires to Santorini" in the sense of "like bringing coals to Newcastle," a redundant act.

Orthodox practices of excommunication bolstered belief in the vampire. When Orthodox Christian priests or bishops issue an order of excommunication, they add the curse "and the earth will not receive your body!" This signifies that the body of the excommunicated person will remain "uncorrupt and entire." The soul will not rest in peace. In this case a nondecaying body is the sign of evil. Those Orthodox Christians who have converted to Roman Catholicism or Islam are doomed to wander the earth and not enter Heaven. It is worth recalling in this context that the historical Dracula, having converted to Roman Catholicism toward the end of his life, "forsook the light of orthodoxy" and "accepted the darkness" of heresy and was hence a candidate to become an undead, a vampire.

One theory about the prevalence of vampire belief in Transylvania suggests that since the Tibetan Mongols had a belief in both the vampire and the bat god, they may have come in contact with those Asians who eventually migrated in large numbers to Transylvania. Both the Hungarians (Magyars) and the Szekelys of Transylvania moved initially from Asia into Europe. In this context it is revealing to note that Stoker has Dracula claim Szekelys descent. Another theory concerning the reasons for the apparent richness of vampire belief in Transylvania comes from the fact that so many different ethnic groups inhabit the area, leading to an elaborate mix of folklore from the Germans, Hungarians, Gypsies, and Romanians.

Romanians in particular have many names for a variety of vampires. For example, the most common term, *strigoi* (or the feminine form, *strigoaica*), is an evil creature who sleeps during the daylight hours, flies at night, can change into animal form such as a wolf, dog, or bird, and sucks the blood from sleeping children. The female is more dangerous than the male. She can also spoil marriages and harvests, stop cows from giving milk, and even cause fatal disease and death. The Romanian *pricolici* is an undead who can appear in human, dog, or wolf forms. Among Romanians vampires are always evil, their journey to the other world has been interrupted, and they are doomed to prey upon the living for a time.

In Transylvania, garlic is the powerful weapon to deter vampires. Windows and doors are anointed with garlic to keep them away. In addition, farm animals, especially sheep, are rubbed with garlic for vampires might just as well attack animals for their blood as humans.

Peasants consider garlic to be a medicinal plant. They eat it to ward off the common cold and various diseases. Anything that wards off disease is considered to be good or "white" magic, hence garlic can ward off devils, werewolves, and vampires.

A vampire's grave can sometimes be detected by holes around the gravesite big enough for a snake to pass through. To prevent the vampire from emerging from the grave, one must fill these holes with water. The thorns of wild roses are sure to keep vampires at bay. Poppy seeds are strewn on the path from the cemetery to the town because vampires are compulsive counters and must pick up all the thorns. This practice can prevent the vampire from reaching the village before dawn, at which time he must return to his coffin.

The ultimate way to destroy a vampire is to drive a stake through the heart or the navel during the daylight hours when the vampire must rest in his coffin. The stake should be made of wood from an ash or an aspen tree. In some areas of Transylvania iron bars—preferably heated red-hot—are used. As an added safeguard, the vampire's body is burned. Sometimes a fir tree is plunged into the body of the vampire in order to keep it in the grave. A derivation of this is the fir tree ornament that one finds over graves in Romania today.

Most Romanians believe that life after death will be much like life on earth. As there is not much faith in a purely spiritual world, it seems reasonable that after death an undead will walk the earth in much the same way as a living person. The walking dead are not always vampires, however. In fact, the Romanian term for undead, *moroi*, is more prevalent than the term for vampire or blood-drinker, *strigoi*. But both the undead and the vampire are killed in the same way. *Strigoi* are literally demon birds of the night. They fly only after sunset, and they eat human flesh and drink blood.

Belief in vampires is still prevalent in Dracula country particularly among the older generation. In 1969, at the foot of Castle Dracula, in the small village of Capatineni, lived a Gypsy named Tinka. She was the *lautar,* or village singer, and was often called upon to sing old stories at weddings, balls, and funerals.

Tinka told us two stories about the undead. One of them concerned her father. When he died thirty years before, he was duly laid out, but the next day the villagers discovered that the old man's face was still ruddy, and his body still flexible, not rigid. The people knew that he was an undead, and a stake was driven through his heart.

The other story concerned an old woman in the village. After her death many of her close relatives died. So did various animals around her home. The people realized that she was an undead and they exhumed her coffin. When the lid was removed, they found that her eyes were open and that she had rolled over. They also noticed that the corpse had a ruddy complexion. The villagers burned her body.

Belief in the walking dead and the blood-sucking vampire may never entirely disappear. It was only in the past century—1823, to be exact—that England outlawed the practice of driving stakes through the hearts of suicides. Today, it is in Transylvania that the vampire legends have their strongest hold. Examining the following superstitions, it is chilling to imagine their potency six hundred years ago.

In Eastern Europe vampires are said to have two hearts or two souls; since one heart or one soul never dies, the vampire remains undead.

Who can become a vampire? In Transylvania, criminals, bastards, witches, magicians, excommunicated people, those born with teeth or a caul, and unbaptized children can all become vampires. The seventh son of a seventh son is doomed to become a vampire.

How can one detect a vampire? Any person who does not eat garlic or who expresses a distinct aversion to garlic is suspect.

Vampires sometimes strike people dumb. They can steal one's beauty or strength, or milk from nursing mothers.

In Romania, peasants believe that the vampires and other specters meet on Saint Andrew's Eve at a place where the cuckoo does not sing and the dog does not bark.

Vampires are frightened by light, so one must build a good fire to ward them off, and torches must be lit and placed outside the houses.

Even if you lock yourself up in your home, you are not safe from the vampire, since he can enter through chimneys and keyholes. Therefore, one must rub the chimney and the keyholes with garlic, and the windows and doors as well. The farm animals must also be rubbed with garlic to protect them.

Crosses made from the thorns of wild roses are effective in keeping the vampire away.

Take a large black dog and paint an extra set of eyes on its forehead with white paint—this repulses vampires.

According to Orthodox Christian belief, the soul does not leave the body to enter the next world until forty days after the body is laid in the grave. Hence the celebrations in Orthodox cemeteries forty days after the burial.

Bodies were once disinterred between three and seven years after burial; if decomposition was not complete, a stake was driven through the heart.

If a cat or other evil animal jumps or flies over a body before it is buried, or if the shadow of a man falls upon the corpse, the deceased may become a vampire.

If the dead body is reflected in a mirror, the reflection helps the spirit to leave the body and become a vampire.

In Hungarian folklore one of the most common ways of identifying a vampire was to choose a child young enough to be a virgin and seat the child on a horse of a solid color that was also a virgin and had never stumbled. The horse was led through the cemetery and over all the graves. If it refused to pass over a grave, a vampire must lie there.

Usually the tomb of a vampire has one or more holes roughly the size through which a serpent can pass.

How to kill a vampire? The stake, made from a wild rosebush, ash or aspen wood, or of heated iron, must be driven through the vampire's body and into the earth in order to hold him securely in his grave. The vampire's body should then be burned, or reburied at the crossroads.

If a vampire is not found and rendered harmless, it first kills all members of its immediate family, then starts on the other inhabitants of the village and the animals.

The vampire cannot stray too far from his grave since he must return to it at sunrise.

If not detected, the vampire climbs up into the belfry of the church and calls out the names of the villagers, who instantly die. Or, in some areas, the vampire rings the death-knell and all who hear it die on the spot.

If the vampire goes undetected for seven years, he can travel to another country or to a place where another language is spoken and become a human again. He or she can marry and have children, but they all become vampires when they die.

Romanians slit the soles of the feet or tie together the legs or knees of suspected vampires to try to keep them from walking. Some bury bodies with sickles around their necks, so that in trying to rise the vampire will cut his own head off.

Whitethorn was sure to keep vampires away since it was believed that Christ's crown of thorns was made from whitethorn. Vampires would become entrapped in the thorns and become disoriented.

Silver, thought to be a pure alloy, was believed to thwart vampires as well as were-wolves. So crosses or icons were often made of silver.

Did the peasants of the fifteenth century consider Vlad Tepes a vampire? When questioned about current beliefs, peasants living in the region around Castle Dracula revealed that there is no longer a connection between Vlad Tepes and the vampire in their folklore. The peasants are not aware of Stoker's *Dracula*. The elderly do believe passionately, however, in vampires and the undead.

As our culture has become more urban, a bias against peasant superstition has evolved. This is reflected in our use of the word "urbane" to describe something positive, broad-minded, and rational, and the word "provincial" to designate something unsophisticated, narrow-minded, and ignorant. One tends to regard peasant culture as primitive and unscientific. Even Karl Marx conceded that capitalism had at least saved a majority of the population from "the idiocy of rural life."

Far from being incessantly preoccupied with doubt and fear, however, peasants spend most of the day in very practical pursuits necessary for their subsistence.

Some evolutionists assume that primitive people have no capacity to comprehend natural explanations, that since primitive man lives at a low technological level he must have a thought process opposite to that of modern man. The assumption is that primitive, rural man is "prelogical," like an innocent or a child.

But not all of modern Western man's beliefs are logical and scientific. Attitudes toward death and life have always been complex for all men, encompassing hate and love, attraction and repulsion, hope and fear. Belief in vampires is a poetic, imaginative way of looking at death and at life beyond death.

Primitive beliefs are not any stranger than modern scientific beliefs. Nightly on our TV sets there is some variation of the man in the white coat who stands amid Bunsen burners and test tubes and declares, "Scientific tests have proved that in nine out of ten cases ..." whereupon everyone in the audience genuflects to the new god Science. If it is scientific then it must be true, and only the scientifically proven fact can be true. Is this any more absurd than primitive peasant beliefs? The vampire belongs to that common store of images which psychologists call symbols. Many people assume a symbol refers to an unreal event, but in fact most symbols are indications of actual occurrences, having universal application. Over time the historical connection is often forgotten and great effort must be made to retrieve its original meaning. As Jung put it, "It [symbol] implies something vague, unknown, hidden in us."

The vampire possesses powers which are similar to those belonging to certain twentieth-century comic book characters. During the day he is helpless and vulnerable like Clark Kent or Bruce Wayne. But just as the mild-mannered Clark Kent becomes Superman when called upon, and the effete Bruce Wayne becomes Batman when needed, so the vampire acquires great powers at night. The British author Clive Leatherdale has characterized Batman as "the count cleansed of his evil and endowed with a social consciousness."

Dracula the vampire-count is a kind of father figure of great potency. In many religions the opposite of God the Father, with his flowing white beard, is Satan, also a father figure, often portrayed with huge, dark, batlike wings.

The connection between Dracula, the devil, the bat, and the vampire becomes clear when one understands that in Romanian folklore the devil can change himself into an animal or a black bird. When he takes wing, he can fly like a bird or a bat. Satan seeks also to be nocturnal. During the day he remains in the quiet of Hell, like the bat in its refuge; when day is done, the night is his empire, just as it is the bat's.

The bat is the only mammal that fulfills one of man's oldest aspirations: it can fly, defying gravity not unlike Superman. Contrary to popular belief, the bat is not a flying rat. The wings of this small animal are actually elongated, webbed hands. The head of the bat is erect like a man's head. And, like man, the bat is one of the most versatile creatures in the world.

Why is the vampire image linked to that of the vampire bat in particular? Vampire bats do not exist anywhere in Europe, yet it is there that belief in the vampire as a night-flying creature that sucks the blood of the living has flourished.

When Cortés came to the New World, he found blood-sucking bats in Mexico. Remembering the mythical vampire, he called them vampire bats. The name stuck. So a word that signified a mythical creature in the Old World became attached to a species of bats particular to the New World. Vampire bats exist only in Central and South America.

The vampire bat, the *Desmodus rotundus,* is marvelously agile. It can fly, walk, dodge swiftly, and turn somersaults, all with swiftness and efficiency. Generally it attacks cattle rather than men. The victim is not awakened during the attack. The vampire bat walks very softly over the victim and, after licking a spot on the flesh, neatly inserts its incisor or canine teeth. As the blood surfaces, the bat licks it up. That the vampire bat subsists on blood alone is a scientific fact.

The once-human vampire's existence is a frightening tragedy, *sans* goodness or hope, repose or satisfaction. In order to survive, he must drink the blood of the living. The possibility of real death is closed to him. Thus he continues, wanting to live, wanting to die; not truly alive and not really dead. The folklore about him is not based on science, yet it is essentially true. As all vampire legends and customs attest, not only does man fear death, man fears some things even more than death. Stoker's notes, now housed at the Rosenbach Foundation in Philadelphia, indicate that he read *The Book of Werewolves* (1865), which had a section on the infamous "Blood Countess," Elizabeth Bathory, written by the Protestant minister and scholar Reverend Sabine Baring-Gould (best remembered for penning the words to the inspiring hymn "Onward, Christian Soldiers"). In fact, Stoker's description of Dracula's hands being squat with hair growing on the palms comes directly from Baring-Gould's book.

The Book of Werewolves recorded the basic legend of a Hungarian countess who killed her young female servants in order to bathe in their blood because she thought that such treatments kept her skin looking young and healthy. In all, she butchered some 650 girls for this purpose. Baring-Gould simply repeated the story popularized by the German scholar Michael Wagner during the late eighteenth century. Our recent investigation revealed hitherto unknown documentation from a court of inquiry which took place before Elizabeth Bathory's court trial in 1611. Testimony by hundreds of witnesses demonstrated that her supposed blood use for cosmetic purpose was a legend, but that she did indeed kill more than 650 girls (she recorded each separate atrocity in her diary). The countess evidently liked to bite and tear the flesh of her young servants. One of her nicknames was "the tiger of Cachtice." Cachtice, the town where her main castle was, once part of northwestern Hungary, is now located in Slovakia, north of Bratislava. Elizabeth Bathory was born in 1560 into one of the most powerful and illustrious Hungarian families of the time.

She tortured and murdered not only at Castle Cachtice but also in Vienna where she had a mansion on Augustinian Street at Lobkowitz Square, near the royal palace in the center of the city. During the trial of 1611 it was recorded that "In Vienna the monks there hurled their pots against the windows when they heard the cries [of the girls being tortured]." These monks must have been in the old Augustinian monastery across from the Bathory mansion. In the cellar, Bathory had a blacksmith construct a kind of iron maiden or cage in which to torture her victims.

Constant intermarriage among the Hungarian noble families, designed to keep the property in the family, led to genetic degeneration; Elizabeth herself was prone to epileptic fits. Also, one of her uncles was a noted Satanist, her aunt Klara an infamous sexual adventurer, her brother Stephen a drunkard and a lecher.

At age eleven Elizabeth was betrothed to the son of another aristocratic Hungarian family, Ferenc Nadasdy. She went to live with the Nadasdy family where, like a tomboy, she evidently enjoyed playing with the peasant boys on the Nadasdy estate. At thirteen she got pregnant by one of them. Her mother spirited her away to a remote Bathory castle where Elizabeth gave birth to a child who was secretly sent out of the country. Shortly before her fifteenth birthday, Elizabeth was married to Ferenc Nadasdy.

Ferenc, who later earned the nickname The Black Knight, was as cruel as his wife. He was off fighting in the wars against the Turks during most of their marriage. When home, he enjoyed torturing Turkish captives. He even taught some torture techniques to Elizabeth. One of them, star-kicking, was a variation of the hotfoot in which bits of oiled paper were put between the toes of lazy servants and set on fire, causing the victim to see stars from the pain and to kick to try to put out the fire. Meanwhile, Elizabeth stuck needles into servant girls' flesh and pins under their fingernails. She also put red-hot coins and keys into servants' hands, or she used an iron to scald the faces of lazy servants. She had other girls hurled out into the snow, where cold water was poured on them until they froze to death.

Ferenc showed Elizabeth how to discipline another of her servants. The girl was taken outside, undressed, and her body smeared with honey. She was then forced to stand outside for twenty-four hours, so as to be bitten by flies, bees, and other insects.

Ferenc died in 1604, leaving his widow free to indulge her morbid sexual fantasies. She set the pubic hair of one of her female servants on fire, according to testimony at the 1611 trial. Elizabeth also liked to have her female servants strip for her. She once pulled a serving girl's mouth until it split at the corners.

Bathory could get away with all this quite easily because she was a Hungarian aristocrat; the servants were Slovaks, to be treated like property or chattel, as cruelly as she wished, for they had no recourse. She lured servants to her castle with promises of wealth and prestige. When that method began to wane, she had her minions raid the surrounding villages and round up the victims.

Bathory finally tired of servant girls and began to entice aristocrats to her nightly games of sadism. That was her first mistake. Elizabeth carried out her atrocities in the company of a mysterious woman who dressed like a man.

Once when Bathory was sick in bed she commanded her elder female servants to bring a young servant girl to her bedside. Bathory rose up "like a bulldog," bit the girl on the cheek, ripped out a piece of her shoulder with her teeth, and then bit the girl's breasts.

Disposing of the innumerable bodies became a growing technical problem: at one point Bathory even stuffed some of the bodies under beds in the castle. The stench became unbearable, and some of the older servants tossed some bodies, naturally drained of blood, in a field. The frightened local villagers believed that vampires were responsible for the blood-drained corpses.

Bathory was much wealthier than the Hungarian king Matthias II. In fact, he owed her a great deal of money. When news reached him that there was mounting evidence that Bathory was molesting girls of noble birth, he decided to act—out of economic reasons, not religious ones. Some scholars wrongly assumed that Matthias, a Catholic, attacked Bathory because she was Protestant. With the support of the nobles in the Hungarian Parliament, Matthias came to Bratislava and ordered Count Thurzo, the local governor, to investigate and ascertain the facts in the Bathory case. The king, who believed in witchcraft, as did most of his peers, was motivated mainly by financial considerations. If Bathory could be accused and found guilty of being a witch, then her vast property could be confiscated, and all of his debts to her nullified.

However, Count Thurzo was a close friend and relative of the Bathory family. Quickly, behind closed doors, the family, including Elizabeth's sons and daughters, agreed to make a deal with Thurzo: there would be a quick trial arranged by Thurzo before the king could act; Bathory would not take the stand, but her accomplices would be put on trial. In that way the property could remain in the Bathory family and not be taken over by the king.

The strategy worked. Thurzo planned his raid for Christmas, when the Hungarian parliament was not in session, so that he could have a free hand. On the night of December 29, 1610, Count Thurzo raided Castle Cachtice and found several mutilated bodies in full view.

Thurzo kept King Matthias II in the dark. The count controlled all the proceedings. The quickly arranged trial convened on January 2, 1611, in the Slovakian town of Bytca at Thurzo's castle north of Cachtice; a second trial took place on January 7. Only petty officials and peasants participated at the first trial, so Thurzo could manipulate everything. Bathory was not allowed to be present in court, even though she wanted to appear and protest her innocence. Her accomplices were formally tried and found guilty at the second trial, during which some twenty jurors and high-level judges heard the testimony. Church officials had been bribed to waive their right to interrogate the accused, even though there were questions of witchcraft. All attempts by the king's representative to place Bathory on the stand failed because of Thurzo's clever maneuvering. He argued that if the Court were to try Bathory it would be a blot on the honor of the Nadasdy and Bathory families and a trauma for the Hungarian nobility.

Bathory's accomplices had their fingers torn out with red-hot pincers by the executioner. They were then tossed alive on the fire. Elizabeth was placed under house arrest, condemned to be walled up in a room in her Castle Cachtice, never again to see the light of day. The property remained safely within the Bathory family's grasp.

Late in August 1614, one of Elizabeth's jailers wanted to get a look at her. Peeking through the small opening through which she received food, he saw the countess lying dead. Hungarian authorities tried to cover up all memory of the "Blood Countess," and they succeeded until her trial documents, kept in official secret archives, were discovered.

There are several links between the Bathory family and Dracula. The commander-in-chief of the expedition that put Dracula back on the throne in 1476 was Prince Stephen Bathory. In addition, a Dracula fiefdom became a Bathory possession during Elizabeth's time. Furthermore, the Hungarian side of Dracula's ancestors might have been related to the Bathory clan.

Accounts of living vampires like Elizabeth Bathory surfaced during the middle of the nineteenth century and were tied strongly to necrophilia. In 1849 at the famous

Père Lachaise cemetery in Paris, where many famous artists and musicians were buried, reports circulated about a mysterious night creature who had disinterred and violated corpses there. The French newspapers named the culprit "the vampire of Paris." Traps were laid, and the authorities tracked down the perpetrator. He turned out to be a seemingly normal, handsome young blond sergeant named Victor Bertrand. At his trial on July 10, 1849, he testified that his obsession began in a village churchyard, where he witnessed a funeral and was seized with an overwhelming desire to dig up the corpse and rip it apart.

During the 1920s German newspapers were filled with stories about the "Hanover Vampire." His name was Fritz Haarmann; he had been in and out of prisons, madhouses, and the army, until he settled down to run a butcher shop in 1918. After World War I, Germany was filled with homeless boys and young men; Haarmann picked them up at the Hanover railroad station. He invited his victims home, where he pinned them down and murdered them by sinking his teeth in their throats. He killed at least twenty-four, and at his trial in 1925 he admitted to twenty-seven murders. Like the infamous Sweeney Todd, Haarmann ground parts of his victims' bodies into sausage meat, some of which he ate and some of which he sold in his store.

An Englishman named George Haigh confessed to drinking the blood of nine victims and then dissolving their bodies in acid during the 1940s. English newspapers dubbed him the "Acid-Bath Vampire."

In the Wisconsin farmhouse of bachelor hermit Eddie Gein during the late 1950s investigators stumbled on a bizarre scene: heads, skins, and other parts of at least ten human bodies were discovered, and Gein had mummified several others. He admitted to two murders and said that he got the other bodies by robbing local graveyards. As a youth he had been fascinated with accounts of Nazi experiments on human flesh in the concentration camps. Gein's story inspired the films *Psycho, Deranged,* and *The Texas Chainsaw Massacre.*

As recently as 1981 a self-proclaimed living vampire named James Riva II was put on trial in Brockton, Massachusetts. His attorney told the jury that his client had "shot his grandmother twice and sucked the blood out of the bullet holes because he believed a vampire told him that was what he had to do." Despite the objection of the assistant district attorney to the defense's plea of "vampire," the judge overruled the objection and the defense continued their line of reasoning. This was undoubtedly the first time in history that vampirism was used in a *defense* plea! The defense's strategy was that if they could prove that Riva believed he was a vampire, there would be grounds for an insanity plea. During the trial, a doctor testified that Riva had killed a cat and drank its blood, and had once mixed horse's blood with crackers and drank it like soup. Riva was found guilty of the murder of his grandmother but was confined to a mental institution.

Medical doctors utilize the clinical classification "living vampire" in diagnosing cases of two types: those with a proven physical need for fresh healthy blood because their own blood is defective, such as in cases of severe anemia and other blood diseases; and those with a psychological need for blood because it provides a sexual or erotic thrill. These latter living vampires get their satisfaction by actually drinking blood.

One theory to explain the living vampire phenomenon is based on an erythropoietic disease, inherited porphyria. A relatively rare blood disorder, it is caused by a recessive gene that leads to the production of an excess of porphyrins, which are components of red blood cells.

The patient suffering from inherited porphyria becomes extremely sensitive to light. In addition, skin lesions may develop, and the teeth become brown or reddish brown because of the excess porphyrins.

This vampire disease may have been prevalent among the Eastern European nobility. Five hundred years ago physicians even recommended that some nobles replenish their blood by drinking the blood of their subjects. So when a peasant declared that there was a vampire living up in the castle, he wasn't referring to folklore but to an actual blood-drinker.

The Need Fire

By James G. Frazer

The fire-festivals hitherto described are all celebrated periodically at certain stated times of the year. But besides these regularly recurring celebrations the peasants in many parts of Europe have been wont from time immemorial to resort to a ritual of fire at irregular intervals in seasons of distress and calamity, above all when their cattle were attacked by epidemic disease. No account of the popular European fire-festivals would be complete without some notice of these remarkable rites, which have all the greater claim on our attention because they may perhaps be regarded as the source and origin of all the other fire-festivals; certainly they must date from a very remote antiquity. The general name by which they are known among the Teutonic peoples is need-fire. Sometimes the need-fire was known as "wild fire," to distinguish it no doubt from the tame fire produced by more ordinary methods. Among Slavonic peoples it is called "living fire." The history of the custom can be traced from the early Middle Ages, when it was denounced by the Church as a heathen superstition, down to the first half of the nineteenth century, when it was still occasionally practised in various parts of Germany, England, Scotland, and Ireland. Among Slavonic peoples it appears to have lingered even longer. The usual occasion for performing the rite was an outbreak of plague or cattle-disease, for which the need-fire was believed to be an infallible remedy. The animals which were subjected to it included cows, pigs, horses, and sometimes geese. As a necessary preliminary to the kindling of the need-fire all other fires and lights in the neighbourhood were extinguished, so that not so much as a spark remained alight; for so long as even a night-light burned in a house, it was imagined that the need-fire could not kindle. Sometimes it was deemed enough to put out all the fires in the village; but sometimes the extinction extended to neighbouring villages or to a whole parish. In some parts of the Highlands of Scotland the rule was that all householders who dwelt within the two nearest running streams should put out their lights and fires on the day appointed. Usually the need-fire was made in the open air, but in some parts of Serbia it was kindled in a dark room; sometimes the place was a cross-way or a hollow in a road. In the Highlands of Scotland the proper places for performing the rite seem to have been knolls or small islands in rivers. The regular method of producing the need-fire was by the friction of two pieces of wood; it might not be struck by flint and steel. Very exceptionally among some South Slavs we read of a practice of kindling a need-fire by striking a piece of iron on an anvil. Where the wood to be employed is specified, it is generally said to be oak; but on the Lower Rhine the fire was kindled by the friction of oak-wood or fir-wood. In Slavonic countries we hear of poplar, pear, and cornel wood being used for the purpose. Often the material is simply described as two pieces of dry wood. Sometimes nine different kinds of wood were deemed necessary, but rather perhaps to be burned in the bonfire than to be rubbed together for the production of the need-fire. The particular mode of kindling the need-fire varied in different districts; a very common one was this. Two poles were driven into the ground about a foot and a half from each other. Each pole had in the side facing the other a socket into which a smooth cross-piece or roller was fitted. The sockets were stuffed with linen, and the two ends of the roller were rammed tightly into the sockets. To make it more inflammable the roller was often coated with tar. A rope was then wound round the roller, and the free ends at both sides were gripped by two or more persons, who by pulling the rope to and fro caused the roller to revolve rapidly, till through the friction the linen in the sockets took fire. The sparks were immediately caught in tow or oakum and waved about in a circle until they burst into a bright glow, when straw was applied to it, and the blazing straw used to kindle the fuel that had been stacked to make the bonfire. Often a wheel, sometimes a cart-wheel or even a spinning-wheel, formed part of the mechanism; in Aberdeenshire it was called "the muckle wheel"; in the island of Mull the wheel was turned from east to west over nine spindles of oak-wood. Sometimes we are merely told that two wooden planks were rubbed together. Sometimes it was prescribed that the cart-wheel used for fire-making and the axle on which it turned should both be new. Similarly it was said that the rope which turned the roller should be new; if possible it should be woven of strands taken from a gallows rope with which people had been hanged, but this was a counsel of perfection rather than a strict necessity.

Various rules were also laid down as to the kind of persons who might or should make the need-fire. Sometimes it was said that the two persons who pulled the rope which twirled the roller should always be brothers or at least bear the same baptismal name; sometimes it was deemed sufficient if they were both chaste young men. In some villages of Brunswick people thought that if everybody who lent a hand in kindling the need-fire did not bear the same Christian name, they would labour in vain. In Silesia the three employed to produce the need-fire used to be felled by a pair of twin brothers. In the western islands of Scotland the fire was kindled by eighty-one married men, who rubbed two great planks against each other, working in relays of nine; in North Uist the nine times nine who made the fire were all first-begotten sons, but we are not told whether they were married or single. Among the Serbians the need-fire is sometimes kindled by a boy and girl between eleven and fourteen years of age, who work stark naked in a dark room; sometimes it is made by an old man and an old woman also in the dark. In Bulgaria, too, the makers of need-fire strip themselves of their clothes; in Caithness they divested themselves of all kinds of metal. If after long rubbing of the wood no fire was elicited they concluded that some fire must still be burning in the village; so a strict search was made from house to house, any fire that might be found was put out, and the negligent householder punished or upbraided; indeed a heavy fine might be inflicted on him.

When the need-fire was at last kindled, the bonfire was lit from it, and as soon as the blaze had somewhat died down, the sick animals were driven over the glowing embers, sometimes in a regular order of precedence, first the pigs, next the cows, and last of all the horses. Sometimes they were driven twice or thrice through the smoke and flames, so that occasionally some of them were scorched to death. As soon as all the beasts were through, the young folk would rush wildly at the ashes and cinders, sprinkling and blackening each other with them; those who were most blackened would march in triumph behind the cattle into the village and would not wash themselves for a long time. From the bonfire people carried live embers home and used them to rekindle the fires in their houses. These brands, after being extinguished in water, they sometimes put in the mangers at which the cattle fed, and kept them there for a while. Ashes from the need-fire were also strewed on the fields to protect the crops against vermin; sometimes they were taken home to be employed as remedies in sickness, being sprinkled on the ailing part or mixed in water and drunk by the patient. In the western islands of Scotland and on the adjoining mainland, as soon as the fire on the domestic hearth had been rekindled from the need-fire, a pot full of water was set on it, and the water thus heated was afterwards sprinkled upon the people infected with the plague or upon the cattle that were tainted by the murrain. Special virtue was attributed to the smoke of the bonfire; in Sweden fruit-trees and nets were fumigated with it, in order that the trees might bear fruit and the nets catch fish. In the Highlands of Scotland the need-fire was accounted a sovereign remedy for witchcraft. In the island of Mull, when the fire was kindled as a cure for the murrain, we hear of the rite being accompanied by the sacrifice of a sick heifer, which was cut in pieces and burnt Slavonian and Bulgarian peasants conceive cattle-plague as a foul fiend or vampyre which can be kept at bay by interposing a barrier of fire between it and the herds. A similar conception may perhaps have originally everywhere underlain the use of the need-fire as a remedy for the murrain. It appears that in some parts of Germany the people did not wait for an outbreak of cattle-plague, but, taking time by the forelock, kindled a need-fire annually to prevent the calamity. Similarly in Poland the peasants are said to kindle fires in the village streets every year on St. Rochus's day and to drive the cattle thrice through them in order to protect the beasts against the murrain. We have seen that in the Hebrides the cattle were in like manner driven annually round the Beltane fires for the same purpose. In some cantons of Switzerland children still kindle a need-fire by the friction of wood for the sake of dispelling a mist.

ON THE FIRE-FESTIVALS IN GENERAL

The foregoing survey of the popular fire-festivals of Europe suggests some general observations. In the first place we can hardly help being struck by the resemblance which the ceremonies bear to each other, at whatever time of the year and in whatever part of Europe they are celebrated. The custom of kindling great bonfires, leaping over them, and driving cattle through or round them would seem to have been practically universal throughout Europe, and the same may be said of the processions or races with blazing torches round fields, orchards, pastures, or cattle-stalls. Less widespread are the customs of hurling lighted discs into the air and trundling a burning wheel downhill. The ceremonial of the Yule log is distinguished from that of the other fire-festivals by the privacy and domesticity which characterise it; but this distinction may well be due simply to the rough weather of midwinter, which is apt not only to render a public assembly in the open air disagreeable, but also at any moment to defeat the object of the assembly by extinguishing the all-important fire under a downpour of rain or a fall of snow. Apart from these local or seasonal differences, the general resemblance between the fire-festivals at all times of the year and in all places is tolerably close. And as the ceremonies themselves resemble each other, so do the benefits which the people expect to reap from them. Whether applied in the form of bonfires blazing at fixed points, or of torches carried about from place to place, or of embers and ashes taken from the smouldering heap of fuel, the fire is believed to promote the growth of the crops and the welfare of man and beast, either positively by stimulating them, or negatively by averting the dangers and calamities which threaten them from such causes as thunder and lightning, conflagration, blight, mildew, vermin, sterility, disease, and not least of all witchcraft.

But we naturally ask, How did it come about that benefits so great and manifold were supposed to be attained by means so simple? In what way did people imagine that they could procure so many goods or avoid so many ills by the application of fire and smoke, of embers and ashes? Two different explanations of the fire-festivals have been given by modern enquirers. On the one hand it has been held that they are sun-charms or magical ceremonies intended, on the principle of Imitative magic, to ensure a needful supply of sunshine for men, animals, and plants by kindling fires which mimic on earth the great source of light and heat in the sky. This was the view of Wilhelm Mannhardt. It may be called the solar theory. On the other hand it has been maintained that the ceremonial fires have no necessary reference to the sun but are simply purificatory in intention, being designed to burn up and destroy all harmful influences, whether these are conceived in a personal form as witches, demons, and monsters, or in an impersonal form as a sort of pervading taint or corruption of the air. This is the view of Dr. Edward Westermarck and apparently of Professor Eugen Mogk. It may be called the purificatory theory. Obviously the two theories postulate two very different conceptions of the fire which plays the principal part in the rites. On the one view, the fire, like sunshine in our latitude, is a genial creative power which fosters the growth of plants and the development of all that makes for health and happiness; on the other view, the fire is a fierce destructive power which blasts and consumes all the noxious elements, whether spiritual or material, that menace the life of men, of animals, and of plants. According to the one theory the fire is a stimulant, according to the other it is a disinfectant; on the one view its virtue is positive, on the other it is negative.

Yet the two explanations, different as they are in the character which they attribute to the fire, are perhaps not wholly irreconcilable. If we assume that the fires kindled at these festivals were primarily intended to imitate the sun's light and heat, may we not regard the purificatory and disinfecting qualities, which popular opinion certainly appears to have ascribed to them, as attributes derived directly from the purificatory and disinfecting qualities of sunshine? In this way we might conclude that, while the limitation of sunshine in these ceremonies was primary and original, the purification attributed to them was secondary and derivative. Such a conclusion, occupying an intermediate position between the two opposing theories and recognising an element of truth in both of them, was adopted by me in earlier editions of this work; but in the meantime Dr. Westermarck has argued powerfully in favour of the purificatory theory alone, and I am bound to say that his arguments carry great weight, and that on a fuller review of the facts the balance of evidence seems to me to incline decidedly in his favour. However, the case is not so clear as to justify us in dismissing the solar theory without discussion, and accordingly I propose to adduce the considerations which tell for it before proceeding to notice those which tell against it. A theory which had the support of so learned and sagacious an investigator as W. Mannhardt is entitled to a respectful hearing.

THE SOLAR THEORY OF THE FIRE-FESTIVALS

In an earlier part of this work we saw that savages resort to charms for making sunshine, and it would be no wonder if primitive man in Europe did the same. Indeed, when we consider the cold and cloudy climate of Europe during a great part of the year, we shall find it natural that sun-charms should have played a much more prominent part among the superstitious practices of European peoples than among those of savages who live nearer the equator and who consequently are apt to get in the course of nature more sunshine than they want. This view of the festivals may be supported by various arguments drawn partly from their dates, partly from the nature of the rites, and partly from the influence which they are believed to exert upon the weather and on vegetation.

First, in regard to the dates of the festivals it can be no mere accident that two of the most important and widely spread of the festivals are timed to coincide more or less exactly with the summer and winter solstices, that is, with the two turning-points in the sun's apparent course in the sky when he reaches respectively his highest and his lowest elevation at noon. Indeed with respect to the midwinter celebration of Christmas we are not left to conjecture; we know from the express testimony of the ancients that it was instituted by the church to supersede an old heathen festival of the birth of the sun, which was apparently conceived to be born again on the shortest day of the year, after which his light and heat were seen to grow till they attained their full maturity at midsummer. Therefore it is no very far-fetched conjecture to suppose that the Yule log, which figures so prominently in the popular celebration of Christmas, was originally designed to help the labouring sun of midwinter to rekindle his seemingly expiring light.

Not only the date of some of the festivals but the manner of their celebration suggests a conscious imitation of the sun. The custom of rolling a burning wheel down a hill, which is often observed at these ceremonies, might well pass for an imitation of the sun's course in the sky, and the imitation would be especially appropriate on Midsummer Day when the sun's annual declension begins. Indeed the custom has been thus interpreted by some of those who have recorded it. Not less graphic, it may be said, is the mimicry of his apparent revolution by swinging a burning tar-barrel round a pole. Again, the common practice of throwing fiery discs, sometimes expressly said to be shaped like suns, into the air at the festivals may well be a piece of imitative magic. In these, as in so many cases, the magic force may be supposed to take effect through mimicry or sympathy: by imitating the desired result you actually produce it: by counterfeiting the sun's progress through the heavens you really help the luminary to pursue his celestial journey with punctuality and despatch. The name "fire of heaven," by which the midsummer fire is sometimes popularly known, clearly implies a consciousness of a connexion between the earthly and the heavenly flame.

Again, the manner in which the fire appears to have been originally kindled on these occasions has been alleged in support of the view that it was intended to be a mock-sun. As some scholars have perceived, it is highly probable that at the periodic festivals in former times fire was universally obtained by the friction of two pieces of wood. It is still so procured in some places both at the Easter and the Midsummer festivals, and it is expressly said to have been formerly so procured at the Beltane celebration both in Scotland and Wales. But what makes it nearly certain that this was once the invariable mode of kindling the fire at these periodic festivals is the analogy of the need-fire, which has almost always been produced by the friction of wood, and sometimes by the revolution of a wheel. It is a plausible conjecture that the wheel employed for this purpose represents the sun, and if the fires at the regularly recurring celebrations were formerly produced in the same way, it might be regarded as a confirmation of the view that they were originally sun-charms. In point of fact there is, as Kuhn has indicated, some evidence to show that the midsummer fire was originally thus produced. We have seen that many Hungarian swine-herds make fire on Midsummer Eve by rotating a wheel round a wooden axle wrapt in hemp, and that they drive their pigs through the fire thus made. At Obermedlingen, in Swabia, the "fire of heaven," as it was called, was made on St. Vitus's Day (the fifteenth of June) by igniting a cart-wheel, which, smeared with pitch and plaited with straw, was fastened on a pole twelve feet high, the top of the pole being inserted in the nave of the wheel. This fire was made on the summit of a mountain, and as the flame ascended, the people uttered a set form of words, with eyes and arms directed heavenward. Here the fixing of a wheel on a pole and igniting it suggests that originally the fire was produced, as in the case of the need-fire, by the revolution of a wheel. The day on which the ceremony takes place (the fifteenth of June) is near midsummer; and we have seen that in Masuren fire is, or used to be, actually made on Midsummer Day by turning a wheel rapidly about an oaken pole, though it is not said that the new fire so obtained is used to light a bonfire. However, we must bear in mind that in all such cases the use of a wheel may be merely a mechanical device to facilitate the operation of fire-making by increasing the friction; it need not have any symbolical significance.

Further, the influence which these fires, whether periodic or occasional, are supposed to exert on the weather and vegetation may be cited in support of the view that they are sun-charms, since the effects ascribed to them resemble those of sunshine. Thus, the French belief that in a rainy June the lighting of the midsummer bonfires will cause the rain to cease appears to assume that they can disperse the dark clouds and make the sun break out in radiant glory, drying the wet earth and dripping trees. Similarly the use of the need-fire by Swiss children on foggy days for the purpose of clearing away the mist may very naturally be interpreted as a sun-charm. In the Vosges Mountains the people believe that the midsummer fires help to preserve the fruits of the earth and ensure good crops. In Sweden the warmth or cold of the coming season is inferred from the direction in which the flames of the May Day bonfire are blown; if they blow to the south, it will be warm, if to the north, cold. No doubt at present the direction of the flames is regarded merely as an augury of the weather, not as a mode of influencing it. But we may be pretty sure that this is one of the cases in which magic has dwindled into divination. So in the Eifel Mountains, when the smoke blows towards the corn-fields, this is an omen that the harvest will be abundant. But the older view may have been not merely that the smoke and flames prognosticated, but that they actually produced an abundant harvest, the heat of the flames acting like sunshine on the corn. Perhaps it was with this view that people in the Isle of Man lit fires to windward of their fields in order that the smoke might blow over them. So in South Africa, about the month of April, the Matabeles light huge fires to the windward of their gardens, "their idea being that the smoke, by passing over the crops, will assist the ripening of them." Among the Zulus also "medicine is burned on a fire placed to windward of the garden, the fumigation which the plants in consequence receive being held to improve the crop." Again, the idea of our European peasants that the corn will grow well as far as the blaze of the bonfire is visible, may be interpreted as a remnant of the belief in the quickening and fertilising power of the bonfires. The same belief, it may be argued, reappears in the notion that embers taken from the bonfires and inserted in the fields will promote the growth of the crops, and it may be thought to underlie the customs of sowing flax-seed in the direction in which the flames blow, of mixing the ashes of the bonfire with the seed-corn at sowing, of scattering the ashes by themselves over the field to fertilise it, and of incorporating a piece of the Yule log in the plough to make the seeds thrive. The opinion that the flax or hemp will grow as high as the flames rise or the people leap over them belongs clearly to the same class of ideas. Again, at Konz, on the banks of the Moselle, if the blazing wheel which was trundled down the hillside reached the river without being extinguished, this was hailed as a proof that the vintage would be abundant. So firmly was this belief held that the successful performance of the ceremony entitled the villagers to levy a tax upon the owners of the neighbouring vineyards. Here the unextinguished wheel might be taken to represent an unclouded sun, which in turn would portend an abundant vintage. So the waggon-load of white wine which the villagers received from the vineyards round about might pass for a payment for the sunshine which they had procured for the grapes. Similarly in the Vale of Glamorgan a blazing wheel used to be trundled downhill on Midsummer Day, and if the fire were extinguished before the wheel reached the foot of the hill, the people expected a bad harvest; whereas if the wheel kept alight all the way down and continued to blaze for a long time, the farmers looked forward to heavy crops that summer. Here, again, it is natural to suppose that the rustic mind traced a direct connexion between the fire of the wheel and the fire of the sun, on which the crops are dependent.

But in popular belief the quickening and fertilising influence of the bonfires is not limited to the vegetable world; it extends also to animals. This plainly appears from the Irish custom of driving barren cattle through the midsummer fires, from the French belief that the Yule log steeped in water helps cows to calve, from the French and Serbian notion that there will be as many chickens, calves, lambs, and kids as there are sparks struck out of the Yule log, from the French custom of putting the ashes of the bonfires in the fowls' nests to make the hens lay eggs, and from the German practice of mixing the ashes of the bonfires with the drink of cattle in order to make the animals thrive. Further, there are clear indications that even human fecundity is supposed to be promoted by the genial heat of the fires. In Morocco the people think that childless couples can obtain offspring by leaping over the midsummer bonfire. It is an Irish belief that a girl who jumps thrice over the midsummer bonfire will soon marry and become the mother of many children; in Flanders women leap over the midsummer fires to ensure an easy delivery; in various parts of France they think that if a girl dances round nine fires she will be sure to marry within the year; and in Bohemia they fancy that she will do so if she merely sees nine of the bonfires. On the other hand, in Lechrain people say that if a young man and woman, leaping over the midsummer fire together, escape unsmirched, the young woman will not become a mother within twelve months; the flames have not touched and fertilised her. In parts of Switzerland and France the lighting of the Yule log is accompanied by a prayer that the women may bear children, the she-goats bring forth kids, and the ewes drop lambs. The rule observed in some places that the bonfires should be kindled by the person who was last married seems to belong to the same class of ideas, whether it be that such a person is supposed to receive from, or to impart to, the fire a generative and fertilising influence. The common practice of lovers leaping over the fires hand in hand may very well have originated in a notion that thereby their marriage would be blessed with offspring; and the like motive would explain the custom which obliges couples married within the year to dance to the light of torches. And the scenes of profligacy which appear to have marked the midsummer celebration among the Esthonians, as they once marked the celebration of May Day among ourselves, may have sprung, not from the mere licence of holiday-makers, but from a crude notion that such orgies were justified, if not required, by some mysterious bond which linked the life of man to the courses of the heavens at this turning-point of the year.

At the festivals which we are considering the custom of kindling bonfires is commonly associated with a custom of carrying lighted torches about the fields, the orchards, the pastures, the flocks and the herds; and we can hardly doubt that the two customs are only two different ways of attaining the same object, namely, the benefits which are believed to flow from the fire, whether it be stationary or portable. Accordingly if we accept the solar theory of the bonfires, we seem bound to apply it also to the torches; we must suppose that the practice of marching or running with blazing torches about the country is simply a means of diffusing far and wide the genial influence of the sunshine of which these flickering flames are a feeble imitation. In favor of this view it may be said that sometimes the torches are carried about the fields for the express purpose of fertilising them, and with the same intention live coals from the bonfires are sometimes placed in the fields to prevent blight. On the eve of Twelfth Day in Normandy men, women, and children run wildly through the fields and orchards with lighted torches, which they wave about the branches and dash against the trunks of the fruit-trees for the sake of burning the moss and driving away the moles and field-mice. "They believe that the ceremony fulfills the double object of exorcising the vermin whose multiplication would be a real calamity, and of imparting fecundity to the trees, the fields, and even the cattle"; and they imagine that the more the ceremony is prolonged, the greater will be the crop of fruit next autumn. In Bohemia they say that the corn will grow as high as they fling the blazing besoms into the air. Nor are such notions confined to Europe. In Corea, a few days before the New Year festival, the eunuchs of the palace swing burning torches, chanting invocations the while, and this is supposed to ensure bountiful crops for the next season. The custom of trundling a burning wheel over the fields, which used to be observed in Poitou for the express purpose of fertilising them, may be thought to embody the same idea in a still more graphic form; since in this way the mock-sun itself, not merely its light and heat represented by torches, is made actually to pass over the ground which is to receive its quickening and kindly influence. Once more, the custom of carrying lighted brands round cattle is plainly equivalent to driving the animals through the bonfire; and if the bonfire is a sun-charm, the torches must be so also.

THE PURIFICATORY THEORY OF THE FIRE-FESTIVALS

Thus far we have considered what may be said for the theory that at the European fire-festivals the fire is kindled as a charm to ensure an abundant supply of sunshine for man and beast, for corn and fruits. It remains to consider what may be said against this theory and in favour of the view that in these rites fire is employed not as a creative but as a cleansing agent, which purifies men, animals, and plants by burning up and consuming the noxious elements, whether material or spiritual, which menace all living things with disease and death.

First, then, it is to be observed that the people who practise the fire-customs appear never to allege the solar theory in explanation of them, while on the contrary they do frequently and emphatically put forward the purificatory theory. This is a strong argument in favour of the purificatory and against the solar theory; for the popular explanation of a popular custom is never to be rejected except for grave cause. And in the present case there seems to be no adequate reason for rejecting it. The conception of fire as a destructive agent, which can be turned to account for the consumption of evil things, is so simple and obvious that it could hardly escape the minds even of the rude peasantry with whom these festivals originated. On the other hand the conception of fire as an emanation of the sun, or at all events as linked to it by a bond of physical sympathy, is far less simple and obvious; and though the use of fire as a charm to produce sunshine appears to be undeniable, nevertheless in attempting to explain popular customs we should never have recourse to a more recondite idea when a simpler one lies to hand and is supported by the explicit testimony of the people themselves. Now in the case of the fire-festivals the destructive aspect of fire is one upon which the people dwell again and again; and it is highly significant that the great evil against which the fire is directed appears to be witchcraft. Again and again we are told that the fires are intended to burn or repel the witches; and the intention is sometimes graphically expressed by burning an effigy of a witch in the fire. Hence, when we remember the great hold which the dread of witchcraft has had on the popular European mind in all ages, we may suspect that the primary intention of all these fire-festivals was simply to destroy or at all events get rid of the witches, who were regarded as the causes of nearly all the misfortunes and calamities that befall men, their cattle, and their crops.

This suspicion is confirmed when we examine the evils for which the bonfires and torches were supposed to provide a remedy. Foremost, perhaps, among these evils we may reckon the diseases of cattle; and of all the ills that witches are believed to work there is probably none which is so constantly insisted on as the harm they do to the herds, particularly by stealing the milk from the cows. Now it is significant that the need-fire, which may perhaps be regarded as the parent of the periodic fire-festivals, is kindled above all as a remedy for a murrain or other disease of cattle; and the circumstance suggests, what on general grounds seems probable, that the custom of kindling the need-fire goes back to a time when the ancestors of the European peoples subsisted chiefly on the products of their herds, and when agriculture as yet played a subordinate part in their lives. Witches and wolves are the two great foes still dreaded by the herdsman in many parts of Europe; and we need not wonder that he should resort to fire as a powerful means of banning them both. Among Slavonic peoples it appears that the foes whom the need-fire is designed to combat are not so much living witches as vampyres and other evil spirits, and the ceremony aims rather at repelling these baleful beings than at actually consuming them in the flames. But for our present purpose these distinctions are immaterial. The important thing to observe is that among the Slavs the need-fire, which is probably the original of all the ceremonial fires now under consideration, is not a sun-charm, but clearly and unmistakably nothing but a means of protecting man and beast against the attacks of maleficent creatures, whom the peasant thinks to burn or scare by the heat of the fire, just as he might burn or scare wild animals.

Again, the bonfires are often supposed to protect the fields against hail and the homestead against thunder and lightning. But both hail and thunderstorms are frequently thought to be caused by witches; hence the fire which bans the witches necessarily serves at the same time as a talisman against hail, thunder, and lightning. Further, brands taken from the bonfires are commonly kept in the houses to guard them against conflagration; and though this may perhaps be done on the principle of homoeopathic magic, one fire being thought to act as a preventive of another, it is also possible that the intention may be to keep witch-incendiaries at bay. Again, people leap over the bonfires as a preventive of colic, and look at the flames steadily in order to preserve their eyes in good health; and both colic and sore eyes are in Germany, and probably elsewhere, set down to the machinations of witches. Once more, to leap over the midsummer fires or to circumambulate them is thought to prevent a person from feeling pains in his back at reaping; and in Germany such pains are called "witch-shots" and ascribed to witchcraft.

But if the bonfires and torches of the fire-festivals are to be regarded primarily as weapons directed against witches and wizards, it becomes probable that the same explanation applies not only to the flaming discs which are hurled into the air, but also to the burning wheels which are rolled down hill on these occasions; discs and wheels, we may suppose, are alike intended to burn the witches who hover invisible in the air or haunt unseen the fields, the orchards, and the vineyards on the hillside. Certainly witches are constantly thought to ride through the air on broomsticks or other equally convenient vehicles; and if they do so, how can you get at them so effectually as by hurling lighted missiles, whether discs, torches, or besoms, after them as they flit past overhead in the gloom? The South Slavonian peasant believes that witches ride in the dark hail-clouds; so he shoots at the clouds to bring down the hags, while he curses them, saying, "Curse, curse Herodias, thy mother is a heathen, damned of God and fettered through the Redeemer's blood." Also he brings out a pot of glowing charcoal on which he has thrown holy oil, laurel leaves, and wormwood to make a smoke. The fumes are supposed to ascend to the clouds and stupefy the witches, so that they tumble down to earth. And in order that they may not fall soft, but may hurt themselves very much, the yokel hastily brings out a chair and tilts it bottom up so that the witch in falling may break her legs on the legs of the chair. Worse than that, he cruelly lays scythes, bill-hooks, and other formidable weapons edge upwards so as to cut and mangle the poor wretches when they drop plump upon them from the clouds.

On this view the fertility supposed to follow the application of fire in the form of bonfires, torches, discs, rolling wheels, and so forth, is not conceived as resulting directly from an increase of solar heat which the fire has magically generated; it is merely an indirect result obtained by freeing the reproductive powers of plants and animals from the fatal obstruction of witchcraft. And what is true of the reproduction of plants and animals may hold good also of the fertility of the human sexes. The bonfires are supposed to promote marriage and to procure offspring for childless couples. This happy effect need not flow directly from any quickening or fertilizing energy in the fire; it may follow indirectly from the power of the fire to remove those obstacles which the spells of witches and wizards notoriously present to the union of man and wife.

On the whole, then, the theory of the purificatory virtue of the ceremonial fires appears more probable and more in accordance with the evidence than the opposing theory of their connexion with the sun.

'Spoiling' and 'Healing'

By Linda Ivanits

Some accounts specify that sorcerers and witches were the most dangerous of the unclean dead, and, indeed, popular opinion attributed great damage to them. They supposedly ate the flesh of living people, caused illnesses, plagues, and epidemics, and brought drought and other harm to grain fields.[107] Many accounts of dead sorcerers and witches concern damage to crops. Russian newspapers from the middle and end of the nineteenth century report a number of instances of digging up the unclean dead, including sorcerers, during droughts. These reports usually note that peasants poured water on the deceased to bring an end to the dry period and make the rain come.[108] From Orel Province comes an ethnographic account of a sorcerer whose daughter, on his instructions, threw a few stalks of freshly harvested rye into his grave during the burial ceremony. A severe thunderstorm with hail immediately destroyed the village's fields, and for years afterward the same thing occurred on the anniversary of his funeral. Finally the peasants resolved to dig up the grave of the sorcerer and remove the dried-up grain.[109]

Everywhere the prospect of meeting a dead sorcerer inspired terror (Narrative 86). An eyewitness from Tula Province told how as a child she and her sister-in-law encountered one when they were forced to spend a night in a neighboring village while waiting their turn at the mill. The narrator's sister-in-law convinced her that a dead man, who reputedly visited his family every night, surely would not come while guests were in the house. The sorcerer, though, made his usual nocturnal visit, and while making himself comfortable near the stove, happened to sit down on the sister-in-law's legs. As a consequence, she became ill and died within a year.[110]

It seems clear that for the broad masses of Russian peasants, dead sorcerers and witches functioned as vampires: they were perceived as "living" corpses that rose from the grave to inflict harm.[111] Russian sources rarely mention, however, that dead sorcerers gained sustenance by sucking the blood of the living, a traditional vampiric activity elsewhere in Eastern Europe; and in Russia, unlike the Balkans, the categories of vampire and werewolf did not merge.[112] The term "vampire" (*upyr*), which occurred in ancient texts, was largely unknown in Great Russia from about the fifteenth century.[113]

As Felix Oinas has demonstrated, this is partly because in the Russian North and a few other places peasants tended to use the term "heretic" (*eretik/eretitsa; eretnik/eretnitsa*) for a dead sorcerer or witch who was still active.[114] Sometimes "heretic" was used in a slightly different sense: in Olonets Region *erestun* designated a dying person who was revived when a sorcerer entered his body; in parts of Tambov Province *eretitsa* designated a type of dead witch who walked around as an ugly old woman in rags, slept in the graves of the unclean dead, and had the power to inflict death by her glance alone,[115] In addition, the term "heretic" was sometimes used for a living sorcerer or witch.[116]

Lilith, Harpies, and *Sirin*

The Epic of Gilgamesh: Prologue

Translated by Samuel N. Kramer

After heaven and earth had been separated
    and mankind had been created,
after Anucircum, Enlil and Ereskigal had taken posession
    of heaven, earth and the underworld;
after Enki had set sail for the underworld
    and the sea ebbed and flowed in honor of its lord;
on this day, a huluppu tree
    which had been planted on the banks of the Euphrates
    and nourished by its waters
was uprooted by the south wind
    and carried away by the Euphrates.
A goddess who was wandering among the banks
    siezed the swaying tree
And—at the behest of Anu and Enlil—
    brought it to Inanna's gardea in Urok.
Inanna tended the tree carefully and lovingly
    she hoped to have a throne and a bed
    made for herself from its wood.
After ten years, the tree had matured.
But in the meantime, she found to her dismay
    that her hopes could not be fulfilled.
because during that time
    a dragon had built its nest at the foot of the tree
    the Zu-bird was raising its young in the crown,
    and the demon Lilith had built her house in the middle.
But Gilgamesh, who had heard of Inanna's plight,
    came to her rescue.

He took his heavy shield
    killed the dragon with his heavy bronze axe,
    which weighed seven talents and seven minas.
Then the Zu-bird flew into the mountains
    with its young,
while Lilith, petrified with fear,
    tore down her house and fled into the wilderness.

Lilith

By Rosemary Ellen Guiley

A winged, long-haired female demon of the night who vampirizes newborn children and seduces sleeping men—especially the newly married—in order to produce demon sons. She is accompanied by a horde of SUCCUBI demons, and she uses tens of thousands of names to disguise herself. Her powers are greatest during the waning MOON. In the late 17th century, she was described as a screech owl blind by day, who sucked the breasts or navels of young children, or the dugs of goats.

Lilith entered Jewish demonology from Babylonian and perhaps Sumerian sources, and then also was adopted into Christian and Islamic lore. In Islamic lore, she is the mother of the *djinn,* a type of demon.

Lilith originally was human. She was the first woman to have sexual relations with Adam, but left him when he refused to treat her as an equal. Adam complained to God, who sent three angels (in some Christian versions, three saints) to return her to Adam. She refused, and God began destroying 100 of her demon offspring every day. She retaliated by attacking women in childbirth and newborn infants.

Another version of her story says that she joined Adam after he and Eve were cast out of Paradise. The two produced demon sons who filled the world. Yet another story tells that Lilith became the bride of the angel Samael, who is equated with Satan.

Lilith can be warded off with magical amulets bearing the names of angels and local patron saints, and by saying one of her many names. Men who have nocturnal emissions have been seduced by Lilith during the night and must say incantations to prevent the offspring from becoming demons.

FURTHER READING:

Guiley, Rosemary Ellen. *The Encyclopedia of Witches and Witchcraft.* 2d ed. New York: Facts On File, 1999.

Tlahuelpuchi

By Rosemary Ellen Guiley

In the lore of rural Tlaxcala, Mexico, a vampire witch who can assume animal form, and who sucks the blood of infants, causing them to die. The *tlahuelpuchi* is not a demon, but a shape-shifting person with supernatural powers. It epitomizes everything that is horrible, evil, and hateful. It can be either male or female, but usually is female; the female is considered to be the more bloodthirsty and evil of the two. At least 100 legends exist about it. The *tlahuelpuchi* provides a supernatural explanation for sudden infant death syndrome, or crib death, and helps to alleviate guilt over the death.

Origins and Characteristics

According to lore, *tlahuelpuchis* are born into their fate; they cannot transmit or teach their powers to others. They are independent agents of evil, but will do the bidding of higher evil forces, such as the devil. For example, they will act as intermediaries (in animal form) in transactions involving selling of the soul to the devil and making pacts with the devil. *Tlahuelpuchis* are more powerful than *nahuales*, a trickster type of supernatural agent.

When a *tlahuelpuchi* is born, it cannot be distinguished from an ordinary infant. Differences do not emerge until puberty, at which point their supernatural powers such as shape-shifting suddenly manifest. For females, this often occurs with the onset of the menses. When the powers manifest, the *tlahuelpuchis* of both sexes begin to have a lifelong, uncontrollable urge to drink human blood, especially that of infants. This causes a great deal of unhappiness and shame to their families, who go to great lengths to cover up their secret in order to avoid being stigmatized and ostracized by the community.

Tlahuelpuchis cannot attack members of their own families, unless they reveal their secret. Although *tlahuelpuchis* cannot transmit their powers to others of their own volition, if they are killed, their powers go into the killer. Hence, family members are reluctant accomplices of sorts.

The *tlahuelpuchis* can shape-shift to numerous animal forms, among them turkey, donkey, dog, CAT, duck, buzzard, crow, ant, and flea. Their preferred forms are fowls, with turkey being the most favored of all. When shape-shifted, they are limited to the abilities of that particular creature, and cannot make it perform in magical ways—with one exception: they can make turkeys fly. When in animal form, they give off a luminescence or phosphorescence that is a telltale sign of their identity.

They prowl about at night—especially between the hours of midnight and four A.M.—but will operate during the day if their blood craving is extreme. *Tlahuelpuchis* are not out every night, but only when they experience their uncontrollable blood cravings, which ranges from one to four times a month. They are more active during rainy and cold weather.

Though they will drink the blood of any human, they overwhelmingly prefer the blood of infants between the ages of three and 10 months, because it is tastier and more invigorating. According to lore, the blood of younger infants is not so palatable to them. The *tlahuelpulchis* have a keen sense of smell and can detect the presence of infants inside a home; thus they identify their best targets.

They steal into a home as a mist, sometimes luminous, that seeps under doors and windowsills, or through keyholes, or they crawl in as an insect. Once inside, they shape-shift into a turkey or buzzard, and hypnotize the occupants into a deep sleep so that they can carry out their attacks.

Tlahuelpuchis can recognize one another in both their human and their shape-shifted forms. However, they do not bond together in any social structure, but remain mostly solitary. They are jealous and aggressive toward their own kind, and protect their territories. Poaching on another's territory may result in a fight (in human form) to the death. They do share a common pact not to harm one another's primary family. They also share news of outside danger with one another.

Bloodsucking Attacks and Remedies

Most *tlahuelpuchi* attacks are made on sleeping infants at night, followed by sleeping or resting infants during the day. The victims are not removed from the home. Occasionally, *tlahuelpuchis* will attack children and adults during the day, hypnotizing them to lure them away from their homes. The bodies are left in ravines and wooded areas.

The *tlahuelpuchi* prefers to suck the blood from the back of an infant's neck, but may take it from the sides of the neck or the cheeks. However, it cannot take blood from the chest or the lower body. Children may be attacked as well. The *tlahuelpuchi* rarely attacks firstborn infants, and even more rarely will attack two infants in a row in the same family.

The relatives of a victim may experience malaise—nausea or headaches—or disturbed sleep on the night of the attack. Sometimes family and neighbors say after the fact that they saw the witch flying through the air in the form of a luminosity or ball of fire, or sitting outside a window, or coming into a house. Almost anything unusual, such as the odd behavior of pets or animals, is considered evidence of the presence of a *tlahuelpuchi.*

The dead infants are discovered either in their cribs or on the floor or even out in the courtyard; doors usually are found ajar or open—a telltale sign that a *tlahuelpuchi* has struck. The bodies have bruises and purple and yellow spots; the faces and necks are purple, and sometimes the bodies have scratch marks. Occasionally there may be dried blood around the mouth. The *tlahuelpuchi* also sometimes leaves marks upon the victim's mother in the form of bruises on one breast, but never both breasts.

Neighbors must be notified immediately so that they can take steps to ward off more attacks on their own children. A victim's corpse must be cleaned immediately and placed in a simple wooden coffin on top of a table in the main room, with lighted candles at the head and feet. Underneath the table, an oblique cross of pinewood ashes is made; pinewood is believed to be especially powerful for warding off evil and for cleansing the environment tainted by a *tlahuelpuchi.* Neighbors handle these activities, for families cannot handle their own dead.

A *tezitlazc,* a helpful sorcerer and healer, is called in to perform ritual cleansings of the corpse, mother, and space where the death took place. A representative cleansing, witnessed by family and friends, is done in the following manner:

The coffin is removed from the table and the table is taken away from the pine cross. The body of the infant is placed on top of the cross, with the head resting on the intersection of the arms. An incense burner is placed at the foot of the cross. The *tezitlazc* takes the incense burner and walks around the cross three times clockwise and three times counterclockwise, reciting litanies in Nahuatl and invoking the protection of local saints. He places the incense burner back at the foot of the cross. He takes a bundle of herbs and roots, including capulin branches, ocoxoxhiti leaves, and century roots, and brushes the body of the infant from feet to head and hand to hand three times, invoking for the infant the protection of Our Lord, the Holy Virgin, and a local patron saint. The corpse is then returned to the coffin, and the table is placed back over the cross.

The mother is made to stand against a wall with her arms spread in the form of a cross. The *tezitlazc* brushes her with the same cleansing brush three times from feet to head and from hand to hand, but in complete silence. The mother bares her breasts, which the *tezitlazc* brushes with zoapatl leaves. She kisses the foot of the oblique cross. The *tezitlazc* cleanses the entire room where the infant died by brushing the floor, walls, ceilings, doors, and windows. He recites litanies and prayers in Nahuatl while he does so. He buries the cleansing brush in a hole that he previously dug outside the house while praying in Nahuatl and facing north.

The *tezitlazc* may also instruct the mother to rub her breasts on something touched by the *tlahuelpuchi,* such as the floor.

The *tezitlazc* is likely to be needed later as well, to help alleviate the ensuing symptoms of grieving and psychological stress, such as seizures, headaches, nausea and vomiting, depression, and excessive weeping. These also are blamed on the *tlahuelpuchi* as the secondary results of the attack.

Funeral rites for victims of *tlahuelpuchis* are conducted in complete silence, save for a commendation of the soul of the infant when a cross is planted at the foot of the tomb. The pinewood ashes of the oblique cross are buried. The dead infant is to be completely forgotten, as though he or she never existed. The tomb is not visited, nor are flowers placed upon it, nor is the infant remembered at the family altar on All Saints Day and All Souls Day.

Preventative measures against the *tlahuelpuchi* include the use of garlic, onions, metals, and even pieces of tortilla, which have a similar function as sand and seeds. Infants can be protected with silver medals, pins, an open pair of scissors near the crib, metal crosses, and mirrors.

Cases of *tlahuelpuchi* attacks have been recorded in modern times, with some being identified, tried, and executed. While almost every extended Tlaxacalan family suffers multiple bloodsuckings over the course of generations, the accusations of bloodsucking witchcraft that result in trial and execution historically have not been common, and have declined considerably since the late 19th and early 20th centuries. The last known execution of a *tlahuelpuchi*, a woman, occurred in 1973.

Other Forms of Attacks

In addition to sucking the blood of infants, *tlahuelpuchis* can exercise evil powers over adults who are their enemies or who have offended them in some way. They can hypnotize sleeping victims and make them go to high places and jump to their deaths. They can injure and kill domestic and farm animals, and can ruin crops. There are no ways to protect against the destruction of one's animals and crops. Adults can prevent *tlahuelpuchis* from taking control of them by several ways: wearing raw garlic in one's scapular or rubbing the scapular periodically with garlic; pinning undergarments with safety pins in the form of a cross; wearing a blessed cross or St. Christopher's medal; attaching a pin or needle to the inside of one's hat.

Killing Tlahuelpuchis

Tlahuelpuchis almost always are killed in their animal forms, for that is when they are most likely to be detected. Confrontation with one in its human form is rare. There are three principal ways to immobilize one, in the order of preference:

- take one's pants off, turn one leg inside out and throw the pants at the vampire

- knot three corners of a white handkerchief, wrap it around a stone, and throw it to the *tlahuelpuchi*
- take off one's hat, throw it on the ground, and drive a knife or machete through it

If any of these touch the *tlahuelpuchi* or fall within 10 meters, it will be immediately immobilized and can be clubbed or stoned to death. Directly touching a *tlahuelpuchi* is considered unclean. The body is retrieved by other *tlahuelpuchis* and returned to its home, where family members bury it in secret.

The vampire killers must be ritually cleansed with a brushing of capulin branches. Some people are particularly adept at killing *tlahuelpuchis* and acquire a good reputation for it.

If a *tlahuelpuchi* is killed in human form—by immobilization and clubbing or stoning—the corpse is symbolically killed again by the destruction of the sense organs: The eyes are torn out of their sockets, all the fingers are cut off, and the ears, nose, tongue, and lips are severed.

FURTHER READING

Nutini, Hugo G., and John M. Roberts. *Bloodsucking Witchcraft: An Epistemological Study of Anthropomorphic Supernaturalism in Rural Tlaxcala.* Tucson, Ariz.: University of Tucson Press, 1993.

Sirin

Translated by Thomas J. Garza

Sí - rin [from the Greek seiren , cf. sirena]—bird-woman.

In Russian liturgical verse, once coming down from heaven, she charms people with her song; in western European legends she is the incarnation of an evil spirit. It originates from the Greek sirens. In Slavic mythology, it is a miraculous bird, whose song repels sadness and longing; she appears only to happy people. Sirin is a heavenly bird, even whose name sounds like the name for heaven: Irij. However, she is in no way the bright Alkonost and Gamajun. Sirin is a dark bird, a dark force, messenger of the ruler of the underworld.

Sometimes the beautiful bird Sirin is found in the form of a real bird, without any human characteristics. An invisible mass, symbolizing Nature, covers her feathers. "Her wings were white with blue and red stripes, like a candy, her beak was a soft violet, sharp, blade-like, but her eyes were bright, green, the colors of young leaves, and wise and gracious."

The Werewolf vs. the Vampire

Lycanthropy Among the Ancients

By Sabine Baring-Gould

Definition of Lycanthropy—Marcellus Sidetes—Virgil—Herodotus—Ovid— Pliny—Agriopas—Story from Petronius—Arcadian Legends—Explanation offered.

What is lycanthropy? The change of man or woman into the form of a wolf, either through magical means, so as to enable him or her to gratify the taste for human flesh, or through judgment of the gods in punishment for some great offence.

This is the popular definition. Truly it consists in a form of madness, such as may be found in most asylums.

Among the ancients this kind of insanity went by the names of Lycanthropy, Kuanthropy, or Boanthropy, because those afflicted with it believed themselves to be turned into wolves, dogs, or cows. But in the North of Europe, as we shall see, the shape of a bear, and in Africa that of a hyæna, were often selected in preference. A mere matter of taste! According to Marcellus Sidetes, of whose poem πεςί λυκανθδωπου a fragment exists, men are attacked with this madness chiefly in the beginning of the year, and become most furious in February; retiring for the night to lone cemeteries, and living precisely in the manner of dogs and wolves.

Virgil writes in his eighth Eclogue:—

Has herbas, atque hæc Ponto mihi lecta venena
Ipse dedit Mœris; nascuntur plurima Ponto.
His ego sæpe lupum fieri, et se conducere sylvis
Mœrim, sæpe animas imis excire sepulchris,
Atque satas alio vidi traducere messes.

And Herodotus:—"It seems that the Neuri are sorcerers, if one is to believe the Scythians and the Greeks established in Scythia; for each Neurian changes himself, once in the year, into the form of a wolf, and he continues in that form for several days, after which he resumes his former shape."—(Lib. iv. c. 105.)

See also Pomponius Mela (lib. ii. c. 1): "There is a fixed time for each Neurian, at which they change, if they like, into wolves, and back again into their former condition."

But the most remarkable story among the ancients is that related by Ovid in his "Metamorphoses," of Lycaon, king of Arcadia, who, entertaining Jupiter one day, set before him a hash of human flesh, to prove his omniscience, whereupon the god transferred him into a wolf:—[1]

> In vain lie attempted to speak; from that very instant
> His jaws were bespluttered with foam, and only he thirsted
> For blood, as he raged amongst flocks and panted for slaughter.
> His vesture was changed into hair, his limbs became crooked;
> A wolf,—he retains yet large trace of his ancient expression,
> Hoary he is as afore, his countenance rabid,
> His eyes glitter savagely still, the picture of fury.

Pliny relates from Evanthes, that on the festival of Jupiter Lycæus, one of the family of Antæus was selected by lot, and conducted to the brink of the Arcadian lake. He then hung his clothes on a tree and plunged into the water, whereupon he was transformed into a wolf. Nine years after, if he had not tasted human flesh, he was at liberty to swim back and resume his former shape, which had in the meantime become aged, as though he had worn it for nine years.

Agriopas relates, that Demænetus, having assisted at an Arcadian human sacrifice to Jupiter Lycæus, ate of the fleshy and was at once transformed into a wolf, in which shape he prowled about for ten years, after which he recovered his human form, and took part in the Olympic games.

The following story is from Petronius:—

"My master had gone to Capua to sell some old clothes. I seized the opportunity, and persuaded our guest to bear me company about five miles out of town; for he was a soldier, and as bold as death. We set out about cockcrow, and the moon shone bright, as day, when, coming among some monuments, my man began to converse with the stars, whilst I jogged along singing and counting them. Presently I looked back after him, and saw him strip and lay his clothes by the side of the road. My heart was in my mouth in an instant, I stood like a corpse; when, in a crack, he was turned into a wolf. Don't think I'm joking: I would not tell you a lie for the finest fortune in the world.

---

1   * OVID, Met. i. 237; Pausanias, viii. 2, § 1; Tzetze ad Lycoph.
481; Eratosth. Catas. i. 8.

"But to continue: after he was turned into a wolf, he set up a howl and made straight for the woods. At first I did not know whether I was on my head or my heels; but at last going to take up his clothes, I found them turned into stone. The sweat streamed from me, and I never expected to get over it. Melissa began to wonder why I walked so late. 'Had you come a little sooner,' she said, 'you might at least have lent us a hand; for a wolf broke into the farm and has butchered all our cattle; but though he got off, It was no laughing matter for him, for a servant of ours ran him through with a pike' Hearing this I could not close an eye; but as soon as it was daylight, I ran home like a pedlar that has been eased of his pack. Coming to the place where the clothes had been turned into stone, I saw nothing but a pool of blood; and when I got home, I found my soldier lying in bed, like an ox in a stall, and a surgeon dressing his neck. I saw at once that he was a fellow who could change his skin (*versipellis*), and never after could I eat bread with him, no, not if you would have killed me. Those who would have taken a different view of the case are welcome to their opinion; if I tell you a lie, may your genii confound me !"

As everyone knows, Jupiter changed himself into a bull; Hecuba became a bitch; Actæon a stag; the comrades of Ulysses were transformed into swine; and the daughters of Prœtus fled through the fields believing themselves to be cows, and would not allow any one to come near them, lest they should be caught and yoked.

S. Augustine declared, in his *De Civitate Dei*, that he knew an old woman who was said to turn men into asses by her enchantments.

Apuleius has left us his charming romance of the *Golden Ass*, in which the hero, through injudicious use of a magical salve, is transformed into that long-eared animal.

It is to be observed that the chief seat of Lycanthropy was Arcadia, and it has been very plausibly suggested that the cause might be traced to the following circumstance:— The natives were a pastoral people, and would consequently suffer very severely from the attacks and depredations of wolves. They would naturally institute a sacrifice to obtain deliverance from this pest, and security for their flocks. This sacrifice consisted in the offering of a child, and it was instituted by Lycaon. From the circumstance of the sacrifice being human, and from the peculiarity of the name of its originator, rose the myth.

But, on the other hand, the story is far too widely spread for us to attribute it to an accidental origin, or to trace it to a local source.

Half the world believes, or believed in, were-wolves, and they were supposed to haunt the Norwegian forests by those who had never remotely been connected with Arcadia: and the superstition had probably struck deep its roots into the Scandinavian and Teutonic minds, ages before Lycaon existed; and we have only to glance at Oriental literature, to see it as firmly engrafted in the imagination of the Easterns.

Among the Bulgarians and Slovakians the were-wolf is called *vrkolak*, a name resembling that given it by the modern Greeks βςύκολακας. The Greek were-wolf is closely related to the vampire. The lycanthropist falls into a cataleptic trance, during which his soul leaves his body, enters that of a wolf and ravens for blood. On the return of the soul, the body is exhausted and aches as though it had been put through violent exercise. After death lycanthropists become vampires. They are believed to frequent battlefields in wolf or hyæna shapes, and to suck the breath from dying soldiers, or to enter houses and steal the infants from their cradles. Modern Greeks call any savage-looking man, with dark complexion, and with distorted, misshapen limbs, a βςúκολακας, and suppose him to be invested with power of running in wolf-form.

The Serbs connect the vampire and the were-wolf together, and call them by one name *vlkoslak*. These rage chiefly in the depths of winter: they hold their annual gatherings, and at them divest themselves of their wolf-skins, which they hang on the trees around them. If anyone succeeds in obtaining the skin and burning it, the vlkoslak is thenceforth disenchanted.

The power to become a were-wolf is obtained by drinking the water which settles in a foot-print left in clay by a wolf.

Among the White Russians the *wawkalak* is a man who has incurred the wrath of the devil, and the evil one punishes him by transforming him into a wolf and sending him among his relations, who recognize him and feed him well. He is a most amiably disposed were-wolf, for he does no mischief, and testifies his affection for his kindred by licking their hands. He cannot, however, remain long in any place, but is driven from house to house, and from hamlet to hamlet, by an irresistible passion for change of scene. This is an ugly superstition, for it sets a premium on standing well with the evil one.

The Slovakians merrily term a drunkard a vlkodlak, because, forsooth, he makes a beast of himself. A Slovakian household were-wolf tale closes this chapter.

The Poles have their were-wolves, which rage twice in the year—at Christmas and at midsummer.

According to a Polish story, if a witch lays a girdle of human skin on the threshold of a house in which a marriage is being celebrated, the bride and bridegroom, and bridesmaids and groomsmen, should they step across it, are transformed into wolves. After three years, however, the witch will cover them with skins with the hair turned outward; immediately they will recover their natural form. On one occasion a witch cast a skin of too scanty dimensions over the bridegroom, so that his tail was left uncovered: he resumed his human form, but retained his lupine caudal appendage.

The Russians call the were-wolf *oborot*, which signifies "one transformed." The following receipt is given by them for becoming one.

"He who desires to become an oborot, let him seek in the forest a hewn-down tree; let him stab it with a small copper knife, and walk round the tree, repeating the following incantation:—

On the *sea*, on the ocean, on the island, on Bujan,
On the empty pasture gleams the moon, on an ashstock lying

In a green wood, in a gloomy vale.
Toward the stock wandereth a shaggy wolf,
Horned cattle seeking for his sharp white fangs;
But the wolf enters not the forest,
But the wolf dives not into the shadowy vale,
Moon, moon, gold-horned moon,
Check the flight of bullets, blunt the hunters' knives,
Break the shepherds' cudgels,
Cast wild fear upon all cattle,
On men, on all creeping things,
That they may not catch the grey wolf,
That they may not rend his warm skin!
My word is binding, more binding than sleep,
More binding than the promise of a hero!

"Then he springs thrice over the tree and runs into the forest, transformed into a wolf."[2]

In the ancient Bohemian Lexicon of Vacerad (A.D. 1202) the were-wolf is called *vilkodlak,* and is explained as faunus. Safarik says under that head,—

"Incubi sepe improbi existunt mulieribus, et earum peragunt concubitum, quos demones Galli *dusios* nuncupant." And in another place: " Vilkodlaci, incubi,

sive invidi, ab inviando passim cum animalibus, unde et incubi dicuntur ab incubando homines, i. e. stuprando, quos Romani faunos ficarios dicunt."

That the same belief in lycanthropy exists in Armenia is evident from the following story told by Haxthausen, in his *Trans-Caucasia* (Leipzig, i. 322):—" A man once saw a wolf, which had carried off a child, dash past him. He pursued it hastily, but was unable to overtake it. At last he came upon the hands and feet of a child, and a little further on he found a cave, in which lay a wolf-skin. This he cast into a fire, and immediately a woman appeared, who howled and tried to rescue the skin from the flames. The man, however, resisted, and, as soon as the hide was consumed, the woman had vanished in the smoke."

---

2 Sacharow: Inland, 1838, No. 17.

The Werewolf: An Introduction

By Leonard R.N. Ashley

STARTING WITH THE STARTLING

To begin, here is a *pot pourri* of werewolf lore to whet your appetite. In later chapters we examine the werewolf in Europe, in the Americas, in the rest of the world, on the screen (cinema, television, video, computer), and sample werewolf fiction, concluding with the werewolf myth in literature and folklore. Here is Everything You Wanted to Know about The Werewolf—But Were Afraid to Ask. Or didn't know to ask. However, *Complete* in the title is an exaggeration. Everything about the werewolf is exaggerated, usually.

BECOME A WOLF

The werewolf is an outcast, shunned. Medieval laws stated that for certain crimes against society the offender must "become a wolf." That meant that the offender was placed outside the protection of law (outlaw) and could be hunted and killed with impunity, just as one would kill a dangerous wolf.

The werewolf has attracted the sympathy of all sorts of outsiders today. They identify with its problems. Some feel they bear some kind of disability, discrimination or a curse themselves.

SUPERCILIOUS

Do your heavy eyebrows grow together between your eyes? Superstition says you may be on your way to becoming a werewolf. Were you born with a tiny tail? (Some people are.) Do you have a tiny lock of hair between your shoulder blades?

HOW TO BECOME A WEREWOLF

You can, as you see in this book, become a werewolf without wanting to be one. (You can even, if teen movies know anything—which I doubt—turn it on and off at will.) People like rituals, however, and if you think simply throwing on a wolf's skin is too quick and easy, see Thomas G. Aylesworth's *Werewolves and Other Monsters* (1971). He suggests two concentric circles, one three feet in diameter, one seven. (Actually, the circle for ritual magic is nine.)

Full moon. Midnight. Magic cauldron containing "henbane, opium, hemlock, parsley," several doggerel incantations:

> Spirits from the deep
> Who never sleep,
> Be kind to me.
> Spirits from the grave
> Without a soul to save,
> Be kind to me. ...

And so on for (too) many stanzas to:

> Wolves, vampires, satyrs, ghosts!
> Elect of all the devillish hosts!
> I pray you send hither,
> Send hither, send hither!
> The great gray shape that makes men shiver!
> Shiver, shiver, shiver!
> Come! Come! Come!

For good measure anoint the naked body with magical ointment, put on the wolf-skin, don the magic belt (three fingers wide, "made from the skin of a criminal hung or tortured on the wheel"), recite more bad verse, and add a pledge of loyalty to the Devil. One becomes a werewolf by striking the head on the ground three times. Aylesworth also offers a briefer ceremony with a single incantation:

> Make me a werewolf! Make me a man-eater!
> Make me a werewolf! Make me a woman-eater!
> Make me a werewolf! Make me a child-eater!
> I pine for blood! Human blood!
> Give it me! Give it me tonight!
> Great Wolf Spirit! Give it me, and
> Heart, body, and soul, I am yours.

Aylesworth adds:

"Then what happens? There are those who said that a long, deep silence would come before the transformation. Others talked of crashes and bangs, groaning and shrieking. Anyway, it seemed that the subject felt a deathlike cold and was terrified." Who wouldn't be?

Aylesworth's book is better than most, I suppose, but poorly researched albeit well illustrated. Books on werewolves, aimed mostly at juveniles, are quite worthless.

TIMING IS EVERYTHING

The best time for werewolfery is on a Saturday and the best month is February, so tradition says. Well, at least February is the shortest month!

LYCANTHROPY

The Rev. Montague Summers (whose 1933 book was reprinted in 1966 and is still consulted) actually believed in werewolves. You may or may not. Consider whether you would define lycanthropy as a magical transformation of man into wolf or as a term of abnormal psychology for people who a) imagine they have turned themselves into wolves or b) are under the delusion that it can be done.

Do sufferers require spiritual or psychiatric treatment? Are people who believe in werewolves crazy? Would you describe such people as religious, superstitious, irrational—or what?

IN A NUTSHELL

The werewolf myth is a prime example of the power of the movies to shape our ideas. That's where you first heard of werewolves, isn't it? Kevin Jackson speaks of "The Werewolf as Social-Climber" in *The Independent* 10578 (25 August 1994, p. 25) and others have commented on werewolves in culture.

Here I select the best information for you, old and new, fact and fiction. This is the first attempt at a "complete" description of all aspects of werewolfery. It's a catholicon, if you want to be fancy, and a hodgepodge if you don't. Of course it doesn't have everything: *bonus Bernardus non videt omnia,* people used to say. "Even the good St. Bernard doesn't see everything."

That was in the Middle Ages, when most people believed in werewolves. Some still do. The myth's endurance interests me the most. What's in this?

Some fan is sure to ask how I could have missed a werewolf skit in some TV comedy from decades ago; or a film which they will insist is an essential (if tremendously obscure) werewolf movie. Cultists are quite capable (as I learned penning this series) of pouncing on an error amongst thousands upon thousands of correctly presented facts. I content myself with the question: have I told you something you didn't know that is worth knowing? Expertise can be enjoyable. Even trivia is fun.

In which werewolf movie was Allen Ginsberg's *Howl* (though it has nothing to do with wolves howling) in evidence? In what movie was Jacinto Molina (expert werewolfologists will instantly register "Paul Naschy") recalled by the character name Jack Molina? List thirteen ways in which werewolves are created or dispatched in the movies. Make a list of actors who played a Wolf Man only once.

For less trivial information (and some trivia too) keep on reading.

EARLY MENTIONS AND CONTINUING RELEVANCE

In Turkey, I have seen Kultepec (Pile of Ashes), a ruined city with cave drawings of leopard men. Whether men were supposed to have turned into leopards or merely dressed in their skins for magical reasons no one can say. *Gilgamesh* takes place thousands of years after those decorations, but thousands before our time. So a wer-animal—a man turned into an animal—appears early in the written record.

Early Egyptian art is full of man/monster combinations. Classical writings document Greek and Roman belief in metamorphosis (shape-shifting) and metempsychosis (transmigration of souls). The question is what references to werewolves exist in non-Western literature, and how do they compare to that of Homer, Herodotus, Virgil, Petronius, Apuleius, Pausanias, and other writers of an age that contained much more fantasy than today's.

So far we know that the literature of the east is rich in wer-animals but that werewolves are few and far between. Still, there are *some* werewolves. "From China to Peru," as Pope said, mankind is one.

In the werewolf myth mankind has toyed with definitions of the relationship of mankind to other animals, and the relationship of our world to possible other worlds, natural and supernatural. No matter how obscure, old texts tell us something about our current selves. We see with shocking recognition the print of a prehistoric hand; we realize that history and pre-history are not so long ago. Human existence is but a tick of the great clock old.

Werewolves were always part of magical belief, of ferocious laws, of art and literature and the life they reflect. They are an integral part of us—the natural and the supernatural.

THE DAMNED THING EXPLAINED

Ambrose Bierce (1842–*c.* 1914) provides a sort of explanation of the supernatural in a short story:

I have the solution of the mystery; it came to me last night—suddenly, as by revelation. How simple—how terribly simple! There are sounds that we cannot hear. At either end of the scale there are notes that stir no chord of that imperfect instrument, the human ear. They are too high or too grave. … As with sounds, so with colors. At each end of the solar spectrum the chemist can detect the presence of what are known as "actinic" rays. They represent colors—integral colors of the composition of light—which we are unable to discern. The human eye is an imperfect instrument. … I am not mad; there are colors we cannot see. And, God help me! The Damned Thing is of such a color!

DO YOU BELIEVE IN THE PARANORMAL?

Belief in the paranormal is normal in America in the sense that it is very common, but regarded as kooky. Superstition is only slightly more embarrassing to Americans than devout religious practice. Almost all say they believe in some sort of god, and, despite their actions during the rest of the week, a great many attend some kind of service. There is a buffet of religions, yet Stephen Carter of Yale thinks ours is a "culture of disbelief."

Nonetheless people believe in the presence of extraterrestrials. This includes God, the Devil and angels. I think this comes from traditional American resistance to authority. Who are *they* to tell *us* what to believe? Also, there is a pronounced dissatisfaction with reality (and a noticeable flight from it) in many areas of American thought. Conspiracy theories, doubts and suspicions, persist in the modern world. In the words of the New York Lottery, "Hey, you never know!"

As Pascal remarked, it is best to bet on the existence of God. I say, bet on the paranormal as well. It does not claim to have all the answers but it tries to be accurate in reporting (a standard religions do not always achieve). There can be no assertion of authority in a subject as chancy as the paranormal. This author's aversion to dogmatism is evident throughout these pages, I hope, and accounts for his light-hearted style. On the subject of werewolves, one should not become extremely serious.

VERSE FROM THE WOLF MAN (CURT SIODMAK)

Even the man who is pure in heart
And says his prayers by night
May become a wolf when the wolfbane blows
And the moon is pure and bright.

AN EARLY MENTION OF LYCANTHROPY

It is sobering to think that the medical knowledge of the ancient Greek Discorides and the surgical techniques of the Renaissance's Ambrose Paré did not much improve over many centuries. The use of anesthetic, phenomenal advances like surgery took place in nineteenth-century medicine. The industrial age made great leaps forward with Pasteur.

(Ever hear of Crawford Williamson Long of Jefferson, Georgia? He used anesthesia in 1841 and was promptly forgotten.)

In psychology and psychiatry there have been a number of advances since Charcot and Breuer, owing to an enlightened attitude that talks of mental illness rather than demonic possession. Paulus Ægineta, a physician of ancient times, wrote of werewolf myths. Paulus described what we now call obsession (which sounds better than possession) and depression (a vague term replacing the equally vague "melancholia").

He did not sort out all the types. That was left to Burton's *The Anatomy of Melancholy* during the seventeenth century. Paulus did, however, single out physical diseases like rabies (with the terrible symptoms of hydrophobia) and mental diseases such as lycanthropy (the Wolf Man delusion).

Today Paulus is an extremely obscure footnote in the history of medicine. His case reminds us that modern progress is so swift and extensive that we merely brush past what was once a grave mystery. Paulus does not even have a disease or "syndrome" named for him! We resurrect him here as an early commentator on the werewolf.

F. Adams edited the *Seven Books of Paulus Æginet* (1844) but I am certain your modern clinician or even professor of medicine never heard of poor Paulus. He was there before the Wolf Man somehow became an adversarial figure, or lycanthropy became associated with demonology.

CAN YOU BELIEVE IN WEREWOLVES?

If you subscribe to a religion that tells you exactly what to believe—and which does not?—you had best check its teachings on werewolves. Maybe you're free to hold an opinion. Maybe there is a party line that says certain opinions remove you from the congregation.

In my *Complete Book of Devils and Demons* I stated that, for Roman Catholics, the Devil is a person, not a symbol, as real as you and I. A twentieth-century pope has settled the matter once and for all. That's it, for them.

Roman Catholics regard werewolves not so much as persons but as demons in possession of the person. Werewolves are part of their doctrine of demonic possession. It is incumbent on Roman Catholics to believe that werewolves are possible, you are advised to have no truck with them, and it is heresy to say they cannot be cured.

I don't know what your synagogue, church, or mosque says about werewolves if, indeed, they are noticed at all. But Catholics have spoken of them for a long time.

Winfrith, a Benedictine monk from England, was sent off by Pope Gregory to convert the Germans in AD 718. Winfrith became St. Boniface (the do-gooder) and "The Apostle of Germany."

In his *De Abrenuntiatione in baptismate* (Concerning what We Must Renounce at Baptism), St. Boniface insists Christians must not only renounce sin and Satan but the Devil's witches and werewolves as well. Most believed werewolves were in the grip of the evil one. Now, this is not exactly the same as demonic possession, but close enough.

St. Boniface, however, reasons that it is wrong to think Satan could create werewolves, and a sin to think God could not correct the problem. Naturally, the general populace strongly disagreed with the holy man. Eventually he was martyred.

Where do you stand? Have werewolves made a pact with the Devil? Do you believe a werewolf is, like God, a person? Christians say God is three people in one: The Trinity. Furthermore, are God and the adversary (which is what "Satan" means) locked in a continual struggle? If you believe they are equal in power, by the way, that's a heresy. People got burned at the stake for that.

Do werewolves exist? Have they ever existed? Are they to be pitied, exorcised or destroyed? Would you suggest the couch or burning stake?

PUTTING IT SIMPLY

My late, distinguished friend Perkin (D.P.) Walker wrote *Unclean Spirits: Possession and Exorcism in France and England in the Late Sixteenth and Early Seventeenth Centuries* (1981). The period he covered was the height of the European werewolf craze, a time when most people believed werewolves were possessed.

"Faced with a case of supposed possession," wrote Walker, "a sixteenth-century observer had the choice of three possible explanations: first, a supernatural cause, a devil; second, disease ['dissociative disease']; third, fraud." Walker diagnosed cases as disease or fraud, ruling out the cacode-monomaniacal (a lovely word meaning "bad-demon craziness"). The Church did not share his view.

In Elizabethan England, Reginald Scot published *The Discouerie of Witchcraft* (1597) and argued that it was all mental disease or deliberate fraud. Scot was a member of a line, hailing back to classical times, in which physicians pooh-poohed the idea of possession, although he was not in the majority.

In the nineteenth century P. Janet in his *L'Automatisme psychologique* (Psychological Automatism, 1889) got rid of the popular belief in demonic possession and came up with what now we regard as delusion, the *idée fixe*. Oddly, throughout the centuries the number of cases attributed to fraud has been small.

The main argument against demonic possession, unless you believe the Devil can possess an innocent person (why would God let that happen?), is that being a werewolf is not a great deal. Witches do better. In exchange for their immortal souls they get the power to turn into all sorts of animals plus frequent-flier miles and orgies, although the sex is said to be unpleasant.

Lying under torture must have occurred frequently. Today, I think, there is a great deal of fraud in multiple-personality cases and other dubious disabilities. Instead of demons in their heads, people lie about a gaggle of extremely boring personalities.

A proper werewolf has to effect a visible transformation into animal. I really would like to see that, but I do not expect to ... except in the movies.

POSSESSION

The average psychiatrist would refuse to discuss demonic possession with you. (I don't know what a Roman Catholic psychiatrist would do. Call a priest?) But anthropologist Erika Bourguignon of Ohio State examined 488 selected societies and found that 74% believed in spiritual possession. Over 50% of the societies she studied have some sort of possession trance (as in voodoo or bible-thumping healers) not characterized as mental illness. In *Possession* (1976) she writes:

> Possession ... is a belief, a cultural belief, a shared and not an idiosyncratic belief. Insofar as the behavior involves acting out a personality ... [is] believed in, concerning which there are shared expectations, to that extent surely "possession states" cannot exist in societies where such beliefs are absent.
>
> Nevertheless, if we speak in very general terms about dissociation ... multiple personalities, fainting, functional epileptic seizures and other behavior of an apparently hysterical type, then the behavior is probably universal and occurs in all societies; however, it should not be properly referred to as "possession states."

As I said before, orthodox Judeo-Christian theology would not call states of possession a belief. They would call them a fact. Jews tell unmarried men not to live alone lest demons come to possess them. Christians read of Christ personally casting out devils, not to mention the legions of devils cast out in His name.

Demonologists would say that the werewolf is possessed by a demon, and that possession is not just in societies with scripts for behavior of the possessed. The Devil at work is the same everywhere.

One thing is certain: werewolves in historical records certainly knew how werewolves were supposed to behave. Was the Devil driving them? Was there a demon at work? Is there any society in which the Devil—who is universal, you know—acts any differently, or has werewolves behave in a manner different from the rest?

This is deep stuff. For a better understanding look into to T. K. Oesterreich's *Possession by Spirits Both Good and Evil in Oriental and Occidental Spiritualism and Occultism Among Primitive Races, In Antiquity, the Middle Ages and Modern Times.*

(That's the title page of the 1930 English translation of the 1921 German original. It gives you some idea of the nature of this ponderous tome.)

Almost any widespread folk belief, no matter how frivolous, will connect you to the most fundamental questions of theology and philosophy. The werewolf myth illustrates what "gets into people" who act strangely. It analogizes the minds of men and women to other animals and the nature of the relationship between the Creator and the creations.

It delves into the truth about our concepts of good and evil; free will and predestination; sin and the goodness of God; sanity and insanity; shamanism and magic; madness and the delusions of crowds—to name a few!

THE DEAD RETURN

A lot of people think so. See my previous book in this series, *The Complete Book of Ghosts and Poltergeists* (1999). But here's one piece of good news: the dead do not return as werewolves. Werewolves are living human beings. Kill a werewolf and you have no further trouble with him. In fact, as he dies (only occasionally is it a she), the werewolf is said to resume human shape and look like any other dead human being.

ARE THERE ANY WOLF MEN?

Learned doctors of the Roman Catholic Church cannot say the Devil has power like God the Creator's, to make creatures or to transform them, certainly not against the will of The Almighty.

At the same time, Catholics must recognize the existence of the supernatural. The basic approach has been that the Devil can only make it seem a new creature or change, by casting a *glamour* over things. It's a false impression, by the Master of Lies.

This glamour, the Church taught, deceives human beings into thinking that men have become wolves when they have not. Therefore, are there any real werewolves? Actually no. Here is St. Augustine in *De Civitate Dei* (Concerning the City of God), 18:18:

> Nor can the devils create anything … but … cast a changed shape over that which God has made, altering only … appearance. Nor do I think The Devil can form any soul or body into bestial or brute members … however, they have an unspeakable way of transporting the fantasies of men into bodily shapes, unto other senses … while the bodies of the men lie thus affected somewhere else, still alive … yet in an ecstasy far deeper than any sleep.
>
> Now, this fantasy may appear to other senses to have a bodily shape, and a man may seem even to himself to be what he often thinks himself to be in

his dream state, and to bear burdens ... it is the devils who bear them, thus to delude men's eyes with the appearance of real burdens and false shapes. ...

Do you—let us be upfront about this—believe that St. Augustine knew anything at all? Read it again. Give him another chance and then make up your own mind.

When someone speaks dogmatically, always ask, "Can you prove that, or just assert it?"

"Where did you get that idea?" is an important question to ask, especially in matters of theology. Theology fascinates me, but the chief amusement in its study is how people strive to answer problems they cannot truly understand, let alone solve. There is a statement that compares philosophy to theology: philosophy consists of blind men looking for a black cat in a dark cellar while theology consists of the same blind men searching, only the cat is not there.

WHAT IS PROBABLE?

Peter Doskoch (*Psychology Today*), Dr. Stephen Manson (*Skeptical Inquirer*), "Randi" (Occult Buster), and Nathan Myhrold (Microsoft guru) were asked by the now defunct *Spy* (July/August 1997, p. 43) to rank America's beliefs in the paranormal from the most to least likely. The results:

1.   In baseball, whoever ends an inning with a great defensive play will invariably bat first in the next
2.   The Loch Ness monster
3.   UFOs
4.   Spontaneous Human Combustion
5.   A human face carved into the surface of Mars
6.   Bigfoot/Sasquatch
7.   Something odd about the Bermuda Triangle
8.   ESP
9.   Elvis or JFK or Jim Morrison still alive
10.   Voodoo/Sympathetic Magic
11.   Telekinesis
12.   Werewolves
13.   Crop circles caused by something other than humans
14.   Astrology
15.   Nostradamus
16.   Reincarnation
17.   Ghosts
18.   Out-of-body experiences
19.   Angels

This list infuriates people. Try it on a friend. You can, if you like, add the Devil, the Blessed Virgin, psychics, numerology, vampirism, etc. In my view, most Americans would move angels to the top of the probable and put astrology higher than twelve.

One who would place werewolves at the bottom is the American insurance company who, at this writing, is accepting small premiums to insure anyone against becoming a werewolf or a vampire. They are said also to offer a policy against Immaculate Conception and to have only recently withdrawn the offer of insurance against reincarnation. It would be a bit easier to collect on the werewolf policy than on the vampire one. Some people have in fact sworn they were vampires but no one, as far as I can tell, has been legally convicted.

BY ANY OTHER NAME, IT STILL SMELLS

There have been (as you will see) a host of pretty awful werewolf movies, from *An American Werewolf in Paris* (U.S. 1997, partly redeemed by special effects), to the much worse *El Charro de los calvaros* (The Cowboy of the Skulls, Mexico 1966), which could not be saved by vampires, werewolves or the headless horsemen.

There was also the absolutely awful takeoff of *The Maltese Falcon,* called *The Maltese Bippy.* In production this had a series of dumb names. Among them were: *The Strange Case of … #*%, The Incredible Werewolf Murders* and *Who Killed Cock Robin?* Miss it if you can. You very likely can.

WHAT'S IN A NAME?

I have a book of that title (revised 1995), about onomastics (the study of names). Regarding the werewolf, note that Scandinavian names such as Ulf (Wolf) and Bjørn (Bear) may just as easily point to wer-animals or totem animals.

German has Wolf, Wolfgang, Wolfram, Ulric, and Ursula. Among Jews, Wolf is common (related to the tribe of Benjamin, described as ravening wolf in *Genesis* 49:27) as both forename and surname.

One "wolf name" translation under question is Adolf. Is it Father Wolf, Noble Wolf, or Wolf of the Land? Linguists debate it. Since Hitler, few will use it, whatever it means.

Lykos appeared in both life and fiction. In the ancient world there were names such as Lyakon and Lupus. From the Latin, the forename Lupe and the surname López are common in the Spanish language. Among the British are both Wolfe Tone and Wolf Mankowitz.

British surnames include Wolf, Wolfe, Woolf, not to mention the Anglo-Saxon, Randall (House Wolf), Randolph (Wolf, Shield), and a great many others. There are Rankin (Little Randy), Beowulf, Ethelwulf, Wul-fric … you get the picture.

When named, some may have exhibited the qualities of the wolf. Or naming them as such may have been an attempt to write a script for their lives, a desire to evoke the lupine. The Romans said *nomen est omen* and bestowed such names as Felix (Happy) and Victor.

Gazi (a military title) Mustafa Kemal was given the name Attatürk (Father of the Turks) by a grateful nation, but was also known as Bozkürt (Grey Wolf), a popular surname in Turkey.

Tradition says that if you call a werewolf three times by his real name he will revert to his human shape. Or you can just touch him with a key. Of course, his real name is the key to his identity, and would "bring him back to himself."

WRONG ETYMOLOGY

George Turberville (1540?–1610) in *Noble Art of Venerie* (1575) gets the meaning of "werewolf" all wrong. He is copying from a *Booke of Huntynge* (*c.* 1400) that if ever a wolf kills and eats a human being the wolf will be satisfied thereafter with no other food.

"Such Wolues are called War-woIues, bicause a man had needed to beware of them." The fact is that werewolf comes from Old English, which stresses that it is a man-wolf, not a wolf that eats men. (Think of the Latin *vir,* man.) A werewolf is a Wolf Man, not a wolf. One must be wary of a Wolf Man, too.

Wes Whirresley, "On the Etiology of Werewolves," *New York Folklore 22* (1966), 261–268, gives us this passage from John Aubrey's *Remaines of Gentilisme and Judaisme:*

> This is the Lycanthropos; the French call it Garloup: and doe believe that some wicked men can transforme themselves into Woolves and bite, and worry people and doe mischiefe to mankind: When I was at Orleans I sawe in the Hospitall there a young fellow in cure whose left Cheeke was eaten (he sayde by this Garloup) for sayde he had it been a woolfe he would have killed me out right and eaten me up. No doubt heretofore this opinion was in this island [Britain].

THE CREATION OF WEREWOLVES

Tradition dictates werewolf transformation as punishment for one's own actions, from foul deeds or eating a lamb slaughtered by a wolf to being cursed or demonically possessed. The world is a dangerous place. Before scientific knowledge, it was a more frightening place.

Religion offered compassionate deities to bestow help and protection. There was some consolation in The Age of Faith, but it also held threats of evil forces, and claimed the very air was full of demons. Religion thrived on the belief that everyone was in constant peril from the supernatural. To the myths of the pagans Christianity added horrors as well as hope.

God Himself, we are told by the pious, can be naughty. He permits calamities that descend upon the innocent as well as the guilty. He allowed Satan to torment poor Job, an innocent man. Of course He is the very essence of good and everything will turn out right, but you can understand why Job was tempted to "curse God, and die."

So the fear of the Lord was the beginning of wisdom, and the more ignorant you were the more likely to add the burdens of superstition to the threats of religion. Religion compelled followers to believe in the werewolf threat. It provided guidance and holy water for protection, which, against werewolves anyway, looked pretty weak.

In fact the Church was responsible for inventing the oddest way to become a werewolf. It was believed that if a saint lost their temper they might make you one. That is not a kind or saintly thing to do but righteousness, as you may have noticed, can get particularly nasty. St. Patrick is the most famous saint credited with turning a person into a werewolf. According to tradition, a British chieftain crossed him and St. Patrick demonstrated his wrath in that way.

The ordinary way to become a werewolf was to be bitten by one. Evil is contagious. Not everyone bitten by vampires becomes one but *all* who are bitten by werewolves become werewolves.

If you recall, that is what happened to Lawrence Talbot, The Wolf Man of the movies. (Who has not seen Lon Chaney in *The Wolf Man*, the classic werewolf movie from Universal Studios in 1941?) In Curt Siodmak's screenplay, Talbot returns to his ancestral home in Wales. He runs into a gypsy werewolf called Béla, played by Lugosi. In a battle between them, Béla is killed, but not before he has bitten Larry and transferred the werewolf taint.

After that, Talbot, now The Wolf Man, dreads every full moon.

French trial records of the early modern period document alleged causes of werewolfery. If you have the misfortune to be the bastard of a priest, watch out. If you commit incest or some other heinous crime, you bring it on yourself. The same goes for black magic, which involves abjuring God.

The literature of werewolves reflects superstitions and exaggerated history. There is the famous novel by Guy Endore, based on the true story of the French necrophile François Bertrand. He was called Sgt. Bertrand because he was in the French Army when he ghoulishly raided graves and munched on corpses. In it the werewolf is the bastard son of a priest from Périgord and for good measure the author accuses Bertrand of incest with his mother. Actually, neither of these charges was preferred against Sgt. Bertrand.

Endore's Bertrand ends up in a madhouse. The real Sgt. Bertrand (brace yourself!) got off with serving one year in jail. Years later he was reported, in the San Francisco

Daily Bulletin (27 June 1874), on what authority no one knows, as "alive and well, cured of his hideous disease ... a model of gentleness and propriety."

THE WEREWOLF AND THE FAIRYTALES

A fascinating psychological aspect of the werewolf myth is the act of transformation. Transformations from human to animal occur in fairytales like Beauty and the Beast, which contain many human archetypes.

There is the savage monster in Bluebeard, and the Wolf in Little Red Riding Hood. American writer Tanith Lee, who has written about the vampire, weaves together werewolves and fairytales too. Read her *Heart-Beast* (1992).

We mustn't forget the Cursed Object. It's nicely depicted in Lord Dun-sany's *The Idol's Eye* (a cursed jewel, like the Hope Diamond). Stolen not from an idol but a tomb, a cursed gem gives David Velmund terrible werewolf urges when he gets his hands on it.

Like the dreaded object in the chilling W.W.Jacobs story of *The Monkey's Paw,* it cannot simply be discarded. Lee's diamond does fall into other hands, and the curse spreads. Young Laura (the sweet Cinderella with the wicked family) is married off to a rich man. A shady magician persuades the rich husband to buy Laura David's cursed jewel. Thus the lives of Laura and David are linked by the werewolf curse.

See also Janet Garton, "Little Red Riding Hood Comes of Age," pp. 289–294 in *Essays in Memory of Michael Parkinson and Jayne Dakins* (edited by Christopher Smith, 1996).

SCIENCE AND THE WEREWOLF; SOME "LYC" READING

Patrick G. Coll, Geraldine O'Sullivan, Patrick A. Browne, *British Journal of Psychiatry* 147 (1975), 201–202.

Robert Eisler, *Man into Wolf: An Anthropological Study of Sadism, Masochism, and Lycanthropy* (1978)

Richard Noll, ed., *Vampires, Werewolves, and Demons: Twentieth Century Reports in The Psychiatric Literature* (1992)

William M. S. Russell, Claire Russell, *"The Social Biology of Werewolves,"* pp. 143–182 *in Animals in Folklore* (ed. J. R. Porter & W.M.S. Russell, 1978)

Ian Woodward, *The Werewolf Delusion* (1978)

Dorothy Yamamoto, *The Boundaries of the Human in Medieval English Literature* (2000)

RELIGION AND MYTHOLOGY

Mary G. Gerstein, *Warg: The Outlaw as Werewolf in Germanic Myth, Law, and Medicine,* UCLA Dissertation (1972). See *Dissertation Abstracts* 33 (1972), 1681 A.

Klaus Völker, ed., *Von Wervölfen und anderen Tiermenschen* (Of Werewolves and Other Animal Men, 1972)

Gerald James Larsen *et al.*, Eds. *Myth in Indo-European Antiquity* (1974)

Jean Przyluski, *"Les Confiries de loupe-garous dans les sociétés indo-Européenes,"* *Revue de l'Histoire des Religions* 121 (1940), 128–145

H. Krappe, *Etudés des mythologie et de folklore* (1928)

Konrad Müller, *Die Werwölfssage: Studien zum Begriff der Volkssage* (1937)

Wes Whirresley, "On the Etiology of Werewolves," *New York Folklore 22* (1966), 261–268

Stig Wikander, *Der arische Männerbund* (1938)

Lycanthropy and the Undead Corpse

By David Keyworth

According to the historiographical sources, a pronounced antipathy existed between canines and revenants. An undead-corpse that roamed twelfth-century Berwick, on the English-Scottish border, was described as being constantly pursued by a pack of barking dogs,[1] and after their unsuccessful attempt to stake the undead shepherd of fourteenth-century Blow, Bohemia, the revenant thanked the villagers for such a fine stick to drive away the dogs that continually harassed him.[2]

Similarly, Cuntius the sixteenth-century *spectrum*, was always accompanied by the unusual barking and howling of the village dogs and would supposedly catch them in the street and bash their brains out.[3] In a Romanian tale, for instance, a young man returning from military service entered a village one night and, seeing a house with a light on, went inside to seek lodging.[4] But the house was empty, except for a table with a corpse lying upon it. Nonetheless, he decided to stay for the night and climbed into the loft to sleep. But at eleven o'clock, a huge dog rushed into the house and attacked the corpse, which rose up from the table and began to wrestle with the dog. At midnight, however, the dog departed and the revenant lay back upon the table. Inquiring into the matter the next morning, the young man was simply told that the deceased was so evil that nobody wanted to watch over the corpse before burial, as per the usual custom, and that the events that transpired simply confirmed the evil nature of the deceased.

Wolves in particular took a special dislike to vampires. According to the Serbian Gypsies, even though horses could sense a vampire and dogs warn of a vampire's approach and thereby hamper its movement, only a wolf was strong enough to rip apart and devour a vampire, leaving nothing behind but a bloody mess[5]—given that the Gypsy vampire (*mullo*) lacked a skeleton and was little more than a bag of blood and 'jelly'.[6] Similarly, in Greece, once villagers had identified the grave of a *vrykolakas*, they would trace the image of a wolf on the outer wall of the local church, and then 'take earth from the grave of that *vrykolakas* and strew it all the way to the image of the wolf, so that the wolf would go and eat the *vrykolakas*.[7]

Despite the apparent enmity between vampires and wolves, however, and by extension werewolves, there were also similarities. In Greek folklore, for example, a werewolf was thought likely to become a revenant after death,[8] and so too whoever ate the flesh of a sheep killed by wolves.[9] Similarly, in some Slavic countries a vampire could reputedly be killed with a silver bullet that had been blessed by a priest, akin to that of the traditional werewolf.[10] While in Ukrainian folklore, not only werewolves but revenants were affected by the moon in that a corpse left outside would be revived by the action of the moonbeams, which would explain why Ukrainian vampires were supposedly most active during the full moon.[11] And in nineteenth-century Serbia and Herzegovina, as evidenced by the following extract from *Les Slaves de Turquie, Serbes, Montenegrins, Bosniaques, Albanais et Bulgares* (1844), vampires and werewolves had merged to become one and the same, at least in the popular imagination:

'The people of Servia [Serbia] and Herzegovina have preserved more than one dark tradition of unhappy souls who after death are condemned to wander hither and thither over the earth to expiate their sins, or who live a horrid life in death in the tomb as *voukodlaks* or vampires. The *voukodlak* (literally *loup-garou*, werewolf) sleeps in his grave with open staring eyes; his nails and hair grow to an excessive length, the warm blood pulses in his veins. When the moon is at her full he issues forth to run his course, to suck the blood of living men by biting deep into their dorsal vein. When a dead man is suspected of leaving his place of sepulchre thus, the corpse is solemnly exhumed; if it be in a state of putrefaction and decay sufficient for the priest to sprinkle it with holy water; if it be ruddy and fresh-complexioned it is exorcised, and placed in the earth again, where before it is covered a sharp stake is thrust through the carcass lest it stir forth once more. ... In Thessaly, in Epirus, and among the *Vlachi* of the Pindus district the country-folk believe in another kind of vampire, one which their fathers also well know in days of old. These *vampires* are living men who in a kind of somnambulistic trance are seized by a thirst for blood and prowl forth at night from their poor shepherd's huts to scour the whole countryside, biting and fiercely tearing with their teeth all whom they meet, man or beast ... [and] are especially eager to quaff the hot blood of young girls ...'[12]

Unlike the victims of a vampire, who inevitably became vampires in turn, those wounded by a werewolf generally did not become a werewolf as a result,[13] despite that depicted in horror movies and the like. According to European folklore, there were numerous mundane ways to become a werewolf, ranging from eating the brain of a wolf or the flesh of an animal killed by wolves, wearing a certain white flower that grew in the Balkans, or even drinking from certain streams in the Harz Mountains, although the results of such methods could be unpredictable and even uncontrollable.[14] Becoming a werewolf could also result by undertaking a particular magical ceremony, which required the initiate to draw a magic circle and place at its centre a boiling cauldron of specified herbs that included hemlock, opium and other ingredients.[15] After an incantation is recited over the cauldron, the initiate then smears his/her body with an unguent of animal fat mixed with similar herbs, and then fastens a wolf-skin about his waist and awaits the imminent arrival of an unnamed, demonic spirit that would possess the initiate and transform him into a wolf.

More commonly, though, an individual chose to become a werewolf through a pact with the Devil. In his *Demonomanie des Sorciers* [*On the Demon-Mania of Witches*], Jean Bodin, a late sixteenth-century French jurist and demonologist, tells us that Pierre Bourgot, burnt at the stake at Poligny in 1521 for being a werewolf, confessed to the slaughter and cannibalism of numerous children, and even to copulation with real wolves while in the guise of a werewolf.[16] Accordingly, he had sworn allegiance to the Devil and attended a sabbat where he had been given a salve to smear over his naked body, which would transform him into a werewolf, although the effects of the salve only lasted for a short period of time. On one occasion, Bourgot had fallen upon a young boy to devour him when he suddenly began to revert to human form and was obliged to retreat to nearby bushes where he had hidden his clothes, and smear himself again with the salve in order to recover his wolf form and escape.

Indeed, it was commonly believed that the werewolf form was superimposed upon the human frame, like donning a suit of clothes. In the thirteenth-century *Saga of the Volsungs,* two outlaws, Sigmund and Sinfjotli, broke into a house in the forest and found a pair of wolf-skins hanging on the wall, and decided to try them on.[17] The wolf-skins, however, were enchanted and once donned could not be removed until an obligatory ten days had passed. Subsequently, Sigmund and Sinfjotli became fearsome werewolves and roamed the forest seeking prey, and although Sigmund warned Sinfjotli not to attack any more than seven men at once, and to howl for him if he needed help, Sinfjotli stumbled upon a group of eleven men and slew them all but was badly wounded as a result. When Sigmund later came upon Sinfjotli, he was so furious with his recklessness that he attacked Sinfjotli and tore out his throat. Nonetheless, Sigmund miraculously healed him with a particular magical herb he had found and once ten days had passed, the pair removed the wolf-skins and burnt them lest someone else meet the same misfortune.

The most oft-quoted werewolf, however, is Peter Stubbe of late sixteenth-century Germany, who for twenty-five years killed and mutilated dozens of people, supposedly in the form of a fearsome wolf.[18] Accused of witchcraft and sorcery, Stubbe confessed to have received a magical girdle from the Devil that, when tied around his waist, transformed him into a werewolf. Subsequently, livestock were killed and mutilated, women raped and butchered, pregnant mothers had their babies ripped from the womb, and many victims had evidently been cannibalized. Stubbe even killed his own son and ate his brains. Eventually, though, a group of hunters tracked down the so-called werewolf and had almost trapped the beast when Stubbe removed his girdle, reverted to human form and pretended to be a simple traveller upon his way. The hunters, however, became suspicious and took Stubbe to the authorities for further interrogation. And after confessing his crimes, Stubbe was sentenced to having the flesh torn from his body with red-hot pincers, and his limbs smashed with a hammer, before being decapitated and cremated.

Hence, vampires and werewolves were entirely different folkloric beings, even though a vampire might be able to take on canine form. Whereas the vampire was an undead-corpse that wandered about and consumed the blood of the living, the latter was a *living* individual who transformed into a fearsome wolf, and in that guise, mutilated and cannibalized his victims.

Given that revenants like the *spectrums* of sixteenth-century Silesia were supposedly able to metamorphose into various types of animal, at least in the popular imagination, it is worthwhile to examine the actual mechanics of lycanthropy, and explore what this can tell us about the bodily transformation of so-called undead-corpses. During the sixteenth and seventeenth century, however, opinion on the matter of lycanthropy differed immensely. Johann Weyer, a Protestant physician, for example, portrayed werewolves in his *De Praestigiis Daemonum* (1563) as delusional individuals with a mental disease that could be cured by the appropriate medical intervention, be it the letting of blood or dietary change:

'As a result of sootiness of their black bile, the victims of this disease [i.e. lycanthropy] believe that they have changed into wolves or dogs in their very action. They are pale and their eyes sunken and dry. They see but dimly and have a dry tongue and a great thirst, while their mouth lacks saliva. Their legs are so covered with sores that they cannot be healed—because of frequent injuries and dog bites. These individuals are cured by the letting of blood … and also by good juicy foods, fresh water baths, buttermilk … and all the other remedies [i.e. herbal concoctions] useful against melancholia.'[19]

By contrast, Casper Peucer in his *Commentarius de Praecipibus Generibus Divinationum* (1572), argued that while the physical transmutation of man into wolf did not actually take place, at the exact moment of their so-called transformation such individuals would fall down to the ground in a stupor, during which time the astral 'double' of the so-called werewolf would leave their physical body and roam the countryside in the semi-corporeal form of a wolf, battling witches and other evil beings.[20] Peucer reported that, near Riga, a peasant having supper with his foreman fell into a deep stupor that the latter recognized as that of a werewolf, and promptly had him incarcerated until he regained his senses. At his subsequent interrogation, the peasant admitted that he was responsible for a horse found dead the next morning in a neighbouring field, apparently cut in half:

'... he confessed that he had pursued a witch [or rather her 'double'] who was flying around in the shape of a fiery butterfly (for lycanthropes boast that they are hired to drive away witches); to escape him she had hidden under the horse, which was pasturing, and in striking at the witch with a sickle he had cut open the horse.'[21]

Similarly, in *The Kingdom of Darkness* (1688), Richard Burton tells us about a certain witch who boasted that she could send forth her double in the form of a wolf to slay livestock, and demonstrated her supposed lycanthropy before the magistrate:

'... a certain woman being in prison on suspicion of witchcraft, pretending to be able to turn herself into a wolf, the magistrate before whom she was brought promised her that she should not be put to death in case she would then in his presence thus transform herself, which she readily consented to, accordingly she anointed her head, neck and armpits, immediately upon which she fell into a most profound sleep for three hours, after which she suddenly rose up, declaring that she had been turned into a wolf, and had been at a place some miles distant, and there killed first a sheep and then a cow. The magistrates presently sent to the place and found that first a sheep and then a cow had then been killed.'[22]

Henry Boguet, however, dismissed any such notion that the soul could conveniently leave the body, let alone take on the form of a wolf and attack livestock in the field. In his *Discours des Sorciers* (1602), Boguet noted that when the 'soul is separated from the body, death must necessarily ensue', given that it is impossible for Satan to bring the body back to life once the soul had departed.[23] Indeed, the same argument was used by King James in his book, *Daemonologie* (1597), when it came to the belief that the soul of a witch could leave her body and wander about:

'... as to their forme of extasie and spitituall transporting, it is certaine the soules going out of the bodie, is the onely difinition of naturall death: and who are once dead, God forbid wee should thinke that it should lie in the power of all the Devills in Hell, to restore them to their life againe: Although he can put his own spirite in a dead bodie, which the *Necromancers* commonlie practise, as ye have heard. For that is the office properly belonging to God; and besides that, the soule once parting from the bodie, cannot wander anie longer in the worlde, but to the owne resting place must it goe immediatelie, abiding the conjunction of the bodie againe, at the latter daie [i.e. the Resurrection].'[24]

Boguet's preferred explanation for incidents involving the apparent use of lycanthropy was simply that the Devil befuddled the senses of particular individuals, to such an extent that they perceived themselves to be a wolf, even though their physical form remained unchanged:

> 'My opinion is that Satan leaves the witch asleep behind a bush, and himself goes and performs that which the witch has in mind to do, giving himself the appearance of a wolf; but that he so confuses the witch's imagination that he believes that he has really been a wolf and has run about and killed men and beasts … And when it happens that they find themselves wounded, it is Satan who immediately transfers to them the blow which he has received in his assumed body. Notwithstanding, I maintain that for the most part it is the witch himself who runs about slaying: not that he is metamorphosed into a wolf, but that it appears to him that he is so. And this comes from the Devil confusing the four humours, of which he is composed, so that he represents whatever he will to his fantasy and imagination. This will be easier to believe when it is considered that there are natural maladies of such a nature that they cause the sick to believe that they are cocks, or pigs, or oxen.'[25]

Furthermore, Boguet gives various examples in which alleged werewolves had killed their victims with knives and swords, or by strangulation, and undressed children before they killed and ate them,[26] hardly the work of a savage beast. In fact, many of the werewolf incidents reported at the time can be favourably compared to contemporary serial killers that kill, mutilate and even cannibalize their victims, so much so, that serial killers have even been described as modern-day 'werewolves'.[27]

Guazzo also doubted that actual bodily transformation could ever take place, and in his *Compendium Maleficarum* (1608) noted that 'no one can doubt but that all the arts and metamorphoses by which witches change men into beasts are deceptive illusions and opposed to all nature … any one who holds the contrary opinion is in danger of anathema'.[28] Accordingly, the Devil himself would take on the form of a wolf and commit the atrocities attributed to a particular werewolf, and then beguile the individual into thinking that they themselves were responsible for the ensuing bloodshed:

> '… no one must let himself think that a man can really be changed into a beast, or a beast into a real man; for these are magic portents and illusions, having the form but not the reality of those things which they present to our sight. … Sometimes he [the Devil] substitutes another body, while the witches themselves are absent or hidden apart in some secret place, and himself assumes the body of a wolf formed from the air and wrapped about him, and does those actions which men think are done by the wretched absent

witch who is asleep … [and if wounded] the devil wounds her in that part of her absent body corresponding to the wound which he knows to have been received by the beast's body …'[29]

Similarly, in his *Demonolatry* (1595), Nicholas Remy declared that it was 'absurd and incredible that anyone can truly be changed from a man into a wolf'.[30] Nonetheless, demons could so 'confuse the imagination of a man that he believes himself to be changed and then the man behaves and conducts himself not as a man but as the beast which he fancies himself to be'.[31] Empowered by demonic agencies, these individuals 'imitated' the preternatural 'faculties, powers and actions' of their chosen beast to such an extent that they acquired fleetness of foot, stupendous strength, ravenous ferocity and other corresponding characteristics far beyond that of human ability.[32] Alternatively, such 'illusions can be caused extrinsically, when the Demon causes an actual object to assume the apparent shape which suits his purpose, and so deludes a man's senses into the belief that an object has been changed into a different form [i.e. glamour]'.[33]

The Devil might also manipulate the inner faculties of the witnesses themselves through 'prestidigitation' so that they too perceived a wolf in place of the actual individual,[34] as explained by the authors of the *Malleus Maleficarum* (1484):

'… devils can, with God's permission, enter our bodies; and they can then make impressions on the inner faculties … the Devil can draw out some image retained in a faculty corresponding to one of the senses; as he draws from the memory, which is in the back part of the head, an image of a horse, and locally moves that phantasm to the middle part of the head, where are the cells of imaginative power; and finally to the sense of reason, which is in the front of the head. And he causes such a sudden change and confusion that such objects are necessarily thought to be actual things seen with the eyes.'[35]

According to the *Compendium Maleficarum* (1608), however, the Devil could also encase the physical form of a particular individual in a blanket of congealed air, which could be manipulated to create the external appearance of a fearsome wolf:

'Sometimes in accordance with his pact, he [the Devil] surrounds a witch with an aerial effigy of a beast, each part of the witch's body, head to head, mouth to mouth, belly to belly, foot to foot, and arm to arm but this only happens when they use certain ointments and words … and then they leave the footprints of a wolf upon the ground … it is no matter for wonder if they are afterwards found with an actual wound in those parts of their human body where they were wounded when in the appearance of a beast; for the enveloping air easily yields, and the true body receives the wound.'[36]

Similarly, in his *Disquisitiones Magicae* (1599), Del Rio explains that the outer covering of congealed air could be reshaped into various shapes and forms, even more gigantic than the real animal:

'... [evil spirits] can surround a real living body with this elemental body so that it seems to be a human body [i.e. take on the appearance of other people], or an animal bigger and more gigantic than the real one. I see no reason why this cannot be, for the argument that air has the ability to expand and become less solid, or to thicken and become dense is persuasive.'[37]

By contrast, William Drage in his *Daimonomageia* (1665) declared that witches could actually take on whatever zoomorphic form they pleased, be it an insect or a fearsome wolf, and later return to human form:

'It would be too tedious here to describe how Witches can thus alter their bodies, or in a manner annihilate them. This worlde was made of nothing, by Spiritual Power, and may be resolved into nothing again by the same Power; and we can resolve dense Bodies into Air, and coagulate Air into Water; and the Devil [being a spirit] ... can do that, that a Spirit can do. ... Let us not doubt of the Transformation of Witches and how they are sensible in the shapes of Wolves, Cats, Mice, Dogs, Hoggs [Flyes, Bees etc.] ... and Copulate with the creatures of the shape they assume, and sometimes eat such meat and devour Children in the shape of Wolves ... [and] through Diabolical power given them, to transform and metamorphose any men or women they have power to hurt into what shape they please. ... And in the shape of Wolves have divers Witches lacerated in [and?] eaten those that they thirsted to be revenged, or those that casually fell into their hands, I should rather say their claws ...'[38]

As proof that the body underwent an actual physical transformation, many authors cited what is known as 'repercussion'. Accordingly, once a werewolf had been struck down and suffered the loss of a limb, he would be without that limb once human form had been regained.[39] In Auvergne, 1588, for example, a huntsman was attacked by a large, ferocious wolf and after a long struggle, managed to cut off its paw and drive it away.[40] Subsequently, the hunter recounted the incident to the local laird and pulled the paw out of the bag to show him but much to their surprise, the paw had reportedly become a woman's hand with a ring on it, which the laird recognized as belonging to his own wife, who upon investigation, was found to be missing her hand. Needless to say, she was subsequently burnt at the stake as a witch.

Likewise, in the village of Thiecourt, a witch developed a hatred for a particular shepherd and would change into a wolf to mercilessly decimate his flocks.[41] One day, though, the shepherd managed to wound the wolf with his axe and tracked the injured beast to a clump of bushes where he found the witch, nursing the wound she had received in the form of a wolf, and after binding her injuries, he handed her over to the authorities for due punishment.

Henry More, the English Platonist, concurred with this scenario, and in his *Antidote against Atheism* (1655), argued that the Devil could soften up a physical body and knead it into whatever shape and form he so desired, and afterwards return the body to its original state of being:

> 'For I conceive the Devil gets into their body, and by his subtle substance, more operative and searching than any fire or putrefying liquor, melts the yielding *compages* [components?] of the body to such a consistency, and so much of it as is fit for his purpose, and makes it pliable to his imagination; and then it is as easy for him to work it into what shape he pleaseth, as it is to work the Aire into such forms and figures as he ordinarily doth. Nor is it any more difficulty for him to mollify what is hard, than it is to harden what is so soft and fluid as the Aire.[42]
>
> 'The first philosophical objection is against the transformation of a human body into the shape, suppose of a wolf or any such like creature. For it is conceived that it cannot be done without a great deal of pain to the transformed. To which I answer, that although this transformation be made in a very short time, yet it may be performed without any pain at all. ... So that he may soften all the parts of the body besides into what consistency he please, and work it into any form [that] he can his own vehicle of Aire, and the party not be sensible thereof all the time. And there is the same reason of reducing the body into its own shape again, which is as painless to the party that suffers it. Nor is there any fear that the body once loosened thus will ever after be in his loose melting condition: for it is acknowledged even by those that oppose Bodin, whose cause I undertake, that a Spirit can as well stop and fix a body as move it. Wherefore I say when the Devil has fixed again the body in its pristine shape, it will according to the undeniable laws of nature remain in that state ...'[43]

More, however, does not discuss what happens to the extra body mass when such transformations takes place, given the obvious difference in size and bulk between a human body and that of a wolf, or even some smaller animal like an insect, nor where the extra body mass comes from when the reversal occurs. But if we accept that the Devil can rearrange and sculpt living flesh, then the shrinking and compression of solid matter should pose no problem, nor returning condensed matter to its original shape and form. More also argued that the soul could temporarily separate itself from the body while undergoing physical transformation, and then reunite with the body thereafter:

> 'The second objection is against our acknowledging an actual separation of soul and body without death, death being properly, as we define it, a disjunction of the soul from the body by reason of the bodies unfitness any longer to entertain the soul ... the answer is easy, That any separation by violence is not death, but such violence in separation as makes the body unfit to entertain the soul again, as it is in letting the blood run by wounding the body, and in hindering the course of the spirits by strangling it, or drowning, it or the like. For to revive such a body as this, would be a miracle indeed, in such cases as these, death having seized upon the body in a true and proper sense ...'[44]

Such arguments, however, rely heavily on the concept of Cartesian dualism, a philosophical notion introduced by Rene Descartes in his *Meditations on First Philosophy* (1641).[45] Accordingly, a distinct separation exists between the physical body and the mind or what Descartes called 'soul', and that the body and mind can exist and function quite independently of each other.[46] Similarly, More argued that:

> 'It remains therefore that we conclude that that which impresses *Spontaneous Motion* upon the Body, or more immediately upon the Animal Spirits, that which *imagines*, *remembers* and *reasons*, is an *Immaterial Substance distinct* from the *Body*, which uses the Animal Spirits and the Brains for Instruments in such and such Operations: and thus we have found a *Spirit* in a proper Notion and signification that has apparently these faculties in it, it can both *understand* and *move* Corporeal Matter.'[47]

Cartesian dualism, therefore, lent support to lycanthropy in that the mind itself could retain its memory and other faculties, and remain unaltered, while the body supposedly underwent physical transformation. By contrast, earlier thinkers like Boguet had argued that the body and soul were the same substance and could not exist independently of each other, and any severe trauma to the body, exemplified by lycanthropy, would no doubt scramble and macerate the brain itself during the process, and inevitably cause dislocation of the soul and result in the death of the individual.

But whereas Boguet and other commentators loathed the very notion of physical transmutation, they were more than willing to believe in wandering corpses. In his *Discours des Sorciers* (1602), Boguet, declared that the 'metamorphosis of a man into a beast is impossible', and that 'lycanthropy is an illusion', given that it would be impossible for a man who is changed into a beast and to 'keep his soul and power of reasoning' at the same time.[48] Nonetheless, Boguet readily accepted the notion that the Devil could possess and reanimate a corpse.[49]

Similarly, even though Remy argued that such 'transformations are magical portents and glamours, which have the form but not the reality of their appearance',[50] he accepted that demons could 'enter into the bodies of the dead and from within give them motion like that of the living'.[51] Furthermore, King James, the Protestant ruler of early seventeenth-century England, attributed lycanthropy to a 'naturall superabundance of melancholy',[52] yet promoted the existence of flesh-and-blood revenants, albeit empowered by the Devil.

Hence, bearing in mind More's contention that the Devil could refashion living flesh into whatever shape and form he chose, it could be assumed that the Devil also had the ability to remodel the dead flesh of a corpse, which would explain how revenants like the *spectrums* of sixteenth-century Silesia could reportedly transform into the shape and form of an animal.

A different scenario, however, could be that undead-corpses did not actually undergo a miraculous transformation at all, but rather that the undead-corpse surrounded itself with a malleable cloak of congealed air, as suggested by the *Compendium Maleficarum* (1608), which could be kneaded into the shape and form of its choosing, and thus appear to transform into an animal. And given Del Rio's notion that such a cloak of congealed air could be transformed into 'an animal bigger and more gigantic than the real one', this might explain why the undead maid of sixteenth-century Breslau, could supposedly take on the form of a 'hen that grew into an immense bigness'.[53] Alternatively, we could simply dismiss such notions and attribute the supposed shapeshifting ability of undead-corpses, and even their very existence, to prestidigitation, glamour and devilish illusion.

NOTES

1. *Historia Rerum Anglicarum* (Book 5: Chapter 23 & 24), Internet Medieval Source Book.
2. Perkowski (1989), pp. 105-06.
3. More (1655), pp. 218, 223.
4. Senn(1982), pp. 4–5.
5. Vukanovic (1976), p. 229.
6. Ibid, pp. 209–210. Similarly, in Macedonia, the *vrykolakas* was thought of as a 'bull-skin full of blood, with a pair of eyes on side gleaming like fire' [Abbott (1969), p. 217].
7. Lee (1936), pp. 304–05.
8. Lawson (1910), p. 385 (&) Masters (1972), pp. 29–31.
9. Lawson(1910), p. 376.
10. Summers (1991), p. 209.
11. Koenig(1938), p. 272.
12. Montague Summers, *The Werewolf in Lore and Legend* (New York: Dover Books, 2003), p. 148.
13. Elliott O'Donnell, *Werewolves*, 1912 (Royston: Oracle Books, 1996), p. 134.

14. O'Donnell (1996), 59–70, 161–73, 174–80 (&) Jim Haskins, *Werewolves* (New York: Franklin Watts, 1981), 74–81.

15. Ian Woodward, *The Werewolf Delusion* (New York: Paddington Press, 1979), pp. 113–20. Indeed, many of these ingredients had obvious psychotropic properties.

16. Jean Bodin, *On the Demon-Mania of Witches: De la Demonomanie des Sorciers*, 1580 (trs.) R. Scott (Toronto: Centre for Reformation and Renaissance Studies, 1995), pp. 122–23. Furthermore, it was absurd to cite illness as the cause of lycanthropy, given that illness would 'only be in the Lycanthrope and not affect those who see the man change into a beast and then return to his own shape' (p. 128).

17. *Saga of the Volsungs* (trs.) J. Byock (London: Penguin, 1990), pp. 44–45.

18. Anon. *A True Discourse: Declaring the Damnable Life and Death of one Stubbe Peeter, a Most Wicked Sorcerer who in the Likeness of a Woolfe, Committed many Murders* (London, 1590) [Early English Books Online].

19. Weyer (1998), pp. 181–82.

20. Lea (1957), Volume 2: pp. 426–27.

21. Ibid, p. 427. Indeed, such notions were voiced by St. Augustine in the early fifth century. In his *City of God* [(trs.) H. Withan (London: Penguin, 1984), pp. 782–83], Augustine declared that: '… I do not believe, on any consideration, that the body—to say nothing of the soul—can be converted into the limbs and features of animals by the craft or power of demons. Instead, I believe that a person has a phantom [i.e. double] which in his imagination or in his dreams takes on various forms. … This phantom is not a material body, and yet with amazing speed it takes on shapes like material bodies; and it is this phantom, I hold, that can in some inexplicable fashion be presented in bodily form to the apprehension of other people. … This means that the actual bodies of the people concerned are lying somewhere else, still alive, to be sure, but with their senses suspended in lethargy far more deep and oppressive than that of sleep. Meanwhile the phantom may appear to the senses of others as embodied in the likeness of some animal …'

22. Burton (1688), pp. 69–70.

23. Boguet (1929), p. 146.

24. (King) James (1597), p. 41.

25. Boguet (1929), p. 146.

26. Ibid, pp. 151, 153.

27. Anastasia Toufexis, 'Dances with Werewolves', *Time* April 4th (1994), pp. 54–56.

28. Guazzo (1988), p. 50.

29. Ibid, pp. 50–51.

30. Remy (1970), p. 111.

31. Ibid, p. 111.

32. Ibid, pp. 112–13.

33. Ibid, pp. 111–12.

34. Ibid, pp. 111–12.

35. Kramer, & Sprenger (1971), p. 125.

36. Guazzo (1988), pp. 50–51.

37. Del Rio (2000), p. 110.

38. Drage (1665), pp.18–19.

39. Olaus Magnus, *Description of the Northern Peoples*, 1555 (ed.) P. Foote (London: The Hakluyt Society, 1998), Vol. 3, p. 931. Accordingly, if such a creature were to be killed by dogs or hunters, he will never again appear as a man.

40. Boguet (1929), pp. 140–41.

41. Remy (1970), pp. 108–09.

42. More (1655), pp. 235–36.

43. Ibid, pp. 384–85.

44. Ibid, pp. 385–86.

45. René Descartes, 'Meditation 6: The Real Distinction between Mind and Body', *Meditations on First Philosophy*, 1641 (in) *Meditations on First Philosophy, with Selections from the Objections and Replies* (ed.) J. Cottingham (Cambridge: Cambridge University Press, 1996), pp. 107–15.

46. John Cottingham, 'Soul' (in) *A Descartes Dictionary* (Oxford: Blackwell, 1993), p. 158.

47. More (1655), p. 61.

48. Boguet (1929), pp. 143–44.

49. Ibid, p. 33.

50. Remy (1970), p. 111.

51. Ibid, p. 86.

52. (King) James (1597), p. 61.

53. More(1655), p. 214.

The "Real" Dracula: Vlad Tepes Dracula

A Journey into Dracula Country

By Manuella Dunn Manscetti

To embark upon the vampire trail is to undertake a journey of mystery and danger that leads us to a country that looks and feels like those lands we dream of in fairy tales: great expanses of dark and thick forest, across the Carpathian mountains, and into the misty and remote valleys of Transylvania on the hills of which stands Dracula's castle, eerie with the memories written on its walls of past impalements, torture, and cruel and bloody deeds.

We provide here a guide for the journeyer, warning him and her that this should on no account be treated like a "holiday" for it will open doors to matters that mankind has never seen or lived through before.

From New York or London, or indeed, any other city in the world, the first stop must be Munich, that beautiful city in Bavaria, Germany. On arrival in Munich the best hotel to stay at is the Hotel of the Four Seasons (Vierjahrzeiten Hotel): Jonathan Harker, the main character in Bram Stoker's novel, stayed there, as did all the other explorers and vampire hunters of history. The hotel is one of the main stepping stones in the vampire trail: its glorious rooms invite one to collect one's thoughts and to prepare for the adventure into the wilderness.

From Munich we climb aboard the express train to Austria's capital city –Vienna. The journey takes us through some of Europe's most startling and beautiful country, and from Vienna we continue on to Budapest, in Hungary. Vienna and Budapest sit on opposite banks of the Danube and the train journey follows the large and slow curves of this great flowing river. The magnificent city of Budapest is the gateway to eastern Europe, the new and more open world following the recent fall of communist suppression. It is also the last post of central Europe, and from here on the traveler enters the real eastern borders of the continent, quickly becoming enveloped in an atmosphere of romance and mystery, for this part of Europe is truly and recognizably different from any other, drawing the traveler back into a time when vampires really did have sway over the villages and people. Primitive, basic times filled with high winds and strong fears which still live in these often bleak lands.

From Budapest the journey continues to Cluj in Romania, approximately six hours by train to the largest city of Transylvania. In Stoker's novel, Cluj is named "Klausenburgh," the Anglicized German spelling of the name, since in his time, this area was within the jurisdiction of the Habsburg Empire. Jonathan Harker, the hero of Stoker's novel, stayed at the Hotel Royal, today called the Continental.

Cluj represents the heart of Transylvania, a city of extremely ancient ethnic mixes of population: the Saxons in the south, the Wallachians (or Romanians), the Magyars (or Hungarians) in the west, and the Szekelys in the east and north, who claim to be descended from Attila and the Huns. The name Romania originates in the ethnic origin of its population, for this area was the easternmost province of the Roman Empire. The native language of the Roman soldiers stationed there was Latin, and the Romanians take pride in their Latin roots, a unique heritage in eastern Europe, where the spoken tongues are largely Slavonic. The Romanians are strangely cautious, shy people who have very largely retained their gentle peasant ways, particularly in the countryside. The recently ended dictatorship under the dreaded Ceausescu family has left its mark on the land and the people, holding them almost as though in a frozen state of development. Ceausescu himself was thought perhaps to have been a vampire, perhaps, according to the continued stories of outlying areas, still walking the nights in search of victims. In any event the atmosphere of Romania satisfies the vampire hunter's desire of uncertainty and adventure—the glorious scenic value of the land somehow undercut with shadow.

After a good night's rest, the traveler will take heart in tasting the local *mamaliga*: "a sort of porridge of maize flour" which remains the national and very nutrient dish of the Romanian peasant. For his lunch in Cluj, Jonathan Harker partook of paprika chicken and "umplutura," an eggplant dish. These three dishes are so much part of the culinary fare of Transylvania, that it is said that even Count Dracula offers them to his guests, while he remains seated in the inimitable stillness of the meditating vampire without tasting anything, of course, for his diet is somewhat restricted.

From Cluj it is possible to enter Dracula country only by car. The journey to Bistrita is about a day long. The surrounding area is largely forests of oak, beech, and pine. Gentle streams break the greenness of the valleys and altogether the view is so pleasing to the eye that it is hard to imagine how movie makers depicted it as a sinister, bleak, primeval, and dangerous landscape. Every now and then, one can see a castle or a hill-fort perched on top of a steep hill. Haystacks are neatly piled by the landworkers on the edge of the cultivated fields, and the farms can be identified by their fuming chimneys in midafternoon, when the work is finished and the men and women return home for a cup of warm soup after their hard day.

The people of Transylvania are both deeply religious and superstitious: by the side of the road the traveler will notice many crosses to protect the road and the fields on the side, but also to bless and protect the worker and journeyer.

Students of folklore will assert that superstitions abound in this northern part of the country, where the local villagers still believe that the forces of good and evil are constantly fighting for supremacy, taking in their stride human destiny and action. There is little science here to break the pattern of mystery.

The peasants believe, for instance, in *nosferatu*, or *necuratul*, which literally means the "unclean one" and in Romanian applies to the devil. The *Ordog*—in Hungarian meaning Satan—is believed to roam around the dark forests at night. It would be inadvisable to utter the word *strigoiaca*—meaning female vampire in Romanian—for it is believed that, being more mischievous than her male counterpart, she will appear as soon as she is summoned and take a life with her. The word "vampire" derives from the Slavic *vampyr*, and for sure this creature is well known to the Romanian peasant. The villagers have recourse to the powers of the church (holy water, the cross, and prayers), as well as herbs such as garlic, wolfbane, and petals of wild roses that are locally grown to combat their fears and to send away the evil creatures when they appear. There is nothing in this that

The ultimate and living Prince Dracul was truly the real thing. His escapades around the beleaguered kingdoms of eastern Europe were echoed by the sounds of dreadful torture and slaughter.

the Romanian farmer would laugh at, for the conditioning of history is too long and unbroken to be termed superstition. It is only we in the West who term it so, degrading its value. One visit to this extraordinary country is enough to convince anyone that there are more things in heaven and earth than we could possibly be aware of in our restricted western philosophy. For this is the land of the vampire first and before all else.

Bistrita is located in the extreme east of the country and near the border with Moldavia and the Soviet Union, amid the Carpathian mountains. From Bistrita we can proceed across the pass of Prundul-Bargaului. The description of the area in Bram Stoker's novel is still accurate today.

> *Before us lay a green sloping land full of forests and woods, with here and there steep hills, crowned with clumps of trees or with farmhouses, the blank gable end to the road. There was everywhere a bewildering mass of fruit blossom—apple, plum, pear, cherry; and as we drove by I could see the green grass under the trees spangled with the fallen petals.*

The ultimate and living Prince Dracul was truly the real thing. His escapades around the beleaguered kingdoms of eastern Europe were echoed by the sounds of dreadful torture and slaughter.

Hie facht sich an gar ein grausen

liche erschröckenliche hystorien. von dem wilden wütrich Dracole weyde Wie er die leüt gespist hot vnd
gepraten vñ mit den haußtern yn einē kessel gesotten

The Historical Dracula: Tyrant from Transylvania

By Raymond T. MacNally and Radu Florescu

In a broad sense, Stoker was quite correct in setting his Dracula story in Transylvania, even though he located his fictional castle to the northeast, miles away from the authentic one on the southern border. The real Dracula was born in 1431 in Transylvania, in the old German fortified town of Schassburg (Sighisoara in Romanian). One of the most enchanting Saxon burghs, certainly the most medieval, Schassburg is located about sixty-five miles south of Bistrita. Its castle lies on the strategic hillside location which dominates the valley of the Tirnava River. It is surrounded by thick defensive walls of stone and brick three thousand feet long, with fourteen battlement-capped towers, each named for the guild which bore its cost—the tailors, jewellers, furriers, butchers, goldsmiths, blacksmiths, barbers, and ropemakers. With its narrow, tortuous, cobblestone streets and innumerable stairways linking the famous clock tower to the higher towers on the crest of the hill, the fortified town served the needs of a prosperous German merchant community that traded with Nuremberg and other German cities. The town functioned as a depot for goods moving back and forth between the German West and Constantinople; in addition it served the northeast trade route to Poland, the Baltic Sea, and the German cities linked to the Hanseatic Customs Union. The house in which Dracula and his brother Radu were born is identified by a small plaque mentioning the fact that their father, Dracul, lived there from 1431 to 1435. The building is a three-story stone construction of dark yellowish hue with a tiled roof and small windows and openings suitable for the small garrison assigned to Vlad Dracul. Recent restoration on the second floor revealed a painted mural depicting three men and a woman seated at a table. Only the central figure has survived fully intact. The portrait is that of a rotund man with a double chin, a long, well-waxed moustache, arched eyebrows, and a finely chiseled nose. The similarity of the brown, almond-shaped eyes to those of the

Dracula's birthplace in Sighisoara, Transylvania.
The plaque on the house states that Vlad Dracul, Dracula's father, lived here in 1431.

famous portrait of Dracula preserved at Ambras Castle suggests that this may be the only surviving portrait of Dracula's father, Vlad Dracul.

Dracula's mother, Princess Cneajna, of the Musatin dynasty of neighboring Moldavia, raised young Dracula with the help of her ladies-in-waiting within the household. His father's mistress, Caltuna, bore Dracul a second son named Vlad. She eventually entered a monastery and took the name Eupraxia. Her son later became known as Vlad the Monk, because he followed in his mother's footsteps, pursuing a religious vocation.

Dracula thus spent his youth in a peculiarly Germanic atmosphere; his father exercised authority over all the local German townships and defended all of Transylvania against potential Turkish attacks. Vlad Dracul owed his authority to the Holy Roman Emperor Sigismund of Luxembourg, at whose court in Nuremberg he was educated by Catholic monks. His political ambitions took shape when on February 8, 1431, two important events took place in Nuremberg: his induction into the prestigious Order of

Views of present-day Sighisoara.

the Dragon, along with King Ladislas of Poland and Prince Lazarevic of Serbia, and his investiture as Prince of Wallachia. The German Emperor Sigismund of Luxembourg and his second wife, Barbara von Cilli, had founded the Order of the Dragon in 1387 as a secret military and religious confraternity with the goal of protecting the Catholic Church against heretics, such as the Hussites who then posed a threat to Central Europe. Another objective of the Order was the organization of a crusade against the Turks, who had overrun most of the Balkan peninsula. The second investiture, presided over by the Emperor himself, bound Dracul to the hazardous task of seeking the insecure Wallachian throne (which included the Transylvanian duchies of Amlas and Fagaras) ruled at the time by Prince Alexandru Aldea, Dracula's half brother. This was to mark the beginning of a lengthy feud between rival members of the princely Basarab family, one featuring numerous crimes.

When the recently invested "Dragon" was finally able to make good his title of prince by expelling Alexandru Aldea from Wallachia during the winter of 1436–37, the seat of Wallachian power continued to be close to the Transylvanian border, where Dracul drew his support. Historically, Transylvania had always been linked to both the Moldavian and the Wallachian principalities. After the Roman legions evacuated the more recently conquered province of Dacia in A.D. 271, the bulk of the Romanized population withdrew to the mountains, seeking escape from the turmoils of eastern invasion in the Transylvanian plateau. In this way, the Daco-Romans survived untouched by the Gothic, Hunnish, Slavic, or even Hungarian and Bulgarian avalanches, which would surely have destroyed their Latin language and customs had they remained in the plain. Only after the torrent of invasions had receded did these Romanians descend into the plain, but cautiously, maintaining their mountain hideout. Each generation of Romanians from the thirteenth century onward advanced a little farther into the plain. Eventually they reached the Danube and the Black Sea to the south, the Prut and the Dniester to the northeast—in other words, the limits of modern Romania, and also in part the former limits of ancient Dacia. In the case of Wallachia, nothing is more typical of its tendency to turn to Transylvania for security, and nothing better demonstrates the reticence in abandoning the mountains as a haven of shelter, than the choice of the early capitals of the principality. The first, early fourteenth-century capital, Cimpulung, borders the Transylvanian Alps.

Dracula's capital, Tirgoviste, lies somewhat lower in the hills, but still provides easy access to the mountains. The choice of this site marks a period of increased self-confidence in the country's history. Rumor had it that Dracula's younger brother, Radu the Handsome, owing to his lengthy sojourn in the Turkish capital, also wanted to be close to Constantinople, as he was not immune to the pleasures of the sultan's harem. Gossip accused him, largely because of his good looks, of being one of the minions in the male harem of Mehmed, heir to the Ottoman throne, thus requiring him to be constantly at his master's disposal. In any case, Radu's reign marked the reversal of the heroic stage in Wallachia's history and the beginning of conditional surrender to the sultan. It was conditional, since the relationship of Wallachia to Constantinople continued to be regulated by treaty, with the local princes as vassals to the sultan.

When secure on his throne, Dracul, a wily politician, sensed that the tenuous balance of power was rapidly shifting to the advantage of the ambitious Turkish sultan Murad II. By now the Turks had destroyed both Serbs and Bulgars and the sultan was contemplating a final blow against the Greeks. Thus, Dracul began the first of his numerous deceptions, treacherously signing an alliance with the Turks against the successors of his patron, the Holy Roman Emperor Sigismund, who died in 1437. In 1438, in admittedly difficult circumstances, Dracul and his son Mircea accompanied Sultan Murad II on one of his frequent incursions of Transylvania, murdering, looting, and burning on the way, as was the Turkish practice. This was the first of many occasions when the Draculas, who considered themselves Transylvanians, returned to their homeland as enemies rather than as friends. But the Transylvanian cities and towns, though cruelly raided and pillaged, still believed that they could get a better deal from a fellow citizen than from the Turks. This provides an explanation for the eagerness of the mayor and burghers of the town of Sebes to surrender

Dracula's main palace at Tirgoviste. The city of Tirgoviste was his capital.

The Chindia watchtower at Tirgoviste; a nineteenth-century reconstruction. Apart from its role as an observation post, it also enabled Dracula to watch the impalements in the courtyard below.

specifically to the Draculas, on condition that their lives be spared and that they not be carried into Turkish slavery. Dracul, sworn to protect the Christians, was at least on this occasion able to save one town from complete destruction.

Many such incidents made the Turks suspect the true allegiance of the Romanian prince. Accordingly, Sultan Murad II beguiled Dracul into a personal confrontation in the spring of 1442. Insensitive to the snare, Dracul crossed the Danube with his second son, Dracula, and his youngest son, Radu, only to be "bound in iron chains" and brought into the presence of the sultan, who accused him of disloyalty. In order to save his neck and regain his throne, after a brief imprisonment at Gallipoli, Dracul swore renewed fidelity to Murad II, and as proof of his loyalty, he left Dracula and Radu as hostages. The two boys were placed under house arrest in the Sultan's palace at Gallipoli and were later sent, for security reasons, to far off Egrigoz in Asia Minor. Dracula remained a Turkish captive until 1448; Radu stayed on and became the ally of Murad II and, because of his weaker nature, submitted more easily to the refined indoctrination techniques of his so-called jailors. He became a minion of the future Sultan Mehmed II and eventually the official Turkish candidate to the Wallachian throne, to which, in due course, he succeeded his brother, Dracula.

Dracula's reaction to these dangerous years was quite the reverse. In fact, his years of Turkish imprisonment offer a clue to his shifty nature and perverse personality. From that time onward Dracula held human nature in low esteem. Life was cheap—after all, his own life was in danger should his father prove disloyal to the sultan—and morality was not essential in matters of state. He needed no Machiavelli to instruct him in the amorality of politics. The Turks taught Dracula the Turkish language, among other things, which he mastered like a native; acquainted him with the pleasures of the harem, for the terms of confinement were not too strict; and completed his training in Byzantine cynicism, which the Turks had inherited from the Greeks.

As related by his Turkish captors during those years, he also developed a reputation for trickery, cunning, insubordination, and brutality, and inspired fright in his own guards. This was in sharp contrast to his brother's sheepish subservience. Two other traits were entrenched in Dracula's psyche because of the plot into which father and sons had been ensnared. One was suspicion; never again would he trust himself to the Turks or to any man. The other was a taste for revenge; Dracula would not forget, nor forgive, those who crossed him—indeed, this became a family trait.

In December 1447, Dracul the father died, a victim of his own plotting. His murder was ordered by John Hunyadi, who had become angered by the Dragon's flirtations with the Turks. Dracul's pro-Turkish policies are easily accountable, if for no other basis than to save his sons from inevitable reprisals and possible death. Dracul's eldest son, Mircea, was blinded with red-hot iron stakes and buried alive by his political enemies in Tirgoviste. These killings and the particularly vicious circumstances attending his brother's death made a profound impression on young Prince Dracula shortly after his ascent to power. The assassination of Dracul had taken place in the marshes of Balteni near the site of an ancient monastery that still exists. There was, however, some justification for the Hunyadi-engineered assassination.

At the time of his imprisonment at Adrianople, Dracul had sworn that he would never bear arms against the Turks, a flagrant violation of his previous oath as a member of the Order of the Dragon. Once safely restored to his position as prince, and in spite of the fact that his two sons were hostages of the Turks, Dracul hesitantly resumed his oath to the Holy Roman Emperor and joined the anti-Turkish struggle. He was even absolved of his Turkish oath by the Papacy. This implied that he could participate in the Balkan crusades organized by Hunyadi against Sultan Murad II. Serbian Prince Brankovic's two sons were blinded by the Turks when Brankovic was disloyal to the sultan, and Dracul anticipated the same tragic fate awaited his own sons. He wrote disconsolately to the city elders of Brasov at the end of 1443: "Please understand that I have allowed my children to be butchered for the sake of the Christian peace, in order that both I and my country might continue to be vassals to the Holy Roman Empire." Indeed, it is little short of a miracle that the Turks did not behead Dracula and Radu. Dracula's elder brother, Mircea, not Dracul, had actually taken a more active lead in what is described as "the long campaign" of 1443. From the Wallachian point of view, this campaign proved an outstanding success. It led to the capture of the citadel of Giurgiu (built at great cost to Wallachia by Dracula's grandfather) and threatened Turkish power in Bulgaria. However, Hunyadi's Varna campaign of 1444, organized on a far more ambitious scale and reaching the Black Sea, was a disaster. The young, inexperienced King of Poland, Ladislas III, fell to his death along with the papal legate Juliano Cesarini. Hunyadi was able to flee and survived only because the Wallachians knew the terrain well enough to lead him to safety. In the inevitable recriminations which followed, both Dracul and Mircea held Hunyadi personally responsible for the magnitude of the debacle. A council of war held somewhere in the Dobrogea judged Hunyadi responsible for the Christians' defeat, and, largely upon the entreaties of Mircea, sentenced him to death. But Hunyadi's past services and his widespread reputation as the white knight of the Christian forces saved his life, and Dracul ensured him safe passage to his Transylvanian homeland.

Nonetheless, from that moment on the Hunyadis bore the Draculas and particularly Mircea a deep hatred. This vindictiveness was finally satisfied with Dracul and Mircea's assassinations. After 1447, Hunyadi placed the Wallachian crown in the more reliable hands of a Danesti claimant, Vladislav II. (The rival Danesti family traced back to Prince Dan, one of Dracula's great-uncles.)

What is far more difficult to account for is Dracula's attitude upon his escape from Turkish captivity in 1448. We know that the Turks, undoubtedly impressed by Dracula's ferocity and bravery and obviously opposed to the Danesti princes since they were thoroughly identified with the Hungarian court, tried to place Dracula on the Wallachian throne as early as 1448, while Vladislav II and Hunyadi were crusading south of the Danube. This bold coup succeeded for merely two months. Dracula, then about twenty years old, fearful of his father's Transylvanian assassins and equally reluctant to return to his Turkish captors, fled to Moldavia, the northernmost Romanian principality, ruled at that time by Prince Bogdan, whose son, Prince Stephen, was Dracula's cousin. During these years of Moldavian exile, Dracula and Stephen developed a close and lasting friendship, each promising the other that whoever succeeded to the throne of his principality first would help the other to power swiftly—by force of arms if necessary. The Moldavian princely residence was then at Suceava, an ancient city where Dracula and Stephen continued their scholarly Byzantine ecclesiastical education under the supervision of erudite monks.

Dracula stayed in Moldavia until October 1451, when Bogdan was brutally assassinated by his rival, Petru Aron. Perhaps because of a lack of alternatives, Dracula then reappeared in Transylvania, where he threw himself upon the mercy of John Hunyadi. He was undoubtedly taking a chance, though by that time, owing to Turkish pressure, the reigning Danesti prince of Wallachia, Vladislav II, had adopted a pro-Turkish policy, thus estranging him from his Hungarian patrons. It was essentially history repeating itself at the expense of the Danesti.

It was in Hunyadi's interests once again to have a pliable tool, a prince in reserve, just in case the Danesti prince might turn to the Turks completely. Thus, mutual interest rather than any degree of confidence bound Dracula and John Hunyadi together from 1451 until 1456, when Hunyadi died at Belgrade. During this time, Hunyadi was Dracula's last tutor, political mentor, and, most important, military educator. Hunyadi introduced his protégé at the court of the Hapsburg king of Hungary, Ladislas V. He also met Hunyadi's son Matthias, his future political foe. Dracula could have had no finer instruction in anti-Turkish strategy. Like a chivalrous vassal he personally took part in many of Hunyadi's anti-Turkish campaigns fought in what became twentieth-century Yugoslavia. He was invested, as his father Dracul had been, with the duchies of Fagaras and Almas. In addition, Dracula also became the official claimant to the Wallachian throne. It was for this reason that he did not accompany his suzerain in the Belgrade campaign of 1456, when Hunyadi was finally felled by the plague. At the time Dracula

John Hunyadi (1387–1456), prince of Transylvania, hereditary count of Timisoara and Bistrita, governor-general and regent of Hungary. Father of King Matthias Corvinus, he was known as the white knight of the crusaders.

had finally been granted permission to cross the Transylvanian mountains to oust the unfaithful Danesti prince from the Wallachian throne.

During the years 1451–56 Dracula once again resided in Transylvania. Abandoning the family home at Sighisoara, he took up residence in Sibiu, mainly to be closer to the Wallachian border. In Sibiu, Dracula was informed by the mayor of Sibiu and by many other refugees from the beleaguered capital of the Greek empire about an event which had the effect of a bombshell in the Christian world: Constantinople had fallen to the Turks and Emperor Constantine XI Paleologus (at whose court Dracula may briefly have been sent as a page in the 1430s) died in hand-to-hand combat defending the walls of his capital. One Romanian refugee, Bishop Samuil, informed Dracula that Sultan Mehmed II's next objective was the conquest of Transylvania and that he planned an attack on Sibiu itself, a strategic location that could serve as a base for later conquest of the Hungarian kingdom. Dracula at least could take comfort in the fact that Sibiu was considered the most impregnable city in Transylvania. This may have influenced his decision to stay there. Yet, in one of those acts that make a riddle of his personality, in 1460, barely four years after he left the city of Sibiu, Dracula mercilessly raided this region with a Wallachian contingent of twenty thousand men and killed, maimed, impaled, and tortured some ten thousand of his former fellow citizens and neighbors. He considered that the Germans of Sibiu had engaged in unfair trade practices at the expense of Wallachian merchants. Pillaging and looting took place on a more ferocious scale than had been the case with the Turks in 1438.

This leads us to consider one of the most ambivalent aspects of Dracula's Transylvanian career, when from friend he turned foe toward his former kinsmen and allies. (These will be described in detail in the review of the German horror stories.) This feud lasted roughly three years, from 1457 to 1460, during which Dracula was prince in neighboring Wallachia. The first lightning raid in the Sibiu area took place in 1457, when Dracula burned and pillaged townships and villages, destroying everything in his way. Only the city of Sibiu itself, at least that portion within its powerful defensive walls, was spared destruction. The purpose of the raid may have been to capture Dracula's half brother and political rival Vlad, the Monk, and to serve as a warning to the citizens of Sibiu not to give shelter and protection to rival candidates.

Another Transylvanian town that is linked with Dracula's name is Brasov (Kronstadt in German). Brasov has the dubious distinction of having witnessed on its surrounding hills more stakes bearing Dracula's victims rotting in the sun or chewed and mangled by Carpathian vultures than any other place in the principality. It was likely on one of the hills that Dracula is said to have wined and dined among the cadavers. It was likely on the same occasion that Dracula exemplified his perverted sense of humor. A Russian narrative tells of a *boyar* attending the Brasov festivity who, apparently unable to endure the smell of coagulating blood any longer, held his nose in a gesture of revulsion. Dracula ordered an unusually long stake prepared and presented it to him, saying: "You live up there yonder, where the stench cannot reach you." He was immediately impaled. After the Brasov raid, Dracula continued burning and terrorizing other villages in the vicinity of the city. He was not able, however, to capture the fortress of Zeyding (Codlea in Romanian), still partially standing today, but he executed the captain responsible for his failure.

During the winter of 1458–59 Dracula's relations with the Transylvanian Saxons took a turn for the worse in Wallachia. Dracula decided to increase the tariffs of Transylvanian goods to favor native manufacturers, in violation of the treaty he had signed at the beginning of his reign. He also obligated the Germans to revert to the previous custom of opening their wares only in certain specified towns, such as Cimpulung, Tirgoviste, and Tirgsor. This action suddenly closed many towns to German trade where the Saxons had made a profitable business, including those on the traditional road to the Danube. Since the Brasovians ignored these measures, Dracula proceeded to another act of terrorism.

Dracula's vindictiveness and violence extended through the spring and summer of 1460. In April he was finally able to catch and kill his opponent Dan III; only seven of Dan's followers were able to escape. In early July, Dracula captured the fortress of Fagaras and impaled its citizens—men, women, and children. Although statistics for that period are very difficult to establish (and the German figures must be viewed with caution), in the town of Amlas twenty thousand may have perished on the night of Saint Bartholomew, August 24, 1460, more than were butchered by Catherine de Médicis in Paris over a century later. Somehow Dracula's Saint Bartholomew massacre has escaped the eye of the historian while that of Catherine de Médicis has made her the object of great moral reprobation.

After 1460, Transylvanian raids and actions against the Germans in Wallachia subsided, and renewed treaties granting the Germans trading privileges were signed in accordance with previous obligations, as events conspired to turn Dracula's attention elsewhere. However, the Saxons exercised their revenge by being instrumental in Dracula's arrest "as an enemy of humanity" in the autumn of 1462, and more permanently by ruining his reputation for posterity.

In reviewing this catalog of horrors one must bear in mind that there were two sides to Dracula's personality. One was the torturer and inquisitor who used terror deliberately as an instrument of policy while turning to piety to liberate his conscience. The other reveals a precursor of Machiavelli, an early nationalist, and an amazingly modern statesman who justified his actions in accordance with *raison d'état*. The citizens of Brasov and Sibiu were after all foreigners who attempted to perpetuate their monopoly of trade in the Romanian principalities. They were intriguers as well. The Saxons, conscious of Dracula's authoritarianism, were eager to subvert his authority, in Transylvania and grant asylum to would-be contenders to the Wallachian throne. It is far too easy to explain Dracula's personality, as some have done, on the basis of cruelty alone. There was a method to his apparent madness.

Although Dracula ruled the Romanian principality of Wallachia on three separate occasions and died near the citadel of Bucharest, his place of birth, his family homestead, and the two feudal duchies under his allegiance—Amlas and Fagaras—anchored his name to Transylvania. Dracula loved the country of his birth and ultimately took residence in Sibiu after making peace with the Germans. Even his famous castle on the Arges River, though technically located on the Wallachian side of the border, skirts the Transylvanian Alps. To this extent the tradition borne out in Stoker's story is quite correct. Dracula's name is inexorably and historically connected with romantic Transylvania.

Crusader Against the Turks

By Raymond T. MacNally and Radu Florescu

During the winter of 1461, Dracula hurled a challenge at none other than the proud conqueror of Constantinople, Sultan Mehmed II. The subsequent Danubian and Wallachian campaigns, which lasted from the winter of 1461 through the fall of 1462, undoubtedly constitute the most-discussed episode in Dracula's fascinating career. His resourcefulness, his feats of valor, his tactics and strategy brought him as much notoriety in Europe as his gruesome treatment of his own subjects. Whereas his impalements were recorded in popular narratives, his acts of heroism during the crusades against the Turks were enshrined in the official records of the time.

With the death of the great Hunyadi in 1456, the remaining Christian forces desperately needed leadership. The bitter squabbles that had led to Dracula's father's assassination continued unabated. This absence of Christian unity greatly helped the Turkish cause and contributed to the capture of Constantinople in 1453, three years before Dracula's second accession to the Wallachian throne.

With the disappearance of the last vestiges of Serbian and Bulgarian independence and the fall of the Greek Empire, circumstances of geography placed Wallachia at the forefront of the anti-Turkish crusade. Moldavia, Wallachia's ally, lay safely in the hands of Dracula's cousin Stephen, who emerged as a hero in the post-Hunyadi Christian world. Following the assassination of his father, Bogdan, Stephen had accompanied Dracula to his exile in Transylvania. There, while both were sojourning in the castle of the Hunyadis at Hunedoara, Dracula made a formal compact with Stephen: whoever succeeded to the throne first would help the other gain the sister principality. In 1457, exactly one year after his accession to the throne, Dracula, true to his promise, sent a Wallachian contingent to help Stephen reconquer the crown of his ancestors. In this way, Dracula helped launch the brilliant career of the greatest soldier, statesman, and man of culture that the Romanian Renaissance produced. For Stephen the Great, or Saint Stephen as he is now called following his canonization by the Orthodox Church in 1972, was both a soldier and a lover of the arts. The number of monasteries that still survive in the region of Suceava, Stephen's capital, are eloquent testimony to the cultural and architectural brilliance of his age.

When Dracula finally ascended the throne in June 1456, both Chinese and European astronomers documented an unusual celestial appearance—a comet "as long as half the sky with two tails, one pointing west the other east, colored gold and looking like an undulated flame in the distant horizon." The comet later became an object of study for British astronomer Edmund Halley and has been known ever since as Halley's comet. In the fifteenth century, as today, superstitious people looked upon the sighting of a comet as a warning of natural catastrophies, plagues, or threats of invasions. With the death of Hunyadi at Belgrade, such auguries seemed likely to be fulfilled. Yet Dracula's seers and astrologers interpreted the comet as a symbol of victory. A Romanian numismatic specialist recently discovered a small silver coin minted by the prince showing the Wallachian eagle on one side and a star trailing six undulating rays on the other, a crude depiction of the famous comet.

After the fall of Constantinople, the surviving powers of Central and Eastern Europe were all committed to liberating the Balkan lands conquered by the Turks. One of the great Renaissance figures, Enea Silvio Piccolomini, an astute diplomat and expert on Eastern Europe, became Pope Pius II in 1458. He saw the portents of danger for the whole Christian world in the imperialist ambitions of Sultan Mehmed II. Pius II launched his crusade at the council of Mantua in 1459, warning the incredulous rulers in attendance that unless Christians banded together to oppose Mehmed, the Sultan would destroy his enemies one by one. The pope asked Christians to take up the cross and raise 100,000 gold ducats.

Following the death of Hunyadi and the assassination of his eldest son, Ladislaus, a struggle for the Hungarian crown ensued between the Hunyadis and the Hapsburgs. Dracula had remained loyal to the Hunyadis throughout his struggles with the Transylvanian Germans, initially to Ladislaus and after his assassination to Hunyadi's younger son, Matthias, and brother-in-law, Michael Szilagy. On the opposing side were the Hapsburgs: Albert I who had ruled briefly, his wife Elizabeth, and Ladislaus V. The sacred Crown of Saint Stephen, hidden at the Fortress of Visegrad, waited for the next legitimate Hapsburg to claim it. The Holy Roman Emperor Frederick III was so preoccupied with internal affairs that his empire was not likely to respond to the papal appeal. Hunyadi's son, Matthias, managed to become king of Hungary in 1458. Dracula, who had met Matthias as a young man, had expected him to join the crusade. He was as disappointed in that respect as the pope. Matthias never gave his full support to the papal crusade against the Turks because of his shaky hold on the Hungarian throne. The Holy Roman Emperor Frederick III; George of Podebrady, king of Bohemia; Casimir IV of Poland; the grand duke of Moscow, Ivan III; the rulers of the Italian republics; and a number of Eastern potentates, all of whom had attended the council, merely sent kind words of encouragement to the pope. All were embroiled in their own petty squabbles and chose to dismiss the papal appeal out of hand.

Dracula was the only sovereign who responded immediately to the papal plea. His courageous action was rewarded with favorable comments from the official representatives of Venice, Genoa, Milan, Ferrara, and even Pope Pius II. While still disapproving of some of the cruel tactics he used, they all admired Dracula's courage and praised his willingness to fight for Christianity.

In spite of his oath to the Hungarian king and the pope, Dracula's relationship with the Turks remained accommodating. He fulfilled his obligation of vassalage, which included payment of the tribute and an occasional visit to Constantinople. The first indication that there might be problems in preserving amicable relations came from Dracula himself. In a letter dated September 10, 1456, written to the city elders of Brasov, Dracula revealed his real thinking, only days after his inauguration as prince:

I am giving you the news ... that an Embassy from the Turks has now come to us. Bear in mind and firmly retain what I have previously transacted with you about brotherhood and peace ... the time and the hour has now come, concerning what I have previously spoken of. The Turks wish to place on our shoulders ... unbearable burdens and ... to compel us not to live peaceably [with you]. ... They are seeking a way to loot your country passing through ours. In addition, they force us ... to work against your Catholic faith. Our wish is to do no evil against you, not to abandon you, as I have told you and sworn. I trust I will remain your brother and faithful friend. This is why I have retained the Turkish envoys here, so that I have time to send you the news.

Vlad the Impaler and the Turkish Envoys, as depicted in a nineteenth century painting by Theodor Aman.

There follows a typical precept which anticipates Machiavelli:

You have to reflect ... when a prince is powerful and brave, he can make peace as he wishes. If, however, he is powerless, some more powerful than he will conquer him and dictate as he pleases.

Taking into account the overall tense Turkish-Wallachlan situation resulting from Dracula's double allegiance, the reasons for the final breakdown of relations and for the opening of hostilities must be sought in Turkish attempts to turn infringements of existing treaties to their advantage. The tribute had been paid regularly by Dracula only during the first three years of his reign. From 1459 to 1461 and onward, however, because he was preoccupied with the problems of the Transylvanian Saxons, Dracula had violated his obligation and failed to appear at the Turkish court. This is why when negotiations resumed, the Turks asked for the payment of the unpaid tax.

There was another surprising new demand which had never been stipulated before and represented a clear infraction of previous treaties. This entailed a request for child tribute—no fewer than five hundred young boys destined for the janissary corps. This infantry elite was composed of recruits from various provinces of the Balkans under the Sultan's control. Indeed, Turkish recruiting officers had occasionally invaded the Wallachian plain, where they felt the quality of young men was best. Dracula had resisted such incursions with a force of arms, and any Turks who were caught were apt to find themselves on the stake. Such violations of territory by both sides were added provocations and only embittered Turkish-Wallachian relations. Raiding, pillaging, and looting were endemic from Giurgiu to the Black Sea. The Turks had also succeeded in securing control of various fortresses and townships on the Romanian side of the Danube.

Further complicating matters, Radu the Handsome, who had faithfully resided at Constantinople since his liberation in 1447, was encouraged by the Turks to consider himself a candidate to the Wallachian throne. Before relations broke down, Sultan Mehmed II gave Dracula a final chance. He invited him to come to Nicopolis on the Danube to meet Isaac Pasha, the ruler of Rumelia and the sultan's representative, who was instructed to persuade Dracula to come to Constantinople in person and explain his vassalage violations of the last few years. Dracula said he was prepared to come with gifts to Constantinople, agreed to discuss nonpayment of the tribute and the frontier adjustments, but was still unwilling to contribute the child levy. In truth, under no circumstance would he proceed to the Sultan's court because he remembered how his father had been tricked. The official pretext for his refusal to go to Constantinople was fear that if he did his enemies in Transylvania would seize power in his absence.

Since there was no basis for genuine and sincere negotiations, one must view the sultan's reaction with a certain understanding. Dracula's refusal to go to Constantinople confirmed the Turks' suspicions that he was simultaneously negotiating an alliance with the Hungarians. Thus the Turks laid plans for an ambush. The men entrusted to carry out the plot could not have been better chosen—a clever Greek devil, Thomas Catavolinos, and Hamza Pasha, the chief court falconer, governor of Nicopolis, a man known for his subtle mind. Their ostensible pretext was to meet with Dracula to discuss a mutually acceptable frontier and to persuade him to come to Constantinople. Since they knew Dracula would refuse the latter, their secret instructions were to capture the Wallachian prince dead or alive.

We are fortunate to possess a comprehensive and dramatic account of the precise circumstances by which Dracula outfoxed his opponents. The story is told by Dracula himself in a letter dated February 11, 1462, addressed to King Matthias Corvinus:

In other letters I have written to Your Highness the way in which the Turks, the cruel enemies of the Cross of Christ, have sent their envoys to me, in order to break our mutual peace and alliance and to spoil our marriage, so that I may be allied only with them and that I travel to the Turkish sovereign, that is to say, to his court, and, should I refuse to abandon the peace, and the treaties, and the marriage with Your Highness, the Turks will not keep the peace with me. They also sent a leading counselor of the Sultan, Hamza Pasha of Nicopolis, to determine the Danubian frontier, with the intent that Hamza Pasha should, if he could, take me in some manner by trickery or good faith, or in some other manner, to the Port and if not, to try and take me in captivity. But by the grace of God, as I was journeying towards their frontier, I found out about their trickery and slyness and I was the one who captured Hamza Pasha in the Turkish district and land, close to a fortress called Giurgiu. As the Turks opened the gates of the fortress, on the orders of our men, with the thought that only their men would enter, our soldiers mixing with theirs entered the fortress and conquered the city which I then set on fire.

In that same letter Dracula describes the subsequent campaign that took place along the Danube up to the Black Sea during the winter of 1461, which constituted a de facto opening of hostilities without so much as a formal declaration of war: Thus, Dracula can be looked upon as the aggressor.

The Danubian campaign was the initial successful phase of the Turkish-Wallachian wan Dracula was on the offensive, attempting to duplicate Hunyadi's successful amphibious warfare of the 1440s. Much of the campaign took place on Bulgarian soil controlled by the Turks. From the mention of place names it is possible to reconstruct the progress of Dracula's forces along the Danube, and Dracula tells precisely the number of casualties inflicted:

> I have killed men and women, old and young, who lived at Oblucitza and Novoselo where the Danube flows into the sea up to Rahova which is located near Chilia from the lower [Danube] up to such places as Samovit and Ghighen [both located in modern Bulgaria]. [We killed] 23,884 Turks and Bulgars without counting those whom we burned in homes or whose heads were not cut by our soldiers ... thus Your Highness must know that I have broken the peace with the sultan.

There follow some startling statistics of people killed: at Oblucitza and Novoselo, 1,350; at Dirstor (Durostor, Silistria), Girtal, and Dridopotrom, 6,840; at Orsova, 343; at Vectrem, 840; at Turtucaia, 630; at Marotim, 210; at Giurgiu itself, 6,414; at Turnu, Batin, and Novigrad, 384; at Sistov, 410; at Nicopolis, Samovit, and Ghighen,

1,138; at Rahova, 1,460. To further impress King Matthias with the accuracy of this account, Dracula sent to him his envoy, Radu Farma, with two bags of heads, noses, and ears.

The winter campaign ended on the Black Sea coast, within sight of the powerful Turkish invasion force that had crossed the Bosporus for a full-scale invasion of Wallachia. With his flank unprotected, Dracula was compelled to abandon the offensive. He had burned all the Turkish fortresses he could not actually occupy. Beyond that he could not go; the momentum of the offensive had been spent.

The Danubian campaign had established Dracula's reputation as a crusader and warrior for Christianity. Throughout Central and Western Europe Te Deums were sung, and bells tolled from Genoa to Paris in gratitude for endowing the crusade with a new lease on life and taking over the leadership of the great Hunyadi. Dracula's bold offensive also sent a new hope of liberation to the enslaved peoples of Bulgaria, Serbia, and Greece. At Constantinople there was an atmosphere of consternation, gloom, and fear, and some of the Turkish leaders, fearing the Impaler, contemplated flight across the Bosporus into Asia Minor.

Mehmed II decided to launch his invasion of Wallachia during the spring of 1462; Dracula had given the sultan no alternative. To defy the sultan by spoiling a probable assassination plot was one thing; to ridicule him and instill hopes of liberation among his Christian subjects was quite another, one far more dangerous to his recently established empire. In any event, Mehmed wished to reduce Wallachia to a Turkish province. With this formidable task in mind, the sultan gathered the largest Turkish force that had been amassed since the fall of Constantinople in 1453. The main contingent, led by the sultan himself, was carried across the Bosporus by a vast flotilla of barges. The other major force, collected at Nicopolis in Bulgaria, was to cross the Danube, recapture the fortress of Giurgiu, and then unite with the main force in a combined attack on Tirgoviste.

Dracula hoped for reinforcements from Matthias of Hungary in order to correct the disparity of numbers; he had, according to the Slavic narrative, no more than 30,900 men. Dracula appealed to his countrymen; as was the custom when the independence of the country was threatened, able-bodied men, including boys from age twelve upward, and even women were conscripted. An eyewitness Turkish chronicler states that the crossing of the Danube was completed on the night of the sixth day of the fast of Ramadan (Friday, June 4, 1462), the Turkish soldiers being transported in seventy boats and barges. Other Turkish eyewitnesses give us detailed and graphic accounts of the whole operation. The crossing was made possible by Turkish cannon fire being directed against Wallachian emplacements on the right bank:

> [When night began to fall,] we climbed into the boats and floated down the Danube and crossed to the other side several leagues lower from the place where Dracula's army was standing. There we dug ourselves in trenches

setting the cannons around us. We dug ourselves into the trenches so that the horsemen could not injure us. After that we crossed back to the other side and thus transported other soldiers across the Danube. And when the whole of the infantry crossed over, we prepared and set out gradually against the army of Dracula, together with the artillery and other impedimenta we had taken with us. Having stopped, we set up the cannon, but until we could succeed in doing this, 300 soldiers were killed. The Sultan was very saddened by this affair, seeing a great battle from the other side of the Danube and being unable personally to come there. He was fearful lest all the soldiers be killed, since the Emperor had personally not crossed. After that, seeing that our side was weakening greatly, having transported 120 guns, we defended ourselves with them and fired often, so that we repelled the army of the prince from that place and we strengthened ourselves. Then the Emperor having gained reassurance, transported other soldiers. And Dracula seeing he could not prevent the crossing, withdrew from us. Then, after the Emperor had crossed the Danube following us with a whole army, he gave us 30,000 gold coins to be divided among us.

Soon after, there were preliminary skirmishes along the marshes of the Danube, aimed essentially at delaying the juncture of the two great Turkish armies. Dracula abandoned the river and began his withdrawal northward. From this point, Dracula resorted to what is known as strategic retreat, a device invariably used by an outnumbered army. The idea was to draw the enemy force deep into Dracula's territory. The Romanians depended on the varieties of the terrain for their defense: the marshy soil near the Danube, the dense Vlasie forest extending deep into the plain, and the impenetrable mountains. According to Romanian tradition, the "mad" forest and the mountains were "brothers of the people" that ensured survival of the nation through the ages. As the Wallachian troops gave up their native soil to the Turks, Dracula used scorched-earth tactics in wearing down his enemies, creating a vast desert in the path of the invading army. As Dracula's army withdrew northward, abandoning territory to the Turks, they depopulated the area, burned their own villages, and set fire to the cities, reducing them to ghost towns. *Boyars*, peasants, and townspeople alike accompanied the retreating armies, unless they could find shelter in isolated mountain hideouts or inaccessible island monasteries such as Snagov, where the wealthy sought refuge. In addition, Dracula ordered the crops systematically burned, poisoned all the wells, and destroyed the cattle and all other domestic animals that could not be herded away into the mountains. His people dug huge pits and covered them with timber and leaves in order to trap men, camels, and horses. Dracula even ordered dams to be built to divert the waters of small rivers to create marshes that might impede the progress of the Turkish cannons by miring them down. Contemporary sources confirm the scenario of desolation that greeted the Turkish armies. For instance, a Greek historian states,

"Dracula removed his entire population to the mountains and forest regions, and he left the fields deserted. He had all beasts of burden herded up into the mountains. Thus, after having crossed the Danube and advancing for seven days, [Mehmed] II found no man, nor any significant animal, and nothing to eat or drink." A compatriot added, "Dracula had hidden the women and children in a very marshy area, protected by natural defenses, covered with dense oak forest. And he ordered his men to hide themselves in this forest, which was difficult for any newcomer to penetrate." On the Turkish side, the comments are very much the same. A veteran of the campaign complained that "the best of the Turks could find no springs … [no] drinkable water." Mahmud Pasha, one of the commanders who was sent ahead of the main army with a small contingent, thought that he had finally found a place to rest. "But even here," the veteran wrote, "for a distance of six leagues there was not a drop of water to be found. The intensity of the heat caused by the scorching sun was so great that the armor seemed as if it would melt like a lighted candle. In this parched plain, the lips of the fighters for Islam dried up. The Africans and Asians, used to desert conditions, used their shields to roast meat." Certainly a factor contributing to the sufferings and death endured by the Turkish army was the fact that the summer of 1462 was one of the hottest on record.

Along with the scorched-earth measures, Dracula used guerrilla tactics in which the element of surprise and intimate knowledge of the terrain were the keys to success. An Italian traveler reported that Dracula's cavalry would often emerge from relatively unknown paths and attack foraging Turkish stragglers who had departed from the main force. At times Dracula would even attack the main force when it least expected and, before they could rally, he would return to the forest without giving his enemy an opportunity to give battle on equal terms. Stragglers who remained behind the main body of the Turkish force were invariably isolated and killed, most likely by impalement. A most insidious tactic, almost unheard of in this period, was a fifteenth-century form of germ warfare. Dracula would encourage all those affected by diseases, such as leprosy, tuberculosis, and the bubonic plague, to dress in Turkish fashion and intermingle with the soldiers. Should they somehow survive their illness after successfully contaminating and killing Turks, the infected Wallachians would be richly rewarded. In that same vein, Dracula set free hardened criminals, who were then encouraged to kill Turkish stragglers.

The attack known as the Night of Terror is a dramatic example of Dracula's daring and mastery of surprise tactics. In one of the many villages leading to Tirgoviste, near the forest encampment of the Turks, Dracula held a council of war. The situation of Tirgoviste was desperate, and Dracula presented a bold plan for saving his indefensible capital. The council agreed that only the assassination of the sultan would sufficiently demoralize the Turkish army to effect a speedy withdrawal.

The outcome of this plan was admirably recorded by a Serbian soldier who experienced the whole impact of Dracula's audacious onslaught. His account described the complex Turkish camp: the sound of vigilant guards occasionally called to order, the smell of lamb roasting over glowing fires, the noise of departing soldiers, the laughter of women and other visitors, the plaintive chant of Turkish slaves, the noise of the camels, the countless tents, and finally, the elaborate gold-embroidered tent of the sleeping sultan in the very heart of the camp. Mehmed had just retired after a heavy meal. Suddenly came the hooting of an owl, Dracula's signal to attack, followed by the onrush of cavalry. The invaders penetrated the defensive layers of guards, frantically galloping through the tents housing half-asleep soldiers. The Wallachian sword and lance—with Dracula in the lead—cut a bloody swath. *"Kaziklu Bey!"*—"the Impaler!"—cried rows of awestruck Turkish soldiers, moaning and dying in the path of the Romanian avalanche. Finally Turkish trumpets called the men to arms. A body of determined elite guardsmen gradually assembled around the sultan's tent. Dracula had calculated that the sheer surprise and impetus of the attack would carry his cavalry to the sultan's bed. But as he was within sight of his goal, the sultan's guard rallied, held the Wallachian offensive, and actually began to push the attackers back. Realizing that he was in danger of being surrounded and captured, Dracula reluctantly gave the orders to retreat. He had killed several thousand Turks, wounded countless more, created havoc, chaos, and terror within the Turkish camp; but he had lost several hundred of his bravest warriors and the attack had failed. Sultan Mehmed had survived and the road to Tirgoviste lay open.

The grand vizier Machumet caught a Wallachian and, threatening him with torture, began to question him as to Dracula's whereabouts and ultimate plans. The prisoner remained silent and was eventually sawed in half. Overawed by such a display of courage, the grand vizier told the sultan, "If this man had been in command of an army he could have achieved great power."

The Turks eventually reached Tirgoviste but found neither men nor cattle, food nor drink. Indeed, the Wallachian capital presented a desolate spectacle to the incoming Turks. The gates of the city had been left open, and a thick blanket of smoke shut out the dawning light. The city had been stripped of virtually all its holy relics and treasures, the palace emptied of all that could be taken, and the rest burned. Here, as elsewhere, all the wells had been poisoned. The Turks were greeted by a few desultory cannon shots fired by the few Wallachian defenders who still manned the battlements. Mehmed II chose not to secure the capital but continued on his march in quest of the elusive Impaler. Just a few miles to the north, the sultan was greeted by an even more desolate spectacle: in a narrow gorge, one mile long, he found a veritable "forest of impaled cadavers, perhaps 20,000 in all." The sultan caught sight of the mangled, rotting remains of men, women, and children, the flesh eaten by blackbirds that nested in the skulls and rib cages. In addition, the sultan found the corpses of prisoners Dracula had caught at the beginning of the campaign the preceding winter. On a much higher pike lay the carcasses of the two assassins who had tried to ensnare Dracula before hostilities had begun. Over the course of several months the elements and the blackbirds had done their work. It was a scene horrible enough to discourage even the most hardhearted. Overawed by this spectacle, Mehmed II ordered the Turkish camp to be surrounded by a deep trench that very night. Soon, reflecting on what he had seen, the sultan lost heart. As one historian recorded it, "Even the sultan, overcome by amazement, admitted that he could not win the land from a man who does such things, and above all knows how to exploit his rule and that of his subjects in this way. A man who performs such deeds would be capable of even more awesome things!" The sultan then gave orders for the retreat of the main Turkish force and started eastward for a port on the Danube where the fleet had anchored.

After the withdrawal of Mehmed's contingent, the character of the war changed radically. Indeed this last chapter should be described more properly as a civil rather than a foreign war, even though Turkish soldiers were still involved. Before departing, Sultan Mehmed formally appointed Radu as commander-in-chief with the mission of destroying Dracula and taking over the princely office. The Turkish contingent, under the command of the pasha of Silistria, was to support Radu's actions, but the new commander was to rely primarily upon native support. The Turks had deliberately fostered this conflict in order to confuse the Wallachians and avoid the impression of a national war against a common foe, in effect abandoning their erstwhile plan to conquer Wallachia by reducing it to an obedient vassal state. What they had failed to do by force of arms they accomplished by diplomacy. Thus, in the final analysis, it was less a matter of tactics than of politics. The last battles pitted Dracula not so much against the Turks as against the powerful Romanian *boyars* who ultimately and decisively rallied to the cause of Radu. "The Romanian *boyars* realizing that the Turks were stronger, abandoned Dracula and associated themselves with his brother who was with the Turkish Sultan." So ended an account by a Serbian janissary.

There was another more compelling reason for the Turkish withdrawal. The plague had made its appearance within the sultan's ranks and the first victims of the dreaded disease were recorded at Tirgoviste. Perhaps Dracula's attempt at bacterial warfare had worked.

Dracula's desperate appeal for help from his kinsman Stephen was answered with treachery. In June, the Moldavian ruler attacked the crucial Wallachian fortress of Chilia from the north, while powerful Turkish contingents attacked it from the south simultaneously. Yet this extraordinary double assault was unsuccessful. The Turks abandoned the siege. Stephen was wounded by gunfire from the fortress and withdrew to Moldavia. He did not renew the attack on Chilia until 1465, and that time he captured it, while his cousin Dracula was safely in a Hungarian jail many miles farther up the Danube at Visegrad.

During the last phase of the Turkish-Wallachian war, Dracula ruled from his castle on the upper Arges, the prince's final place of refuge from the advancing Turks. Since the primary chronicler of the Turkish campaign returned to Constantinople with the sultan and the main bulk of the army, historians must rely on popular ballads from the castle region for information.

The peasants in the villages surrounding Castle Dracula relate numerous tales concerning the end of Dracula's second reign in the fall of 1462. All these stories end when Dracula crossed the border into Transylvania and became prisoner of the Hungarian king. They start anew around 1476, when Dracula returned to Wallachia for this third reign. One of the more classic narrations of Dracula's last moments of resistance to the Turks in 1462 runs as follows: after the fall of Tirgoviste, Dracula and a few faithful followers headed northward; avoiding the more obvious passes leading to Transylvania, they reached his mountain retreat. The Turks who had been sent in pursuit encamped on the bluff of Poenari, which commanded an admirable view of Dracula's castle on the opposite bank of the Arges. Here they set up their cherrywood cannons. The bulk of the Turkish soldiers descended to the river, forded it, and camped on the other side. The bombardment of Dracula's castle began, but it had little success owing to the small caliber of the Turkish guns and the solidity of the castle walls. Orders for the final assault upon the castle were set for the next day.

That night, a Romanian slave in the Turkish corps who, according to local tale, was a distant relative of Dracula, forewarned the Wallachian prince of the great danger that lay ahead. Undetected in the moonless night, the slave climbed the bluff of Poenari and, taking careful aim, he shot an arrow at one of the distant, dimly lit openings in the main tower, which he knew contained Dracula's quarters. Attached to the arrow was a message advising Dracula to escape while there was still time. The arrow extinguished a candle within the tower opening. When it was relit, the slave could see the shadow of Dracula's wife, and could faintly discern that she was reading the message.

The remainder of this story could only have been passed down by Dracula's intimate advisors within the castle. Dracula's wife apprised her husband of the warning. She told him she would rather have her body eaten by the fish in the Arges River below than be led into captivity by the Turks. Dracula knew from his own experience at Egrigoz what that imprisonment would entail. Realizing how desperate their situation was and before anyone could intervene, Dracula's wife rushed up the winding staircase and hurled herself from the tower. Today this point of the river is known as *Riul Doamnei,* the Princess's River. This tragic folktale is practically the only mention of Dracula's first wife.

Dracula immediately made plans for his own escape; no matter how unfavorable the circumstances, suicide was not an option. He ordered the bravest leaders from the neighboring village of Arefu to be brought to the castle, and during the night they discussed the various routes of escape to Transylvania. It was Dracula's hope that Matthias of Hungary, to whom he had sent many appeals since that first letter in February 1462, would greet him as an ally and support his reinstatement on the Wallachian throne. Indeed, it was known that the Hungarian king, along with a powerful army, had established headquarters just across the mountains at Brasov. To reach him was a matter of crossing the Transylvanian Alps at a point where there were no roads or passes. The upper slopes of these mountains are rocky, treacherous, often covered with snow or ice throughout the summer. Dracula could not have attempted such a crossing without the help of local experts. Popular folklore still identifies various rivers, clearings, forested areas, even rocks which were along Dracula's escape route. We have tried to use them to reconstruct Dracula's actual passage, but the task has been difficult since many of the place names have changed over the years. As far as we have been able to reconstruct the escape, Dracula, a dozen attendants, his illegitimate son, and five guides left the castle before dawn by way of a staircase which spiraled down into the bowels of the mountain and led to a cave on the banks of the river. Here the fleeing party could hear the noises of the Turkish camp just a mile to the south. Some of the fastest mounts were then brought from the village; the horses were equipped with inverted horseshoes so as to leave false signs of an approaching cavalry.

During the night the castle guns were repeatedly fired to detract attention from the escape party. The Turks at Poenari replied in kind. Because of the noise, so the story goes, Dracula's own mount began to shy, and his son, who had been tied to the saddle, fell to the ground and in the confusion was lost. The situation was far too desperate for anyone to begin a search, and Dracula was both too battle-hardened and too coldhearted to sacrifice himself for his son.

This tragic little vignette had a happy outcome, though. The boy, not yet in his teens, was found the next morning by a shepherd who took him to his hut and raised him as though he were one of his own family. When Dracula returned as prince fourteen years later, the peasant, who had found out the true identity of his ward, brought the boy to the castle. By that time he had developed into a splendid young man. He told his father all that the shepherd had done for him, and in gratitude Dracula richly recompensed the peasant with tracts of land in the surrounding mountains. It is possible that the son stayed on in the area and eventually became governor of the castle.

When the fleeing party finally reached the crests of the mountains, they were able to view the Turks' final assault to the south, which partially destroyed Castle Dracula. To the north lay the fortified walls and towers of Brasov, where it was hoped the armies of King Matthias were maneuvering to come to Dracula's aid. At a place called Plaiul Oilor, or Plain of the Sheep, Dracula's party, now quite safe from the Turks, retired and made plans for the northward descent.

Summoning his brave companions, Dracula asked them how best he could recompense them for saving his life. They answered that they had simply done their duty for prince and country. The prince, however, insisted: "What do you wish? Money or land?" They answered: "Give us land, Your Highness." On a slab of stone known as the Prince's Table, Dracula fulfilled their wishes, writing upon the skin of some hares caught the day before. He bestowed upon the five guides vast tracts of land on the slope of the mountain as far as the eye could see. This included sixteen mountains and a rich supply of timber, fish, and sheep, all in all perhaps 20,000 acres. He further stipulated in the deed that none of this land could ever be taken away from them by prince, *boyar*, or ecclesiastical leaders; it was for their families to enjoy through the generations.

Ancient tradition has it that these rabbit skins are still carefully hidden by the five men's descendants, but despite many efforts and inducements, no descendant has been willing to shed light on the exact whereabouts of these alleged documents. Still, we have reason to suppose that somewhere hidden in an attic or buried underground, the Dracula rabbit skins still exist. One Romanian historian attempted to find the scrolls, but the peasants of the area remained secretive and intractable. Even large sums of money would not persuade them to share such precious souvenirs of Dracula's heroic age.

Vlad Tepes depicted in a German engraving

The Imprisonment and Final Reign of Dracula

By Kurt W. Treplow

We have faith in God that we shall again be that which we once were, and much more.

—Petru Rareș, 1540[1]

Afterhisarrestandimprisonmentin1462, Draculawouldnotbeheardfromagain for thirteen years. During this time, a legend was born which over the centuries would be transformed into the vampire myth of today. The forged letter used to justify Matthias Corvinus's imprisonment of the brave prince who defied the sultan was only the beginning; the Hungarian court, aided by Vlad's Saxon enemies, promoted the spread of legends about the evil deeds of the prince. They were aided in their efforts by a new technological development of the fifteenth century, the invention of moveable type.

As a result, these stories were published in a variety of editions and spread throughout the German speaking world during the late fifteenth and early sixteenth centuries;[2] first as political propaganda against the Wallachian prince to justify the actions of Matthias Corvinus, and later as popular literature that would be among the first bestsellers in Europe. These stories would also form the basis for a similar set of tales that circulated

---

1   Letter of Petru Rareș, prince of Moldavia (1527–1528 and 1541–1546), as he prepared to take the throne of Moldavia for a second time, see Iorga, Scrisori de boieri, scrisori de domni, p. 201.

2   On the German Stories about Dracula see P.P. Panaitescu, "The German Stories about Vlad Țepeș" pp. 185–196, in Treptow, *Dracula: Essays ...* See appendix IV which contains a complete English translation of the tales; and Anton Balotă, "An Analysis of the Dracula Tales," in *Ibidem,* pp. 153–184. See also the long poem of the court bard Michel Beheim, "Von Ainem Wutrich der Hiess Trakle Waida," pp. 104–153, in Cazacu, *L'histoire du prince Dracula.* These tales present an extremely negative image of Dracula in order to justify Saxon political opposition to the prince, as well as his arrest and imprisonment by Matthias Corvinus.

in the Slavic world, first appearing in 1486.[3] These tales all helped to create the image of the ruthless and bloody tyrant that centuries later would be transformed into a diabolical vampire; the nature of these tales and the purpose for which they were written demand that they be used with great caution by historians. In this way the legend of Dracula was born even before the death of the Wallachian prince.

During this missing period in the career of Vlad III Dracula he was held prisoner at the castle of Visegrad, near Buda. Meanwhile, his brother, Radu cel Frumos, enjoyed relatively good relations with both the Ottoman Empire and Hungary, apart from the usual conflicts with the Saxon cities of Transylvania. The greatest threat faced by Wallachia during his reign came from Stephen the Great, who, as he began to assert his independence more and more, tried to dominate the neighboring Romanian principality. The first conflict between the two occurred in 1465 when Stephen succeeded in seizing Chilia.[4] After this attack, peaceful relations between Moldavia and Wallachia resumed,[5] until Stephen again launched an attack on his neighbor, pillaging and burning Brăila, Târgul Floci, and Ialomița in 1470.[6] These attacks had an economic character as the localities pillaged and burned were important commercial centers of eastern Wallachia, and craftsmen and Gypsy slaves were taken in the raids. The Moldavian prince hoped to destroy Wallachian commerce in the Danube region in favor of his principality.[7] This marked the beginning of a series of border wars between the two Romanian states.

During this period Stephen the Great began to support Basarab Laiotă, a pretender to the Wallachian throne.[8] At the end of 1473 Stephen invaded Wallachia and installed Laiotă on the throne, capturing part of the princely treasure along with Radu's wife and his young daughter, Maria Voichița, who would later become his wife. Less than a month later, Radu, with Ottoman assistance, would regain the throne.[9] The throne would alternate a number of times over the next year between Radu cel Frumos

---

3   See P.P. Panaitescu, "Viața lui Vlad Țepeș: Povestire despre Dracula voievod," pp. 195–214, in *Cronicile slavo-romîne*; Pan dele Olteanu, *Limba povestirilor slave despre Vlad Țepeș*, and Balotă, "An Analysis of the Dracula Tales," pp. 153–184, in Treptow, *Dracula: Essays*. … The Slavic Stories present the image of a cruel but just prince, unlike the German tales that stress his excessive cruelty. Some have gone so far as to suggest that these stories could be considered as a Slavic version of Machiavelli's *The Prince*.

4   "Cronica moldo-germană," in Panaitescu, *Cronicile slavo-romîne*, p. 29.

5   See the treaty between Moldavia and Poland from 1468 in which Stephen the Great does not list Wallachia among his enemies. See Bogdan, *Documentele lui Ștefan cel Mare*, vol. II, pp. 300–304.

6   Costăchescu, *Arderea Târgului Floci și a Ialomiței în 1470*, pp. 1–3.

7   Panaitescu, "Comunele medievale în principatele romîne," in *Interpretări românești*, pp. 151–152.

8   See Costăchescu, *Arderea Târgului Floci și a Ialomiței în 1470*, pp. 99–105. This is the same pretender that had established himself in Sighișoara in 1459–1460 during the reign of Dracula.

9   "Letopisețul anonim al Moldovei," p. 17, and "Letopisețul de la Putna II," p. 63, in Panaitescu, *Cronicile slavo-romîne*.

and Basarab Laiotă, until Stephen finally succeeded in establishing his protege on the Wallachian throne at the beginning of 1475. At the same time, Stephen broke off relations with the Ottomans in 1474, refusing to pay tribute any longer. The Ottomans responded by invading Moldavia early in 1475, but suffered a great defeat at the hands of the Moldavian army at Podul Înalt near Vaslui on 10 January.[10]

It is during this period that we again hear news of Dracula. Stephen's ally, Basarab Laiotă, after seizing the throne from Radu cel Frumos, turned his back on the Moldavian prince and cooperated with the Turks during their invasion of Moldavia. The Moldavian prince knew that the sultan would not be content to leave the humiliating defeat of his forces at Vaslui unpunished, and that he would soon prepare a campaign against Moldavia. Under these circumstances Stephen now entered into an alliance with his former enemy, Matthias Corvinus,[11] and looked for a new pretender to the throne of Wallachia:

> I asked that Prince Basarab be removed from the other Romanian land and that another Christian prince be put on its throne, Dracula by name, with whom we can cooperate; I requested of His Majesty, the king of Hungary to allow Vlad Dracula to become prince.[12]

It is reasonable that Stephen would ask for Vlad's restoration to the throne at this time. Like Dracula in 1462, the Moldavian prince was now an ally of the Hungarian king and at war with the Ottomans. Under these circumstances Matthias Corvinus released Vlad from prison. The Slavic Stories about Vlad Țepeș, which contain information about his imprisonment at Buda, relate that:

> the king sent a messenger to him in prison, telling him that if he wished to again be prince of Wallachia, as before, then he must accept the Latin faith [Catholicism]. If he refused he would die in prison. Dracula preferred the sweetness of temporal life more than eternal life, and he abandoned Orthodoxy and the truth, and left light for darkness. He did not have the patience to endure the passing hardships of prison and he prepared himself for eternal suffering by abandoning our Orthodox faith and receiving the

---

10 "This event is mentioned in all the Moldavian chronicles of the time, see Panaitescu, *Cronicile slavo-romîne*, pp. 18, 33, 50, 63, and 72. News of this remarkable victory circulated throughout Europe. See, for example, the letter of the rector of Raguza to the doge of Venice, dated 12 February 1475, doc. V in Bianu, "Ștefanu cel Mare: Câteva documente din archivulu de statu dela Milanu," pp. 41–42.

11 Bogdan, *Documentele lui Ștefan cel Mare*, vol. II, p. 332.

12 Bogdan, *Documentele lui Ștefan cel Mare*, vol. II, p. 349.

Latin heresy. The king not only made him prince of Wallachia, but he also gave his sister to him to be his wife.[13]

Essentially, in return for his release from prison, Vlad was required to accept the terms of the agreement he concluded with Matthias at the end of 1461. Dracula accepted these terms and was released from prison in 1475; he then prepared to take the throne of Wallachia for the third time.

In August, 1475, Matthias Corvinus sought to reconcile the two princes who had been enemies in 1462, announcing that:

> we bring about an agreement between the two princes, Stephen of Moldavia and Vlad of Wallachia, based upon the agreements that had been concluded between Alexander the Good and Mircea the Old, princes of these two countries.[14]

It would still be some time, however, before Vlad would be allowed to reclaim his heritage. As usual, Matthias Corvinus was indecisive. Being occupied during this time with affairs in Serbia and Bosnia, he delayed preparations for an attack on Wallachia. Meanwhile, Vlad served as a commander in the royal army; together with the Serbian Prince Vuk Brankovic, he led an attack on the Ottomans in Bosnia in February-March, 1476, seizing Srebrenica and other towns, capturing great booty, and spreading terror among the Turks.[15]

In the summer of 1476 the sultan, accompanied by Basarab Laiotă, personally led an expedition against the prince of Moldavia. The Ottoman forces plundered Moldavia, reaching as far as the capital of Suceava. The two armies met in a great battle at Războieni on 26 July where the Moldavian army was defeated, but Stephen the Great escaped. The sultan then besieged the fortress of Neamț, an important Moldavian stronghold, but he was unable to capture it. The Ottomans, suffering from a lack of provisions and an outbreak of the plague, were forced to retreat; a German chronicler, Jakob Unrest, recalls that, around the time of the sultan's retreat from Moldavia, Stephen was joined by forces commanded by Dracula and Vuk Brankovic who helped him regain control of Moldavia.[16] As they withdrew from the country, the Ottoman troops were harassed

---

13   "Viat;a lui Vlad Țepeș," in Panaitescu, *Cronicele slavo-romine,* p. 212; and Olteanu, *Limba po vests rile slave despre Vlad Țepeș,* p. 363.

14   Bogdan, *Documentele lui Ștefen sel Mare,* vol. II, pp. 334–335.

15   Ștefan Andreescu, "Military Actions of Vlad Țepeș Southeastern Europe in 1476," in Treptow, *Dracula: Essays …,* pp. 139–140.

16   Jakob Unrest, "Osterreichische Chronik," in Karl Grossman, ed., *Monumenta Germaniae Historica, Scriptores Rerum Germanicarum, Nova Series,* XI (Weimar, 1957), p. 68. On this question see Andreescu, "Military Actions of Vlad Țepeș in Southeastern Europe in 1476," in Treptow, *Dracula: Essays …,* pp. 145–146.

all along their way by the regrouped Moldavian forces.[17] Thus, the Byzantine chronicler George Sphrantzes recorded:

In the summer of 6984 [1476] the Sultan advanced against Greater Wallachia [Moldavia] with all his forces. He returned in September ... he had suffered more defeats than victories.[18]

After the failure of the Ottomans to remove Stephen from the throne of Moldavia, both the Hungarian king and the Moldavian prince began to make preparations to oust Basarab Laiotă and return Vlad III Dracula to the throne of Wallachia. On 7 October 1476 he was in Braşov where he emitted the decree previously discussed, reestablishing economic relations between Wallachia and the Saxon lands, as it was in earlier days, in the time of the great Mircea voievod, until the days of My Majesty's father, the great Vlad voievod, and then also during my reign.[19]

By early November preparations for the invasion of Wallachia had been completed. Vlad, aided by Hungarian troops, set out from Braşov, while Stephen the Great simultaneously launched an invasion from the northeast. Victory came swiftly for the invading forces led by Dracula, who, on 8 November, wrote to the councilors of Braşov announcing:

Herewith I give you news that I have overthrown our foe Laiotă, who fled to the Turks. Thus, God has given you a free path. Come with bread and goods, and you will eat now that God has given us a single country.[20]

After having captured the capital of Wallachia, the next important objective was the fortress of Bucharest; here troops led by Stephen the Great would join Vlad's army in their attack on this key fortress. News of this battle reached Braşov in a letter sent by Cârstian, the *pârcălab* of Târgovişte, on 17 November:

I send you news that the fortress of Bucharest was won this past Saturday [16 November]. Therefore, I ask you to give praise to the Almighty God with

---

17   See the Moldavian chronicles from the time contained in Panaitescu, *Cronicile slavo-romîne*, pp. 18, 33–34, 50, 63, and 72; Nicolae Iorga, *Istoria lui Ştefan cel Mare povestită neamului românesc* (Bucureşti, 1904), pp. 174–181; Ion Ursu, *Şefan cel Mare şi turcii* (Bucureşti, 1914), pp. 71–72; and Ilie Minea, *Cetatea Neamţului*(Iasj, 1943), p. 8.

18   Sphrantzes, *The Fall of the Byzantine Empire*, p. 94 [XLVII.6].

19   Doc. LXXIV in Bogdan, *Documente privitoare la relapile Ţării Româneşti cu Braşovul şi Ţara Ungurească*, pp. 95–97; doc. 100 in Tocilescu, *534 documente istorice slavo-române*, pp. 95–97.

20   Doc. LXXV in Bogdan, *Documente privitoare la relapile Ţării Româneşti cu Braşovulşi Ţara Ungurească*, pp. 97–98; and doc. 101 in Tocilescu, *534 documente istorice slavo- române*, p. 97.

organs, songs, and bells, as we have done in our country which is also yours. And you must know that all the boyars of the country have sworn allegiance to Vlad vodă.[21]

Vlad III Dracula had succeeded in gaining the throne of Wallachia for a third time. In a report sent to the duke of Milan by Giustiniano Cavitello, his representative in Buda, dated 4 December 1476, we learn that:

the people [the assembly of boyars that proclaimed Dracula as prince] asked both of the voievods [Vlad and Stephen] to swear love and allegiance to one another so that all of the country could be certain that the Turks would no longer harm them.[22]

Although we have little information about his third reign, we do know that Vlad respected the promises contained in his decree of 7 October and restored free trade between Wallachia and the Saxon lands. Shortly after regaining the throne for a third time, Dracula informed the officials and councilors of Braşov and Ţara Bârsei:

My Majesty gives you news that, with the help of God, all of Wallachia and its boyars have submitted to me; and God has opened the roads to you everywhere, to Rucăr, Prahova, Teleajin, and Buzău. Therefore go now freely where you like and feed yourselves. And God will be pleased.[23]

Although it seemed as if his former power and glory had been restored to him, Dracula's reign would come to an abrupt end. Little over a month after his third reign began, Basarab Laiotă, joined by an Ottoman army, invaded Wallachia and seized the

---

21   Doc. CCCXII in Bogdan, *Documente privitoare la relaţiile Ţării Româneşti cu Braşovul şi Ţara Ungurească*, pp. 357–358. In a letter to the pope, dated 8 December 1476, Matthias Corvinus wrote:

My army, which numbered 60,000 men, besieged the fortress [Bucharest] and conquered it, taking control of the country through which the Turks had easy entry into Moldavia, while Vlad Dracula, my captain, a fierce warrior ... in accordance with my wishes and desire was received as prince by the inhabitants of the country.

See Hurmuzaki, *Documente*, vol. VIII, pp. 22–23. The Hungarian king's estimation of the size of his forces is an exaggeration, probably to impress upon the pope the great expense he incurred, as diplomatic sources indicate that Vlad had 25,000 troops, while Stephen led a force of 15,000 (see the letter of Giustiniano Cavitello to the Duke of Milan, dated 4 December 1476, in Iorga, *Acte şi fragmente cu privire la istoria rominilor*, pp. 58–59).

22   Iorga, *Acte şi fragmente cu privire la istoria rominilor*, pp. 58–59.

23   Doc. LXXVI in Bogdan, *Documente privitoare la relaţiile Ţării Româneşti cu Braşovul şi Ţara Ungurească*, p. 98; and doc. 102 in Tocilescu, *534 documente istorice slavo- române*, pp. 97–98.

throne from Vlad III who perished in the fighting. In early January, 1477, news of Vlad's death reached Moldavia. In a letter dated 10 January, Stephen recounted that:

> the disloyal Basarab returned, and finding Vlad voievod alone, killed him along with all my men; only ten of them escaped with their lives.[24]

Additional information is provided in a letter, dated 1 February 1477, to the duke of Milan from his ambassador to Buda, Leonardo Botta:

> the Turks entered Wallachia and again conquered the country and cut to pieces Dracula, the captain of the king of Hungary, with approximately 4,000 of his men.[25]

Thus the life of Vlad III Dracula came to an end. The legend surrounding this enigmatic figure, however, would continue to grow, making him one of the most famous Romanian princes in all of history. While many consider him a villainous tyrant or a heroic crusader for the cause of Christianity against the Turkish Infidels, what can be said of Dracula for certain is that he was a prince driven by the desire to strengthen and protect his country's independence. "We do not want to leave unfinished that which we began," he wrote to Matthias Corvinus in 1462, "but to follow it through to the end."[26] His failure to do so would be symbolic of the fate of the Romanian principalities that would endure centuries of foreign domination.

---

24   See doc. CLIV in Bogdan, *Documentele lui Ştefan cel Mare*, vol. II, p. 345. At Vlad's request, Stephen had left a guard of 200 Moldavian troops to help protect the Wallachian prince.

25   "Quoted in Xenopol, "Lupta dintre Dăneşti şi Draculeşti," p. 33 (215).

26   Iorga, *Scrisori de boieri, season de domni*, pp. 166–170.

The Female Vampire: Elizabeth Bathory

Elizabeth Bathory (1560–1614)
from *The Vampire Book*

Edited by J. Gordon Melton

Elizabeth Bathory was the countess who tortured and murdered numerous young women and, because of these acts, became known as one of the "true" vampires in history. She was born in 1560, the daughter of George and Anna Bathory. Though frequently cited as Hungarian, due in large part to the shifting borders of the Hungarian Empire, she was in fact more closely associated with what is now the Slovak Republic. Most of her adult life was spent at Castle Cachtrice, near the town of Vishine, northeast of present-day Bratslava, where Austria, Hungary, and the Slovak Republic come together. (The castle was mistakenly cited by Raymond T. McNally as being in Transylvania.) Bathory grew up in an era when much of Hungary had been overrun by the Turkish forces of the Ottoman empire and was a battleground between Turkish and Austrian (Hapsburg) armies. The area was also split by religious differences. Her family sided with the new wave of Protestantism that opposed the traditional Roman Catholicism. She was raised on the Bathory family estate at Ecsed in Transylvania. As a child she was subject to seizures accompanied by intense rage and uncontrollable behavior. In 1571, her cousin Stephen became Prince of Transylvania and, later in the decade, additionally assumed the throne of Poland. He was one of the most effective rulers of his day, though his plans for uniting Europe against the Turks were somewhat foiled by having to turn his attention toward fighting Ivan the Terrible, who desired Stephen's territory.

In 1574, Elizabeth became pregnant as a result of a brief affair with a peasant man. When her condition became evident, she was sequestered until the baby arrived because she was engaged to marry Count Ferenc Nadasdy. The marriage took place in May 1575. Count Nadasdy was a soldier and frequently away from home for long periods. Meanwhile, Elizabeth assumed the duties of managing the affairs at Castle Sarvar, the Nadasdy family estate. It was here that her career of evil really began—with the disciplining of the large household staff, particularly the young girls.

Elizabeth Bathory, known as the "female Dracula."

In a time period in which cruel and arbitrary behavior by those in power toward those who were servants was common, Elizabeth's level of cruelty was noteworthy. She did not just punish infringements on her rules, but found excuses to inflict punishments and delighted in the torture and death of her victims far beyond what her contemporaries could accept. She would stick pins in various sensitive body parts, such as under the fingernails. In the winter she would execute victims by having them stripped, led out into the snow, and doused with water until they were frozen.

Elizabeth's husband joined in some of the sadistic behavior and actually taught his wife some new varieties of punishment. For example, he showed her a summertime version of her freezing exercise—he had a woman stripped, covered with honey, then left outside to be bitten by numerous insects. He died in 1604, and Elizabeth moved to Vienna soon after his burial. She also began to spend time at her estate at Beckov and at a manor house at Cachtice, both located in the present-day country of Slovakia. These were the scenes of her most famous and vicious acts.

In the years immediately after her husband's death, Elizabeth's main cohort in crime was a woman named Anna Darvulia, about whom little is known. When Darvulia's health failed in 1609, Elizabeth turned to Erzsi Majorova, the widow of a local tenant farmer. It was Majorova who seems to have been responsible for Elizabeth's eventual downfall by encouraging her to include a few women of noble birth among her victims. Because she was having trouble procuring more young servant girls as rumors of her activities spread through the countryside, Elizabeth followed Majorova's advice. At some point in 1609, she killed a young noble woman and covered it by charges of suicide.

As early as the summer of 1610, an initial inquiry had begun into Elizabeth's crimes. Underlying the inquiry, quite apart from the steadily increasing number of victims, were political concerns. The crown hoped to confiscate Elizabeth's large land-holdings and escape having to pay back the extensive loan that her husband had made to the king. With these things in mind, Elizabeth was arrested on December 29, 1610.

Elizabeth was placed on trial a few days later. It was conducted by Count Thurzo as an agent of the king. As noted, the trial (rightly characterized as a show trial by Bathory's biographer Raymond T. McNally) was initiated to not only obtain a conviction, but to also confiscate her lands. A week after the first trial, a second trial was convened on January 7, 1611. At this trial, a register found in Elizabeth's living quarters was introduced as evidence. It noted the names of 650 victims, all recorded in her handwriting. Her accomplices were sentenced to be executed, the manner determined by their roles in the tortures. Elizabeth was sentenced to life imprisonment in solitary confinement. She was placed in a room in her castle at Cachtice without windows or doors and only a small opening for food and a few slits for air. There she remained for the next three years until her death on August 21, 1614. She was buried in the Bathory land at Ecsed.

Above and beyond Elizabeth's reputation as a sadistic killer with more than 600 victims, she has been accused of being both a werewolf and a vampire. During her trials, testimony was presented that on occasion, she bit the flesh of the girls while torturing them. These accusations became the basis of her connection with were-wolfism. The connection between Elizabeth and vampirism is somewhat more tenuous. Of course, it was a popular belief in Slavic lands that people who were werewolves in life became vampires in death, but that was not the accusation leveled at Elizabeth. Rather, she was accused of draining the blood of her victims and bathing in it to retain her youthful beauty, and she was by all accounts a most attractive woman.

RECOVERING ELIZABETH'S STORY

No testimony to this activity was offered at her trial, and in fact, there was no contemporary testimony that she engaged in such a practice. Following her death, the records of the trials were sealed because the revelations of her activities were quite scandalous for the Hungarian ruling community. Hungarian King Matthias II forbade the mention of her name in polite society. It was not until 100 years later that a Jesuit priest, Laszlo Turoczy, located copies of some of the original trial documents and gathered stories circulating among the people of Cachtice, the site of Elizabeth's castle. Turoczy included an account of her life in a book he wrote on Hungarian history. His book initially suggested the possibility that she bathed in blood. Published in the 1720s, it appeared during the wave of vampirism in Eastern Europe that excited the interest of the continent. Later writers would pick up and embellish the story. Two stories illustrate the legends that had gathered around Elizabeth in the absence of the court records of her life and the attempts to remove any mention of her from Hungarian history:

It was said that one day, the aging countess was having her hair combed by a young servant girl. The girl accidently pulled her hair, and Elizabeth turned and slapped the servant. Blood was drawn, and some of it spurted onto Elizabeth's hands. As she rubbed it on her hands, they seemed to take on the girl's youthful appearance. It was from this incident that Elizabeth developed her reputation for desiring the blood of young virgins.

The second story involves Elizabeth's behavior after her husband's death, when it was said she associated herself with younger men. On one occasion when she was with one of those men, she saw an old woman. She remarked, "What would you do if you had to kiss that old hag?" He responded with expected words of distaste. The old woman, however, on hearing the exchange, accused Elizabeth of excessive vanity and noted that such an aged appearance was inescapable, even for the countess. Several historians have tied the death of Bathory's husband and this story into the hypothesized concern with her own aging, and thus, the bathing in blood.

Elizabeth has not been accused of being a traditional blood-drinking or blood-sucking vampire, though her attempts to take and use the blood to make herself more youthful would certainly qualify her as at least a vampire by metaphor. Previously a little known historical figure, she was rediscovered when interest in vampires rose sharply in the 1970s; since that time she has repeatedly been tied to vampirism in popular culture. Noticeable interest in Elizabeth was evident in the publication of a series of books in the early 1970s beginning with Valentine Penrose's *Erzsebet Bathory, La Comtesse Sanglante*, a 1962 French volume whose English translation, *The Bloody Countess*, was published in 1970. It was followed by Donald Glut's *True Vampires of History* (1971) and Gabriel Ronay's *The Truth about Dracula* (1972). Penrose's book inspired the first of the Bathory films; the movie in turn, inspired a novel based on its screenplay, *Countess Dracula* by Michael Parry. The celebration of the mythical countess in the 1970s motivated Dracula scholar Raymond McNally to produce by far the most authoritative book on Elizabeth to date—*Dracula was a Woman: In Search of the Blood Countess of Transylvania*—which appeared in 1984. Based on a new search through the original court documents, and a broad understanding of Eastern European history and folklore, McNally thoroughly demythologized the legend and explained many of the problems that had baffled previous researchers. Recently, Elaine Bergstrom authored a novel, *Daughter of the Night* (1992), that drew inspiration from McNally's study.

BATHORY ON FILM

The first movie inspired by the Bathory legend was the now largely forgotten *I Vampiri* (released in the United States as *The Devil's Commande-ment*), notable today because of the work of future director Mario Bava as the film's cameraman. A decade later, as part of its vampire cycle, Hammer Films released what is possibly the best of the several movies based on Elizabeth's life, *Countess Dracula* (1970). Ingrid Pitt starred in the title role. The film was built around the mythical blood baths and portrayed her as going increasingly crazy as she continued her murderous career.

Daughters of Darkness (1971), one of the most artistic of all vampire films, brought the countess into the twentieth-century in a tale with strong lesbian overtones. In the movie, Elizabeth and her companion Iona check into an almost empty hotel where they meet a newlywed couple. When it is revealed that the husband has a violent streak, the stage is set for Elizabeth and Iona to move in and "help" the new bride. A series of vampiric encounters ensues, and in the end, the wife (the newest vampire) emerges as the only survivor.

Elizabeth, (or a character modeled on her) also appeared in *Legend of Blood Castle* (1972), *Curse of the* Devil (1973), and *Immoral Tales* (1974), all films of lesser note. In

1981, a full-length animated version of Elizabeth's story was released in Czechoslovakia. More recent films include *Thirst* (1980) and *The Mysterious Death of Nina Chereau* (1987).

BATHORY AND DRACULA

Bram Stoker, the author of *Dracula* (1897), read of Elizabeth in *The Book of Werewolves* by Sabine Baring-Gould (1865) where the first lengthy English-language account of Elizabeth's life appeared. McNally has suggested that the description of Elizabeth might have influenced Stoker to shift the site of his novel from Austria (Styria), where he initially seemed to have set it, to Transylvania. In like measure, McNally noted that Dracula became younger and younger as the novel proceeded, an obvious allusion to the stories of Elizabeth bathing in blood to retain her youth. He made a strong case that the legends about her "played a major role in the creation of the character of Count Dracula in the midst of Bram Stoker."

SOURCES

Baring-Gould, Sabine. *The Book of Werewolves*. London: Smith, Elder, 1865. Reprint. New York: Causeway Books, 1973.

Glut, Donald F. *True Vampires of History*. New York: HC Publishers, 1971.

McNally, Raymond T. *Dracula was a Woman: In Search of the Blood Countess of Transylvania*. New York: McGraw-Hill, 1983. Reprint. London: Robert Hale, 1984. Reprint. London: Hamlyn, 1984.

Parry, Michel. *Countess Dracula*. London: Sphere Books, 1971. Reprint. New York: Beagle Books, 1971.

Penrose, Valentine. *Erzsebet Bathory, La Comtesse Sanglante*. Paris: Mercure du Paris, 1962. English translation as: *The Bloody Countess*. London: Calder & Boyars, 1970. Rept: London: Creation Books, 1996. 157 pp.

Ronay, Gabriel. *The Truth about Dracula*. London: Gallancz, 1972. Reprint. New York: Stein and Day, 1972. Thorne, Tony. Countess Dracula: *The Life and Times of Elisabeth Báthory, the Blood Countess*. London: Bloomsbury, 1997. 274 pp.

Elizabeth Bathory from
The Vampire Encyclopedia

By Matthew Bunson

Hungarian noblewoman (1560–1614) and member of the powerful Bathory family who became known as the "Bloody Countess" for her multiple murders and obsession with blood. Married to the warrior count Ferenz Nadasdy, Bathory spent many nights alone while her husband was fighting the Turks. She developed obsessive interests in her own beauty, in pleasure, in the occult, and in the most depraved kinds of sadism, which were normally manifested toward her serving girls, with whom she engaged in orgies before murdering them with the help of her lieutenants. Bathory became convinced that blood was a useful cosmetic and restorative when she hit a victim so hard that her blood splashed onto the countess's face and arms; when she washed off the blood she believed that her skin felt smoother and younger. Henceforth she drank, bathed, and showered in the blood of maidens, murdering hundreds of young girls who were brought into her service.

Exact figures on the number of her victims vary, but some accounts put the number at 610, others as few as 50. Inevitably, however, the truth became known, and in 1610 the countess and her henchmen were arrested, tried, and convicted. Her accomplices were executed or imprisoned, and Bathory was walled up in her bedroom at Castle Csejthe. Four years later the guards who attended her looked through the tiny slot used to provide her with food and discovered that she was dead. The "living vampire" was no more, although her memory was kept alive by legends and tales. Several films were made about her, including *Daughters of Darkness* (1970), *Countess Dracula* (1971), *Blood Castle* (1972), *Ceremonia Sangrienta* (1972), and *La Noche de Walpurgis* (1972). (See *Aging; Baths, Blood; Blood; Historical Vampires; Hematomania;* and *Sex and Love.*)

The Passion of Elizabeth Bathory: Bloody Christmas 1610

By Raymond T. McNally

Times were changing—and not in Elizabeth's favor. After 1606 when the Austrians concluded peace with the Turks at Zsitva-Török (where the Zsitva River flows into the Danube) the era of great turmoil was drawing to an end. The lawlessness and the extraordinary power of the local nobles were slowly coming to an end. Archduke Matthias, brother of the Holy Roman emperor Rudolf II, who had wrested control of Hungary from his brother's hands, was intent upon restoring order in the Hungarian lands. Matthias saw to it that the city of Bratislava (called Pozsony in Hungarian and Pressburg in German) became acknowledged as the new capital of Hungary. Rudolf retreated deeper and deeper into his castle in order to avoid learning about his hated brother's triumphs. He eventually went insane and died on January 20, 1612.

Matthias II started an investigation of his own into the allegations which had reached his court about the inhuman and ferocious acts of Elizabeth Bathory. The king expressed special displeasure that some of these acts had been committed against daughters of the nobility.

No previous historian has pointed out the existence of an important document which demonstrates that, as early as 1610, the king had arranged for a court of inquiry to be set up by Count Thurzo. From the end of March to the beginning of July the chief notary Andrei of Keresztur recorded the testimonies of thirty-four witnesses from the town of Novoe Mesto on the Vah River. Their statements were set down in a formal document dated September 19, 1610. (See Appendix for summary translation. The original document is in the State Archives in Budapest, which kindly provided me with a copy.) In short, we know now that there was abundant testimony by reliable witnesses, some of whom were nobles, to convict Elizabeth of murder. In particular, some witnesses stated that she bit the bodies of some of her victims. Such bestial behavior inspired legends to characterize her as a witch and a heretic, and more to our point, a kind of werewolf.

Some historians have wrongly assumed that the king went after Elizabeth because she was a Protestant and he a Roman Catholic. Although it is true that the Catholic Hapsburgs had stepped up their anti-Protestant campaign, Matthias II remained relatively tolerant in religious matters. His motives were largely economic, not religious in the Bathory case. If Elizabeth could be found guilty, her property would be confiscated and, most important of all, her claims to the debt which the crown owed her would be canceled.

The deceased Lutheran paster of Cachtice, Reverend Andreas Berthoni, had long suspected foul play at the castle. He had seen too many girls disappear behind those gray walls. He had denounced Elizabeth from his pulpit, and he had also composed an extensive report on what the countess had been doing. His successor, the Reverend Jan Ponikenusz, finally succeeded in smuggling the secret report written by the late Paster Berthoni to Count George Thurzo, Palatine Prince of Transylvania. The title "Palatine" allowed the Count to act with the full authority of the king himself in the absence of the king. This put the Lord Palatine, George Thurzo, in a very delicate position. As the widow of one of the leading lords in the realm, she could not be arrested without a special act of Parliament.

But evidence against Elizabeth was mounting; some of her crimes were serious enough to warrant the death penalty. Count Thurzo ordered a court of inquiry to be held at Bratislava, and the proceedings were duly recorded by the judge, Moiysis Cziraky, on October 27, 1610. The evidence directly implicated personnel from Sarvar Castle (where more murders had taken place than anywhere else) in the killings.

In the winter of 1610 Elizabeth evidently still felt that her social position made her virtually untouchable before the law, since she had her servants toss four murdered girls from the ramparts of Castle Cachtice into the path of roaming wolves. This was done in full view of the Cachtice villagers, who reported this latest atrocity to the king's officials.

During the pre-Christmas season in 1610, Thurzo questioned Elizabeth herself specifically about the deaths of the nine virgins mentioned in the report of the late Pastor Berthoni. Elizabeth was undaunted; she explained to Count Thruzo that the nine girls had been victims of an epidemic whose spread had to be halted at any cost, so their burials had to have been held in secret in order to prevent further infection and panic among the common people. Rumors circulated among the local Cachtice villagers that the Countess was a witch. Though not formally ever officially convicted of witchcraft, like many of her contemporaries Elizabeth Bathory was very superstitious. During the late sixteenth and early seventeenth centuries superstition was widespread. For example, a work entitled *A Complete Home and Country Library* by Andreas Glorez, was published in Regensburg from 1668 to 1671. It was a best seller in its day. Glorez warned about the diseases caused by witches, and claimed that witches made wax figures with the faces of those whom they wished to make ill; they would then place the wax figures on meat skewers and roast the skewers over an open fire; the person depicted on them invariably took sick, and some died. The author asserted that almost all unexplainable illnesses were caused by witches, and he added a list of herbs and plants as antidotes.

As Mrs. Istvan Kovacs was to state under oath during Elizabeth's trial, the countess herself was very deft in poisoning and sorcery. In particular, she supposedly employed sorcery and incantations against the king, the Lord Palatine, Megyery and others. Ficzko also testified to one of Elizabeth's attempts at poisoning. Her female servant Majorova had acquired a reputation for being a great concocter of magic potions. During the Christmas season in 1610 Elizabeth set in motion her plan to poison the "plotters" against her.

She had Majorova mix up a batch of a potion with which to make a coffee cake. The peasant woman arrived with her concoction four hours ahead of the deadline set by Elizabeth. It was poured into a huge kneading trough. The countess herself took a bath in the mixture; part of the bath water was then taken down to the river; Elizabeth took a second bath in the remaining solution, out of which a special seed cake was made. Her plan was to serve the cake to the king and the Lord Palatine who were expected at Castle Cachtice. But first Elizabeth decided that it had to be tried out on some live subjects. Some of her retainers were forced to eat the cake, but evidently something had gone wrong with the secret formula, because all they got were bad stomachaches. For the moment Elizabeth abandoned her plans for the poisoning and did not dare to try it again, since the lords were becoming suspicious. (See Appendix, A, Trial Document, Question Eleven, Answer of Ficzko).

It was Ficzko who had apparently introduced Elizabeth to the occult. In an early letter to her husband after 1594 the Countess had written about her servant Ficzko whom she called Thorko: "Thorko has taught me a lovely new one. Catch a black hen and beat it to death with a white cane. Keep the blood and smear a little of it on your enemy. If you get no chance to smear it on his body, then get one of his articles of clothing and smear the hen's blood on it."

The local Lutheran pastor at Cachtice Jan Ponikenusz was convinced that Elizabeth had sent black cats and dogs against him by magic. He wrote to his religious superior Elias Lanyi that on the last day of December in the year 1610 after praying and talking with his wife at home, he heard the mewing of cats coming from the upper floor of his house. "This was not the noise made by ordinary cats," he asserted. He went upstairs to investigate and found nothing. Then his servants told him that the mice were squeaking in the boxroom. He ran there and again found nothing. As he was about the leave the house, six cats and dogs began to bite his right leg. The good pastor grabbed a stick and beat at them; they dashed into the yard as he shouted, "You devils go to hell!" His servant Janos ran after the creatures but could not see a single one. "As you can see," the minister wrote, "this was the doing of the devil." (The entire account reads like an immense fantasy; and I suspect that the clergyman simply came across a dog chasing some cats at night: obviously his feeling about the countess ran high.)

Elizabeth had her own special kind of charming prayer; it was not in Hungarian but in Slovak, the language of her peasants. According to Reverend Ponikenusz, Elizabeth had lost one of her most precious lucky charms, an incantation written on a slip of paper, the day before her arrest. So she hurried to the local forest sorceress Erzsi Majorova, the one who had helped her mix the potion for the ill-fated poisonous cake, to get a new incantation, which Ponikenusz quoted in one of his letters:

"Help me, O Clouds! O Clouds, stay by me! Don't let any harm come to Elizabeth Bathory, let her remain healthy and invincible! Send, O send, you powerful Clouds, ninety cats. I command you, O King of the Cats, I pray you, may you gather together, even if you are in the mountains, waters, or on the roofs, or on the other side of the ocean! May these ninety cats appear to lacerate and destroy the hearts of the king Matthias and of the Palatine Prince and in the same way the hearts of the red Megyery and of the Judge Cziraky, so that they many not harm Elizabeth Bathory! Holy Trinity, protect me!" (The text was published in Budapest on March 18, 1891 in a pamphlet by an author who only gave his name as Junius and did not mention the exact source of it; it was republished by George von Marcziani in another pamphlet entitled "Elizabeth Bathory" in Vienna on March 26, 1891. See the Foreign Pamphlets Section [Fremdenblatt], no. 87 in the State Archives, Vienna.)

The specific reference to the Judge Moysis Cziraky is worthy of note, because the countess's son Paul, who was evidently in on the deal to arrest Elizabeth, later on married one of the daughters of Moysis Cziraky. The reader may be perhaps surprised at the combination of pagan and Christian elements in Elizabeth's incantation, since the Christian Trinity took a back seat to the Clouds and the King of the Cats. But such practices were quite common at the time. Better to call up pagan support than to restrict yourself to Christian gods; better safe than sorry.

The Hungarians, who had originated in Asia, had once believed in an animistic religion known as Shamanism. The shamans were evidently some sort of augurs, magicians, soothsayers, and sorcerers. They had their secret incantations to the forces of nature. Inspection of the innards of slaughtered animals was part of their ritual, as it was in ancient Greece and Rome. Some of them believed in a Supreme Being called *Isten,* a word probably borrowed from the Persians, meaning "God." (In Bram Stoker's novel *Dracula* the reader may recall that one of the passengers in the coach bringing Jonathan Marker to Castle Dracula sees a tall mountain peak covered with snow and calls it *Isten szek* meaning "God's Seat," as Stoker points out in the text.) But besides this Supreme Being, ancient Hungarians also adored numerous other deities, such as those of the mountains, springs, rivers, clouds, fire, thunder, etc., and sacrifices were made to these lesser gods. In a way, Elizabeth represents an example of how the pre-Christian beliefs continued to persist for over five hundred years after the formal adoption of Christianity in the area.

Under pressure from the Hungarian Catholic nobles, most of whom envied the Protestant countess's land-holdings, Parliament was summoned to Bratislava, Hungary's temporary capital after the old capital of Budapest had fallen to the Turks. The nobles in solemn session listened to the complaints from the Cachtice villagers, presented formally by knights from the village. They also heard testimony from Imre Megyery, the tutor of Elizabeth Bathory's son Paul. In particular, Megyery offered evidence in the case of a girl whose murder he had seen. The Catholic nobles in Parliament especially registered their indignation at these acts of cruelty and bestiality by Elizabeth Bathory, and cited the fact that Elizabeth had tortured and killed girls of *noble birth,* not only peasant girls. The Protestant Count Thurzo was in a quandary. In the midst of his vain attempts to find some face-saving device and preserve Elizabeth's family properties from possible confiscation by the Catholic king, an emissary from King Matthias II came to Bratislava with specific instructions for Thurzo to go to Castle Cachtice, ascertain the exact facts, and punish the guilty—under royal command.

Count Thurzo took the assignment seriously since, under the Hungarian constitution, he was second only to King Matthias himself and hence top executive of the Hapsburg power in Transylvania. This put Count Thurzo in a difficult position, however, as he was trying to come to terms with Gabor Bathory, the ruling prince of Transylvania, who was a relative of Elizabeth. He had hoped to avoid a confrontation between the interests of Protestant and Catholic noble families in this area.

But George Thurzo also believed, as did most people of the age, in witches. If Elizabeth were to be accused and to be found guilty of witchcraft, she would have to be properly punished. Only a few years before his raid on Elizabeth's castle, the count had had three of his own peasant women tried and convicted of being witches in league with the devil (who, by the way, was also condemned *in absentia*). One hundred and seventeen witnesses had been called up and had confirmed his worst suspicions about those women. All three were tortured and burned at the stake. It was the only way that God and justice could be served.

Count Thurzo planned his raid on Elizabeth Bathory carefully. He decided to act over the Christmas holiday while the Hungarian Parliament was not in session. With the Parliament not in session he figured that he might just be able to arrange things in the way that he wanted.

As Count Thurzo planned to make his surprise attack on Castle Cachtice, one of Elizabeth's servants reported to her that a girl named Doricza had stolen a pear. This incited Elizabeth's righteous wrath: imagine stealing a pear at Christmas time! This servant girl Doricza had only worked at the castle for only a month or so, and evidently did not know about the strict house rules concerning stealing.

Doricza, who was a buxom, powerfully built girl from the small Croatian town of Rednek, would prove to be one of Elizabeth's most long-lasting victims. The countess ordered the culprit to appear in the manorhouse laundry room.

Once the servant Doricza came to the laundry room, the usual "home justice" treatment typical of the countess was applied. The girl was first made to undress, then her hands were tied behind her back. Next her cheeks were slapped several times in preparation for the arrival of the countess with her club. The countess proceeded to beat the girl with the club, until Elizabeth became so tired that she could no longer raise her arms to strike. So Dorka had to take over the task. (Ordinarily Helena Jo would have done the job, but she was suffering from a stiff arm at this time.) After Dorka finished as much beating as she could, Elizabeth, somewhat refreshed, grabbed the club again and started in on the groaning Doricza. Elizabeth's shirt was so covered with blood that she changed into a fresh one.

But Doricza refused to die. Dorka then rose to the occasion. She grabbed a pair of scissors and stabbed Doricza again and again. By 11:00 P.M., according to the witnesses at the trial held on January 2, 1611, the girl at last expired; a twisted lump of flesh was about all that remained of her.

The famous raid led by Count Thurzo, which took place on the night of December 29, 1610 (in some accounts the date is given as December 30), has inspired a large number of legends incorporated in several novels. Most previously published works have claimed that the Palatine Prince surprised Elizabeth *in flagrante delicto* the night when she had just killed the young servant Doricza Szalaiova. One story goes that Count Thurzo and his raiding party arrived at Castle Cachtice shortly after midnight, just an hour after Doricza had died. The count supposedly leaped from his carriage and demanded to see the mistress of the castle at once. The servants were confused. Elizabeth had issued strict orders that no one should be allowed to disturb her "work." Whom should the servants obey? One of the frightened castle guards finally led the count's party through the castle. The group moved rapidly through the main court-yard and reached the room with its ten-foot thick impregnable walls. Suddenly Count Thurzo stumbled over something in the dark. He ordered the guard to bring his torch closer. In the dim light Thurzo could see the mangled body of a fair-haired girl about sixteen years old. She was lying naked in the snow. Her body had been cut and torn to shreds. It was still warm. Stepping over the body in the open courtyard, the count burst into the tower through its main door. Without waiting for the others, Count Thurzo quickly descended the winding tower staircase. Below he found yet another passageway. He went down about 150 feet. Then he heard muffled voices. He tripped, stumbled, and almost fell headfirst into a spiked door which would have probably killed him; fortunately his right hand caught the iron handle and the door swung open.

The air was damp and fetid, a combination of stale smoke and vapor. Through the haze he noticed a fifty-year-old woman crouching over a stool. She turned towards the count in a state of frenzy. It was Elizabeth. At first, not recognizing the intruder and thinking him one of the servants, the countess shrieked: "You shall pay for this intrusion!" The count noticed a female victim at the feet of the countess.

The girl's body had been mangled, and she was dead. In the far corner of the room the count discerned three other girls bound and gagged. "Not so, my lady," the Palatine Lord is said to have shouted back at Elizabeth, "this is not one of your servants, but the Palatine Prince of Hungary who stands before you and has come in the name of the king to bring justice to these accursed walls!" Meanwhile the count's companions, Barons Zrinyi and Drugeth, along with Imre Megyery, had crowded into the tower room and bore witness to the terrible scene. They began rounding up Elizabeth's cohorts there, the three women—Helena, Jo, Dorothea Szentes, and Katharina Beneczky—as well as the young manservant Ficzko. Elizabeth herself was dispatched to her rooms. Further immediate investigation led to the discovery of a mass grave of murdered girls lower down in the tower.

The above account of the capture of the Blood Countess has been repeated with some incidental variation in several novels written about the Elizabeth Bathory case. Unfortunately for those interested in the sensational, although his companions were the same, the facts were different: The count and his party (the two sons-in-law and Megyery) had set out from Bratislava, the temporary capital of Hungary after the fall of Budapest, sometime around December 27, 1610. The trip from Bratislava to Cachtice took at least two days of continuous driving in those days. By the early evening of December 29, 1610, the party reached Novoe Mesto on the Vah River.

There was no midnight raid on Elizabeth's castle, because there was no need for any. Over the years there had been abundant evidence built up against the countess. When the raiding party arrived at Elizabeth's manorhouse in Cachtice, they found the beaten body of Doricza before the door. Elizabeth and her cohorts had not yet bothered to bury the body. Inside the house the nobles found two other female victims.

Another legend, still repeated by the local peasants, is that the actions of a young male peasant were at the root of the raid. One day he supposedly saw his beloved, a girl who lived in the Cachtice market area, go to the castle in order to get drinking water and bring it home in the usual two buckets. She never returned. After waiting for two days, the young lad became worried. He asked around and found out that the girl had been detained at the castle of evil reputation. He knew what that meant, so he hastened to Bratislava to the prince Palatine George Thurzo with the demand that Countess Elizabeth Bathory be brought to justice. But it is unreasonable to assume that Count Thurzo would have listened to a complaint from a peasant against one of his own aristocratic relatives.

The Calvinist preacher Elias Laszlo, who generally kept a very detailed diary, wrote only a laconic note in this regard: "1610. 29 December. Elizabeth Bathory was put in the tower behind four walls, because in her rage she killed some of her female servants."

* * *

A lot has been written about what caused the December raid on Elizabeth Bathory, and what really led to her downfall. Some have suggested that because she had committed such terrible atrocities she was bound to be found out, and that the wheels of justice simply finally caught up with her. Others (of a somewhat Freudian persuasion) have claimed that she actually brought it all in upon herself, because she unconsciously wanted to get caught—hence her lack of proper caution. Still others have written that it was *solely* because she began to pick on aristocratic girls, instead of confining her interests to peasants, that she ran into deep trouble. (There is some truth to that last analysis, as the reader will see, but it is not the whole story.) The most honest appraisal came from the pen of the authoritative biography by R. von Elsberg, who stated simply that the real reasons behind her capture and trial remain "unknown." Today, thanks to the newly found documentation at the Bytca archives, especially some private letters written by Count George Thurzo, we have much fuller information as to how and why action was finally taken.

First of all, Elizabeth's trial was totally planned before it took place. It was similar to the "show trials" in Moscow during the 1930s. The entire affair was based upon economic and political considerations, in which the question of what Elizabeth actually did or did not do played no role. She was merely a pawn in a vast economic and political power play. Gabor Bathory, Prince of Transylvania and cousin to Elizabeth Bathory, reigning at the time of Elizabeth's capture and subsequent trial, had unfortunately for her, already made his move against the power of the Hapsburg monarchy. He wanted to topple King Matthias II and expand Transylvania in order to absorb some of the Hapsburg land. As a member of the Bathory clan, Elizabeth was automatically a part of this conflict, got caught in the political crossfire and suffered the consequences. Her family feared that they would lose their property rights if she were to be found guilty of crimes warranting confiscation of her properties and cancellation of the debts owed to her by the crown, so her relatives became active accomplices in her capture and subsequent trial—to protect their own position.

Elizabeth's son Paul and his tutor at Sarvar, Imre Megyery, had been looking for a way to put a stop to this Hapsburg threat to the inheritance. The Hungarian king wanted to put Elizabeth on trial on capital charges leading to the expropriation of her estates. This had to be stopped at any cost. As we showed at the end of the previous chapter, Count Thurzo was enticed reluctantly into the whole affair, and only informed Elizabeth's immediate family about what was going on. Baron Drugeth in Vienna protected Elizabeth's son Paul from any direct involvement in the affair. The Hungarian king Matthias II was kept deliberately in the dark. Thurzo called together a small group of the Bathory family and made a backstairs political deal. He would control the judicial proceedings and see to it that the Bathory family properties could not be confiscated. In return, they would all pay him back at a later date.

The role of Count George Thurzo was so central in all these secret negotiations that it requires some clarification. His first wife, Sophia Forgacs, had died in 1590.

Thurzo's second wife was Elizabeth Czobor; through that marriage he became related to Elizabeth Bathory. Rumors also circulated that Thurzo had even had a short-lived sexual affair with Elizabeth, so that his motives were probably far from pure.

Thurzo's letters to his wife after the famous raid on Elizabeth's mansion indicated that, as soon as he had the "damned woman" transferred from her manorhouse to the fortress at Cachtice, he was in a hurry to get to Bytca and set up the trial. He paused only long enough to spend New Year's Day with his wife. The count was intent upon arranging a very speedy "legal" process in his town of Bytca. If he could get things wrapped up while the Hungarian Parliament was not in session, he could present them with a *fait accompli.* His letters to his wife show that he had already decided that the subsequent verdict should be "in perpetuis carceribus" (life imprisonment) for the countess. Anything else he would not tolerate, especially any suggestions of having her property confiscated so that her heirs could not get it.

The otherwise reliable biographer of Elizabeth Bathory, R. von Elsberg, is at a loss to explain why Count Thurzo did not stay a while at Cachtice in order to take the time to ascertain all the facts and details in the case. But Thurzo knew all he wanted to already. Facts were not going to change his idea of what had to be done.

After his raid on Elizabeth's castle Count Thurzo wrote to his wife: "I took the Nadasdy woman into custody; she was immediately taken to her fortress ... She will be well watched and held in strict imprisonment until God and the law decide about her ... As we directly came then upon certain men and female servants in the manorhouse, we found a dead girl at the house, a second one was also dead due to many wounds and torture. I await only until the accursed woman has been deposited in the fortress and a suitable room found for her. Tomorrow I ride further ..." Count Thurzo was obviously intent upon moving the juridical process as fast as he possibly could.

Vampires and the Slavs

Vampires and the Slavs

Edited by J. Gordon Melton

While vampires and vampirelike creatures appeared in the mythology of many of the world's peoples, nowhere were they more prevalent than among the Slavs of eastern and central Europe. Because of their belief in vampires, the Slavs experienced several panic-stricken "vampire" outbreaks in the late seventeenth and early eighteenth centuries that resulted in the opening and desecration of numerous graves. This belief system brought the vampire to the attention of the West and led directly to the development of the contemporary vampire myth.

The Slavic people include most eastern Europeans, from Russia to Bulgaria, from Serbia to the Czech Republic and Poland. Pouring into the region between the Danube and the Adriatic Sea, the people known collectively as the southern Slavs created several countries—Serbia, Croatia, Bosnia and Herzegovina, and Macedonia. In the midst of the Slavic lands are two non-Slavic countries, Romania and Hungary, though each has shared much of its language and lore with its Slavic neighbors. Gypsies have been a persistent minority throughout the Slavic lands, though much of the Gypsy community was decimated by the Nazi holocaust.

The exact origin of the Slavs is a matter of continuing historical debate, but most scholars agree that they came from river valleys north of the Black Sea and were closely associated with the Iranians, with whom they shared a religious perspective that gave a central place to a sun deity. At some point prior to the eighth-century A.D., the Slavs, made up of numerous tribes, migrated north and west into the lands they now inhabit. Once settled in their new homes, they began to unite into national groups.

The most important event to give direction to the Slavs was the introduction of Christianity. Initial penetration of the church into Slavic lands began as soon as the Slavs occupied the lands formerly in the hands of the Byzantine empire. However, systematic conversion attempts emerged as an outcome of the extensive reforms instituted during the long reign of Charlemagne (768–814). Charlemagne saw to the development of missions among the Moravians and the Croatians and had a bishop placed at Salzburg to further the Christianization of the Slavs. Most Slavs, however, recognize the work of the brothers Cyril (827–869) and Methodius (825–885) as the real beginning of Slavic Christianity. The brothers developed a Slavic alphabet capable of expressing all of the sounds in the Slavic language in its various dialects. They borrowed letters from Greek, Hebrew, and Armenian and created a new literary language that included Greek loan-words and new Slavic words that expressed some of the subtleties of Greek. This new literary language, most closely resembling Old Bulgarian, became Old Church Slavonic and influenced the various new national languages (from Bulgarian and Serbian to Polish and Russian) that were beginning to emerge from the older common language of the Slavic tribes. Cyril and Methodius translated the Bible and Greek liturgy into Old Church Slavonic. Out of their missions grew the several national eastern Orthodox communions, autonomous churches affiliated with the Ecumenical Patriarch in Constantinople (now Istanbul), the spiritual (though not administrative) head of eastern Orthodoxy.

Through the ninth and tenth centuries, the Eastern Orthodox church and the Western Roman church engaged in a fight over policy and administrative matters that were to lead to their break and mutual excommunication of each other in 1054 A.D. That break had immense significance for the Slavic people, as the Bulgarians, the Russians, and the Serbians adhered to the Eastern church, while the Poles, Czechs, and Croatians gave their loyalties to the Roman church. This split had great significance in the development of vampire lore, as the two churches disagreed over their understanding of the noncorruption of the body of a dead person. In the West, the noncorruption of the body of some saintly people was seen as an additional sign of their sanctity, while in the East, the incorruptibility of the body was viewed as a sign of God's disfavor resting upon the dead person, and hence, the likelihood of the individual's becoming a vampire.

ORIGIN OF THE SLAVIC VAMPIRE

Jan L. Perkowski, who has done the most thorough study of Slavic vampirism, concluded that it originated in the Balkans. Beginning around the ninth century, speculation on vampires evolved as a result of the confrontation between pre-Christian paganism and Christianity. Bogomilism, a dualistic religion with roots in Iran that emerged in Macedonia in the tenth century, added yet another element to the developing concept. Eventually Christianity won over the other religions, and pagan and Bogomil ideas, including the belief in vampires, survived as elements of popular demonology. As the concept of the vampire evolved in Slavic mythology, several terms emerged to designate it. (*Author's note: The discussion of terminology quickly brings even the most accomplished scholar into an area of possible confusion, simply because of the dynamic nature of language in which words are constantly shifting in meaning or connotation. There is a major disagreement among authorities over the primacy of older Slavic origins or Turkish origins. Perkowski favors a Slavic origin and his approach has been accepted as a framework for this discussion.)*

The most widely used term was one or the other of many variants of the original Slavic term that lay behind our modern word *vampire,* which seems to have evolved from the common form *obyri* or *obiri.* Each language group has a cognate form of the older root word—*upirina* (Serbo-Croatian), *upirbi* (Ukrainian), *upír* (Byelo-Russian, Czech, Slovak), *upiór* (Polish), *wupji* (Kashubian), *lampir* (Bosnian), and *vampir* (Bulgarian, also *vbpir, vepir,* or *vapir.* There is a wide range of opinion on the origin of the root term *opyrb,* an unsolvable problem because the history of the early Slavic tribes has been lost.

The second popular term, especially among the Greeks and southern Slavs is *vrykola-kas* (which, like vampire, possessed a number of forms in the different Slavic languages). This term seems to have derived from the older Serbian compound word, *vblkb* plus *dlaka,* meaning one who wore wolf pelts. Perkowski argues that the term designated someone who wore a wolfskin in a ritual situation. By the thirteenth century, when the word first appeared in a written text, the earlier meaning had been dropped and *vlbkodlaci* referred to a mythological monster who chased the clouds and ate the sun and moon (causing eclipses). Still later, by the sixteenth century, it had come to refer to vampires and as such had passed into both Greek and Romanian culture. The older southern Slavic term appears today as *vrykolakas* (Greek), *vircolac* (Romanian), *vbkolak* (Macedonian, Bulgarian), and *vukodlak* (Serbo-Croatian, sometimes shortened to *kudlak*). Because of the root meaning of the term, *vudkolak* has become part of the discussion of the relation of werewolves and the vampire.

Three other words have assumed some importance in the literature as designations of the vampire. *Strigoi* (female: *strigoaica*) is the popular Romanian word for witch. Harry Senn, author of *Were-Wolf and Vampire in Romania,* found a variant, *strigoi mort* (dead witch), as a common term for a vampire. *Strigoi* is derived from the Latin *strix* (screech owl) that had also come to refer to a night demon that attacked children. Russians commonly replaced *upír,* their older Slavic term for a vampire, with *eretik* (or *heretic*), a Greek ecclesiastical word for one who has departed from the true faith. *Vjesci* (alternate spellings *vjeszczi* and *vjeszcey*) is a term employed by the Kashubs of northern Poland.

THE SLAVIC VAMPIRE

The vampire found its place within the world view of the people of eastern and central Europe. It was associated with death and was an entity to be avoided. However, it was not the all-pervasive symbol of evil it would come to be in nineteenth-century western European literature. Within the prescientific world of village life, the role of the vampire was to explain various forms of unpredicted and undeserved evil that befell people.

The Slavic vampire differed considerably from the popular image of the creature that evolved in twentieth-century novels and movies. First, it generally appeared without any prior contact with another vampire. The vampire was the product of an irregularity in the community life, most commonly a problem with the process of either death and burial or of birth. People who met a violent death, which cut them off from the normal completion of their lives could become vampires. Thus, people who committed suicide or died as the result of an accident might become vampires. Most Slavic cultures had a precise set of ritualized activities to be followed after someone's death and even for some days following the interment of the body. Deviation from that procedure could result in the deceased becoming a vampire. In a community where the church was integral to social life, and deviation from the church a matter of serious concern, to die in a state of excommunication was seen as a cause of vampirism.

Vampirism also could result from problems associated with birth. For example, most Slavic communities had certain days of the year when intercourse was frowned upon. Children conceived by parents who had violated such taboos could become vampires. Bulgarians believed that an infant who died before it was baptized could become a *ustrel,* a vampire that would attack and drink the blood of cows and sheep. Among the Kashubs, a child born with teeth or with a membrane cap (a caul) on its head could become a vampire after its death.

Thus, Slavic society offered many reasons why vampires could appear. Of course, part of the horror felt toward vampires was the possibility of its passing on its condition to others. The vampire tended to attack its family, neighbors, friends, and people with whom it had unfinished business. Those attacked assumed the possibility of also becoming a vampire. The belief that a number of community members might become vampires contemporaneously brought on waves of vampire hysteria experienced in Slavic communities.

In the cases where a deceased person was suspected of becoming a vampire, a wide variety of pre-burial actions were reportedly taken as precautions. Among the most widespread was the placing of various materials into the coffin that were believed to inhibit a vampire's activity. Religious objects such as the crucifix were the most common. Such plants as the mountain ash were believed to stop the vampire from leaving its grave. Since vampires had a fascination with counting, seeds (millet or poppyseed) were spilled in the grave, on top of the grave, and on the road from the graveyard. The vampire slowly counted the seeds before it assumed the privilege of engaging in any vampiric activity. On occasion, in more extreme cases, the body might be pierced with thorns or a stake, different groups having preferences for wood (hawthorn, aspen, or oak) or iron. Believing that vampires would first attack and eat their burial garments every effort was made to keep the clothes away from the corpse's mouth. A wooden block might be placed under the chin, or the clothes might be nailed to the side of the coffin.

While there were many possible causes for the creation of a vampire, the existence of one became apparent through the negative effects of its activities. Most commonly, the unexplained death of sheep and cattle (a community's food supply) was attributed to vampires. Strange experiences of the kind usually studied by para-psychologists also suggested the presence of vampires. Included in the stories of vampires were accounts of poltergeist activity, the visitation of an incubus/succubus, or the appearance of the specter of a recently deceased person to a relative or friend. The sudden illness or death of a person, especially a relative or friend, soon after the death of an individual suggested that the person had become a vampire. Vampires also were associated with epidemics.

Once the suggestion that a community was under attack by a vampire was taken seriously by several residents, the discovery and designation of the vampire proceeded. The most likely candidate was a person who had recently died, especially in the previous 40 days. (Derived from the 40 days between Jesus' death and ascension.) The body of the suspected vampire might then be exhumed and examined for characteristic signs. The body of a vampire was believed to appear lifelike and to show signs of continued growth and change. It would possess pliable joints and blood would ooze from its mouth or other body openings. It might have swelled up like a drum filled with blood. Its hair may have continued to grow and new fingernails may have appeared.

When the supposed vampire was located, it had to be destroyed. Destroying the vampire usually involved action against the corpse—most commonly, the body was staked using a variety of wood or metal materials. The stake was driven into the head, heart, or stomach. In some instances decapitation might occur. The Kashub people placed the severed head between the feet of the corpse before reburial. In the most extreme cases, the body was destroyed by burning. These actions were accompanied, where the services of a priest could be obtained, by such ritual activity as the repeating of the funeral service, the sprinkling of holy water, or even an exorcism.

While the belief in vampires was quite widespread, especially in rural eastern Europe, the cases of a community detecting a vampire and taking action against the corpse of the suspect were relatively rare. This was true especially after the widely reported incidents of vampires in the eighteenth-century and the subsequent institution of legal penalties, both secular and ecclesiastical, against people who desecrated the bodies of the dead. However, besides the reports of contemporary vampires, a large body of vampire folktales set in the indefinite past circulated in Slavic lands. Like Aesop's fables, these stories functioned as moral tales to teach behavioral norms to members of the community. Among the more famous was one titled simply "The Vampire," originally collected by A. N. Afanas'ev in Russia in the nineteenth century. It told of a young girl, Marusia, who became infatuated with a handsome young man who ventured into her town. He was rich, personable, and mannered, but he was also a vampire. Even after she discovered his nature, she did not act, and as a result several members of her family died. She finally learned what to do from her grandmother. The story offered the listener a number of guidelines. For example, it taught that wisdom was to be sought from one's elders, and that young people should beware attractive strangers, as they might be the source of evil. Other stories offered similar advice.

THE SLAVIC VAMPIRE TODAY

Folklorists such as Harry Senn have had little difficulty collecting vampire stories, both folktales and accounts of the apparent actual vampires, among Slavic populations throughout the twentieth century, though increasingly they have had to travel to the more isolated rural communities to find such accounts. Governments hostile to any form of supernaturalism have had a marked influence on the loss of belief in vampires, effectively eradicating most such beliefs in the urban areas and among more educated persons. Also assisting in the decline of belief has been the rise of the modern undertaker, who has assumed the burial functions previously done by the family of the deceased. The removal of the burial ceremony from the people has caused a certain distancing from the experience of death, which has contributed to the decline of many beliefs about human interaction with the dead.

SOURCES

Dvornik, Francis. *The Slavs: Their Early History and Civilization.* Boston: American Academy of Arts and Sciences, 1956. 394 pp.

Perkowski, Jan L. *The Darkling: A Treatise on Slavic Vampirism.* Columbus, OH: Slavica Publishers, 1989. 174 pp.

——, ed. *Vampires of the Slavs.* Cambridge, MA: Slavica Publishers, 1976. 294 pp.

Senn, Harry. *Were-Wolf and Vampire in Romania.* New York: Columbia University Press, 1982. 148 pp.

Summers, Montague. *The Vampire in Europe.* New York: Routledge, Kegan Paul, Trench, Trubner, & Co., 1929. 329 pp. Reprint. New Hyde Park, NY: University Books, 1961. 329 pp.

Wilson, Katherina M. "The History of the Word 'Vampire.'" *Journal of the History of Ideas* 46, 4 (October–December 1985): 577–83.

Of Magic, Witches, and Vampires
in the Balkans

By M. Edith Durham

I n all the Balkan lands which I have visited there is still a strong belief in the existence of many supernatural beings, for the most part harmful to man, and also in the existence of many human beings who have the power to communicate with the evil spirits and cause them to work harmfully.

MONTENEGRO.—Here, as in other South Slav lands, the Vila was widely believed in, and I found the belief not yet quite extinct. Vilas were female spirits and therefore usually evil. They were very beautiful and lived in the numerous underground caverns frequent in limestone rocks. But since the coming of artillery they have disappeared. Sometimes they would swear sisterhood with a warrior and be of great service in protecting him from foes. But they were excessively jealous and, should he marry, almost certainly slew his bride. They made love also to male animals. I rode up country upon a white stallion, a pretty little beast. It was turned out to pasture at night. Next morning, before mounting, I began to disentangle the knots in the mane. The owner at once intervened and prayed me not to touch them. The Vilas, he said, had been with the horse all night, he was covered with sweat in the morning. They had knotted the mane as a sign, and if I undid it they would certainly cause an accident *en route*. I was told a tale that "happened a longtime ago" of a Vila who, disguised as a beautiful maiden, caused two brothers to fall in love with her. She urged them on to fight and promised herself to the victor. They fought. One killed the other. The Vila laughed and flew away. The luckless survivor then stabbed himself and died. The sympathies of the Vilas were on the whole Slavonic, for they frequently in former days warned the Montenegrins of the approach of the Turks. The phrase "beautiful as a Vila" is still in everyday use. The references to Vilas in the ballads are very numerous.

Ghosts.—As in other lands, there is a very general belief that churchyards after dark are uncanny places and should be avoided. And it is as well to carry a knife. This probably is not to kill ghosts with, but that the iron may serve as a protection. My usual guide, Krsto, firmly believed in the evil power of ghosts.

Vampires.—In Montenegro the vampire is called "tenatz." To become a vampire is "potentzio se." I did not hear of anyone in Montenegro being a vampire during his lifetime, though they used to be formerly. But I heard of recent cases in which they had arisen at night from the grave and caused deaths. A weird tale was told, in the Tzermnitza valley. A young man was in love with a girl, but was not allowed to marry her, as her parents had betrothed her elsewhere. She was forced against her will to marry her betrothed. Her lover left Montenegro in despair and died. After death he returned as a vampire and visited the woman at night. She told the neighbours of his visit and was much alarmed. She bore a child by him which, so my guide, who had seen it, assured me, was so exactly like the deceased man that there could be no possible doubt of the paternity. As the man had died abroad nothing could be done to lay the vampire. A corpse suspected of being a vampire can be stopped from rising from the grave either by the usual method of transfixing the body with a stake—a ceremony at which the priest must assist—or by hamstringing the corpse, or by burning it. When a corpse is awaiting burial it is most necessary that it should be constantly watched. If a cat should jump over it, it is sure to become a vampire.

In Bosnia there was, I found, plenty of belief in vampires. Here they are called "lampir" or "vukodlak" (lit.: wolf's hair). I was told by several of the local Austrian governors that when the Austrians first occupied the country (1878) the cases of disinterring bodies and burning them were numerous. The Government forbade the practice. A recent case (told me in 1906) was when there was an outbreak of typhus (they always called enteric, typhus. I never saw spotted typhus) in a village near Vlasenitza. A young man was the first to die. His wife sickened and swore that her husband had returned in the night and sucked her blood, and said "He is a lampir!" The neighbours, filled with fear, begged the authorities to permit them to dig up and burn his body. Permission was refused and a panic ensued. The lampir was seen and heard by many people and there were fifteen deaths. It would be interesting to know how many of these died because they believed they must die, owing to the lampir. The peasants all through Albania, and Macedonia are extraordinarily affected mentally if they believe they must die, and seem to make no effort whatever to live. In Albania, I heard of more than one case in which a man's death having been foretold by reading the future in fowls' bones, he proceeded to sicken and died. There was no suspicion whatever of poison and the tale appeared to be true.

A patient under such circumstances refuses all food, believing it to be useless.

During the last few weeks a case of burning a vampire's body has been reported from Bosnia.

Witches.—These in Montenegro are called Vjeshtitza. I was told that they do not now exist, but that they did formerly. There was, however, a belief in them, for I saw people kill moths, saying "Perhaps it is a vjeshtitza." Vjeshtitzas were in the habit of changing themselves to moths or flies and entering at night through the keyhole and sucking peoples' blood. The person got more and more pallid and had fever and died. I suggest that the gnat and malaria may be the origin of this belief.

Witches could sail on the sea in a boat made of the shell of an egg eaten on the first of March. My guide's wife, however, used to smash all egg shells. She would not say why, except that it was better to do so. Petar Jovitchevitch, Montenegrin Consul at Scutari, told me that his grandmother always, on the first of March, stirred the ashes on the hearth with two horns (goat's or of cattle), thrusting the horns right through the ash heap, which is usually large. This was to preserve the house from witches, who hold their yearly gathering on that day. On the next day a heap of rubbish was always burnt. He did not know why, except that it was part of the protective ceremony.

In various parts of the country, I was told that in former days the punishment for a witch was stoning to death and that this actually took place. As in other lands, the test for witches was to throw them in water, to see if they sank or floated. Medakovitch, writing in 1860, tells of a case where a woman of the Raichevitches was condemned to be ducked. Her relatives came to the rescue. In the fight four men were killed and a blood feud started.

When I was in Montenegro, it was customary for the bride's brothers to guard her carefully till the groomsmen came to fetch her away, in order to see that no evil-minded person tied knots in the fringe of her strukka (long straight garment worn like a plaid), for, if so, she would either miscarry or bear a deformed child.

ALBANIA.—Albania was in a more primitive state, and belief in witchcraft and magic universal. People spoke of it as a matter of course and did not pretend not to believe it as in Montenegro.

Weakness and pallor were commonly ascribed to the night attack of a witch (shtriga) in the form of a fly, bee, or moth. But shtrigas are difficult to detect. They, however, always vomit the blood they have sucked. If you follow one at night whom you suspect, you may see her do so, but you must not let her see you. Some of this vomited blood will make an amulet to protect you against shtrigas.

If a woman's hair turns white when she is twenty it is a sure sign she is a shtriga. Garlic is a good protection against shtrigas and often tied round the necks of children.

Shtrigas can be caught if you make a cross with pigs' bones and fasten it to the door on a feast day when the church is crowded with people. If a Shtriga is in church she cannot get out because of this bone cross and will run wildly round and round trying to escape and so can be captured. They used to be killed "in former days." I did not hear of any recent execution, but gathered that they were sometimes terrorised and maltreated, and sometimes excommunicated by the priest.

As in Montenegro, the Shtrigas are especially powerful in the first week in March. I was told that in Shala it is customary to hang at the doors of the houses at this date—scissors, the comb for carding wool, a black thread tied in knots and an acid fruit (species unidentified), and this not only protects the house but prevents Shtrigas from working evil to mankind in general.

If you catch a Shtriga who has been sucking someone's blood you can save the life of the patient by making the Shtriga spit in his mouth. An Albanian friend of mine described dramatically how he had seen his father thus save the life of a child who was already unconscious and cold. Fortunately he found the right Shtriga. She denied guilt, but he dragged her to the dying child and clapped his pistol to her head, crying, "Spit or I shoot." She spat into the child's mouth and it gradually recovered consciousness and ultimately got quite well, which, as my friend said, clearly proved the guilt of the Shtriga. At one time a large number of the women of the Nikaj tribe were Shtrigas and those also of the Djakova district.

I was once annoyed by a Shtriga myself. I lived at the house of my guide, Marko Shantoya. Riding home from Mirdita, I saw a corn-dolly in an inn, admired it and was presented with it. I hung it on the wall of the room I lived in. At night a number of mice came; I heard them nibbling and found two eating the corn-dolly. Next day I told Marko to buy me a mouse-trap. At night I asked for it and found he had not got one. I again told him and said "Don't forget this time." After several days there was still no trap. Then his wife came to me and said "Please do not ask Marko for a trap. He does not wish to catch the mice." "But why?" "Because he believes they are sent." "Sent? But by whom?" "The woman next door is very bad. We think she is a Shtriga. It is she who has sent the mice. They are not natural. They have come all of a sudden. And if we catch them Marko says she will send something worse." "But what?" "Bats perhaps? We do not know. But it is better to suffer the mice." (Than fly to evils that you know not of.) So I suffered mice till I had the brilliant idea of importing a cat. After much consideration they decided that a cat by its own nature catches mice and that we should not be responsible for its actions. Thus we successfully dodged the wickedness of the woman next door. Marko when asked how it was possible to "send mice" only groaned and said "With the devil all things are possible." And that probably she was in direct communication with Beelzebub or Belial.

Albania is haunted at night by spirits called "Ore" (pl. Ort). Like the Slav Vilas they are female and very mischievous. But they differ in habit. Their chief occupation now, is to appear at night as sparks in the air and to stop travellers from proceeding further by circling around them. This happened to an Albanian friend of mine who could get no further till the first cock crowed, when they disappeared. Cocks are very valuable against evil spirits and under the old mountain laws the theft of a cock was more heavily punished than that of an ordinary fowl.

These "ort" also guard hidden treasure, of which there is a great deal hidden in caves. The "orts" kill all intruders. I was told of such a cave near Djakova where there is an underground bazaar of fabulous wealth, but could not induce anyone to guide me to it. The tale no doubt originates from foul air in the cave, It is possible that the man who saw the bazaar in question and just escaped with his life, dreamed the bazaar while unconscious under the influence of the gas. None of the people who told of supernatural adventures were lying, they all believed firmly in what they told. I used to give entertainments by casting shadows of animals, etc., on the walls at night with my hands. When I made a horned creature which was supposed to resemble the devil, folk crossed themselves and I was asked not to make this figure again. A Franciscan was very much troubled by it. This was up country. They were also frightened by one or two of the simplest conjuring tricks done by old Marko, who once had to explain his trick to convince the simple people that the devil had nothing to do with it.

Treasure can be guarded also magically by entrusting it to the earth (amanet) and bidding the earth to yield it only when certain ceremonies are performed. If these be not done you may dig in vain at the right spot and find nothing; the earth guards it faithfully.

Belief in the Evil Eye was universal. A good amulet is the head of a snake, cut off with silver (the sharpened edge of a coin). This is dried, and fastened between two medals or images of St. George and blessed by a priest. This represents the destruction of the Evil power by the good one.

The Vampire also exists in Albania and is called "Kukuthi" or "Lugat." Its habits are the same as in other lands and the corpse from which it rises can be rendered harmless by turning or ham-stringing. I came across no examples.

Insanity is always ascribed to the presence of an evil spirit, or several of them. The ceremony of casting out of devils is performed over the insane in church and I have seen Turkish gendarmes bring in a Moslem and lay him before the altar to be exorcised. In order to drive out the devil, great cruelty is sometimes inflicted. In an orthodox monastery, I once saw a wretched lunatic stark naked, tied to a kennel out of doors like a dog and in great misery, but could do nothing to alleviate his lot. The monks were trying to drive out the evil spirits.

There is a grain of truth at the bottom of all strange and primitive beliefs. Modern science and the microscope have revealed the presence of the "evil spirits," the strepto-, staphylo- and other cocci, which are the cause of a very large proportion of physical and mental diseases. Primitive races throughout the world have made a good attempt at diagnosis. It is in treatment that they have failed.

Vampires in Bulgaria

Edited by J. Gordon Melton

Bulgaria is one of the oldest areas of Slavic settlement. It is located south of Romania and sandwiched between the Black Sea and Macedonia. In the seventh-century A.D., the Bulgar tribes arrived in the area of modern Bulgaria and established a military aristocracy over the Slavic tribes of the region. The Bulgars were only a small percentage of the population, and they eventually adopted the Slavic language.

Christianity arrived with force among the Bulgarians in the ninth-century when Pope Nicholas I (858–67) claimed jurisdiction over the lands of the former Roman province of Illyricum. He sent missionaries into Bulgaria and brought it under Roman hegemony. The Bulgarian ruler, Boris-Michael, was baptized in 865, and the country officially accepted Christianity. The pope sent two bishops but would not send an archbishop or appoint a patriarch, causing Boris to switch his allegiance to the eastern church in Constantinople. A Slavic liturgy was introduced to the church and has remained its rite to the present.

Among the many side effects of Byzantine influence in Bulgaria was the growth of a new rival religious group, the Bogomils. The Bogomils grew directly out of an older group, the Paulicians, whose roots went back to the dualistic Maniceans. The Paulicians had been moved into Bulgaria from Asia Minor in order to prevent their alignment with the Muslim Arabs. The Bogomils believed that the world had been created by the rejected son of God, Satanael. While the earthly bodies of humans were created by Satanael, the soul came from God. It was seen by the church as a rebirth of the old gnostic heresy. Perkowski has argued at length that it was in the conflict of Bogomil ideas, surviving Paganism, and emerging Christianity that the mature idea of the Slavic vampire developed and evolved. However, his argument was not entirely convincing in that vampires developed in quite similar ways in countries without any Bogomilism. When the Christian Church split in 1054, the Bulgarians adhered to the orthodoxy of Constantinople.

The Bulgarians gained their independence at the end of the twelfth century, but were overrun by the Ottomans in 1396. They remained under Ottoman rule until

1878, when Turkish control was restricted by the Congress of Berlin, but did not become independent until 1908.

THE BULGARIAN VAMPIRE

The Bulgarian words for the vampire, a variety of the Slavic vampire, derived from the original Slavic opyrb/opirb. Its modern form appears variously as *vipir, vepir,* or *vapir,* or even more commonly as *vampir,* a borrowing from Russian. The modern idea of the vampire in Bulgaria evolved over several centuries. Most commonly, the Bulgarian vampire was associated with problems of death and burial, and the emergence of vampires was embedded in the very elaborate myth and ritual surrounding death. At the heart of the myth was a belief that the spirits of the dead went on a journey immediately after death. Guided by their guardian angel, they traveled to all of the places they had visited during their earthly life. At the completion of their journey, which occurred in the 40 days after their death, the spirit then journeyed to the next life. However, if the burial routine was done improperly, the dead might find their passage to the next world blocked. Generally, in Bulgaria, the family was responsible for preparing the body for burial. There were a number of ways in which the family could err or become negligent in their preparation. Also, the body had to be guarded against a dog or cat jumping over it or a shadow falling on it prior to burial. The body had to be properly washed. Even with proper burial, a person who died a violent death might return as a vampire.

As in other Slavic countries, certain people were likely candidates to become vampires. Those who died while under excommunication from the church might become a vampire. Drunkards, thieves, murderers, and witches were also to be watched. Bulgaria was a source of tales of vampires who had returned to life, taken up residence in a town where they were not known, and lived for many years as if alive. They even married and fathered children. Such people were detected after many years because of some unusual event which occurred. Apart from their nightly journeys in search of blood, the vampire would appear normal, even eating a normal diet.

Among the Gagauz people—Bulgarians who speak their own language, Gagauzi— the vampire was called *obur,* possibly a borrowing from the Turkish word for glutton. As with other vampires among the southern Slavs, the *obur* was noted as a gluttonous blood drinker. As part of the efforts to get rid of it, it would be enticed by the offerings of rich food or excrement. The *obur* was also loud, capable of creating noises like firecrackers, and could move objects like a poltergeist.

James Frazer noted the existence of a particular Bulgarian vampire, the *ustrel.* The *ustrel* was described as the spirit of a child who had been born on a Saturday but who died before receiving baptism. On the ninth day after its burial, a *ustrel* was believed to work its way out of its grave and attack cattle or sheep by draining their blood. After feasting all night, it returned to its grave before dawn. After some 10 days of feeding, the *ustrel* was believed to be strong enough that it did not need to return to its grave. It found a place to rest during the day either between the horns of a calf or ram or between the hind legs of a milch-cow. It was able to pick out a large herd and begin to work its way through it, the fattest animals first. The animals it attacked—as many as five a night—would die the same night. If a dead animal was cut open, the signs of the wound that the vampire made would be evident.

As might be suspected, the unexplained death of cows and sheep was the primary sign that a vampire was present in the community. If a *ustrel* was believed to be present, the owner of the herd could hire a *vampirdzhija,* or vampire hunter, a special person who had the ability to see them, so that all doubt as to its presence was put aside. Once it was detected, the village would go through a particular ritual known throughout Europe as the lighting of a needfire. Beginning on a Saturday morning, all the fires in the village were put out. The cattle and sheep were gathered in an open space. They were then marched to a nearby crossroads where two bonfires had been constructed. The bonfires were lit by a new fire created by rubbing sticks together. The herds were guided between the fires. Those who performed this ritual believed that the vampire dropped from the animal on whose body it had made its home and remained at the crossroads where wolves devoured it. Before the bonfires burned out, someone took the flame into the village and used it to rekindle all the household fires.

Other vampires, those that originated from the corpse of an improperly buried person or a person who died a violent death, were handled with the traditional stake. There were also reports from Bulgaria of a unique method of dealing with the vampire: bottling. This practice required a specialist, the *djadadjii,* who had mastered the art. The *djadadjii's* major asset was an icon, a holy picture of Jesus, Mary, or one of the Christian saints. The vampire hunter took his icon and waited where the suspected vampire was likely to appear. Once he saw the vampire, he chased it, icon in hand. The vampire was driven toward a bottle that had been stuffed with its favorite food. Once the vampire entered the bottle, it was corked and then thrown into the fire.

The folklore of the vampire has suffered in recent decades. The government manifested great hostility toward all it considered superstitious beliefs, which included both vampires and the church. As the church was suppressed, so was the unity of village life that provided a place for tales of vampires to exist.

SOURCES

Abbott, G. F. *Macedonian Folklore.* Chicago: Argonaut, Inc., Publishers, 1986.

Blum, Richard, and Eva Blum. *The Dangerous Hour: The Lore of Crisis and Mystery in Rural Greece.* London: Chatto & Windus, 1970. 410 pp.

Brautigam, Rob. "Vampires in Bulgaria." *International Vampire* 1, 2 (Winter 91): 16–17.

Frazer, James G. *The Golden Bough.* Vol. 10. *Balder the Beautiful: The Fire-Festivals of Europe and the Doctrine of the External Soul.* London: Macmillan and Co., 1930. 346 pp.

Georgieva, Ivanichka. *Bulgarian Mythology.* Sofia: Svyet, 1985. Nicoloff, Assen. *Bulgarian Folklore* Cleveland, OH: The Author, 1975. 133 pp.

———. *Bulgarian Folktales.* Cleveland, OH: The Author, 1979. 296 pp.

Perkowski, Jan L. *The Darkling: A Treatise on Slavic Vampirism.* Columbus, OH: Slavica Publishers, 1989. 174 pp.

St. Clair, Stanislas Graham Bower, and Charles A. Brophy. *Twelve Years Study of the Eastern Question in Bulgaria.* London: Chapman & Hall, 1877. 319 pp.

Summers, Montague. *The Vampire in Europe.* 1929. New Hyde Park, NY: University Books, 1961. 329 pp.

Vampires and the Southern Slavs

Edited by J. Gordon Melton

The region consisting of what was formerly Yugoslavia and Albania, now comprises seven countries of diverse religious, ethnic, and linguistic backgrounds. Although very diverse in some respects, these seven nations share a common folk heritage that becomes quite evident upon examination of the reports of vampires and vampire beliefs in the area. Thus, it became fitting to treat vampires and vampirism in these lands as a whole phenomenon.

BACKGROUND

Albania traced its history to ancient Illyria, a Roman province which reached from present-day Albania north and east across Croatia to Romania. Beginning in the fourth-century A.D., it was successfully invaded and occupied by Goths, Bulgars, Slavs, and Normans, successively. Albanians, much like Romanians, asserted their Roman ties. In the twelfth-century Albania was conquered by the Ottoman Turks and remained in the empire until after World War I. As a legacy, the retreating Ottoman rulers left a population that had primarily been converted to Islam. Albania gained a measure of independence following World War I but was occupied by Italy during World War II. After the war, it became an independent nation. Under dictator Enver Hoxha, it was an independent Communist nation with a repressive government that was officially atheist and hostile to religion. Following Hoxha's death the country regained some degree of freedom.

Today, the majority of ethnic Albaniac live outside the boundaries of their homeland. There is a small but important Albanian community in the United States, and many live in Italy. The largest number of Albanians outside of Albania live in Serbia and constitute more than 90 percent of the autonomous region of Kosmet (Kosovo-Metohija).

Yugoslavia was created in 1918, following World War I, as a centralized state uniting the former independent countries of Serbia, Bosnia and Herzegovina, Croatia, and Montenegro. To these countries a part of Macedonia, previously a part of the Ottoman Empire, and Slovenia, a part of the Austrian (Hapsburg) Empire, were added to the new country. Slavic tribes had first moved into the Balkan peninsula in the sixth-century and by the eighth-century had established themselves as the dominant influence in the area. Some unity was brought by the expansive Bulgar Empire at the beginning of the tenth century, which controlled most of present-day Serbia, Macedonia and Bosnia-Herzegovina.

Christianity moved into the Balkans in strength through the ninth century. Following the division of the Christian movement in 1054 A.D., Serbia, Montenegro, and Macedonia became largely Eastern Orthodox while Croatia and Slovenia were Roman Catholic. Bosnia-Herzegovina was split between the two groups of Christians with a significant Moslem minority. The Bosnia Muslims derive largely from the surviving remnants of the Bogomils, who had persisted to the time of the Turkish conquest and chose Islam over both Orthodoxy or Catholicism.

In 1389 the Turks defeated the combined Slavic forces at the Battle of Kosovo, following which the Ottoman Empire established itself across the southern Balkans. Only Slovenia, controlled by the Germanic Kingdom (and after the thirteenth-century the Austrian) remained free of Ottoman control. During the years of Muslim control, proselytization occurred most strongly in Bosnia and Croatia. At the end of the seventeenth-century the Hapsburgs pushed further south across Croatia to the Sava River which flowed into the Danube at Belgrade. This territory was formally ceded to Austria in 1699. Through the next two centuries the line between the Ottoman and Hapsburg Empire continued to fluctuate. Serbians began to assert their political independence which was formally granted in 1878.

Following World War II, strongman Josef Broz Tito ruled Yugoslavia until his death in 1980. A decade of weakened central control led to the break-up of the country at the end of the decade. Six separate countries emerged in the early 1990s. (As this volume goes to press, the central region of the former Yugoslavia remains in a state of war and the exact configuration of the new national boundaries remains very much in doubt. The partition or division of Bosnia remains an attractive option to many.)

THE SOUTHERN SLAVIC VAMPIRE

The southern Slavic vampire was a variation of the Slavic vampire, and the beliefs and practices related to it were influenced by those of their neighbors in every direction. The lands of the former Yugoslavia have been cited as the most likely land of origin of the Slavic vampire. Jan L. Perkowski has suggested that the peculiar shape assumed by the vampire originated through a combination of Pagan and Bogomil beliefs (religious ideas dominant in the region at the end of the tenth-century) that were pushed aside by the conquest of Christianity, though he has found little support for his hypothesis. In any case, through the centuries, Christian leaders attempted to destroy the belief of vampires, but were often forced to accommodate to them as they remained strong among the people. Islam proved quite accommodating to the belief in vampires.

Perkowski also traced the origin of the modern word vampire to an old Slavic form *obyrbi* or *obirbi*. Among the various Slavic groups and their neighbors, different forms of the word evolved. Dominant in the region in the modern era was *upirina*, a Serbo-Croatian word. The word *vampir*, with the addition of an "m" sound, was also present, and in Bosnia *lampir* was used. Also present was *vukodlak* (Croatian) or *vurvulak* (Albanian), words similar to the Greek designation of the vampire, *vrykolakas*. *Vukodlak* was often shortened to *kudlak*. In the late nineteenth century, in Istria near the Italian border, a *kudlak* was believed to be attached to each clan. It was considered an evil being that attacked people at night. It was opposed by another entity, the *krsnik*, which often interrupted a *kudlak's* attack and fought it.

In addition to the more ubiquitous words, the term *tenatz* has been found in Montenegro. This was used interchangeably with *lampir*, the local variation on *vampir*. It was believed to be the body of a deceased person that had been taken over by evil spirits. The *tenatz* wandered the night and sucked the blood of the sleeping. They transformed themselves into mice to reenter their burial place. A primary means of detecting a vampire in Montenegro was to take a black horse to the cemetery. The horse would be repelled by the grave of the vampire and refuse to walk across it. Once detected, the body would be disinterred and if, upon further determination, the vampire hunters decided it was a vampire, the corpse would be impaled with a stake and burned.

In Croatia one also might find *kosac, prikosac, tenjac,* and *lupi manari* as terms for a vampire. Albanian names for a vampire included *kukuthi* or *lugat*. The *strigon* (Slovenian) and shtriga (Albanian, Macedonian) are blood-sucking witches related to the Romanian *strigoi*.

Another blood-sucking witch related to the *strigoi* was the *vjeshtitza* (also spelled *veshtitza*). During her field work in Montenegro early in this century, Edith Durham discovered that people no longer believed that *vjeshtitza* existed but retained a rich lore about them. *Vjeshtitza* were older women who were hostile to men, other women, and all children. Possessed by an evil spirit, the sleeping witch's soul wandered at night and inhabited either a moth or a fly. Using the flying animal, the witch entered into the homes of neighbors and sucked the blood of victims. The victim, over a period of time, grew pale, developed a fever, and died. The witches were especially powerful during the first week of March, and protective measures would be taken against them. The protective ceremony, performed the first day of March each year, included the stirring the ashes in the family hearth with two horns, which were then stuck into the ash heap. Garlic was also a common protective substance.

The vampire was a revenant, a body that returned from the grave with some semblance of life. Some believed that it was a body inhabited by an evil spirit. A person was believed to become a vampire in several ways, but a sudden, unexpected, and/or violent accidental death, a wasting sickness, or suicide were seen as primary causes. M. Edith Durham, for example, recorded the story in Bosnia of an epidemic of vampirism associated with a typhus epidemic. Vampirism was also associated, in a day prior to professional undertakers, with the need to follow a prescribed process of preparation of the body of a deceased person and its subsequent burial. Irregularities in the process could cause a person to turn into a vampire. In particular, it had to be watched so that animals, especially cats, did not jump over the body prior to burial. In Macedonia, if a cat did jump over the body, the corpse would then be pierced with two needles. Vampirism was also assumed to be contagious—an attack by a vampire would lead to vampirism.

The *shtriga* and *vjeshtitza* were blood-sucking witches. Although not revenants, the witches were members of the community believed to be living incognito. They were difficult to identify, although a sure sign was a young girl's hair turning white. *Shtriga* attacked in the night, usually in the form of an animal such as a moth, fly, or bee. In fact, the word *shtriga* was derived from the Latin strix, screech owl, that referred to a flying demon that attacked in the night. The Albanian *shtriga* could be detected by placing a cross made with pig bones on the church door when it was crowded with people. The witch was unable to leave the church and would be seen running around the church trying to find a safe exit. The *shtrega* traveled at night and, often in the form of an animal, attacked people and sucked their blood. If a *shtriga* was sighted, it could be followed and positively identified because it had to stop and vomit up the blood it had sucked. The vomited blood could then be used to make an amulet to protect one from witchcraft and vampirism.

The *strigon* of Slovenia was also a bloodsucking witch. The term was derived from the Latin *striga* (witch), which in turn was derived from *strix,* originally a screech owl that was perceived as a demon that attacked infants in the night. The term was also used more generally to describe a vampire.

Slovenian historian Baron Jan Vajkart Valvasor (1641–93) recounted the killing of a *strigon* in Istria (western Slovenia). A person who was the suspected vampire had recently died and was seen by several people walking around the town. His suspected vampirism was reported by his wife after he returned home and had sexual relations with her. The *strigon* was killed by a hawthorn stake driven into its stomach while a priest read an exorcism. The corpse was then decapitated. All the while, the corpse re-acted as if it were alive—it recoiled as the stake was driven in, cried while the exorcism was pronounced, and screamed out as its head was severed. After the decapitation, it bled profusely.

Vampires attacked people it had strong emotional attachments to—both positive (family and friends) and negative (those with whom it had quarreled in life)—and sucked their blood. A sure sign of a vampire was an outbreak of various kinds of contagious illnesses. People who became sick and died from what were then unknown causes were often ascribed to vampiric activity. The vampire could also attack the village livestock in a similar manner.

The southern Slavic vampire was, like that among the Gypsies, capable of having sex with a spouse or lover. Durham related the story of a girl in Montenegro who was forced to marry the man chosen by her parents rather than her true love. Her beloved left the country and, in his despair, died. He returned from the grave as a vampire and visited the girl who eventually became pregnant by him. In appearance, the child closely resembled the deceased man. The villagers were frustrated because the man had died abroad, and thus they could not destroy him. Bodies of males uncovered in the search for a vampire would often have an erect sex organ.

The existence of a vampire could be detected by a variety of means. In Montenegro, for example, a black horse (in Albania, a white horse was used) would be led to a local cemetery—the horse would be repelled by a vampire's grave. The horse usually had to be ridden by a boy who had not yet experienced puberty or a virginal girl. In Croatia, there were reports of strange animal sounds coming from the grave of someone later determined to be a vampire. The body was then disinterred. The discovery of a body turned face down or bloated to the point that the skin was stretched like a drum indicated that the correct body had been uncovered. If only bones remained in the grave, it was not considered a vampire. The Serbians and Bosnians shared the belief with Gypsies in the *dhampir,* the son of a vampire. The offspring of a vampire was considered to have the power to both see and destroy his father and other vampires. In Macedonia, there was the belief in the power of people born on Saturday. Such Sabbatarians, as they were termed, were thought to have a great influence over vampires including the power to lure them into traps where they could be destroyed. On Saturdays, the Sabbatarians could see and kill vampires. For average people, protection from vampires was secured by barricading their homes with thorn bushes (an old remedy for witches).

Once discovered, the vampire could be rendered harmless or destroyed by the traditional means of fixing the body to the ground with a stake and/or decapitation.

In the most severe cases, the body might be dismembered or burned. In general, a priest was asked to be present to repeat the funeral prayers over the person who was perceived to be dying a second time. (As part of an attempt to stop the mutilation of dead bodies, the church in Serbia and Montenegro threatened any priest who cooperated in such activity with excommunication.) In both Montenegro and Albania, it was believed that a vampire could be stopped by hamstringing the corpse. G.F. Abbott reported observing the destruction of a vampire by scalding it with boiling water and driving a long nail in its navel. The body was returned to the ground and the grave covered with millet seeds so if the vampire was not destroyed, it would waste its time counting the millet until dawn. In Croatia, it was believed that a stake driven into the ground over the grave prevented the vampire from rising. In Serbia, a white-thorn or hawthorn stake or other sharp objects might be stuck into the ground over a vampire, or a sickle placed over the neck of the corpse when it was reburied.

It was common among the southern Slavs (as among the Greeks) to dig up bodies some years after their burial, to cleanse the bones, and rebury them in a permanent location. It was important that the soft tissue be completely decomposed by that time—delays in decomposition were cause for concern and could lead to suggestions of vampirism.

THE VAMPIRE EPIDEMICS, 1727–32

The beliefs and practices of the southern Slavs concerning vampires were brought to the attention of western Europe primarily through two spectacular cases that were publicized due to official inquiries into the cases by Austrian authorities. Both cases occurred in a region of Serbia north of Belgrade that had been taken over by Austria from the Ottoman Empire at the end of the seventeenth-century and, subsequently, incorporated into the Hungarian province. One incident began with the sudden death of Peter Plogojowitz. He was seen by his family several nights after his death. Shortly thereafter, Plogojowitz appeared to several people in their dreams. In one week, nine people died of no known cause. When the local army commander arrived to investigate, Plogojowitz's body was taken from the grave. It was found to be as fresh as it had been when buried. The eyes were open and the complexion was ruddy. His mouth was smeared with fresh blood. Fresh skin appeared just below an old layer of dead skin he appeared to be shedding, and his hair and nails had grown. It was concluded that he was a vampire. Plogojowitz's body was staked and burned.

More famous than the Plogojowitz incident was the case of Arnold Paul. Paul lived in the village of Medvegia (spelled in numerous ways in different sources), Serbia, north of Paracin. He told his neighbors that while he had been serving in the army in Turkey, he had been bitten by a vampire. A week later he died. Several weeks after his death, people began to report seeing him, and four such people died. On the fourtieth day after his burial, the grave was opened and he was found in a lifelike condition. When his body was cut, he bled freely. When staked, it was later reported that he groaned aloud. He and the four people he reportedly vampirized were decapitated and their bodies burned.

The Arnold Paul case should have ended with his funeral pyre. However, in 1731, some 17 people in the village died of an unknown cause. Vampirism was suggested.

Word of the unusual occurrences reached all the way to Vienna, and the emperor ordered an official inquiry. Following the arrival of Johannes Fluckinger in Medvegia, the body of a new suspected vampire was disinterred. He was also found to be in a healthy state. After some further investigation, it was discovered that Paul had vampirized several cows. Those who ate the meat from the cows were infected with a vampiric condition. The bodies of the recently dead were then disinterred and all were staked and burned.

Fluckinger returned to Vienna and presented the emperor with a complete report. During 1732, the report and several journalistic versions of it became bestsellers throughout Europe. The two cases became the basis of a heated debate in German universities, and after a decade of arguing, the participants concluded that vampires did not exist. However, the debate spurred the interest of Dom Augustin Calmet, a French biblical scholar, who, in 1746, completed a most important treatise on the subject published in England as *The Phantom World*.

The fame of Plogojowitz and Paul should have focused attention on Serbia and the southern Slavic countries. Instead, from mere geographical ignorance, many involved in the debate placed the occurrences in Hungary, and thus Hungary—which has the least vampire mythology of all the Eastern European countries—became known for vampirism. As a result, scrutiny of vampire beliefs was directed away from Serbia and its southern Slavic neighbors. The misdirection given vampire phenomena by Calmet was reinforced by the writings of Montague Summers and number of writers on vampires who essentially copied him.

The vampire has had a long and interesting history in what is now the independent country of Slovenia. Largely Roman Catholic in background, the country existed for many centuries as an Austrian province; however, south of the Drava River, especially in rural areas, Slovenes resisted Germanization and retained their own language and folklore. One of the earliest books to deal with vampires was Count Valvasor's *Die Ehre des Herzogthums Krain* (1689), which told the story of Grando, a peasant of the district of Kranj. A quiet man in life, in death Grando began to attack his neighbors and his body was ordered exhumed. His body was found with ruddy complexion and he appeared to have a smile on his face. A priest called upon the vampire to look to his savior Jesus Christ, at which the body took on a sad expression and tears were flowing down his cheek. The body was then decapitated and reburied. A more general account of vampires in the region was given in the famous 1734 travelogue, *The Travels of Three English Gentlemen*.

MODERN VAMPIRES AMONG THE SOUTHERN SLAVS

Vampire beliefs have continued into the twentieth century, in spite of several generations of hostile governments that denounced both religion and superstitions. Folklorists have had no trouble locating vampire stories. The depth and persistence of the vampire belief was vividly illustrated in a most unexpected manner early in 1993, in the midst of the most violent era experienced directly by Serbia following the break-up of the former Yugoslavia. During that year, a man made a number of appearances on Serbia's state-controlled television station at the height of the country's conflict. He, in all seriousness, argued that at the moment when final destruction threatened the Serbian nation, a fleet of vampires would arise from the cemeteries to defeat Serbia's enemies.

In preparation for this event, he advised viewers to keep a supply of garlic at hand lest the vampires attack them by mistake.

SOURCES

Abbott, G. F. *Macedonian Folklore.* Chicago: Argonaut Inc., 1969. 372 pp.

Barber, Paul. *Vampires, Burial, and Death: Folklore and Reality.* New Haven, CT: Yale University Press, 1988. 236 pp.

D'Assier, Adolphe. *Posthumous Humanity: A Study of Phantoms.* San Diego, CA: Wizards Bookshelf, 1981. 360 pp.

Durham, M. Edith. "Of Magic, Witches and Vampires in the Balkans." *Man* 121 (December 1923): 189–92.

Kinzer, Stephen. "At Root of Mayhem: A Bizarre Dream World Called Serbia." *Star Tribune* (Minneapolis) (May 16, 1993): 11A.

Perkowski, Jan L. *The Darkling: A Treatise on Slavic Vampirism.* Columbus, OH: Slavica Publishers, 1989. 174 pp.

———, ed. *Vampires of the Slavs.* Cambridge, MA: Slavica Publishers, 1976. 294 pp.

Petrovitch, Woislav M. *Hero Tales and Legends of the Serbians.* London: George G. Harrap, 1914. 393 pp. Reprint. New York: Kraus Reprint Co., 1972. 393 pp.

Vampires and the Gypsies

Edited by J. Gordon Melton

In the opening chapters of Bram Stoker's novel *Dracula*, Jonathan Barker discovered that he was a prisoner in Castle Dracula, but he was given hope by the appearance of a band of Gypsies:

> A band of Szgany have come to the castle, and are encamped in the courtyard. These Szgany are gypsies; I have notes of them in my book. They are peculiar to this part of the world, though allied to the ordinary gypsies all the world over. There are thousands of them in Hungary and Transylvania who are almost outside all law. They attach themselves as a rule to some great noble or boyar, and call themselves by his name. They are fearless and without religion, save superstition, and they talk only their own varieties of the many tongues.

He soon discovered that the Gypsies were allied to the Count. The letters he attempted to have the Gypsies mail for him were returned to Dracula. The Gypsies were overseeing the preparation of the boxes of native soil that Dracula took to England. The Gypsies then reappeared at the end of the novel, accompanying the fleeing Dracula on his return to his castle. In the end, they stepped aside and allowed their vampire master to be killed by Abraham Van Helsing and his cohorts.

THE EMERGENCE OF THE GYPSIES

Since the fourteenth century, the Gypsies have formed a distinct ethnic minority group in the Balkan countries. Within the next two centuries, they were found across all of Europe. While they received their name from an early hypothesis that placed their origin in Egypt, it is now known that they originated in India and were related to similar nomadic tribes that survive to this day in northern India. At some point, around 1000 A.D., some of these tribes wandered westward. A large group settled for a period in

Turkey and incorporated many words from that country into their distinctive Romany language. Crossing the Bosporous, the Gypsies found their way to Serbia and traveled as far north as Bohemia through the fourteenth century. They were noted as being in Crete as early as 1322. In the next century, a short time before the emergence of Vlad Dracul and Vlad the Impaler as rulers in Wallachia, they moved into what are now Romania and Hungary. The Gypsies fanned out across Europe throughout the next century. They were in Russia and Poland, eventually making their way to France and Great Britain.

In Romania and Hungary, Gypsies were often enslaved and persecuted. Their nomadic, nonliterary culture left them vulnerable to accusations of wrongdoing, and they became known not only as traveling entertainers but as thieves, con artists, and stealers of infants; this latter charge often was made about despised minority groups in Europe. During World War II, simultaneously with their attack upon the Jews, the Nazis attempted an extermination of the Gypsies as a "final solution" to what they had defined as the Gypsy problem.

GYPSIES AND THE SUPERNATURAL

Gypsies developed a sophisticated and complicated supernatural religious world view, made more difficult to describe by the diversity of the different bands in various countries and the reluctance of Gypsies to talk to outsiders about their most sacred beliefs. Only the most diligent and persistent effort by a small band of scholars yielded a picture of the world view, which varied from country to country.

Gypsy theology affirmed the existence of *o Del* (literally, the God), who appeared one day on Earth (the Earth being the eternally present uncreated world). Beside *o Del,* the principle of Good, was *o Bengh,* or Evil, *o Del* and *o Bengh* competed in the creation of humanity. *O Bengh* formed two statuettes out of earth, and *o Del* breathed life into them. Again, with no written text, the account differed from tribe to tribe. The expanded world of the Gypsies was alive with the forces of Good and Evil contending with each other throughout nature. Wise Gypsies learned to read the signs and omens to make the forces work for them and to prevent evil forces from doing them harm.

Gypsies kept a living relationship with the dead (some have called it a cult of the dead), to whom they had a great loyalty. Gypsies regularly left offerings of food, especially milk, with the goal of having the dead serve a protective function for living family members. E. B. Trigg, in *Gypsy Demons & Divinities: The Magical and Supernatural Practices of the Gypsies,* described this practice as a form of worship vampire gods, which he compared to the activity of Indian worshippers toward the vampire figures of Indian mythology.

What happened to the dead? Among the Gypsies of the Balkans, there was a belief that the soul entered a world very much like this one, except there was no death. Bosnian Gypsies, influenced by Islam, believed in a literal paradise, a land of milk and honey. Others, however, believed that the soul hovered around the grave and resided in the corpse. As such, the soul might grow restless and the corpse might develop a desire to return to this world. To keep the dead content, funeral rites were elaborate and families made annual visits to the grave sites. Within this larger world there was ample room for the living dead, or vampires. This belief was found among Gypsies across Europe, but was especially pronounced, as might be expected, in Hungary, Romania, and the Slavic lands.

Questions have been posed as to the origins of Gypsy vampire beliefs. In India, the Gypsies' land of origin, there were a variety of acknowledged vampire creatures. For example, the *bhuta,* found in western India, was believed to be the soul of a man who died in an untimely fashion (such as an accident or suicide). The bhuta wandered around at night, and among its attributes was the ability to animate dead bodies, which in turn attacked the living in ghoulish fashion. In northern India, from whence the Gypsies probably started their journey to the West, the *brahmaparusha* was a vampire-like creature who was pictured with a head encircled by intestines and a skull filled with blood from which it drank. Gypsies also had a belief in Sara, the Black Virgin, a figure derived from the bloodthirsty goddess Kali. Thus, Gypsies may have brought a belief in vampires, or at least a disposition to believe in them, to the Balkan Peninsula. Once in the area, however, they obviously interacted with the native populations and developed the belief of what became a variety of the Slavic vampire.

The Gypsy vampire was called a *mulo* (or *mullo*; plural, *mulé*), and means literally "one who is dead." Gypsies viewed death essentially as unnatural, hence any death was an affront and viewed as being caused by evil forces attacking the individual. Thus, any individual—but especially anyone who died an untimely death (by suicide or an accident)—might become a vampire and search out the person or persons who caused the death. Given the clannish nature of Gypsy life, these people were most likely those close to the deceased. Prime candidates would be relatives who did not destroy the belongings of the deceased (according to Gypsy custom) but kept them for themselves. The vampire also might have a grudge against any who did not properly observe the elaborate burial and funeral rites.

The vampire usually appeared quite normal, but often could be detected by some sign in its physical body. For example, the creature might have a finger missing, or have animal-like appendages. Easier to detect was the vampire that took on a horrific appearance. This involved certain individuals who could only be viewed under special conditions. Vampires might be seen at any time of day or night, though some believed them to be strictly nocturnal creatures. Others thought that vampires could appear precisely at noon when they would cast no shadow. Slavic and German Gypsies believed that vampires had no bones in their bodies, a belief based upon the observation that a vampire's bones are often left behind in the grave.

Upon their return from the dead, Gypsies believed that vampires engaged in various forms of malicious activity. They attacked relatives and attempted to suck their blood.

They destroyed property and became a general nuisance by throwing things around and making noises in the night. Male vampires were known to have a strong sexual appetite and returned from the dead to have sexual relations with a wife, girlfriend, or other women. Female vampires were thought to be able to return from the dead and assume a normal life, even to the point of marrying—though her husband would become exhausted from satisfying her sexual demands.

Gypsies thought that animals and, on occasion, even plants became vampires. Dead snakes, horses, chickens, dogs, cats, and sheep were reported as returning as vampires, especially in Bosnia. In Slavic lands it was thought that if an animal such as a cat jumped over a corpse prior to burial, the corpse would become a vampire. Gypsies believed that the animal might become a vampire at the time of its death. Plants such as the pumpkin or watermelon could, if kept in the house too long, begin to stir, make noises, and show a trace of blood; they would then cause trouble, in a limited way, for both people and cattle. In the most extreme cases, family tools might become vampires. The wooden knot for a yoke or the wooden rods for binding sheaves of wheat became vampires if left undone for more than three years.

It was believed that action could be taken to prevent a dead person from returning as a vampire. As a first step, the victim of a vampire called upon a *dhampir,* the son of a vampire. Gypsies believed that intercourse between a vampire and his widow might produce a male offspring. This child would develop unusual powers for detecting vampires, and a *dhampir* might actually hire out his services in the case of vampire attacks. There was some belief that the *dhampir* had a jelly like body (remembering that some thought that vampires had no bones) and hence would have a shorter life span.

Many Gypsies thought that iron had special powers to keep away evil. To ward off vampires, at the time of burial a steel needle was driven into the heart of the corpse, and bits of steel were placed in the mouth, over the ears and nose, and between the fingers. The heel of the shoe could be removed and hawthorn placed in the sock, or hawthorn stake could be driven through the leg. If a vampire was loose in a village, one might find protection in different charms, such as a necklace with an iron nail. A ring of thorn could be set around one's living quarters. Christian Gypsies used a crucifix. Slavic Gypsies prized the presence of a set of twins, one male and one female, who were born on a Saturday and who were willing to wear their underclothes inside out. From such the vampire would flee immediately.

The grave site might be the focus of a suspected vampire. Gypsies have been known to drive stakes of ash or hawthorn into a grave, or pour boiling water over it. In more problematic cases, coffins were opened and the corpse examined to see if it had shifted in the coffin or not properly decomposed. In the case of a body thought to be a vampire, Gypsies followed the practices of their neighbors by having the Christian prayers for the dead said; staking it in either the stomach, heart, or head; decapitation; and/or in extreme cases, cremation.

The need to destroy the vampire was slight among some Gypsies who believed its life span was only 40 days. However, some granted it a longer life and sought specific means to kill it. An iron needle in the stomach often would be enough. In Eastern Orthodox countries, such as Romania, holy water would be thrown on the vampire. If these less intrusive means did not work, Gypsies might resort to more conventional weapons. If captured, a vampire might be nailed to a piece of wood. If one was available, a *dhampir* might be called upon to carry out the destruction. Black dogs and wolves were known to attack vampires, and some Romanian Gypsies believed that white wolves stayed around the grave sites to attack vampires and that without their work the world would be overrun with the dead.

Numerous reports on the *mulo* have been collected and show significant variance among geographically separated Gypsy groups. There has been some speculation that their vampire beliefs originated in India, from whence the Gypsies themselves seemed to have derived and which had a rich vampiric lore. The notions have become differentiated over the centuries as Gypsies dispersed around Europe and North America and interacted with various local cultures.

CONCLUSION

The belief in vampires has survived among Gypsies, but, like all supernatural beliefs, it has shown signs of disappearing. Secular schooling, modern burial practices, and governments hostile to actions (such as mutilating bodies) taken in response to vampires have affected the strength of this belief.

SOURCES

Clebert, Jean-Paul. *The Gypsies.* Harmondsworth, Middlesex, U.K.: Penguin Books, 1963. 282 pp.

Leland, G. G. *Gypsy Sorcery.* New York Tower Books, n.d. 267 pp.

Trigg, E. B. *Gypsy Demons & Divinities: The Magical and Supernatural Practices of the Gypsies.* London: Sheldon Press, 1973. 238 pp.

Vukanovic, T. P. "The Vampire." In Jan L. Perkowski, ed. *Vampires of the Slavs.* Cambridge, MA: Slavica Publishers, 1976, 201–34.

Vampires in Russia

Edited by J. Gordon Melton

The former Soviet Union, including Russia, Siberia, the Ukraine, and Byelorussia, has been one of the homelands of the Slavic vampire. The first mention of the word "vampir" in a Slavic document was in a Russian one, *The Book of Prophecy* written in 1047 A.D. for Vladimir Jaroslav, Prince of Novgorod, in northwest Russia. The text was written in what is generally thought of as proto-Russian, a form of the language that had evolved from the older, common Slavonic language but had not yet become distinctive Russian language of the modern era. The text gave a priest the unsavory label "Upir Lichy," literally "wicked vampire" or "extortionate vampire," an unscrupulous prelate. The term—if not the concept—was most likely introduced from the southern Slavs, possibly the Bulgarians. The Russians of Kiev had adopted Eastern Christianity in 988 A.D. and had drawn heavily on Bulgaria for Christian leadership.

Those areas of Russia under Prince Vladimir, centered around the city of Kiev (the Ukraine), accepted Christianity in 988, at which time Vladimir declared war on paganism. Christianity then spread from Kiev northward and westward. For several centuries Christianity existed side by side with existing tribal faiths, but became an integral part of the amalgamation of the tribal cultures into unified states. The invasion of Mongols in the 1240s, including their destruction of Kiev, and their decade of rule, led to a shift of power to Novgorod under Alexander Nevsky. During the fourteenth century, power began to shift to the princedom of Muskovy and the chief Christian cleric established himself in Moscow, though still titled as the metropolitan of "Kiev and all Rus." Westernmost Russia, including the Ukraine and Byelorussia, came under the expanded Lithuanian empire. Thus modern Russia emerged by pushing back the Mongols in the East and the Lithuanians (and Poles) in the West.

While the state fought back foreign territorial rivals, Orthodox Christianity was in the very process of driving out the pre-Christian religions. That process was accompanied by the rise of new heretical religious movements, some being amalgamations of Christian and pagan practices. With the emergence of a strong central state in Moscow in the fourteenth century, the state periodically moved against dissident movements. Surviving through this entire period into modern times were people who practiced (or who were believed to practice) magic. They were known as witches and sorcerers.

During the long reign of Vasili II in the mid-fifteenth century, vast changes occurred in Russia, including an expansion of its territory. In 1448, following the breakup of the Roman Catholic and Eastern Orthodox union to combat Islam, and just five years before the fall of Constantinople, the bishop in Moscow declared his autonomous status. There followed a period of expansion, both secular and ecclesiastical. The Russian church assumed many of the prerogatives formerly held by Constantinople, and early in the sixteenth-century there arose the concept of Moscow as the "third Rome," the new center of Christian faith. Under Ivan III the Great, territorial expansion reached new heights with the incorporation of Finland and movement to the east across the Urals. Thus the stage was set for the expansion into the Volga River valley under Ivan the Terrible, and the incorporation of Siberia and lands all the way to the Pacific Ocean in the seventeenth century. During the several centuries of Romanov rule, Russia continued westward into the Baltic states, Byelorussia, and the Ukraine, though its most impressive conquests were southward to the Caspian Sea and the Persian border. By the time of the Russian revolution in 1917, the country had assumed the proportions it has today.

The Russian revolution of 1917 brought the Union of Soviet Socialist Republics (USSR) into existence. The USSR collapsed in December 1991 and has been replaced by the Commonwealth of Independent States (CIS), though a number of the former Soviet states did not join the CIS and chose to become new and independent countries. This essay deals with the lands of the CIS, primarily Russia, Byelorussia, and the Ukraine.

THE RUSSIAN VAMPIRE

In modern Russia the most common term for a vampire is *uppyr*, a term probably borrowed from the Ukrainian *upyr*. In Russia, the idea of the vampire became closely associated with that of the witch or sorcerer, which in turn had been tied to the concept of heresy. Heresy is defined as the deviation on matters considered essential to orthodox faith, in this case, Eastern Orthodox Christianity. This idea can be viewed as an extension of the Eastern Orthodox belief that a body would not decay normally if death occurred when the individual was outside the communion of the church. The person could be in an excommunicated state due either to immoral behavior or to heresy. Thus a heretic (i.e., *eretik*, or, in related dialects and languages, *eretnik, eretica, eretnica*, or *erestun*) might become a vampire after death. In Russian thought, the relationship between heresy and the existence of vampires was simply strengthened to the point of identifying one with the other.

The person who was a heretic in this life might become a vampire after death. The most likely heretic to turn into a vampire was the practitioner of magic, under a variety of names—*kudesnik, porcelnik, koldun,* or *snaxar.* The method of transformation into a vampire varied widely.

An *eretik* was also associated with sorcery, a practice that also led to one's becoming a vampire. Over the years and across the very large territory comprising Russia, the *eretik* assumed a number of additional connotations. At time it referred to members of the many sectarian groups that drew people from the true faith. It also referred to witches who had sold their soul to the devil. The vampire *eretik* possessed an evil eye that could draw a person caught in the vampire's gaze into the grave.

Dmitrij Zelenin has traced the emergence of the *eretik* vampire from the fight conducted by the Orthodox against the medieval religious sectarians. Sectarians were designated *inovercy* (i.e., persons who adhere to a different faith). Upon death the *inovercy* were associated with the *zaloznye pokojniki,* or unclean dead, and thus were not buried in cemeteries. They had died without confession and thus were seen as dying in sin. Since they did not believe in the true God, possibly they had served the devil, and hence were considered sorcerers.

Eretiks generally were destroyed by the use of an aspen stake driven into the back or by fire.

In the Olonecian region, accounts suggested that any person, including a pious Christian, could become a vampire if a sorcerer entered and took over the body at the moment of death. The peasant would appear to have recovered, but in fact had become a *erestuny* (vampire) who would begin to feed on members of the family. People in the nearby village would start to die mysteriously. In the Elatomsk district of east-central Russia, there were even reports of the *ereticy*—women who sold their soul to the devil. After their death, these women roamed the earth in an attempt to turn people from the true faith. They might be found near graveyards, as they slept at night in the graves of the impious. They could be identified by their appearance at the local bathhouse, where they made an unseemly noise.

VAMPIRE FOLKTALES

The vampire has been the subject of many Russian folk stories collected in the nineteenth and early twentieth centuries beginning with the work of A. N. Afanas'ev in the 1860s. As was common with many folktales, they served to promote community values and encouraged specific kinds of behavior. The tale "Death at the Wedding," for example, related the adventure of a soldier proud of his service to God and the emperor. When he returned to his home town on a visit, he encountered a sorcerer/vampire. Unknowingly, the soldier took the vampire to a wedding, where the vampire began to drain the blood of the newlyweds. Horrified, the soldier nevertheless engaged the sorcerer in conversation until he discovered the secret of stopping him. First, he stole some of the blood the vampire had collected into two vials and poured the blood back into the wounds the vampire had made on the couple's bodies. He next led the villagers out to the cemetery, where they dug up the vampire's body and burned it. The soldier was generously rewarded for his actions and his display of courage in service to God and emperor.

The dispatch of the Russian vampire followed traditional means known throughout Slavic countries. The body of a suspected vampire was first disinterred. Often a stake (aspen was a preferred wood) was driven through the heart. Sometimes the body would be burned (Afanes'ev's account mentioned that aspen wood was used in the cremation of the vampire). In the account from the Olonecian region, the corpse was whipped before the stake was driven through the heart.

THE VAMPIRE IN RUSSIAN LITERATURE

During the nineteenth century, the vampire entered the world of Russian literature, seemingly through the popularity of the German romantic stories of E. T. A. Hoffmann and the writings of Goethe. In the 1840s Alexey K. Tolstoy (1817–75) combined the vampire of popular Russian folklore with the literary vampire that had emerged in Germany and France. His two stories, "Upyr" and "The Family of the Vourdalak," became classics of both the horror genre and Russian literature. The latter was brought to the movie screen by Italian producer Mario Bava as part of his horror anthology *Black Sabbath*. More recently, "The Family of the Vourdalak" has become the subject of a Russian-made movie released in the United States as *Father, Santa Claus Has Died* (1992). At least two other Russian vampire stories have been translated and given worldwide distribution, "Vij" (or "Viv") by Nikolai Gogol and "Phantoms" by Ivan Turgenev. The former became the basis of two movies, *La Maschera del Demonio* (released in the United States as *Black Sunday*), also directed by Mario Bava, and a 1990 remake with the same name by Mario's son Lamberto Bava. A Russian version of *Vij* was filmed in 1967.

What was possibly the first vampire film, *The Secret of House No. 5*, was made in Russia in 1912. An unauthorized version of *Dracula*, the first screen adaptation of the Bram Stoker novel, was filmed in Russia two years before *Nosferatu, Eine Symphonie des Garuens*, the more famous film by Freidrich Wilhelm Murnau. However, the vampire has not been a consistent topic for movies in Russia over the years.

SOURCES

Coxwell, C. Fillingham. *Siberian and Other Folk-Tales*. London: C. W. Daniel Company, 1925. 1056 pp. Reprint. New York: AMS Press, 1983. 1056 pp.

Oinas, Felix J. "Heretics as Vampires and Demons in Russia." *Slavic and East European Journal* 22, 4 (Winter 1978): 433–41.

Perkowski, Jan L. *The Darkling: A Treatise on Slavic Vampirism.* Columbus, OH: Slavica Publishers, 1989. 174 pp.

Tale of a Russian Vampire

By Helena P. Blavatsky
(1877)

ABOUT THE AUTHOR

Helena Petrovna "Madame" Blavatsky (1831–1891) was, and remains, a highly controversial figure in the history of philosophy and religion. Born in Russia to an aristocratic family, Blavatsky showed an early talent for languages, music, and art, but, after a failed marriage, embarked on extensive spiritual pilgrimages throughout the world. Settling in New York, she cofounded the Theosophical Society in 1875 and rapidly became a fixture of Manhattan society, then enthralled with the spiritualist craze sweeping the country. Blavatsky attempted to give spiritualism a philosophical pedigree through an eclectic synthesis of her esoteric studies and personal claims of occult power.

Although she was widely denounced as a fraud for her carnivalesque exhibitions of table rapping, ectoplasm, and other mediumistic displays, she nonetheless was a major force in the introduction of Eastern philosophy to America, especially concepts of reincarnation, karma, and the presence of life and consciousness in all matter.

The selection presented here is taken from Blavatsky's first major work, *Isis Unveiled*, first published in 1877.

About the beginning of the present century, there occurred in Russia, one of the most frightful cases of vampirism on record. The governor of the province of Tch—was a man of about sixty years, of a malicious, tyrannical, cruel and jealous disposition. Clothed with despotic authority, he exercised it without stint, as his brutal instincts prompted. He fell in love with the pretty daughter of a subordinate official. Although the girl was betrothed to a young man whom she loved, and, the tyrant forced her father to consent to his having her marry him; and the poor victim, despite her despair, became his wife. His jealous disposition exhibited itself. He beat her, confined her to her room for weeks together, and prevented

Helena P. Blavatsky (1887).

her seeing any one except in his presence. He finally fell sick and died. Finding his end approaching, he made her swear never to marry again; and with fearful oaths, threatened that, in case she did, he would return from his grave and kill her. He was buried in the cemetery across the river, and the young widow experienced no further annoyance, until, nature getting the better of her fears, she listened to the importunities of her former lover, and they were again betrothed.

On the night of the customary betrothal-feast, when all had retired, the old mansion was aroused by shrieks proceeding from her room. The doors were burst open, and the unhappy woman was found lying on her bed, in a swoon. At the same time a carriage was heard rumbling out of the courtyard. Her body was found to be black and blue in places, as from the effect of pinches, and from a slight puncture on her neck drops of blood were oozing. Upon recovering, she stated that her deceased husband had suddenly entered her room, appearing exactly as in life, with the exception of a dreadful pallor; that he had upbraided her for her inconstancy, and then beaten and pinched her most cruelly. Her story was disbelieved; but the next morning, the guard stationed at the other end of the bridge which spans the river, reported that, just before midnight, a black coach and six had driven furiously past them, toward the town, without answering their challenge.

The new governor, who disbelieved the story of the apparition, took nevertheless the precaution of doubling the guards across the bridge. The same thing happened, however, night after night; the soldiers declaring that the toll-bar at their station near the bridge would rise of itself, and the spectral equipage sweep by them despite their efforts to stop it. At the same time every night, the coach would rumble into the courtyard of the house; the watchers, including the widow's family, and the servants, would be thrown into a heavy sleep; and every morning the victim would be found bruised, bleeding and swooning as before. The town was thrown into consternation. The physicians had no explanations to offer; priests came to pass the night in prayer, but as midnight approached, all would be seized with the terrible lethargy. Finally, the archbishop of the province came, and performed the ceremony of exorcism in person, but the following morning the governor's widow was found worse than even. She was now brought to death's door.

The governor was finally driven to take the severest measures to stop the ever-increasing panic in the town. He stationed fifty Cossacks along the bridge, with orders to stop the spectre-carriage at all hazards. Promptly at the usual hour, it was heard and seen approaching from the direction of the cemetery. The officer of the guard, and a priest bearing a crucifix, planted themselves in front of the toll-bar, and together shouted: "In the name of God, and the Czar, who goes there?" Out of the coach-window was thrust a well-remembered head, and a familiar voice responded: "The Privy Councillor of State and Governor, C_____!" At the same moment, the officer, the priest, and the soldiers were flung aside as by an electric shock, and the ghostly equipage passed by them, before they could recover breath.

The archbishop then resolved, as a last expedient, to resort to the time-honored plan of exhuming the body, and pinning it to the earth with a stake driven through its heart. This was done with great religious ceremony in the presence of the whole populace. The story is that the body was found gorged with blood, and with red cheeks and lips. At the instance that the first blow was struck upon the stake, a groan issued from the corpse, and a jet of blood spurted high into the air. The archbishop pronounced the usual exorcism, the body was reinterred, and from that time no more was heard of the vampire.

How far the facts of this case may have been exaggerated by tradition, we cannot say. But we had it years ago from an eye-witness; and at the present day there are families in Russia whose elder members will recall the dreadful tale.

Russia, Roumania, and Bulgaria

By Montague Summers

I t is no matter for surprise that in so sad and sick a country as Russia the tradition of the vampire should assume, if it be possible, an even intenser darkness. We find, indeed, a note of something deformed, as it were, something cariously diseased and unclean, a rank wealth of grotesque and fetid details which but serve to intensify the loathliness and horror.

There are still to be observed in Russia very distinct traces of survival from the old rites with which the ancient Slavonians, whilst yet Pagans, celebrated the obsequies of their dead. Concerning these we are fortunate enough to possess a considerable amount of detailed information. Important references to various customs that prevailed at Slavonic funerals may be found in such early writers as the Emperor Maurice[1], who in his *Strategica* comments upon the fact that the wives of Slavonian warriors refused to survive their lords. Theophylactus Simocatta, the Byzantine historian who died 629 A.D.[2] relates that the Roman general Priscus invaded the Slavonic territory, and captured Mousokios, "the king of the Barbarians," who was lewdly intoxicated with wine after the celebrations with which he had honoured the funeral of one of his brothers. This gives evidence of the savage revelry that took place during these ancient burials, and the passage was incorporated by Theophanes Isaurus[3] in his *Chronicon*, which comes down to the year 811, and hence it has been copied by Anastasius the Librarian about 886. In the eighth century S. Boniface who was martyred 5 June, 755 (754), remarked that among the Slavonic Winedi, or Wends, the bonds of matrimony were considered to be so strong that it was usual for wives to kill themselves upon the death of their husbands, a custom to which reference will again be made a little later. During the first half of the tenth century those acute and observant Arabian travellers, Ibn Dosta, Masudi, and Ibn Fozlan, gave very striking accounts of Slavonic burials, drawing particular attention to the extraordinary nature of the sacrifices which were then offered. This material was largely drawn upon by Leo Diaconus, a Byzantine historian of the tenth century, whose chronicle[4] includes the period from the Cretan expedition of Nicephoras Phocas, in the reign of the Emperor Romanus II, A.D, 959, to the death of Joannes I Zimisces, 975. Dithmar (Thietmar), Bishop of Merseburg,[5] in his famous

Chronicon Thielmari which comprises in eight books the reigns of the Saxon Emperors Henry I (the Fowler), the three Ottos, and S. Henry II, gives much valuable information regarding the contemporary history and civilization of the Slavonic tribes east of the river Elbe. In his encyclicals S. Otto, Bishop of Bamburg, (*circa* 1060,–30 June, 1139), reproves many Pagan customs which were beginning again to assert themselves, and amongst others he particularly forbids obscure burials in lonely woods and fields which were afterwards regarded as haunted, if not accursed spots. The "Herodotus of Bohemia," Cosmas of Prague, whose *Chronica Bohemorum* commences with the earliest times and brings the narrative down to 1125, affords very copious information upon this very subject, and his work is particularly valuable since as a historian Cosmas is truthful and conscientious, distinguishing between what is certain and what is based on tradition and generally indicating his sources of information.[6] Rather more than four centuries later, a Latin poem by Klonowicz, *Roxolania*, Cracow, 1584, contains a vivid picture of Ruthenian obsequies in the sixteenth century. Even better known is the account given by Meletius (or Menetius) in a letter dated 1551, *De Sacrificiis et ydolatria ueterum Borussorum*, which was largely reproduced by Lasicius in his study *De Diis Samogitarum*. A summary of all that is valuable and pertinent in these authors will be found in the erudite if somewhat old-fashioned treatise by Kotlyarevsky, *O Pogrebal'nuikh Obuichayakh Yazuicheshikh Slavyan* (*On the Funeral Customs of the Heathen Slavonians*), Moscow, 1868.

Many scholars have debated the question whether the Old Slavonians buried their dead or burned them in funeral pyres. Some writers have maintained the first, and others as stoutly asserted the second. Again, it has been supposed that those Slavonians who led a nomadic life cremated their dead, but when they settled down in hamlets and villages the custom of inhumation was adopted. It has been suggested that among these Pagans there were two religious sects or parties each of which disposed of the dead in its own particular way. Not a few writers, moreover, have thought that the wealthy Slavonians were burned, whilst the poor were merely interred. Further it has been held that the Slavonians whilst they were yet Heathen used to incinerate the dead, but that upon their conversion they abandoned this practice. Kotlyarevsky after a general review of the many arguments reaches the conclusion that there was in fact no fixed rule, that some Slavonians buried the dead, and that others first cremated the bodies and then acting in accordance with an old family tradition interred the ashes. It has been pointed out that during excavations it is by no means unusual to find traces of both customs in the one tomb; for near the remains of a corpse which has been interred without cremation lie the ashes of a body that has been calcined.

It may be noted that no ancient word for "cemetery" occurs in any Slavonic dialect, and general burying-grounds do not seem to have been known, for research has shown that almost always the tombs stand singly or in family groups. Sometimes hills, and especially caves in hills, were chosen for the graves of the departed. The tribes who lived around the shores of the Baltic especially favoured lonely fields and the depths of the forest. In common with many another savage race when a corpse was burned or buried various objects suffered the same fate. Warriors had passed before, and so their favourite chargers were generally slain; their armour, dress, ornaments, and even household utensils, were destroyed to serve them beyond the grave. But the most important of the companions of the dead were the human beings who either killed themselves or were put to death upon the occasion of a chieftain's funeral. The Arabian traveller Ibn Dosta, to whom reference has already been made, tells us that in some cases it was customary for the dead man's wife to hang herself in order that her body might be cremated with that of her lord; in other districts she was expected to allow herself to be buried alive with him.[7] To this practice there are constant allusions in the songs and customs of the people, and this explains the so-called "marriages" between the living and the dead. Among such songs are those Moravian laments in which the dead are described as rising from their graves, and carrying off their wives or the betrothed. In one *Builina* or metrical romance the dead Potok is buried together with his living wife. Writing in 1872 Ralston[8] says: "Marriage and death were often brought into strange fellowship by at least some of the Old Slavonians. Strongly impressed with the idea that those whom the nuptial bond had united in this world were destined to live together also in the world to come they so sincerely pitied the lot of the unmarried dead, that, before committing their bodies to the grave they were in the habit of finding them partners for eternity. The fact that, among some Slavonian peoples, if a man died a bachelor a wife was allotted to him after his death, rests on the authority of several witnesses, and in a modified form the practice has been retained in some places up to the present day. In Little-Russia, for instance, a dead maiden is dressed in nuptial attire, and friends come to her funeral as to a wedding, and a similar custom is observed on the death of a lad. In Podolia, also, a young girl's funeral is conducted after the fashion of a wedding, a youth being chosen as the bridegroom who attends her to the grave, with the nuptial kerchief twined around his arm. From that time her family considered him their relative, and the rest of the community look upon him as a widower. In some parts of Servia when a lad dies, a girl dressed as a bride follows him to the tomb, carrying two crowns; one of these is thrown to the corpse, and the other she keeps at least for a time.

Ibn Fozlan[9] relates that certain "Russian" merchants with whom he became acquainted in Bulgaria loudly blamed their Arabian friend as belonging to a race who buried their dead to rot and be consumed of worms, in which case it was impossible to tell what might not befall the deceased, whereas they themselves at once cremated their dead, and so without delay the departed passed on to Paradise. It seems uncertain who were these "Russians," and Rasmussen the translator of the narrative into Danish roundly denies that they were Scandinavians, but most authorities are agreed that they must have been Varangian traders.

It may be noticed that the heathen Slavonians set up upon the mound which covers a grave a little hut or tent in which the soul might find rest and shelter when it came to revisit the body where it once inhabited, and hither also the relatives of the dead resorted when they desired to mourn over his remains. Half a century ago traces of this custom still persisted in Russia. In spite of the strictest ecclesiastical prohibition the White-Russians were wont to build over graves a kind of log-house. In some districts these were known as a *Golubets,* a term more properly applied to the roofed cross which is generally erected in God's acre. As may well be imagined, it was popularly supposed that these little lodgements, banned by the Church, were most fearfully haunted and were often the lurking places of werewolves and Vampires.

The Pagan Slavonians also encouraged the practice of burying in one tomb as many generations of a family as possible, and the more tenants there were in a grave the more their respect for it increased, since it was protected by so many "Fathers," whose abiding place it had become. It would appear that some remnant of this custom, prevails in Bulgaria to-day, where, it is said, that if no relative dies within the space of three years the family tomb is opened, and any stranger who happens to pass away in the vicinity is buried in it, which no doubt is due to the old superstition that the grave required a victim.

Even to-day there persist practices which are obviously derived from this idea, and the connexion between the dead and the living must be broken for fear that the deceased may else return to claim some of those who are left. Thus in parts of Russia the bed upon which a dying person has lain, or at least the mattress, must be destroyed. In England to-day the same custom is not wholly extinct, for in certain counties it is held to be unlucky for any person belonging to the family, any relative, or any one of the household to sleep in the bed where a person has died, and accordingly this piece of furniture is disposed of as soon as possible. The ill omen is not held to affect any person save those who have been in some way intimate with the deceased or who have lived in the same house. In Russia, the cottage whence there has just set forth a funeral, or at any rate the principal room, is strewed with corn. In England, in some houses the chamber in which a person has died is kept locked for seven days after the burial. The reason for this has entirely disappeared, but the original idea seems to be to prevent the spirit returning to the room. I have heard that the door is secured lest the ghost should issue from the room, and this seems to point to an old belief that after a period of seven days the power of an apparition wanes and fades.

There existed a former custom among the Bohemians that when returning from a funeral none of the party must look back, and it was considered lucky that they should throw sticks and stones over their shoulders behind them. This was obviously to keep off the dead man and prevent him from following in their track. An even more elaborate precaution was that of the mourners putting on masks and behaving in a strange and extraordinary manner as they came back from the churchyard.[10] They intended, in fact, to disguise themselves so that the dead man would fail to recognize them, and therefore could not follow them home. In most countries it is considered terribly untoward if a corpse is carried out of the house head foremost, as then he will see the door and assuredly find his way back again. This reason is definitely assigned for the practice in parts of the world so far distant from one another as various provinces of Germany and among the Indians of Chile.[11] Not many years ago it was still the custom in the north of England to carry a body to the graveyard by an unusual and roundabout way, and although the reason for this is entirely forgotten it was undoubtedly in order that the deceased should not discover the way to revisit the house. It is more than probable that the old practice of burying at night which to name but a few countries was practised in ancient Rome, in Scotland, in Germany, in Hawai'i and among the Mandingos, was originally intended to conceal from the deceased the path to the tomb.[12] It was also thought that the ghost could not penetrate through fire, and therefore the South Slavonians on their return from a funeral are met by an old woman who carries a brazier containing live coals. In some parts they take the glowing embers from the hearth and with a pair of tongs cast these backward over their shoulders. In Ruthenia this custom has so entirely lost all signification that they do no more than gaze steadfastly at the house stove and touch it with their hands. In other districts the idea prevailed that the spirit cannot cross a stream, and the Lusatian Wends are most scrupulous to pour out water in front of the house when they have returned from a burial. No doubt some belief in a lustral purification is not altogether unconcerned with this, and the necessity for some symbolism of cleansing is particularly marked among the Serbians. With them neither the spade that dug the grave nor the cart that carried the coffin may be brought into the farmyard. Even the horses which drew the bier must be turned loose into the pastures, and thus for a space of three days every instrument and accessory of burial must needs be left without, otherwise they might bring death into the house.

It is obvious from the above details, and very many more might be added, that throughout Russia, as in the other countries we have mentioned, there is a very marked dread of the return of the deceased. The power of the dead to inflict injury upon the living is not merely confined to any ghostly affrightment, but strikes something deeper. The dead may come back in their own bodies as malignant monsters eager to carry off the living to the shadowy realm where they have gone before. Hence all these elaborate ceremonials and semi-heathen rites to prevent such a visitation. This terror of the departed is a gloomy and terrible thing and it stands out in sad contrast to the gentle thoughts of the Departed, the prayers and Requiems that solace the Holy Souls as the Catholic Church so sweetly teaches and enjoins.

The figure of the Vampire logically evolved from such dark superstitions. Although his pronouncement is in fact far from correct, it is easy to see why Hertz wrote: "The belief in vampires is the specific Slavonian form of the universal belief in spectres (*Gespenster*)." Concerning the Russian Vampire W. R. S. Ralston remarks[13]:

"The districts of the Russian Empire in which a belief in vampires mostly prevails are White Russia and the Ukraine. But the ghastly blood-sucker, the *Upir*, whose name has become naturalized in so many alien lands under forms resembling our 'Vampire,' disturbs the peasant-mind in many other parts of Russia, though not perhaps with the same intense fear which it spreads among the inhabitants of the above-named districts, or of some other Slavonic lands. The numerous traditions which have gathered around the original idea vary to some extent according to their locality, but they are never radically inconsistent.

"Some of the details are curious. The Little-Russians hold that if a vampire's hands have grown numb from remaining long crossed in the grave, he makes use of his teeth, which are like steel. When he has gnawed his way with these through all obstacles, he first destroys the babes he finds in a house, and then the older inmates. If fine salt be scattered on the floor of a room, the vampire's footsteps may be traced to his grave, in which he will be found resting with rosy cheek and gory mouth.

"The Kashoubes say that when a *Vieszcy,* as they call the Vampire, wakes from his sleep within the grave, he begins to gnaw his hands and feet; and as he gnaws, one after another, first his relations, then his other neighbours, sicken and die. When he has finished his own store of flesh, he rises at midnight and destroys cattle, or climbs a belfry and sounds the bell. All who hear the ill-omened tones will soon die. But generally he sucks the blood of sleepers. Those on whom he has operated will be found next morning dead, with a very small wound on the left side of the breast, exactly over the heart. The Lusatian Wends hold that when a corpse chews its shroud or sucks its own breast, all its kin will soon follow it to the grave. The Wallachians say that a *murony*—a sort of cross between a werewolf and a vampire, connected by name with our nightmare—can take the form of a dog, a cat, or a toad, and also of any blood-sucking insect. When he is exhumed, he is found to have long nails of recent growth on his hands and feet, and blood is streaming from his eyes, ears, nose and mouth."

Ralston tells us that he has drawn his information concerning Russian Vampires for the most part from a study by the eminent authority Alexander Afanasief, *Poeticheskiya Vozzryeniya Slavyan na Prirodu (Poetic Views of the Slavonians about Nature)*[14], which was published in three volumes, Moscow, 1865–1869, and accordingly the best illustration of popular Russian tradition will be given by a consideration of those stories which Ralston has translated.

The following tale[15] is reported to have been heard in the Tambof Government:—

A peasant was driving past a grave-yard, after it had grown dark. After him came running a stranger, dressed in a red shirt and a new jacket, who cried,

"Stop! take me as your companion."

"Pray take a seat."

They enter a village, drive up to this and that house. Though the gates are wide open, yet the stranger says, "Shut tight!" for on those gates crosses have been branded. They drive on to the very last house; the gates are barred, and from them hangs a padlock weighing a score of pounds; but there is no cross there, and the gates open of their own accord.

They go into the house; there on the bench lie two sleepers—an old man and a lad. The stranger takes a pail, places it near the youth, and strikes him on the back; immediately the back opens, and forth flows rosy blood. The stranger fills the pail full, and drinks it dry. Then he fills another pail with blood from the old man, slakes his brutal thirst, and says to the peasant:

"It begins to grow light! let us go back to my dwelling,"

In a twinkling they found themselves at the grave-yard. The vampire would have clasped the peasant in its arms, but luckily for him the cocks began to crow, and the corpse disappeared. The next morning, when folks came and looked, the old man and the lad were both dead.

The four very striking stories I now give are also from Afanasief, and Ralston's versions in *Russian Folk-Tales* have been used.

THE COFFIN-LID[16]. A moujik was driving along one night with a load of pots. His horse grew tired, and all of a sudden it came to a stand-still alongside of a graveyard. The moujik unharnessed his horse and set it free to graze; meanwhile he laid himself down on one of the graves. But somehow he didn't go to sleep.

He remained lying there some time. Suddenly the grave began to open beneath him: he felt the movement and sprang to his feet. The grave opened, and out of it came a corpse—wrapped in a white shroud, and holding a coffin-lid—came out and ran to the church, laid the coffin-lid at the door, and then set off for the village.

The moujik was a daring fellow. He picked up the coffin-lid and remained standing beside his cart, waiting to see what would happen. After a short delay the dead man came back, and was going to snatch up his coffin-lid—but it was not to be seen. Then the corpse began to track it out, traced it up to the moujik, and said:

"Give me my lid: if you don't, I'll tear you to bits!"

"And my hatchet, how about that?" answers the moujik. "Why, it's I who'll be chopping you into small pieces!"

"Do give it back to me, good man!" begs the corpse.

"I'll give it when you tell me where you've been and what you've done."

"Well, I've been in the village, and there I've killed a couple of youngsters."

"Well then, now tell me how they can be brought back to life."

The corpse reluctantly made answer:

"Cut off the left skirt of my shroud, and take it with you. When you come into the house where the youngsters were killed, pour some live coals into a pot and put the piece of the shroud in with them, and then lock the door. The lads will be revived by the smoke immediately."

The moujik cut off the left skirt of the shroud, and gave up the coffin-lid. The corpse went to its grave—the grave opened. But just as the dead man was descending into it, all of a sudden the cocks began to crow, and he hadn't time to get properly covered over. One end of the coffin-lid remained sticking out of the ground.

The moujik saw all this and made a note of it. The day began to dawn; he harnessed his horse and drove into the village. In one of the houses he heard cries and wailing. In he went—there lay two dead lads.

"Don't cry," says he, "I can bring them to life!"

"Do bring them to life, kinsman," say their relatives. "We'll give you half of all we possess."

The moujik did everything as the corpse had instructed him, and the lads came back to life. Their relatives were delighted, but they immediately seized the moujik and bound him with cords, saying:

"No, no, trickster! Well hand you over to the authorities. Since you knew how to bring them back to life, maybe it was you who killed them!"

"What are you thinking about, true believers! Have the fear of God before your eyes!" cried the moujik.

Then he told them everything that had happened to him during the night. Well, they spread the news through the village; the whole population assembled and swarmed into the graveyard. They found out the grave from which the dead man had come out, they tore it open, and they drove an aspen stake right into the heart of the corpse, so that it might no more rise up and slay. But they rewarded the moujik richly, and sent him away home with great honour.

THE TWO CORPSES[17]. A Soldier had obtained leave to go home on furlough—to pray to the holy images, and to bow down before his parents. And as he was going his way, at a time when the sun had long set, and all was dark around, it chanced that he had to pass by a graveyard. Just then he heard that some one was running after him, and crying:

"Stop ! you can't escape!"

He looked back and there was a corpse running and gnashing its teeth. The Soldier sprang on one side with all his might to get away from it, caught sight of a little chapel, and bolted straight into it.

There wasn't a soul in the chapel, but stretched out on a table there lay another corpse, with tapers burning in front of it. The Soldier hid himself in a corner, and remained there hardly knowing whether he was alive or dead, but waiting to see what would happen. Presently up ran the first corpse—the one that had chased the Soldier—and dashed into the chapel. Thereupon the one that was lying on the table jumped up, and cried to it!

"What hast them come here for?"

"I've chased a soldier in here, so I'm going to eat him."

"Come now, brother! he's run into my house. I shall eat him myself."

"No, I shall!"

"No, I shall!"

And they set to work fighting; the dust flew like anything. They'd have gone on fighting ever so much longer, only the cocks began to crow.[18] Then both the corpses fell lifeless to the ground, and the Soldier went on his way homeward in peace, saying:

"Glory be to Thee, O Lord! I am saved from the wizards!"

THE DOG AND THE CORPSE. A moujik went out in pursuit of game one day, and took a favourite dog with him. He walked and walked through the woods and bogs, but got nothing for his pains. At last the darkness of night surprised him. At an uncanny hour he passed by a graveyard, and there, at a place where two roads met, he saw standing a corpse in a white shroud. The moujik was horrified, and knew not which way to go—whether to keep on or to turn back.

"Well, whatever happens, I'll go on," he thought; and on he went, his dog running at his heels. When the corpse perceived him, it came to meet him; not touching the earth with its feet, but keeping about a foot above it—the shroud fluttering after it. When it had come up with the sportsman, it made a rush at him; but the dog seized hold of it by its bare calves, and began a tussle with it. When the moujik saw his dog and the corpse grappling with each other, he was delighted that things had turned out so well for himself, and he set off running home with all his might. The dog kept up the struggle until cock-crow, when the corpse fell motionless to the ground. Then the dog ran off in pursuit of its master, caught him up just as he reached home, and rushed at him, furiously trying to bite and to rend him. So savage was it, and so persistent, that it was as much as the people of the house could do to beat it off.

"Whatever has come over the dog?" asked the moujik's old mother. "Why should it hate its master so?"

The moujik told her all that had happened.

"A bad piece of work, my son!" said the old woman.

"The dog was disgusted at your not helping it. There it was fighting with the corpse—and you deserted it, and thought only of saving yourself! Now it will owe you a grudge for ever so long."

Next morning, while the family were going about the farmyard, the dog was perfectly quiet. But the moment its master made his appearance, it began to growl like anything.

They fastened it to a chain; for a whole year they kept it chained up. But in spite of that, it never forgot how its master had offended it. One day it got loose, flew straight at him, and began trying to throttle him.

So they had to kill it.

THE SOLDIER AND THE VAMPIRE. A certain soldier was allowed to go home on furlough. Well, he walked and walked, and after a time he began to draw near to his native village. Not far off from that village lived a miller in his mill. In old times the Soldier had been very intimate with him; why shouldn't he go and see his friend? He went. The Miller received him cordially, and at once brought out liquor; and the two began drinking and chattering about their ways and doings. All this took place towards nightfall, and the Soldier stopped so long at the Miller's that it grew quite dark.

When he proposed to start for his village, his host exclaimed:

"Spend the night here, trooper! It's very late now, and perhaps you might run into mischief."

"How so?"

"God is punishing us! A terrible warlock has died among us, and by night he rises from his grave, wanders through the village, and does such things as bring fear upon the very boldest! How could even you help being afraid of him?"

"Not a bit of it! A soldier is a man who belongs to the crown, and 'crown property cannot be drowned in water nor burnt in fire.' I'll be off: I'm tremendously anxious to see my people as soon as possible."

Off he set. His road lay in front of a graveyard. On one of the graves he saw a great fire blazing. "What's that?" thinks he. "Let's have a look." When he drew near, he saw that the Warlock was sitting by the fire, sewing boots.

"Hail, brother!" calls out the Soldier.

The Warlock looked up and said:

"What have you come here for?"

"Why, I wanted to see what you're doing."

The Warlock threw his work aside and invited the Soldier to a wedding.

"Come along, brother," says he, "let's enjoy ourselves. There's a wedding going on in the village."

"Come along!" says the Soldier.

They came to where the wedding was; there they were given drink, and treated with the utmost hospitality. The Warlock drank and drank, revelled and revelled, and then grew angry. He chased all the guests and relatives out of the house, threw the wedded pair into a slumber, took out two phials and an awl, pierced the hands of the bride and bridegroom with the awl, and began drawing off their blood. Having done this, he said to the Soldier:

"Now let's be off!"

Well, they went off. On the way the Soldier said:

"Tell me; why did you draw off their blood in those phials?"

"Why, in order that the bride and bridegroom might die. To-morrow morning no one will be able to wake them. I alone know how to bring them back to life."

"How's that managed?"

"The bride and bridegroom must have cuts made in their heels, and some of their own blood must then be poured back into those wounds. I've got the bridegroom's blood stowed away in my right-hand pocket, and the bride's in my left."

The Soldier listened to this without letting a single word escape him. Then the Warlock began boasting again.

"Whatever I wish," says he, "that I can do!"

"I suppose it's quite impossible to get the better of you?" says the Soldier.

"Why impossible? If anyone were to make a pyre of aspen boughs, a hundred loads of them, and were to burn me on that pyre, then he'd be able to get the better of me. Only he'd have to look out sharp in burning me; for snakes and worms and different kinds of reptiles would creep out of my inside, and crows and magpies and jackdaws would come flying up. All these must be caught and flung on the pyre. If so much as a single maggot were to escape, then there'd be no help for it, in that maggot I should slip away!"

The Soldier listened to all this and did not forget it. He and the Warlock talked and talked, and at last they arrived at the grave.

"Well, brother," said the Warlock, "now I'll tear you to pieces. Otherwise you'd be telling all this."

"What are you talking about? Don't you deceive yourself; I serve God and the Emperor."

The Warlock gnashed his teeth, howled aloud, and sprang at the Soldier—who drew his sword and began laying about him with sweeping blows. They struggled and struggled; the Soldier was all but at the end of his strength. "Ah!" thinks he, "I'm a lost man—and all for nothing!" Suddenly the cocks began to crow. The Warlock fell lifeless to the ground

The Soldier took the phials of the blood out of the Warlock's pockets, and went on to the house of his own people. When he had got there, and had exchanged greetings with his relatives, they said:

"Did you see any disturbance. Soldier?"

"No, I saw none."

"There now! Why we've a terrible piece of work going on in the village. A Warlock has taken to haunting it!"

After talking a while, they lay down to sleep. Next morning the Soldier awoke, and began asking:

"I'm told you've got a wedding going on somewhere here?"

"There was a wedding in the house of a rich moujik," replied his relatives, "but the bride and bridegroom have died this very night—what from, nobody knows."

"Where does this moujik live?"

They showed him the house. Thither he went without speaking a word. When he got there, he found the whole family in tears.

"What are you mourning about?" says he.

"Such and such is the state of things, Soldier," say they.

"I can bring your young people to life again. What will you give me if I do?"

"Take what you like, even were it half of what we've got!"

The Soldier did as the Warlock had instructed him, and brought the young people back to life. Instead of weeping there began to be happiness and rejoicing; the Soldier was hospitably treated and well rewarded. Then—left about face! off he marched to the

Starosta, and told him to call the peasants together and to get ready a hundred loads of aspen wood. Well, they took the wood into the graveyard, dragged the Warlock out of his grave, placed him on the pyre, and set it alight—the people all standing round in a circle with brooms, shovels and fire-irons. The pyre became wrapped in flames, the Warlock began to burn. His corpse burst, and out of it crept snakes, worms and all sorts of reptiles, and up came flying crows, magpies, and jackdaws. The peasants knocked them down and flung them into the fire, not allowing so much as a single maggot to creep away! And so the Warlock was thoroughly consumed, and the Soldier collected his ashes and strewed them to the winds. From that time forth there was peace in the village.

The Soldier received the thanks of the whole community. He stayed at home some time, enjoying himself thoroughly. Then he went back to the Tsar's service with money in his pocket. When he had served his time, he retired from the army, and began to live at his ease.

"The stories of this class," Ralston tells us, "are very numerous, all of them based on the same belief—that in certain cases the dead, in a material shape, leave their graves in order to destroy and prey upon the living. The belief is not peculiar to the Slavonians, but it is one of the characteristic features of their spiritual creed."[19]

Passing from folk-tales, which none the less contain more than a grain or two of truth, we enter the realms of fact. In that famous work *Isis Unveiled* by Madame Blavatsky the following account is given of a Russian vampire, and it is stated that the details were told by an eye-witness of these terrible happenings. "About the beginning of the present century, there occurred in Russia, one of the most frightful cases of Vampirism on record. The governor of the Province Tch——was a man of about sixty years, of a malicious, tyrannical, cruel, and jealous disposition. Clothed with despotic authority, he exercised it without stint, as his brutal instincts prompted. He fell in love with the pretty daughter of a subordinate official. Although the girl was betrothed to a young man whom she loved, the tyrant forced her father to consent to his having her marry him; and the poor victim, despite her despair, became his wife. His jealous disposition exhibited itself. He beat her, confined her to her room for weeks together, and prevented her seeing anyone except in his presence. He finally fell sick and died. Finding his end approaching, he made her swear never to marry again; and with fearful oaths threatened that, in case she did, he would return from his grave and kill her. He was buried in the cemetery across the river, and the young widow experienced no further annoyance, until, nature getting the better of her fears, she listened to the importunities of her former lover, and they were again betrothed.

On the night of the customary betrothal-feast, when all had returned, the old mansion was aroused by shrieks proceeding from her room. The doors were burst open and the unhappy woman was found lying on her bed in a swoon. At the same time a carriage was heard rumbling out of the courtyard. Her body was found to be black and blue in places, as from the effect of pinches, and from a slight puncture on her neck drops of blood were oozing. Upon recovering she stated that her deceased husband had suddenly entered her room, appearing exactly as in life, with the exception of a dreadful pallor; that he had upbraided her for her inconstancy, and then beaten and pinched her most cruelly. Her story was disbelieved; but the next morning the guard stationed at the other end of the bridge which spans the river, reported that, just before midnight, a black coach and six had driven furiously past them, towards the town, without answering their challenge.

The new governor, who disbelieved the story of the apparition, took nevertheless the precaution of doubling the guards across the bridge. The same thing happened, however night after night; the soldiers declaring that the toll-bar at their station near the bridge would rise of itself, and the spectral equipage sweep by them despite their efforts to stop it. At the same time every night the coach would rumble into the court-yard of the house; the watchers, including the widow's family, and the servants, would be thrown into a heavy sleep, and every morning the young victim would be found bruised, bleeding and swooning as before. The town was thrown into consternation. The physicians had no explanation to offer; priests came to pass the night in prayer, but as midnight approached, all would be seized with the terrible lethargy. Finally, the archbishop of the province came, and performed the ceremony of exorcism in person, but the following morning the governor's widow was found worse than ever. She was now brought to death's door.

The governor was now driven to take the severest measures to stop the ever-increasing panic in the town. He stationed fifty Cossacks along the bridge, with orders to stop the spectre-carriage at all hazards. Promptly at the usual hour, it was heard and seen approaching from the direction of the cemetery. The officer of the guard, and a priest bearing a crucifix, planted themselves in front of the toll-bar, and together shouted: "In the name of God and the Czar, who goes there?" Out of the coach window was thrust a well-remembered head, and a familiar voice responded: "The Privy Councillor of State and Governor C——!" At the same moment, the officer, the priest, and the soldiers were flung aside as by an electric shock, and the ghostly equippage passed by them, before they could recover breath.

The archbishop then resolved as a last expedient to resort to the time-honoured plan of exhuming the body, and pinning it to the earth with an oaken stake driven through its heart. This was done with great religious ceremony in the presence of the whole populace. The story is that the body was found gorged with blood, and with red cheeks and lips. At the instant that the first blow was struck upon the stake, a groan issued from the corpse, and a jet of blood spurted high in the air. The archbishop pronounced the usual exorcism, the body was re-interred, and from that time no more was heard of the Vampire."

Here we see that a strong individuality, cruelty and devilish hate are energized by the jealousy of lust—not love—and are perpetuated in this horrid manner even beyond the grave.

The following instance of vampirism was related to me by a friend who himself had it from Captain Pokrovsky in 1905, Captain Pokrovsky, a Russian-Lithuanian Guards officer, had been for a time relegated to his estates in Lithuania on account of some political indiscretion, but a little later he was allowed to spend a week or two with his uncle. His cousin, this nobleman's daughter, one morning invited him to go round with her while she was visiting her peasants. One man was pointed out to them as having mysteriously begun to fail in health and fade away since he had married his second wife. "He seems to shrivel from day to day, yet he is a rich farmer and eats meats ravenously at his meals." The man's sister, who lived with him, said, "Since he has re-married he cries out in the night." Captain Pokrovsky, who saw the man, described him as being pale and listless, not at all what a peasant of that stamp ought to appear, and accordingly he asked his cousin what actually was the matter with the fellow. The girl answered: "I do not know, but the villagers all declare that a vampire is getting at him." The Captain was so interested in the case that he sent for a doctor who came from a considerable distance. The doctor after a careful examination reported that the man, whilst not anæmic in a medical sense, seemed to have lost a great deal of blood, but no wound could be found serious enough to account for such a drain. There was, however, a small puncture in the neck with inflamed edges, yet no swelling as might have been expected in the case of the bite of an insect. Tonics were promptly prescribed, and strengthening food was given to the invalid.

In due course Pokrovsky went back to his own home, but some time afterwards he inquired of his cousin concerning the anæmic peasant. She replied that in spite of the meat juice and red wine she had given him, the man had died, and that the wound in his neck at the time of death was far larger than when Pokrovsky had seen it. Further, the village was so entirely convinced that the man had been vampirized, that his wife, although she had frequently eaten heartily of food in public, had been seen to cross herself devoutly, and was a frequent attendant at Mass, immediately found it advisable, nay necessary, to leave the district. It should be remembered that as this took place in Lithuania, the peasants were probably not Slavs or Orthodox, but Lithuanians and Latins. Pokrovsky suggested that the woman may have played vampire subconsciously, whilst asleep; or that it may have been a case of vampiric possession. Either of these is possible, and it seems certain that one must be the correct explanation. Which of the two could only have been determined by an investigator upon the spot, an eye-witness. We have here then an indubitable history of vampirism, an instance of very recent date.

In the following narrative of an Armenian vampire, which is related by Baron August von Haxthausen in his *Transcaucasia*, London, Chapman and Hall, 1854[20] (pp. 190–191), we return to folk-lore and legend. The travellers were approaching Mt. Ararat and he writes: "Ararat is more than half covered with eternal snow, and now under the "bright morning sun it was lighted up with various colours—crimson; orange, and violet … on our right rose the glaciers of Allagas, and at two miles from

Erivan commenced the mountains of Ultmish Altotem, stretching to a distance of forty or fifty versts. They are said to have 366 valleys, respecting which Peter related the following Armenian legend. There once dwelt in a cavern in this country a vampire, called Dakhanavar, who could not endure any one to penetrate into these mountains or count their valleys. Every one who attempted this, had in the night his blood sucked by the monster, from the soles of his feet, until he died. The vampyre was however at last outwitted by two cunning fellows: they began to count the valleys, and when night came on they lay down to sleep, taking care to place themselves with the feet of the one under the head of the other. In the night the monster came, felt as usual, and found a head: then he felt at the other end, and found a head there also. 'Well,' cried he, 'I have gone through the whole 366 valleys of these mountains, and have sucked the blood of people without end, but never yet did I find any one with two heads and no feet!' So saying he ran away, and was never more seen in that country; but ever after the people have known that the mountain has 366 valleys."

In Roumania the vampire tradition extends back far into the centuries, and there is perhaps no supernatural belief which is so strongly prevalent both in city and market-town as in the villages and remoter country districts. Moreover the tradition is amplified and complicated by local legends and peculiarly romantic ideas of rustic fancy, which often proves poetical enough and not without a certain macabre beauty, but often exhibits itself as materially gross and saturnine. It is hardly too much to say that in Roumania we find gathered together around the Vampire almost all the beliefs and superstitions that prevail throughout the whole of Eastern Europe. Although, as will be noted later, a certain species of vampire may tend to merge into a mere mythical imagination (the *vârcolac*), and again although he may be at times identified with the witch who in her turn is frequently no more than the *baba* or wise woman of some hamlet, yet when he preserves his own horrid qualities he is a being much dreaded and feared throughout the whole country even at the present day.

The old folk tale says: "There was once a time when vampires were as common as blades of grass, or berries in a pail, and they never kept still, but wandered round at night among the people."[21] Although nowadays the appearance of a vampire may be regarded as exceptional, none the less it is a very distinct and a very terrible possibility, and against such visitations it is well to be on one's guard, and should any such suspicion arise wise heads will not neglect every remedy and precaution.

In Roumania also there is a belief which, however vaguely expressed when put into words, is very definite and clear in the peasant mind to the effect that after death the soul is not finally separated from the body and cannot enter Paradise until full forty days have passed. Accordingly if there be any presumption that the deceased is or may become a vampire this interval is one of great anxiety and distress. In actual practice bodies are religiously exhumed three years after death, if it be a child; four or five years if it be a young person; and seven years in the case of those who are elderly or full grown. Should the body not have fallen to putrefaction then it is assuredly a vampire.

If the bones however are white and dry the soul has passed to its eternal reward. The atomy is ceremonially washed in wine and water, it is wrapped in a fair linen shroud, a requiem is sung, and it is devoutly reinterred.

As in all other countries, so in Roumanian the suicide, the witch, he who has trafficked in goetry and dark spells or led a life of cruelty and wickedness, each one of these will certainly become a vampire after death. Should a hapless child die before it is baptized, it will become a vampire when seven years have passed, and the spot where it is buried is unhallowed ground. Men who seek material gain by perjury, who bear false witness to the hurt of others, will become vampires six months after death. When there are seven children of the same sex the seventh will have a little tail and must become a vampire. This is a remarkably curious idea and would seem to be in complete contradiction to the general belief that a seventh child is the child of luck. In Devonshire and in Scotland,[22] for example, a seventh son and even a seventh daughter were both credited with natural gifts of healing, and their aid was often sought by sufferers. Occult powers and the faculty of a close communion with the spiritual world are generally attributed to a seventh son, or—more rarely—to a seventh child of either sex. It is remarkable that this idea should appear in a somewhat degraded and inverted form, so to speak, among the Roumanians. It is perhaps remotely connected with the primitive thought that offerings to the dead must always be seven in number or a multiple of seven survivals of which custom may yet be remotely traced.[28]

A man born with a caul becomes a vampire in less than the fortieth day after he has been interred. This again is in contradiction to the belief in other countries. Cotgrave remarks that to be born with a caul is a sign of good luck: "Il est né colffé. Born rich, honorable, fortunate; born with his mother's kerchief about his head." The Italians name a caul "la camicia della Madonna," and in his *Usi e Pregiudizi della Romagna* (p. 25) Miohele Placucci tells us: "Credono invulnerabile il detto uomo della camicia, ma solo però riguardo al piombo, e perciô in caso di rissa il competitor sostituisce alle palle di piombo altre di cera, od'argento, oppure mitraglia e così credono eludere la virtù portata dalla ripetuta camicia." The same idea is recorded by the author of *Superstitions Anciennes et Modernes* (Amsterdam, 1736, ii): "Non seulement, dit on encore, l'enfant qui est né coiffé est heureux; il a même le privilege d'être invulnerable, pourvu qu'il la porte toute sa vie sur soi et encore mieux c'est s'il la mange." William Henderson in his *Notes on the Folk-lore of the Northern Counties of England and the Borders,* London, 1866, says: "On the borders persons born with cauls are supposed to possess special powers of healing, but with this restriction—that the virtue is held to be so much abstracted from their own vital energy, and if much drawn upon they pine away and die of exhaustion," an idea which very definitely partakes of an exercise of vampirism, the *né coiffé* being the subject whose vitality may be sucked and drained by others. The caul was regarded as a lucky charm, and in the Malvern *Advertiser,* March, 1872, a child's caul was advertised for sale. There are many literary references to this old belief. Thus in *Oberon's Palace, Hesperides,* 444, Herrick writes of Queen Mab's bed:

For either sheet was spread the caul
That doth the infant's face enthral.
When it is born (by some enstyl'd
The lucky omen of the child).

In Act V of the comedy, *Elvira ; or, The Worst not always true,* by George Digby, Earl of Bristol, produced at Lincoln's Inn Fields in 1663; 4to, 1667; Zancho cries:

Were, we not born with cauls upon our heads?
Think'st thou, Chichon, to come off twice arow
Thus rarely from such dangerous adventures?

It is said that sometimes in Roumania a man who knows that he was born with a caul will when he dies leave instructions to his family to treat his body as that of a vampire and so avert any future danger.

If a vampire cast his cold grey eyes upon a pregnant woman, especially if she be past her sixth month, and the spell be not undone by the blessing of the Church, the child she carries will become a vampire. If a pregnant woman does not take salt she is big with vampire.

A notable mark of vampirism is if a man does not eat garlic, for this plant has great virtue and is hateful to the vampire. Should a cat jump over a dead body, or a man step over it, or even the shadow of a living man fall upon it, the deceased will become a vampire. In many districts of Roumania it is thought that persons are doomed to become vampires and that they cannot escape their destiny. Whilst they lie asleep their soul comes out of their mouth like a little fly. If the body were to be turned round so that the head reposed where the feet had lain the soul would not be able to find its way back and the man dies.

That the soul of a sleeper wanders away from his body and often actually visits the places and performs the acts of which he may dream is a belief which has been held the whole world over. In the account of a trial for witchcraft at Mühlbach in the year 1746 it appeared that a woman had engaged two men to work in her vineyard. About noon all took the usual repose from the heat of the day. After an hour had passed the labourers got up and tried to wake the woman so that they might duly proceed to work. However, she was stretched out motionless and stark with her mouth wide open. Towards eventide when the sun was setting they returned but she still lay inert, scarce seeming to breathe, as though she were dead. Just then a large fly buzzed past and this was caught by one of the men who put it in his leather pouch. They then again endeavoured to wake the woman but without success. Afterwards they released the fly which flew straight into the woman's mouth and she instantly awoke. Upon seeing this the men could no further doubt that she was indeed a witch.[24]

The Serbians hold that the soul of a sleeping witch leaves her body in the form of a butterfly. If during its absence her body be turned round and her head placed in another position the butterfly soul will not be able to find its way back to the mouth, and the witch will die.[25] A precisely similar belief prevails among the Esthonians,[26] and in Livonia it is common knowledge that when the soul of a werewolf is abroad on his particular business his body lies dead as stock or stone. If during this time the body were moved to another place, or even if the position were accidentally shifted, the soul could not find its way back, but must perforce remain in the body of a wolf until death.[27] This is a particularly striking tradition when we bear in mind the intimate connexion that prevails between the werewolf and the vampire. There is a story of Languedoc which tells how a woman who was suspected of being a witch one day fell asleep in the hot summer sun among the reapers in the field. Scenting a fine opportunity to prove their suspicions the reapers carried her whilst she slumbered to another part of the field, and exactly upon the spot where she had first lain they set a large empty kilderkin. When her soul returned it entered the vessel which it adroitly rolled along at great speed until the moving pitcher actually came into contact with her body, of which it immediately once more took possession.[28]

Amongst some races it is not even necessary to alter the position of a sleeper's body for the soul to be thwarted in its return. The Coreans are convinced that during sleep "the soul goes out of the body, and if a piece of paper is put over the face of the sleeper he will assuredly die, for his soul cannot find its way back into him again."[29] The Malays declare that if a person's face be daubed or blackened while he sleeps the soul which has gone forth will not recognize its home and the man will sleep on until his face be washed.[30] In Bombay indeed it was considered nothing less than murder to disguise or in any way paint the face of a sleeper, for if the aspect of the countenance be changed the soul upon its return cannot recognise its body and the individual must shortly expire.[31]

In Transylvania a child should never be allowed to sleep with its mouth open lest the soul might slip out in the shape of a mouse and the child never waken again.[32] So in Brunswick, the country folk say that the soul issues from a sleeper's mouth as a white mouse or a little bird and that to catch the mysterious animal or bird would kill the sleeping person.[33] This theme occurs innumerable times in saga and legend. In an East Indian story the soul comes forth as a cricket[34]; in a Scotch story it is a bumble bee[35]; and in Germany again it is a white mouse[36] or a red mouse[37].

In Roumania the vampire is generally of two kinds and Mrs. Agnes Murgoçi differentiates the "dead-vampire type" from the "live-vampire type."[38] The "dead-vampire" is the re-animated corpse, energized by the return of the soul. The corpse possessed by some demon seems unknown, or at any rate of the rarest, for Mrs. Murgoçi says: "I have found so far no instance in which the dead corpse is supposed to be reanimated by a devil and not by its own soul." "People destined to become vampires after death may be able in life to send out their souls, and even their bodies, to wander at cross-roads with reanimated corpses. This type may be called the live-vampire type. It merges into the ordinary witch or wizard, who can meet other witches or wizards either in the body or as a spirit."[39]

A third type of vampire, the *vârcolac,* is entirely mythical, being thought to be an extraordinary creature which eats the sun and moon and thus causes eclipses. A prominent authority I. Otescu in his *Credintele Taranului Romān despre Cer și Stele (Beliefs of the Roumanian peasant concerning the Sky and the Stars)*[40] gives the following account of the *vârcolaci.* "*Vârcolaci* are supposed to be different from any beings on the earth. They cause eclipses of the moon, and even of the sun, by mounting up to heaven and eating the moon or sun. Some think that they are animals smaller than dogs. Others that they are dogs, two in number. ... They have different origins; some say that they are the souls of unbaptized children, or of children of unmarried parents, cursed by God and turned into *vârcolaci.* ... Others again say that *vârcolaci* originate from the air of heaven, when women spin at night, especially at midnight, without a candle, particularly if they cast spells with the thread they spin. Hence it is never good to spin by moonlight, for vampires and *vârcolaci* get up to the sky by the thread and eat the sun and moon. They fasten themselves to the thread, and the thread makes itself into a road for them. As long as the thread does not break the *vârcolaci* have power, and can go where ever they wish. They attack the heavenly bodies, they bite the moon, so that she appears covered with blood, or till none of her is left. But if the thread is broken their power is broken and they go to another part of the sky. ..."

G. F. Ciaușanu, in his *Superstitüle poporului Român* reports that "in Valcea there are said to be beings who are called *vârcolaci,* because their spirit is *vârcolaci.* They are recognized by their pale faces and dry skin, and by the deep sleep into which they fall when they go to the moon to eat it. But they eat it only during an eclipse, and when the disc of the moon is red or copper-coloured. The redness is the blood of the moon, escaping from the mouths of the *vârcolaci* and spreading over the moon.

"When the spirit of the *vârcolaci* wants to eat the moon, the man to whom the spirit belongs begins to nod, falls into a deep sleep as if he had not slept for weeks, and remains as if dead. If he is roused or moved sleep becomes eternal, for, when the spirit returns from its journey, it cannot find the mouth out of which it came, and so cannot go in again. ..."

"Some say that God orders the *vârcolaci* to eat the moon so that men may repent and turn from evil."

With reference to the various Roumanian terms for a vampire, Mrs. Murgoçi writes as follows: "As regards the names used for vampires, dead and alive, *strigoi* (fem. *strigoica*) is the most common Roumanian term, and *moroii* is perhaps the next most usual. *Moroii* is less often used alone than *strigoi.* Usually we have *strigoi* and *moroii* consorting together but the *moroii* are subject to the *strigoi.* We find also *strigoi, moroii* and *vârcolaci,* and *strigoi* and *pricolici* used as if all were birds of the same feather. A Transilvanian term is *șișcoi.* *Vârcolaci* (*svârcolaci*) and *pricolici* are sometimes dead vampires, and sometimes animals which eat the moon. *Oper* is the Ruthenian word for dead vampire. In Bukovina, *vidme* is used for a witch; it covers much the same ground as *strigoi* (used for a live vampire), but it is never used for a dead vampire."

The "live-vampires" are said to meet the "dead-vampires" on certain nights in old and forlorn cemeteries, in deserted houses, in the haunted depths of the forest and in other ill-boding places, where from the deceased who are the more powerful they learn the runes of black magic. In some country districts it is supposed that the "live-vampires" form covens, and at the head of each company is a master or a mistress as the case may be, the men following their officer, and the women together with their moderatrix. This arrangement exactly resembles that of the historical witch society, and it is plain that the "live-vampire" and the witch in rustic credence are identical. We are not surprised to learn that in the Mihalcea district it is supposed that chiefly women are vampires. They possess a certain control which enables them to extract the "power" of animals and objects for their own use. Thus they are able in some mysterious way to absorb or collect the vitality of fowls and bees, for example, and to concentrate this upon their own farm-yards and hives, so that their hens will become plump and lay abundantly; their hives be exceedingly rich in honeycomb, whilst the poultry of the neighbours sickens and dies, and the aparies of the village contain no store of golden sweetness. It is told that one woman baked bread which was so light and good in the eating that half the country-side came to buy her loaves, and before long her pockets were well filled. The other wives in the village could not get their dough to rise, do what they would. Their bread seemed always mouldy and stale. Now this happened because the bakeress was a vampire, and knew how to obtain the essential goodness of bread from all the other ovens.

Some of these vampires can control the rain, and to them secret resort is constantly made by the farmers. They can also gather the "power" of beauty, which they sell for money, and here in fact we have the regular love-charms. These female vampires are generally of a dry burning skin and a notably florid complexion. The men are bald and distinguished by peculiarly piercing eyes. It is supposed that they can assume the shapes of various animals, and they particularly favour the form of a cat. When a vampire washes rain will soon fall, and it is said that in the olden days during a drought the great landowners and nobles would cause all the peasants of their estates to bathe in the river hoping that there might be a vampire among them. This influence over the weather conditions is generally considered to be the peculiar quality of "live-vampires," but at Zârneşti a series of extraordinarily heavy floods was supposed to be caused by a girl who had been recently buried and who was generally reputed to be a vampire.

The remedies effectually to dispose of a dead man who has become a vampire are much the same as in all other lands. It is strongly advised that precautions of this kind should be taken at burial, or as soon after as possible. A suicide must be put in running water. It may be remembered that running water dissolves all charms, and a witch cannot cross a stream. Water in itself is a holy element and as such has had its place in all religions, nor is the poet's conception of "waters at their priest-like task" without a very real truth. In Vălcea it is usual to thrust a long needle into the heart of the vampire, but the general method is that which is common throughout the whole of Eastern Europe, at one blow to drive a stake through the navel or the heart. Again small pebbles and grains of incense may be placed in the mouth, ears, nose and navel, and in the quicks of the nails, so that the vampire may have something to gnaw at when he wakes. Millet should be scattered over him, for he will delay until he has counted and eaten every grain. Garlic may also be stuffed in the mouth. The body should be arranged face downwards, and a correspondent of the *Times* in June, 1874, writes that burying with the face downwards is resorted to in Maine, U.S.A., as a means of stopping consumption from running through a household. If reburial is necessary the corpse should be turned head to foot. Long garlands of wild roses should be wreathed round the coffin, which further may be confined with stout bands of wood. It may be remembered that on the eve of S. George's day there used not to be a Saxon farm in Transylvania which had not the gates of the yard decorated with branches of wild rose bushes in order to keep out the witches.[41] Since other thorny shrubs were also utilized in this way, the idea originally seems to have been that the evil visitants would get caught in the briars if they attempted to climb through, but this precaution became at least partially obscured and certain magical properties were ascribed to the wild rose of itself.

In the district of Teleorman, on the third day after a death, when people go to the house of mourning in order to burn incense they carry with them nine spindles, and these they thrust deep into the grave. Should the vampire rise he would be pierced by their sharp points. Another method is to take tow, to scatter it upon the grave, and to set fire to it there, for it is believed that the occupant will scarce venture through the flames. Sometimes the anathema of a priest will confine the vampire in his tomb.

In the Romanați district the vampire is stripped and the naked carrion thrust into a stout bag. The clothes and cerements are sprinkled with holy water, replaced in the coffin which is secured and again buried in the grave. The body is taken away to the forest. The heart is first cut out, and then it is hacked piecemeal limb from limb and each gobbet burned in a great fire. Last of all the heart is flung into the flames and those who have assisted come near so that they shall be fumigated with the smoke. But all must be consumed, every shred of flesh, every bone. The veriest scrap if left would be enough to enable the vampire again to materialize. Occasionally the ashes of the heart are collected mingled with water and given to sick people as a powerful potion.

At Zârneşti after a female vampire had been exhumed great iron forks were driven through the heart, eyes, and breast after which the body was buried at a considerable depths face downwards.

In Mehedinti it was once thought a sufficient precaution if the body was carried far away to some remote spot among the mountains and there totally abandoned. But such a method in practice was rarely used, and indeed was seldom found effectual. It is not to be compared with the Greek method of transporting the body to some lonely island, for in the latter case this is done precisely because the vampire is unable to cross the waters of the sea.

It is held to be imperative that the vampire should be traced to his lair and destroyed at the very first opportunity. If he is sufficiently cunning to avoid detection so long at the end of seven years he will become a man again, and then he will be able to pass into another country, or at any rate to a new district, where another language is spoken. He will marry and have children, and these after they die will all go to swell the vampire host.

In Roumania as in Greece and other lands the vampire first attacks his own household and even the animals belonging to his family. Yet he will return in the night and talk with them; he may even help with the housework, fetch and carry, cleave wood and bring it home from a considerable distance. Female vampires persistently return to their children. Sometimes, however, he will be destructive, break dishes, upset jars of water, cause a veritable racket, and abominably plague the whole house. However, whether he be busily helpful or whether he prove a bane all the inhabitants will quickly die off, and even the cattle will fall victims to some strange disease. The village priest is then generally requested to read certain prayers over the graves, but if the horrid molestations persist more drastic measures must speedily be taken. In order precisely to discover which is the tomb that is the source of these fatal distresses a white stallion is led to the cemetery, and the grave over which he refuses to pass, but at the side of which he stands still, shivering with fright and neighing wildly, contains the vampire. In the same way a gander will not walk over the vampire's grave. The body must then be exhumed and if the notable marks of vampirism are found it can be dealt with in the traditional manner.

It may be noted that if the relations of a vampire have died the monster will be found in his coffin, full and foggy as a great leech, his mouth gaping wide and slobbered with rank gouts of fresh crimson blood. If he has only been destructive of pots and pans and eaten what he could find in the larder the mouth will be covered with maize meal. It is believed that very often the vampire will resist when his body is disinterred and utter hideous yells to scare those who are employed upon the business, but if they pluck up good courage and if the priest be there the monster cannot harm them.

In Roumania at certain times during the year when their power is at its height special precautions must be taken against the attacks of the vampire. The two particular periods in a year when the vampire is most active are S. Andrew's Eve and S. George's Eve. There exists however, many variants of this idea in different districts. Thus in some localities they are said to be most troublesome just before Easter; in Mihalcea their operations are confined to the period between S. Andrew's Eve and the Epiphany; in Siret they are given a longer term since they are free to plague living folk from S. Andrew's Day until the Transfiguration, or in some cases from S. George's Day until the feast of S. John.

Generally, however, the particular precautions to safeguard a house or a village are taken on the last day of the year, before Easter Sunday, before S. Andrew's Day and on the eve of S. George. Throughout the whole of Eastern Europe, indeed, the feast of S. George, 23 April, is one of the most important celebrations of the whole year and it has become the occasion of numberless observances and rites which can barely be glanced at here. S. George is the patron or protector of England, Antioch, Bavaria, Venice, Constantinople, Friedberg, Genoa, Gronsfeld, Haguenau, Keldra, Leuchtenberg, Molsheim,

Ochsenhausen, Ratisbon, Rechheim, Ueberlingen, Ulm, Vigevano, of Serbia, Saxony, Russia, and of numberless other countries and towns.[42] S. George, "le trés-loyal Chevalier de la Chrétienneté," has always been honoured in the East as "The Great Martyr," and one of the first churches erected by Constantine, after his profession of Christianity, was in honour of this saint. He is the especial patron of cattle, horses and wolves, and it may not untruly be said that among the herdsmen and shepherds of Eastern Europe the feast of S. George, who will protect their flocks from the ravages of wild beasts has a national, one might almost write an international as well as an ecclesiastical character. At the same time upon the eve of the saint the power of vampires, witches and every evil thing is at its height. Among the Ruthenians of Bukowina and Galicia the farmer's wife gathers great branches of thorn to lay on the threshold of her house and every door is painted with a cross in tar to protect it from witches. The Huzuls kindle large bonfires for their houses for the same reason whilst throughout Transylvania, Walachia and Bulgaria precautions of various kinds are similarly taken. The South Slavs favour bundles of thistles which are placed on the fence, the windows and the doors to prevent the entry of any evil thing. On the morrow, 23 April, the house is garlanded with flowers, chaplets of roses decorate the stalls and the horns of the cows are wreathed with blossom in honour of the saint. Until quite recent years in Swabia all the church bells used to be kept ringing a merry chime from nightfall until dawn on the day of the festival. This no doubt, was often taken to be merely the due ushering in of the celebrations, but originally it had a further signification, for in those parts it was believed that no vampire and no witch can come within the sound of a church bell. Although unfortunately, in many cases as in England,[43] owing to the blameworthy coldness and neglect of the authorities, the cultus of S. George cannot be said to be flourishing or popular, yet in some places the saint is still particularly honoured and it is sad to think that the solemn celebrations which attracted pilgrims from far and near to Ostrotta in Poland and Ertringen in Bavaria have lost much of their popularity.

In Roumania upon these particular days when the vampire is most malicious the country folk anoint the windows with garlic, they tie bundles of garlic on the door and in the cow sheds. All lights throughout the house must be extinguished and it is well that every utensil should "be turned topsy-turvy. Pious people will pass the whole night in prayer, and even those who have not this devotion do their best to keep awake.

If a man must sleep he generally puts a knife unsheathed beneath the pillow. Nor will anyone answer if called by name, at least not until he has been summoned three times, for as in Chios, a vampire may call you once at night but cannot repeat his request, wherefore if one waits to hear the name a third time one may be well assured it is not the horrible intruder.

It is upon record that there have been from time to time in Roumania very grave outbreaks of vampirism, and in consequence of these widespread molestations the peasants, as is not surprising, more than once took the law into their own hand until they were checked by the authorities. Ureche in his *History of Roumania,* records:—"In 1801, on 12 July, the Bishop of Sigen sent a petition to the hospodar of Wallachia, requesting that he should order his provincial waywodes no longer to permit, the peasants of Stroesti to disinter dead people, who had already been twice exhumed, under the idea that they were *vârcolaci.*" Again in the *Biserica Orthodoxa Romana* we find: "The Archbishop Nectarie (1813–19) dispatched an official letter to all his higher clergy (protopopes) exhorting them to inquire in what districts it was thought that the dead might return as vampires. If they came upon a case of vampirism they were not to take it upon themselves immediately to cremate the corpse, but they were rather to instruct the people how to proceed according to the formal canon of the Church."

Dr. Tudor Panfile, one of the most eminent of Roumanian scholars has collected a vast number of vampire stories in *Ion Creanda,* a native periodical of peasant art and literature. Thence I take the following which must serve as typical of very many.[44]

"Some twenty or thirty years ago (from 1914) in the commune Afumati in Dolj, a certain peasant, Mărin Mirea Ociocioc, died. It was noticed that his relations also died, one after the other. A certain Badea Vrajitor (Badea the wizard) dug him up. Badea himself, going later into the forest up to the frontier on a cold wintry night, was eaten by wolves. The bones of Marin were sprinkled with wine, a church service read over them, and replaced in the grave. From that time there were no more deaths in the family.

"Some fifteen years ago, in Amărăşti, in the north of Dolj an old woman, the mother of the peasant Dinu Gheorghita, died. After some months the children of her eldest son began to die, one after the other, and, after that, the children of her youngest son. The sons became anxious, dug her up one night, cut her in two, and buried her again. Still the deaths did not cease. They dug her up a second time, and what did they see? The body was whole without a wound. It was a great marvel. They took her and carried her into the forest, and put her under a great tree in a remote part of the forests. There they disemboweled her, took out her heart, from which blood was flowing, cut it in four, put it on hot cinders, and burnt it. They took the ashes and gave them to children to drink with water. They threw the body on the fire, burnt it, and buried the ashes of the body. Then the deaths ceased.

"Some twenty or thirty years ago, a cripple, an unmarried man, of Cuşmir, in the south of Mehedinţi, died. A little time after, his relations began to die, or to fall ill.

They complained that a leg was drying up. This happened in several places. What could it be? 'Perhaps it is the cripple; let us dig him up.' They dug him up one Saturday night, and found him as red as red, and all drawn up into a corner of the grove. They cut him open, and took the customary measures. They took out the heart and liver, burnt them on red-hot cinders, and gave the ashes to his sister and other relations, who were ill. They drank them with water, and regained their health.

"In the Cușmir, another family began to show very frequent deaths, and suspicion fell on a certain old man, dead long ago. When they dug him up, they found him sitting up like a Turk, and as red as red, just like fire; for had he not eaten up nearly the whole of a family of strong, young men. When they tried to get him out he resisted, unclean and horrible. They gave him some blows with an axe, they got him out, but they could not cut him with a knife. They took a scythe and an axe, cut out his heart and liver, burnt them, and gave them to the sick folk to drink. They drank, and regained their health. The old man was reburied, and the deaths ceased.

"In Văguilești, in Mehedinți, there was a peasant Dimitriu Vaideanu, of Transilvanian origin, who had married a wife in Văguilești and settled there. His children died one after the other; seven died within a few months of birth, and some bigger children had died as well. People began to wonder what the cause of all this could be. They took counsel together, and resolved to take a white horse to the cemetery one night, and see if it would pass over all the graves of the wife's relations. This they did, and the horse jumped over all the graves, until it came to the grave of the mother-in-law, Joana Marta, who had been a witch, renowned far and wide. Then the horse stood still, beating the earth with its feet, neighing and snorting, unable to step over the grave. Probably there was something unholy there. At night Dimitriu and his son took candles and went to dig up the grave. They were seized with horror at what they saw. There she was, sitting like a Turk, with long hair falling over her face, with all her skin red, and with finger nails frightfully long. They got together brushwood, shavings, and bits of old crosses, they poured wine on her, they put in straw and set fire to the whole. Then they shovelled the earth back and went home."

To multiply similar relations of peasant anas and local fable, throughout Eastern Europe would be no difficult but a somewhat superfluous task. It is well to consider the more serious side of tradition, and accordingly the following account of the Bulgarian beliefs as given by St. Clair and Brophy in their *Twelve Years' Study of the Eastern Question in Bulgaria*[45] will not be impertinent here. "By far the most curious superstition in Bulgaria is that of the Vampire, a tradition which is common to all countries of Slavonic origin, but is now to be found in its original loathsomeness only in these provinces. In Dalmatia and Albania, whence the knowledge of this superstition was first imported into Europe, and which were consequently, though wrongly, considered as its mother-countries, the Vampire has been disfigured by poetical embellishments, and has become a mere theatrical being—tricked out in all the tinsel of modern fancy. The Dalmatian youth who, after confessing himself and receiving the Holy Communion as if in preparation for death, plunges a consecrated poniard into the heart of the Vampire slumbering in his tomb; and the supernaturally beautiful Vampire himself, who sucks the life-blood of sleeping maidens, has never been imagined by the people, but fabricated, or at least dressed up, by romancers of the sensational school.

"When that factitious poetry, born from the ashes of a people whose nationality is extinct, and from which civilization has reaped its harvest, replaces the harsh, severe, even terrible poetry which is the offspring of the uncultivated courage or fear of a young and vigorous humanity, legendary lore becomes weak, doubtful, and theatrical. Thus, as in a ballad said to be antique, we recognize a forgery by the smoothness of its rhythm and the nicety of its rhythm; so, when the superstitions of a people naturally uneducated and savaged are distinguished by traits of religion or of sentiment, we trace the defacing hand of the Church or the poet.

"In Dalmatia the Vampire is now no more than a shadow, in which no one believes, or at best in which people pretend to believe;[46] just as a London Scottish volunteer will assure you of his firm faith in the Kelpie and Brounie of Sir Walter Scott, or will endeavour to convince you that he wears a kilt from choice and not for effect. Between the conventional Vampire and the true horror of Slavonic superstition there is as much difference as between the Highland chief who kicked away the ball of snow from under his son's head, reproaching him with southron effiminacy in needing the luxury of a pillow, and the kilted cockney sportsman who shoots down tame deer in an enclosure.

"In Poland the Roman Catholic clergy have laid hold upon this superstition as a means of making war upon the great enemy of the Church, and there the Vampire is merely a corpse possessed by the Evil Spirit,[47] and no longer the true Vampire of the ancient Slavonians. In Bulgaria we find the brute in its original and disgusting form; it is no longer a dead body possessed by a demon, but a soul in revolt against the inevitable principle of corporeal death; the Dalmatian poniard, blessed upon the altar, is powerless here, and its substitute is an Ilatch (literally, medicine) administered by the witch, or some other wise woman, who detects a Vampire by the hole in his tombstone or the hearth which covers him, and stuffs it up with human excrement (his favourite food) mixed with poisonous herbs.

"We will now give the unadulterated Bulgarian superstitions, merely prefacing that we ought to be well acquainted with it, inasmuch as a servant of ours is the son of a noted Vampire, and is doing penance during this present Lent, by neither smoking, nor drinking wine or spirits, in order to expiate the sins of his father and to prevent himself inheriting the propensity.

"When a man who has Vampire blood in his veins—for this condition is not only epidemic and endemic, but hereditary—or who is otherwise predisposed to become a vampire, dies, nine days after his burial he returns to upper earth in an æriform shape. The presence of the Vampire in this his first condition may be easily discerned in the dark by a succession of sparks like those from a flint and steel; in the light, by a shadow projected upon a wall, and varying in density according to the age of the Vampire, in his career. In this stage he is comparatively harmless, and is only able to play the practical jokes of the German Kobold and Gnome, of the Irish Phooka, or the English Puck; he roars in a terrible voice, or amuses himself by calling out the inhabitants of a cottage by the most endearing terms, and then beating them black and blue.

"The father of our servant, Theodore, was a Vampire of this class. One night he seized by the waist (for vampires are capable of exercising considerable physical force) Kodja Keraz, the *Pehlivan,* or champion wrestler, of Derekuoi, crying out, "Now then, old Cherry Tree, see if you can throw me." The village champion put forth all his strength, but the Vampire was so heavy that Kodja Keraz broke his own jaw in throwing, the invisible being who was crushing him to death.

"At the time of this occurrence, five years ago, our village was so infested with Vampires that the inhabitants were forced to assemble together in two or three houses, to bum candles all night, and to watch by turns, in order to avoid the assaults of the Obours, who lit up the streets with their sparkles, and of whom the most enterprising threw their shadows on the walls of the room, where the peasants were dying of fear; whilst others howled, shrieked, and swore outside the door, entered the abandoned houses, spat blood into the flour, turned everything topsy-turvy, and smeared the whole place, even the pictures of the saints, with cow-dung. Happily for Derekuoi, Vola's mother, an old lady suspected for a turn for witchcraft, discovered the Ilatch we have already mentioned, laid the troublesome and troubled spirits, and since then the village has been free from these unpleasant supernatural visitations.

"When the Bulgarian Vampire has finished a forty days' apprenticeship to the realm of shadows, he rises from his tomb in bodily form, and is able to pass himself off as a human being, living honestly and naturally. Thirty years since a stranger arrived in this village, established himself, and married a wife with whom he lived on very good terms, she making but one complaint, that her husband absented himself from the conjugal roof every night and all night. It was soon remarked that (although scavengers were, and are, utterly unknown in Bulgaria) a great deal of scavengers' work was done at night by some unseen being, and that when one branch of this industry was exhausted, the dead horses and buffaloes which lay about the streets were devoured by invisible teeth, much to the prejudice of the village dogs, then the mysterious mouth drained the blood of all cattle that happened to be in any way sickly. These occurrences, and the testimony of the wife, caused the stranger to be suspected of Vampirism; he was examined, found to have only one nostril, and upon this irrefragable evidence was condemned to death. In executing this sentence, our villagers did not think it necessary to send for the priest, to confess themselves, or to take consecrated halters or daggers; they just tied their man hand and foot, led him to a hill a little outside Derekuoi, lit a big fire of wait-a-bit thorns, and burned him alive.

"There is yet another method of abolishing a Vampire—that of *bottling* him. There are certain persons who make a profession of this; and their mode of procedure is as follows: The sorcerer, armed with a picture of some saint, lies in ambush until he sees the Vampire pass, when he pursues him with his *Eikon*; the poor Obour takes refuge in a tree or on the roof of a house, but his persecutor follows him up with the talisman, driving him away from all shelter, in the direction of a bottle specially prepared, in which is placed some of the Vampire's favourite food. Having no other resource, he enters this prison, and is immediately fastened down with a cork, on the interior of which is a fragment of the *Eikon*. The bottle is then thrown into the fire, and the Vampire disappears for ever. This method is curious, as showing the grossly material view of the soul taken by the Bulgarians, who imagine that it is a sort of chemical compound destructible by heat (like sulphuretted hydrogen), in the same manner that they suppose the souls of the dead to have appetites, and to feed after the manner of living beings, 'in the place where they are.'

"To finish the story of the Bulgarian Vampire, we have merely to state that here he does not seem to have that peculiar appetite for human blood which is generally supposed to form his distinguishing and most terrible characteristics, only requiring it when his resources of coarser food are exhausted."

Although I have quoted this account at length I would point out that often the writers have gone astray, not so much perhaps in the presentation of facts as in their interpretation of these. Their scepticism sets ill upon them, and, as all scepticism, is very fallible—yet I have chosen to cite them fairly rather than to emend.

In a note (p. 32) they say: "Since commencing this chapter (III), we have learned that the village of Dervishkuoi, six hours from here, is just now haunted by a Vampire. He appears with a companion who was suppressed by means of the usual remedy, but this one seems to be proof against poison, and as he will shortly have completed his fortieth day as a shadow, the villagers are in terrible alarm lest he should appear as flesh and blood." The allusion to a period of forty days has been fully considered and explained in the previous chapter which deals with the Vampire in modern Greece. It is plain that the writers here fail to appreciate this important point, and indeed although they have set forth a certain number of facts, valuable in themselves, they appear incapable of regarding the subject from the philosophical or even traditional point of view.

The belief that spirits and evil entities could be enclosed in vessels of glass would appear to be of Oriental origin,[48] and amongst other fantasies to have been introduced into Spain by the Morisco. Owing to the notorious trial for witchcraft of Doctor Eugenio Torralda in 1531, the Grand Inquisitor, Don Alfonso Manriquez promulgated certain articles detailing various offences connected with demonolatory which every good Christian was bound to denounce to the Holy Office, and among these appears the following inquiry: "If any person made or caused to be made mirrors, rings, phials of glass or other vessels in order thereby to control or therein to contain some spirit who should reply to his demands and aid his "projects," such a one must be delated to the proper ecclesiastical authorities.

It will be remembered that in *El Diabolo Coxuelo* by Luis Velez de Guevara, which romance was first printed in 1641, the hero Don Cleofas having by chance entered the chamber of an astrologer delivers from a bottle wherein he had been confined by potent charms *El Diabolo Coxuelo* who proves grateful and richly rewards his liberator. The situation will be at once recognized by all as having been used by Le Sage in his *Le Diable Boiteux,* which is so amply conveyed from his Spanish predecessor.

So far as I am aware there is no other country save Bulgaria where it is supposed that a Vampire can be imprisoned in this manner, and even in Bulgaria it cannot be the real Vampire, the dead body returned from the grave, but rather some vampirish wraith which they imagine can be trapped in this manner. There is reason to suppose that this local superstition comes from the Turks, and this, indeed, seems borne out by its very crudity. There does, indeed, exist a belief in Vampires among the Turks, but the Turkish Vampire is almost entirely to be identified with the ghoul, which monster has already been sufficiently considered. Among the people who are grossly materialistic many barbarous horrors are ignorantly believed, and there are corresponding methods, paynim and uncouth, for defending themselves against the goblins and devils which are so very present to them.

It is not too much to say that terrible though he may be in Christian countries the Vampire, when a material reality, may be baffled and destroyed, but upon passing beyond the pale of Christianity the unhappy people become the sport and the prey of fiends and cacodemons who so far from being exorcized and banished are rather attracted by the cantrips and abracadabra of their warlocks and voodoo professors of darkest necromancy.

NOTES

1. The Emperor Maurice was murdered at Chalcedon in 602, when he was succeeded by the centurian Phocas who had revolted against him. There is a study by Adamek, *Beitrage zur Geschichte des Kaisers Mauritius,* Graz, 1891.

2. His chief work is a chronicle of the reign of the Emperor Maurice, in eight books, from the death of Tiberius II and the accession of Maurice in 582 down to the murder of the latter. Ed. by Bekker, Bonn, 1834.

3. He lived during the second half of the eighth century, and the early part of the ninth. In consequence of his resistance to the Iconoclasts he was banished by the tyrant Leo the Armenian to the island of Samothrace, where he died in 818. The *Chronicon* commences with the accession of Diocletian in 277 and concludes in 811. It was edited by De Boor, Leipzig 1883, and may also be found in the Collections of the Byzantine writers Paris, 1055, folio; and Venice, 1729, folio.

4. Edited by Hase, Paris, 1818; and by Migne, 1863.

5. Born 25 July, 975; died 1 December, 1018. Dithmar's original manuscript, with corrections and additions made by himself, is still preserved at Dresden. A facsimile edition of it was prepared by L. Schmidt, Dresden, 1905. The chronicle was also published by Kurze in *Scriptores*

Rerum Germanicarum, Hanover, 1889; and by Lappenberg in *Monumenta Germaniæ Historiæ Scriptorum,* III, 733–871, whence it was reprinted in Migne, *Patres Latini,* CXXXIX, 1183–1422. A German translation was made by Laurent, Berlin, 1848; reprinted Leipzig, 1892.

6. Cosmas was born about 1045 at Prague, and died there, 21 October, 1125. His *Cronica* consists of three books; the first brings the narrative to 1038, the second to 1092, and the third to 1125. The work has been repeatedly edited; Freher, *Scriptores rerum bohemicarum,* Hanover, 1602, 1607, and 1620; Mencke, *Scriptores rerum Germanicarum.* Leipzig, 1728, vol. 11 Pelzl and Dobrowsky, *Scriptores rerum bohemicarum,* Prague, 1783; Koepke, *Monumenta Germaniæ Historiæ Scriptorum,* Hanover, 1851, vol. IX. It is also to be found in Migne, *Patres Latini,* CLXVI; Emler and Tomek, *Fontes rerum bohemicarum,* Prague, 1874, vol. II.

7. One may recall the episode in the Fourth Voyage of Sindbad the Sailor. *Le Livre des' Mille Nuits et Une Nuit:* La trois cent troisiéme nuit et la trois cent quatrième nuit; traduction de Dr. J. C. Mardrus, tome VI, Paris, 1901, pp. 140–153.

8. Ibn Fozlan's narrative was published in 1823 by the Russian Academy of Sciences, with a German translation by C. M. Frahn. Rasmussun had previously translated it into Danish, and an English rendering of his version appeared in the Fourth volume of *Blackwood's Magazine.*

9. Adolf Bastian, *Der Mensch in der Geschichte,* Leipzig, 1860, II, p. 328.

10. A. Wuttke, *Deutscher Aberglaude,* 736. Klemm, *Culturgeschickte,* II, p. 101.

11. Servius on Vergil, *Aeneid,* Ed. G. Thilo and H. Hagen. Leipzig, 1881, I, p. 186. Charles Rogers, *Social Life in Scotland,* Edinburgh, 1884–1886, I, p. 161. F. Schmidt, *Sitten und Gebrauche in Thuringen,* p. 94. The Rev. William Ellis, *Polynesian Researches,* Second Edition, London, 1832–1836, IV, p. 361). (*Cf.* Captain James Cook's, *Voyages,* London, 1809, p. 149 *sqq.*). Mungo Park, *Travels in the Interior Districts of Africa.* Fifth Edition, London, 1807, p. 414.

12. *Russian Folk-Tales,* London, 1873, pp. 320–322.

13. III. Chapter xxvi.

14. Afanasief: *Poeticheskiya Vozzryeniya Slavyan na Peirodu,* III, 558. Translated by Ralston, *Songs of the Russian People,* pp. 411–12.

15. Afanasief. V, pp. 142–4. Ralston, *op. cit.,* pp. 309–311. The tale is from the Tambof Government.

16. Afanasief. V, pp. 324–5. Ralston, p. 312.

17. The crowing of the cock disperses all phantasms of the night and dissolves enchantments. So Prudentius sings:

    Ferunt uagantes Dsemonas

    Lætas tenebras noctium

    Gallo canente exterritos

    Sparsim timere et credere.

    The sabbats of witches concluded at cock-crow, and a witch named Latoma confessed to Nicolas Remy that this bird is the most hateful of all to sorcerers. See my *History of Witchcraft,* pp. 117–118.

18. Afanasief, VI, pp. 321–2. Ralston, pp. 313–14.

19. Afanasief, V, pp. 144–7. Ralston, pp. 314–18. This story is from the Tambof Government.

20. *Op. cit.,* p. 318.

21. London, Chapman and Hall, 1854, pp. 190–191.

22. *Ion Creanga,* vol. iv, p. 202.

23. In *Superstitions anciennes et moderns,* 2 tom, folio, Amsterdam, 1733–36, (I, 1.xvi, p. 107) we have: "On me disoit, il y a quelque tems que les septiemes filles avoient le privilege de gucrir les mules aux talons. Mais ce rare privilege ne subsiste que dans l'imagination des personnes qui veulent railler, non plus qui celin de guerir les louppes, lequel on attribue aux enfants post-humes, et à la main d'un Bourreau fraischement revenu de faire quelque execution de mort." In Devonshire the power to heal is attributed to a seventh daughter; see *Transactions of the Devonshire Association,* ix, 93; also *Notes and Queries,* VII, i, 6, 91, and 475. James Kelly, *Scottish Proverbs,* London, 1721, has: "Or why in England the King cures the Struma by stroking, and why the Seventh Son in Scotland; whether his Temperate complexion conveys a balsom and sucks out the corrupting principles by a frequent warm sanative contact; or whether the parents of the seventh child put forth a more eminent virtue to his production than to all the rest as being the certain meridian and height to which their vigour ascends, and from that forth have a gradual declining into a feebleness of the body and its production." Arthur Mitchell in his *Superstitions of the Highlands and Islands of Scotland,* 1862, records: "In the island of Lewis, the seventh son of a seventh son in curing the King's evil by laying on of hands, gives the patient a sixpenny-piece with a hole in it, through which a string is passed, to wear round the neck. Should this be taken off, a return of the malady may be looked for." The Epilogue, spoken by Doctor Hughball (and Perigrine), to Brome's comedy, *The Antipodes,* acted at Salisbury Court in 1638; quarto 1640; commences thus:

> Whether my cure be perfect yet or no,
>
> It lies not in my doctor-ship to know.
>
> Your approbation may more raise the man,
>
> Then all the Colledge of physitians can;
>
> And more health from your faire hands may be wonne,
>
> Then by the stroakings of the seaventh sonne.

24. There is a vestige of such practices among the mountaineers on the north-west coast of New Guinea. F. S. A. de Clercq, "De Westen Noordkust van Nederiandsch Nieuw-Guinea," *Tijdschrift van het kon, Nederlandsch Aardrijkskundig Genootschap,* Tweede Serie, x (1893), p. 199.

25. F. Müller, *Beitrag zur Geschichte des Hexenglaubens und Hexenprozesses in Siebenbürgen.* Brunswick, 1854.

26. Friebrich S. Krauss, *Volksglaube und religiöser Brauch der Südslaven.* Munster, i, W., 1890, p. 112.

27. J. D. Holzmayer, "Osiliana," *Verhandlungen der Gelehrten Estnischen Gesellschaft zu Dorpat,* vii (Dorpat, 1872), No. 2, p. 53.

28. P. Einhorn, "Wiederlegunge der Abgötterey; der ander Theil." Riga, 1627. Reprinted in *Scriptores rerum Liuonicarum,* ii, 645. Riga and Leipzig, 1848.

29. Alfred de Nore, *Coutumes, Mythes et Traditions des provinces de France,* Paris and Lyons, 1846, p, 88.

30. W. Woodville Rockhill, "Notes on some of the Laws, Customs, and Superstitions of Korea," *The American Anthropologist*, iv, p. 183. Washington, 1891.

31. Nelson Annandale, "Primitive Beliefs and Customs of the Patani Fishermen," *Fasciculi Malayenses, Anthropology*, Part I, April, 1903, p. 94.

32. *Punjab Notes and Queries*, iii, p. 116.

33. H. von Wlislocki, *Volksglaube und Volksbrauch der Siebenbürger Sachsen*, Berlin, 1893, p. 167.

34. Richard Andree, *Braunschweiger Volkskunde*, Brunswick, 1896; p. 266.

35. G. A. Wilken, "Het amimisme bij de volken van den Indischen Archipel," *De Indische Gids*, June, 1884, p. 940. This article was separately reprinted at Leyden in the following year.

36. Hugh Miller, *My Schools and Schoolmasters*, Edinburgh, 1854; Chapter vi, pp. 106 *sqq.*

37. Anton Birlinger, *Volksthümliches aus Schwaben*, Freiburg im Breisgau, 1861–62; I, 303.

38. Eugen Mogk, "Sitten und Gebrauche im Kreislauf des Jahres," in R. Wuttke's *Sachsiche Volkskunde*, Dresden, 1901, Second Edition, p. 318.

39. Mrs. Agnes Murgoçi, "The Vampire in Rumania," *Folk-Lore*, xxxvii, no. 4; pp. 320–21.

40. Mrs. Murgoçi, *op. cit.*, p. 321.

41. As quoted by Mrs. Murgoçi, *op.cit*, p. 335.

42. Josef Haltrich, *Zur Volkskunde der Siebenburger Sachsenv* Vienna, 1885, p. 281.

43. C. D. Frick, *De S. Georgio*, Lipsiæ, 1683; Neuius, *De equite S. Georgio*, Tubingen, 1716; and Joachim Mantzelm, *De Georgiis … claris*, Gustrouisæ, 1712; amongst many other authorities.

44. As early as 1222 the national synod of Oxford ordered S. George's Day to be kept as a lesser holiday. In 1415 the Constitution of Archbishop Chichele raised S. George's Day to the rank of one of the chief feasts of the year in England and prescribed that it should be observed with the same solemnity as Christmas Day itself. In England during the seventeenth and eighteenth centuries S. George's Day remained a Holiday of Obligation.

45. *Ion Creanga*, vol. VII, 1914, p. 165. These particular stories were collected by N. I. Dumitrascu. I give them from the version of Mrs. Murgoçi.

46. London, 1877, pp. 29–33. The book is a revised edition of a *Residence in Bulgaria*, written in 1866–67 and published in 1869.

47. It is almost superfluous to say that this is wholly incorrect. The Vampire tradition still prevails in Dalmatia.

48. This again is wholly mistaken. The authors, perhaps naturally enough, have no knowledge of the terrible facts of possession, and write unwittingly and somewhat flippantly.

49. See my *Geography of Witchcraft*, pp. 603–605, and the corresponding notes.

Vampires in Romania

Edited by J. Gordon Melton

No country is as identified with vampires as Romania. A land of rich folklore concerning vampires, its reputation was really established Bram Stoker, whose novel *Dracula* began and ended in Transylvania. Though at the time Transylvania was a part of Hungary, it is now a part of Romania. Recent scholarship has confirmed that one of the sources from which Stoker created Dracula was Vlad the Impaler, a fifteenth-century prince of Wallachia, a section of modern Romania that lies south of the Carpathian Mountains.

Stoker derived much of his knowledge of Transylvania, where he located Castle Dracula, from Emily Gerard's *The Land Beyond the Forest* (1888). Gerard was a Scottish woman who had married a Polish officer serving the Austrian army. As a brigade commander, he was stationed in Transylvania in the 1880s. The couple resided in Sibiu and Brasov. In describing the several supernatural entities encountered in her research on practices surrounding death, she wrote:

> More decidedly evil is the *nosferatu,* or vampire, in which every Roumanian peasant believes as firmly as he does in heaven or hell. There are two sorts of vampires, living and dead. The living vampire is generally the illegitimate, offspring of two illegitimate persons; but even a flawless pedigree will not insure any one against the intrusion of a vampire into the family vault, since every person killed by a nosferatu becomes likewise a vampire after death, and will continue to suck the blood of other innocent persons till the spirit has been exorcised by opening the grave of the suspected person, and either driving a stake through the corpse, or else firing a pistol-shot into the coffin. To walk smoking around the grave on each anniversary of the death is also supposed to be effective in confining the vampire. In very obstinate cases of vampirism it is recommended to cut off the head, and replace it in the coffin with the mouth filled with garlic, or to extract the heart and burn it, strewing its ashes over the grave. (p. 185)

Bran Castle in Brasov, Romania, which the Romanian government once touted as Castle Dracula.

Romanian concepts concerning the vampire are strongly related to folk beliefs of the Slavic vampire in general, though the Romanians, in spite of being largely surrounded by Slavic peoples are not themselves Slavic. Romanians locate their origins in ancient Dacia, a Roman province that emerged in Transylvania and the surrounding territories after Trajan's capture of the land in the second century A.D. He also brought in thousands of colonists in the sparsely settled area. As the colonists and the indigenous people intermarried, a new ethnic community was born. This new community spoke a form of Latin—the basis for modern Romanian. Their subsequent history, especially over the next century is a matter of great controversy between Romanians and their neighbors, a controversy difficult to resolve due to the paucity of archeological evidence.

Following the abandonment of the territory at the end of the third century, Transylvania became the target of various invaders, including the early Slavic tribes. In the seventh-century it was absorbed into the Bulgar Empire. Though some Romanians had become Christians as early as the fourth century, the systematic conversion of the land began in the ninth-century soon after the conversion of the Bulgarians under the brothers Cyril and Methodius. The Romanian church eventually aligned itself to Eastern Orthodoxy under Bulgarian episcopal authority.

At the end of the tenth century, the Magyars (present-day Hungarians) included Transylvania in their expanding kingdom. The Hungarians were Roman Catholics, and they imposed their faith in the newly conquered land. They also encouraged immigration by, among others, the Szekleys, a branch of Magyars, and Germans. During the thirteenth century, seizing upon a moment of weakened Hungarian authority in Transylvania, a number of Romanian Transylvanians migrated eastward and southward over the Carpathian Mountains found the kingdoms of Moldavia and Wallachia. An Eastern Orthodox bishop was established a century later in Wallachia. From that time to the present day, Transylvania would be an item of contention between Hungary and Wallachia (which grew into the present-day Romania). Ecclesiastically, both Roman Catholics and Eastern Orthodox would compete for the faith of the people.

No sooner had Wallachia and Moldavia been established than a new force arose in the area. The Ottoman Empire expanded into the Balkans and began the steady march across the peninsula that would carry it to the very gates of Vienna in the early sixteenth century. During the fourteenth-century Hungary and the Turks vied for hegemony in Wallachia, thus providing a context for a prince of Wallachia by the name of Vlad to travel to the court of the Emperor Sigismund where he would join the Order of the Dragon, pledged to defend Christian lands against the invading Muslims. The Wallachian prince would become known as Vlad Dracul (1390?–1447). He in turn would be succeeded by his son, Vlad the Impaler (1431?–1476), known as Dracula. Vlad the Impaler is remembered today in Romania as a great patriot and a key person in the development of the Romanian nation. After Vlad's death, Wallachia fell increasingly under Turkish hegemony, and Moldavia soon followed suit. Through the 1530s the Turkish army moved through Transylvania to conquer the Hungarian capital in 1541. The remainder of the Hungarian land fell under the control of the Austrian Hapsburg empire. The incorporation of the Romanian kingdoms into the Turkish empire allowed a degree of religious freedom, and Protestantism made a number of inroads, particularly in Transylvania. Contemporary scholars have emphasized that none of the vampire legends from Romania or the surrounding countries portray Vlad the Impaler as a vampire. In the German and some Slavic manuscripts, Vlad's cruelty and his identification as Dracula and devil was emphasized, however, Dracula as a vampire was a modern literary creation.

Vlad the Impaler's court in Bucharest.

In the seventeenth century, the Hapsburgs began to drive the Ottomans from Europe, and by the end of the century assumed dominance of Transylvania and began to impose a Roman Catholic establishment. Transylvania remained a semiautonomous region until 1863 when it was formally unified with Hungary. For over a century Moldavia survived amid Russians, Greeks, and Turks, each fighting for control until a united Romania came into existence in 1861. Through a series of annexations at the beginning and end of World War I, including that of Transylvania in 1920, Romania, in roughly its present size, came into existence. The Romanian majority exists side-by-side with a significant Hungarian minority in Transylvania, and the Romanian Orthodox Church competes with a strong Roman Catholic and persistent Protestant presence.

THE VAMPIRE IN ROMANIA

The Romanian vampire, in spite of the distinct ethnic origin of the Romanians, is a variation of the Slavic vampire. However, like the vampire in each of the other Slavic regions, the vampire in Romania has acquired some distinguishing elements. That distinctiveness begins with the major term used to label vampires, as found by Harry Senn in his field work in the 1970s. *Strigoi* (female, *strigoaica*) is closely related to the Romanian word *striga* (a witch), which in turn was derived from the Latin *strix*, the word for a screech owl that was extended to refer to a demon that attacked children at night. A second term, *moroi* (female, *moroaica*), also spelled *murony* in older sources, seems to be the common term in Wallachia, as *strigoi* is in Transylvania. The Romanians also distinguish between the *strigoi vii* (plural, *strigoi*), or live vampire, and the *strigoi mort* (plural, *stigoi morti*), or dead vampire. The *strigoi vii* are witches who are destined to become vampires after death and who can send out their souls and/ or bodies at night to cavort with the *strigoi mort*. The live vampires tend to merge in thought with the *striga* (witches), who have the power to send their spirits and bodies to meet at night with other witches. The dead vampires are, of course, the reanimated bodies of the dead who return to life to disturb and suck the blood of their family, livestock, and—if unchecked—their neighbors.

The *strigoi mort* was a variation of the Slavic vampire, although the Romanians were not Slavs and used a Latin word to designate their vampire. The *strigoi* was discovered by an unusual occurrence either at their birth or death, and a living *strigoi* was a person who was born with either a caul or a little tail. A *strigoi vii* may become a *strigoi mort*, as well as other people who died irregularly by suicide or an accident.

Romanians also use the term *vircolac*, but almost exclusively to describe the old mythological wolflike creature who devoured the sun and moon. The closely related terms *pricolici* or *tricolici* were also wolves. *Virolac* is a variation of the Greek *vrykolakas* or the Serbo-Croatian *vukodlak*. Agnes Murgoci, who worked in Romania in the 1920s, found that they still connected the term with its pre-vampiric mythological meaning of a creature who devours the sun and moon. At times when the moon appears reddish, it was believed to be the blood of the *vircolac* flowing over the moon's face. More definitive work was pursued by Harry Senn in Transylvania in the 1970s. He found that popular use of the *vircolac* distinguished it from the *strigoi*. The term *vircolac* described a person who periodically changed into one of several animals, usually a pig, dog, or wolf. As such it was much closer to the popular concept of werewolves than vampires.

Nosferatu is an archaic Old Slavonic term apparently derived from *nosufuratu*, from the Greek *nosophoros*, "plague carrier." From the religious context, the word passed into popular usage. It has been variously and mistakenly cited as a Romanian word meaning either "undead" (Wolf) or the devil (Senn). Through the twentieth-century it seems to have dropped from use in Romania. Stoker's use of the term derived from Gerard. It was used by Freidrich Wilhelm Murnau in his attempt to disguise his movie, *Nosferatu, Eine Symphonie des Gareuns* from Dracula. He tied the story to the great plague that hit Bremen, Germany, in 1838.

In Romania the vampire was believed to come into existence first and foremost as the product of an irregular birth, and any number of conditions have been reported that could predispose a person to become a vampire. Children born out of wedlock, born with a caul, or who died before baptism could become vampires. Pregnant women who did not eat salt or who have allowed themselves to be gazed upon by a vampire could bear a vampiric child. The seventh child of the same sex in one family was likely to have a tail and become a vampire.

Though children with an irregular birth were the prime candidates of vampirism, anyone could become a vampire if bitten by one. Other potential vampires included people who led wicked lives (including men who swore falsely), witches (who had relations with the devil), a corpse over whom a cat had jumped, or a person who committed suicide.

The presence of vampires was usually first noticed when several unexpected deaths in a family and/or of livestock followed the death of either a family member or of someone suspected of being a vampire. The vampire might, on occasion, appear to the family, and female vampires were known to return to their children. The home of a suspected vampire often was disturbed by the its activity, either in throwing things around (poltergeist) or getting into the food supplies. The vampire would first attack the family and its livestock and then move on to others in the village. If not destroyed it might move on to more distant villages and even other countries, where it could reassume a normal role in society.

Vampires were especially active on the eve of St. George's Day (either April 23 or May 5), the day witches and vampires gathered at the edge of the villages to plan their nefarious activities for the next year. Villagers would take special precautions to ward off the influences of supernatural beings on that evening. Stoker's character Jonathan Harker made the last leg of his journey and finally arrived at Dracula's Castle on St. George's Eve. Vampires and witches were also active on St. Andrew's Day. St. Andrew was the patron of wolves and the donor of garlic. In many areas of Romania, vampires were believed to become most active on St. Andrew's Eve, continued to be active through the winter, and ceased their period of activity at Epiphany (in January), Easter, or St. George's Day.

St. George's Day was and is celebrated throughout much of Europe on April 23, hence the Eve of St. George's would be the evening of April 22. St. Andrew's day is November 11, and the eve immediately precedes it. Romania which was on the old Julian Calendar, was 12 days behind the modern Gregorian calendar. Thus in Stoker's day, St. George's Day would have been celebrated in Romania on what was the evening of May 4–5 in western Europe. Likewise, St. Andrew's Eve would have been the evening of November 23–24. The lag time between the Julian and our Gregorian calendar increases one day every century.

The grave of a suspected vampire would be examined for telltale signs. Often a small hole would be found in the ground near the tombstone, a hole by which the vampire could enter and leave the coffin. If there was reason to believe someone was a vampire, the grave was opened. Those opening the coffin would expect to find the corpse red in the face. Often the face would be turned downward and fresh blood on it or, on occasion, corn meal. One foot might have retracted into a corner of the coffin. Senn reported that a vampire in the community could be detected by distributing garlic at church and watching to see who did not eat.

Vlad the Impaler's tower at his palace in Tirgoviste, Romania.

It was the common practice of Romanians to open the graves of the deceased three years after the death of a child, four or five years after the death of a young person and seven years after an adult's death. Normally, only a skeleton would be found, which would be washed and returned to the grave. If, however, the body had not decayed, it was treated as if it were a vampire.

There were a wide variety of precautions that could be taken to prevent a person either from becoming a vampire or doing any damage if they did become one. A caul might be removed from the face of a newborn and quickly destroyed before it was eaten. Careful and exacting preparation of the body of the recently dead also prevented their becoming a vampire. The thorny branch of the wild rose might be placed in the tomb. Garlic was also very useful in driving away vampires. On St. Andrew's and St. George's Eve, the windows (and other openings of the house) were anointed with garlic, and the cows would be given a garlic rubdown.

Once the vampire was in the tomb, distaffs might be driven into the ground above the grave upon which the vampire would impale itself if it were to rise. On the anniversary of the death of a suspected vampire, the family walked around the grave.

Once a vampire began an attack on the community and its identity was discerned, the vampire had to be destroyed. Emily Gerard, author of *The Land Beyond the Forest,* found the emergence of a relatively new tradition in nineteenth-century reports in which a vampire might be killed by firing a bullet into the coffin. The preferred method, however, was to drive a stake into the body, followed by decapitation, and the placing of garlic in the mouth prior to reburial. This method was adopted by Stoker in *Dracula* as a means of destroying the vampiric nature that had taken over Lucy Westenra's body. In Romania, the staking could be done with various materials, including iron or wood, and the stake was impaled either in the heart or the navel. Instead of decapitation, the body could also be turned face downward and reversed in the coffin. Millet seeds might be placed in the coffin to delay the vampire, who must first go through a lengthy process of eating the millet before rising from the grave.

An even more thorough process might be followed in the case of a vampire resistant to other preventive measures. The body might be taken from the grave to the woods and dismembered. First, the heart and liver were removed, and then piece by piece the body was burned. The ashes could then be mixed with water and given to afflicted family members as a curative for the vampire's attack.

VAMPIRE FOLKTALES

The Romanian vampire has also become the subject of a number of folktales. Folklorists have noticed that many relate to the cases of couples in which one has recently died. Frequently reprinted was the story of "The Girl and the Vampire" (which also exists in a Russian variant) in which the boy committed suicide following his failure to gain the marriage blessing of his girlfriend's parents. As a result of his manner of death, he became a vampire and began to visit the girl at night. The girl spoke with a wise elder woman in the village who instructed her to attach a thread to his shirt. She then traced the thread, which led to the graveyard and disappeared into the grave of her late boyfriend.

The vampire continued to visit the girl, and they continued their sexual liaison, when her parents died. She refused the vampire's request for her to tell what she had seen the night she followed him to the graveyard, and the girl soon also died. She was buried according to the wise woman's instruction. A flower grew from her grave, which was seen by the son of the emperor. He ordered it dug up and brought to his castle. There, in the evening, it turned into a maiden. Eventually she and the emperor's son were wed. Some time later, she accompanied her husband to church and had an encounter with the vampire. He followed her into church where she hid behind an icon, which then fell on the vampire and destroyed him.

The story served as a discouragement to out-of-wedlock sexual relations while at the same time reaffirming the wisdom of older people and upholding the church as a bastion against evil. Similar values were affirmed in other stories.

It was once the case, according to one folktale that "vampires were as common as leaves of grass, or berries in a pail." They have, however, become more rare and confined to the rural areas. In the mid-1970s Harry Senn had little trouble locating vampire accounts in a variety of Romanian locations. Admittedly, however, the vampire suffered during recent decades from both the spread of public education and the hostility of the government to tales of the supernatural. The importance of vampires in the overall folk belief of Romanians was also demonstrated in a recent study of a Wallachian immigrant community in Scandinavia.

CONCLUSION

The *strigoi mori*, the Romanian vampire conformed in large part to the popular image of the vampire. It was a revenant of the deceased. It had powers to product poltergeist-like phenomena, especially the bringing to life of common household objects. It was seen as capricious, mischievous, and very debilitating. However, the vampire's attack was rarely seen as fatal. Also, it rarely involved the literal biting and draining of blood from its victim (the crux of the distortion of the vampire's image in films in the eyes of Romanian folklorists). The *strigoi* usually drained the vital energy of a victim by a process of psychic vampirism. The description of the *strigoi*'s attack, described in vivid metaphorical language, was often taken in a literal sense by non-Slavic interpreters who then misunderstood the nature of the Slavic vampire.

Of contemporary note, Mircea Eliade, the outstanding Romanian scholar of world religion, was fascinated with vampires, and among his first books was a vampire novel, *Dominisoara Christina* ("Miss Christina"). This obscure work was rediscovered years later by Eliade fans in France and Italy and republished in both countries.

SOURCES

Eliade, Micea. *Domnisoara Christina Bucharest,* 1935. French ed. as: *Mademoiselle Christiana.* Paris: Editions de l'Herne, 1978. Italian ed. as: *Signorina Christiana.* Milan: Jaca Book, 1984.

Gerard, Emily. *The Land Beyond the Forest.* 2 vols. London: Will Blackwood & Sons, 1888.

Murgoci, Agnes. "The Vampire in Romania." *Folk-Lore* 27, 5 (1926): 320–49.

Perkowski, Jan L. *The Darkling: A Treatise on Slavic Vampirism.* Columbus, OH: Slavica Publishers, 1989. 174 pp.

———, ed. *Vampires of the Slavs.* Cambridge, MA: Slavica Publishers, 1976. 294 pp.

Schierup, Carl-Ulrik. "Why Are Vampires Still Alive?: Wallachian Immigrants in Scandinavia." *Ethnos* 51, 3–4 (1986): 173–98.

Senn, Harry A. *Were-Wolf and Vampire in Romania.* New York: Columbia University Press, 1982. 148 pp.

Summers, Montague. *The Vampire in Europe.* 1929. New Hyde Park, NY: University Books, 1961. 329 pp.

Vampires in Hungary

Edited by J. Gordon Melton

Hungary, the country that gave Bela Lugosi to the world, has a special place in the history of vampires. Vampire historian Montague Summers opened his discussion of the vampire in Hungary by observing, "Hungary, it may not untruly be said, shares with Greece and Slovakia the reputation of being that particular region of the world which is most terribly infested by the Vampire and where he is seen at his ugliest and worst." Bram Stoker's Dracula opened with Jonathan Harker's trip through Hungary. Harker saw Budapest as the place that marked his leaving the (civilized) West and entering the East. He proceeded through Hungary into northeast Transylvania, then a part of Hungary dominated by the Szekelys, a Hungarian people known for their fighting ability. (Dracula was identified as a Szekely.) In the face of Stoker and Summers, and before the Dom Augustin Calmet, Hungarian scholars have argued that the identification of Hungary and vampires was a serious mistake of Western scholars ignorant of Hungarian history. To reach some perspective on this controversy, a brief look at Hungarian history is necessary.

EMERGENCE OF HUNGARY

The history of modern Hungary began in the late ninth-century when the Magyar people under ïrpád occupied the Carpathian Basin. They had moved into the area from the region around the Volga and Kama rivers. They spoke a Finnish-Ugrian language, not Slavic. Their conquest of the land was assisted by Christian allies and, during the tenth century, the Christianization of the Magyars began in earnest. In 1000 A.D., Pope Sylvester crowned István, the first Hungarian king. Later in that century, when the Christians split into Roman Catholic and Eastern Orthodox branches, the Hungarians adhered to the Roman church.

István's descendants moved into Transylvania gradually but had incorporated the area into Hungary by the end of the thirteenth century. The Hungarian rulers established a system by which only Hungarians controlled the land. A Magyar tribe, the Szekleys were given control of the mountain land in the northeast in return for their serving as a buffer between Hungary and any potential enemies to the east. The Romanian people of Transylvania were at the bottom of the social ladder. Above them were the Germans, who were invited into cities in southern Transylvania. In return for their skills in building the economy, the Germans were given a number of special privileges. By the fourteenth century, many Romanians had left Transylvania for Wallachia, south of the Carpathians, where they created the core of what would become the modern state of Romania.

Following the death of the last of István's descendants to wear the crown of Hungary, it was ruled by foreign kings invited into the country by the nobles. The height of prosperity for the nation came in the late fifteenth-century when Matthias Corvinus (1458–1490), a Romanian ethnic and contemporary of Wallachian prince Vlad the Impaler, ruled. He built his summer capital at Visegrád into one of the most palatial centers in eastern Europe.

Hungarian independence ended essentially at the battle of Mohács in 1526, which sealed the Turkish conquest of the land. During the years of Turkish conquest, while Islam was not imposed, Roman Catholic worship was forbidden. The Reformed Church was allowed, however, and remains a relatively strong body to the present. Transylvania existed as a land with an atmosphere of relative religious freedom, and both Calvinist Protestantism and Unitarianism made significant inroads. Unitarianism made significant gains at the end of the sixteenth-century following the death of Roman Catholic Cardinal Bathory at the Battle of Selimbar (1599). The Szekelys were excommunicated and as a group turned to Unitarianism.

The Turks dominated the area until 1686 when they were defeated at the battle of Buda. Hungary was absorbed into the Hapsburg empire and Roman Catholicism rebuilt. The Austrian armies would soon push farther south into Serbia, parts of which were absorbed into the Hungarian province.

The eighteenth-century was characterized by the lengthy rulerships of Karoly III (1711–40) and Maria Theresa (1740–80). Hungarian efforts for independence, signaled by the short-lived revolution in 1848, led to the creation in 1867 of Austria-Hungary. Austria-Hungary survived for a half century, but then entered World War I on Germany's side. In 1919 Austria-Hungary was split into two nations and the large segments of Hungary inhabited by non-Hungarian ethnic minorities were given to Romania, Serbia, and Czechoslovakia. Most importantly, Transylvania was transferred to Romania, a matter of continued tension between the two countries. Hungary was left a smaller but ethnically homogeneous land almost entirely comprised of people of Hungarian ethnicity but with a small but measurable number of Gypsies.

After the wars, Hungary was ruled by Miklós Horthy, a dictator who brought Hungary into an alliance with Hitler and Germany as World War II began. After the

Vlad the Impaler was imprisoned at Visegrad, Hungary, possibly in Solomon's Tower, pictured here from the air and in a nineteenth-century painting.

war, in 1948, the country was taken over and ruled by Communists until the changes of the 1990s led to the creation of a democratic state.

THE VAMPIRE EPIDEMICS

Following the Austrian conquest of Hungary and regions south, reports of vampires began to filter into western Europe. The most significant of these concerned events during 1725–32, their importance due in large measure to the extensive investigations of the reported incidents carried on by Austrian officials. The cases of Peter Plogojowitz and Arnold Paul especially became the focus of a lengthy debate in the German universities. Different versions of the incidents identified the locations of the vampire epidemics as Hungary rather than (more properly) a Serbian province of the Austrian province of Hungary. The debate was summarized in two important treatises, the first of which, *Dissertazione sopre I Vampiri* by Archbishop Giuseppe Davanzati, assumed a skeptical attitude. The second, Dom Augustin Calmet's *Dissertations sur les Apparitiones des Anges des Démons et des Espits, et sur les revenants, et Vampires de Hingrie, de Boheme, de Moravie, et de Silésie*, took a much more accepting attitude.

Calmet's work was soon translated and published in German (1752) and in English (1759) and spread the image of eastern Europe as the home of the vampire. While Calmet featured vampire cases in Silesia (Poland), Bohemia, and Moravia (Czechoslovakia), the "Hungarian" cases of Paul and Plogojowitz were the most spectacular and best documented. The image of Hungary as a land of vampires was reinforced by Stoker and Summers, and later by both Raymond T. McNally and Leonard Wolf, who suggested that the Hungarian word *vampir* was the source of the English word vampire. That theory has more recently been countered by Katerina Wilson, who argued that the first appearance of the word 'vampir' in print in Hungarian postdates the first published use of the term in most Western languages by more than a century (actually by some 50 years). The question remains open, however, in that it is highly possible that someone (for example, a German-speaking person in Hungary in the early eighteenth-century) might have picked up the term in conversation and transmitted it to the West.

Meanwhile, Hungarian scholars confronted the issue. As early as 1854, Roman Catholic bishop and scholar Arnold Ipolyi assembled the first broad description of the beliefs of pre-Christian Hungary. In the course of his treatise he emphasized that there was no belief in vampires among the Hungarians. That observation was also made by other scholars, who wrote their articles and treatises in Hungarian destined never to be translated into Western languages. In current times, the case was again presented by Tekla Dömötör, whose book *Hungarian Folk Beliefs* was translated and published in English in 1982. He asserted, "There is no place in Hungarian folk beliefs for the vampire who rises forth from dead bodies and sucks the blood of the living." The conclusions of the Hungarian scholars have been reinforced by the observations of Western researchers, who have had to concede that few reports of vampires have come from Hungary. Most also assert, however, that in Hungarians' interaction with the Gypsies and their Slavic neighbors, such beliefs likely did drift into the rural regions.

VAMPIRELIKE CREATURES IN HUNGARY

Having denied the existence of the vampire in Hungarian folk culture, the Hungarian scholars from Ipolyi to Dömötör also detailed belief in a vampirelike being, the *lidérc*. The *liderc* was an incubus/succubus figure that took on a number of shapes. It could appear as a woman or a man, an animal, or a shining light. Interestingly, the *lidérc* did not have the power of transformation, but rather was believed to exist in all its shapes at once. Through its magical powers, it caused the human observer to see one form or another. As an incubus/succubus it attacked victims and killed them by exhaustion. It loved them to death. Defensive measures against the *lidérc* included the placing of garters on the bedroom doorknob and the use of the ubiquitous garlic.

Hungarians also noted a belief in the *nora*, an invisible being described by those to whom he appeared as small, humanoid, bald, and running on all fours. He was said to jump on his victims and suck on their breasts. Victims included the same type of person who in Slavic cultures was destined for vampirism, namely the immoral and irreverent. As a result of the *nora*, the breast area swelled. The antidote was to smear garlic on the breasts.

SOURCES

Calmet, Augustine. *The Phantom World.* 2 vols. London: Richard Bentley, 1746, 1850.

Dömötör, Tekla. *Hungarian Folk Beliefs.* Bloomington, IN: Indiana University Press, 1982.

Kabdebo, Thomas. *Hungary.* Santa Barbara, CA: Clio Press, 1980. 280 pp.

McNally, Raymond T. *A Clutch of Vampires.* New York: Bell Publishing Company, 1974. 255 pp.

Summers, Montague. *The Vampire in Europe.* New Hyde Park, NY: University Books, 1961. 329 pp.
"Vampires in Hungary." *International Vampire* 1, 4 (Summer 1991).
Wilson, Katherine M. "The History of the Word 'Vampire.'" *Journal of the History of Ideas* 64, 4 (October–December 1985): 577–83.

Vampires in the Czech Republic
and Slovakia

Edited by J. Gordon Melton

The first historical state in what is now the territory occupied by the Czech Republic and Slovakia was founded by tribes that settled in the mountainous region north of present-day Austria and Hungary. The state founded in the seventh-century would, two centuries later, be united with the Great Moravian empire, which in 836 A.D. invited Cyril and Methodius, the Christian missionaries, into their land. While among the Czechs and Slovaks, the pair preached and taught the people in their native Slavic language. However, Roman Catholicism, not Eastern Orthodoxy, dominated church life, and Latin, not Old Church Slavonic became the language of worship. The Moravian empire disintegrated early in the tenth-century and Slovakia became part of Hungary. After a period under German control, the Czech state reemerged as the Czech (Bohemian) kingdom. Like Poland, both the Czechs and the Slovakians became Roman Catholic.

The Bohemian kingdom survived through the Middle Ages but gradually through the sixteenth-century came under Austrian hegemony and in the next century was incorporated into the Hapsburg empire. At the end of the eighteenth century, a revival of Czech culture led to a revival of Czech nationalism. Finally, in 1918, at the end of World War I, Czechoslovakia was created as an independent state. That country survived through most of the twentieth century, though 1000 years of separate political existence had driven a considerable wedge between the Czechs and Slovaks. After World War II, Communist rule replaced the democratic government that had been put in place in 1918. The Communist system was renounced in 1989 and shortly thereafter, Bohemia and Moravia parted with Slovakia. On January 1, 1993, two separate and independent countries, the Czech Republic and Slovakia, emerged.

THE VAMPIRE IN THE CZECH REPUBLIC AND SLOVAKIA

The Czech and Slovakian vampire—called a *upír,* and to a lesser extent, *nelapsi,* in both Czech and Slovak—was a variety of the Slavic vampire. The *upir* was believed to have two hearts and hence two souls. The presence of the second soul would be indicated by a corpse's flexibility, open eyes, two curls in the hair, and a ruddy complexion. Among the earliest anecdotes concerning Czech vampires were two fourteenth-century stories recounted by E. R Evans in his volume on the *Criminal Prosecution and Capital Punishment of Animals* (1906), as mentioned in Dudley Wright's survey. The first concerned a revenant that terrorized the town of Cadan. The people he attacked seemed destined to become a vampire like him. They retaliated, attacking his corpse and driving a stake through it. That remedy proving ineffective, they finally burned him. In 1345, in Lewin, a woman believed to be a witch died. She returned in various beastly forms and attacked villagers. When uncovered in her grave it was reported that she had swallowed her face cloth; when the cloth was pulled out of the grave, it was stained with blood. She also was staked, which again proved ineffective. She used the stake as a weapon while walking around town. She was finally destroyed by fire. Writing in 1863, Henry More recorded events that occurred in the late 1500s to Johannes Cuntius (or Kunz), a merchant who troubled his family and neighbors following his violent death. Cuntius lived in the town of Pentsch (present-day Horni Benesov). His son lived in Jagerdorf (present-day Krnov) in a part of Moravia dominated by Lutheran Protestants.

Dom Augustin Calmet included reports of vampires from Bohemia and Moravia in his famous 1746 treatise. He noted that in 1706 a treatise on vampires, *Magia Posthuma* by Charles Ferdinand de Schertz, was published in Olmutz (Moravia). *Magia Posthuma* related a number of incidents of vampires who made their first appearance as troublesome spirits that would attack their former neighbors and the village livestock. Some of the reports were of classic nightmare attacks accompanied with pain, a feeling of being suffocated, and squeezing around the neck area. Those so attacked would grow pale and fatigued. Other stories centered on poltergeist effects featuring objects being thrown around the house and possessions of the dead person mysteriously moved. One of the earliest and more spectacular cases concern a man of the Bohemian village of Blow (Blau) in the fourteenth century. As a vampire he called upon his neighbors, and whomever he visited died within eight days. The villagers finally dug up the man's body and drove a stake through it. The man, however, laughed at the people and thanked the people for giving him a stick to fend off the dogs. That night he took the stick out of his body and began again to appear to people. After several more deaths occurred, his body was burned. Only then did the visitations end.

Schertz, a lawyer, was most concerned with the activity of villagers who would take the law into their hands and mutilate and burn bodies. He argued that in cases of severe disturbances, a legal process should be followed before any bodies were desecrated. Included in the process was the examination of the body of any suspected vampire by physicians and theologians. Destruction of the vampire, by burning, should be carried out as an official act by the public executioner.

Montague Summers was most impressed by the evidence of vampirism detailed by the Count de Cadreras, who early in the 1720s was commissioned by the Austrian emperor to look into events at Haidam, a town near the Hungarian border. The count investigated a number of cases of people who had been dead for many years (in one case 30 and another 16 years), and who had reportedly returned to attack their relatives. Upon exhumation each still showed the classic signs of delayed decomposition, including the flow of "fresh" blood when cut. With the Count's consent, each was beheaded (or nails driven into the skull) and then burned. The extensive papers reporting these incidents to the emperor survived, as well as a lengthy narrative given by the count to an official at the University of Fribourg.

It is unlikely that the town of "Haidam" will ever be identified. No place by that name has been recorded. It has been suggested most convincingly that the term derived from the word "haidamak," a Ukrainian term meaning "outlaw" or "freebooter." Haidamak, derived from the Slavic "heyduck" referred to a class of dispossessed who had organized themselves into loose itinerant bands to live off the land. Eventually the Austrian Hapsburg rulers employed them as guardians along their most distant frontiers. This Haidam probably referred to the land of a haidamak rather than a specific town by that name.

As recently as the mid-twentieth century, folklorist Ján Mjartan reported that the belief in vampires was still alive in Slovakia. The vampire was thought to be able to suck the blood of its victims (humans and cattle) and often suffocated them. The vampire also was believed capable of killing with a mere glance (evil eye), thus decimating whole villages. Preventing the rising of a suspected vampire was accomplished by placing various objects in the coffin (coins, Christian symbols, various herbs, the dead person's belongings), putting poppyseed or millet seeds in the body orifices, and nailing the clothes and hair to the coffin. Finally, the head or the heart could be stabbed with an iron wedge, an oak stake, a hat pin, or some thorn such as the hawthorn. The body was carried headfirst to the grave, around which poppyseed or millet was scattered. The seeds also were dropped on the path homeward, and once home various rituals such as washing one's hands and holding them over the stove were followed. The family of the deceased repeated these measures if they proved ineffective the first time.

CONTEMPORARY VAMPIRE LORE

As with other Slavic countries, the belief in. vampires receded to rural areas of the Czech Republic and Slovakia through the twentieth century. It made a brief appearance in the midst of the Czech cultural revival of the nineteenth-century in a famous short story "The Vampire" by Jan Neruda (1834–91). In. recent decades, Josef Nesvadba, a Czech psychiatrist, has emerged as an impressive writer of horror fiction. A collection of his stories in English was published in 1982 as *Vampires Ltd.*

SOURCES

Calmet, Augustine. *The Phantom World.* 2 vols. London: Richard Bentley, 1850. Reprint of English translation of 1746 treatise.

Hrbkova, Sárka B. *Czechoslovak Stories.* Freeport, NY: Books for Libraries Press, 1970. 330 pp.

Nesvadba, Josef. *Vampires Ltd.* Czechoslovakia: Artia Pocket Books, 1982. 225 pp.

Perkowski, Jan L. *The Darkling: A Treatise on Slavic Vampirism.* Columbus, OH: Slavica Publishers, 1989. 174 pp.

———, ed. *Vampires of the Slavs.* Cambridge, MA: Slavica Publishers, 1976. 294 pp.

Summers, Montague. *The Vampire in Europe.* London: Routledge, Kegan Paul, Trench, Trubner, & Co. 1929. 329 pp. Reprint. New Hyde Park, NY: University Books, 1961. 329 pp.

Wright, Dudley. *Vampires and Vampirism.* London: William Rider and Sons, 1914, Rev. ed.: 1924. Reprint. *The Book of Vampires.* New York: Causeway Books, 1973. 217 pp.

The Golem (1920)

By John DeBartolo

Our story takes place in the 17th Century in the Jewish ghetto in the city of Prague. The learned Rabbi Loew (Albert Steinruck) reads in the stars that misfortune and a new oppression threaten the Jews of Prague. The Rabbi approaches the patriarch of the ghetto, Rabbi-Jehuda (Hanns Sturm), and the panic stricken duo summon the elders of the community together to pray for deliverance. Emperor Rudolf II (Otto Gebuhr) upon the advice of counselors who believe that the Jews were responsible for a plague which had swept the city, issues an edict stating that the Jews must leave the Prague before the end of the month.

Wishing to protect his people from persecution, Rabbi Loew builds a Frankenstein-like monster out of clay in a secret cellar in his home. Through alchemy, magic, secret writings and chants the Rabbi is told that if he places the magic word "Aemaet," the Hebrew word for "truth" or "God," in an amulet and then imbeds it in the Golem's breast, the creature will come to life. The Rabbi gives life to the Golem (Paul Wegener) and he becomes the Rabbi's servant doing various chores, chopping firewood, and running errands. However, the Golem's towering figure, granite-like face and lumbering walk repels the residents as he roams the streets of the Ghetto. A little girl who is not frightened befriends the huge man of clay only to unwittingly remove the amulet from his chest immediately rendering him lifeless.

The Rabbi seeks and obtains an audience with the Emperor to inform him that the stars are forecasting danger. He brings the revitalized Golem with him to the emperor's court. The Emperor instructs the Rabbi to perform feats of magic. Loew invokes a panorama of events that appear on the wall. As it portrays the exodus of the Jews from Prague, the building suddenly begins to shake and crumble violently. Terrified, the Emperor turns to the Rabbi for help, promising to rescind his edict against the Jews if the religious man can prevent the building from collapsing upon him. It is the Golem who holds up the ceiling and prevents it from collapsing thus saving the Emperor and his court from being crushed.

This screen adaptation of *The Golem* was made more compelling by the design elements that went into its production. The medieval sets were designed by Hans

Poelzig, whom Wegener had known before WWI. Designer Kurt Richter supervised the construction of 54 structures at UFA's Tempelhof studios. The stylized gabled buildings, portals and fountains with a Gothic flair are quite similar to the expressionist sets used in *The Cabinet of Dr. Caligari* (Decla-Bloscop, 1919). The costumes were created by Rochus Gliese and complement the period setting beautifully. All of this was captured by the lens of master cinematographer Karl Freund (1890–1969) who enjoyed a long and esteemed career through the television era. His artistry conveyed the mood, and in expressionist films, the mood is everything. Contemporary reviews in the U.S. responded favorably to the visual feast set before them:

Photoplay, in September 1921 unequivocally stated, "This new German picture is a masterpiece ... with a sweep and a sincerity of purpose that thrills and amazes. It is racially, Jewish; artistically, it is international."

The *Variety* film review of June 24, 1921, touted, "The production is an impressively dignified one and the scenes of medieval times are well visualized, with some magnificent mob scenes. The cast has been carefully selected with a view to the depiction of ancient types and all are excellent screen players."

The *New York Times*, for June 20, 1921, confirmed, "The black magic of the Middle Ages, sorcery, astrology and all the superstitious realities of people so legendary in appearance and manners that the unnatural seems natural among them, have been brought to the screen of the Criterion in *The Golem*."

The genesis of the Golem has its roots in an old medieval Czech legend and is mentioned in the ancient Jewish *Talmud*. Jewish mystics ascribe the actual creation of this phenomenon to Abraham, who brought about a golem calf, and Joseph's brothers creating both golem animals and golem people. The more one reads about the Golem the more fascinating it becomes. Perhaps the most well-known legend (and the one this film borrows from), is traced from 300 to 600 A.D. God instructed a Jewish religious leader to make a man out of mud from the river Jordan. In the mouth of this mud pile an inscription of the name of God was placed on a bisque, and thus was created a Healing Golem.

The Golem was filmed three times during the silent era by its star Paul Wegener (who also co-director and co-wrote). This version, subtitled "Wie er in de Welt" (*How He Came into the World*), was the third and only surviving film of the trilogy. There were also several sound adaptations of this story, primarily European, but it is this version of *The Golem* that influenced one of the most famous of classic horror films, *Frankenstein* (Universal, 1931). Director James Whale even borrowed the plot device of a little girl befriending the creature for his own masterpiece.

Paul Wegener (1874–1948) born in Bischdorf, Germany, began his acting career in Reinhardt's Deutsches Theater in Berlin. Over the subsequent decades, he became a towering figure in German drama. Entering films in 1913, he soon began working as both an actor and director. He was married five times; one of his wives being actress Lyda Salmonova who had a leading role in *The Golem* (Rabbi Loew's daughter). They

Two scenes from *The Golem* starring Paul Wegener.

appeared together in many films. However, a more dubious recognition for the actor came about during the Nazi regime where he produced propaganda films. He was named an Actor of the State by the Nazi propaganda minister Josef Goebbels. Wegener himself appeared in Nazi feature films up until 1945—quite a turnabout from the homage he paid to a Jewish legend with *The Golem*. Wegener can also be seen in a few available silent films, including *Passion* (a.k.a. *Madame DuBarry*) (UFA, 1919), *One Arabian Night* (UFA, 1920), and *Student of Prague* (H.R. Sokal-Film, 1926), *The Magician* (M-G-M, 1926) and *Mandrake* (Ama-Film, 1928).

The Golem (UFA, 1920)—Cast: Paul Wegener, Albert Steinrack, Lyda Salmonova, Ernst Deutsch, Otto Gebuhr, Dore Paetzold, Lothar Muthel, Greta Schroder and Loni Nest. Directed by Paul Wegener and Carl Boese. B&W. 6 reels. This is a film we would like to see officially released on video.

SOURCES

The Great German Films, by Frederick W. Ott; *The Haunted Screen*, by Lotte H. Eisner; *The UFA Story*, by Klaus Kreimer; *World Film Directors*, by John Wakeman; *The Film Encyclopedia*, by Ephraim Katz; *From Caligari to Hitler*, by Siegfried Kracauer; and *Horror in Silent Films: A Filmography, 1896–1929*, by Roy Kinnard.

Early Vampire Stories

Peter Plogojowitz

By Paul Barber

E uropeans of the early 1700s showed a great deal of interest in the subject of the vampire. Indeed, the word itself entered English in 1734, according to the *Oxford English Dictionary,* at a time when, in Germany especially, many books were being written on the subject.

In retrospect it seems clear that one reason for all the excitement was the Peace of Passarowitz (1718), by which parts of Serbia and Walachia were turned over to Austria. Thereupon the occupying forces, which remained there until 1739, began to notice, and file reports on, a peculiar local practice: that of exhuming bodies and "killing" them.[1] Literate outsiders began to attend such exhumations. The vampire craze, in other words, was an early "media event," in which educated Europeans became aware of practices that were by no means of recent origin, but had simply been provided, for the first time, with effective public-relations representatives. The story of Peter Plogojowitz (1725) illustrates this, in an involuted style characteristic of the bureaucratic German of the eighteenth century. This account is usually paraphrased, not translated, perhaps because its stylized expressions of deference create, in English, a misleading impression of mawkish obsequiousness. (The German, because of its formalistic character, does not give quite the same effect.) I translate it here nonetheless, because efforts to paraphrase the story usually omit important details. As we shall see, it is important to know *exactly* what was being said about vampires. Here, then, is the story of Peter Plogojowitz:

> After a subject by the name of Peter Plogojowitz had died, ten weeks past—he lived in the village of Kisilova, in the Rahm District—and had been buried according to the Raetzian custom, it was revealed that in this same village of Kisilova, within a week, nine people, both old and young, died also, after suffering a twenty-four-hour illness. And they said publicly, while they were yet alive, but on their death-bed, that the above-mentioned Plogojowitz, who had died ten weeks earlier, had come to them in their sleep, laid himself on them, and throttled them, so that they would have to give up the ghost. The other subjects were very distressed and strengthened even more in such [beliefs] by

the fact that the dead Peter Plogojowitz's wife, after saying that her husband had come to her and demanded his opanki, or shoes, had left the village of Kisilova and gone to another. And since with such people (which they call vampires) various signs are to be seen—that is, the body undecomposed, the skin, hair, beard and nails growing—the subjects resolved unanimously to open the grave of Peter Plogojowitz and to see if such above-mentioned signs were really to be found on him. To this end they came here to me and, telling of these events, asked me and the local pope, or parish priest, to be present at the viewing. And although I at first disapproved, telling them that the praiseworthy administration should first be dutifully and humbly informed, and its exalted opinion about this should be heard, they did not want to accommodate themselves to this at all, but rather gave this short answer: I could do what I wanted, but if I did not accord them the viewing and the legal recognition to deal with the body according to their custom, they would have to leave house and home, because by the time a gracious resolution was received from Belgrade, perhaps the entire village—and this was already supposed to have happened in Turkish times—could be destroyed by such an evil spirit, and they did not want to wait for this. Since I could not hold such people from the resolution they had made, either with good words or with threats, I went to the village of Kisilova, taking along the Gradisk pope, and viewed the body of Peter Plogojowitz, just exhumed, finding, in accordance with thorough truthfulness, that first of all I did not detect the slightest odor that is otherwise characteristic of the dead, and the body, except for the nose, which was somewhat fallen away, was completely fresh. The hair and beard—even the nails, of which the old ones had fallen away—had grown on him; the old skin, which was somewhat whitish, had peeled away, and a new fresh one had emerged under it. The face, hands, and feet, and the whole body were so constituted, that they could not have been more complete in his lifetime. Not without astonishment, I saw some fresh blood in his mouth, which, according to the common observation, he had sucked from the people killed by him. In short, all the indications were present that such people (as remarked above) are said to have. After both the pope and I had seen this spectacle, while the people grew more outraged than distressed, all the subjects, with great speed, sharpened a stake—in order to pierce the corpse of the deceased with it—and put this at his heart, whereupon, as he was pierced, not only did much blood, completely fresh, flow also through his ears and mouth, but still other wild signs (which I pass by out of high respect) took place. Finally, according to their usual practice, they burned the often-mentioned body, *in hoc casu,* to ashes, of which I inform the most laudable Administration, and at the same time would like to request, obediently and humbly, that if a mistake was made in this matter, such is to be attributed not to me but to the rabble, who were beside themselves with fear.

Imperial Provisor, Gradisk District.

Thanks be to God, we are by no means
credulous. We avow that all the light which
science can throw on this fact discovers
none of the causes of it. Nevertheless, we
cannot refuse to believe that to be true
which is juridically attested, and by persons
of probity.
—Dom Calmet, 1746

Plogojowitz has a place of honor in any book on vampires, since his case is remarkably complete and shows most of the classic motifs—and some of the misconceptions—of vampirism. Since I shall be discussing these in detail later, I shall merely mention them at this point:

1. Plogojowitz's village is usually identified as Hungarian ("Niederungarn," according to Zedler's *Universal-Lexikon* of 1745), but this is because of the confused political situation of the time. Actually, Kisilova was in Serbia.
2. Characteristically, vampirism occurs as an epidemic, as it does here, and it is typical that Plogojowitz, as the first person who died, is held responsible for the deaths that followed: *post hoc, ergo propter hoc.*
3. Vampirism may cause a lingering death (especially in fictional treatments of the subject), but in folklore we are often told that the victim's death was viewed as sudden and unexpected. Plogojowitz's "victims," for example, died after a one-day illness.
4. Typically, where the vampire is of the ambulatory type—for example, the Yugoslavian vampire—he appears before the victim in the night and either strangles him or sucks blood. In any case, the victim often complains of a feeling of suffocation before death.
5. The body is said to be "completely fresh," but it is not unchanged: the nose has fallen in somewhat, the hair, beard, and nails have grown, and new skin has formed under the old. Our witness does not make nice distinctions as to what he himself saw and what he was told: presumably he could not know whether Plogojowitz's hair and beard had grown. Incidentally, accounts differ as to how long Plogojowitz was in the grave: Horst cites one that has him there for three weeks, rather than ten.

6.	It is not necessarily typical that the body has no unpleasant odor. Indeed, Dom Calmet, the eighteenth-century French ecclesiastic, observed that "when they [vampires] have been taken out of the ground, they have appeared red, with their limbs supple and pliable, without worms or decay; but not without great stench." And de Tournefort, the French botanist who observed a supposed Greek revenant, was so graphic in his description of its stench that later editions of his book, in both French and English, thoroughly bowdlerized that part of his text dealing with the subject.

The stench of the vampire, by the way, is one aspect of the nexus between vampirism and the plague. In European folklore, vampires "cause" epidemics (even in the movies, vampirism is catching).

Now, foul smells were commonly associated with disease, also as a cause, perhaps because people reasoned that, since corpses smelled bad, bad smells must be a cause of disease and death. Typically, by way of combating such smells, people introduced good-smelling (or strong-smelling) substances: "Pleasant smells were important, for they drove away noxious plague fumes. Those threatened by plague were urged to burn aromatic softwoods such as juniper and ash. Oak, pine, rosemary, aloe, amber and musk were other good smells." This account is from a description of fourteenth-century beliefs, but such views have been common over many centuries.[1]

7.	It is clear from the description that Plogojowitz, if our sources are to be believed, was all but caught in flagrante delicto, since he actually had fresh blood in his mouth when he was dug up. Moreover—and this is characteristic of such stories—his own blood was fresh, not coagulated, as one might expect.

8.	The staking of the vampire, so familiar from the movies, is, in south Slavic territory, perhaps the most common method of disposing of him, and when this is done the vampire is usually reported to have bled profusely. It is also typical for the vampire to be burned as well, especially if piercing him with a stake does not end his depredations. Also, while Plogojowitz is not reported to have protested his fate, some vampires were said to scream or groan when pierced by the stake. This was true, for example, of Arnold Paole, the subject of chapter 3.

9.	It is generally assumed that the "wild signs" (*wilde Zeichen*) imply that the corpse was believed to have an erection.[2] The vampire of folklore is a sexual creature,

---

1	In New Orleans, e.g., during the yellow fever epidemics of the nineteenth century, people commonly burned barrels of tar at street corners during the night to purify the air (Duffy, 74). See Ariès, 482, for similar accounts from Paris.

2	Such "erections," according to coroners I have spoken to, actually result from the bloating, with decomposition, of the sexual organs (Svensson, 411). They may have contributed to the common belief that, as Wiedemann ([1917], 29) remarks, the dead are generally regarded as particularly sensual beings. Spitz, 349, discusses physiological aspects of the matter in greater detail.

and his sexuality is obsessive—indeed, in Yugoslavia, when he is not sucking blood, he is apt to wear out his widow with his attentions, so that she too pines away, much like his other victims.

There are a few characteristic things that we are *not* told about Plogojowitz as well. Often people who became vampires were difficult, contentious people while alive. When they died, if anything untoward happened in their vicinity, the suspicion arose that they had something to do with it. Nothing of this sort is reported about Peter Plogojowitz: he seems merely to have been the first person in his village to have caught a good case of vampirism and, by infecting others, to have made a place for himself in the history of folklore. And all this after his own death.

The Shoemaker of Silesia

By Paul Barber

Even before Peter Plogojowitz's death there were detailed accounts of exhumations, and not just from Slavic territory. And if you look at just the exhumation, rather than the folklore associated with the revenant, many of these accounts are very much like the Slavic ones: vampire and *Nachzehrer* (from *nach* [after] and *zehren* [consume, prey upon]: a northern German variety of revenant) seem to be identical in the grave.

We see this in the following account. This particular revenant is referred to in the text simply as a "ghost" (*Gespenst*) and is found in Grässe's collection of Prussian folklore.

THE SHOEMAKER OF BRESLAU

In the year 1591, on the twentieth of September, a Friday, early in the morning in the garden behind his house, a well-to-do shoemaker in the city of Breslau cut his throat—for what reason, no one knew. He had cut the veins of his throat with his knife, and was obliged to die from the wound. When his wife had seen this and told her sisters, they were all most distraught about this sudden misfortune, but sought to conceal it however they could, considering it a great disgrace. She, therefore, told everyone who asked her about her husband's death, that a stroke had taken him. She also had the doors locked, so that no one could see what had happened. But when her neighbors and acquaintances came to speak with her and to console her, the sisters of the widow did not allow it and said that she recognized their love and well-meaning very well, but the dead man had no need of their services and the widow, in her first distress, did not want to accept visitors. They should, therefore, if they liked, come some time later. Then they sent to the church fathers and ordered the burial, the grave site, and the ringing of the bells, which they achieved without hindrance, since the dead man had been considered a rich man. But so that everything would remain secret and no one would learn anything about the murder [that is, suicide], they hired an

Paul Barber, "The Shoemaker of Silesia," from *Vampires, Burial, and Death: Folklore and Reality,* pp. 10–14. Copyright © 1988 Yale University Press. Permission to reprint granted by the publisher.

old woman who had to wash the corpse, which had lost its blood, and tie up the wound so tightly that one could not see anything of it. When she had done that, together they laid him into the coffin. The widow herself, who was recovering from childbirth—she had been lying in for just ten days—had the priest come, so that he could comfort her in this grievous instance. And he did come and comfort the widow, but when he wanted to leave, the sisters of the widow suggested—and he knew nothing of the matter—that he should at least look at the body once. This he did, without any thought that there was anything behind this. For the body was so well wrapped up on all sides with linen, that even someone who was paying close attention would not have noticed anything, and they had placed it so high that the folded and twisted wraps could not arouse suspicion. The third day thereafter—it was on a Sunday—he was buried with great ceremony, in the manner of those who are pious and distinguished. And such a send off and funeral speech were held, as though he had led a holy and guilt-free life and had been a splendid Christian.

If the relatives of the deceased believed that the murder would remain concealed, since they had arranged things so carefully, nonetheless a rumor came about among the people, to the effect that the man had killed himself and had not been killed by a stroke. At first people did not want to believe it, but nonetheless the rumor got stronger and stronger, so that the council saw itself obliged precisely to question those who had been with the deceased, and to demand that they admit, in accordance with the truth, what they had seen or heard and what each of them was aware of. Perhaps because all these people tried to talk their way out of it, and did not stay with one answer, they could soon see that not everything was right. Finally they conceded that he had fallen and had hit a sharp rock and had injured himself in this way. They said also that an awl had been found in his clothing, but they had removed it so that it could never again injure anyone else. The council, since the evidence continued to increase, now considered what was to be done. This too did not remain quiet, and some friends of the widow persuaded her under no circumstances to allow the body of her husband to be dug out or put at a dishonorable location or viewed as a sorcerer or suicide, if they could not come up with stronger proofs. In the meantime a ghost appeared now and again, in just such a form as the shoemaker had in his lifetime, and during the day as well as at night. It scared many people through its very form, awakened others with noises, oppressed others, and others it vexed in other ways, so that early in the morning one heard talk everywhere about the ghost. But the more the ghost appeared, the less the relatives wanted to celebrate. They went to the president of the court and said that too much credence was being placed in the people's unfounded rumors, the honorable man was being abused in his grave, and they found themselves obliged to take the matter to the Kaiser. But now that the matter actually brought about a prohibition, the state of haunting became even worse. For the ghost was there right after sundown, and since no one was free of it, everyone looked around constantly for it. The ones most bothered were those who wanted to rest after heavy work; often it came to their bed, often it actually lay down in it and was like to smother the people. Indeed, it squeezed them so hard that—not without astonishment—people could see the marks left by its fingers, so that one could easily judge the so-called stroke [that the shoemaker was alleged to have died from]. In this manner the people, who were fearful in any case, became yet more fearful, so that they did not remain longer in their houses, but sought for more secure places. Most of them, not secure in their bedchamber, stayed in the rooms, after bringing many others in, so that their fear was dispersed by the crowd. Nonetheless, although they all waked with burning lights, the ghost came anyway. Often everyone saw it, but often just a few, of whom it always harassed some.

As the clamor grew worse from day to day, with the whole city confirming the being, the council decided to do something so that the ghost would stay away. The corpse had lain in the grave now into the eighth month, from September 22, 1591, to April 18, 1592, when the grave was opened, by high command. Present were the entire council, the innkeepers, and other functionaries. In the opened grave they found the body complete and undamaged by decay, but blown up like a drum, except that nothing was changed and the limbs all still hung together. They were—which was remarkable—not stiffened, like those of other dead people, but one could move them easily. On his feet the skin had peeled away, and another had grown, much purer and stronger than the first, and as almost all sorcerers are marked in an out-of-the-way place, so that one does not notice it easily, so did he have on his big toe a mole like a rose. No one knew the meaning of this. There was also no stench to be noticed, except that the cloths in which he was wrapped had a repulsive smell. The wound in his throat gaped open and was reddish and not changed in the slightest. The body was guarded day and night on its bier, from the fourth to the twenty-fourth of April, except that in the day he was put out in the air, whereas in the evening he was put in a house there. Everyone could see him up close, and every day many citizens, and many people from the neighboring areas, went there. Nonetheless the exhumation did not help: the ghost, which they had hoped to banish by this means, caused still more unrest. The corpse was laid under the gallows, but this didn't help either, for the ghost then raged so cruelly that one cannot describe it.

But now, as the ghost was raging so terribly and thereby causing great inconvenience to many citizens as well as his good friends, the widow went to the council and said that she would admit everything, they could deal with her former husband with all strictness. But in the short time from April 24 to May 7, the body had grown much fuller of flesh, which everyone could see who remembered how it had looked before. Whereupon, on the seventh, the council had the hangman take the corpse out of the other grave. Then its head was cut off, its hands and feet dismembered, after which the back was cut open and the heart taken out, which looked as good as that of a freshly slaughtered calf. Everything together was burned on a pyre built up of seven klafters[1] of wood and of many pitch rings. But so that no one would gather the ashes or the bones and keep them for sorcery, as tends to happen otherwise, the guards were not allowed to let anyone near. Early in the morning, when the stack of wood had burned up, the ashes, in a sack, were thrown into the flowing water, whereupon, through God's help, the ghost stayed away and was never seen again.

Much in this story, clearly, is implausible, but, as we shall see later, many details—notably in the description of the dead body—are accurately depicted, leaving us with no choice but to conclude that we are dealing here with an account based on real events, however badly those events have been misinterpreted. The bloated body, for example, and the "new skin" (a phenomenon known to pathologists as "skin slippage") are normal events associated with decomposition and provide convincing proof that an exhumation took place. In general we will find that such accounts are accurate as to their data, inaccurate as to their interpretations. And this particular account conveys much that is typical:

1. The revenant dies as a suicide, murder victim, drowning victim—indeed, in almost any way that causes him to end his days somewhat earlier than expected: he "dies before his time." We do not know, of course, how this particular revenant died—he may have been murdered—but it is clear that his death was out of the ordinary and was therefore viewed as a possible source of disturbance within his community.

2. Such bodies are dealt with differently from "honorable" ones—buried in a different place, often with a very different set of funerary rites—and the resulting disgrace to the survivors of the deceased is such that they typically go to great lengths to prevent such treatment of the body. Klapper gives an account, for example, from Upper Silesia, of a woman who demanded (successfully) that her mother's body be exhumed so that it could be turned right-side-up and various other apotropaic measures could be undone.

---

1   An old measure: one *Klafter* was about three cubic meters of wood.

3. The body, when exhumed, looks rather different than expected (it is bloated, does not show rigor mortis, has a mole on the big toe, does not have a sufficiently rank odor).

4. The body is "killed" in a variety of ways, one after another—dismembered, excoriated, and cremated, then thrown into a river: nothing is left to chance. An accelerant (pitch) is used to encourage the fire: such bodies burn only reluctantly.

5. The account ends, typically, when the ghost is finally laid. The ghost, incidentally, appears to be independent of the corpse in one sense—nothing is said of the *corpse* leaving the grave—yet dependent on it in another, for to kill the ghost, you only need to kill the body in the right way. I stress "in the right way" because sometimes several methods must be tried and the right one selected, finally, by trial and error. In this instance, apparently, the methods were used all at once, to dispense with the nuisance of waiting to see which one worked.

Even this account, however, as detailed as it is, does not present us with such a dramatic juxtaposition of physiological anomalies and compelling testimony as our next account, *Visum et Repertum*, which was written by a doctor who presided over the exhumation and dissection of a graveyard full of Serbian vampires.

Visum et Repertum

By Paul Barber

Perhaps the most notable instance of "vampirism" is that associated with the name of Arnod Paole, who fell off a haywagon and into history in the first quarter of the eighteenth century. Paole, an ex-soldier from Serbia, was the first of a series of vampires that finally attracted the attention of the authorities and led to the investigative report known as *Visum et Repertum* (*Seen and Discovered*). Paole himself, as it happens, was not studied closely: the investigators arrived on the scene several years after he had been exhumed, staked, and burned.

The report itself is a curious document. Hardly a literary masterpiece, it has seldom made its way in complete form into English-language books on the vampire, and this may be because it is difficult to translate: the language is stilted, the author is indifferent to questions of grammatical parallelism, and several versions are extant, each of which, incidentally, gives a different spelling of the author's name, the most innovative of which (Clickstenger) is to be found in the English translation of Calmet (see Bibliography). For my translation I have used a text published in Nuremberg in 1732 and reprinted in Sturm and Völker's excellent anthology, *Von denen Vampiren oder Menschensaugern*. And since I was more concerned with accuracy than with elegance, I make no apologies for the style:

VISUM ET REPERTUM

After it had been reported that in the village of Medvegia the so-called vampires had killed some people by sucking their blood, I was, by high decree of a local Honorable Supreme Command, sent there to investigate the matter thoroughly, along with officers detailed for that purpose and two subordinate medical officers, and therefore carried out and heard the present inquiry in the company of the captain of the Stallath Company of haiduks [a type of soldier], Gorschiz Hadnack, the bariactar [literally: "standard-bearer"] and the oldest haiduk of the village, as follows: who unanimously recount that about five years ago a local haiduk by the name of Arnod Paole broke his neck in a fall from a hay wagon. This man had, during his lifetime, often revealed that, near Gossowa in Turkish Serbia, he had been troubled by a vampire, wherefore he had eaten from the earth of the vampire's grave and had smeared himself with the vampire's blood, in order to be free of the vexation he had suffered. In twenty or thirty days after his death some people complained that they were being bothered by this same Arnod Paole; and in fact four people were killed by him. In order to end this evil, they dug up this Arnod Paole forty days after his death—this on the advice of their Hadnack, who had been present at such events before; and they found that he was quite complete and undecayed, and that fresh blood had flowed from his eyes, nose, mouth, and ears; that the shirt, the covering, and the coffin were completely bloody; that the old nails on his hands and feet, along with the skin, had fallen off, and that new ones had grown; and since they saw from this that he was a true vampire, they drove a stake through his heart, according to their custom, whereby he gave an audible groan and bled copiously. Thereupon they burned the body the same day to ashes and threw these into the grave. These same people say further that all those who were tormented and killed by the vampires must themselves become vampires. Therefore they disinterred the above-mentioned four people in the same way. Then they also add that this Arnod Paole attacked not only the people but also the cattle, and sucked out their blood. And since the people used the flesh of such cattle, it appears that some vampires are again present here, inasmuch as, in a period of three months, seventeen young and old people died, among them some who, with no previous illness, died in two or at the most three days. In addition, the haiduk Jowiza reports that his stepdaughter, by name of Stanacka, lay down to sleep fifteen days ago, fresh and healthy, but at midnight she started up out of her sleep with a terrible cry, fearful and trembling, and complained that she had been throttled by the son of a haiduk by the name of Milloe, who had died nine weeks earlier, whereupon she had experienced a great pain in the chest and became worse hour by hour, until finally she died on the third day. At this we went the same afternoon to the graveyard, along with the often-mentioned oldest haiduks of the village, in order to cause the suspicious graves to be opened and to examine the bodies in them, whereby, after all of them had been dissected, there was found:

1. A woman by the name of Stana, twenty years old, who had died in child-birth two months ago [three in Horst's account], after a three-day illness, and who had herself said, before her death, that she had painted herself with the blood of a vampire, wherefore both she and her child—which had died right after birth and because of a careless burial had been half eaten by dogs—must also become vampires. She was quite complete and

undecayed. After the opening of the body there was found in the *cavitate pectoris* a quantity of fresh extravascular blood. The *vasa* [vessels] of the *arteriae* and *venae,* like the *ventriculis cordis,* were not, as is usual, filled with coagulated blood, and the whole *viscera,* that is, the *pulmo* [lung], *hepar* [liver], *stomachus, lien* [spleen], *et intestina* were quite fresh as they would be in a healthy person. The uterus was however quite enlarged and very inflamed externally, for the placenta and lochia had remained in place, wherefore the same was in complete *putredine.* The skin on her hands and feet, along with the old nails, fell away on their own, but on the other hand completely new nails were evident, along with a fresh and vivid skin.

2. There was a woman by the name of Miliza (sixty years old, incidentally), who had died after a three-month sickness and had been buried ninety-some days earlier. In the chest much liquid blood was found, and the other viscera were, like those mentioned before, in a good condition. During her dissection, all the haiduks who were standing around marveled greatly at her plumpness and perfect body, uniformly stating that they had known the woman well, from her youth, and she had, throughout her life, looked and been very lean and dried up, and they emphasized that she had come to this surprising plumpness in the grave. They also said that it was she who had started the vampires this time, because she had eaten of the flesh of those sheep that had been killed by the previous vampires.

3. There was an eight-day-old child which had lain in the grave for ninety days and was similarly in a condition of vampirism.

4. The son of a haiduk, sixteen years old, was dug up, having lain in the earth for nine weeks, after he had died from a three-day illness, and was found like the other vampires.[1]

5. Joachim, also the son of a haiduk, seventeen years old, had died after a three-day illness. He had been buried eight weeks and four days and, on being dissected, was found in a similar condition.

6. A woman by the name of Ruscha who had died after a ten-day illness and had been buried six weeks previous, in whom there was much fresh blood not only in the chest but also *in fundo ventriculi.* The same showed itself in her child, which was eighteen days old and had died five weeks previously.

---

1   In Mackensen's version of Visum et Repertum, which is taken from a book published in 1751, the name of this youth is given as Milloe (p. 20). It is apparently he, and not the Milloe of #12, who tormented Stanacka in the night.

7. No less did a girl of ten years of age, who had died two months previously, find herself in the above-mentioned condition, quite complete and undecayed, and had much fresh blood in her chest.

8. They caused the wife of the Hadnack to be dug up, along with her child. She had died seven weeks previously, her child—who was eight weeks old—twenty-one days previously, and it was found that both mother and child were completely decomposed, although earth and graves were like those of the vampires lying nearby.

9. A servant of the local corporal of the haiduks, by the name of Rhade, twenty-three years old, died after a three-month-long illness, and after a five-week burial was found completely decomposed.

10. The wife of the local bariactar, along with her child, having died five weeks previously, were also completely decomposed.

11. With Stanche, a haiduk, sixty years old, who had died six weeks previously, I noticed a profuse liquid blood, like the others, in the chest and stomach. The entire body was in the oft-named condition of vampirism.

12. Milloe, a haiduk, twenty-five years old, who had lain for six weeks in the earth, also was found in the condition of vampirism mentioned.

13. Stanoicka [sic], the wife of a haiduk, twenty years old, died after a three-day illness and had been buried eighteen days previously. In the dissection I found that she was in her countenance quite red and of a vivid color, and, as was mentioned above, she had been throttled, at midnight, by Milloe, the son of the haiduk, and there was also to be seen, on the right side under the ear, a bloodshot blue mark, the length of a finger.[2] As she was being taken out of the grave, a quantity of fresh blood flowed from her nose. With the dissection I found, as mentioned often already, a regular fragrant fresh bleeding, not only in the chest cavity but also *in ventriculo cordis*. All the viscera found themselves in a completely good and healthy condition. The hypodermis of the entire body, along with the fresh nails on hands and feet, was as though completely fresh. After the examination had taken place, the heads of the vampires were cut off by the local gypsies and then burned along with the bodies, and then the ashes were thrown into the river Morava. The decomposed bodies, however, were laid back into their own graves. Which I attest along with those assistant medical officers provided for me. *Actum ut supra:*

(L.S.)[3] Johannes Fluchinger, Regiment Medical Officer of the Foot Regiment of the Honorable B. Fürstenbusch.

---

2   That is, the blue mark is taken for evidence that she was throttled.

3   Locus sigilli ("the place of the seal").

(L.S.) J. H. Sigel, Medical Officer of the Honorable Morall Regiment.

(L.S.) Johann Friedrich Baumgarten, Medical Officer of the Foot Regiment of the Honorable B. Fürstenbusch.

The undersigned attest herewith that all that which the Regiment Medical officer of the Honorable Fürstenbusch Regiment had observed in the matter of vampires—along with both of the medical officers who have signed with him—is in every way truthful and has been undertaken, observed, and examined in our own presence. In confirmation thereof is our signature in our own hand, of our own making. Belgrade, January 26, 1732.

(L.S.) Biittener, Lieutenant Colonel of the Honorable Alexandrian Regiment.

(L.S.) J. H. von Lindenfels, Officer of the Honorable Alexandrian Regiment.

A number of motifs here are typical of instances of "vampirism":

1. The authorities step in to deal with a situation that is clearly causing a major disruption in the lives of the local people.
2. In two instances (Arnod Paole and Stana) people are said to have used the blood of the vampire as an antidote to vampirism. In both cases, the remedy appears to have failed.
3. People complain that the (dead) Arnod Paole is terrorizing them.
4. The disinterment takes place forty days after his death. In Slavic tradition, Paole had no business being intact at this point.
5. Paole's body has not decayed, his blood is fresh, and his hair and nails have continued to grow after death.
6. Paole's body is staked, then cremated. Note that the corpse groans and bleeds. Note also that—unfortunately for us—Flückinger does not observe this: Paole's disinterment antedated Flückinger's arrival on the scene by five years.
7. The victims of the vampire must themselves become vampires.
8. The vampire also attacks cattle. Those who eat the flesh of the cattle must also become vampires.
9. Stana's child, which is buried carelessly, is dug up by dogs. This incident suggests that—as one would expect of the time and place—the child, at least, was not in a coffin. The bodies were probably buried in linen shrouds. Coffins, as a medical examiner pointed out to me, are intended to prevent events of this sort.
10. In one instance (Miliza) a vampire has not remained unchanged but is described as plump, even though she was lean when alive. Here it must be stressed that quite different, even contradictory, conditions are believed to indicate vampirism.

11. To demonstrate that the undecayed bodies are unusual, it is noted that other nearby bodies have decayed properly.
12. The woman named Stanoicka is "in her countenance quite red and of a vivid color."

All these are typical observations in the history of vampirism. It would also be useful, however, since Flückinger was an outsider and a medical officer, to separate out what he himself observed that is unusual. Here we must leave Arnod Paole out of consideration: his famous groan is hearsay, and Flückinger mentions no similar event occurring as he dissected the vampires. Here, then, is a list of unusual phenomena observed by Flückinger:

1. Corpses which, after having been buried for lengths of time ranging from eighteen days to three months had not decomposed or showed only slight changes in their appearance.
2. Fresh or liquid blood in these corpses.
3. Two bodies that had fresh skin and nails.
4. Bodies that, under conditions similar to those of the "vampires," had decomposed completely. These bodies, four in number, were similar to those of the vampires, except that one (#9: Rhade) had undergone a lengthy illness, unlike all but one of the vampires (Miliza, who had also changed somewhat, having become plump in the grave). Since this suggests that the duration of the illness might have something to do with the distinction between vampires and nonvampires, it is unfortunate that Flückinger does not mention the length of illness of three of the four decomposed bodies. In fact, according to Glaister and Rentoul, "Bodies of persons dying suddenly in apparent health decompose less quickly than those of persons dying from acute or chronic diseases, especially infective diseases." Presumably this is one reason some of the bodies had not decomposed (another reason is suggested by the date of the report: the exhumations took place in the winter!).
5. One body (#13: Stanoicka) that had the distinctive ruddy face of the typical vampire.
6. One vampire (Stanoicka) who had a mark under the ear. Flückinger apparently takes this for evidence of the "throttling," but since it was customary to look for such a mark on the skin of a witch or vampire, this would in any case have confirmed the belief that something spooky was going on.[4]

---

4 Vampires and witches are not always viewed as distinct species (see chap. 15). Grässe (2:199) quotes an early description of the exhumation and "killing" of a witch (Hexe) who was causing trouble after her death. The body is treated, in other words, like a vampire. And Burkhart, 237, points out that one defends one's self against witches with the same apotropaics as one uses against vampires.

One may see from this list that, however persuaded Flückinger was that something very strange was going on, he confirms little of what we have been told, in folklore, about vampirism. In fact, if we were to attempt a definition of a vampire, based on Flückinger's reported observations, we would come up with something like the following: "A vampire is a body that in all respects appears to be dead except that it does not decay as we expect, its blood does not coagulate, and it may show changes in dimension and in color." Indeed, one of our observers watched the dissection of a revenant and concluded that it was, in fact, merely a dead body.

Hie facht sich an gar ein grausem

liche erschröckenliche Hystorien. von dem wilden wütrich Dracole weyde. Wie er die leüt gespißt hot vnd gepraten vñ mit den haußtern yn einë keffel gesotten

Russian Stories

By Raymond T. McNally and Radu Florescu

Translation by Raymond T. McNally of the oldest Russian manuscript about Dracula: MS 11/1088 in the Kirillov-Belozersky Monastery Collection at the Saltykov-Schredin Public Library, Leningrad. First translation of this document into a Western language.

Among the very few authentic, signed documents which have been preserved from the late fifteenth century is the Russian "Story about Dracula." Copies of it were made from the fifteenth to the eighteenth century in Russia. It is one of the first instances of belletristic writing in Russian literature, and the historian Nicholas Karamzin has called it his country's first historical novel.

This manuscript was written by the monk Efrosin from the Kirillov-Belozersky Monastery in northern Russia in the year 1490. In it the monk states that he copied the story from another manuscript penned in 1486. No one knows who the author of that earlier manuscript was. Most scholarly opinion has focused upon a Russian diplomat who was at the Hungarian court in the 1480s, Fedor Kurytsin; he could have picked up the tale there since Dracula had been a captive of the Hungarian king from 1462 to 1474. Moreover, the monk states that the earlier author had seen one of the sons of Dracula.

Whoever the original author was, he was more disturbed by the prince's abandonment of Orthodoxy than by his cruelties. While in prison Dracula "forsook the light" of the Orthodox Church and accepted the "darkness" of the Roman Church because he was too attracted to the "sweetness" of this earthly life and not motivated enough by concern for the next one. Thus, the story has a marked religious tone.

The manuscript supports the notion of a "cruel but just" autocrat in its presentation of Dracula. However cruel his actions may have appeared they were necessary for the good of the state. In order to ward off not only the Turkish invaders but also the continual threat of opposition from the aristocratic *boyars,* Dracula had to take harsh measures. Obviously, the manuscript was written to indicate support of the autocratic ruler in Russia at the time, Ivan III, known as Ivan the Great. Here is the text:

1. There lived in the Wallachian lands a Christian prince of the Greek faith who was called Dracula in the Wallachian language, which means devil in our language, for he was as cruelly clever as was his name and so was his life.

   Once some ambassadors from the Turkish sultan came to him. When they entered his palace and bowed to him, as was their custom, they did not take their caps from their heads and Dracula asked them: "Why have you acted so? You ambassadors have come to a great sovereign and you have shamed me." The ambassadors answered, "Such is the custom of our land and our sovereign." And Dracula told them, "Well, I want to strengthen you in your custom. Behave bravely." And he ordered that their caps be nailed to their heads with small iron nails. And then he allowed them to go and said, "Go relate this to your sovereign, for he is accustomed to accepting such shame from you, but we are not accustomed to it. Let him not impose his customs upon other sovereigns who do not want them, but let him keep his customs to himself." [This episode confirmed in Romanian and German sources.]

2. The Turkish sultan was very angered because of that, and he set out with an army against Dracula and invaded with overwhelming force. But Dracula assembled all the soldiers he had and attacked the Turks during the night, and he killed a great many of them. But he could not conquer them with his few men against an army so much greater than his, so he retreated.

   He personally examined those who had fought with him against the Turks and who had returned. Those wounded in the front he honored and armed them as knights. But those who were wounded in the back he ordered to be impaled from the bottom up and said: "You are not a man but a woman." And when he marched against the Turks once again, he spoke to his entire army in this way, "Whoever wants to think of death, let him not come with me but let him remain here." And the Turkish sultan, hearing of this, retreated with great shame. He lost an immense army and never dared again to set out against Dracula. [The night attack is confirmed by an eyewitness report.]

3. The sultan sent an ambassador once to Dracula, in order that he be given the yearly tribute. Dracula greatly honored this ambassador, and showing him all that he had, he said, "I not only wish to give the sultan the tribute, but I also wish to place myself at his service with my whole army and with my whole treasury. I shall do as he commands, and you shall announce this to your emperor, so that when I shall come to place myself at his disposal, he will give orders throughout his whole land that no harm should come to me or to my men. And, as for me, I shall come to the emperor after your departure and I shall bring him the tribute, and I shall come in person."

When the sultan heard from his ambassador that Dracula wished to submit his service, the emperor honored this man, gave him gifts and was elated because at that time he was at war with the emperors and lands of the East. Immediately the sultan sent to all his fortified cities and throughout his land the message that when Dracula comes, not only should no one do him any harm but, on the contrary, they should honor Dracula when he comes. Dracula set out with his whole army and with him were officers of the emperor who greatly honored him. And he traveled throughout the Turkish empire for about five days. But then suddenly he turned around and began to rob and attack the cities and the towns. And he captured many prisoners whom he cut into pieces. He impaled some Turks, others he cut in two, and then he burned them. The whole country which he penetrated was laid to waste. He allowed no one to remain alive, not even the babes in arms. But others, those who were Christian, he displaced and installed them in his own lands. After taking much booty, he returned home. And, after having honored the officers, he said, "Go and tell your emperor what you have seen. I served him as much as I could. If my service has been pleasing to him, I am again going to serve him with all my might." And the emperor could do nothing against him but was shamefully vanquished. [This episode confirmed by historical documents.]

4. Dracula so hated evil in his land that if someone committed a misdeed such as theft, robbery, lying, or some injustice, he had no chance of staying alive. Whether he was a nobleman or a priest or a monk or a common man, or even if he had great wealth, he could not escape death. And he was so feared that in a certain place he had a source of water and a fountain where many travelers came from many lands, and many of these people came to drink at the fountain and the source, because the water was cool and sweet. Dracula had put near this fountain in a deserted place a great cup wonderfully wrought in gold; and whoever wished to drink the water could use this cup and put it back in its place. And as long as this cup was there, no one dared steal it. [Romanian folklore stresses Dracula's maintenance of law and order.]

5. Once Dracula ordered throughout the land that whoever was old or sick or poor should come to him. And there gathered at the palace a huge multitude of poor and vagabonds, who expected some great act of charity. And he ordered that all these miserable people be gathered together in a large house which was prepared with this idea in mind. And he ordered that they be given food and drink in accordance with their wishes. Then, after having eaten, they began to amuse themselves. Then Dracula personally came to see them and spoke to them in the following way: "What else do you need?" And they answered him in unison, "Lord, only God and your Highness knows, as God will let you hear." He then said to them, "Do you want me to make

you without any further cares, so that you have no other wants in this world?"
And, as they all expected some great gift, they answered, "We wish it, Lord."
At that point he ordered that the house be locked and set on fire, and all
of them perished in the fire within it. During this time he told his nobles,
"Know that I have done this first of all so that these unfortunate people
will no longer be a burden on others, and so that there should be no more
poor in my land but only rich people, and in the second place, I freed these
people, so that none of them suffers any longer in this world either because of
poverty, or because of some sickness." [Dracula's killing of the sick and poor
is a favorite theme in Romanian folklore. One critic has suggested that the
prince's motive was control of the plague.]

6. Once there came from Hungary two Roman Catholic monks looking for
alms. Dracula ordered them to be housed separately. And he first of all invited one of these monks and showed him in the court countless people on
stakes and spokes of wheels. And he asked the monk, "Have I done well?
How do you judge those on the stakes?" And the monk answered, "No, lord,
you have done badly. You punish without mercy. It is fitting that a master
be merciful, and all these unfortunate people whom you have impaled are
martyrs." Dracula then called the second monk and posed the same question.
The second monk answered, "You have been assigned by God as sovereign to
punish those who do evil and to reward those who do good. Certainly they
have done evil and have received what they deserved." Dracula then recalled
the first monk and told him, "Why have you left your monastery and your
cell, to walk and travel at the courts of great sovereigns, as you know nothing?
Just now you told me that these people are martyrs. I also want to make a
martyr out of you so that you will be together with these other martyrs." And
he ordered that he be impaled from the bottom up. But to the other monk,
he ordered that he be given fifty ducats of gold and told him, "You are a wise
man." And he ordered that a carriage be prepared for him in order that he
be driven with honor to the Hungarian border. [Note different ending in
Romanian story no. 6. Note, too, that the Russian version seems designed to
support one-man rule, however cruel.]

7. Once a merchant, a foreign guest from Hungary, came to Dracula's capital
city. Following his command, the merchant left his carriage on the street of
the city before the palace and his wares in the carriage, and he himself slept
in the house. Someone came and stole 160 golden ducats from the carriage.
The merchant went to Dracula and told him about the loss of the gold. And
Dracula told him, "You may go in peace; this night your gold will be returned." And he issued orders to look for the thief throughout the entire city
and said, "If you do not find the thief, I will destroy the entire city." And he
ordered that the gold be placed in the carriage during the night, but he added

one additional gold coin. The merchant got up in the morning and found his gold and he counted the pieces once, twice, and found the one additional gold coin. He went to Dracula and told him, "Sire, I have found the gold, but look, there is one additional gold coin which does not belong to me." At that moment they brought in the thief who had the original gold with him. And Dracula told the merchant, "Go in peace. If you had not told me about the additional gold coin, I was ready to impale you, together with this thief." [This tale recurs in Romanian folklore. Russian version is obviously meant to stress Dracula's sense of justice.]

8. If a married woman committed adultery Dracula ordered that her shameful parts be cut and she be skinned alive. Then he ordered that her skin be hung on a pole in the middle of the city at the marketplace. He did the same thing with young girls who had not preserved their virginity and also widows [who fornicated]. In some cases he cut the nipples off their breasts. In other cases he took the skins from their vagina and he rammed an iron poker, reddened by fire, up their vaginas so far upwards that the iron bar emerged from their mouths. They remained naked, tied to a pole until the flesh and bones detached themselves or served as food for the birds. [A favorite theme in the German pamphlets is Dracula's austere standards for women.]

9. Once when he was traveling, Dracula saw a poor man with a shirt torn and in bad shape. And he asked that man, "Have you a wife?" And he answered, "I have, sire." Then Dracula said, "Take me to your house, so that I can see her." And in the house of the man he saw a young and healthy wife. Then he asked her husband, "Did you sow grain?" And the husband answered, "Lord, I have much grain." And he showed much grain to him. Then Dracula said to his wife, "Why are you lazy toward your husband? It is his duty to sow and to work and to feed you, but it is your duty to make nice clean clothes for your husband. Only you do not even wish to clean his shirt, though you are quite healthy. You are the guilty one, not your husband. If your husband had not sown the grain, then your husband would be guilty." And Dracula ordered that both her hands be cut off and that she be impaled.

10. Once Dracula was feasting amid the corpses of many men who had been impaled around his table. There amid them he liked to eat and have fun. There was a servant who stood up right in front of him and could not stand the smell of the corpses any longer. He plugged his nose and drew his head to one side. Dracula asked him, "Why are you doing that?" The servant answered, "Sire, I can no longer endure this stench." Dracula immediately ordered that he be impaled, saying, "You must reside way up there, where the stench does not reach you." [Dracula's macabre sense of humor is highlighted in German pamphlets.]

11. On another occasion, Dracula received the visit of an emissary from Matthias the Hungarian king. The ambassador was a great noble of Polish origin. Dracula invited him to stay at his royal table in the midst of the corpses. And set up in front of the table was a very high, completely gilded stake. And Dracula asked the ambassador, "Tell me, why did I set up this stake?" The ambassador was very afraid and said, "Sire, it seems that some nobleman has committed a crime against you and you want to reserve a more honorable death for him than the others." And Dracula said, 'You spoke fairly. You are indeed a royal ambassador of a great sovereign. I have made this stake for you." The ambassador answered, "Sire, if I have committed some crime worthy of death, do what you wish because you are a fair ruler and you would not be guilty of my death but I alone would be." Dracula broke out laughing and said, "If you had not answered me thus, you would really be on that very stake yourself." And he honored him greatly and gave him gifts and allowed him to go, saying, "You truly can go as an envoy from great sovereigns to great sovereigns, because you are well versed in knowing how to talk with great sovereigns. But others let them not dare talk with me, before learning how to speak to great sovereigns."

12. Dracula had the following custom: whenever an ambassador came to him from the sultan or from the king and he was not dressed in a distinguished way or did not know how to answer twisted questions, he impaled them, saying, "I am not guilty of your death but your own sovereign, or you your-self. Don't say anything bad about me. If your sovereign knows that you are slow-witted and that you are not properly versed and has sent you to my court, to me a wise sovereign, then your own sovereign has killed you. And if somehow you dare to come without being properly instructed to my court, then you yourself have committed suicide." For such an ambassador he made a high and wholly gilded stake, and he impaled him in front of all, and to the sovereign of such a foolish ambassador he wrote the following words: "No longer send as an ambassador to a wise sovereign a man with such a weak and ignorant mind."

13. Once artisans made him some iron barrels. He filled the barrels with gold and put them at the bottom of a river. Then he ordered that the artisans be killed, so that no one would know the crime committed by Dracula except for the devil whose name he bore. [The story of the persons who killed the workmen who hid Dracula's treasure occurs the world over, thus this episode can be considered as a mythical one.]

14. On one occasion the Hungarian king Matthias set out with an army to war against Dracula. Dracula met him, they fought, and in the battle they captured Dracula alive, because Dracula was betrayed by his own men. And Dracula was brought to the Hungarian king, who ordered him thrown in

jail. And he remained in jail at Visegrad on the Danube up from Buda for twelve years. And in Wallachia the Hungarian king ordered another prince. [Dracula's presence in Hungary is confirmed by Hungarian sources, reports by papal representatives in Buda, and the memoirs of Pius II.]

15. After the death of this prince, the Hungarian king sent a messenger to Dracula, who was in jail, to ask him whether he would like to become prince in Wallachia again. If so, he must accept the Latin faith, and if he refuses, he must die in jail. But Dracula was more attached to the sweetness of this passing world than life eternal. That is why he abandoned orthodoxy and forsook the truth; he abandoned the light and received the darkness. He could not endure the temporary sufferings of prison, and he was prepared for the eternal sufferings; he abandoned our Orthodox faith and accepted the Latin heresy. The king not only gave him the princedom of Wallachia but even gave him his own sister as a wife. From her he had two sons, he lived for another ten years, and he ended his life in this heresy. [Sources given above confirm Dracula's restoration in 1476, and his heresy in eyes of the Orthodox Church.]

16. It was said about him that even when he was in jail, he could not abandon his bad habits. He caught mice and bought birds in the market. And he tortured them in this way: some he impaled, others he cut their heads off, and others he plucked their feathers out and let them go. And he taught himself to sew, and he fed himself. [This incident is not recorded in any other known sources.]

17. When the king freed him from jail he brought him to Buda where he gave him a house located in Pest across from Buda. At a time before Dracula had seen the king, it so happened that a criminal sought refuge in Dracula's house. And those chasing the criminal came into Dracula's courtyard, began looking for him, and found the criminal. Dracula rose up, took his sword, and cut off the head of the prefect who was holding the criminal and then Dracula liberated the criminal. The other guards fled to the municipal judge and told him what had happened. The judge and his men went to the Hungarian king to complain against Dracula. The king sent a messenger to ask him: "Why have you committed this misdeed?" But Dracula answered in this way: "I did not commit a crime. He committed suicide. Anyone will perish in this way should he thievingly invade the house of a great sovereign. If this judge had come to me and had explained the situation to me, and if I had found the criminal in my own home, I myself would have delivered the criminal to him or would have pardoned him of death." When the king was told about this, he began to laugh and marvel at his courage. [Not found elsewhere.]

18. The end of Dracula came in the following way: while he was ruling Wallachia, the Turks invaded and began to conquer it. Dracula attacked the Turks and

put them to flight. Dracula's army began killing the Turks without mercy. Out of sheer joy Dracula ascended a hill in order to see better his men massacring the Turks. Thus, detached from his army and his men, some took him for a Turk, and one of them struck him with a lance. But Dracula, seeing that he was being attacked by his own men, immediately killed five of his would-be assassins with his own sword; however, he was pierced by many lances and thus he died. [That Dracula died in 1476 is certain; whether he died in the circumstances related here is not known.]

19. The king took his sister with the two sons of Dracula to Buda in Hungary. One of these sons still lives with the king's son, whereas the other who was with the bishop of Oradea has died in our presence. I saw the third son, the eldest, whose name was Mikhail, in Buda. He fled from the Turkish emperor to the king of Hungary. Dracula had him by a certain woman when he was not yet married. Stephen of Moldavia, in accord with the wish of the king, helped establish in Wallachia the prince's son called Vlad. This same Vlad was in his youth a monk, later a priest, and subsequently the abbot of a monastery. He was then defrocked and was set up as prince and married. He married the widow of a prince who ruled a little later after Dracula [Basarab III the Young, 1477–1482], and who was killed by Steven the Vlakh. He took the former's wife and now rules Wallachia—the same Vlad who pre viously had been a monk and abbot. This was first written on February 13, 1486; later, on January 28, 1490, I have transcribed [the text] a second time, I, the sinner Efrosin. [The historical references here are fairly accurate, Dracula's son here called Mikhail was also known as Mihnea. Specific mention of Vlad, "a former monk" as "the present ruler" points to Vlad the Monk (1482–1495) and supports authenticity of the date of the manuscript.]

The Literary Vampire

The Vampyre: A Tale

Edited by D.L. Macdonald and Kathleen Scherf

It happened in the midst of the dissipations attendant upon a London winter, that there appeared at the various parties of the leaders of the *ton* a nobleman, more remarkable for his singularities, than for his rank. He apparently gazed upon the mirth around him, as if he could not participate therein. It seemed as if, the light laughter of the fair only attracted his attention, that he might by a look quell it, and throw fear into those breasts where thoughtlessness reigned. Those who felt this sensation of awe, could not explain whence it arose: some attributed it to the glance of that dead grey eye, which, fixing upon the object's face, seemed not to penetrate, and at one look to pierce through to the inward workings of the heart; but to throw upon the cheek a leaden ray that weighed upon the skin it could not pass. Some however thought that it was caused by their fearing the observation of one, who by his colourless cheek, which never gained a warmer tint from the blush of conscious shame or from any powerful emotion, appeared to be above human feelings and sympathies, the fashionable names for frailties and sins. His peculiarities caused him to be invited to every house; all wished to see him, and those who had been accustomed to violent excitement, and now felt the weight of *ennui*, were pleased at having something In their presence capable of engaging their attention. Nay more in spite of the deadly hue of his finely turned head, many of the female hunters after notoriety attempted to win his attentions, and gain, at least, some marks of what they might term affection. Lady Mercer, who had been the mockery of every monster shewn in drawing-rooms since her marriage, threw herself in his way, and did all but put on the dress of a mountebank, to attract his notice?—but in vain?—when she stood before him, though his eyes were apparently fixed upon hers, still it seemed as if they were unperceived;—even her unappalled impudence was baffled, and she left the field. Yet though the common adultress could not influence even the guidance of his eyes, it was not that the sex was indifferent to him: but such was the caution with which he spoke to the virtuous wife and innocent daughter, that few knew he ever addressed himself to females. He had, however, the reputation of a winning tongue; and whether it was that this even overcame the dread of his singular character, or that they were moved by his apparent hatred of vice, he was as often among those females who adorn the sex by their domestic virtues, as among those who sully it by their vices.

About the same time, there came to London a young gentleman of the name of Aubreys: he was an orphan left with an only sister in the possession of great wealth, by parents who died whilst he was yet in childhood. Left also to himself by guardians, who thought it their duty merely to take care of his fortune, while they relinquished the more important charge of his mind to the care of mercenary and negligent sub-alterns, he cultivated more his imagination than his judgment. He had, hence, that high romantic feeling of honour and candour, which daily ruins so many milliners' apprentices. He believed all to sympathise with virtue, and thought that vice was thrown in by Providence as by authors in Romances merely for the picturesque effect of the scene: he thought that the misery of a cottage merely consisted in the vesting of clothes, which were as warm, perhaps warmer than the thin naked draperies of a drawing room, but which were more pleasing to the painter's eye by their irregular folds and various coloured patches. He thought, in fine, that the dreams of poets were the realities of life. He was handsome, frank, and rich: for these reasons, upon his entering into the gay circles, many mothers surrounded him, striving which should describe with least truth their languishing or romping favourites: many daughters at the same time, by their brightening countenances when he approached, and by their sparkling eyes, when he opened his lips, soon led him into false notions of his talents and his merit. Attached as he was to the romance of his solitary hours, he was startled at finding, that, except in the tallow and wax candles flickering not from the presence of a ghost, but from a draught of air breaking through his golden leathered doors and felted floors, there was no foundation in real life for any of that congeries of pleasing horrors and descriptions contained in the volumes, which had formed the occupation of his midnight vigils. Finding, however, some compensation in his gratified vanity, he was about to relinquish his dreams, when the extraordinary being we have above described, crossed him in his career.

He watched him; the very impossibility of forming an idea of the character of a man entirely absorbed in himself, of one who gave few other signs of his observation of external objects, than the tacit assent to their existence, implied by the avoidance of their contact: at last allowed his imagination to picture some thing that flattered its propensity to extravagant ideas. He soon formed this person into the hero of a romance, and determined to observe the offspring of his fancy, rather than the individual before him. He became acquainted with him, paid him attentions, and so far advanced upon his notice, that his presence was always acknowledged. He gradually learnt that Lord Strongmore's affairs were embarrassed, and soon found, from the notes of prepara-tion in——Street, that he was about to travel. Desirous of gaining some information respecting this singular character, who, till now, had only whetted his curiosity, he hinted to his guardians, that it was time for him to perform the grand tour, a tour which for many generations had been thought necessary to enable the young to take some important steps in the career of vice, put themselves upon an equality with the aged, and not allow them to appear as if fallen from the skies, whenever scandalous intrigues are mentioned as the subjects of pleasantry or of praise, according to the degree of skill shewn in their conduct. They consented: and Aubrey immediately mentioning his intentions to Lord Strongmore, was surprised to receive from him a proposal that they should travel together. Flattered by such a mark of esteem from him, who, apparently, had nothing in common with other men, he gladly accepted the invitation, and in a few days they had passed the circling waters.

Hitherto, Aubrey had had no opportunity of studying Lord Strongmore's character, and now he found, that, though many more of his actions were exposed to his view, the results offered different conclusions from the apparent motives to his conduct. His companion was profuse in his liberality;—the idle, the vagabond, and the beggar, received from his hand more than enough to relieve their immediate wants. But Aubrey could not avoid remarking, that it was not upon the virtuous, reduced to indigence by the misfortunes attendant even upon virtue, that he bestowed his alms. These were sent from the door with hardly suppressed sneers; but when the profligate came to ask something, not to relieve his wants, but to allow him to wallow in his lust, or to sink him still deeper in his iniquity, he was sent away with rich charity. This was, however, attributed by him to the greater importunity of the vicious, which generally prevails over the retiring bashfulness of the virtuous indigent. There was one circumstance about the charity of his Lordship, which was however still more deeply impressed upon his mind: all those upon whom it was bestowed, inevitably found that there was a curse upon it, for they were all either led to the scaffold, or sunk to the lowest and the most abject misery. At Brussels and other towns through which they passed, Aubrey was surprised at the apparent eagerness, with which his companion sought for the centres of all fashionable vice; there he entered into all the spirit of the faro table. He betted, and always gambled with success, except when the known sharper was his antagonist, and then he lost even more than he gained; but it was always with the same unchanging face, with which he generally watched the society around. It was not, however, so when he encountered the rash youthful novice, or the luckless father of a numerous family; then his very wish seemed fortune's law—his apparent abstractedness of mind was laid aside, and his eyes sparkled with vivid fire. In every town, he left the formerly affluent youth, torn from the circle he adorned, cursing, in the solitude of a dungeon, the fate that had drawn him within the reach of this fiend; whilst many a father sat frantic, amidst the speaking looks of mute hungry children, without a single florin of his late immense wealth, wherewith to buy even sufficient to satisfy their present craving. Yet he took no money from the gambling table; but immediately lost, to the ruiner of many, the last gilder he had just snatched from the convulsive grasp of the innocent. This might but be the result of a certain degree of knowledge, which was not, however, capable of combating the cunning of the more experienced. Aubrey often wished to represent this to his friend, and beg him to resign that charity and pleasure which proved the ruin of all, and did not tend to his own profit;—but he delayed it—for each day he hoped his friend would give him some opportunity of speaking frankly and openly to him; this, however, never occurred. Lord Strongmore in his carriage, and amidst the various wild and rich scenes of nature, was always the same: his eye spoke less than his lip; and though Aubrey was near the object of his curiosity, he obtained no greater gratification from it than the constant excitement of vainly wishing to break that mystery, which to his exalted imagination began to assume the appearance of something supernatural.

They soon arrived at Rome, and Aubrey for a time lost sight of his companion; he left him in daily attendance upon the morning circle of an Italian countess, whilst he went in search of the memorials of another almost deserted city. Whilst he was thus engaged, letters arrived from England, which he opened with eager impatience; the first was from his sister, breathing nothing but affection; the others were from his guardians, these astonished him; if it had before entered into his imagination, that, there was an evil power resident in his companion, these seemed to give him almost sufficient reason for the belief. His guardians insisted upon his immediately leaving his friend, and urged, that such a character was to be dreaded, for the possession of irresistible powers of seduction, rendered his licentious habits too dangerous to society. It had been discovered, that his contempt for the adultress had not originated in hatred of her character; but that he had required, to enhance his gratification, that his victim, the partner of his guilt, should be hurled from the pinnacle of unsullied virtue, down to the lowest abyss of infamy and degradation: in fine, that all those females whom he had sought, apparently on account of their virtue, had, since his departure, thrown even the mask aside, and had not scrupled to expose the whole deformity of their vices to the public view.

Aubrey determined upon leaving one, whose character had not yet shown a single bright point on which to rest the eye. He resolved to invent some plausible pretext for abandoning him altogether, purposing, in the mean while, to watch him more closely, and to let no slight circumstances pass by unnoticed. He entered into the same circle, and soon perceived, that his Lordship was endeavouring to work upon the inexperience of the daughter of the lady whose house he chiefly frequented. In Italy, it is seldom that an unmarried female is met with in society; he was therefore obliged to carry on his plans in secret; but Aubrey's eye followed him in all his windings, and soon discovered that an assignation had been made, which would most likely end in the rain of an innocent, though thoughtless girl. Losing no time, he entered the apartment of Lord Strongmore, and abruptly asked him his intentions with respect to the lady, informing him at the same time that he was aware of his being about to meet her that very night. Lord Strongmore answered, that his intentions were such as he supposed all would have upon such an occasion; and upon being pressed whether he intended to marry her, merely laughed. Aubrey retired; and, immediately writing a note, to say, that from that moment he must decline accompanying his Lordship in the remainder of their purposed tour, he ordered his servant to seek other apartments, and calling upon the mother of the lady, informed her of all he knew, not only with regard to her daughter, but also with regard to the character of his Lordship. The meeting was prevented. Lord Strongmore next day merely sent his servant to notify his complete assent to a separation; but did not hint any suspicion of his plans having been foiled by Aubrey's interposition.

Having left Rome, Aubrey directed his steps towards Greece, and crossing the Peninsula, soon found himself at Athens. He there fixed his residence in the house of a Greek; and was soon occupied in tracing the faded records of ancient glory upon monuments that apparently, ashamed of chronicling the deeds of freemen only before slaves, had hidden themselves beneath the sheltering soil or many coloured lichen. Under the same roof as himself, existed a being, so beautiful and delicate, that she might have formed the model for a painter wishing to portray on canvass the promised hope of the faithful in Mahomet's paradise, save that her eyes spoke too much mind for any one to think she could belong to those beings who had no souls. As she danced upon the plain, or tripped along the mountain's side, one would have thought the gazelle a poor type of her beauties, for who would have exchanged her eye, apparently the eye of animated nature, for that sleepy luxurious look of the animal suited but to the taste of an epicure. The light step of Ianthe often accompanied Aubrey in his search after antiquities, and often would the unconscious girl, engaged in the pursuit of a Kashmere butterfly, show the whole beauty of her form, floating as it were upon the wind, to the eager gaze of him, who forgot, in the contemplation of her sylph-like figure, the letters he had just decyphered upon an almost effaced tablet. Often would her tresses falling, as she flitted around, exhibit in the sun's ray such delicately brilliant and swiftly fading hues, as might well excuse the forgetfulness of the antiquary, who let escape from his mind the very object he had before thought of vital importance to the proper interpretation of a passage in Pausanias. But why attempt to describe charms which all feel, but none can appreciate?—It was innocence, youth, and beauty, unaffected by crowded drawing-rooms and stifling balls. Whilst he drew those remains of which he wished to preserve a memorial for his future hours, she would stand by, and watch the magic effects of his pencil, in tracing the scenes of her native place; she would then describe to him the circling dance upon the open plain, would paint to him in all the glowing colours of youthful memory, the marriage pomp she remembered viewing in her infancy; and then, turning to subjects that had evidently made a greater impression upon her mind, would tell him all the supernatural tales of her nurse. Her earnestness and apparent belief of what she narrated, excited the interest even of Aubrey; and often as she told him the tale of the living vampyre, who had passed years amidst his friends, and dearest ties, forced every year, by feeding upon the life of a lovely female to prolong his existence for the ensuing months, his blood would run cold, whilst he attempted to laugh her out of such idle and horrible fantasies. But Ianthe cited to him the names of old men, who had at last detected one living among themselves, after several of their near relatives and children had been found marked with the stamp of the fiend's appetite. When she found him incredulous, she begged of him to believe her, for it had been remarked, that those who had dared to question their existence, always had some proof given, which obliged them, with grief and heartbreaking, to confess its truth. She detailed to him the traditional appearance of these monsters, and his horror was increased, upon hearing a pretty accurate description of Lord Strongmore. He, however, still persisted in persuading her, that there could be no truth in her fears, though at the same time he wondered at the many coincidences which had all tended to excite a belief in the supernatural power of Lord Strongmore.

Aubrey began to attach himself more and more to Ianthe; her innocence, so contrasted with all the affected virtues of the women amongst whom he had sought for his vision, of romance, won his heart; and while he ridiculed the idea of a young man of English habits, marrying an uneducated Greek girl, still he found himself more and more attached to the almost fairy form before him. He would tear himself at times from her, and, forming a plan for some antiquarian research, he would depart, determined not to return until his object was attained; but he always found it impossible to fix his attention upon the ruins around him, whilst in his mind he retained an image that seemed alone the rightful possessor of his thoughts. Ianthe was unconscious of his love, and was ever the same frank infantile being he had first known. She always seemed to part from him with reluctance; but it was because she had no longer any one with whom she could visit her favourite haunts, to whom she could point out the beauties of the spots so dear to her infantile memory, whilst he was occupied in sketching or uncovering some fragment which had yet escaped the destructive hand of time. She had appealed to her parents on the subject of Vampyres, and they both, with several present, affirmed their existence, pale with horror at the very name. Soon after, Aubrey determined to proceed upon one of his excursions, which was to detain him for a few hours; when his hosts heard the name of the place, they all at once begged of him not to return at night, as he must necessarily pass through a wood, where no Greek would ever remain, after the day had closed, upon any consideration. They described it as the resort of the vampyres in their nocturnal orgies, and denounced the most heavy evils as impending upon him who dared to cross their path, Aubrey made light of their representations, and tried to laugh them out of the idea; but when he saw them shudder at his daring thus to mock a superior, infernal power, the very name of which apparently made their blood freeze, he was silent.

Next morning Aubrey set off upon his excursion unattended; he was surprised to observe the melancholy face of his host, and was concerned to find that his words, mocking the belief of these horrible fiends, had inspired them with such terror. When he was about to depart, Ianthe came to the side of his horse, and earnestly begged of him to return, ere night allowed the power of these beings to be put in action;—he promised. He was, however, so occupied in his research that he did not perceive that day-light would soon end, and that in the horizon there was one of those specks which, in the warmer climates, so rapidly gather into a tremendous mass, and pour all their rage upon the devoted country.—He at last, however, mounted his horse, determined to make up by speed for his delay: but it was too late. Twilight, in these southern climates, is almost unknown; immediately the sun sets, night begins: and ere he had advanced far, the power of the storm was above—its echoing thunders had scarcely an interval of rest—its thick heavy rain forced its way through the canopying foliage, whilst the blue forked lightning seemed to fall and radiate at his very feet. Suddenly his horse took fright, and he was carried with dreadful rapidity through the entangled forest. The animal at last, through fatigue, fell, and he found, by the glare of lightning, that he was in the neighbourhood of a hovel which hardly lifted itself up from the masses of dead leaves and brushwood surrounding it. Dismounting, he approached, hoping to find some one to guide him to the town, or at least trusting to obtain shelter from the pelting of the storm When near the door, the thunders, for a moment silent, allowed him to hear the dreadful shrieks of a woman mingling with the stifled, exultant mockery of a laugh, continued in one almost unbroken sound;—he was startled: but, roused by the thunder which again rolled over his head, he, with a sudden effort, forced open the door of the hut. He found himself in utter darkness: the sound, however, guided him. He was apparently unperceived; for, though he called, still the sounds continued, and no notice was taken of him. He found himself in contact with some one, whom he immediately seized; when a voice cried, 'Again baffled!' to which a loud laugh succeeded; and he felt himself grappled by one whose strength seemed superhuman: determined to sell his life as dearly as he could, he straggled; but it was in vain: he was lifted from his feet and hurled with enormous force against the ground.—His enemy threw himself upon him, and kneeling upon his breast, had placed his hands upon his throat—when the glare of many torches penetrating through the hole that gave light in the day, disturbed him.—He instantly rose, leaving his prey, he rushed through the door, and in a moment the crashing of the branches, as he broke through the wood, was no longer heard. The storm was now still; and Aubrey, incapable of moving, was soon heard by those without. They entered; the light of their torches fell upon nothing but the mud walls, and the thatch loaded on every individual straw with heavy flakes of soot, though at this moment it was apparently untenanted. There was one spot slippery with blood but it was hardly visible on the black floor. No other trace was seen of human presence having disturbed its solitude for many years. At the desire of Aubrey they searched for her who had attracted him by her cries; he was again left in darkness; but what was his horror, when the light of the torches once more burst upon him, to perceive the airy form of his fair conductress brought in a lifeless corpse. He shut his eyes, hoping that it was but a vision arising from his disturbed imagination; but he again saw the same form, when he unclosed them, stretched by his side. There was no colour upon her cheek, not even upon her lip; yet there was a stillness about her face that seemed almost as attaching as the life that once dwelt there:—upon her neck and breast was blood, and upon her throat were the marks of teeth having opened the vein of the neck:—to this the men pointed, crying, simultaneously struck with horror, 'A Vampyre! a Vampyre!'

A litter was quickly formed, and Aubrey was laid by the side of her who had lately been to him the object of so many bright and fairy visions, now fallen with the flower of life that had died within her. He knew not what his thoughts were—his mind was benumbed and seemed to shun reflection, and take refuge in vacancy—he held almost unconsciously in his hand a naked dagger of a particular construction, which had been found in the hut. They were soon met by different parties who had been engaged in the search of her whom a mother had missed. Their lamentable cries, as they approached the city, forewarned the parents of some dreadful catastrophe.—To describe their grief would be impossible; but when they ascertained the cause of their child's death, they looked at Aubrey, and pointed to the corpse. They were inconsolable; both died broken-hearted.

Aubrey being put to bed was seized with a most violent fever, and was often delirious; in these intervals he would call upon Lord Strongmore and upon Ianthe—by some unaccountable combination he seemed to beg of his former companion to spare the being he loved. At other times he would imprecate maledictions upon his head, and curse him as her destroyer. Lord Strongmore chanced at this time to arrive at Athens, and, from whatever motive, upon hearing of the state of Aubrey, immediately placed himself in the same house, and became his constant attendant. When the latter recovered from his delirium, he was horrified and startled at the sight of him whose image he had now combined with that of a Vampyre; but Lord Strongmore, by his kind words, implying almost repentance for the fault that had caused their separation, and still more by the attention, anxiety, and care which he showed, soon reconciled him to his presence. His Lordship seemed quite changed; he no longer appeared that apathetic being who had so astonished Aubrey; but as soon as his convalescence began to be rapid, he again gradually retired into the same state of mind, and Aubrey perceived no difference from the former man, except that at times he was surprised to meet his gaze fixed intently upon him, with a smile of malicious exultation playing upon his lips: he knew not why, but this smile haunted him. During the last stage of the invalid's recovery, Lord Strongmore was apparently engaged in watching the tideless waves raised by the cooling breeze, or in marking the progress of those orbs, circling, like our world, the moveless sun; - indeed, he appeared to wish to avoid the eyes of all.

Aubrey's mind, by this shock, was much weakened, and that elasticity of spirit which had once so distinguished him now seemed to have fled for ever. He was now as much a lover of solitude and silence as Lord Strongmore; but much as he wished for solitude, his mind could not find it in the neighbourhood of Athens; if he sought it amidst the ruins he had formerly frequented, Ianthe's form stood by his side—if he sought it in the woods, her light step would sound wandering amidst the underwood, in quest of the modest violet; and often she would suddenly turning round, show, to his wild imagination, her pale face and wounded throat, while a meek smile played upon her lips. He determined to fly scenes, every feature of which created such bitter associations in his mind. He proposed to Lord Strongmore, to whom he held himself bound by the tender care he had taken of him during his illness, that they should visit those parts of Greece neither had yet seen. They travelled in every direction, and sought every spot to which a recollection could be attached: but though they thus hastened from place to place, yet they seemed not to heed what they gazed upon. They heard much of robbers, but they gradually began to slight these reports, which they imagined were only the invention of individuals, whose interest it was to excite the generosity of those, whom they defended from pretended dangers. In consequence of thus neglecting the advice of the inhabitants, they travelled on one occasion with only a few guards, more to serve as guides than as a defence. Upon entering, however, a narrow defile, at the bottom of which was the bed of a torrent, with large masses of rock brought down from the neighbouring precipices, they had reason to repent their negligence; for scarcely were the whole of the party engaged in the narrow pass, when they were startled by the echoed report of several guns, and by the whistling of bullets close to their heads. In an instant their guards had left them, and, placing themselves behind rocks, had begun to fire in the direction whence the report came. Lord Strongmore and Aubrey, imitating their example, retired for a moment behind the sheltering turn of the defile: but ashamed of being thus detained by a foe, who with insulting shouts bade them advance, and being exposed to unresisting slaughter, if any of the robbers should climb above and take them in the rear, they determined at once to rush forward in search of the enemy. Hardly had they lost the shelter of the rock, when Lord Strongmore received a shot in the shoulder, which brought him to the ground. Aubrey hastened to his assistance; and, no longer heeding the contest or his own peril, was soon surprised by seeing the robbers' faces around him—his guards having, upon Lord Strongmore's being wounded, immediately thrown up their arms and surrendered.

By promises of great reward, Aubrey soon induced them to convey his wounded friend to a neighbouring cabin; and having agreed upon a ransom, he was no more disturbed by their presence—they being content merely to guard the entrance until their comrade should return with the promised sum, for which he had an order. Lord Strongmore's strength rapidly decreased; in two days mortification ensued, and death seemed advancing with hasty steps. His conduct and appearance had not changed; he seemed as unconscious of pain as he had been of the objects about him: but towards the close of the last evening, his mind became apparently uneasy, and his eye often fixed upon Aubrey, who was induced to offer his assistance with more than usual earnestness—'Assist me! you may save me—you may do more than that—I mean not my life, I heed the death of my existence as little as that of the passing day; but you may save my honour, your friend's honour.'—'How? tell me how? I would do any thing,' replied Aubrey.—'I need but little—my life ebbs apace—I cannot explain the whole—but if you would conceal all you know of me, my honour were free from stain in the world's mouth—and if my death were unknown for some time in England—I—I—but life.'—'It shall not be known.'—'Swear!' cried the dying man, raising himself with exultant violence, 'Swear by all your soul reveres, by all your nature dreads, swear that for a year and a day you will not impart your knowledge of my crimes or death to any living being, in any way, whatever may happen, or whatever you may see.'—His eyes seemed bursting from their sockets: 'I swear!' said Aubrey; he sunk laughing upon his pillow, and breathed no more.

Aubrey retired to rest, but did not sleep; the many circumstances attending his acquaintance with this man arose upon his mind, and, he knew not why, when he remembered his oath a cold shivering came over him, as if from the presentiment of something horrible awaiting him. Rising early in the morning, he was about to enter the hovel, in which he had left the corpse, when a robber met him, and informed him that it was no longer there, having been conveyed by himself and comrades, upon his retiring, to the pinnacle of a neighbouring mount, according to a promise they had given his Lordship, that it should be exposed to the first cold ray of the moon that rose after his death, Aubrey was astonished, but taking several of the men, he determined to go and bury it upon the spot where it lay. When however he reached the summit he found no trace of the corpse, nor could he discover any remnant of the clothes, though the robbers assured him that they pointed out the identical rock on which they had laid the body. For a time his mind was bewildered in conjectures, but he at last returned, convinced that they had secretly buried his friend's remains for the sake of the dress in which he died.

Weary of a country in which he had met with such terrible misfortunes, and in which all apparently conspired to heighten that superstitious melancholy which had seized upon his mind, he resolved to leave it, and he soon arrived at Smyrna. While waiting for a vessel to convey him to Otranto, or to Naples, he occupied himself in arranging those effects he had with him belonging to Lord Strongmore. Amongst other things there was a case containing several weapons of offence, more or less adapted to ensure the death of the victim. There were several daggers and ataghans. Whilst turning these over, and examining their curious forms, what was his surprise at finding a sheath apparently ornamented in the same style as the dagger discovered in the fatal hut—he shuddered—hastening to gain further proof, he found the weapon, and his horror may be imagined, when he discovered that it fitted, though peculiarly shaped, the sheath he held in his hand. His eyes seemed to need no further certainty—they seemed gazing to be bound to the dagger; yet still he wished not to believe his sight; but the particular form, the varying tints upon the haft and sheath were alike, and left no room for doubt; there were also drops of blood on each.

He left Smyrna, and on his way home, at Rome, he inquired concerning the lady he had attempted to snatch from Lord Strongmore's seductive arts. Her parents were in distress, their fortune ruined, and she had not been heard of since the departure of his Lordship. Aubrey's mind became almost broken under so many repeated horrors; he was afraid that this lady had fallen a victim to the destroyer of Ianthe. He became morose and silent; and his only thought seemed to be how to urge the speed of the postilions, as if he were hastening to save the life of some one he held dean. He arrived at Calais; a breeze, which seemed obedient to his will, soon wafted him to the English shores. He hastened to the mansion of his fathers, and there, for a moment, he appeared to lose, in the embraces and caresses of his sister, all memory of the past. If she before, by her infantine caresses, had gained his affection, now that the woman began to appear, she was still more attaching as a companion.

Miss Aubrey had not that winning grace which gains the gaze and applause of the drawing-room assemblies. There was none of that ephemeral brilliancy which can only exist in the heated atmosphere of a crowded apartment. Her blue eye was never lit up by the levity of the mind beneath. There was a melancholy charm about it which did not seem to arise from misfortune, but from some feeling within, that appeared to indicate a soul conscious of a brighter realm. Her step was not that light footing, which strays where'er a butterfly or a colour may attract—it was sedate and pensive. When alone, her face was never brightened by the smile of joy; but when her brother breathed to her his affection, and would in her presence forget those griefs she knew destroyed his rest, who would have exchanged her smile for that of the voluptuary? It seemed as if those eyes,—that face were then playing in the light of their own native sphere. She was yet only eighteen, and had not yet been presented to the world, her guardians having thought proper to delay her presentation at court until her brother's return from the continent, when he might be her protector. It was now, therefore, resolved that the next drawing-room, which was fast approaching, should be the epoch of her entry into the 'busy scene,' Aubrey would rather have remained in the mansion of his fathers, to feed upon the melancholy which overpowered him. He could not feel interest about the frivolities of fashionable strangers, when his mind had been so torn by the events he had witnessed; but he determined to sacrifice his own comfort to the protection of his sister. They therefore soon arrived in town, and prepared for the day, which had been announced as the one on which a drawing-room was to be held.

The crowd was excessive—a drawing-room had not been held for a long time, and all who were anxious to bask in the smile of royalty, hastened thither. Aubrey was there with his sister. While he was standing in a corner by himself, heedless of all around him, engaged in the recollection that the first time he had seen Lord Strongmore was in this very place—he felt himself suddenly seized by the arm, and a voice he recognized too well, sounded in his ear—'Remember your oath,' He had hardly courage to turn, fearful of seeing a spectre, that would blast him, when he perceived, at a little distance, the same figure which had attracted his notice on this spot upon his first entry into society. He gazed till his limbs almost refusing to bear their weight, he was obliged to take the arm of a friend, and forcing a passage through the crowd, to throw himself into his carriage, and be driven home. He paced the room with hurried steps, and fixed his hands upon his head, as if he were afraid his thoughts were bursting from his brain. Lord Strongmore again before him—circumstances started up in dreadful array—the dagger—his oath.—He roused himself, he could not believe it possible—the dead rise again!—He thought his imagination had conjured up the image his mind was resting upon. It was impossible that it could be real—he determined, therefore, to go again into society; for though he attempted to ask concerning Lord Strongmore, the name hung upon his lips, and he could not succeed in gaining information. He went a few nights after with his sister to the assembly of a near relation. Leaving her under the protection of a matron, he retired into a recess, and there gave himself up to his own devouring thoughts. Perceiving, at last, that many were retiring, he roused himself, and entering another room, found his sister surrounded by several gentlemen, apparently in earnest conversation; he attempted to pass and get near her, when one, whom he requested to move, turned round, and revealed to him those features he most abhorred. He sprang forward, seized his sister's arm, and, with a hurried step, forced her towards the street: at the door he found himself impeded by the crowd of servants, who were waiting for their lords; and while he was engaged in passing them, he again heard that voice whisper close to him—'Remember your oath!'—He did not dare to turn, but, hurrying his sister, he soon reached home.

Aubrey became almost distracted. If before his mind had been absorbed by one subject, how much more completely was it engrossed now, that the certainty of the monster's living again pressed upon his thoughts. His sister's attentions were now unheeded, and it was in vain that she intreated him to explain to her what had caused his abrupt conduct. He only uttered a few words, and those terrified her. The more he thought, the more he was bewildered. His oath startled him;—was he then to allow this monster to roam, bearing rain upon his breath, amidst all he held dear, and not avert its progress? His very sister might have been touched by him. But even if he were to break his oath, and disclose his suspicions, who would believe him? He thought of employing his own hand to free the world from such a wretch; but death, he remembered, had been already mocked. For days he remained in this state; shut up in his room, he saw no one, and eat only when his sister came, who, her eyes streaming with tears, besought him, for her sake, to support nature. At last, no longer capable of bearing stillness and solitude, he left his house, roamed from street to street, anxious to fly that image which haunted him. His dress became neglected, and he wandered, as often exposed to the noon-day sun as to the mid-night damps. He was no longer to be recognized; at first he returned with the evening to his home; but at last he laid him down to rest wherever fatigue overtook him. His sister, anxious for his safety, employed people to follow him; but they were soon distanced by him, who fled from a pursuer swifter than any—from thought. His conduct, however, suddenly changed. Struck with the idea that he left by his absence the whole of his friends, with a fiend amongst them, of whose presence they were unconscious, he determined to enter again into society, and watch him closely, anxious to forewarn, in spite of his oath, all whom Lord Strongmore should approach with intimacy. But when he entered into a room, his haggard and suspicious looks were so striking, his inward shudderings so visible, that his sister was at last obliged to beg of him to abstain from seeking, for her sake, a society, which affected him so strongly. When, however, remonstrance proved unavailing, the guardians thought proper to interpose, and, fearing that his mind was becoming alienated, they thought it high time to resume again that trust, which had been before imposed upon them by Aubrey's parents.

Desirous of saving him from the injuries and sufferings he had daily encountered in his wanderings, and of preventing him from exposing to the general eye those marks of what they considered folly, they engaged a physician to reside in the house, and take constant care of him. He hardly appeared to notice it, so completely was his mind absorbed by one terrible subject. His incoherence became at last so great, that he was confined to his chamber. There he would often lie for days, incapable of being roused. He had become emaciated, his eyes had attained a glassy lustre;—the only sign of affection and recollection remaining displayed itself upon the entry of his sister; then he would sometimes start, and, seizing her hands, with looks that severely afflicted her, he would desire her not to touch him. 'Oh, do not touch him—if your love for me is aught, do not go near him!' When, however, she inquired to whom he referred, his only answer was; 'True! true!' and again he sank into a state, whence not even she could rouse him. This lasted many months: gradually, however, as the year was passing, his incoherences became less frequent, and his mind threw off a portion of its gloom, whilst his guardians observed, that several times in the day he would count upon his fingers a definite number, and then smile.

The time had nearly elapsed, when, upon the last day of the year, one of his guardians entering his room, began to converse with his physician upon the melancholy circumstance of Aubrey's being in so awful a situation, when his sister was going next day to be married. Instantly Aubrey's attention was attracted; he asked anxiously to whom. Glad of this mark of returning intellect, of which they feared he had been deprived, they mentioned the name of the Earl of Marsden. Thinking this was a young Earl whom he had met with in society, Aubrey seemed pleased, and astonished them still more by expressing his intention to be present at the nuptials, and by desiring to see his sister. They answered not, but in a few minutes his sister was with him. He was apparently again capable of being affected by the influence of her lovely smile; for he pressed her to his breast, and kissed her cheek, wet with tears, flowing at the thought of her brother's being once more alive to the feelings of affection. He began to speak with all his wonted warmth, and to congratulate her upon her marriage with a person so distinguished for rank and every accomplishment; but he suddenly perceived a locket upon her breast; having opened it, what was his surprise at beholding the features of the monster who had so long influenced his life. He seized the portrait in a paroxysm of rage, and trampled it under foot. Upon her asking him, why he thus destroyed the resemblance of her future husband, he looked as if he did not understand her—then seizing her hands, and gazing on her with a frantic expression of countenance, he bade her swear that she would never wed this monster, for he—But he could not continue—it seemed as if that voice again bade him remember his oath—he turned suddenly round, thinking Lord Strongmore was near him but he saw no one. In the meantime the guardians and physician, who had heard the whole, and thought this was but a return of his disorder, entered, and forcing him from Miss Aubrey, desired her to leave him. He fell upon his knees to them, he implored, he begged of them to delay but for one day. They, attributing this to the insanity, they imagined had taken possession of his mind, endeavoured to pacify him, and retired.

Lord Strongmore had called the morning after the drawing-room, and had been refused with every one else. When he heard of Aubrey's ill health, he readily under-stood himself to be the cause of it; but, when he learned that he was deemed insane, his exultation and pleasure could hardly be concealed from those, among whom he had gained this information. He hastened to the house of his former companion, and, by constant attendance, and the pretence of great affection for her brother and interest in his fate, he gradually won the ear of Miss Aubrey. Who could resist his power? His tongue had dangers and toils to recount—could speak of himself as of an individual having no sympathy with any being on the crowded earth, save with her, to whom he addressed himself;—could tell how, since he knew her, his existence had begun to seem worthy of preservation, if it were merely that he might listen to her soothing accents.—In fine, he knew so well how to use the serpent's art, or such was the will of fate, that he gained her affections. The title of the elder branch falling at length to him, he obtained an important embassy, which served as an excuse (in spite of her brother's deranged state,) for hastening the marriage, which was to take place the very day before his departure for the continent.

Aubrey, when he was left by the physician and his guardians, attempted to bribe the servants, but in vain. He asked for pen and paper; it was given him; he wrote a letter to his sister, conjuring her, as she valued her own happiness, her own honour, and the honour of those now in the grave, who once held her in their arms as their hope and the hope of their house, to delay but for a few hours that marriage, on which he denounced the most heavy curses. The servants promised they would deliver it; but giving it to the physician, he thought it better not to harass any more the mind of Miss Aubrey by, what he considered, the ravings of a maniac. Night passed on without rest to the busy inmates of the house; and Aubrey heard, with a horror that may more easily be conceived than described, the notes of busy preparation. Morning came, and the sound of carriages broke upon his ear, Aubrey grew almost frantic. The curiosity of the servants at last overcame their vigilance, they gradually stole away, leaving him in the custody of an helpless old woman. He seized the opportunity, with one bound was out of the room, and in a moment found himself in the apartment where all were nearly assembled. Lord Strongmore was the first to perceive him: he immediately approached, and, taking his arm by force, hurried him from the room, speechless with rage. When on the staircase, Lord Strongmore whispered in his ear—'Remember your oath, and know, if not my bride to day, your sister is dishonoured. Women are frail!' So saying, he pushed him towards his attendants, who, roused by the old woman, had come in search of him. Aubrey could no longer support himself; his rage not finding vent, had broken a blood-vessel, and he was conveyed to bed. This was not mentioned to his sister, who was not present when he entered, as the physician was afraid of agitating her. The marriage was solemnized, and the bride and bridegroom left London.

Aubrey's weakness increased; the effusion of blood produced symptoms of the near approach of death. He desired his sister's guardians might be called, and, when the midnight hour had struck, he related composedly the substance of what the reader has perused—and died immediately after.

The guardians hastened to protect Miss Aubrey; but when they arrived, it was too late. Lord Strongmore had disappeared, and Aubrey's sister had glutted the thirst of a VAMPYRE!

The Essential Dracula

By Bram Stoker

JONATHAN HARKER'S JOURNAL—*continued.*

5 May.—I must have been asleep, for certainly if I had been fully awake I must have noticed the approach to such a remarkable place. In the gloom the courtyard looked of considerable size, and as several dark ways led from it under great round arches it perhaps seemed bigger than it really is. I have not yet been able to see it by daylight.

When the calèche stopped the driver jumped down, and held out his hand to assist me to alight. Again I could not but notice his prodigious strength. His hand actually seemed like a steel vice that could have crushed mine if he had chosen. Then he took out my traps,[1] and placed them on the ground beside me as I stood close to a great door, old and studded with large iron nails, and set in a projecting doorway of massive stone. I could see even in the dim light that the stone was massively carved, but that the carving had been much worn by time and weather. As I stood, the driver jumped again into his seat and shook the reins; the horses started forward, and trap and all disappeared down one of the dark openings.

I stood in silence where I was, for I did not know what to do. Of bell or knocker there was no sign; through these frowning walls and dark window openings it was not likely that my voice could penetrate. The time I waited seemed endless, and I felt doubts and fears crowding upon me. What sort of place had I come to, and among what kind of people? What sort of grim adventure was it on which I had embarked? Was this a customary incident in the life of a solicitor's clerk sent out to explain the purchase of a London estate to a foreigner? Solicitor's clerk! Mina would not like that. Solicitor,[2]—for just before leaving London I got word that my examination was successful; and I am now a full-blown solicitor! I began to rub my eyes and pinch myself to see if I were awake. It all seemed like a horrible nightmare to me, and I expected that I should suddenly awake, and find myself at home, with the dawn struggling in through the windows, as I had now and again felt in the morning after a day of overwork. But my flesh answered the pinching test, and my eyes were not to be deceived. I was indeed awake and among the Carpathians. All I could do now was to be patient, and to wait the coming of the morning.

Just as I had come to this conclusion I heard a heavy step approaching behind the great door, and saw through the chinks the gleam of a coming light. Then there was the sound of rattling chains and the clanking of massive bolts drawn back. A key was turned with the loud grating noise of long disuse, and the great door swung back.

Within, stood a tall old man,[3] clean shaven save for a long white moustache, and clad in black from head to foot, without a single speck of colour about him anywhere. He held in his hand an antique silver lamp, in which the flame burned without chimney or globe of any kind, throwing long quivering shadows as it flickered in the draught of the open door. The old man motioned me in with his right hand with a courtly gesture, saying in excellent English, but with a strange intonation:—

"Welcome to my house! Enter freely and of your own will!" He made no motion of stepping to meet me, but stood like a statue, as though his gesture of welcome had fixed him into stone. The instant, however, that I had stepped over the threshold, he moved impulsively forward, and holding out his hand grasped mine with a strength which made me wince, an effect which was not lessened by the fact that it seemed as cold as ice—more like the hand of a dead than a living man. Again he said:—

"Welcome to my house. Come freely. Go safely; and leave something of the happiness you bring!"[5] The strength of the handshake was so much akin to that which I had noticed in the driver, whose face I had not seen, that for a moment I doubted if it were not the same person to whom I was speaking; so to make sure, I said interrogatively:—

"Count Dracula?" He bowed in a courtly way as he replied:—

"I am Dracula; and I bid you welcome, Mr. Harker, to my house. Come in; the night air is chill, and you must need to eat and rest." As he was speaking, he put the lamp on a bracket on the wall, and stepping out, took my luggage; he had carried it in before I could forestall him. I protested but he insisted:—

"Nay, sir, you are my guest. It is late, and my people are not available. Let me see to your comfort myself." He insisted on carrying my traps along the passage, and then up a great winding stair, and along another great passage, on whose stone floor our steps rang heavily. At the end of this he threw open a heavy door, and I rejoiced to see within a well-lit room in which a table was spread for supper, and on whose mighty hearth a great fire of logs, flamed and flared.

The Count halted, putting down my bags, closed the door, and crossing the room, opened another door, which led into a small octagonal room lit by a single lamp, and seemingly without a window of any sort. Passing through this, he opened another door, and motioned me to enter. It was a welcome sight; for here was a great bedroom well lighted and warmed with another log fire, which sent a hollow roar up the wide chimney. The Count himself left my luggage inside and withdrew, saying, before he closed the door:—

"You will need, after your journey, to refresh yourself by making your toilet. I trust you will find all you wish. When you are ready come into the other room, where you will find your supper prepared."

The light and warmth and the Count's courteous welcome seemed to have dissipated all my doubts and fears. Having then reached my normal state, I discovered that I was half famished with hunger; so making a hasty toilet, I went into the other room.

I found supper already laid out. My host, who stood on one side of the great fireplace, leaning against the stonework, made a graceful wave of his hand to the table, and said:—

"I pray you, be seated and sup how you please. You will, I trust, excuse me that I do not join you; but I have dined already, and I do not sup."[6]

I handed to him the sealed letter which Mr. Hawkins had entrusted to me. He opened it and read it gravely; then, with a charming smile, he handed it to me to read. One passage of it, at least, gave me a thrill of pleasure:

"I must regret that an attack of gout, from which malady I am a constant sufferer, forbids absolutely any travelling on my part for some time to come; but I am happy to say I can send a sufficient substitute, one in whom I have every possible confidence. He is a young man, full of energy and talent in his own way, and of a very faithful disposition. He is discreet and silent, and has grown into manhood in my service. He shall be ready to attend on you when you will during his stay, and shall take your instructions in all matters."

The Count himself came forward and took off the cover of a dish, and I fell to at once on an excellent roast chicken. This, with some cheese and a salad and a bottle of old Tokay, of which I had two glasses, was my supper. During the time I was eating it the Count asked me many questions as to my journey, and I told him by degrees all I had experienced.

By this time I had finished my supper, and by my host's desire had drawn up a chair by the fire and begun to smoke a cigar which he offered me, at the same time excusing himself that he did not smoke. I had now an opportunity of observing him, and found him of a very marked physiognomy.

His face was a strong—a very strong—aquiline, with high bridge of the thin nose and peculiarly arched nostrils; with lofty domed forehead, and hair growing scantily round the temples, but profusely elsewhere. His eyebrows were very massive, almost meeting over the nose, and with bushy hair that seemed to curl in its own profusion. The mouth, so far as I could see it under the heavy moustache, was fixed and rather cruel-looking, with peculiarly sharp white teeth; these protruded over the lips, whose remarkable ruddiness showed astonishing vitality in a man of his years. For the rest, his ears were pale and at the tops extremely pointed; the chin was broad and strong, and the cheeks firm though thin. The general effect was one of extraordinary pallor.

Hitherto I had noticed the backs of his hands as they lay on his knees in the firelight, and they had seemed rather white and fine; but seeing them now close to me, I could not but notice that they were rather coarse—broad, with squat fingers. Strange to say, there were hairs in the centre of the palm.[7] The nails were long and fine, and cut to a sharp point. As the Count leaned over me and his hands touched me, I could not repress a shudder. It may have been that his breath was rank, but a horrible feeling of nausea came over me, which, do what I would, I could not conceal. The Count, evidently noticing it, drew back; and with a grim sort of smile, which showed more than he had yet done his protuberant teeth, sat himself down again on his own side of the fireplace. We were both silent for a while; and as I looked towards the window I saw the first dim streak of the coming dawn. There seemed a strange stillness over everything; but as I listened I heard as if from down below in the valley the howling of many wolves. The Count's eyes gleamed, and he said:—

"Listen to them—the children of the night. What music they make!"[8] Seeing, I suppose, some expression in my face strange to him, he added:—

"Ah, sir, you dwellers in the city cannot enter into the feelings of the hunter." Then he rose and said:—

"But you must be tired. Your bedroom is all ready, and to-morrow you shall sleep as late as you will. I have to be away till the afternoon; so sleep well and dream well!" and, with a courteous bow, he opened for me himself the door to the octagonal room, and I entered my bedroom. …

I am all in a sea of wonders. I doubt; I fear; I think strange things, which I dare not confess to my own soul. God keep me, if only for the sake of those dear to me!

NOTES

1. My luggage. My bags.
2. In British legal practice there are two kinds of lawyers. The solicitor prepares cases for the barrister to try, and usually appears, if at all, only in the lower courts. The barrister may plead in any court.
3. Dracula is clean-shaven; the "coachman" had a brown beard. Stoker's portrait is an amalgam of Polidori's Lord Ruthven in *The Vampyre*, Prest's *Varney the Vampyre* and an anonymous author's *The Mysterious Stranger*.

   That Dracula is an old man at the beginning of the story has been persistently forgotten in all but one of the many film versions of the tale.

   For his description of Dracula Stoker has added folklore material regarding the appearance of vampires. The traditional elements are summarized both in Montague Summers's *The Vampire: His Kith and Kin* and in Ornella Volta's *The Vampire*. Summers writes (p. 179):

   "A Vampire is generally described as being exceedingly gaunt and lean with a hideous countenance and eyes wherein are glinting the red fire of perdition.

When, however, he has satiated his lust for warm human blood his body becomes horribly puffed and bloated, as though he were some great leech gorged and replete to bursting. Cold as ice, or it may be fevered and burning as a hot coal, the skin is deathly pale, but the lips are very full and rich, blub and red; the teeth white and gleaming, and the canine teeth, wherewith he bites deep into the neck of his prey to suck thence the vital streams which re-animate his body and invigorate all his forces, appear notably sharp and pointed."

And Volta's composite portrait (p. 145) is no more enticing:

"Vampires differ according to regions in which they are found ... but they all have certain characteristics in common such as an emaciated face, with a phosphorescent pallor. ... The vampire has many thick hairs on his body which are often reddish in colour, and often has hair in the palms of his hands ... and blue eyes. ... The vampire also has swollen, sensual lips covering sharp canine teeth ... Vampires also have extremely long finger nails, pointed ears like bats, foetid breath, and move jerkily, showing a tendency to suffer from epilepsy. Their bite has anaesthetizing powers."

One should take both of these descriptions with some caution. Volta and Summers occasionally use Stoker as their source for folklore. The "hair in the palms," for example, cited by Volta, is found, as far as I can tell, only in Dracula.

It is likely, too, that Stoker had read an anonymous German tale called (in nglish) *The Mysterious Stranger* (1860). The structural parallels between *Dracula* and the German tale are remarkable. There is no question of plagiarism. At the same time sheer coincidence isn't enough to account for the similarity of moments in the two stories. Perhaps "inspired borrowing" is one way to describe what happened.

4. This is an interesting moment. Stoker is making use of the tradition that the Devil can only do his business with willing clients. In Coleridge's "Cristabel" the monstrous Lady Geraldine must be invited into Cristabel's ancestral home. In Goethe's *Faust* Mephistopheles in the guise of a poodle is called by Faust to him and later is introduced into the scholar's home. See, too, *The Mysterious Stranger:*

"You wish it?—You press the invitation?" asked the stranger earnestly and decidedly.

"To be sure, for otherwise you will not come," replied the young lady shortly.
"Well, then, come I will!" said the other, again fixing his gaze on her. "If my company does not please you at any time, you will have yourself to blame for an acquaintance with one who seldom forces himself, but is difficult to shake off."

Free will is of the essence in these implied contracts between good and evil.

5. If this splendid greeting is based on a Central European formula, I have been unable to find its source.

6. To the British (and on the continent) dinner was formerly the large meal of the day taken at mid-afternoon. Supper was a light evening repast. There is no doubt some play on the words dine and, particularly, on sup as implying sip.

7. Very strange. There does exist a medical condition known as hypertrichosis, an excessive hairiness that may be purely localized or so extreme that sufferers from the condition may be exhibited as hairy monsters. There was a Peter Gonzales born with such long hair in 1556 in the Canary Islands. He was later sent to the court of King Henry II of France. Gonzales married, and several of his children, too, were hairy. Hypertrichosis is an exceedingly rare condition, occurring only once in a billion births.

   Though Summers does not give other instances of palm hair, he does quote the Frenchman Venette as saying that very hairy men are "usually amorous."

   One wonders whether Stoker knew the American boys' entrapment game in which one boy says "If you masturbate, you'll grow hair on your palms," and watches to see which of his listeners looks guiltily down at his hands.

   Finally, following this lead a moment longer, it is worth noting that the description of Dracula given here has certain similarities with the standard nineteenth-century image of the masturbator. Wayland Young, in *Eros Denied* (p. 236) quotes from William Acton's *Functions and Disorders of the Reproductive Organs* (1857) in which Claude-Francois Lallemand's description of the effects of masturbation on children is given as follows:

   "However young the children may be, they become thin, pale and irritable, and their features assume a haggard appearance. We notice the sunken eye, the long, cadaverous-looking countenance, the downcast look which seems to arise from a consciousness in the boy that his habits are suspected, and, at a later period, from the ascertained fact that his virility is lost. … Habitual masturbators have a dank, moist, cold hand, very characteristic of vital exhaustion; their sleep is short, and most complete marasmus [wasting of the body] comes on; they may gradually waste away if the evil passion is not got the better of, nervous exhaustion sets in, such as spasmodic contraction, or partial or entire convulsive movements, together with epilepsy, eclampsy, and a species of paralysis accompanied with contraction of the limbs."

   If this is a portrait that does not suggest the power that Dracula manifests, one needs only to remember the inert, pale cataleptic figure of the vampire in his daytime coffin.

8. This line, spoken by Bela Lugosi in the Tod Browning film version of *Dracula* (1931), has achieved something of a classic life of its own. There is hardly a schoolchild who does not achieve a moment's illusory greatness by imitating the inimitable Master.

9. The octagonal room is, one suspects, a visual pun. Coffins, particularly nineteenth-century coffins, were frequently octagonal in shape. Poe, too, plays this game. See the five-sided room in *Ligeia*.

From Dracula to Nosferatu

By S.S. Prawer

Like Mary Shelley's *Frankenstein* and Stevenson's *The Strange Case of Dr Jekyll and Mr Hyde,* Stoker's late Victorian novel belongs to a cherished class nineteenth-century fictions in which 'an unusual individual in touch with private fears at a time when these fears were shared by the outside world consciously or unconsciously exploited the link between the *two*'.[1] *Dracula,* never out of print since its first publication, is also a filter through which folk beliefs, rural and urban myths, and historically conditioned as well as perennial psychological experiences, have passed into the ken of successive generations. Much of this is sexual: vampirism, as Stoker presents it, involves sadistic and masochistic practices, symbolic rapes of men, women and children, sudden changes from virgin to whore, and violations of jealously protected inner and outer spaces by vampire-hunters; neither the bodies of men and women, nor bedrooms, tombs, asylums, chapels, are sacrosanct.[2]

Social implications involve aristocratic violations of bourgeois proprieties, disastrous incursions of eastern strangers into western cities, capitalists 'sucking blood'—a metaphoric usage that Stoker's contemporary Karl Marx made peculiarly his own.[3] Freudians could detect instances of 'the return of the repressed', ancient fears returning to life—the dead coming back to plague the living, revenants and ghouls, succubi and succubae, lamias, empusas and striges—while Jungians could have a field-day searching for denizens of the collective unconscious where Shadow battled Anima. Medical fears also found an echo in such works: vampiric incursions could recall outbreaks of bubonic plague, smallpox, venereal disease (Stoker himself, like many of his contemporaries, may have suffered from syphilis), cholera, influenza and, more recently, SARS and AIDS. *Dracula* enshrines a version of the *Doppelgänger,* the spectral double beloved of German writers and film-makers: the vampiric Count may be seen as Jonathan Harker's double, acting out repressed desires that come to the surface when Jonathan is confronted by three vampire women (one of whom seems strangely familiar!) before Dracula chases them back with his homoerotic 'This man is mine!' And vampirism, as we meet it in Stoker's novel, is spilt religion: it parodies the Eucharist and needs a

S.S. Prawer, "From Dracula to Nosferatu," from *Nosferatu: Phantom der Nacht*, pp. 7–11. Copyright © 2004 by BFI Publishing. Permission to reprint granted by the publisher.

Bram Stoker

panoply of crucifixes and communion wafers (along with garlic and pointed stakes) for its defeat.

Dracula derives his name from a historic figure: Vlad Dracula, a fifteenth-century ruler of Wallachia, named after the Order of the Dragon into which his father had been received—though 'Dracul' (dragon) also meant 'Devil' in Romanian, an appropriate sobriquet in view of his legendary cruelty that involved impaling hundreds of victims at a time. Many of his brutal deeds took place in neighbouring Transylvania, famous for the exploits of Countess Elisabet Bathory, who sought to rejuvenate herself by bathing in the blood of freshly killed young girls—just as Stoker's Dracula grows younger as he sates himself on the blood of his male and female victims.[4]

Stoker spent six years studying vampire lore, in the British Museum and in other libraries, through conversations with Arminius Vambery, a Hungarian professor of Oriental Languages whom he met and befriended in London in 1890, and through extensive acquaintance with many vampire-plays performed in London (often translated from French Grand Guignol), penny-dreadfuls like *Varney the Vampyre, or, The Feast of Blood*, travel writings and a rich Romantic tradition that was very much alive in Victorian England. There were poems by Goethe, Coleridge, Byron, Southey and Keats, featuring vampiric beings of both sexes, 'Gothic' novels by Anne Radcliffe, 'Monk' Lewis and Charles Maturin, and one story in particular, penned by Stoker's fellow-Irishman Sheridan Le Fanu, 'Carmilla', which had taken its place in a remarkable collection of Le Fanu's short stories entitled *In a Glass Darkly* (1872). The influence of Le Fanu's tale is most clearly visible in the chapter from *Dracula* which Stoker later excised and which was published separately as 'Dracula's Guest'. The most powerful influence of all, however, was the work of Wilkie Collins, especially *The Woman in White* of 1860, whose multi-narrator and multi-document structure *Dracula* mirrors, and whose plot includes a wicked foreign nobleman and scenes in a Victorian lunatic asylum. The appearance, in *Dracula*, of a ghostly 'Lady in Black' is a nod to Collins as surely as a child's invocation of a 'boofer lady' echoes the 'boofer lady' of Dickens's *Our Mutual Friend*.

Stoker's novel has perennial appeal; but it is firmly rooted in Victorian soil. It shows a bourgeois businessman travelling into foreign regions in quest of improved sales and in a spirit of enterprise. An English aristocrat, a wealthy American and a spirited woman who is more than a swooning invalid or her complement, the 'Angel in the House', all join him in the task of foiling a foreign danger that is threatening the stability of Victorian marriage and Victorian society. In this task of thwarting an invader from eastern lands they are helped by a scientist and occultist from a friendly western power, the Netherlands. The setting is London, which had, by the 1890s, become the biggest city in the world; battening on its teeming life, Dracula becomes an ancestor of more recent power-hungry figures like Blofeld or Goldfinger or the controllers of SMERSH.

Stoker firmly sketches in a background of scientific discovery and technological innovation; information is imparted, collected and stored not only in handwritten diaries but also in documents produced on typewriters and speech recorded on phonographs. Van Helsing, the Dutch vampire-hunter, is a disciple of Jean-Martin Charcot and adopts his guru's theories of hysteria along with his experimental practice of hypnotism. In fact, Van Helsing and other male characters are themselves subject to hysterical attacks, proving that one need not have a womb (*hustera*) to be so afflicted. There is much talk of medical theories, their limitations and the gradual crossing of frontiers that formerly guarded unknown territories of body and mind, as well as the application of recent medical practices like blood transfusion.[5]

Above all, *Dracula* enshrines in its two principal female figures, Mina and Lucy, two conceptions of women that complemented one another towards the end of the nineteenth century. On the one hand there is fear of the disruptive effects female sexuality might have within a patriarchal society: Lucy, who begins as a girlishly gushing, well-brought-up young lady, has 'polyandrist' fantasies when she is courted by three eligible young men at the same time; under the vampire's bite, she turns into a polymorphously perverse sexual predator and paedophile who has to be hunted down as mercilessly as the foreign Count who changed her from Victorian virgin to voluptuous devourer of blood. 'The blood is the life', quotes the mad Renfield from Deuteronomy 12:23, tempting us post-Freudians to equate blood and semen.

Mina, on the other hand, is the male vampire-hunters' invaluable helpmeet: she is more steady and intelligent than any of the British and American males, and by keeping and assembling all the relevant records, she becomes the putative author of the novel in which she is a character. One of her principal weapons is that typewriter which transformed the career prospects of so many women at the end of the century; and though, like Lucy, she is bitten by the vampire, her help enables the male hunters with their fearful panoply of phallic weapons, ranging from scalpel to stake, to track the attacker to his lair and, by defeating him, restore Mina to her admirable self. The only one of the fearless vampire-hunters who dies is the American; and after Van Helsing, his task completed, has returned to the Netherlands, three happy English couples are left to raise their families. As Martin Tropp has commented:

> All the distortions of the maternal role, the gruesome tastes of Dracula's women, Lucy's nocturnal activities, Mina's nursing of grown men, and even Dracula's opening a vein in his chest and forcing Mina to drink his blood—are answered by the birth of Mina's child. Mina becomes a wife and mother who is useful, competent and independent. ... Though they set out to save her, at the end of the book it is Mina who leads the reluctant band of men into the twentieth century.[6]

The movie Nosferatu *was premiered in 1922 at the marble room in the Zoologischer Garten, Berlin.*

Stoker's *Dracula* completed a process begun, in England, by the Byronic Lord Ruthven of John Polidori's *The Vampyre,* written in 1816 but first published in 1819: the transformation of the evil-smelling revenant of peasant folklore, come from the grave to torment his fellow-villagers until they staked him or cut off his head, into the aristocratic being who could travel to distant parts (provided he carried with him some of his native earth) to work his mischief. He remained a shape-shifter, assuming the garb and manners of the sophisticated society he invaded as easily as changing into a bat or some other beast—though he could be recognised for what he was by his failure to cast a shadow or appear as a reflection in a mirror. The novel of which he is the central character has been subject to the most varied interpretations, many of which have been summarised in Maud Ellmann's admirable edition:

> Dracula has been interpreted as a figure for perversion, menstruation, venereal disease, female sexuality, male homosexuality, feudal aristocracy, monopoly capitalism, the proletariat, the Jew, the primal father, the Antichrist, and the typewriter. But Dracula is all these things, and more: he stands for the return of the repressed, the contents of which are forever shifting. For this reason he can never be pinned down: he continues to change shape, beyond the covers of Bram Stoker's book, in the minds of his insatiable interpreters.[7]

Among these interpreters and reinventors, filmmakers of many nations have been prominent—none more so than one of the greatest German directors of silent films, F. W Murnau (Friedrich Wilhelm Plumpe, 1888–1931). Murnau and his scriptwriter Henrik Galeen plucked out a term Stoker had found for the undead, 'Nosferatu', placed it in their title—*Nosferatu. Eine Symphonie des Grauens*—and had the chronicler who acted as narrator give it a resonance it has never since lost:

Nosferatu, does not this word sound in your ear like a call of the bird of death. Beware of uttering it, or the images of life will fade into shadows, spectral dreams will arise in your heart and feed on your blood ...[8]

This cinematic 'symphony' of 1921–2, in its turn, inspired Werner Herzog to another set of variations, to be considered in Chapter 4, which were as significant for the Germany of the Western Republic that followed World War II as Murnau's had been for that which had its all-too-brief life after World War I. Both, however, drew freely on the late Victorian novel whose author uncovered, partly unconsciously, deep-seated desires and apprehensions, and had, in the process, transformed a peasant superstition into a potent modern myth.[9]

Dracula and the
Eastern Question

By Matthew Gibson

BRITISH AND FRENCH VAMPIRE NARRATIVES
OF THE NINETEENTH-CENTURY NEAR EAST

In his amusing travel book of 1875, the mysteriously initialled R.H.R. describes how he decided to relax after what he considered to have been one of the best meals of his life at the Russian consulate in Cattaro, Dalmatia: 'I got another chair, and stretched my legs on it; the natives stared—no Oriental ever thinks of stretching his legs—the acme of comfort for him is to tuck them under him.' This distinction between an 'Oriental' and a Western custom is designed to show the exotic nature of his location—what can be more exotic than a difference of custom in a function which for most of us seems natural, not cultural?—but also to define the area in which the traveller finds himself: it is a part of the Orient, and he is amongst Orientals. Few people today would define the Dalmatian coast (now southern Croatia and Montenegro) as 'Oriental', although they would not hesitate, I should think, to describe it as 'Balkan', and a part of 'Eastern Europe'.

However, the idea of the South Eastern European countries of the Balkans as being not merely Eastern (in the sense of a Slavic Eastern Europe to which, as Larry Wolff has shown, they have also variously been perceived as belonging since Venetian times) but 'Oriental' (i.e., part of the East that not does include North Eastern Europe and Russia, and is mainly non-Christian) is a common one throughout the nineteenth century and up until the first Balkan war. In *Eothen* (1835), Alexander Kinglake declared that having left Austro-Hungarian Semlin for Turkish-occupied Belgrade 'I had come, as it were, to the end of this wheel-going Europe, and now my eyes would see the splendour and Havoc of the East.' Europe ends at Belgrade for Kinglake, although in his travels to Constantinople he is almost oblivious of the Christian Slavs and interested only in the Turks, even though he would have travelled through Southern Serbia, an area by then independent of Ottoman rule. H. Charles Woods, in his long and ominous warning *The Danger Zone of Europe: Changes and Problems in the Near East* (1911), defines the Near East as the Balkan Peninsular and Asia Minor, and justifies a decision to include chapters on the history of Turkey itself only because 'as Asia Minor is ruled by and is dependent upon the Government of Constantinople, the conditions actually prevailing in this part of the Ottoman Empire actually influence the fate of European Turkey, and thus affect the question as to whether or not the Balkan Peninsula is "the Danger Zone of Europe"'. Most strikingly, the important London monthly magazine, *The Near East* included articles on Bosnia (at the time under Austrian rule, but titularly part of the Ottoman Empire), Montenegro and Serbia along with reports from Yemen and Morocco. Thus, although classifactions of the Orient always appear to have been nebulous, and the identity of South Eastern Europe—including on occasions some parts of what we might now term 'Middle Europe', like Hungary—was somewhat 'overdetermined' in Western eyes (as 'Eastern Europe', 'the Balkans', 'the East', 'not Europe' and 'le Monde Slave'), the area was nevertheless characterised as belonging to an 'Oriental' East and 'The Near East' up until the first Balkan War of 1912. In the nineteenth century these particular regions of the Near East form the area around which politicians framed 'the Eastern Question': namely, the problem of how to resolve what to do with them once, as appeared inevitable, the Ottoman Empire would fall. Thanks to British interference, as we shall see, this inevitability was postponed for a very long time. We shall also see that the British and French vampire story is a fertile means of political commentary upon the Eastern Question.

Maria Todorova has classified this area as being a separate one to the Oriental East in the minds and vision of eighteenth- and nineteenth-century Western Europeans and Americans, called either 'the Balkans' or 'Haemus'. Unlike the 'Orientalism' of Said, she understands the concept of 'Balkanism' as 'being a discourse about an imputed ambiguity' (Todorova, p. 16). Her understanding of Balkanism as being a Western means of representing South Eastern Europe results from both her objection to the simplistic and ideally reconstituted binary of Edward Said's concept of 'Orientalism', and from her own detailed study of the writings about the region by travellers and diplomats from many different countries over five centuries. She observes that Said has allowed the Ottoman Orient to be confused with the Arab Orient (p. 12), and furthermore that his acceptance of the Foucauldian idea of 'discourse' over and above examining the history of representations more rigorously (p. 9), has meant that there is no space for other contradictory discourses within this Gramscian 'hegemony'—a hegemony which Said has perhaps invented more than he has described.

Although I accept that Todorova's understanding of the Balkans as 'an imputed ambiguity' of Eastern and Western traditions over what is an 'Ottomanised' region of Europe is true, I do not accept that we cannot in some ways see the region as being part of the Old Near East, and thus as 'Oriental'. This is because it strikes me that the Near East, as both a cultural and a political concept (i.e., the area which had been or was still under Ottoman power) does not negate the narrower cultural construct of the Balkans. For a nineteenth-century Englishman the Levant and the Gulf are distinct parts of the Near East, just as is French North Africa: all were, in different ways and to varying degrees, engaged with an Islamic system of government, past or still current, and were crucially either involved in trade routes with India, or else with preventing Russia or Austria-Hungary from spreading their wings and destroying those trade routes. They are all separate regions and yet are joined by history, geographical proximity and social organisation, and are also, in a political sense, an important factor in the perpetuation of Britain's and France's economic health. All are therefore capable at different times and by different factions as being seen as part of 'The Near East', something which cannot be said of the Balkan nations *after* 1912, when Turks left the region *en masse,* and the different peoples tried to solidify themselves as European nation states, away from the aegis of either Austria or the Ottoman Empire.

Where I thoroughly agree with Todorova is that Said has been woefully lacking in attempting to define 'Orientalism' without looking at British and French attitudes to the Turks: the people whom, as she is quick to point out, did control most of what the British and French considered to be the Near East for some six centuries ([Todorova, p. 12] up until the twentieth, in many areas), as opposed to the few decades in which Britain controlled her old Near Eastern (modern Middle Eastern) colonies. Following from Todorova's own critique of Said's omissions and inability to align ideological positions with factual reality, three major objections to Said's ideas must be addressed before we can begin to observe political attitudes to the Eastern Question in a more objective and plural light, and as they are represented in the vampire narrative.

The first is that Orientalism was a hegemonic discourse, which, in Said's view, perfused all areas of British and French attitudes to the Orient, and created the boundaries for knowledge about an area that contained a complexity ignored by the Europeans. Maria Todorova's own examinations of the accounts of British travellers like David Urquhart and Jonathan Morritt demonstrate that attitudes towards Ottoman rulers, and indeed Ottoman customs, were often favourable in contrast to the contempt felt for the Greek or Slavic peasants under their control. Thus the idea of a hegemonic discourse seeing 'Orientals' as 'irrational, depraved (fallen), childlike "different"' as opposed to the European who is 'rational, virtuous, mature, "normal"' (p. 40), which Said discerns everywhere in the discourse he understands as 'Orientalism', (Said, p. 51), in all its areas of knowledge, is grossly simplistic since English aristocrats who discerned the nobility of Turks on their travels through Roumelia invert this binary entirely.

A second contention of Said is that this discourse was a justification for rule and imperialism. 'To say simply that Orientalism was a rationalisation of colonial rule', he writes, 'is to ignore the extent to which colonial rule was justified in advance by Orientalism.' (Said, p. 39). As well as arguing that Orientalism was an inclusive discourse which equated knowledge with power and created both the object of knowledge and the method of knowing, Said argued that it was a means of justifying control: by defining Orientals as irrational and childlike, Orientalist scholars were constructing an object of knowledge which justified the actions of colonisers from Napoleon to Lord Balfour with the right to impose their rule. This movement from the ideal to the real, from discourse to actuality, is characterised as follows:

> at the outset one can say that so far as the West was concerned during the nineteenth century and twentieth centuries, an assumption had been made that the Orient and everything in it was, if not patently inferior to, then in need of corrective study by the West. The Orient was viewed as if framed by the classroom, the criminal court, the prison, the illustrated manual. Orientalism, then, is knowledge of the Orient that places things Oriental in class, court, prison, or manual for scrutiny, study, judgement, discipline, or governing. (pp. 40–1)

The body of knowledge, Orientalism, seeps to the justification of rule and rule itself, further reinforcing Said idea that the discourse was hegemenonic and transcended civil societies (schools, families, clubs, newspapers etc, which disseminate ideology) and political societies (law courts, governments, police forces, think-tanks etc, which make and implement policies).

However, such a claim needs a wider proof. If Orientalism is a hegemonic discourse held by the British and French about the Orient in relation to Europe, and if it justifies and helps to enforce power over it, then that should be manifest throughout its history. What one finds puzzling on leaving *Orientalism* is that at no point in the book does Edward Said mention Sir Stratford Canning. Canning was Britain's intermittent ambassador to the Ottoman Empire from 1809–61, and a Turcophile, who saved the Turks from extinction in 1812 when he helped them broke the Treaty of Bucharest against the advancing Russians, and who was an instrumental support to Turkish concerns during the Crimean war. Even at the time of the Russo-Turkish war (1876–78) he was arguing that the Turks, despite the misrule in their region, should be supported by Britain in the continued possession of their Balkan and Central Asian provinces as a bulwark against Russia. Nor do we find any reference in *Orientalism* to the Treaty of Berlin (1878), in which Disraeli, with French support, ensured that large parts of the Balkans were returned to the Ottoman Sultan, Abdul Hamid II, in order to make sure that the Russians could not nestle in Roumelia and threaten the Mediterranean. Just as British aristocrats like Morritt and Urquhart saw the nobility of the Turks as being traduced by the barbarism of their European subjects, and found much to admire in Turkish rulers (Todorova, p. 94), so also politicians supported an Islamic oriental state against the interests of Christian Europeans, when they saw that it was in their own interests to do so.

A final objection is to Said's use of this Gramscian idea of hegemony between civil and political societies: that all areas of society, whilst appearing to be independent and autonomous, are in fact complicit in the same hegemony, and that the political societies of imperial nations 'impart to their civil societies a sense of urgency' which interferes with the civil societies and circumscribes their knowledge (p. 11). While I do not wish to attack Gramsci's excellent and useful distinctions per se, I believe that we can see a very real fissure between different ideas about Orientals (which as Todorova has shown are in any case extremely varied) and the crudely self-interested decisions made at treaties by politicians and the justifications that they give. While there may, I do not deny, be relations between the ideas prevalent in a 'free' society and the secret wishes of a government, at moments of crisis political societies may verge very widely from the ideas of civil societies. This is no more true than in Disraeli's open support for Turkey at the Treaty of Berlin, justified by his famous 'Peace with Honour' speech, which led to the British electorate punishing him in 1880: areas of the civil society clearly differed with him as regards the British government's behaviour in the Near East, as the marvellous Tenniel cartoons of the time also demonstrate. Similarly, his own absorption in the civil societies (which, as we can see in the accounts of men like George Stoker, Urquhart and Morrit, were not part of a 'hegemony' at all), that he reflects to some extent in his novel *Tancred* (where Orientals are indeed portrayed in keeping with certain negative stereotypes) clearly did not affect his policy-making at the Treaty of Berlin: pure commercial self-interest did instead. As Linda Colley has shown, while Said may be justified in 'investigating the minds and myths of empire makers, and not just their weaponry and economic muscle', nevertheless 'material factors did matter, and were bound to matter' (Colley, p. 132). This is an extremely important point since, as shall be shown with regard to *Dracula,* the vampire narrative with Near Eastern setting can encode 'Orientalist' assumptions about a society while also suggesting a political solution which refutes entirely the idea that Oriental power should be diminished; the cultural and political meanings diverging from each other widely.

In post-Napoleonic Europe, British and French policy towards the Near East and attitudes to the Eastern Question, are in constant flux. At a representational level this also has an effect, as Ottoman and Balkan peoples are frequently recast according to different stereotypes in different media. Thus one must observe Britain's and France's relations with the Near East in terms of their material and wider economic interest, rather than fall into the trap of hegemony, to understand that representations of Orientals in Britain and France are plural, varied, and reactive to real situations involving other imperial powers like Russia and Germany, rather than being a simplistic, self-perpetuating binary.

In dealing with how vampire stories set in the old Near East actually confront the Eastern Question, the intention here is to look at literature in the light of genuine political events, balancing sections of literary analysis, biography, and detailed historical context. The assumption in each case is that the story is connected to a referential context upon which the author is either commenting codedly, or is discussing in ways which his unconscious prejudices determine. While in certain cases stock stereotypes about the Orient are used for political reasons (as is the case in the work of Le Fanu), other contradictory stereotypes (e.g., the Turks as noble and civilised rulers; the Venetians as despotic and medieval) also raise their head, making absolute patterns of consistency hard to discern. It is thus only through analysing the concrete political circumstances against which they were written that we can be confident of why particular representations arise.

Interpretations of the Vampire

The vampire, as literary phenomenon, has its origins in Near Eastern traditions, and its fame in the West is almost entirely attributable to the collection of accounts made by Dom Calmet for his *Treatise on Revenants* (1746). Hence it has a local habitation and a name, although its transformations into the literary vampire depend upon attitudes in the West rather than in the region from which the superstition itself hails.

To begin with, the vampire as a *literary* theme has its precursor in the Graveyard Poetry which induced both terror and horror in the hearts of readers more used to (and bored by) the rationalism of Augustan literature. It is one of several Gothic and Romantic themes that caused the terror mingled with delight that Burke, in his famous philosophical essay, considered the essence of the sublime in taste. David Punter sees the vampire as being, like the undead Wanderer, a specific Romantic Gothic type in its literary manifestation, and understands it politically as being a bourgeois anxiety about the resurgence of the old aristocratic class which the newly dominant would like to suppress. Similarly, Judith Barbour understands the vampire story as being the 'aerial battle of locked divinities' between the old master and his suffering servant, and the result of a moment when the old regime returned after the restoration of the Bourbon dynasty in 1815.

Perhaps in keeping with this notion of struggle with the past, many critics have seen the original vampire stories as proof of the primal horde theory of Freud, in which the father harasses the sons and the sons have to combine in order finally to overcome the father. James Twitchell records how in Calmet vampires are portrayed as preying upon their own, and how the 'dhampire', who eventually stakes the vampire through the heart, is often a younger, sonlike figure. In later literary adaptations of the vampire, as Leatherdale notes, the vampires' sucking blood from their own may be seen as the sublimation of an incest anxiety (a potential in both *Carmilla* and *Dracula*) as well as a possible sublimation of homosexual anxieties. The female vampire can also be seen as representing male fears about the new woman (Leatherdale, pp. 145–8). Thus the superstition of the vampire along with its sucking blood, constant resurgence as living dead and nocturnal life-style, presents a plethora of political and sexual meanings.

More recently, the concept of vampirism has been understood as signifying degeneration from the unknown, in particular from the racial 'other' of Eastern Europe.

Indeed, the vampire has been seen as the metaphoric representation of Eastern Europe's unresolved racial mixture. Stephen D. Arata has discerned in it the British public's fear of reverse colonisation, thus constituting an anxiety caused by guilt at their own colonialism. However, as William Hughes has pointed out, the post-colonial Gothic with regard to Eastern Europe must be treated with some caution, given that the British possessed no colonies there, the closest they came to this being in the novels of Anthony Hope!

I would agree that the Eastern European setting for the vampire is important, but not in the way that Arata believes. To see *Dracula* as a representation of the racial other, a repository of anxieties by a colonial elite who harbour a reverse Orientalism, or Occidentalism, about the West which he invades (*Victorian Studies,* 33: 621–45, at 634), is too imprecise. Less than simply a fear of reverse colonialism from an all purpose Oriental 'Other', it is in fact a very detailed and complex reaction to a recent set of events in the Balkans, in particular the Treaty of Berlin and Russian interference. In fact all of the writers to be discussed—Polidori, Le Fanu, Stoker, Nodier, Mérimée and Verne—were dependent upon scholarship and research into the politics of the region: all were reacting against recent events as opposed to general, over-arching discourses, and in several cases were trying to capitalise upon topicality. Furthermore, in Le Fanu's and Stoker's case that topicality is less to do with their Irishness, as many recent critics have believed, than it is with a more wholly British attitude to the area in which their tales are set—although this is not to deny that the Irish political situation could not in addition affect their attitude towards it.

Thus the time is rife for reconsidering vampire narratives set in the Balkans and Near East as being discussions of the region itself.

Political Allegory

A question arises as to how these works are capable of 'encoding' political attitudes to the Near East in relation to their authors' home countries. Whether the attitudes are unconscious or intended is a question that will immediately strike the reader. My contention is that in the majority of cases, the vampire narrative set in the Near East is a deliberate and coded practice, which makes use of either careful dating, or else literary and contemporary allusion, to embed certain political ideas. If one takes into account that the very first of these narratives, John Polidori's *The Vampire,* was written as a careful indication of Polidori's own relation with Lord Byron, and that he takes Lord Byron's own rhetoric and inverts its meaning (he was, after all, rewriting Byron's *Fragment,* but adding his own emphasis), then it does not seem too fanciful to see later aristocratic vampire stories as using both the myth and the symbolism to suggest other topical ideas not present at a literal level.

Furthermore, in Polidori's case the rejection was political as well as personal, express-ing ideas that would not have been fashionable at the time amongst circles in which he moved (particularly the philhellene aristocrats who would have read his story). Likewise Le Fanu's *Carmilla* also presents quite extreme attitudes to topical politics in Austria-Hungary, using vampirism as symbolism. For Mérimée too the vampire is used in various ways both to condemn the earlier colonisations of Dalmatia, but also to praise the Napoleonic project, while the work of Verne uses literary allusion to create metaphorical resonance beyond the literal meaning of the work in a comment upon the political situation in Transylvania. In all cases the vampire has an allegorical, political meaning that is created either through intertext (as in the case of Polidori and Verne), or else through relation to recent events (as in Le Fanu's, Stoker's and Mérimée's work), and in each case it represents an extreme or marginal position that was more comfortably suggested than openly avowed.

The way in which such allegory works can best be explained through reference to the work of two literary theorists who have looked at the novel, Paul de Man and Fredric Jameson, de Man understood the figures of literary works as frequently imposing 'allegories of reading' upon the reader by using metaphor in order to prioritise certain passages, and thus certain readings, over others. Hence he saw the interpretation of texts as dependent upon certain strategies understood by the reader and facilitated by the text itself. These strategies depended upon the notion that reading was a kind of 'getting inside' the text, which 'unite[s] outer meaning with inner understanding, action with reflection, into one single totality', as opposed to the more 'external' mode of reading the text by its literal relation to a concept. Our reading is organised by assumptions (de Man, p. 15), which prioritise rhetoric over grammar, and metaphor over metonymy, allowing the reader to think that they are unravelling the mystery of the text at certain key points. Thus metaphorical passages were themselves metaphors of the process of reading, involving, as they do, a privileged sense of moving within.

Such priority, often accepted by semioticians without question, involves the assumption of a controlling, metaphysical presence to the text, whose removal allows immediate conflicts here. By using deconstructive techniques, de Man shows that this allegory of reading can easily be inverted, and the text can become a site of contradiction. In particular, he shows how a passage from Proust's *A la Recherche du Temps Perdu* presents Swann's act of reading as a cool antidote to the heat of the exterior, but most importantly uses metaphor to express its superiority through the figure 'torrent d'activité' (p. 66) as though reading replaces the motion of heat with the fast motion of cool water, and also invites us to prioritise the passage. However, as de Man explains, the phrase 'torrent d'activité' has become a dead metaphor, to the extent that it is more like a literal figure for physical exertion which causes heat, thus implying, through a more deconstructive reading, that there has been no replacement of heat with coolness at all, nor any figural superiority of one activity over another. An interpretation which divorces self-presence from the text, and exposes 'reading' to a plethora of new figural interpretations, presents such contradictions as being a central element of the text itself.

In the following analyses there are, needless to say, fundamental differences to de Man's study. To begin with, all of these readings attempt to locate the political symbolism either within the intention or, at the very least, within the latent and historically demonstrable prejudices of the author, rather than to see the text purely as an autotelic but self-contradictory plane. The lesson of de Man is nevertheless a useful one, not least because he shows how figures can be simultaneously metonymical and metaphorical, and also contradict each other in a way designed to refute the 'organic' theory implicit to much humanist and common sense criticsm. However, where he invariably sees metonymy as undercutting metaphor, in the vampire novel set in the Near East we shall see the opposite: implicit metaphor, constructed through intertext or allusion, undercutting the literal naming of the narrator, and allowing reactionary or extreme views to refute the surface meaning. Whereas de Man sees the text as deconstructing itself through this ludic combat between two modes of representation, the present study discerns instead a combat between acceptable expression and implicit feeling, or on occasions conscious intention and subconscious anxieties which are located both within history and the personal predilections of the authors.

This brings us to Jameson's understanding of allegory (not of reading, but of allegory itself) as an element in the developmental stages of fiction, and as thus being an important aspect of Third World literature. According to Jameson, in contradistinction to the literature of the high capitalist West, literature of the Third World is inescapably public, and thus national allegory rather than a literal exploration of individual character. For him, this means that stories in the Third World are 'figural' rather than 'literal' (Jameson, p. 321), and that their characters take on the identities of entire communities. He recognises this process as being 'tribal' rather than individual, and formed by the peculiar sense of class and national identity which is entirely at odds with the construction of identity among the liberal bourgeoisie of the West:

> Third-world texts, even those which are seemingly private and invested with a properly libidinal dynamic—necessarily project a political dimension in the form of national allegory: *the story of the private individual destiny is always an allegory of the embattled situation of the public third-world culture and society.* (p. 320)

He further insists that, unlike in Western conceptions of allegory, meaning can shift in a way that does not adhere to the classical unities expected by pedantic critics of the developed nations (p. 324), and that a work can have more than one allegorical meaning.

Jameson's theory of national allegory finds its absolute inverse in the vampire tale with Near Eastern setting. To understand this one must first take into account that allegory, a form which he says was discredited in the Romantic era in the West (p. 324), is initially a result of popular myths and superstitions becoming more philosophically understood once a belief in their literal reality begins to wane (as in Spenser's *Fairie Queene* or *The Romance of the Rose*: works which take once literal beliefs like the existence of monsters or a material paradise and convert them into the representation of metaphysical or abstract ideas). The accounts originally collected by Calmet and adapted by Byron, Polidori, Le Fanu, Mérimée and others are themselves examples of a set of tribal beliefs (although filtered entirely through Western media) which are ripe for a political or social explanation once the superstition fades (or rather, when exposed to the West, where they are purely superstitions). At that point the superstition can become either a metaphor for the primitiveness of the society or else an allegory of a political situation.

In this sense the vampire novel represents the conversion of an East European or Near Eastern superstitition to a West European political comment about East European society. The superstition is filtered through Western ideas—and also the forms of literary representation, namely the bourgeois novel—to create Gothic: a genre which already depends upon a tension between naturalism and the supernatural, and reason and terror, and so involves a contradiciton of modes of representation. Thus, whereas in Jameson's understanding of Third World narrative the literal and the allegorical are seamlessly combined in the same story, in the Western vampire novel there is normally a contradiction between the open narration (which is usually naturalistic in the initial expectations it provokes), and the political opinions presented by its embedded allegory once the shock of the supernatural has been accepted, in keeping with the collision between two types of literature (naturalism and allegory) and two political opinions (open liberalism and embedded conservatism). In this way the national allegory of the tribe's folk beliefs and continuing superstitions have become part of the Western observer's rhetoric of either denunciation or of sympathy.

It is partly for this reason that I have chosen to steer from attributing recent post-colonial theory to these works. Not only are the political opinions towards the Balkans of these works for the most part far from colonial in aspiration, but the two main strands of post-colonial criticism—the binarism of Said which observes Western texts discerning the Orient as racial other, and the more complex Bhabba notion of the 'hybrid', in which the narrative work of the Third World culture adopts the language of the aggressor in order to articulate its local content,—imply do not apply. The first method has been rejected for reasons already given, namely the need to observe the real circumstances against which texts are written and understand its complexities. The reason for rejecting the second is also obvious, since the text envelops Near Eastern superstitions into a Western articulation that gives the Near Eastern myth no true voice of its own, and whose 'otherness' is in fact controlled by already existent Gothic traditions. There is no space for hybridity of any kind (with the exception of Mérimée, whose *La Guzla* is a more complex work entirely, as shall be shown), especially since the texts which informed the writers of the superstition (whether Fortis, Calmet, Wagener or Emily Gerard) were all Western, and for the most part were not actually reliable.

Thus in the Near Eastern vampire story the Western novel envelops the already modified superstition with its own narrative techniques for presenting character and material realism, and in doing so exploits the superstition for psychological terror while allowing its supernatural elements to become allegory. The allegory or metaphor to which it turns the vampire, in its relation to the culture it either threatens or is threatened by (which has the dominant voice), is also rarely one which argues for British or French colonialism: the political purpose of the vampire figure, while always directed towards the culture from which it is presumed to have come, and which is presumed to have originally articulated it, is too varied to admit of a simple political relation from West to East. As was said above, in relation to the ideas of Edward Said, in each case its meaning can only be understood by research into the exact historical context alone.

Paul Féval

One obvious omission from this work is the early vampire stories of Paul Féval, the Feuilletonier who wrote three vampire novels with an Near Eastern basis, *La Vampire* (1856), *Les Chevaliers Ténèbreux* (1860), and *La Ville-Vampire* (1875), which, like the historical novel, weave in private events around known public figures. The reason for this exclusion is that they relate vampirism to the political history of France as a means of commenting upon France's domestic problems rather than upon the Near East itself. Nevertheless, they deserve to be mentioned briefly, not simply due to their merits, but because explaining why they have been excluded will also define the scope of this project, and the similarities between the texts to be considered.

The first novel relates the story of a beautiful Hungarian, female vampire, Addhéma, who has been causing bodies to be thrown down the river Seine in the Spring of 1804, just before the first consul declares himself Emperor and as the Breton, Georges Cadoudal, is plotting to assasinate him. The second, set some years later during the Bourbon dynasty, deals with two Hungarian vampires (really East End villains), who journey round Europe robbing and pillaging the aristocracy before turning up at the palace of the Archbishop of Paris. In both novels the vampire has a Near Eastern origin, and a partial Near Eastern setting. In the first, Addhéma has her tomb in an islet in the Save in Southern Hungary (now Northern Serbia) near to Semlin and Szeged. She is really a Bulgarian who came and settled in the region, indicating an even closer relation to the Ottomans ([Féval, *La Vampire*, 101] at the time of the 1804 setting, this bordered upon what was simply European Turkeyland, as Southern Serbia was a full part of the Ottoman Empire until 1814). Her origins are thus on the edge of the Ottoman Orient, and the history and geography of that region is described as faithfully as is the history of revolutionary France. In *Le Chevalier Ténèbre*, the tomb of the chevaliers is also described as being near Szeged in Southern Hungary, and is within sights of Belgrade. The exotic location, in these political and historical vampire novels, would seem to be important.

However, what is most striking in both cases is that the political allegory of vampirism, whilst taken from the Near East, applies entirely to domestic French situations. In both cases there are two offered resolutions, one naturalistic, one supernatural: one related to brigandry the other to vampirism proper, making the allegory very obvious, and drawing upon Voltaire's joke in *Dictionnaire philosophique* that although Paris and London did not appear to have vampires like the Serbs, the Hungarians and the Poles, they in fact did in the form of bankers and businessmen. In both cases the vampire is related to corruption and greed resurging in French society, with the Near Eastern origin being a convenient smokescreen for an author writing during a time of intense censorship, the Second Empire of Napoleon III (1851–70), nephew of Napoleon I. In relating vampirism to brigandage in *La Vampire*, Féval is commenting on the bourgeois greed that was to plague France from the first Empire on, resurfacing after the 1830 revolution and the accession of King Louis-Phillipe (Orleans) and the bourgeois constitution. In *Le Chevalier Ténèbre*, Féval shows class warfare, and the resurgence of greed and kleptocracy during the restoration era, since the vampires, whose multiplicity of ethnic origins only serves to negate their importance as specific national types, represent the danger the aristocracy faced from the lower orders.

Thus, regardless of his actual political position, Féval uses the vampire story of the Near East as an allegory of political corruption in the context of genuine history, weaving the Gothic elements in and around real events and people in France, and furthermore to symbolise domestic situations (the rising bourgeoisie under Napoleon; the reemergence of class war under the Bourbons), so that allegorically the vampires constitute subversive comments about the realities of the past, and of the present under Napoleon III's dictatorship. Here, therefore, the vampire superstition is not only used to create a submerged national allegory, but is also disguised as a comment on the East itself, in an attempt to obfuscate the internal as external and avoid the attentions of the authorities. The concealment is, in other words, affected by external censorship.

The same cannot be said of Polidori, Le Fanu, Stoker, Verne, and even Mérimée. Their use of a Near Eastern superstition is a comment upon the Near East in relation to their own countries, and one concealed by self-censorship rather than the curtailment of the state. The vampire is thus a national allegory of the 'other', but one which is against the attitudes of the time, or the personae which the authors would otherwise like to promote. However, in keeping with the complexity and variety of the representations of the Near East, that national allegory is continually changing, continually reappropriating both praise and blame.

The Vampire

By Jan Neruda

The unpretentious steamer which plies daily between Constantinople and the Princes Islands landed us at Prinkipo, and we went ashore. There were only a few passengers, we two and a Polish family, father, mother, and the daughter with her fiancé. But no … there was some one else. A young fellow, a Greek, had joined the boat at Stamboul on the wooden bridge across the Golden Horn. We concluded, from the sketch-book which he was carrying, that he was an artist. He had long black curls down to his shoulders; his face was pale, and his dark eyes deeply set. At first I was interested in him; he was very obliging, and able to give a good deal of information about the country we were travelling in. But he talked too much, and after ten minutes I left him alone.

The Polish family, on the contrary, was very attractive. The old people were kindly and gave themselves no airs, the fiancé was young and distinguished-looking, a man of the word. They were going to spend the summer at Prinkipo; the daughter was delicate and needed the air of the South. The beautiful, pale, girl looked as if she had just recovered from or just fallen a prey to a severe illness. She leant on her fiancé's arm, frequently stood still to catch her breath and now and then a dry cough interrupted her whispered conversation. Whenever she coughed, her companion stopped and looked at her sympathetically, and when she returned his look, her eyes seemed to say: 'It is nothing. … I am quite happy.'

They believed in her recovery and their happiness.

The Greek, who had parted from us at the landing-stage, had recommended an hotel belonging to a Frenchman, and the family decided to take rooms there. The situation was not too high, the view exquisite, and the hotel offered every European comfort.

We lunched together and when the midday heat had passed off a little, we all slowly walked up the slope to reach a pinewood and enjoy the view. We had no sooner found a suitable spot to rest in, when the Greek reappeared. He only bowed to us, looked round for a convenient place and sat down at a few steps' distance from us, opened his sketch-book and began to draw.

'I believe he is sitting with his back to the rock so that we should not see his drawing,' I said.

'We don't want, to,' said the young Pole, 'we have plenty of other things to look at.'

After a while he added: 'I believe he is using us as a foreground. … I don't mind.'

Indeed, we had enough to look at. I do not think there can be a lovelier or happier place in the world than Prinkipo. Irene, the political martyr, a contemporary of Charlemagne, lived in exile here for a month. If I could have spent a month in this place, I should have felt enriched in memories for the rest of my life. Even the one day is unforgettable. The air was so pure and soft and clear that the eye soared as on downy wings from distance to distance. On the right the brown rocks of Asia rose from the sea, on the left, in the distance, were the blue, steep shores of Europe; near us Chalki, one of the nine islands of the Princes Archipelago, lay mute and eerie, with somber cypress groves; it looked like a haunting dream. A huge building crowns the summit of the isle…it is a lunatic asylum.

The surface of the Sea of Marmora was covered with ripples, and played in all colours like a giant opal. In the distance it looked white as milk, near us it had a rosy shimmer and between the two islands it glowed like a golden orange; the depth below was sapphire blue. Its loveliness was untroubled, no large ships were moving on it; only close to the shore two small boats, carrying the British flag, were cruising to and fro, a steam launch, about the size of a signalman's box, and a boat rowed by sailors; liquid silver seemed to drip from their oars when they lifted them rhythmically. Fearless dolphins tumbled about close to the craft, or leapt in long semicircles across the water. From time to time huge eagles sailed from continent to continent in noiseless flights.

The slope below our seat was covered with roses in full bloom, the air was saturated with their scent. Sounds of music, vague and dreamy, rose to us from the arcades of the café on the shore.

We were all deeply affected; our conversation stopped and we gave ourselves up entirely to the emotions called forth by the contemplation of this Paradise. The young Polish girl was lying on the grass with her head resting on her fiancé's breast. The delicate oval face took on a faint flush of colour, and suddenly tears welled forth from her blue eyes. Her fiancé understood her emotion, bent down and kissed them away, one by one. The mother saw it and wept like her daughter, and I … looking at the girl, I also felt as though my heart was too full.

'Here body and soul must recover,' whispered the girl, 'what a wonderful spot!'

'God knows, I have no enemies,' said her father, 'but if I had, and met them here, I should forgive them.'

His voice was trembling. Again there was silence; we all felt an unspeakably sweet emotion. Every one was conscious of a world of happiness within him which he longed to share with all the world. As we all understood what the others felt, none of us talked.

We had hardly noticed that the Greek had closed his sketch book after about an hour's work, taken himself off with a slight acknowledgment of our presence. We remained.

When several hours had passed, and the sky had begun to take on the purple tint which makes the South so attractive, the mother reminded us that it was time to go in. We descended in the direction of the hotel slowly but with buoyant steps, like children free from care.

We sat down in an open veranda in front of the hotel. We had no sooner settled down when we heard sounds of quarrelling and abuse below us. Our Greek seemed to have an altercation with the landlord, and we listened to amuse ourselves. The conversation did not last long.

'If it weren't that I had to consider other guests …' said the landlord, while he came up the veranda steps.

'Pray,' said the young Pole, when he came neat to our table, 'who is that gentleman? What is his name?'

'Oh, God knows what the fellow may call himself,' said the landlord bad-temperedly, and looking daggers over the balustrade, 'we call him the Vampire.'

'An artist, I suppose?'

'Nice sort of an artist … paints nothing but corpses. No sooner has any one died hereabouts or in Constantinople, when the fellow is ready with his death mask, the very same day. That's because he draws in advance … but the devil knows, he never makes a mistake the vulture!'

The old Polish lady gave a shriek; her daughter had dropped into her arms in a dead faint, looking like death itself.

Her fiancé leapt down the steps at one bound, seized the Greek with one hand and his sketchbook with the other.

We ran down after him; both men were rolling in the dust.

The sketch-book flew open, the leaves were scattered, and we saw on one of them a striking portrait of the young girl. Her eyes were closed; a myrtle-wreath encircled her forehead.

The Island of Bornholm

By Nikolai Karamzin

1793

Friends! Beautiful summer has passed; golden autumn has paled; the greenery has faded; trees stand without fruit and without leaves; the misty sky surges like a sullen sea; the wintry down falls on the cold earth—let us bid farewell to Nature until the joyous vernal meeting; let us take shelter from blizzards and snowstorms—let us take shelter in our quiet study! Time should not burden us; we know a remedy for boredom. Friends! The oak and birch are ablaze in our hearth—let the wind rage and pile up our windows with white snow. Let us sit around the crimson fire and tell one another fairy tales, stories, and all sorts of true happenings.

You know that I have wandered in foreign lands, far, far from my fatherland, far from you, dear ones of my heart; I have seen many wonderful things, heard many amazing things; I have told you much, but could not tell you everything that happened to me. Listen—I will tell you a story—I will tell you a true story, not a figment of my imagination.

England was the farthest compass of my journey. There I said to myself: "Your fatherland and friends are waiting for you; it is time to rest in their embraces; it is time to dedicate your pilgrim's staff to the son of Maia*; it is time to hang it on the heaviest branch of that tree beneath which you frolicked in your youth"—I said this and boarded the ship "Britannia" in London to sail to the dear lands of Russia.[1]

Under white sails we moved rapidly along the flowering banks of the majestic Thames. Soon the limitless sea loomed blue before us; soon we heard the noise of its surging—but suddenly the wind shifted and our ship had to stop opposite the small town of Gravesend to await a more propitious time.

Together the captain and I went ashore; with peace of heart I roamed over green meadows adorned by Nature and diligence—sites rare and picturesque; finally, fatigued by the sun's heat, I lay down on the grass, beneath a century-old elm, near the seashore and looked at the watery expanse, at the foamy billows which in countless lines from

---

1 In ancient times wanderers, upon returning to their fatherland, dedicated their staffs to Mercury.

the obscured distance rushed with a dull roar to the island. This doleful noise and view of the boundless waters began to induce a drowsiness in me, that pleasurable quiescence of the soul in which all ideas and feelings stop and become rigid, like the streams of a spring which are frozen suddenly, and which is the most striking and the most poetic image of death; but suddenly the branches shook above my head. … I glanced up and saw—a young man, thin, pale, languid—more specter than man. In one hand he held a guitar, with the other he plucked leaflets from the tree and looked at the dark-blue sea with his motionless dark eyes, in which shone the last ray of a flickering life. My gaze could not meet his; his feelings were dead to external objects; he stood two paces from me, but saw nothing, heard nothing. "Unfortunate young man!" thought I. "You have been destroyed by fate. I know neither your name nor your origin; but I do know that you are unhappy."

He sighed, raised his eyes heavenward—lowered them again to the waves of the sea—walked away from the tree, sat upon the grass, began to play a sad prelude upon his guitar while looking continually at the sea, and he began to sing softly the following song (In Danish, which my friend, Doctor N.N.,[2] had taught me in Geneva):

The laws condemn
The object of my love;
But who, O heart! can Oppose you?

What law is more sacred
Than your innate feelings?
What power is stronger
Than love and beauty?

I love—I shall love forever;
Curse my passion.
Pitiless souls,
Cruel hearts!

Holy Nature!
Your tender friend and son
Is innocent before you.
You gave me a heart;

---

2   In his first letter from Basel (*Letters of a Russian Traveler*), Karamzin describes his meeting with Gottfried Becker (1767–1845), who had studied medicine and chemistry in Germany. Becker, the son of the apothecary to the Danish court, was wandering through Europe on foot. Later, in Geneva, Karamzin met him again and they passed most of the autumn and winter of 1789–90 in close company.

Your righteous gifts
Do adorn it—
Nature! You desired
That I love Lila!

Your thunder rumbled over us,
But did not strike us,
When we delighted
In the embrace of love.

O Bornholm, sweet Bornholm!
My soul craves
For thee incessantly;
But I shed tears in vain,

I languish and sigh!
I have been forced,
By a parental oath, to withdraw
Forever from your shores!

Do you still, O Lila!
Live with your anguish?
Or have you ended this evil life
In the roaring waves?

Appear before me, appear, Dearest shade!
I shall be buried with you
In the roaring waves.

Here an involuntary, inner urge made me want to throw myself on the stranger and press him to my heart, but at that very moment my captain took me by the arm and said that a favorable wind had billowed our sails and that we should not lose any time.—We sailed. The young man, guitar put aside and arms folded, watched us—watched the dark-blue sea.

The waves foamed under the helm of our ship, the Gravesend shore was hidden in the distance, the northern provinces of England grew dark on the other edge of the horizon—finally everything vanished, and the birds, which had hovered over us a long time, flew back to the shore, as if frightened by the boundlessness of the sea. The surge of the noisy waters and the misty sky were the only objects of our eyes, objects majestic and terrible.—My friends! In order to feel intensely all the audacity of the human spirit, one has to be on the open sea, where only *a small; thin plank,* as Wieland says, *separates us from a watery deaths* but where the skillful sailor, unfurling the sails, flies on and in his mind already sees the glitter of gold with which his daring enterprise will be rewarded in another part of the world. *"Nil mortalibus arduum est—nothing is impossible for mortals"*—I thought with Horace, losing my gaze in the infinity of Neptune's kingdom.

But soon a severe attack of seasickness deprived me of consciousness. For six days my eyes were not opened, my languid heart, washed by the foam of stormy waves,[3] barely beat in my chest. On the seventh day I revived and went on deck with a pale but happy face. The sun had already moved through the clear, azure vault of heaven toward the west; the sea, lighted by its golden rays, roared; under full sail the ship flew on over the masses of sundered billows, which vainly endeavored to outstrip it. Around us, at various distances, fluttered white, blue, and pink flags, but on the right something like land loomed dark.

"Where are we?" I asked the captain.

"Our voyage has been successful," he said; "we have passed Zund; the shores of Sweden have disappeared from view. On the right you see the Danish island of Bornholm, a dangerous place for ships; shoals and rocks are concealed there on the sea floor. When night falls, we shall drop anchor."

"The island of Bornholm, the island of Bornholm," I repeated in my thoughts, and the image of the young Gravesend stranger revived in my soul. The sad sounds and words of his song echoed in my ear. "They contain the secret of his heart," I thought; "but who is he? What laws condemn the love of the unfortunate? What oath forced him to leave the shores of Bornholm, so sweet to him? Shall I, sometime, find out his story?"

Meanwhile a strong wind carried us straight toward the island. Its threatening crags had already appeared, whence seething streams, roaring and foaming, hurtled into the sea's depth. It seemed inaccessible on all sides, protected on all sides by the majestic hand of Nature; nothing but the terrible appeared on those gray cliffs. With horror, I saw there the image of cold, silent eternity, the image of implacable death and that indescribably creative power before which everything mortal must tremble.

The sun sank in the waves—and we cast anchor. The wind had fallen, and the sea scarcely moved. I looked at the island, which drew me with an inexplicable force to its shores; a vague foreboding spoke to me: "There you can satisfy your curiosity, and Bornholm will remain indelibly in your memory!"—Finally, having discovered that there were fishermen's huts not far from the shore, I decided to ask the captain for a dinghy and go to the island with two or three seamen. He spoke of the danger, the submerged rocks, but, seeing the inflexibility of his passenger, he agreed to satisfy my demand on the condition that I return to the ship early the next morning.

We set off and safely pulled up to the shore of a small, quiet cove. Here we were greeted by fishermen, coarse and primitive people, reared by the cold elements in the

---

3   Indeed, the foam of the waves often washed over me, as I lay almost unconscious on the deck.

noise of the sea's billows and unacquainted with the smile of friendly greeting; on the other hand, they were neither crafty nor evil people. When they heard that we wished to look over the island and spend the night in their huts, they tied up our boat and led us over a crumbling siliceous hill toward their dwellings. In half an hour we came out on an expansive green plain where, as in Alpine valleys, were scattered low-slung little wooden houses, small groves, and masses of stone. Here I left the seamen and went on alone in order to enjoy a little longer the pleasantness of the evening; a boy of some thirteen years was my guide.

The crimson glow had not yet faded in the bright sky; its pink light fell on the white granite and, in the distance, behind a high hill, lighted the spired towers of an ancient castle. The boy was not able to tell me to whom this castle belonged.

"We do not go there," he said, "God only knows what goes on there!"

I doubled my pace and soon drew near a large Gothic building, which was encircled by a deep moat and a high wall. Silence reigned everywhere, in the distance the sea roared, the last ray of the evening light had died out on the copper spires of the towers.

I walked around the castle—the gates were locked, the bridges drawn. My guide was afraid of something, he himself did not know of what, and implored me to go back to the huts, but could a curious man comply with such a request?

Night came, and suddenly a voice rang out—an echo repeated it, and again all was silent. In fear, the boy grabbed me with both arms and trembled like a criminal at the moment of execution. In a minute a voice rang out again asking: "Who is there?"

"A foreigner," I said, "led to this island by curiosity, and if hospitality is considered a virtue in the walls of your castle, then you will shelter a wanderer during the dark of night."

There was no answer, but in a few minutes the drawbridge began to clank and was lowered from the top of the tower, and the gates opened noisily—a tall man in a long black dress met me, took me by the hand, and led me into the castle. I turned around but the boy who had accompanied me had disappeared.

The gates slammed behind us; the bridge clanked and was raised. We walked across a vast courtyard, overgrown with bushes, nettles, and wormwood, toward a huge house in which a light glowed. A high peristyle in an antique manner led to an iron porch whose steps rang beneath our feet. It was gloomy and deserted everywhere. In the first hall, encircled within by a Gothic colonnade, hung a lamp and it shed a weak, dim light upon a row of gilded pillars which had begun to crumble, worn by time; pieces of the cornice lay in one spot, fragments of the pilasters in another; in still another, entire fallen columns. My guide glanced at me several times with his penetrating eyes, but spoke not a word.

All this made a strange impression on my heart, mixed in part with horror, in part with a secret inexplicable pleasure or, better, with the pleasant expectation of something extraordinary.

We passed through two or three more halls, similar to the first and lighted by the same kind of lamps. Then a door opened to the right—in a corner of the small room sat a venerable, gray-haired old man, leaning upon a table where two white wax candles burned. He raised his head, glanced at me with a kind of sad tenderness, offered me his feeble hand, and said in a soft, pleasant voice: "Although eternal grief dwells within the walls of this castle, yet the wanderer, who demands hospitality, will always find a peaceful refuge here. Foreigner! I do not know you, but you are a man—in my dying heart love still exists for people—my house, my embraces are open to you." He embraced me, seated me, and, trying to enliven his gloomy visage, he seemed like a clear but cold autumn day, recalling rather a grieving winter than joyous summer. He seemed to want to be kind—to want by a smile to inspire in me trust and pleasant feelings of friendliness, but the marks of spiritual sorrow which furrowed his face could not disappear at once.

"You must, young man," said he, "you must inform me of the events of a world which I have abandoned but not entirely forgotten. Long have I lived in solitude, long have I heard nothing of the fate of people. Tell me, does love reign on the terrestrial sphere? Does incense burn on altars of virtue? Do the people of lands you have seen prosper?" "The light of science," I answered, "extends further and further, but human blood still flows on the earth—the tears of the unfortunate flow—they praise the name of virtue and argue about its essence." The old man sighed and shrugged his shoulders.

Having found out that I was a Russian, he said: "We are descended from the same people as you. The ancient inhabitants of the islands Rügen and Bornholm were Slavs. But you were enlightened by the light of Christianity before us. Magnificent temples, dedicated to one God, had already risen to the clouds in your lands, but we in the darkness of idolatry were offering bloody sacrifices to insensate images. In solemn hymns you had already glorified the great creator of the universe, but we, blinded by error, praised in dissonant songs the idols of mythology." The old man spoke with me about the history of northern peoples, about events of antiquity and modern times; he spoke in such a way that I was amazed at his mind, knowledge, and even his eloquence.

In half an hour he got up and wished me a good night. The servant in the dark dress, having taken a candle from the table, led me through long narrow passages—and we entered a large room, hung with ancient weapons, swords, lances, cuirasses, and spiked helmets. In a corner under a golden canopy stood a high bedstead, adorned with fretwork and antique bas-relief.

I wanted to pose many questions to this man, but he, without waiting for them, bowed and left; the iron door slammed—the sound reverberated terribly within the empty walls—and all became quiet. I lay down on the bed—looked at the ancient weapons, which through the small window were lighted by the faint ray of the moon—thought about my host, about his first words: "Here dwells eternal grief"—dreamed about times past, about those adventures which this ancient castle had witnessed—dreamed like a man who amid coffins and graves gazes at the dust of the dead and revives them in his imagination.—Finally the image of the sad Gravesend stranger rose in my soul, and I fell asleep.

But my sleep was not peaceful. It seemed to me that all the cuirasses hanging on the wall had changed into knights, that these knights approached me with drawn swords, and with angry looks said, "Unfortunate man! How dare you land on our island? Do not seafarers grow pale at the sight of its granite shores? How dare you enter the terrible sanctuary of the castle? Is not its horror known through all the environs? Does not the wanderer retreat from its menacing towers? Daring man! Die for this baleful curiosity!" The swords began to bang above me, blows rained down on my chest—but suddenly everything vanished—I awoke and in a minute again fell asleep. Here a new dream disturbed my spirit. It seemed to me that a terrible thunder resounded through the castle, the iron doors banged, windows rattled, the floor shook, and a horrible winged monster, which I do not know how to describe, with a roar and a shriek flew toward my bed. The vision disappeared but I could no longer sleep, felt the need for some fresh air, approached the window, saw beside it a small door, opened it, and by a steep staircase—descended into the garden.

The night was clear, the light of the full moon silvered the dark greenery of ancient oaks and elms, which formed a dense long lane. The noise of the ocean waves joined the noise of the leaves, rustled by the wind. In the distance were whitened rocky masses, which, like a crenelated wall, encircled the island of Bornholm; between these and the walls of the castle could be seen a large forest on one side—an open plain and small groves on the other.

My heart was still pounding from the terrible visions and my blood had not ceased its agitated pulsating. I entered the dark lane, beneath the cover of the rustling oaks, and with a feeling of deep reverence walked deeper into its darkness. A thought of Druids stirred in my soul—and it seemed to me that I was approaching that sanctuary where all the mysteries and all the horrors of their worship are preserved. At last this long lane led me to rosemary shrubs, behind which a sandy hill towered. I wanted to ascend its summit in order to look at the panorama of the sea and the island in the clear moonlight, but here an opening into the hill became visible: a man could with difficulty enter it. An irresistible curiosity drew me into this cavern, which seemed more the work of human hands than a product of wild Nature. I entered—I felt a dampness and coldness but decided to go farther and, having taken some ten steps forward, discerned several descending steps and a wide iron door; to my astonishment, it was not locked. My hand opened it, seemingly without my will—here behind an iron grating, on which a large lock hung, there burned a lamp, attached to the vault, while in a corner on a straw bed lay a pale young woman in a black dress. She was sleeping; her light-brown hair, entangled with yellow straws, covered her high bosom, which was just barely moving; one hand, white but emaciated, lay on the ground, while the head of the sleeping woman rested on the other. Had an artist wished to portray a languishing, endless, constant grief, strewn with the poppies of Morpheus, then this woman could have served as a beautiful model for his brush.

My friends! Who is not touched by the sight of an unfortunate? But the sight of a young woman, suffering in a dungeon—the sight of the weakest and most beloved of all beings oppressed by fate—could infuse the very stone with feeling. I looked at her with grief and thought to myself: "What barbarian hand has deprived you of the light of day? Is it possible, for some serious crime? But your comely face, but the soft movement of your bosom, but my own heart assure me of your innocence!"

At this very moment she awoke—glanced at the grating, saw me—was dumfounded—raised her head—arose—drew near—lowered her eyes to the ground, as if collecting her thoughts—again fixed her eyes on me, wanted to speak and—did not begin.

"If the sensitivity of a wanderer," I said after some moments of silence, "who has been led to this castle and to this cavern by the hand of fate, can ease your lot, if his sincere compassion merits your trust, demand his help!" She looked at me with motionless eyes, in which astonishment was apparent and a certain curiosity, indecision, and doubt. Finally, after an intense inner turmoil, which seemed to shake her bosom as with an electric shock, she answered me in a firm voice: "Whoever you might be, whatever circumstance brought you here—foreigner, I cannot demand of you anything except commiseration. It is not within your power to change my lot. I kiss the hand which punishes me." "But your heart is innocent?" said I. "It, of course, does not merit such cruel punishment?" "My heart," she answered, "could have erred. God will forgive the weak I hope that my life will soon end. Leave me, stranger!" Here she approached the grating, looked at me tenderly, and with a low voice repeated: "For God's sake, leave me! … If he himself sent you—he whose terrible curse thunders constantly in my ear—tell him that I am suffering, suffering day and night, that my heart has wasted away from grief, that tears no longer ease my anguish. Tell him that I shall endure my imprisonment without murmur, without complaints, that I shall die as his tender, unfortunate. …"—She suddenly became silent, became pensive, withdrew from the grating, knelt and covered her face with her hands; in a minute she looked at me, again lowered her eyes to the ground, and said with tender shyness: "You, perhaps, know my story, but if you do not, then do not ask me—for God's sake, do not ask! … Foreigner, farewell!" Having said a few words to her that flowed straight from my soul, I wanted to go, but my gaze once again met her gaze—and it seemed to me that she wanted to find out from me something of significance to her heart. I stopped—awaiting her question, but after a deep sigh it died on her pale lips. We parted.

I did not close the iron door on leaving the cavern in order that the fresh, clean air might penetrate the dungeon through the grating and ease the breathing of the unfortunate woman. Dawn crimsoned the sky, the little birds awakened, a little breeze blew the dew from the bushes and from the little flowers which grew about the sandy hill. "My God!" I thought. "My God! how grievous to be excluded from the society of living, free, joyous creatures, who everywhere inhabit the boundless expanse of Nature! In the very north, among tall, mossy crags, horrible to behold, the creation of your hand is beautiful—the creation of your hand delights the spirit and heart. Even here, where frothy waves have straggled with the granite cliffs since the beginning of the world—even here your hand has impressed the living signs of creative love and goodness, even here in the morning hours roses bloom beneath the azure sky, even here tender zephyrs exhale fragrances, even here green carpets spread like soft velvet beneath the foot of man, even here the little birds sing—they sing gaily for the gay, sadly for the sad, and pleasantly for all, even here the sorrowing heart can ease its burdens of grief in the embraces of sensitive nature! But—the poor girl, imprisoned in the dungeon, does not have this consolation: the dew of morning does not moisten her languishing heart, the little breeze does not freshen her consumed bosom; the rays of the sun do not light her beclouded eyes; the soft, balsamic effusions of the moon do not nourish her spirit with gentle visions and pleasant dreams. Creator! Why have you bestowed on people the destructive power to make one another and themselves miserable?" Beneath the branches of a tall oak, on the soft greenery, my strength ebbed and my eyes closed.

My sleep lasted some two hours.

"The door had been opened; the foreigner entered the cavern"—that is what I heard on awakening—I opened my eyes and saw the old man, my host; he sat pensively on a turf bench some five feet from me; beside him stood the servant who had led me into the castle. I walked up to them. The old man looked at me with a certain severity, arose, clasped my hand—and his expression became kinder. Together we entered the dense lane; not a word was spoken. It seemed that at heart he wavered and was undecided, but suddenly he stopped and, fixing his penetrating, fiery gaze on me, asked in a firm voice: "Did you see her?" "I saw her," I answered, "I saw, without knowing who she was and why she suffers in the dungeon." "You will find out," he said, "you will find out, young man, and your heart will be drenched in blood. Then you will ask yourself: why has Heaven poured out the whole cup of its wrath on this weak, gray-haired old man, an old man who loved virtue, who honored its sacred laws?"

We sat beneath the tree and the old man told me a most horrible story—a story which you will not hear now, my friends; it will wait until another time. This time I shall tell you one thing only, that I have found the secret of the Gravesend stranger—a terrible secret!

The sailors awaited me at the gates of the castle. ... We returned to the ship, set sail, and Bornholm disappeared from sight.

The sea roared. In grieving pensiveness I stood on the deck, grasping the mast with my hand. Sighs crowded my chest—finally I glanced at the sky—and the wind blew my tear into the sea.

1793

The Bridegroom
from *The Bronze Horseman*

By Aleksandr Pushkin

For three days Natasha,
The merchant's daughter,
Was missing. The third night,
She ran in, distraught.
Her father and mother
Plied her with questions.
She did not hear them,
She could hardly breathe.

Stricken with foreboding
They pleaded, got angry,
But still she was silent;
At last they gave up.
Natasha's cheeks regained
Their rosy colour,
And cheerfully again
She sat with her sisters.

Once at the shingle-gate
She sat with her friends
—And a swift troika
Flashed by before them;
A handsome young man
Stood driving the horses;
Snow and mud went flying,
Splashing the girls.

Aleksandr Pushkin, "The Bridegroom," from *The Bronze Horseman: Selected Poems of Alexander Pushkin,* translated by D.M. Thomas, pp. 129–135. Copyright © Viking Press. Permission to reprint granted by the publisher.

He gazed as he flew past,
And Natasha gazed.
He flew on. Natasha froze.
Headlong she ran home.
'It was he! It was he!'
She cried, 'I know it!'
I recognized him! Papa,
Mama, save me from him!'

Full of grief and fear,
They shake their heads, sighing.
Her father says: 'My child,
Tell me everything.
If someone has harmed you,
Tell us … even a hint.'
She weeps again and
Her lips remain sealed.

The next morning, the old
Matchmaking woman
Unexpectedly calls and
Sings the girl's praises;
Says to the father: 'You
Have the goods and I
A buyer for them:
A handsome young man.

'He bows low to no one,
He lives like a lord
With no debts nor worries;
He's rich and he's generous,
Says he will give his bride,
On their wedding-day,
A fox-fur coat, a pearl,
Gold rings, brocaded dresses.

'Yesterday, out driving,
He saw your Natasha;
Shall we shake hands
And get her to church?'
The woman starts to eat

A pie, and talks in riddles,
While the poor girl
Does not know where to look.

'Agreed,' says her father;
'Go in happiness
To the altar, Natasha;
It's dull for you here;
A swallow should not spend
All its time singing,
It's time for you to build
A nest for your children.'

Natasha leaned against
The wall and tried
To speak—but found herself
Sobbing; she was shuddering
And laughing. The matchmaker
Poured out a cup of water,
Gave her some to drink,
Splashed some in her face.

Her parents are distressed.
Then Natasha recovered,
And calmly she said:
'Your will be done. Call
My bridegroom to the feast,
Bake loaves for the whole world,
Brew sweet mead and call
The law to the feast.'

'Of course, Natasha, angel!
You know we'd give our lives
To make you happy!'
They bake and they brew;
The worthy guests come,
The bride is led to the feast,
Her maids sing and weep;
Then horses and a sledge

With the groom—and all sit.
The glasses ring and clatter,
The toasting-cup is passed
From hand to hand in tumult,
The guests are drunk.

BRIDEGROOM
'Friends, why is my fair bride
Sad, why is she not
Feasting and serving?'

The bride answers the groom:
'I will tell you why
As best I can. My soul
Knows no rest, day and night
I weep; an evil dream
Oppresses me.' Her father
Says: 'My dear child, tell us
What your dream is.'

'I dreamed,' she says, 'that I
Went into a forest,
It was late and dark;
The moon was faintly
Shining behind a cloud;
I strayed from the path;
Nothing stirred except
The tops of the pine-trees.

'And suddenly, as if
I was awake, I saw
A hut. I approach the hut
And knock at the door
—Silence. A prayer on my lips
I open the door and enter.
A candle burns. All
Is silver and gold.'

BRIDEGROOM
'What is bad about that?
It promises wealth.'

BRIDE

'Wait, sir, I've not finished.
Silently I gazed
On the silver and gold,
The cloths, the rags, the silks
From Novgorod, and I
Was lost in wonder.

'Then I heard a shout
And a clatter of hoofs …
Someone has driven up
To the porch. Quickly
I slammed the door and hid
Behind the stove. Now
I hear many voices …
Twelve young men come in,

'And with them is a girl,
Pure and beautiful
They've taken no notice
Of the ikons, they sit
To the table without
Praying or taking off
Their hats. At the head,
The eldest brother,

At his right, the youngest;
At his left, the girl.
Shouts, laughs, drunken clamour …'

BRIDEGROOM

'That betokens merriment.'

BRIDE

'Wait, sir, I've not finished.
The drunken din goes on
And grows louder still.
Only the girl is sad.

'She sits silent, neither
Eating nor drinking;
But sheds tears in plenty;
The eldest brother
Takes his knife and, whistling,
Sharpens it; seizing her by
The hair he kills her
And cuts off her right hand.'

'Why,' says the groom, 'this
Is nonsense! Believe me,
My love, your dream is not evil.'
She looks him in the eyes.
'And from whose hand
Does this ring come?'
The bride said. The whole throng
Rose in the silence.

With a clatter the ring
Falls, and rolls along
The floor. The groom blanches,
Trembles. Confusion …
'Seize him!' the law commands.
He's bound, judged, put to death.
Natasha is famous!
Our song at an end.

[1825]

The Bridegroom
from Alexander Pushkin: Collective Narrative and Lyrical Poetry

By Aleksandr Pushkin

INTRODUCTION

The stanza of this ballad (1825), with its haunting alternation of dreamy singsong, hearty rollick, and ominous gallop, is, of course, borrowed *in toto* from G. A. Bürger's (1747–94) famous "Lenore," perhaps the most impressive work of infant Romanticism. Lenore's ghostly ride bewitched both Goethe and Schiller and scored an international triumph second only to the noble vapors spread by Goethe's own *Werther*. A characteristic stanza of "Lenore" goes as follows:

> Schön Liebchen schürzte, sprang und schwang
> Sich auf das Ross behende;
> Wohl urn den trauten Reiter schlang
> Sie ihre Lilienhände;
> Und hurre hurre, hopp hopp hopp!
> Ging's fort in sausendem Galopp,
> Dass Ross und Reiter schnoben,
> Und Kies und Funken stoben.

It is interesting to note also that Natasha's "nightmare" in "The Bridegroom" in atmosphere and some particulars closely prefigures Tatyana's dream in *Eugene Onegin* V, 11–21, which was written in the same period.

THE BRIDEGROOM

Three days Natasha'd been astray,
Who was a merchant's daughter,
When running home in wild dismay
At last the third night brought her.
Her mother and her father plied
The maid with questions, tried and tried;
She cannot hear for quaking,
All out of breath and shaking.

But fret and wonder as they did
And stubbornly insisted,
They could not fathom what she hid,
And in the end desisted.
And soon Natasha grieved no more,
But flushed and merry as before
Went with her sisters walking
Beyond the gate and talking.

Once at the gate of shingled ash
The maidens sat together,
Natasha too, when in a flash
Past speeded, hell-for-leather,
A dashing troika with a youth;
And rug-clad roans he drove, forsooth,
Drove standing up, bespattered
All in his path and scattered.

He, drawing closer, glanced upon
The maid; her glance replying,
He like the whirlwind galloped on,
The maid was nigh to dying.
And arrow-straight she homeward fled,
"It's he, I knew him well!" she said,
"Stop him, it's he, no other,
Oh, save me, friend and brother!"

Her kinfolk listened, grave and sad,
And shook their heads with ruing:
"Speak out, my lass," her father bade,
"And tell us how you knew him.

If something untoward occurred,
Speak openly, say just a word."
Natasha's back to crying,
No further word replying.

Next day a marriage-gossip came,
Came unexpected rather,
She spoke Natasha fair by name,
Fell talking to her father:
"You have the wares, we want to trade;
My buyer is a fine young blade,
Is lithely made and comely,
Not evil-famed or grumbly.

"Has wealth and wits, to never a man
In low obeisance bending,
But rather, like a nobleman
He lives with easy spending.
He's like to give his chosen girl
A fur of fox-skin and a pearl,
Gold hoops for golden tresses,
And stiff brocaded dresses.

"Last night he saw her on his ride
Out by the town-gate linger;
Let's shake, take ikons and the bride
And to the altar bring her!"
There over tea and cake she sits
And hints and yarns and snares their wits,
While the poor bride's uneasy,
All fidgeting and queasy.

"So be it, then," her father said,
"Go forth, God speed you, dearie,
Take wreath, Natasha, and be wed,
Alone upstairs it's dreary.
Comes time for maids no more to flit,
For swallows, too, their chirps to quit,
It's time to nest, to nourish
Young bairns at home and cherish."

Natasha tried to have her say,
Her back to wall and rafter,
But all ashudder sobbed away,
Now racked with tears, now laughter.
The gossip in dismay runs up,
Makes her sip water from a cup,
And all the rest she dashes
And on her forehead splashes.

Natasha's kinfolk moaned and wept.
But she, back in her senses,
Announced: "I honor and accept
What your high will dispenses.
It's time that to the feast you bade
The groom, and many loaves were made,
Mead choice of brew and hearty,
The Judge bid to the party."

"Command, Natasha, angel child,
To please you, I am ready
To give my life!" A feast is piled,
Prodigious, rich, and heady.
Now worthy guests arrive apace,
They lead the bride to take her place;
As bridesmaids sing with weeping,
A sledge and team come leaping.

Here is the bridegroom—all sit down,
Cup touches cup with ringing,
The toasting bowl goes round and round
To drunken shouts and singing.

THE BRIDEGROOM

"I say, my merry friends, abide,
I say, why is my pretty bride
Not serving, eating, drinking,
All lost in mournful thinking?"

Said bride to groom: 'I'll tell my plight
As best I may be able:
I find no rest by day or night,
I weep abed, at table.
A horrid nightmare wears me out."
Her father wonders: "What about?
Whatever kind it may be.
Tell us, my own dear baby!"

The maiden said: "I dream that I
Walk where the wood grows thickly,
It's late, and from a cloudy sky
The moonlight glimmers sickly.
I've lost my way; in pine and fir
No living creature is astir,
The trees alone are brushing
Their crowns with wispy rushing.

"But clear as day I now make out
Ahead a hut emerging;
I reach it, knock: no answer, shout:
No sound; I hail the Virgin,
I lift the latch, go in, advance,
Inside a candle burns; I glance—
All gleams with heaping measure
Of gold and silver treasure."

THE BRIDEGROOM

"What is so bad about your dream?
It means you'll be in clover."

THE BRIDE

"I ask your leave, sir, it would seem
The dream is not yet over.
On gold and silver, rugs untrod,
Brocade and silks from Novgorod,
I stood in silence gazing
With wonder and amazing.

"Now hoofbeats clatter, voices roar,
Here someone comes a-riding;
I quickly up and slam the door,
Behind the chimney hiding.
Then voices swell in mingled din,
Twelve lusty lads come trooping in;
With them in modest duty
A fair and pure young beauty.

"Without a bow they throng the place,
The ikons never heeding,
Sit down to dine without a grace,
And, cap on head, start feeding.
The eldest brother at the head,
The youngest at his right hand fed,
At left in modest duty
There sat the pure young beauty.

"Hubbub and clink, guffaw and scream,
Exuberant carousal. ..."

THE BRIDEGROOM

"What is so bad about your dream?
It bodes a gay espousal."

THE BRIDE

"Your pardon, sir, it is not done.
The drunken dit goes roaring on,
But as they cheer and riot,
The maid sits sad and quiet.

"Sat mute and neither ate nor sipped,
In bitter tears and fretting,
The eldest brother, whistling, gripped
His knife and fell to whetting;
The fiend glanced at the maiden fair,
And sprang and seized her by the hair:
I saw him kill and fling her
To chop off hand and finger."

"Sheer raving, fancy run amuck,
I would not let it grieve me!
Yet," said the groom, "it bodes good luck,
My tender maid, believe me!"
She gazed at him both hard and long:
"To whom, pray, did this ring belong?"
She asked, and, half-arising,

All stared with dread surmising.
The trinket, slipping, clinked and bounced,
The bridegroom blanched and trembled.
The guests stood awed. The Judge pronounced:
"Stop, bind him, all assembled!"
The fiend was tried, in fetters strung,
And shortly from the gallows hung.
Natasha rose to glory!
And therewith ends my story.

Evil Spirits

By Aleksandr Pushkin

Бесы

Мчатся тучи, вьются тучи;
Невидимкою луна
Освещает снег летучий;
Мутно небо, ночь мутна.
Еду, еду в чистом поле;
Колокольчик дин-дин-дин . . .
Страшно, страшно поневоле
Средь неведомых равнин!

«Эй, пошёл, ямщик! . . .» – «Нет мочи:
Коням, барин, тяжело;
Вьюга мне слипает очи;
Все дороги занесло;
Хоть убей, следа не видно;
Сбились мы. Что делать нам!

В поле бес нас водит, видно,
Да кружит по сторонам.

Посмотри: вон, вон играет,
Дует, плюет на меня;
Вон – теперь в овраг толкает
Одичалого коня;
Там верстою небывалой
Он торчал передо мной;

EVIL SPIRITS

The clouds scurry, the clouds whirl; the moon, invisible, lights up the flying snow; the sky is turbid, and so is the night. On and on I drive in the open plain; ding-ding-ding rings the little bell. ... I can't help feeling frightened amid the unknown expanses.

'Drive on, coachman! ... 'I can't, sir: the horses are hard put to it, the blizzard is blinding me, all the roads are snowed up; strike me dead, but I can't see the track; we've lost our way. What are we to do? ...

It seems that an evil spirit is leading us through the plain and making us go round and round in circles.

Look! There he is, over there, playing, blowing,

Там сверкнул он искрой малой
И пропал во тьме пустой».

Мчатся тучи, вьются тучи;
Невидимкою луна
Освещает снег летучий;
Мутно небо, ночь мутна.
Сил нам нет кружиться доле;
Колокольчик вдруг умолк;
Кони стали . . . «Что там в поле ?»
– «Кто их знает ? пень иль волк ?»

Вьюга злится, вьюга плачет;
Кони чуткие храпят;
Вон уж он далече скачет;
Лишь глаза во мгле горят;

Кони снова понеслися;
Колокольчик дин-дин-дин. . . .
Вижу: духи собралися
Средь белеющих равнин.

Бесконечны, безобразны,
В мутной месяца игре
Закружились бесы разны,
Будто листья в ноябре . . .
Сколько их! куда их гонят ?
Что так жалобно поют ?
Домового ли хоронят,
Ведьму ль замуж выдают ?

Мчатся тучи, вьются тучи;
Невидимкою луна
Освещает снег летучий;
Мутно небо, ночь мутна.
Мчатся бесы рой за роем
В беспредельной вышине,
Визгом жалобным и воем
Надрывая сердце мне . . .

spitting at me; there he is—now he is pushing into a ravine our horse which is running wild; here he loomed before me like a fantastic milestone; there he flashed like a tiny spark and vanished into the empty night.'

The clouds scurry, the clouds whirl; the moon, invisible, lights up the flying snow; the sky is turbid, and so is the night. We've no strength left to circle any longer; suddenly the bell falls silent; the horses halt. … 'What's that, out there in the plain?'—'Who knows? —the stump of a tree, or a wolf?'

The blizzard rages, the blizzard wails; the sensitive horses snort; there he is now, scurrying off into the distance—only his eyes are burning in the dark. …

The horses have dashed off again; ding-ding-ding rings the little bell. … I see the phantoms assembled in the white plain.

Countless, hideous, the manifold spirits are whirling in the dim moonlight, like leaves in November. … Legions of them! Where are they being driven? Why are they singing so plaintively? Are they burying a house-sprite? Celebrating a witche's wedding?

The clouds scurry, the clouds whirl; the moon, invisible, lights up the flying snow; the sky is turbid, and so is the night. The spirits, swarms of them, scurry in the boundless height, rending my heart with their plaintive screeching and howling …

The Drowned Man

1828

By Aleksandr Pushkin

УТОПЛЕННИК

Прибежали в избу дети,
Второпях зовут отца:
«Тятя! тятя! наши сети
Притащили мертвеца».
«Врите, врите, бесенята, –
Заворчал на них отец; –
Ох, уж эти мне робята!
Будет вам ужо мертвец!

Суд наедет, отвечай-ка;
С ним я ввек не разберусь;
Делать нечего; хозяйка,
Дай кафтан: уж поплетусь . . .
Где ж мертвец?» – «Вон, тятя, э-вот!»
В самом деле, при реке,
Где разостлан мокрый невод,
Мертвый виден на песке.

Безобразно труп ужасный
Посинел и весь распух.

Горемыка ли несчастный
Погубил свой грешный дух,
Рыболов ли взят волнами,
Али хмельный молодец,
Аль ограбленный ворами
Недогадливый купец?

THE DROWNED MAN

The children ran into the hut and hastily called their father: 'Father, father! Our nets have dragged up a dead man.' 'You're fibbing, you little devils,' their father growled at them. 'Oh these children of mine! I'll give you a dead man, indeed!

'The law will descend on us—and I'll be the one to answer for it! I'll never be done with them. Well, can't be helped; wife, give me my *kaftan:* I suppose I'd better go … But where's the dead man?' 'There, father, just over there.' And, indeed, by the river's edge, where the damp net lay spread out, the dead man could be seen on the sand.

The dreadful corpse had turned a hideous blue and was all swollen. Was it some unhappy wretch who had destroyed his sinful spirit? Was it a fisherman caught by the waves? Or some drunken young fellow, or some slow-witted merchant robbed by thieves?

What does the *muzhik* care? Looking all around him, he hastens; he drags the drowned body

Мужику какое дело?
Озираясь, он спешит;
Он потопленное тело
В воду за ноги тащит,
И от берега крутого
Оттолкнул его веслом,
И мертвец вниз поплыл снова
За могилой и крестом.

Долго мертвый меж волнами
Плыл качаясь, как живой;
Проводив его глазами,
Наш мужик пошел домой.
«Вы, щенки! за мной ступайте!
Будет вам по калачу,
Да смотрите ж, не болтайте,
А не то поколочу».

В ночь погода зашумела,
Взволновалася река,
Уж лучина догорела
В дымной хате мужика,
Дети спят, хозяйка дремлет,
На полатях муж лежит,
Буря воет; вдруг он внемлет:
Кто-то там в окно стучит.

«Кто там?» – «Эй, впусти, хозяин!» –
«Ну, какая там беда?
Что ты ночью бродишь, Каин?
Черт занес тебя сюда;
Где возиться мне с тобою?
Дома тесно и темно».
И ленивою рукою
Подымает он окно.

Из-за туч луна катится –
Что же? голый перед ним:
С бороды вода струится,
Взор открыт и недвижим,

by the legs into the water, and pushed it away from the steep bank with an oar, and the dead man floated off again downstream, in search of a grave, in search of a cross.

For long the dead man floated, swaying amidst the waves like a living person; having watched him float away, our *muzhik* set off home. 'Hey, you pups! Follow me! You'll get a bun each; but mind, no blabbing, otherwise you'll get a thrashing.'

During the night the weather worsened and the wind whipped up the river; already the splinter has burned out in the *muzhik's* smoky hut; the children are asleep, the wife slumbers; aloft on his bed of planks the husband lies. The storm howls. Suddenly he hears someone knocking at the window.

'Who's there?' 'Eh, let me in, master!' 'Well, what's the matter there? Why do you wander about at night, Cain? The devil's brought you here; why should I bother with you? Here inside it's crowded and dark.' And with lazy hand he raises the window.

The moon rolls from behind the clouds—what does he see? A naked figure stands before him: water streams from his beard,

his eyes are open and immobile; everything about him is fearfully lifeless—his hands hang down, and black crabs have dug into his swollen body.

And the *muzhik* slammed the window: when he recognized the naked visitor, he was struck with terror: 'A plague upon you!' he whispered, trembling. His thoughts became confused with terror; the whole night long he

Все в нем страшно онемело,
Опустились руки вниз,
И в распухнувшее тело
Раки черные впились.

И мужик окно захлопнул:
Гостя голого узнав,
Так и обмер: «Чтоб ты лопнул!»
Прошептал он, задрожав.
Страшно мысли в нем мешались,
Трясся ночь он напролет,
И до утра всё стучались
Под окном и у ворот.

Есть в народе слух ужасный:
Говорят, что каждый год
С той поры мужик несчастный
В день урочный гостя ждет;
Уж с утра погода злится,
Ночью буря настает,
И утопленник стучится
Под окном и у ворот.

shuddered, and till the dawn the knocking went on beneath the window and at the gate.

There is a fearful tale among the people: it is said that since that time every year the wretched *muzhik* awaits his visitor on the appointed day; from morning on the weather rages; at night there comes a storm; and the drowned man knocks beneath the window and at the gate.

[1828]

The Family of a Vourdalak

1847

By Alexis Tolstoy

Gathered in Vienna in the year 1815 was the cream of Europe's intellectuals, the elite of the international diplomatic set and all the towering social figures of the day. The congress was coming to an end. Royalist émigrés were preparing to return to their restored châteaux, and Russian fighters to their forsaken homes, while a number of discontented Poles were scheming to bring to Cracow their dreams of liberty and freedom, dubiously promised them by Prince Metternich, Prince Gartenberg and Count Nesselrode.

The scene resembled the aftermath of an animated social ball. For, in those late hours, after the fanfare and revelry had subsided, there remained a small core of people who, still possessing a taste for amusement and the delightful company of the Austrian ladies, were delaying their departures. This congenial circle, of which I was a member, gathered twice weekly in the manor of the Dowager Princess Schwartzenberg, several miles from the city on the outskirts of the tiny village, Gitzing, The aristocratic bearing of the mistress of the manor, her gracious amiability and her astute intellect held for her guests a magnetic attraction. On these blissful occasions, the mornings were devoted to promenades, and the afternoons to lunching in the manor or its environs. Evenings we spent luxuriating by the hearth, chatting—but never about politics, which was strictly forbidden. We surely had had our fill of that. Sometimes we related tales, either the superstitions and legends of our mother countries or our own experiences.

One evening, after a round of story-telling which left everyone in that strained condition relieved only by the enveloping semidarkness, the Marquis d'Urfé, an elderly émigré who was loved for his youthful gaiety and penetrating wit, interrupted the ensuing silence.

"Your tales, gentlemen, are unusual of course, but each, it seems to me, lacks the critical ingredient of personal involvement. I don't know whether any of you has ever actually witnessed the supernatural phenomenon of which you speak or if you can back it up with your word of honor."

Since not one of us could comply, the old man continued, decorously straightening his jabot.

"As for myself, gentlemen, I know of only one case similar to yours, but so strange, horrible and, what is most essential, authentic is it that even the most incredulous man will be left horror-stricken. I unfortunately was both witness and actor, and though I rarely like to recall the experience, I will do so if our charming ladies will only grant me their permission."

General consent followed immediately. A few apprehensive faces glanced toward the moonlit squares on the parquet marble of the hall where we were assembled. Slowly our small circle drew closer together, silently awaiting the tale. The marquis took out his gold snuffbox, drew a pinch, languorously inhaled and thus began.

"First of all, mesdames, I wish to ask your forgiveness if during my story I allude to my affairs of the heart more often than is agreeable for a man my age. But, as you will see, they are essential for the clarity of my story. And since it is excusable in old age to forget oneself, I hope none of you will mind if I imagine myself a young man again. It was in 1769 that I fell hopelessly in love with the exquisite Duchesse de Gramont. This passion, which at the time I considered deep indeed, left me no peace either day or night, and the duchess, like most beautiful women, prolonged my anguish. In a moment of extreme agitation, I requested and received a diplomatic mission to the Gospodar of Moldavia, where negotiations were being held with Versailles on matters of great importance to France. Before my departure, I visited the duchess. She greeted me less mockingly than ever before; in fact, with genuine concern.

"'D'Urfé, you are acting like a madman. But I know you, and I know you will never change your mind. And so, I beg you for only one thing. Please accept this small cross as a token of my frendship. Wear it until you return. It's a family relic which we value highly,'

"With gallantry perhaps misplaced at that moment, I kissed not the family relic but the delicate hand and fastened the cross around my neck. I have never removed it since.

"I shan't tire you, mesdames, with the details of my trip, with my observations about the Hungarians and Serbs—those poor but brave and honest people who, in spite of Turkish enslavement, had forsaken neither their dignity nor their former independence. It's enough to tell you that having learned Polish during my extended stay in Warsaw, I also managed to acquire some Serbian. Thus, I was able to make myself understood when I finally came upon a particular village, the name of which does not matter. Upon arriving at my quarters, I found my hosts in a state of profound confusion. This seemed especially strange since it was Sunday, the day Serbs abandon themselves to such amusements as dancing, sharp-shooting, wrestling and the like. Ascribing their mood to some recent misfortune, I was about to depart when an imposing young man approached and took my hand.

"'Enter. Enter, foreigner,' he urged. 'Don't be upset by our sadness. You will understand when I explain its origin.'

"He told me that his elderly father, Gorcha, a restless and wild-tempered man, arose one morning and took a long Turkish rifle from the wall.

"'Childen,' said he to his two sons, George and Peter, 'I'm going up in the mountains to join the brave ones who are chasing the scoundrel, Ali Beg.'

"Such was called the Turkish bandit who continued to harass the neighborhood.

"'Wait ten days for me, and if by then I do not return, have a priest say a funeral Mass, for it will mean that I have been killed; But,' added old Gorcha sternly, 'if, and may God save you, I should return after those ten days, then, for your own sakes, do not permit me to enter the house. I order you to pierce me with a stake made of ash, regardless of what I will say or do. Because then I will no longer be myself, but rather a cursed vourdalak come to suck your blood.'

"I must digress, mesdames, to explain that the vourdalaks, or vampires, are, according to local opinion in Slavic nations, dead bodies that rise from graves in order to suck blood from the living. Although their habits are similar to vampires of other countries, vourdalaks prefer to suck the blood of close relatives and friends, who die and become vampires also. In Estonia and Herzegovina entire villages may be composed of vourdalaks. Indeed, the Abbot Augustine Colliné, in his curious book on ghosts, indicates terrible examples of this phenomenon. Moreover, commissioners appointed by German emperors to investigate cases of vampirism have printed evidence of vourdalaks, who, being pierced through the heart with ash stakes, were buried in the village squares. Testimony offered by those officials who had been present at the piercings assure us that they heard the corpses moaning as the stakes struck their hearts. I might add that all such testimony was delivered under oath and backed by signatures and authoritative seals.

"Keeping this in mind, it should be easy, mesdames, for you to comprehend the effect of Gorcha's words upon his sons. Both threw themselves at his feet, pleading that he let them go to the mountains in his place. Gorcha didn't even reply. He simply turned his back on them and set forth, whistling an old ballad.

"The day I arrived in this village was the day appointed by Gorcha for his return, so it was not difficult for me to appreciate his family's alarm. Also, this was a fine family. George, the elder of the two sons, married and with two children, seemed to be the serious and firm one. His brother, Peter, a handsome eighteen-year-old youth, had a gentle manner. He was obviously a favorite of his younger sister, Zdenka, a true Slavic beauty. I was immediately struck by her resemblance to the Duchesse de Gramont, particularly with respect to one characteristic, a delicate line on her forehead. To this day, I have never seen it on anyone other than those two. This faint line, which did not seem appealing at first, became irresistible once you had noticed it a few times.

"Perhaps I was too impressionable then, or maybe this characteristic resemblance combined with Zdenka's charming naïveté was, in fact, irresistible. Having spoken to her briefly, I felt an affection that was destined to become even more tender.

"I remember we were all sitting at the table that was set with farmer's cheese and a jug of milk. Zdenka was weaving; her sister-in-law was preparing supper for the children who were playing in the sand at her feet. Peter was lightheartedly whistling as he cleaned his *jitagan,* a long Turkish dagger. George, who was leaning his elbows on the table with his chin in his hands, could not take his eyes off the main road. He sat there brooding.

"I, also confused by the melancholy atmosphere, stared at the evening clouds and at the monastery rising above the pines of a nearby forest. This monastery, as I later discovered, had been famous at one time for its miraculous icon of the Holy Virgin which, according to legend, was brought by the angels and hung on the branches of an oak tree. During the preceding century, the invading Turks had slaughtered the monks and destroyed this cloister. Now there remained only the walls and a shrine where a mysterious hermit served Mass. He also guided travelers through the ruins and sheltered pilgrims who, journeying from shrine to shrine, preferred to stop at Our Lady under the Oak. Of course, I learned all of this later, since that evening my thoughts were hardly on the archeology of Serbia. As often happens when one gives free rein to thought, I became engrossed with memories of earlier days, with the enchanting period of my childhood and with friends whom I had left for this remote and uncivilized country. And I was dreaming about the Duchesse de Gramont, and—but what is the use of hiding my sinful thoughts?—I mused, mesdames, about several other contemporaries of your grandmothers', whose beauty, in spite of my will, reminded me, each in turn, of the charming duchess. Thus obsessed, I was soon oblivious to my hosts and their anxiety.

"Suddenly, George broke the silence to ask his wife about the exact time the old man had left.

"'At eight o'clock,' she replied. 'I remember hearing the monastery bell strike then.'

"'Well, now it must be no later than half past seven,' he said, becoming pensive and gazing again at the long road leading into the forest.

"I failed to mention, mesdames, that when the Serbs suspect someone of vampirism, they avoid referring to him directly. Otherwise they would call him forth from his grave. Consequently, George alluded to his father as the 'old man.'

"Several minutes of silence lasted until one of the boys pulled Zdenka by the apron, asking, 'Auntie, when is Grandfather coming home?'

"George responded to this question with a violent slap. The child began to cry, whereupon his younger brother asked, surprised and frightened, 'Why do you forbid us, Father, to speak of Grandfather?' Another slap silenced him instantly. Then both began to howl as the rest of the family made a sign of the cross. At that very moment, the monastery clock struck the first chime of eight and a human figure emerged from the forest.

"'It's he, thank God!' exclaimed Zdenka, Peter and their sister-in-law all at once.

"'God protect us!' George cried. 'And how are we to tell if the ten days appointed by him have passed or not?'

"Everyone gazed at him in horror. Meanwhile, the human figure was approaching closer, closer, closer. A tall old man with a gray mustache and a pale and stern face dragged himself with the aid of a stick. The closer he drew, the gloomier George became. Finally, the newcomer stopped and circled his family with a look that seemed oblivious, so glazed and distant were his eyes.

"'Well,' he said in a timbreless voice, 'why does no one meet me? What does this silence mean? Don't you see I'm wounded ?'

"Then we all noticed that the old man's left side was drenched with blood.

"'Hold your father up,' I motioned to George. 'And you, Zdenka, give him something to strengthen him; otherwise, he will collapse.'

"'Father,' said George approaching Gorcha, 'show me your wound. I know about wounds and I'll bandage it for you.' But as soon as the son attempted to take off his coat, the old man pushed him away viciously, clasping his side with both hands.

"'Let go, clumsy one. You are hurting me.'

"'That means you're wounded in the heart!' George exclaimed, his face blanching. 'Take off your coat! Take it off, do you hear! It's crucial, do you hear me!'

"The old man rose to his full height. 'Watch out!' he warned, in that same flat voice. 'If you touch me, I shall curse you.'

"Peter placed himself between George and his father. 'Let him be. You must see he's suffering,'

"'Don't go against his will,' his wife advised. 'You know he'll never tolerate such a thing.'

"At that moment we saw the herd heading toward the house in a cloud of dust. It was not certain whether the dog escorting them did not recognize her old master or if something else influenced her, for as soon as she spied Gorcha, she halted. Her fur bristled. She growled, shivering in her tracks as if she were seeing something extraordinary.

"'What's the matter with the dog?' the old man asked, his frown deepening. 'Have I become a stranger to my own family? Did the ten days in the mountain change me so much that my own dog does not recognize me?'

"'Do you hear?' George nudged his wife.

"'What, George?'

"'He said himself that ten days have passed.'

"'Oh, no! And did he not come at the appointed hour?'

"'Yes, yes. It's clear what has to be done.'

"'The accursed dog is still howling. Shoot her!' Gorcha commanded. 'Do you hear me?'

"George didn't move. But Peter, with tears in his eyes, arose, lifted his father's rifle and shot the dog which whimpered, rolling in the dust. 'This one was my favorite, he said huskily. 'I don't know why my father had to have her killed.'

"'Because that's all she was worth,' Gorcha snapped, 'But it has grown cool. I want to be under the roof.'

"While all this took place, Zdenka prepared a drink of vodka with pears, honey and raisins for the old man, which he pushed away with disgust. He displayed the same loathing for the lamb and rice that George placed before him. Then he went to sit in a corner, muttering unintelligibly.

"The pine logs were flaming in the fireplace, their flicker illuminating the old man's gaunt and pallid face. Were it not for the fire's glow, he could have been taken for a dead man. Zdenka sat down beside him.

"'Father, you do not eat or rest. But do tell us about your adventures in the mountain.'

"By saying this, the girl knew she was striking the most sensitive cord in the old man's heart. He loved to recount his battles and exploits against the Turks. A faint smile crossed his livid lips, though his eyes remained unexpressive. He responded by stroking his daughter's lovely blond hair.

"'Zdenka,' he said, 'I will tell you what I saw in the mountain, but not now, not today. I am tired after all. I can tell you one thing. Ali Beg is dead. He perished by your father's stroke. If anyone doubts it, here is the proof!' He pulled open the bag which was slung across his shoulder, removing a bloody head, not much less cadaverous than his own. We all turned away with a shudder. Gorcha, handing it to Peter, said, 'Hang it over the door of our house so that all those who pass may know that Ali Beg is dead, that the roads are free of villains—unless one counts the Yanychars of the Sultan!'

"Peter obeyed, though with obvious aversion. 'Now everything's clear to me,' he reflected. 'The poor dog was growling because she smelled dead flesh.'

"'Yes, she smelled dead flesh ...' George mumbled, after having returned unobtrusively with something in his hand which he rested in a nearby corner. It looked like a sharply pointed pole.

"'George,' whispered his wife, 'you don't mean you intend to ...'

"'Brother,' murmured Zdenka, what do you have in mind? No, no, no. You're not going to do this! It's inconceivable!'

"'Let me be,' warned George. 'I know what I'm doing and it won't be anything rash.'

"Meanwhile, night had fallen and the family wandered off to sleep in that part of the house which was separated from my own room by a thin partition. I must confess that everything I had observed affected me strangely. I snuffed out the candle. The moon shone through my window, casting bluish reflections on the floor—similar to those, mesdames, you see before your very own eyes. I felt sleepy, but, needless to say, I could not fall asleep. Attributing it to the moonlight, I searched for something to drape across the window. But I couldn't find anything. I was startled by voices coming from the other side of the partition and strained to hear what they were saying.

"'Lie down, wife,' George said soothingly. 'You, Peter, and you, Zdenka, don't worry about anything. I'll stand watch.'

"'No, George,' answered his wife. 'It's I who should not be sleeping. You worked all last night; you're exhausted. Besides, I have to attend our elder son who's been ill since yesterday. Don't worry. Lie down. I'll watch for you.'

"'Brother,' Zdenka said in her caressing voice, 'it seems that nobody has to watch for anything. See how peacefully Father sleeps.'

"'Not my wife, nor you, nor anyone seems to have much sense,' George replied in a voice that left no room for contradiction. 'Now I've told you to go to sleep. I'll be the guard!'

"Complete silence followed. Soon, my eyelids grew heavy, and I too fell asleep. The slow creaking of my door awakened me. The old man, Gorcha was entering. I could feel his presence through the pitch darkness. He seemed to be observing me through his vacant eyes. He lifted one foot after another, stealthily, until he was by my side. Consumed with terror, I nevertheless managed to remain still. The old man bent over me, his livid face so close to mine that I could feel his corpselike breath. Then, exerting superhuman effort, I discovered myself sitting up in bed, perspiring profusely. No one was in the room. But through the window I detected Gorcha, his face pressed against the pane, his uncanny eyes riveted upon me, I didn't have the strength to cry out, only enough composure to remain in bed and pretend I saw nothing. The old man was evidently reassuring himself that I was asleep, for, having stared at me thus, he slowly moved away from the window. George was snoring so loudly that the walls rattled. Then I heard Gorcha's voice in the next room. The sick child coughed.

"'You're not asleep, my little boy?' Gorcha asked.

"'No, Grandfather, and I'd like very much to talk to you.'

"'Ah, you want to talk with me. And what will it be about?'

"'I'd like you to tell me how you fought the Turks because I also want to fight them.'

"'I thought you would, my dear child. Tomorrow, I will give you the small dagger I've been saving.'

"'Oh, Grandfather, please give it to me now.'

"'Well, my little one, why didn't you talk with me earlier today?'

"'Because … because Father wouldn't let me.'

"'Your father is very cautious. But you want the dagger very much. …'

"'Yes, I want it *very* much. Only not here because Father might wake up.'

"'Where, then?'

"'Well, let's go outside quietly, Grandfather, so no one can hear us.'

"Gorcha seemed to laugh as the boy got out of bed. I didn't believe in vampires. But my nerves had been so shattered by my nightmare that I got up and slammed my fist against the partition lest I reproach myself later. No one woke, though my blow sounded loud enough to waken the seven sleepers in the Arabian fairy tale. Determined to save the child, I hurled myself against the door, but it was locked from the outside. To intensify my frustration, the old man was already passing the window with the child in his arms.

"'Get up! Get up!' I screamed with all my might, shaking the partition vehemently. Only then did George awaken.

"'Hurry,' I cried. 'He's carrying your child away.' With one swift kick, George broke down the door and darted toward the forest. With some trouble I wakened Peter, then his sister-in-law and Zdenka. Huddled in front of the house, we saw George a few minutes later returning with the boy in his arms. The child had already fainted when George stumbled upon him on the main highway. We revived him, though he appeared no sicker than before. To our anxious interrogation, he explained that Grandfather had done him no harm, that they had strolled together, quietly chatting; that once they were in the fresh air, he had fainted, though he couldn't remember how or why.

"Gorcha was nowhere to be found so the remainder of the night was spent in hushed consultation.

"The next morning I learned that ice was floating in the river, preventing anyone from crossing to the mainland for several days. Even if it were possible for me to leave, however, I could not have done so. The more I saw Zdenka, the more I craved her. And, mesdames, I am not, mind you, one of those who believe in sudden, uncontrollable passion, the kind exalted in novels. Yet I do believe that love can sometimes develop more quickly than is usual. In Zdenka's remarkable beauty I encountered the Duchesse de Gramont, the duchess transformed by pastoral garb and melodious foreign speech. The characteristic line both had on their foreheads was the *coup de grâce.* Yet perhaps it really was the incredible situation in which I had become an actor that ignited my intense passion.

"During that day I overheard Zdenka speaking with her younger brother. What do you think about Father, Peter?' she asked. 'I can't believe you suspect him.'

"'I dare not suspect him, especially since the boy assured us that Father didn't harm him. As for his sudden disappearance, well, you know he has done this before and never explained his activities and departures.'

"'I know,' Zdenka agreed. 'But you know that George is—'

"'Yes, I know. I know. It's useless talking to him.106I'm afraid we'll have to hide the stake. He won't be able to get another one. There are no ash trees on this side of the mountain.'

"'Yes, let's hide it. But don't tell the children, for they'll surely tell George.'

"'We must be cautious,' Peter urged, and they separated.

"Night came, and still not a trace of the old man, Gorcha. Like the previous night, I was in bed, distracted by the moonbeams that illuminated my room. Sleep was beginning to distort my thoughts when I instinctively felt the presence of the old man. Opening my eyes, I saw his deathlike face pressed against the pane. This time I tried to get up, but my limbs were paralyzed. I heard the old man go around the house and knock on George's window. The child tossed and moaned in his sleep. For a while, silence prevailed. Then there was a knock at the child's window. He moaned again and woke up.

"'Is that you, Grandfather?'

"'It's me,' he answered solemnly. 'I brought you the little dagger.'

"'I don't dare come out. Father has forbidden it.'

"'But you don't have to. Just open the window and kiss me.'

"As the window was being opened, I summoned all my nerve, jumped off the bed and began knocking on the partition. George was immediately up. I heard him cursing and his wife screaming. A minute later the entire household clustered around the fainted child. As before, Gorcha had vanished. We revived the child, though he was weak and could barely breathe. The poor little thing didn't understand why he had fainted. His mother and Zdenka ascribed it to the child's fear of being caught in a forbidden conversation with his grandfather. I said nothing. When the boy grew quiet, everyone but George went to sleep. At dawn, I heard him awaken his wife. They were whispering, Zdenka joined them. The women were crying.

"The child died. I shall not elaborate on the family's despair, except to mention that, peculiarly enough, nobody attributed his death to Gorcha. At least not publicly.

"George remained reticent, his gloomy expression menacing. For two days the old man did not reappear. The third night, on the day of the little one's burial, I sensed that somebody was roaming through the house murmuring the name of the child who was still alive. It even seemed to me, momentarily, that Gorcha glanced into my window. I couldn't be sure, since the moon was obscured by clouds. Nevertheless, I reported this to George. He questioned the child, who acknowledged that he had heard his grandfather calling him and had seen him at the window outside his room. George commanded his son to awaken him the next time the old man appeared.

"These events curiously intensified my tenderness for Zdenka. I existed in constant agitation. During the day it was impossible to speak with her alone. At night, I was tormented by the prospect of my imminent departure.

"Zdenka's room was separated from mine by a hall which led on one side to the street, on the other to the yard. On my way for a walk before sleeping, I passed through the hall and noticed her door slightly ajar. In spite of myself, I stood behind it, listening. The familiar rustle of her dress made my heart pound. She was singing a song about a Serbian knight saying farewell to his girl.

"Oh, my young poplar," the old king said, "I am off to the wars and you will forget me. The trees that grow at the foot of the mountain are slender and easily bent, but your young body is even more slender and even more easily bent. Bittersweet berries are red. They are effortlessly blown by the wind. But your lips are redder than the berries. And I am like the old oak without leaves; my beard whiter than the Danube's foam. You will forget me, little heart, and I will perish from longing, for the enemy will not dare to kill the old king." Then the beautiful girl answered. "I swear to remain faithful to you, never to forget you. If I break my oath, then return after death to suck my heart's blood." To which the old king replied, "Amen." He went off to war and the beautiful girl forgot him.

"Here Zdenka stopped as if afraid to finish the song. I could no longer contain myself. Her soft eloquence was an echo of the Duchesse de Gramont. Disregarding the consequences, I flung open the door. My intrusion made her blush, for she had just removed her outer garment and was wearing only a gold-embroidered red silk blouse and a richly colored petticoat. The outline of her supple limbs was visible, her abundant blond hair unbraided. In this state of half-undress, she looked more ravishing than ever.

" 'Zdenka, my life, please do not fear me,' I implored. 'Everybody is asleep. Only the crickets in the grass and the dragonfly in the air can hear what I'm going to tell you.'

"'Go away, go away, my dearest. If my brother sees us, I'm lost.'

"'Zdenka, I will not leave until you promise to love me as the lovely maiden in your song promised to love the king. Zdenka, I soon will have to depart. Who knows whether we shall ever see each other again. I love you more than my own soul, more than my salvation. My life and my blood are yours. Won't you give me but an hour?'

"'Too much can happen in an hour,' Zdenka said softly, leaving her hand in mine. 'You don't know my brother. I have a premonition that he will see us.'

"'Don't worry, Zdenka, my darling Zdenka. Your brother is exhausted by these sleepless nights. He is lulled by the wind rustling through the trees. His slumber is deep. Our night is long, and I beg you for only one hour, whereas the farewell may last forever.'

"'No, no. Not forever!'

"'Perhaps, Zdenka. Yet I see only you, hear only you. I am no longer master over my own fate. It's as if I were compelled by a superior power. Forgive me!' and like a madman I pressed her to my heart.

"'You're not a friend to me, no, no, no,' she gasped, breaking away from my arms and hiding in a corner.

"I don't recall what I replied to her at that moment, for my sudden boldness alarmed me, though not because I was inhibited in the past, but because, in spite of my passion, I deeply respected Zdenka's purity. Thus, my gallant manner, so successful with the beautiful maidens of the time, shamed me. I realized that the young girl, in all her simplicity, had not fathomed the intent of my artful words, though, mesdames, judging from your smiles, I can see it is readily apparent to you. I stood before her bewildered, when unexpectedly she pointed toward the window, shivering. There was

Gorcha peering at us. A heavy arm grabbed my shoulder. I turned around. It was George.

"'What are you doing here?'" he scowled.

"Embarrassed by this turn of events, I directed his attention toward his father, who was still standing at the window but who vanished once George saw him.

"'I heard the old man and came to warn your sister,' I explained. George stared as if to penetrate my innermost thoughts. Taking my arm, he walked me to my room and left without a word.

"The next day the family was gathered in front of the house at a table set with dairy foods.

"'Where is the boy?' asked George.

"'In the yard,' his wife answered. 'He's playing his favorite game, imagining that he's fighting against the Turks.'

"No sooner had she said this than to our great surprise we detected the hulking form of old Gorcha lumbering toward us from the forest, in a manner reminiscent of his initial arrival.

"'You are most welcome, Father,' said his daughter-in-law in a low tone,

"'We are happy to see you, Father,' chorused Zdenka and Peter.

"'Father,' George said, 'we were expecting you. Will you say grace?'

"The old man turned away, frowning.

"'Say grace this very minute,' urged George, 'and make the sign of the cross. Or, I swear by St. George …'

"Zdenka and her sister-in-law begged the old man to say grace.

"'No,' insisted Gorcha. 'He doesn't dare give me orders. If he tries to force me, I will curse him.'

"George darted into the house, returning in a fury. Where is the stake?' he cried. 'Where did you put the stake?'

"Zdenka and Peter glanced at each other furtively.

"'You corpse!' George shouted at his father. 'What have you done with my elder son? Give me my son, you dead man!'

"Speaking this way, he turned more and more pale as rage burned in his eyes. The old man stood motionless, an evil sneer on his lips.

"'Where in heaven's name is the stake? Where is that stake?' George continued. 'Let misery befall those who have hidden it, all the misery possible in one lifetime.'

"Then the most terrible thing occurred. Riding toward us on an enormous stake was the younger son, his blood-curdling laughter resounding in our ears. As he neared us, he screeched the Serbian battle cry.

"George flushed, grabbing the stake away from the child. The youngster threw himself on his father, who let forth a howl, and then darted away in the direction of the forest with a speed that seemed supernatural. George chased him across the field and also faded out of sight. The sun had already set when George, pale as death, his hair on end, came back. As he sat by the fire, his teeth seemed to be chattering. Nobody dared question him. As bedtime approached, he regained his self-control and, calling me to his side, spoke in a casual manner,

"'My dear guest, I just saw that the river is cleared of ice. Nothing detains you any longer. No need to say good-bye to my family,' he added, glancing at Zdenka. 'She wishes you well and hopes you remember us kindly. At dawn, you will find your horse saddled and a guide to direct you out of the village. Farewell, and forgive your hosts for the difficult times you spent with them.'

"George seemed almost friendly as he accompanied me to my room and shook my hand for the last time. Then he shuddered and his teeth chattered as if from the cold.

"Once alone, I thought of the despair I had suffered over former love affairs, the tenderness, jealousy and rage. Yet never until that moment, not even during encounters with the Duchesse de Gramont, had I experienced such despondence. I changed into my traveling clothes before the sun had risen, hoping to see Zdenka before my departure. But George was already awaiting me in the hall.

"I spurred my horse on, promising myself that I would stop at the village when returning from Yassa. Although this was a long time off, the prospect relieved my sadness. I was already contemplating a pleasurable return, and my imagination was working out the sweet details, when my horse bolted, almost hurling me from the saddle. She stopped, stretched out her forelegs and snorted as if in danger. I looked about in every direction until I noticed a wolf about a hundred steps ahead of us, digging in the ground. Seeing us, it raced away. I rode over and found a freshly dug hole, with a stake sticking out a few inches above the ground. Yet I couldn't be sure of this, since I rode by swiftly.

At this point, the marquis stopped talking and took a pinch of snuff.

"Is that all?" the ladies asked.

"Oh, no, not at all," assured d'Urfé. "It's very painful for me to recall what I am about to relate. Gladly would I forfeit worldly pleasures to free my mind forever of these memories.

"It took me about half a year to conclude my affairs in Yassa, much longer than anticipated. How can I tell you what I experienced through that stretch of time? It's the sad truth that stable emotions do not exist in this world. The success of my negotiations regarding the revolting politics which have recently caused so much trouble brought me strong praise from Versailles. But my tormenting memories of Zdenka were intensified. Even the ladies, particularly the wife of the Seigneur of Moldavia—a beauty who spoke our language to perfection and who singled me out from all the other young foreigners in Yassa—could not relieve my pain. Yet, reared according to French gallantry and ruled by the Gallic blood in my veins, I, of course, could not refuse this lady's flattering approaches. Moreover, considering that I was the French representative at the court of her husband, I regarded it my singular duty to satisfy the desires of the seigneur's noble wife. As you can see, mesdames, I always put the interests of my country above all else. …

"Upon my return home, I journeyed by the same road I had taken to Yassa, By then I had forgotten Zdenka and her family and was reminded of them while riding through a field where I heard a bell ring eight times. Its ring was familiar. My guide informed me that it came from a nearby shrine, the Monastery of Our Lady under the Oak. With this, I headed for the guest house which was swarming with pilgrims. A monk assured me I could find lodging practically anywhere, that, due to "damned Gorcha," there were many empty houses.

"'Do you mean,' I gasped, 'that the old man is still alive?'

"'No. Apparently, he is lying quietly in the earth with a stake through his heart. He sucked the blood of his grandson, the younger child of George. One night, the little boy knocked at the house begging to be admitted, crying that he was cold. His foolish mother, though she herself had buried him that very day, was unable to summon the courage to send her son back to his grave. No sooner had she let him in than he threw himself upon her, sucking her life's blood. After she was buried, she in turn came for the blood of her husband and her brother-in-law. They all shared the same fate.'

"'And Zdenka? What happened to her?' I asked, trembling.

"'Well, as for her, the poor thing went mad from sorrow. It's really better we don't speak of her.'

"The monk's comments were puzzling, but I had no heart to pursue them further.

"'Still,' he continued, 'vampirism is contagious. Many families in the village suffer from it. If you accept my advice, you'll remain in the monastery for the night. Out there, whether the vourdalaks get you or not, you'll undergo such terror that your hair will turn snow white before I ring for early Mass. Of course, I'm only a poor monk, yet the generosity of the travelers enables me to care for their needs. I can offer you such excellent farmer's cheese and currants that your mouth will water at the sight of them. There are a few bottles of Tokay wine which are as fine as those served at the table of His Holiness.'

"I seemed to be speaking with an innkeeper rather than a monk, and his purpose in relating these horror stories appeared bent upon coercing me into imitating the generosity of the other travelers who provided the holy man with the means of gratifying their needs. Aside from this, the word 'terror' never fails to affect me like a trumpet affects a war horse. How ashamed I would have been had I not proceeded instantly to investigate the rumors!

"My shivering guide begged permission, which I granted, to remain at the monastery. I thus arrived alone at the deserted village. No lights were on; no songs sung. Through the eerie silence, I passed those familiar houses until I reached George's. Whether I was influenced by a romantic whim or simply by youthful boldness, I resolved to spend the night, though no one answered my knock at the gates. Pushing, I managed to get them open. I tied my saddled horse to the shed and crept up to the house. Not a single door was locked, yet the house seemed abandoned. Zdenka's room appeared to have been forsaken that very day. Several dresses lay across the bed. A few pieces of jewelry, gifts from me, were scattered on the bureau. A small enamel cross, which. I had purchased in Budapest, sparkled in the moonlight.

"My heart pounded at a dreadful speed. Regardless of my waning love, I sighed, wrapped myself in my cape, stretched out on the bed and slept I can't recall the precise details, but I do remember envisioning Zdenka as a charming, ingenuous, devoted creature shamed by my fickleness. How, I agonized, could I have forgotten the sweet maiden who had loved me so very much? The vision of her became intertwined with my memories of the Duchesse de Gramont, and, in those two silhouettes, I saw one and the same person. Kneeling at Zdenka's feet, I prayed for her forgiveness. My entire being, my very soul, became infused with both sadness and happiness. Thus, I continued to dream until gently wakened by wheat stalks waving in the wind. I heard the distant chirping of birds, the rushing of a waterfall and the brushing of leaves, when it seemed that all those sounds could actually have emanated from the rustling of a lady's dress. With this notion, I opened my eyes and beheld Zdenka by my bedside. So bright was the moon that I could distinguish every feature, each more enchanting than I remembered. She was dressed in the garb she had worn on the eve of our farewell: her silk peasant blouse embroidered in gold and dirndl skirt gathered tightly around her slim waist.

"'Zdenka,' I cried, rising quickly from the bed. 'Is it you?'

"'Yes, it is me,' she responded in a small, pathetic voice. 'Yes, it is your forgotten Zdenka. Why didn't you return sooner? Now everything is ended and you must leave at once. A moment's delay and you are lost. Farewell, my friend. Farewell forever.'

"'Zdenka. Zdenka, you have been through so much sorrow. Please speak with me at least. It will relieve your anxiety.'

"'My friend, do not believe all you hear about us. But do go. Go quickly, or else you will die without reprieve.'

"'But Zdenka, what is there to fear? Is it possible you will not grant me an hour?' She shuddered and for a second seemed almost imperceptibly transformed.

"'All right. An hour—just one. Is it not the same request you made the night you overheard me singing about the old king? So be it again. I'll permit you this hour…But no, no,' she screamed, as if coming to her senses, 'Go. Run. Run far away, I'm telling you to hurry while you still have the chance.'

"A wild frenzy distorted her features. I couldn't understand what forced her to speak this way. I only knew how lovely she was and decided to remain in spite of her wishes. Finally, complying with my request, she sat beside me and confessed that she had loved me at first sight. As she spoke, the change in her became gradually more and more distinct. Her eyes glinted boldly. Her movements challenged me provocatively. Indeed, she was emerging as someone quite unmaidenly, even wicked, completely different from the reserved young virgin of my memories.

"Is it possible, I asked myself, that Zdenka was never the chaste girl she appeared to be six months ago? Is it possible that being afraid of her brother, she had assumed a convenient disguise? Had I been tricked by a modest façade? But then, I countered, why did she urge me to leave? Was this simply a coy move? I imagined for the moment that I saw the former Zdenka … But no, she was still transfigured. … If Zdenka is not the Diana I thought she was, could she not be compared to another goddess at least as charming? Anyway, I prefer the fate of Adonis to that of Acteon.* If this classical reference seems out of place, mesdames, please remember that I am relating events of 1769. At that time, mythology was à la mode, and I made the pretense of being avant-garde. Since then, times have changed, for the revolution has eclipsed both paganism and Christianity. The new religion, reason, is erected in their place. I never favored this cult, reason, especially in the company of women. As my story was transpiring, I was particularly unwilling to worship this deity. Quite naturally, I abandoned myself to Zdenka, responding pleasurably to her irresistible advances. Some time passed in sweet forgetfulness. Zdenka amused me by trying on one piece of jewelry after another, until it occurred to me to place the enamel cross around her swanlike neck. Anticipating my intention, Zdenka withdrew with a shudder.

"'Enough of this foolishness, my love,' she smiled, regaining her composure. 'Let us leave all these trinkets and discuss you and your intentions.'

"In spite of my feelings, Zdenka's odd behavior forced me to study her more closely. Unlike the past, she did not have on the holy medals and relics which Serbians commonly wear from childhood to death. I questioned her about this.

"'I lost them,' she answered, impatient to change the subject.

"A sense of foreboding came over me. I decided to leave, but Zdenka stood in my way.

"'What's the meaning of this?' she scowled. 'You begged me for an hour of my time, and now you're leaving so abruptly.'

"'Zdenka, you were right in convincing me to leave. I just heard a noise. I'm afraid we will be discovered together,' I said, attempting to conciliate her.

"'Don't worry, my friend. Everyone around us is asleep. Only the cricket in the grass and the dragonfly in the air can hear what we say.'

"'No, no, Zdenka, this won't do. I must go.'

"'Please wait,' she implored. 'I love you more than my own soul, more than my salvation. You once told me that your life and blood were mine.'

"'But your brother! I have the feeling he is about to arrive.'

"'Be still, my heart. My brother is asleep, too, lulled by the wind that is rustling in the trees. His sleep is deep and the night is long. I am requesting but a moment longer.'

---

* Adonis, after being slain by a wild boar, spent four months out of every year with Persephone, four with Aphrodite, and four wherever he chose; Acteon was transformed into a stag after he saw the goddess of chastity bathing.—Ed.

"As she said this, Zdenka looked so beautiful that the anxiety that had gripped me vanished with my desire to remain by her side. A strange mixture of fright and rapture filled me. Slowly, as my will weakened, Zdenka became increasingly tender. I resolved to give in to her while I maintained my guard. But alas! I was only half sensible, as usual. Noticing my reserve, she offered me a few drafts of wine to warm myself, saying that she had purchased it from the good monk. My compliance elicited a smile, and the wine surely produced its intended effect. After the second glass, my reservations over the little cross and holy medals were completely erased from my consciousness. Zdenka, in her informal attire, her blond hair unbraided, her bracelets gleaming in the moonlight, was hopelessly enticing. I could not restrain myself and impulsively embraced her.

"Then, mesdames, then one of those inexplicable signs appeared. I have never been able to explain it to myself. In fact, at that time I was inclined not to believe in it at all. Nevertheless, when I pressed Zdenka's body to my own, one of the points of the cross, which the Duchesse de Gramont had given me, stuck into my chest. That momentary pain served as a bolt from heaven. Glancing at Zdenka, I saw that her features, though beautiful, were imprinted with death, that her eyes were glazed and that her smile was convulsed with the agony of a condemned prisoner. Simultaneously, I sensed in the room a putrid odor like some half-opened tomb. The loathsome truth stunned me. Only too late did I recall the monk's warning. What a desperate situation I was in! Everything depended upon boldness and cunning. Not wanting her to notice my doubt, I turned away. My gaze passed for a second across the window where Gorcha was leaning on a bloody stake, peering at me with the eyes of a hyena. In the other window stood George, looking exactly like his father. They were both following my movements closely. Undoubtedly they would descend upon me at my slightest effort to escape. So I pretended not to have seen them but continued, with all my will, to caress Zdenka as if nothing unusual were happening. My mind raced through plans of escape. The wailing of women and children floated in from the yard, piercing the silence like the howling of wild cats.

"It is time to escape, I said to myself, and the sooner the better. Turning to Zdenka, I spoke loudly enough for her ghastly relatives to hear. 'I am tired, my dearest, and must lie down for a while. Yet, first, my horse should be fed. I beg you not to leave. Wait for me,' I said, kissing her cold mouth. Outside, my horse was covered with foam, trying vainly to gallop out of the shed. Her neighing made me wary lest she give me away. But the vourdalaks who overheard my conversation with Zdenka did not move. Certain that the gates were ajar, I jumped onto the saddle and spurred my horse on. Having passed swiftly through the gates, I barely noticed the crowd gathered round the house, gaping through the windows. My sudden departure must have startled them. Yet for those first few moments I only concentrated on the rhythmic clatter of my horse's hoofs as they resounded in the unearthly silence.

"On the verge of congratulating myself on a safe escape, I was interrupted by a noise that resembled a hurricane. Voices moaned, howled and argued with one another.

Silence. Then a resounding beat as if a corps of infantrymen were in hot pursuit, I spurred on until my horse spurted blood and my veins almost burst from the fire within. A voice was calling me.

"Wait, wait, my dear. I love you more than my soul, more than my salvation. Wait, wait. Your blood is mine.'

"A cold breath touched my ears as Zdenka leaped upon my horse from behind.

"'My heart, my soul,' she whispered to me. 'I see only you. I want only you. I have no power over myself. I obey a superior force. Forgive me, my dear one, forgive me.' Placing her arms around me, she bit my neck and tried to throw me from my horse.

"A terrible struggle ensued between us. Mustering all my energy, I managed to grab Zdenka with one arm around her waist, the other hand on her braids. Lifting myself in the stirrups, I hurled her to the ground. My strength drained, I became delirious. Gruesome images menaced me. First George, then Peter, was running along the road's edge trying to veer me off course. Neither one succeeded. I was rejoicing over this victory when, turning back, I saw old man Gorcha leaning on his stake, making incredible leaps with it as the Tyroleans do when they jump over crevices. But even he remained behind. His daughter-in-law, who was dragging the two children, threw one of them to him. He caught it on the sharp point, then, operating the stake like a slingshot, hurled the child at me. I avoided the blow, but the child, like a fierce bulldog, set his teeth in the neck of my horse. With some effort, I tore him away. Gorcha discharged the other one at me, but he was crushed under my horse's hoofs. I don't know what happened next. When I regained consciousness, it was already daylight, and I was sprawled at the edge of the road, my horse dying nearby.

"And so, mesdames, ended the love affair which, it would seem, should have numbed all my subsequent desires to search for others among your grandmothers. Those who still survive will testify that I did become far more sensible.

"The events I have related to you this evening are strange indeed. To this very day I shiver at the thought that I had fallen into the power of my enemies. I might have become a vampire in turn. But Providence did not permit this, and I, mesdames, am not thirsty for your blood. And, though an old man, I am prepared to defend you till the last drop of blood courses from my veins."

Viy*

By Nikolai Gogol

As soon as the rather loud seminary bell, hanging at the gates of the Bratsky Monastery, rang out in the morning in Kiev, crowds of schoolboys and seminarists would come hurrying there from all over the town. Seminarists of the lower forms, known as grammarians and rhetoricians, and those of the higher forms, known as philosophers and theologians, trudged to their classrooms with their exercise books under their arms. The grammarians were still small boys and, as they walked along, they pushed each other and swore at one another in shrill treble voices; they almost all wore filthy, tattered clothes and their pockets were always full of all sorts of rubbish, such as knucklebones, whistles made out of feathers, a half-eaten pie, and sometimes even tiny sparrow chicks, one of whom suddenly chirruping in the dead silence of the classroom earned its patron sound blows with a ruler on both hands and, occasionally, a thrashing with cherry twigs. The rhetoricians walked more sedately: their clothes were quite often decent, but their faces almost invariably wore some adornment in the shape of a rhetorical trope: either one eye had disappeared right under the forehead, or there was a huge blister in place of a lip, or some other distinctive mark; these talked and swore among themselves in tenor voices. The philosophers went a whole octave lower; there was nothing in their pockets except strong tobacco made of the crushed roots of the plants. They kept nothing to eat later, but ate everything they came across there and then; they reeked of pipes and vodka so strongly that a passing workman would stop in his tracks and sniff the air for a long time like a setter dog.

The market, as a rule, was only beginning to stir at that time, and the market-women with thick, ring-shaped rolls, ordinary rolls, water-melon seeds and poppy-cakes vied with each other in pulling at the skirts of those whose coats were of fine cloth or some cotton material.

---

* Viy is a colossal creature of popular imagination. The Ukrainians give this name to the chief of the gnomes whose eyelids reach down to the ground. The whole story is a folk legend. I did not wish to change it and I tell it almost in the same simple way as I heard it.

Nikolai Gogol, "Viy," from *Mirgorod*, translated by David Magarshack, pp. 175–219. Copyright © 1962 by Minerva Press. Permission to reprint granted by the publisher.

This way, young gentlemen, this way!" they would say from all sides. "Here are thick-rolls, poppy-cakes, twists, good white rolls! Good ones! Really good ones! Made with honey! I baked them myself!"

Another market-woman, lifting something long made out of twisted dough, would yell: "Here's a bread-stick! Buy a bread-stick, young gentlemen!"

"Don't buy anything from her! See what a nasty woman she is—look at her ugly nose and dirty hands!!"

But they were afraid to accost the philosophers and theologians, for the philosophers and theologians always liked to taste things first and they usually helped themselves to handfuls.

On their arrival at the seminary, the crowd made their way to their low-pitched but fairly large classrooms with little windows, wide doors and dirty benches. The class-room was immediately filled with all sorts of buzzing sounds: the "auditors," mostly students from the higher classes, heard their pupils repeat their lessons: the treble of the grammarian rang so loudly that it evoked almost the same note from the window pane; in a corner a rhetorician, whose mouth and thick lips ought really to have belonged to a philosopher, was droning in a bass voice and all that could be heard at a distance was: "Boo, boo, boo. ..." The auditor, while hearing the lesson, would glance with one eye under the bench, where a role or fruit dumpling or some melon seeds were peeping out of the pocket of the seminarist placed under his supervision.

When this erudite crowd managed to arrive a little early and when they knew that the professors would be later than usual, then by general consent they got up a fight. In this fight everyone had to take part, including the monitors whose duty it was to look after the good behavior and the morals of all this learned profession. The theolo-gians usually made the arrangements for the battle: whether each class had to defend itself separately or whether all were to be divided into two parties: the bursars and the seminarists. In any case, the grammarians were the first to start fighting, but as soon as the rhetoricians entered into the fray, they ran away and took up a position on top of the desks to watch the battle. Next the philosophers, with long, black moustaches, joined in, and finally the thick-necked theologians in their awe-inspiring wide trousers. As a rule, it all ended by theology routing the rest, and philosophy, rubbing its ribs, was forced back into its classroom and sat down on the benches to rest. The professor, who had himself at one time taken part in similar engagements could, on entering the class, see in a flash from the red faces of his students that the fight had been a good one, and while he was caning the rhetoricians on the fingers, in another classroom another professor would be administering punishment to philosophy's hands with a ruler. The theologians were dealt with in quite a different way: they were each served, to use the expression of a professor of theology, a measure of *large peas* in the shape of short leather thongs.

On holidays and festive occasions the seminarists and the bursars went from house to house with their puppet shows. Sometimes they acted a play, in which case some theologian, almost as tall as the Kiev belfry, would distinguish himself in the part of Herodias or Potiphar's wife. As a reward they received a piece of linen or sack of millet or half a boiled goose, or something of that sort.

All that learned crowd, both the seminarists and the bursars, who conducted a sort of hereditary feud among themselves, were very hard up and could ill afford the bare necessities of life, and yet they were at the same time terrible gluttons; indeed, it was quite impossible to add up the number of dumplings each of them bolted during an evening meal and, therefore, the voluntary contributions of the well-to-do citizens could not be sufficient for them. It was then that the "senate" of philosophers and theologians sent the grammarians and rhetoricians, under the supervision of a philosopher, who sometimes joined them, with sacks on their shoulders to lay waste the kitchengardens—and pumpkin porridge made its appearance in the seminary. The "senators" gorged themselves on melons and water-melons, so that next day their "auditors" heard two lessons from them instead of one: one issuing from their lips and another growling from their stomachs. The bursars and the seminarists wore long garments resembling frock coats, reaching *to the present time,* a technical term, signifying below the heels.

The most solemn occasion for the seminary was the advent of the vacation, which began in June, when the students were usually sent back to their homes. Then the whole highroad was dotted with grammarians, philosophers and theologians. Those who had no homes of their own usually went to stay with one of their classmates. The philosophers and theologians usually got jobs as *temporary* tutors, that is to say, they undertook to teach children of well-to-do families so as to prepare them for the entrance examinations and received in payment a pair of new boots, and sometimes even a coat. The whole gang trailed along together like some gypsy encampment, cooked their porridge and slept in the open. Everyone carried a sack in which he had one shirt and a pair of leg-wrappers. The theologians were particularly thrifty and careful: anxious not to wear out their boots, they took them off, hung them on sticks and carried them on their shoulders, especially if it was muddy; rolling up their trousers above their knees, they then strode splashing through the puddles regardless of anything. The moment they caught sight of a hamlet in the distance they would turn off the highway and approaching a cottage which looked a little better kept than the rest, stood in a row in front of the windows and begin singing hymns at the top of their voices. The master of the house, some old Cossack villager, would listen to them for a long time, his head propped up on his hands, then he would weep bitterly and turn to his wife and say: "Wife, what the scholars are singing must be very wise: give them some bacon or anything else we have." And a whole bowl of dumplings were emptied into the sack, followed by a big lump of bacon, several white loaves, and sometimes even a trussed hen. Fortified with such a supply of food, the grammarians, rhetoricians, philosophers and theologians carried on with their journey. The further they went, however, the more their numbers dwindled. Most of them dispersed to their homes and only those remained whose parents lived further away.

Once, during such a journey, three bursars turned off the highway to replenish their supply of provisions at the first hamlet they came across, for their sacks had long been empty. They were the theologian Khalyava, the philosopher Khoma Brut and the rhetorician Tibery Gorobets.

The theologian was a tall, broad-shouldered fellow, and had an extremely odd habit: whatever lay within his reach, he was sure to steal, otherwise he was of an exceedingly gloomy disposition. When he got drunk he used to hide in the tall weeds, and it gave the seminary a great deal of trouble to find him there.

The philosopher Khoma Brut was of a merry disposition. He was fond of lying on his back and smoking a pipe. If ever he went on a drinking spree, he engaged musicians and danced the tropak. He often had a taste of the *large peas,* but he took it with perfect philosophical *insouciance,* saying that what had to be, had to be.

The rhetorician Tibery Gorobets had not yet qualified to wear a moustache, to drink vodka or to smoke a pipe. He only wore a long forelock on his shaven head and hence his character does not seem to have been sufficiently formed at that time, but to judge from the big bumps on his forehead with which he often appeared in class, one could safely assume that one day he would become a first-class warrior. The theologian Khalyava and the philosopher Khoma often pulled him by the forelock as a sign of their patronage and employed him as their errand boy.

It was evening when they turned off the highway. The sun had only just set and the warmth of the day still lingered in the air. The theologian and the philosopher walked along in silence smoking their pipes; the rhetorician Tibery Gorobets decapitated with his stick the thistles growing by the wayside. The road ran between scattered clumps of oak and nut-trees, growing in the meadow. Small, undulating hills, green and round like cupolas, sometimes intersected the plain. A cornfield with ripening wheat which appeared in two places showed that some village must be near. But it was more than an hour since they had passed the cornfield and still they had not come upon any dwelling. Dusk had fallen, the sky had grown completely dark, only in the west the faint scarlet glow of sunset was still visible.

"What the hell!" said the philosopher Khoma Brut. "I could have sworn we'd come across a hamlet any minute!"

The theologian said nothing, looked round at the surrounding countryside, then put the pipe back into his mouth, and they all continued on their way.

"Hell," said the philosopher, stopping again, "can't see a damn thing."

"Well, perhaps we shall come across some hamlet further on," said the theologian, without removing his pipe.

Meanwhile night had fallen, and a rather dark night too, it was. Small clouds increased the darkness and, as far as they could judge, they could expect neither stars nor moon. The seminarists noticed that they had lost their way and had for a long time been walking off the road.

The philosopher, after shuffling about with his feet in every direction, said at last abruptly: "But where is the road?"

The theologian said nothing and, after pondering for a while remarked: "Yes, it's a dark night all right."

The rhetorician walked off to one side and tried to feel for the road on all fours, but his hands only came upon foxes' holes. All round them was the steppe and it seemed that there was no one travelling across it just then. Our travellers made another attempt to carry on, but there was the same wilderness everywhere. The philosopher tried shouting, but his voice died away in the distance and met with no reply. A few moments later, though, they heard a faint moaning like that of a wolf.

"What the hell are we going to do?" said the philosopher.

"To do? Why, stay here and spend the night in the open," said the theologian, feeling in his pocket for the flint to light his pipe again.

But the philosopher would not agree to this. He had always been in the habit of tucking away for the night a thick slice of bread and four pounds of fat bacon and this time he had an insufferable feeling of loneliness in his stomach. Besides, in spite of his cheerful character, the philosopher was rather afraid of wolves.

"No, Khalyava," he said, "it's no good. How on earth can you expect anyone to stretch out and lie down on the bare ground like a dog without having first fortified himself properly. Let's try again. Maybe we'll come across some house and get at least a glass of vodka before turning in."

At the word "vodka" the theologian spat and said: "Why, of course. It's no use staying in the open."

The seminarists walked on and to their intense delight, they thought they could hear the sound of barking in the distance. Listening which direction it came from, they went ahead more boldly and after a little distance saw a light.

"A hamlet, damned if it's not a hamlet!" said the philosopher.

He was not wrong in his supposition: a few moments later they indeed caught sight of a little homestead, consisting of two cottages in one and the same courtyard. There was a light in the windows. A dozen plum-trees could be seen near the fence. Looking through the gates made of paling, they saw a yard filled with the ox-carts of traders who took grain to the Crimea and brought back dried fish and salt to the Ukraine. At that moment a few stars could be seen twinkling in the sky here and there.

"Now then, fellows, remember not to be put off. We must get a night's lodging at any cost!"

The three learned men knocked on the gates all together and shouted: "Open up!"

The door of one of the cottages creaked and a moment later the seminarists saw before them an old woman in an unlined sheepskin coat.

"Who's there?" she shouted with a hollow cough.

"Let's have a night's lodging, Granny. We've lost our way. A night in the open is as bad as an empty belly."

"What sort of people are you?"

"Why, we're humble fellows: Khalyava, a theologian. Brut, a philosopher, and Gorobets, a rhetorician."

"Sorry, I can't let you in," grumbled the old woman. "I've a lot of people in the house, every comer is full. Where am I to put you? And such big, hulking men too! Why, my cottage will fall to pieces if I put fellows like you in it. I know these philosophers and theologians! If I started taking in such drunkards, there'd soon be nothing left of my house and home. Be off with you! Be off! There's no place for you here."

"Take pity on us, granny. You wouldn't let Christian souls be lost for no reason at all, would you? Put us where you please. And if we do anything—anything at all—you understand—then may our arms be withered and may God punish us as He only knows how. Yes, ma'am!"

The old woman seemed a little mollified.

"All right," she said, as though considering what to do with them, "I'll let you in, only I'll put you all in different places. For if you're all together I shan't have a moment's peace of mind."

"You can do as you please," replied the seminarists. "We won't raise any objections."

The gates creaked and they went into the yard. "Look here granny, what about—er as they say—I mean, my stomach feels as though someone was driving a cart though it. Haven't had a bite since morning, you see. ..."

"I see, so that's what you want," said the old woman. "Sorry, I've nothing, nothing at all to give you. Haven't even had my oven heated today."

"Why," said, the philosopher, "we'd pay you for everything tomorrow morning in hard cash. Yes," he added in an undertone, "the devil a bit you'll get."

"Go in, go in, and be satisfied with what you're given. What fastidious young gentle-men the devil has brought us, to be sure!"

Khoma, the philosopher, was thrown into utter dejection by these words. But suddenly his nose perceived the smell of dried fish. He glanced at the wide trousers of the theologian who was walking beside him, and saw a huge fishtail sticking out of his pocket. The theologian had already succeeded in filching a whole carp from one of the oxcarts. And as he had done this from no motive of self interest, but simply from habit and forgetting his carp, was already looking for something else to filch, having no intention of missing even a broken wheel, Khoma, the philosopher, put his hand into the theologian's pocket, as if it were his own, and pulled out the carp.

The old woman put the seminarists in their several places: She found a place for the rhetorician in the cottage, she locked the theologian in an empty closet, and showed the philosopher to a sheep's pen, which was also empty.

Left by himself, the philosopher at once ate the carp, examined the wattled walls of the pen, kicked an inquisitive pig, which woke up, in the snout which it thrust in from the next pen, and turned over on the other side, intending to fall into a sound sleep. Suddenly the low door opened and the old woman, bending down stepped into the pen.

"Why, Granny, what do you want?" said the philosopher.

But the old woman was coming straight towards him with outstretched arms.

"Oho," thought the philosopher, "so that's it! No, my sweet you're too old for that kind of lark!" and he moved away a little, but the old woman unceremoniously, came up to him again.

"Now, listen, Granny," said the philosopher, "it's a fast day today, and I'm not the sort of man who would do anything sinful on a fast day for a thousand gold pieces."

But, without uttering a word, the old woman was stretching out her arms in an attempt to catch him.

The philosopher got scared, especially when he noticed her eyes flash with a strange glitter.

"Granny, what's the matter with you? Go—go—in peace!" he shouted.

But the old woman uttered no word, but continued trying to catch him with her hands.

He jumped to his feet intending to run, but the old woman stood in the doorway, fixing her glittering eyes on him, and again began approaching him.

The philosopher wanted to push her away with his hands, but to his surprise he noticed that he could not lift his arms, that his legs would not move, and he perceived with horror that even his voice would not obey him: words stirred on his lips without a sound escaping them. All he heard was the pounding of his heart; he saw the old woman come up to him, she folded his arms, bent his head down, leapt with the alacrity of a cat upon his back, struck him with a besom on his side and, prancing like a saddle-horse, he carried her on his shoulders. All this happened so quickly that before he knew what he was doing, the philosopher clutched his knees with both hands, trying to stop his legs from moving; but, to his intense astonishment, they lifted against his will and leapt forward more swiftly than a Circassian racer. It was only when they had left the farm behind them and an open plain stretched before them with a forest, black as coal (on one side of it), that he said to himself: "Good Lord, she's a witch!"

The waning crescent of the moon was shining in the sky. The shy radiance of midnight lay, like a transparent veil, in a light haze over the earth. The woods, the meadows, the sky, the valleys—everything seemed to be slumbering with open eyes. Not a breeze fluttered anywhere even for a fleeting moment. There was something moistly warm in the freshness of the night. The shadows of the trees and bushes fell like comets in the pointed wedges of the sloping plain. Such was the night when Khoma Brut galloped along with the mysterious rider on his back. He felt a kind of exhausting, unpleasant and, at the same time, voluptuous sensation spreading to his heart. He lowered his head and saw the grass, which had been almost under his feet, growing far below him. Above it lay a sheet of water, as transparent as a mountain stream, and the grass seemed to be at the bottom of a lambent sea, limpid to its very depths—at least he saw himself and the old woman sitting on his back clearly reflected in it. It was a sun instead of a moon that he saw shining there. He heard the blue harebells ringing as they inclined their little heads. He saw a water nymph swimming out from behind the reeds. He caught a glimpse of her back and her leg—curved and supple, all made of brightness and shimmering. She turned towards him—there was her face, with its bright, sparkling, keen eyes. … She was singing and her song went straight to his heart. … Now her face was coming nearer and nearer, it was already on the surface, but, shaking with sparkling laughter, it moved further and further away. A moment later she turned on her back and her cloudlike breasts, matte like unglazed porcelain, gleamed in the sun round their white, supple, soft circumambience. The water in the shape of tiny bubbles covered them as with beads. She was all quivering and laughing in the water. …

Did he see it or did he not? Was it really happening or was he dreaming? But what was that? Wind or music? It was ringing and ringing and reverberating and coming nearer and nearer and piercing his heart with a kind of unendurable trill.

"What's all this?" thought the philosopher Khoma Brut, looking down as he galloped along at full speed. He was dripping with sweat. He was overcome by a fiendishly voluptuous sensation, by a kind of stabbing, a kind of exhaustingly thrilling pleasure. He often felt as though he had no heart at all any more and he clutched at it with terror. Worn out, confused, he tried to recall any prayer he knew. He called to mind all the exorcisms against evil spirits and, suddenly, he felt a little refreshed; he felt that his step was growing slower and that the witch's hold on his back was getting weaker. The thick grass touched him and he no longer saw anything in it. The bright crescent of the moon was shining in the sky.

"All right!" thought the philosopher Khoma to himself and began saying the exorcisms almost aloud. At last, quick as lightning, he sprang from under the old woman and in his turn leapt on her back. The old woman, with short, invisible steps, ran so fast that the rider could scarcely catch his breath. The ground seemed to flash by under him. He could see everything clearly in the moonlight, though the moon was not full. The valleys were smooth, but at that quick pace everything flashed by indistinctly and confusedly before his eyes. He snatched up a piece of wood that lay on the ground and began to rain blows on the old woman with all his might. She uttered wild cries; at first they were angry and menacing, then they grew fainter, sweeter, clearer, and then rang out softly like delicate silver bells, and went straight to his heart. Involuntarily the thought flashed through his mind: was it really an old woman?

"Oh, I can't any more!" she murmured, and collapsed exhausted on the ground.

He stood up and looked into her eyes: the sun was rising and in the distance the golden domes of the Kiev churches were gleaming. Before him lay a beautiful young girl, her lovely plait of hair undone and in disorder and her eyelashes as long as arrows. Her lean white arms were thrown back lifelessly and she kept moaning, her eyes staring upwards and full of tears.

Khoma trembled like a leaf on a tree: he was overcome by pity and a strange feeling of excitement and timidity he had never known before; he started running as fast as his legs would carry him. His heart throbbed uneasily as he ran and, try as he might, he could not explain to himself the new strange sensation that had taken possession of him. He no longer wanted to go begging at farms and hastened back to Kiev, thinking all the way about this incomprehensible adventure of his.

There were hardly any seminarists left in the town: they were dispersed about the farms, either taking jobs as tutors or simply wandering from one farm to another, for at the Ukrainian farms one could get dumplings, cheese, sour cream and curd or fruit puddings as big as a hat without paying a groat for them. The large, dilapidated house in which the bursars were lodged was quite empty and however much the philosopher rummaged in every corner and felt in all the holes, he could find neither a piece of bacon nor a stale white roll which were usually hidden away by the bursars.

However, our philosopher soon found a way of mending his affairs: he walked whistling three times through the market, winked at last at a young widow in a yellow bonnet, who was selling ribbons, shot and wheels—and was that very day fed on wheat dumplings, a chicken and—in short, it is quite impossible to enumerate the dishes on the table laid for him in the little mud house in the middle of a cherry orchard. The same evening our philosopher was seen in a tavern: he was lying on a bench, smoking, as was his habit, his pipe, and in the sight of all, flung the Jewish landlord half a gold ducat. A mug stood before him. He gazed at the people who came in and went out with cool, contented eyes and thought no longer about his extraordinary adventure.

Meanwhile rumours were circulating everywhere that the daughter of one of the richest Cossack captains, who lived about fifty miles from Kiev, had one day returned home from a walk beaten black and blue. She had hardly the strength to drag herself to her father's house and was lying at the point of death. But she had expressed the wish that one of the Kiev seminarists, Khoma Brut, should read the prayer for the dying over her and the psalms for three days after her death.

Our philosopher heard of it from the rector himself who had summoned him to his room and told him that he should set off on the journey without delay, for the distinguished Cossack captain had sent servants and a carriage to fetch him.

The philosopher shuddered from some unaccountable feeling which he could not explain to himself. A dark foreboding told him that something evil was in store for him. Without knowing himself why, he declared bluntly that he would not go.

"Listen, dominus Khoma," said the rector, who in certain contingencies talked very civilly to those under his authority, "I'm damned well not asking you whether you want to go or not. All I have to say to you is that if you go on showing off your cleverness and obstinacy, I'll have you so thoroughly flogged with green birch twigs all over your back and everywhere else that there will be no need for you to go to the bathhouse afterwards!"

The philosopher, scratching lightly behind his ear, went out without uttering a word, intending at the first favourable opportunity to put his trust in his heels. Sunk in thought, he went down the steep staircase leading into the yard, planted round with poplars, and stopped for a moment as he heard quite distinctly the voice of the rector giving orders to his butler and someone else, probably one of the servants sent to fetch him by the Cossack captain.

"Thank your master for the grain and the eggs," said the rector, "and tell him I will send him the books he writes about as soon as they are ready: I have already given them to a scribe to be copied. And don't forget, my dear fellow, to mention to your master that I know there are excellent fish on his farm, especially sturgeon, and I'd be glad if he'd send some when opportunity offers. Here in the market they are bad and dear. And you, Yavtukh, let the lads have a glass of vodka each, and tie up the philosopher or he'll ran off."

"The dirty dog," the philosopher thought to himself. "Guessed it, the long-legged mountebank."

He went down and saw a covered waggon which he nearly mistook for a barn for drying crops on wheels. And indeed it was deep as a brick kiln. It was only an ordinary Cracow carriage in which about a score of Jews travel together with their wares to all the towns where their noses smell out a fair. Six healthy and stalwart Cossacks of early middle age were waiting for him. Their Ukranian tunics of fine cloth with tassels showed that they belonged to a rather important and wealthy master. Small scars on their faces bore evidence that at some time they had been in battle, not without glory.

"What's to be done?" thought the philosopher. "One cannot escape one's destiny!" And turning to the Cossacks, he said: "Good day to you, my friends."

"Good health to you, master philosopher," some of the Cossacks replied.

"So I shall be travelling with you?" he asked, clambering into the carriage. "A lovely carriage!" he went on. "You could hire some musicians and have a dance in it."

"Yes, sir, a regular chariot," said one of the Cossacks, seating himself on the box next to the driver, who had tied a rag over his head in place of the cap he had managed to leave behind in a pot-house. The other five and the philosopher got inside the waggon and settled themselves on sacks filled with the various purchases they had made in the town.

"It would be interesting to know," said the philosopher, "how many horses would be needed if this carriage were loaded with goods of some sort—say, salt or iron tires."

"Aye," said the Cossack on the box after a pause, "I expect it would need a fairish number of horses."

After such a satisfactory answer the Cossack considered that he was entitled not to utter another word for the rest of the journey.

The philosopher was very anxious to find out more about who the Cossack captain was, what kind of man he was, what was the latest news about his daughter who had returned home in so strange a way and was at the point of death and whose story was now connected with his own, how they all were and what was going on in their house. He plied them with questions, but the Cossacks, too, must have been philosophers, for they made no answer, but went on smoking their pipes as they lay on the sacks. Only one of them turned to the driver on the box with a brief order. "Mind, Overko, you old buzzard, when you get near the tavern on the Chukhraylovsky road, don't forget to stop and waken me and the other lads if any should happen to be asleep." After which he fell asleep, snoring loudly. However, these instructions were quite unnecessary, for as soon as this gigantic carriage drew near the tavern on the Chukhraylovsky road, they all cried in one voice: "Stop!" Besides, Overko's horses were already trained to stop at every tavern. In spite of the hot July day they all got out of the waggon and went into the dirty low-pitched room where the Jewish landlord rushed to welcome his old friends with every sign of delight. The Jew produced from under the skirts of his coat some ham and sausages and, after putting them on the table, at once turned away from this food forbidden by the Talmud. They all sat down round the table. Earthenware mugs appeared before each of the guests. The philosopher Khoma had to take part in the general merry-making and, as Ukrainians, when tipsy, invariably start kissing each other or crying, the whole cottage soon resounded with kisses. "Well, Spirid, let's kiss!" "Come here, Dorosh, I want to embrace you!"

A Cossack with a grey moustache, who was older than the rest, propped his head on his cheek and began sobbing bitterly because he had no father and no mother and was all alone in the world. Another, a great one for argument, kept consoling him, saying: "Don't cry, please, don't I mean to say, God alone knows how it is and what it is all about …" The one who was called Dorosh became very inquisitive and, addressing the philosopher Khoma, kept asking him: "What do they teach you at your seminary? Is it the same as what the deacon reads in the church or something else?"

"Don't ask," the moraliser drawled. "Let it be just as it is. God knows what is wanted. God knows everything."

"But I want to know," Dorosh said, "what's written in them books. Maybe it's quite different from the deacon's."

"Oh dear, oh dear," the worthy preceptor exclaimed, "Why go on like this. It's God's will. What He has decided cannot be altered."

"I want to know all that's written. I'll join the seminary, I will. You don't suppose I can't learn, do you? I'll learn everything, I will."

"Oh dear, oh dear," muttered the comforter as he dropped his head on the table, for he was quite incapable of supporting it on his shoulders any longer.

The other Cossacks were discussing their masters and then questioned why the moon was shining in the sky.

The philosopher Khoma, seeing the sort of state they were in, decided to take advantage of it and make his escape. He first addressed the greyheaded Cossack who was bemoaning the loss of his father and mother.

"What are you crying about, Uncle?" he said. "Look at me: I, too, am an orphan. Let me go, lads. What do you want with me?"

"Yes, let him go," several Cossacks agreed, "He's an orphan, isn't he? Let him go where he likes!"

"Oh Lord, oh Lord," said the comforter, raising his head, "Let him go. Let him go where he likes!"

And the Cossacks were indeed about to lead him outside to let him go, but the one who had been so inquisitive stopped them.

"Don't touch him," he said, "I want to talk to him about the seminary. I'm going to join it myself ...!"

The escape could hardly have taken place in any case, for when the philosopher made up his mind to get up from the table, his legs felt as if they were made of wood and he began to see such a multitude of doors in the room that it is doubtful if he could have discovered the real one.

Not before evening did the entire company wake up to the fact that it was time to resume their journey. Hoisting themselves up into the waggon, they drove slowly along the road, urging on the horses and singing a song, the words and the meaning of which no one could have made out. After driving aimlessly all over the countryside for most of the night, losing their way again and again, though they knew every inch of the road, they drove at last down a steep hill into a valley, and the philosopher noticed a palisade or wattle fence running alongside it with low trees and roofs peeping out behind them. This was the big village belonging to the Cossack captain. It was long past midnight; the sky was dark and there were little stars twinkling here and there. No light was to be seen in a single cottage. They drove into the yard to the accompaniment of the barking of dogs. Thatched barns and little cottages could be seen on both sides. One of them, standing exactly in the middle opposite the gates was larger than the others and was apparently the residence of the Cossack landowner. The carriage pulled up before a small shed that seemed to serve for a barn and our travellers went off to bed. The philosopher, however, wished to have a closer look at the outside of the manor house, but hard as he stared, he could make out nothing distinctly: instead of a house he fancied a bear, and the chimney turned into the rector. The philosopher gave up his idea of making his escape and went to bed.

When the philosopher woke up the whole house was in an uproar: the daughter of the Cossack captain had died in the night. Servants were running to and fro; some old women were crying; a crowd of peasants were peering through the fence at the house as though they might see something there.

The philosopher began inspecting at his leisure the things he had not been able to make out at night. The manor house was a small low-pitched building such as were usually erected in the Ukraine in the old days. The roof was thatched. A small, high, pointed pediment with a little window, looking like an eye turned upwards, was all painted in blue and yellow flowers and red crescents. It rested on small oak pillars, round above and hexagonal below, with a fanciful carving at the top. Under this pediment was a little porch with benches on each side. At either side of the house were awnings resting on similar pillars with spiral carvings on some of them. A tall pear-tree with a pyramidal top and trembling green leaves grew in front of the house. Two rows of grain barns in the middle of the yard formed a sort of wide street leading to the house. Behind the barns and next to the gate two triangular storehouses stood facing each other; they, too, were thatched. Each triangular wall had a little door and all sorts of pictures painted on it. On one of them was painted a Cossack sitting on a barrel and holding a mug over his head with this inscription: "I'll drink it all." On another was painted a bottle, a number of flagons, and at the sides as a special ornament a horse upside down, a pipe, a tambourine, with the inscription: "Vodka is the Cossack's delight." Through the huge window of the loft of one of the barns could be seen a drum and brass trumpets. Two cannons stood at the gates. Everything pointed to the fact that the master of the house was fond of merrymaking and that the courtyard often resounded with the cries of revellers. There were two windmills outside the gate. Behind the house were orchards and all that could be glimpsed through the tops of the trees were the dark caps of the chimneys of the cottages which were hidden in a green thicket. The whole village lay in the broad and level terrace of a hill. From the north everything was screened by the steep side of the hill. The courtyard lay at its very foot. Looked at from below, the hill seemed even steeper, and here and there on its tall top irregular stalks of gaunt weeds stood out black against the clear sky. The sight of its bare loamy surface was, somehow, depressing; it was all gashed with gullies and ravines scooped out by the rains. In two places on its steep slope stood two cottages; a spreading apple-tree, banked up with earth and supported with short stakes near the roots, extended its branches over one of them. Knocked off by the wind, the apples rolled down right into the yard of the manor house. The road, meandering down the hill from its very top, ran past the courtyard to the village. When the philosopher surveyed its terrible steepness and recalled their journey of the previous night, he came to the conclusion that either the master had very clever horses or the Cossacks had very strong heads to have known even while in an alcoholic daze how to avoid crashing down head over heels with the enormous waggon and the goods in it. The philosopher was standing on the highest point in the yard; when he turned and looked in the opposite direction, the view that met his eyes was quite different. The village and the remaining slope of the hill abutted upon a plain. Boundless meadows stretched as far as the eye could see, their brilliant verdure growing darker the further away they were; whole rows of villages could be clearly seen in the blue distance, though they must have been at least fifteen miles away. On the right side of the meadows was a range of hills and far, far away the Dnieper gleamed intermittently—a barely perceptible streak of light and darkness.

"Oh, what a glorious spot!" said the philosopher. "How I wish I could live here, fishing in the Dnieper and the ponds, catching birds with nets or shooting little bustards or king-snipe. There must be lots of great bustard, too, in those meadows, I shouldn't wonder. One could also dry lots of fruit and sell it in the town, or, better still, make vodka of it, for vodka distilled out of fruit is incomparably superior to any grain vodka. Still, I might as well consider how to slip away from here."

He noticed a little path behind the fence completely hidden by tall weeds. He set his foot on it mechanically, intending first to go for a walk, make his way quietly between the cottages, and then dash into the open country, when he suddenly felt a rather heavy hand on his shoulder. Behind him stood the old Cossack who on the previous evening had so bitterly bewailed the death of his father and mother and his own loneliness.

"You're not thinking, Mr. Philosopher, of giving us the slip, are you?" he said. "This is not the sort of place you can run away from, and the roads too are bad for one on foot. You'd better come with me to the master: he's been expecting you for some time in the parlour."

"Let's go by all means," said the philosopher. "I don't mind I'm sure," and he followed the Cossack.

The cavalry captain, an elderly man with a grey moustache and an expression of gloomy sadness, was sitting at a table in the parlour, his head propped up on his hands. He was about fifty, but the deep despondency on his face and a kind of gaunt pallor showed that his soul had been crushed and shattered all at once, in one moment, and all his old gaiety and noisy life had vanished forever. When Khoma and the old Cossack came in, he removed one hand and nodded slightly in response to their bow.

Khoma and the old Cossack stopped respectfully at the door.

"Who are you, where do you come from, and what is your calling, my good man?" said the captain neither affably nor sternly.

"I'm a bursar, sir. Philosopher Khoma Brut."

"Who was your father?"

"I don't know sir,"

"And your mother?"

"I don't know my mother, either. It is reasonable to suppose, of course, that I had a mother. But who she was, where she came from and when she lived, that, sir, I simply don't know."

The captain was silent and for a minute seemed to ponder.

"How did you get to know my daughter?"

"I didn't know her, sir. On my word of honor, I didn't. I have never had anything to do with young ladies, sir. Never in my life. Never went near them, sir. Beshrew them, saving your presence, sir."

"Why, then, did she want you and no one else to read the psalms over her?"

The philosopher shrugged his shoulders. "Goodness only knows. I can't explain it. It's a well-known thing, sir, that the gentry sometimes get something into their heads that the most learned men could not explain. As the proverb says, sir: The devil skips as the master bids."

"You're not telling me lies, philosopher, are you?"

"May I be struck by lightning on this very spot, sir, if I'm lying."

"If only she had lived one minute longer," the captain said sadly, "I'd have found out everything. Don't let anyone read over me, Daddy" she said to me, "but send at once to the Kiev seminary and fetch the bursar Khoma Brut. Let him pray three nights for my sinful soul. He knows … But what he knows I did not hear. That's all she, poor darling, could say before she died. I expect you must be known for your holy life and your pious works and she may have heard of you."

"Me?" said the philosopher, stepping back in amazement. "Holy life?" he ejaculated, staring straight in the captain's face. "Good Lord, sir, what are you saying? Why, though it's hardly decent to mention it, I paid a visit to the baker's wife last Maundy Thursday."

"Well … I suppose there must be some good reason for it. You will begin your duties from this very day."

"If you don't mind, sir, I'd rather—er—I mean to say, sir, every man versed in holy scripture may—er—as far as—er—it's in his power, of course—but, you see, sir, in this case a deacon or at least a sacristan would—er—be much more fitted for it. They have had plenty of experience of this sort of thing and they know what to do, while I … You see, sir, I haven't got the right voice for it and, besides, I'm just no damn good myself—I mean, I haven't got the proper figure for it, have I?"

"I don't know about that, but I shall carry out my darling's last wish without regard for anything. If for three nights from today you say the prayers over her in the way that is customary, I will reward you. If not, well, I shouldn't advise the devil himself to anger me."

The last words were uttered with such vigour that the philosopher fully grasped their meaning.

"Follow me," said the captain.

They went out into the entrance hall. The captain opened the door into another room, opposite the first. The philosopher paused for a minute in the hall to blow his nose and crossed the threshold in inexpressible panic. The whole floor was covered with red cotton material. On a high table in the corner under the icons lay the body of the dead girl on a coverlet of blue velvet adorned with a gold fringe and tassels. Tall wax candles, entwined with sprigs of guelder rose, stood at her feet and head, shedding their dim light, lost in the daylight. The dead girl's face was hidden from him by the disconsolate father, who sat facing her with his back to the door. The philosopher was struck by the words he heard.

"What grieves me so much, my dearly beloved daughter, is not that, to my great sorrow and affliction, you have left this earth in the flower of your age, without living the rest of your allotted days, but that, my darling, I don't know the man—my mortal enemy—who was the cause of your death. For if I knew the man who as much as thought of hurting you or of even saying anything offensive to you, I swear to God he should not see his children again, were he as old as I, nor his father and mother, were he still in the prime of life, and his body would have been thrown out to be devoured by birds and beasts of the steppe. But what's so awful, my wild little marigold, my sweet little quail, my poor darling, is that I shall spend the rest of my days without joy, wiping away with the skirt of my coat the tears flowing out of my old eyes, while my enemy will be making merry and secretly laughing at a feeble old man. ..."

He stopped short, for his unendurable grief dissolved in a flood of tears.

The philosopher was touched by such inconsolable sorrow He coughed and uttered a hollow groan in an effort to clear his throat.

The captain turned round and motioned him to a place at the head of the dead girl, in front of a small lectern with books on it.

"I'll do it for three nights somehow or other," thought the philosopher, "for I'm sure the old fellow will stuff my pockets with gold pieces for it."

He drew near and, clearing his throat again, began reading, paying no attention to anything and not daring to glance at the face of the dead girl.

A profound silence reigned in the room. He noticed that the captain had gone out. Slowly he turned his head to glance at the dead girl and ...

A shudder ran through his veins; before him lay a girl so beautiful that there was no one like her in the world. It seemed that never could a face have been formed of such striking and yet harmonious beauty. She lay as though she were alive. Her forehead, fair and delicate as snow, as silver, seemed to be deep in thought; her eyebrows were like a night amid a sunny day, fine and even, raised proudly over the closed eyes, and her eyelashes, falling like arrows on her cheeks, glowed with the warmth of secret desires; her lips were like rubies, ready to break into a smile. ... But in them, in those very same features, he saw something terribly poignant. He felt his heart beginning to ache painfully, just as though in the midst of a whirl of gaiety and dancing crowds someone had struck up a song about an oppressed people. The rubies of her lips seemed to brim over with blood from her very heart. Suddenly something horribly familiar appeared on her face.

"The witch!" he cried in a frenzied voice. He looked away, turned deathly pale and began reading his prayers.

It was the witch he had killed.

When the sun was setting, they carried the dead girl to the church. The philosopher supported the coffin, covered with a black cloth of mourning, and he felt something cold as ice on his shoulder. The dead girl's father walked in front, supporting on his arm the right side of her narrow coffin.

The wooden church, grown black and adorned with green lichen, with its three cone-shaped cupolas, stood dismally near the end of the village. It was quite obvious that no service had been held in it for a long time. Candles had been lighted before almost every icon. The coffin was placed in the centre opposite the altar. The old Cossack captain kissed the dead girl once more, prostrated himself and went out together with the coffin-bearers, giving orders that the philosopher should have a good meal and be taken to the church after supper. Back in the kitchen the men who had carried the coffin began touching the stove with their hands, something the Ukrainians usually do after seeing a dead body.

The hunger which the philosopher began to feel at that moment made him for a few moments forget all about the dead girl. Soon all the house-serfs began gradually to assemble in the kitchen. In the captain's house the kitchen was something of a club, where all the inhabitants of the yard gathered together, including even the dogs who, wagging their tails, came to the door for bones and slops. Wherever anyone was sent and on whatever business, he first of all went to the kitchen to have a rest on the bench even for no more than a few minutes, and smoke a pipe. All the unmarried men in their smart Cossack tunics lay there almost all day long on the bench. Under the bench, on the stove—anywhere, in short, where a comfortable place could be found to lie on. Besides, everyone invariably left behind in the kitchen his cap, or a whip for stray dogs, or something of the kind. But the largest company gathered there at supper-time, including the coachman, who had driven the horses into their paddock, and the herdsman who had taken the cows to be milked and everyone else who was not to be seen during the day. At supper the most taciturn tongues wagged happily. Everything was usually discussed there: who had got himself new breeches, what was to be found in the interior of the earth, and who had seen a wolf. There were lots of witty fellows there, of whom there is no lack among Ukrainians.

The philosopher found a place among them in the large circle in the open air in front of the kitchen door. Soon a woman in a red bonnet appeared at the door holding in both hands a steaming pot of dumplings and she set it down in the midst of those who came to have their supper. Each pulled a wooden spoon out of his pocket, or for want of a spoon, a wooden stick. As soon as their jaws began to move slowly and the wolfish appetite of the assembled crowd was somewhat assuraged, many of them started talking. The conversation naturally turned on the dead girl.

"Is it true," said a young shepherd, who had put so many buttons and brass discs on the strap on which his pipe hung that he looked like a small village shop, "is it true that any young lady—may the Lord forgive me for saying it about her, was familiar with the evil one?"

"Who? our young lady?" said Dorosh, whom our philosopher already knew. "Why, she was a regular witch! I'll take my oath she was a witch!"

"Really, really, Dorosh," said the man, who had shown a great readiness to console everybody on the journey, "it's no business of ours. Let it be. No good talking about it."

But Dorosh was not disposed to hold his tongue. He had a little earlier gone to the storehouse with the butler on some urgent business and, having once or twice bent over two or three barrels, had come out exceedingly merry and talked without stopping.

"What do you want me to do? Hold my tongue?" he said. "Why, she had a ride on me herself. She had, I tell you."

"I say, Uncle," said the young shepherd with the buttons, "can you tell a witch by some signs?"

"No, you can't," replied Dorosh. "Quite impossible to tell. Even if you read through all the psalter you wouldn't be able to tell."

"You can tell, Dorosh, you can," said the former comforter, "Don't say that. It's not for nothing that God has given every living creature its own special habit. Scholars say that a witch has a little tail."

"When a woman's old, she's a witch," a grey-headed Cossack said coolly.

"You're a fine lot too, I must say," put in the woman who was at that moment pouring fresh dumplings into the empty pot. "Regular fat hogs."

A smile of satisfaction appeared on the lips of the old Cossack, whose name was Yavtukh and nickname Kovtun, when he observed the effect his words had had on the peasant woman, while the cow-man guffawed so loudly that it sounded like the bellowing of two bulls as they stood facing each other.

The conversation had aroused the philosopher's curiosity. He felt an irresistible desire to find out more particulars about the dead girl. Wishing to bring the conversation back to that subject, he addressed his neighbour as follows: "I'd very much like to know why this whole company sitting at supper here thinks that the young mistress was a witch? Did she cause any mischief to anyone or was she the undoing of anyone?"

"There were all sorts of things," replied one of the company, whose face was so flat that it resembled a spade.

"Why, there was that huntsman Mikita and. ..."

"Wait, let me tell about the huntsman Mikita," said Dorosh.

"No, let me," said Spirid.

"Let Spirid tell it! Let Spirid tell it!" the crowd shouted.

"You, Mr. Philosopher Khoma," Spirid began, "did not know Mikita. Oh, he was a man in a thousand, he was. He knew every dog as if it was his own father. The huntsman we have now, Mikola, that fellow next to me but one, isn't fit to hold a candle to him. Mind you, he knows his job all right, but compared to the other he's nothing but trash, nothing but slops."

"Aye," said Dorosh, nodding his head approvingly, "you're telling the story well enough."

"He'd see a hare quicker than you'd wipe the snuff from your nose," Spirid went on. "He'd only to whistle: 'Come on, Roby! Come on, Speedy!' while he himself was off like lightning on his horse, and it was impossible to say who'd outstrip the other: he the dogs or the dogs him. Why, he'd knock back a pint of vodka without winking. A fine huntsman he was! Now, some little time back he began staring at the young mistress a little too much. Whether he'd fallen head over ears in love with her, or whether she'd bewitched him—whatever it was, the poor lad was done for, grown soft, turned into goodness only knows what—oh, it's too disgusting to talk about."

"Aye," said Dorosh.

"As soon as the young mistress looked at him, he dropped the bridle out of his hand, couldn't remember the name of his dogs, stumbled and didn't know what he was doing. One day the young mistress came into the stables when he was rubbing down a horse. 'Would you mind, Mikita,' she said, 'if I put my foot on you?' And the damned fool looked as pleased as Punch: 'Not only your foot,' said he, 'you can sit on me, if you like.' The young mistress raised her foot, and as soon as he saw her bare, plump white leg, her witchery knocked him completely silly, so Mikita said. He bent his back, the damn fool, and clasping her bare legs in his hands, went galloping like a horse over the countryside. He could not for the life of him say where they had been, but he came back more dead than alive and since that day he withered like a chip of wood, and one morning when they went into the stable, all they could find was a heap of ashes and an empty pail: he had burnt up, burnt up by himself. And what a fine huntsman he was! You couldn't find another like him anywhere in the world."

When Spirid had finished his story, all sorts of opinions about the fine qualities of the late huntsman were expressed on all sides.

"You haven't heard of Sheptun's wife, have you?" Dorosh said, addressing Khoma.

"No."

"Good Lord, they don't teach you a great deal at the seminary, do they? Well, then, listen. There's a Cossack called Sheptun in our village. A good Cossack, he sometimes tells lies without rhyme or reason, and he sometimes likes to pinch something, but he's a good Cossack! His cottage is not far from here. Just about the time we sat down to have our supper, Sheptun and his wife, having had theirs, went to bed, and as the weather was fine, his wife lay down in the yard and Sheptun on the bench in the cottage—no, no! I'm sorry, it was his wife who lay on the bench in the cottage and Sheptun in the yard. …"

"Not on the bench, she lay down on the floor," the peasant woman, standing in the doorway with her cheek propped up on her hand, corrected him.

Dorosh looked at her, looked down, then again looked at her.

"When I strip you of your petticoat before everybody," he said after a short pause, "you won't like it."

This warning had its effect. The old woman fell silent and did not interrupt again.

"And in the cradle hanging in the middle of the cottage," Dorosh went on, "lay their one-year-old child—boy or girl, I don't know which. As Sheptun's wife lay there, she suddenly heard a dog scratching at the door and howling fit to make you run out of the cottage. She got frightened, for women are so silly that if you put out your tongue at one in the evening from behind a door, her heart's in her mouth. 'However,' she thought, 'I'd better give that damned dog a good whack on the nose and perhaps he'll stop howling,' and picking up the poker, she went to open the door. She had scarcely time to open it properly when the dog rushed in between her legs and headed straight for the baby's cradle. At that moment Sheptun's wife saw that it was not really a dog, but the young mistress. Now, if it had been the young mistress as she knew her, it would not have been so bad. The extraordinary thing is that she was all blue and that her eyes glowed like coal. She snatched up the baby, bit its throat and began sucking its blood. All poor Mrs. Sheptun could do was to scream, 'Oh, a werewolf!' and she rushed out of the room. But the front door in the passage was locked, so she ran up to the loft. There she sat shaking with terror, the silly woman. After a little while she saw the young mistress coming up to the loft to her; a moment later she pounced on the silly woman and began biting her. It was not till the morning that Sheptun dragged his wife down from the loft, bitten black and blue all over. The next day the silly woman died. So that's the sort of monstrous and passing strange things that happen in this world! You see, she may be a highborn young lady, but once a witch, always a witch!"

After such a story Dorosh looked round self-complacently and thrust a finger into his pipe in preparation for filling it. The subject of the witch seemed inexhaustible. Everyone hastened to tell some story about her in turn. One of them had seen the witch come right up to the door of his cottage in the shape of a haystack; another had had his cap or pipe stolen by her; many village girls had had their plaits cut off by her; others had had several pints of blood sucked from them by her.

At last the whole company came to their senses and realised that they had been chattering too long because it was quite dark in the yard. They all began dispersing to the places they usually went to sleep in at night, such as the kitchen or the barns or the courtyard.

"Well, sir," said the greyheaded Cossack, addressing Khoma the philosopher, "it's time we too went to our deceased mistress."

The four of them, including Spirid and Dorosh, set off for the church, lashing out with their whips at the great multitude of dogs in the street, which gnawed their sticks furiously.

Though he had fortified himself with a good glassful of vodka, the philosopher secretly felt more and more frightened the nearer they got to the lighted church. The stories and strange occurrences he had heard helped to work on his imagination. The darkness under the paling and the trees grew less dense; the place was getting more open. At last they entered the small churchyard behind its ramshackle fence, beyond which not a tree was to be seen, nothing but open country and meadows swallowed up in the darkness and night. The three Cossacks walked up the steep steps to the porch and entered the church. There they left the philosopher after wishing him to carry out his duties satisfactorily and, at the request of their master, locked the door after them.

The philosopher was left alone. At first he yawned, then he stretched himself, then blew into both his hands, and at last looked round. In the middle of the church stood the black coffin. The candles glimmered before the dark icons; the light from them lit up only the icon-case and faintly the middle of the church. The distant corners of the nave were wrapped in darkness. The tall, ancient icon-case already showed signs of fall-ing into decay; its open fretwork, once gilt, only glittered here and there. In one place the gilt had peeled off, in another it had grown altogether black; the faces of the saints completely darkened, gazed somewhat dismally from their frames. The philosopher cast another look around him.

"Well," he said, "what is there to be afraid of? No living man can come in here and as for the dead and apparitions from the other world I have such prayers for them that I have only to read them and they won't lay a finger on me. I don't care," he said, dismissing the subject, "let's read!"

As he went up to the lectern, he noticed several bundles of candles.

"That's good," thought the philosopher "I'd better light up the whole church so that everything will be visible as in daytime. What a pity one can't smoke a pipe in God's temple!"

And he proceeded to stick wax candles to all cornices, lecterns and icons, without regard to expense, and soon the whole church was filled with light. Only overhead the darkness seemed to have grown more intense and the sombre icons looked even more sullenly out of their ancient carved frames, which glittered here and there with specks of gilt. He went up to the coffin, looked timidly at the face of the dead girl and could not help screwing up his eyes with a faint shudder: such terrible, brilliant beauty!

He turned away, intending to move off, but urged on by strange curiosity, by a strange self-contradictory feeling that does not leave a man especially in a moment of panic, he could not resist casting another look at her as he was going away and then, feeling another cold shiver running down his spine, he looked at her again. The striking beauty of the dead girl certainly seemed terrible. Perhaps she would not have instilled such panic fear in him if she had been a little less beautiful. But there was nothing dull, torpid, lifeless in her features; that face was alive, and the philosopher could not help feeling that she was looking at him with closed eyes. He even imagined that a tear rolled down from under her right eyelid, and when it rested on her cheek, he saw distinctly that it was a drop of blood.

He walked away hastily to the lectern, opened the book and, to cheer up his spirits, began reading in a very loud voice. His voice resounded from the wooden church walls, so long deaf and silent, forlornly and without an echo in the absolute dead stillness that it struck him as a little queer.

"What's there to be afraid of?" he was thinking meanwhile to himself. "She won't get out of her coffin, for she will hear the word of God. Let her lie there! And what sort of Cossack am I to be afraid? Well, I've had a drop too much and that's why it seems so terrifying. Let's have a pinch of snuff! Lovely snuff, good snuff!"

However, as he turned over the pages, he kept throwing a sidelong glance at the coffin, and an involuntary feeling seemed whispering to him: "She's going to get up! There! She's going to rise! She's going to look out from the coffin! Any minute now! There! There!"

But the silence was deathlike. The coffin stood motionless. The candles shed a perfect flood of light. What could be more terrifying than a church lit up at night with a dead body in it and not a living soul anywhere near!

Raising his voice, he began singing in different keys in an attempt to drown his still lurking fears. But every minute he turned his eyes to the coffin, as though asking himself involuntarily. "What if she should rise? What if she should get up?"

But the coffin did not stir. If only there'd be some sound, some living creature—a cricket chirping in a corner! All he could hear was the faint sputter of a candle from some distant corner of the church, and the light, slightly reverberating, sound of a drop of wax falling on the floor.

"What if she should get up? …"

She raised her head.

He gave her a wild look and rubbed his eyes. But she was indeed not lying down any more, but sitting up in the coffin. He turned away his eyes and then once more turned them with horror on the coffin. She got up. … She was walking about the church with closed eyes, continually stretching out her arms, as if trying to catch someone.

She was coming straight towards him. In a panic he drew a circle round him and began reading the prayers with an effort and pronouncing exorcisms he had been taught by a monk who had seen witches and evil spirits all his life.

She stood almost on the very line, but it was evident that she had not the power to step over it, and she turned livid all over like one who had been dead for several days. Khoma had not the courage to look at her. She was terrifying. She gnashed her teeth and opened her dead eyes. But unable to see anything she turned with fury—this was apparent from her twitching face—in another direction, stretching out her arms, clasping every pillar and corner with them, trying to catch hold of Khoma. At last she stopped dead and, after shaking a finger at him, lay down in her coffin. The philosopher could not recover his senses and he kept gazing with horror at the narrow habitation of the witch. At last the coffin suddenly broke loose from its place and began flying with a whistling sound all over the church, criss-crossing the air in all directions. The philosopher saw it almost over his head, but at the same time noticed that it could not cross the circle he had drawn, and he went on with his exorcisms with redoubled strength. The coffin came down with a crash in the middle of the church and remained there motionless. The corpse again rose from it, livid and green. But at that moment the crowing of the cock was heard in the distance. The corpse dropped back into the coffin slamming the lid.

The philosopher's heart was pounding and he was dripping wet with sweat. But, heartened by the cock's crowing, he read more rapidly the pages he should have read before. At the first break of dawn the sacristan and greyheaded Yavtukh, at that time performing the duties of a beadle, came to relieve him.

On reaching his distant lodging-place, the philosopher could not fall asleep for a long time, but his fatigue got the better of him and he slept on till dinner-time. When he woke up, the events of the previous night seemed to him to have happened in a dream. To keep up his strength he was given a pint of vodka at dinner, during which he felt more at ease, joining in the conversation once or twice and eating a rather aged sucking pig almost by himself. However, for some inexplicable feeling, he could not bring himself to say anything about what had happened to him in the church and to the questions of the inquisitive he replied: "Yes, there were sorts of wonders!" The philosopher was one of those people who. if they are well fed, display quite an extraordinary degree of philanthropy. Lying down with his pipe between his teeth, he gazed at all of them with honied eyes and kept spitting to one side.

After dinner the philosopher was in excellent spirits. He managed to go round the whole village and make the acquaintance of almost everyone. He was even thrown out of two cottages, one good-looking young woman catching him a painful blow on the back with a spade when he took it into his head to feel her chemise and skirt to find out the material they were made of. But at the approach of evening the philosopher grew more pensive. An hour before supper almost all the house-serfs gathered to play a game of skittles in which long sticks are used instead of balls and the winner has the right to have a ride on the loser's back. This game became highly entertaining for the onlookers, for often the coachman, who was as broad as a pancake, was mounted on the swineherd, a feeble little man, who was all wrinkles. Another time the coachman had to bend his back and, leaping on it, Dorosh always said: "What a strong bull!" Those who were more stolid sat at the door of the kitchen. They looked on very gravely, smoking their pipes, even when the young people laughed heartily at some witty remark by the coachman or Spirid. Khoma tried in vain to take an interest in this game: some kind of sombre thought stuck in his head like a nail. However much he tried to cheer himself up at supper, panic spread in him with the growing darkness over the sky.

"Now then, seminarist, it's time we went!" said the greyheaded Cossack he had got to know so well, getting up from the table together with Dorosh.

Khoma was taken to the church again in the same way; he was again left there alone and the door was locked behind him. As soon as he was alone, apprehension once more began stealing into his breast. Again he saw the dark icons, the flashing frames and the familiar black coffin, standing motionless in the middle of the church, in the menacing stillness.

"Well," he said to himself, "now there's nothing surprising in this uncanny business. It's only terrifying the first time. Yes, it's just a little terrifying the first time, but now it's no longer terrifying. Why, it's not terrifying at all!"

He took his stand at the lectern hastily, drew a circle round him, uttered a few conjurations and began reading aloud, deciding not to raise his eyes from the book and to pay no attention to anything. He had been reading for about an hour and was beginning to feel a little tired and to cough. He took his horn out of his pocket and, before putting the snuff to his nose, stole a timid glance at the coffin. His heart turned cold.

The corpse was already standing before him on the line he had drawn and stared at him with her dead, greenish eyes. The seminarist shuddered and a cold shiver ran down his limbs. Dropping his eyes on the book, he began reading his prayers and exorcisms more loudly and heard the corpse gritting her teeth and waving her arms in an attempt to catch him. But he noticed out of the corner of his eye that the corpse was trying to catch him where he was not standing and that she evidently could not see him. She began muttering hollowly and uttering terrible words with her dead lips; they blubbered hoarsely like the bubbling of boiling pitch. He could not tell what they meant, but there was something terrifying in them. The philosopher realised with horror that she was uttering incantations.

A wind blew through the church at her words and he heard the noise of a multitude of flying wings. He heard the beating of wings on the panes of the church windows and on the iron window frames, and the whining and the scratching of claws upon the iron, and countless numbers of evil spirits trying to smash the door and break into the church. His heart was pounding violently all this time, but, half closing his eyes, he went on reading prayers and exorcisms. At last a shrill sound was suddenly heard in the distance: it was a distant cock crowing. The philosopher, utterly exhausted, stopped and breathed freely again.

The people who came to relieve the philosopher found him more dead than alive. He was leaning with his back against the wall and stared motionless at the Cossacks who were trying to push him out of the church. He was almost carried out of it and he had to be supported all the way back. On arriving at the courtyard, he shook himself and demanded to be given a pint of vodka. When he had drunk it, he smoothed down the hair on his head and said:

"There's a lot of trash of every kind in this world. As for the different kinds of terror—well! …" The philosopher dismissed it all with a wave of a hand.

The group of people who gathered round him bowed their heads when they heard it. Even the small boy whom all the servants felt entitled to depute in their place when it came to mucking out the stable or fetching water, even that poor boy gaped at the philosopher.

At that moment a good-looking and still quite young woman, the old cook's assistant, happened to pass by in a tightly fitting hempen dress, which showed off her round, firm figure, a terrible flirt, who always found something to pin to her cap, a bit of a ribbon, a carnation, or even a piece of paper, if she could find nothing better.

"Good morning, Khoma," she said, seeing the philosopher.

"Good heavens, what's the matter with you?" she cried, clasping her hands.

"Why, what is it, you silly woman?"

"Why, you've gone all grey!"

"Dear me," said Spirid, staring attentively at the philosopher, "she's right! You *have* gone grey, as grey as our old Yavtukh."

Hearing this, the philosopher rushed headlong into the kitchen, where he had noticed a flyblown triangular bit of a looking-glass glued to the wall before which were stuck forget-me-nots, periwinkles and even a wreath of marigold, showing that it was used for her toilet by the flirtatious assistant cook who was fond of showing off her fineries. He was horrified to see the truth of their words: half of his hair had indeed gone white.

Khoma Brut hung his head and sunk into thought.

"I'll go to the master," he said at last, "tell him everything and explain that I can't carry on with the reading. Let him send me back to Kiev at once."

With these thoughts in his mind he turned to go up the front steps of the manor-house.

The Cossack captain sat almost motionless in his parlor. The hopeless grief the philosopher had seen in his face was still there, except that his cheeks were more sunken than before. It was obvious that he did not eat sufficiently or, indeed, did not touch any food at all. His extraordinary pallor gave him a look of almost stony immobility.

"Good morning, old fellow," he said on seeing Khoma standing cap in hand at the door. "How are things with you? Everything satisfactory?"

"It's satisfactory, I suppose, sir, except that there are such devilish things going on that the best you can do is pick up your cap and run as fast as your legs will carry you."

"Oh?"

"Well, you see, sir, it's that daughter of yours I mean, if you look at it sensibly she's, of course, a well-born girl. No one can deny that. But I hope you don't mind my saying so, sir, your daughter, may she rest in peace. ..."

"Well, what about my daughter?"

"Your daughter, sir, is in league with Satan. She is the cause of such horrors that reading of Scripture is of no avail at all."

"Keep on reading! It was not for nothing she sent for you. She was worried, poor darling, about her soul and was anxious to drive away with prayers all evil thoughts."

"It's for you to say, of course, sir, but I tell you I simply can't go on with it."

"Read, read!" the Cossack captain went on in the same admonishing voice. "You've only one night left. You'll do a Christian deed and I'll reward you."

"It's not a question of reward. You can do as you please, sir," Khoma declared firmly, "I will not read."

"Now, listen to me, philosopher," said the Cossack captain and his voice grew firm and menacing, "I don't like these tricks. You can do it in your seminary but not with me: if I give you a flogging, it will not at all be the same thing as when your rector gives you one. Do you know what good leather thongs are like?"

"Of course, I do, sir," said the philosopher, lowering his voice. "Everyone knows what leather thongs are like: in a large dose, it's quite unendurable."

"Aye, only what you don't know is how my lads can thrash," said the Cossack captain sternly, rising to his feet, and his face assumed an imperious and fierce expression, revealing the unbridled violence of his character, restrained only for a time by his grief. "Here they first give you a thrashing, then sprinkle you with vodka, and then begin all over again. Run along, run along, and get on with your task. If you don't, you won't get up again: if you do—a thousand gold pieces."

"Oh-ho! Why, he's a fire-eater!" thought the philosopher as he went out. "He's not to be trifled with. But, wait, wait, my friend, I'll show you such a clean pair of heels that you and your hounds will never catch me."

And Khoma made up his mind definitely to run away. He was only waiting for the servants to get under the hay in the barns, which they usually did after dinner, and then break into such snores and whistling that the courtyard of the manor-house sounded more like a factory. The time at last arrived, even Yavtukh closed his eyes as he lay stretched out in the sun. The philosopher made his way with fear and trembling into the captain's garden from where he thought he could escape into the open country more easily and without being observed. This garden, as usual, was terribly neglected and was therefore extremely useful for any secret undertaking. With the exception of only one path, trodden by the servants for their pressing needs, everything else was hidden by overgrown cherry trees, elders and burdock, which pushed up to the very top its tall stalks with their clinging pink burrs. Wild hops covered as with a net this motley assemblage of trees and bushes, forming a roof over them, got on to the fence and, falling from it, mingled in coiling snakes with the bluebells. Beyond the fence, which formed the boundary of the garden came a perfect forest of tall weeds, which apparently no one was interested enough to look into, and indeed a scythe would have been smashed into smithereens if it attempted to touch with its blade their thick, stout stalks.

When the philosopher tried to step over the fence, his teeth chattered and his heart beat so violently that he was frightened. The skirts of his long loose garment seemed to cling to the ground as though someone had nailed them down. As he was climbing over the fence a voice seemed to shout in his ears with a deafening hiss: "Where? Where?" The philosopher darted into the weeds and took to his heels, constantly stumbling over old roots and trampling on moles. He saw that on emerging from the weeds, he had only to run across a field, beyond which lay a thicket of blackthorn, in which he thought himself safe. For on getting through the thicket, he should, according to his calculation, come upon the Kiev highway. He crossed the field at a run and found himself in the blackthorn thicket. He crawled through the blackthorn bushes, leaving by way of a toll bits of his coat on every thorn, and came out into a small hollow. The spreading branches of a willow tree bent down here and there almost to the ground. A little stream sparkled, pure as silver. The first thing the philosopher did was to lie down and drink, for he was terribly thirsty.

"Lovely water!" he said, wiping his lips. "I'd better rest here."

"No, sir, we'd better run on or they'll be after you."

These words resounded above his ears. He looked up: before him stood Yavtukh.

"Damn Yavtukh," thought the philosopher angrily to himself. "I've a good mind to take you by the feet and ... I'd like to bash in your ugly face, too, and the rest of you with an oaken log."

"You shouldn't have gone such a long way round," went on Yavtukh. "You ought to have taken the road I took: straight by the stable. Besides, it's such a pity about your coat. It's good cloth. How much was it a yard? But we've had a good walk: it's time to go home."

The philosopher scratched himself and trudged after Yavtukh. "The damned witch will give it to me good and proper now," he thought. "Though what the hell am I so worried about? What am I afraid of? Am I not a Cossack? Why, I've been reading for two nights and with God's help I'll do it for the third night too. I suppose that damned witch committed a good number of sins for the evil powers to stand up for her so much."

Such were the reflections that occupied him as he stepped into the courtyard of the manor-house. Having reassured himself by these remarks, he asked Dorosh, who through the patronage of the butler sometimes had access to his master's storehouses, to get out a keg of raw brandy, and the two friends sat down by the barn and drank no less than half a pailful, so that the philosopher, getting up, shouted: "Musicians! Let's have musicians!" Without waiting for the musicians, he was off dancing a tropak in a clear space in the middle of the yard. He danced till it was time for the twelve o'clock meal, and the servants who stood round him in a circle, as is the custom on such occasions, got bored at last and walked away, saying: "Fancy a man dancing such a long time!" At last the philosopher lay down and fell asleep on the spot and it took a pail of cold water to wake him up for supper. At supper he talked about what a Cossack was and how he should not be afraid of anything in the world.

"Come on," said Yavtukh, "it's time to go."

"A splinter through your tongue, you damned boar!" thought the philosopher and, getting up, said: "Let's go!"

On the way to the church the philosopher kept looking from side to side and tried to engage his companions in conversation. But Yavtukh was silent and Dorosh was not very talkative, either. It was a hellish night. Whole packs of wolves could be heard howling in the distance. Even the barking of the dogs, somehow, sounded dreadful.

"It seems as if something else is howling," said Dorosh, "That's not a wolf."

Yavtukh said nothing; the philosopher could not think of anything to say, either.

They came to the church and entered under its decaying wooden vaults which showed how little the owner of the estate cared for God and his own soul. Yavtukh and Dorosh withdrew as before and the philosopher was left alone. Everything was the same. Everything had the same familiar and menacing aspect. He stood still for a minute. The coffin of the horrifying witch was still standing motionless in the middle of the church. "I won't be afraid, I swear I won't be afraid!" he said, and, drawing a circle around him as before, he began calling to mind all his exorcisms. The silence was awful; the candles flickered and flooded the whole church with light. The philosopher turned over one page, then another and noticed that he was not reading what was written in the book. In a panic, he crossed himself and began chanting. This put some heart into him; the reading progressed and page followed page with lightning rapidity. Suddenly—amid the stillness—the iron lid of the coffin burst open with a crash and the corpse rose up. It was more terrible than the first time. Its teeth knocked horribly against each other, its lips twitched convulsively and, screeching wildly, incantations poured from its mouth. A whirlwind swept through the church, the icons fell to the ground, broken glass came flying down from the windows. The doors broke loose from their hinges and a countless multitude of monsters flew into the church of God. The whole church was filled with the terrible noise of wings and scratching claws. All flew and rushed about looking for the philosopher.

The last traces of intoxication disappeared from Khoma's head. He kept crossing himself and repeating any prayers he could remember. At the same time he heard the evil spirits rushing round him, almost touching him with the tips of their wings and their repulsive nails. He had not the courage to take a look at them; all he saw was that a kind of enormous monster filled the whole width of the wall in its tangle of hair as in a forest; two eyes glared horribly through the meshes of hair, their eyebrows raised a little. Above it something in the shape of a huge bubble was hanging in the air and a thousand claws and scorpion stings extended from its centre. Black earth hung from them in clods. They were all gazing at him, looking for him, but, surrounded by his magic circle, could not see him.

"Bring Viy! Go and fetch Viy!" resounded the words of the corpse.

And suddenly a stillness fell upon the church; the howling of wolves was heard in the distance and soon heavy footsteps resounded throughout the church; glancing out of the corner of his eye, the philosopher saw that they were bringing in a huge, squat, bandylegged creature. He was covered all over with black earth. His arms and legs were sprinkled with earth and protruded like strong sinewy roots. He trod heavily, stumbling at every step. His long eyelids hung down to the very ground. Khoma noticed with horror that he had an iron face. Supported under the arms, he was led straight to where Khoma was standing.

"Raise my eyelids; I can't see!" said Viy in a subterranean voice.

And the whole crowd of devils rushed to lift his eyelids.

"Don't look," an inner voice whispered to the philosopher. But he could not contain himself and looked.

"There he is!" cried Viy and pointed an iron finger at him. And all of them rushed upon the philosopher. Breathless he fell to the ground and right there his soul flew from his body with terror.

There was a sound of a cock crowing. It was the second cock crow; the gnomes had missed the first one. The frightened spirits rushed helter-skelter to the windows and doors, but it was too late, and there they remained, stuck in the doors and windows. When the priest arrived he stopped dead at the sight of such a desecration of God's holy place. And so the church was left forever, with monsters stuck fast in the doors and windows, and it was overgrown with trees, roots, tall weeds, and blackthorn bushes; and no one can now find the way to it.

When the rumours of this reached Kiev and the theologian Khalyava heard at last of the fate of the philosopher Khoma, he spent an hour in meditation. Great changes had befallen him during that time. Fortune had smiled on him; at the conclusion of his course of studies, he was appointed bellringer of the highest belfry in Kiev and he almost always walked about with a bruised nose because the wooden staircase to the belfry had been extremely carelessly made.

"Have you heard what happened to Khoma?" Tibery Gorobets who had by now become a philosopher and sported a newly grown moustache, asked, coming up to him.

"It's God's will," said Khalyava the bellringer. "Let's go to a tavern and drink to his memory."

The young philosopher who was beginning to make use of his privileges with the ardour of an enthusiast, so that his wide trousers, his coat, and even his cap reeked of spirits and cheap tobacco, at once gave his consent.

"A jolly good fellow Khoma," said the bellringer as the lame landlord put down the third mug before him. "An excellent fellow and came to a bad end for nothing!"

"I know why he came to a bad end. It was because he was afraid. Had he not been afraid, the witch could not have done anything to him. All you have to do is to cross yourself and spit on her tail. Then nothing will happen. I know all about it. You see, all the market women in Kiev are witches, all of them."

To this the bellringer nodded in token of agreement. But noticing that his tongue was incapable of uttering a single word, he carefully rose from the table and, reeling from side to side, went to hide himself away in the remotest spot in the tall weeds. From force of habit, however, he did not forget to carry off the sole of an old boot that was lying about on the bench.

Phantoms

By Iván Turgénieff

A FANTASY

One instant … and the magic tale is o'er—
And with the possible the soul is filled once more.

A. FET.[1]

I

I could not get to sleep for a long time, and kept tossing incessantly from side to side. "May the devil take those table-tipping follies!"—I thought:—"they only upset the nerves."—Drowsiness began to overpower me …

Suddenly it seemed to me as though a chord had twanged faintly and lugubriously in the room.

I raised my head. The moon was hanging low in the sky, and staring me straight in the eye. White as chalk its light lay on the floor. … The strange sound was clearly repeated.

I leaned on my elbow. A slight alarm nipped at my heart.—One minute passed, then another. … A cock crowed somewhere in the distance; still further away another answered.

I dropped my head on my pillow. "Just see to what one can bring one's self," I began my reflections again:—"my ears will begin to ring."

A little later I fell asleep—or it seemed to me that I did. I had a remarkable dream. It seemed to me as though I were lying in my bedroom, in my bed, but I was not asleep, and could not close my eyes. … I turned over. … The streak of moonlight on the floor

---

1 The pseudonym of Afanásy Afanásievitch Shénshin

(1820–1892).—Translator.

softly began to rise up, to straighten itself, to become slightly rounded at the top. ... Before me, transparent as mist, a white woman stood motionless.

"Who art thou?"—I asked with an effort.

The voice which replied was like the rustling of leaves.—"It is I. ... I. ... I. ... I have come for thee."

"For me? But who art thou?"

"Come by night to the corner of the forest, where the old oak stands. I shall be there."

I tried to get a good look at the features of the mysterious woman—and suddenly I gave an involuntary start: I felt a chill breath on me. And now I was no longer lying in my bed, but sitting on it—and there, where the spectre had seemed to stand, the moonlight lay in a long streak on the floor.

II

The day passed after a fashion. I remember that I tried to read, to work . ... it came to nothing. Night arrived. My heart beat violently within me, as though I were expecting something. I went to bed and turned my face to the wall.

"Why didst thou not come?"—an audible whisper rang out in the room.

I glanced round swiftly.

It was she again. ... the mysterious phantom. Motionless eyes in a motionless face, and a gaze full of grief.

"Come!"—the whisper made itself heard again.

"I will come,"—I replied, with involuntary terror. The phantom quietly swayed forward, and became all mixed up, undulating lightly like smoke;—and the moonlight again lay white upon the polished floor.

III

I passed the day in a state of agitation. At supper I drank almost a whole bottle of wine, and started to go out on the porch; but returned, and flung myself on my bed. My blood was surging heavily through my veins.

Again a sound made itself heard. ... I shuddered, but did not look round. Suddenly I felt some one clasp me in a close embrace from behind, and whisper in my ear: "Come, come, come!" ... Trembling with fright I groaned:

"I will come!"—and straightened myself up.

The woman stood bending over me, close beside the head of my bed. She smiled faintly and vanished. But I had succeeded in scrutinising her face. It seemed to me that I had seen her before;—but where? when? I rose late and roamed about the fields all day long, approached the old oak-tree on the border of the forest, and made an attentive inspection of the surroundings.

Toward evening I seated myself at an open window in my study. The old housekeeper set a cup of tea before me—but I did not taste it … I kept wondering and asking myself: "Am not I losing my mind?" The sun had only just set—and not only did the sky grow red, but the whole air suddenly became suffused with an almost unnatural crimson; the leaves and grass, as though covered with fresh varnish, did not stir; in their stony immobility, in the sharp brilliancy of their outlines, in that commingling of a strong glow and death-like tranquillity, there was something strange, enigmatical A rather large grey bird flew up without any sound, and alighted on the very edge of the window. … I looked at it—and it looked at me askance with its round, dark eye. "I wonder if she did not send thee in order to remind me?"—I thought.

The bird immediately fluttered its soft wings, and flew away, as before, without any noise. I sat for a long time still at the window, but I not longer gave myself up to wonder: I seemed to have got into a charmed circle, and an irresistible though quiet power was drawing me on, as the onrush of the torrent draws the boat while still far away from the falls. At last I gave a start. The crimson had long since disappeared from the air, the hues had darkened, and the enchanted silence had ceased. A breeze was beginning to flutter about, the moon stood out with ever-increasing distinctness in the sky which was turning darkly blue,—and soon the leaves on the trees began to gleam silver and black in its cold rays. My old woman entered my study with a lighted candle, but the draught from the window blew on it and extinguished the flame, I could endure it no longer; I sprang to my feet, banged, my cap down on my head, and set out for the corner of the forest, for the aged oak.

IV

Many years before, this oak had been struck by lightning; its crest had been shattered and had withered away, but it still retained life enough for several centuries. As I began to draw near to it, a dark cloud floated across the moon: it was very dark under its wide-spreading boughs. At first I did not notice anything peculiar; but I glanced to one side—and my heart sank within me; a white figure was standing motionless beside a tall bush, between the oak-tree and the forest. My hair rose slightly on my head; but I summoned my courage, and advanced toward the forest.

Yes, it was she, my nocturnal visitor. As I approached her, the moon shone forth again. She seemed all woven of semi-transparent, milky vapour,—through her face I could see a branch softly waving in the wind,—only her hair and eyes shone dimly-black, and on one of the fingers of her clasped hands gleamed a narrow gold ring. I halted in front of her, and tried to speak; but my voice died in my breast, although I no longer felt any real terror. Her eyes were turned upon me; their gaze expressed neither grief nor joy, but a certain lifeless attention. I waited to see whether she would utter a word; but she stood motionless and dumb, and kept gazing at me with her deadly-intent look. Again I began to feel uneasy.

"I have come!"—I exclaimed at last with an effort. My voice had a dull, queer ring.

"I love thee,"—a whisper became audible.

"Thou lovest me!"—I repeated in amazement.

"Give thyself to me"—rustled the voice again in reply to me.

"Give myself to thee! But thou art a phantom—thou hast no body."—A strange sensation over powered me,—"What art thou,—smoke, air, vapour? Give myself to thee! Answer me first—who art thou? Hast thou lived upon earth? Whence hast thou revealed thyself?"

"Give thyself to me. I will do thee no harm. Say only two words: 'Take me.'"

I looked at her, "What is that she is saying?" I thought. "What is the meaning of all this? And how will she take me? Shall I try the experiment?"

"Well, very good,"—I uttered aloud, and with unexpected force, as though some one had given me a push from behind. "Take me!"

Before I had finished uttering these words, the mysterious figure, with a sort of inward laugh, which made her face quiver for an instant, swayed forward, her arms separated and were outstretched. ... I tried to spring aside; but I was already in her power. She clasped me in her embrace, my body rose about fourteen inches from the earth—and we both soared off, smoothly and not too swiftly, over the wet, motionless grass.

V

At first my head reeled, and I involuntarily closed my eyes ... A minute later, I opened them again. We were floating on as before. But the forest was no longer visible; beneath us lay outspread a level plain dotted with dark spots. With terror I convinced myself that we had risen to a fearful height.

"I am lost—I am in the power of Satan," flashed through me like lightning. Up to that moment, the thought of obsession by an unclean power, of the possibility of damnation, had not entered my head. We continued to dash headlong onward, and seemed to be soaring ever higher and higher.

"Whither art thou carrying me?"—I moaned at last.

"Wherever thou wishest,"—replied my fellow traveller. She was sticking close to me all over; her face almost rested on my face. Nevertheless, I barely felt her touch.

"Let me down to the earth; I feel giddy at this height."

"Good; only shut your eyes and do not take breath."

I obeyed—and immediately felt myself falling, like a stone which has been hurled … the wind whistled through my hair. When I came to myself, we were again floating close above the ground, so that we caught in the tips of the tall plants.

"Set me on my feet,"—I began.—"What. pleasure is there in flying? I am not a bird."

"I thought it would be agreeable to you. We have no other occupation."

"You have not? But who are you?"

There was no answer.

"Thou dost not dare to tell me that?"

A plaintive sound, like that which had awakened me on the first night, trembled on my ear. In the meantime, we continued to move almost imperceptibly through the night air.

"Let me go!"—I said. My companion bent backward, and I found myself on my feet. She came to a halt in front of me and again clasped her hands. I recovered my equanimity and looked her in the face: as before, it expressed submissive grief.

"Where are we?"—I queried. I did not recognise my surroundings.

"Far from thy home, but thou mayest be there in one moment."

"In what manner? Am I to trust myself to thee again?"

"I have not done and will not do thee any harm. We shall float together until dawn, that is all. I can carry thee whithersoever thou wishest—to all the ends of the earth. Give thyself to me; say again: 'Take me!'"

"Well, then … take me!"

Again she fell upon my neck, again my feet left the earth—and away we flew.

VI

"Whither?"—she asked me.

"Straight ahead, ever straight ahead."

"But the forest lies in that direction."

"Let us rise above the forest—only, very gently."

We soared aloft, like wood-snipe flying upon a birch-tree, and again floated on in a straight line. Instead of grass, the crests of the trees flitted past under our feet. It was wonderful to see the forest from above, its bristling spine all illuminated by the moon. It seemed some sort of a vast slumbering wild beast, and accompanied us with a broad, incessant rustling resembling an unintelligible growl. Here and there we came across small glades; a dentated strip of shadow stood out finely in black on one side of them. … Now and then a hare cried pitifully below; up above, an owl whistled, also in plaintive wise; there was an odour of mushrooms, of buds, of lovage abroad in the air; the moonlight fairly poured in a flood in all directions—coldly and severely; the myriad stars glittered directly above our heads.

And now the forest was left behind; athwart the plain stretched a strip of mist; a river flowed there. We floated along one of its shores, above the bushes, rendered heavy and immovable by humidity. The waves on the river now glistened with a blue gleam, now rolled on darkly and as though they were vicious. In places a thin vapour moved strangely above it, and the cups of the water-lilies shone out with the virginal and sumptuous whiteness of all their unfolded petals, as though they knew that they were inaccessible, I took it into my head to pluck one of them—and lo! I immediately found myself directly over the smooth surface of the river. ... The dampness struck me unpleasantly in the face as soon as I had broken the strong stem of a large blossom. We began to flit from shore to shore, like the sand-pipers, which we kept waking, and which we pursued. More than once it happened that we flew down upon a little family of wild ducks, disposed in a circle on a clear spot among the reeds—but they did not stir; perhaps one of them would hastily take its head out from under its wing, look and look, and then anxiously thrust its bill back again into its downy feathers; or another would quack faintly. Its whole body quivering the while. We frightened one heron; it rose out of a willow bush, with dangling legs, and flapped its wings with awkward vigour; it really did seem to me then to resemble a German. Not a fish splashed anywhere—they, too, were asleep. I began to get used to the sensation of flying, and even found a certain pleasure in it; any one who has chanced to fly in his sleep will understand me. I took to watching with great attention the strange being, thanks to whom such improbable events were happening to me.

VII

She was a woman with a small, non-Russian face. Greyish-white, semi-transparent, with barely-defined shadows. It reminded one of the figures on an alabaster vase illuminated from within—and again it seemed to be familiar to me.

"May I talk with thee?"—I said.

"Speak."

"I see that thou hast a ring on thy finger; so thou hast dwelt on earth—thou hast been married?"

I paused. ... There was no reply.

"What is thy name—or what was thy name, at least?"

"Call me Ellis."

"Ellis! That is an English name? Art thou an English woman? Thou hast known me before?"

"No."

"Why didst thou reveal thyself to me in particular?"

"I love thee."

"And art thou content?"

"Yes; we are floating, we are circling, you and I, through the pure air."

"Ellis!"—I said suddenly,—"perchance thou art a guilty, a damned soul?"

My companion's head dropped.—"I do not understand thee,"—she whispered.

"I adjure thee, in God's name. ..." I was beginning.

"What art thou saying?"—she said with surprise.—"I do not understand."—It seemed to me that the arm which lay about my waist like a girdle, was moving gently. ...

"Fear not,"—said Ellis,—"fear not, my dear one!"—Her face turned and moved closer to my face. ... I felt on my lips a strange sensation, like the touch of a soft, delicate sting. ... Leeches which are not vicious take hold in that way.

VIII

I glanced downward. We had again managed to rise to a very considerable height. We were flying over a county capital with which I was unfamiliar, situated on the slope of a broad hill. The churches reared themselves amid a dark mass of wooden roofs and fruit orchards; a long bridge lowered black at a curve in the river; everything was silent, overwhelmed with sleep. The very domes and crosses seemed to glitter with a dumb gleam; dumbly the tall poles of the wells reared themselves aloft beside the round clumps of willows; the whitish highway dumbly plunged, like a narrow dart, into one end of the town—and dumbly emerged from the other side upon the gloomy expanse of the monotonous fields.

"What town is that? "—I queried.

"***off, in the *** Government."

"***off, in the *** Government?"

"Yes."

"Well, I am very far from home!"

"For us distance is nothing."

"Really?" Sudden boldness flashed up within me.—"Then carry me to South America!"

"I cannot go to America. It is day there now."

"While you and I are night birds? Well, somewhere or other, only as far off as possible."

"Close thine eyes and do not draw breath,"—replied Ellis,—and we dashed headlong onward with the swiftness of the whirlwind. The wind rushed into my ears with a crashing noise.

We halted, but the noise did not cease. On the contrary, it had become converted into a sort of menacing roar, a thunderous din. ...

"Now thou mayest open thine eyes,"—said Ellis.

IX

I obeyed … My God, where was I?

Overhead were heavy, smoky clouds; they were crowding together, and flying like a herd of vicious monsters. … and yonder, below, was another monster: the raging, just that,—raging sea. … The white foam was glistening convulsively, and seething in it in mounds,—and rearing aloft in shaggy billows, it was pounding with harsh thunder on the pitch-black cliffs. The howling of the storm, the icy breath of the heaving deep, the heavy dashing of the surf, in which, at times, one seemed to hear something resembling howls, the distant firing of cannon, the ringing of bells, the torturing shriek, and the grinding of the pebbles on the shore, the sudden scream of an invisible gull, on the troubled horizon the reeling remains of a ship—everywhere death, death and horror. … My head began to reel, and swooning, I again closed my eyes. …

"What is this? Where are we?"

"On the southern shore of the Isle of Wight, in front of the Blackgang Cliff, where ships are so frequently dashed to pieces,"—said Ellis, this time with peculiar distinctness and, as it seemed to me, not without malicious joy. …

"Take me away, away from here … home! Home!"

I shrank together utterly, I clutched my face in my hands. … I felt that we were floating still more swiftly than before; the wind no longer howled nor whistled—it shrieked through my hair, in my garments … I gasped for breath …

"Now stand on thy feet,"—rang out the voice of Ellis.

I tried to control myself, my consciousness. …

I felt the ground under foot, but heard nothing, as though everything round about had died. … only the blood beat irregularly in my temples, and my head still reeled with a faint, internal sound. I straightened myself up and opened my eyes.

X

We were on the dam of my pond. Directly in front of me, athwart the pointed leaves of the willows, its broad expanse was visible with filaments of feathery mist clinging to it here and there. On the right a field of rye glinted dully; on the left the trees of the garden reared themselves aloft, long, motionless, and damp in appearance. … Morning had not yet breathed upon them. Across the sky two or three clouds were stretched, obliquely, like wreaths of smoke; they seemed yellowish, and the first faint reflection of the dawn fell on them, God knows whence: the eye could not yet detect on the whitening horizon the spot from which it must be borrowed. The stars had disappeared; nothing was stirring yet, although everything was already awake in the enchanted stillness of early morning.

"The morning! Yonder is the morning!"—exclaimed Ellis in my very ear ..."
Farewell! until to-morrow!"

I turned. ... Lightly quitting the ground, she floated past,—and suddenly raised both arms above her head. The head, and the arms, and the shoulders instantly flushed with warm, corporeal light; in the dark eyes quivered living sparks; a smile of mysterious delicacy flitted across the reddening lips. ... A charming woman suddenly made her appearance before me. ... But she instantly threw herself backward, as though falling into a swoon, and melted away like vapour.

I stood motionless.

When I came to my senses and looked about me, it seemed to me that the corporeal, pale-rosy flush which had coursed over the figure of my phantom had not yet vanished and, dispersed through the air, was flooding me on all sides. ... It was the dawn flushing red. I suddenly became conscious of extreme fatigue and wended my way homeward. As I passed the poultry-yard I heard the first matutinal quacking of the goslings (no bird wakes earlier than they); along the roof, at the tip of each projecting stake, perched a daw; and all of them were diligently and silently pluming themselves, distinctly outlined against the milky sky. From time to time, they all rose into the air simultaneously and, after flying about a little while, alighted again in a row, without croaking. ... From the forest near at hand was wafted, twice, the hoarsely-fresh cry of the black-cock, which had just flown up from the dewy grass all overgrown with berries. ... With a light shiver all over my body, I gained my bed and speedily sank into a sound sleep.

XI

On the following night, when I began to draw near to the ancient oak, Ellis floated to meet me, as to a friend. I was not afraid of her as on the preceding day; I was almost delighted to see her. I did not even attempt to understand what had happened with me: all I cared about was to fly as far as possible, through curious places.

Again Ellis's arm was wound about me—and again we darted off.

"Let us go to Italy,"—I whispered in her ear.

"Whithersoever thou wilt, my dear one,"—she replied solemnly and softly—and softly and solemnly she turned her face toward me. It seemed to me to be less transparent than on the day before; more feminine and more dignified; it reminded me of that beautiful creature who had flashed before my vision in the dawn before our parting.

"To-night is a great night,"—went on Ellis.—"It rarely comes,—only when seven times thirteen . ...."

At this point I lost several words.

"Now that can be seen which is invisible at other times."

"Ellis!"—I pleaded," who art thou? Tell me!"

She silently raised her long, white hand.

In the dark heaven, at the point to which her finger pointed, in the midst of tiny stars, a comet gleamed in a reddish streak.

"How am I to understand thee?"—I began.—"Dost thou mean that thou soarest like that comet, between the planets and the sun,—that thou soarest among men … and how?"

But Ellis's hand was suddenly clapped over my eyes. … Something akin to the grey mist from a damp valley enveloped me. …

"To Italy! to Italy! "—I heard her whisper.—"This night is a great night!"

XII

The mist disappeared from before my eyes, and I beheld beneath me an interminable plain. But I was able to understand, from the very touch of the warm, soft air on my cheeks, that I was not in Russia; and neither did that plain resemble our Russian plains. It was a vast, dim expanse, apparently devoid of grass and empty; here and there, throughout its entire length, gleamed small stagnant pools, like tiny fragments of a mirror; far away the inaudible, motionless sea was visible. Great stars glittered in the intervals between the large, beautiful clouds; a thousand-voiced, unceasing, yet not clamorous trill, arose in all directions; and wonderful was that penetrating and dreamy rumble, that voice of the nocturnal desert. …

"The Pontine Marshes,"—said Ellis.—"Dost thou hear the frogs? Dost thou discern the odour of sulphur?"

"The Pontine Marshes. …" I repeated, and a sensation of majestic sadness took possession of me.—"But why hast thou brought me hither, to this mournful, deserted region? Let us rather fly to Rome."

"Rome is close at hand,"—replied Ellis. … "Prepare thyself!"

We descended and dashed along the ancient Roman road. A buffalo slowly raised from the ooze his shaggy, monstrous head with short whorls of bristles between the crooked horns which curved backward. He rolled the whites of his eyes sideways and snorted heavily with his wet nostrils, as though he scented us.

"Rome, Rome is near," … whispered Ellis.—"Look, look ahead."

I raised my eyes.

What was that which rose darkly against the night sky? The lofty arches of a huge bridge? What river did it span? Why was it rent in places? No, it was not a bridge, it was an ancient aqueduct. Round about lay the sacred land of Campania, and yonder, far away, were the Alban Hills; and their crests and the great back of the ancient aqueduct gleamed faintly in the rays of the moon which had just risen. …

We suddenly soared upward and hung suspended in the air before an isolated ruin. No one could have told what it had formerly been: a tomb, a palace, a tower. … Black ivy enveloped the whole of it with its deadly power—and below; a half-ruined arch yawned like jaws. A heavy, cellar-like odour was wafted in my face from that heap of small, closely-packed stones, from which the granite facing of the wall had long since fallen off.

"Here,"—said Ellis, raising her hand;—"here!—Utter loudly, thrice in succession, the name of a great Roman."

"But what will happen?"

"Thou shalt see."

I reflected.—"Divus Cajus Julius Caesar!"—I suddenly exclaimed:—"Divus Cajus Julius Caesar!" I repeated slowly:—"Caesar!"

XIII

Before the last echoes of my voice had had time to die away I heard. ...

It is difficult to say precisely what. At first I heard a confused burst of trumpet notes and of hand-clapping, barely perceptible to the ear, but endlessly repeated. It seemed as though somewhere, immensely far away, in some bottomless abyss, an innumerable throng were suddenly beginning to stir, and rise, rise, undulating and exchanging barely audible shouts, as though athwart a dream, athwart an oppressive dream many ages in duration. Then the air began to blow and darken above the ruin. ... Shadows began to flit past me, myriads of shadows, millions of outlines, now rounded like helmets now long like spears; the rays of the moon were shivered into many bluish sparks on these spears and helmets—and the whole of that army, that throng, moved nearer and nearer, grew greater, surged mightily. ... An indescribable effort, a tense effort sufficient to lift the whole world, could be felt in it; but not, a single figure stood out distinctly. ... And suddenly it seemed to me as though a tremor ran through it all, as though certain huge billows had surged back and parted. ... " Caesar! Caesar venit!"—rustled voices like the leaves of the forest upon which a whirl-wind has suddenly descended ... a dull shock surged along, and a pallid, stern head in a laurel wreath, with drooping lids,—the head of the emperor,—began slowly to move forward from the rain. ...

There are no words of mortal tongue to express the dread which gripped my heart. It seemed to me that if that head were to open its eyes, to unseal its lips, I should fall dead on the spot—"Ellis!"—I moaned:—"I do not wish it, I cannot, I do not want Rome, coarse, menacing Rome. ... Away, away from here!"—"Pusillanimous!"—she whispered, and we dashed headlong away. Once more I heard behind me the iron shout of the legions, like thunder now ... then all grew dark.

XIV

"Look about thee,"—said Ellis to me,—"and calm thyself."

I obeyed; and I remember that my first impression was so sweet that I could only heave a sigh. Something smoky-blue, silvery-soft encompassed me on every side. At first I could distinguish nothing: that azure splendour blinded me, But lo! little by little the outlines of beautiful mountains and forests began to start forth before me; a lake lay outspread before me, with stars quivering in its depths, and the caressing murmur of the surge. The fragrance of orange-blossoms enveloped me in a billow and along with it, also in a billow as it were, the strong, pure tones of a youthful feminine voice reached my ears. That fragrance, those sounds fairly drew me downward, and I began to descend ... to descend to a luxurious marble palace, which gleamed white and in friendlywise amid a cypress grove. The sounds were welling forth from its wide-open windows; the waves of the lake, dotted with a dust of flowers, plashed against its walls—and directly opposite, all clothed in the dark-green of orange-trees and laurels, all bathed in radiant mist, all studded with statues, slender columns, and porticoes of temples, a circular island rose from the bosom of the lake. ...

"Isola Bella!"—said Ellis. ... "Lago Maggiore. ..."

I articulated only: "Ah!" and continued to descend. The feminine voice rang out ever more loudly, ever more clearly in the palace; I was irresistibly drawn to it. ... I wanted to gaze into the face of the songstress who was warbling such strains on such a night. We halted in front of a window.

In the middle of a room decorated in Pompeian style, and more resembling an ancient temple than the newest sort of a ball, surrounded by Greek statues, Etruscan vases, rare plants, precious stuffs, and lighted from above by the soft rays of two lamps enclosed in crystal globes, sat a young woman at the piano. With her head thrown slightly backward, and her eyes halfclosed she was singing an Italian aria; she was singing and smiling, and, at the same time, her features were expressive of seriousness, even of severity ... a sign of complete enjoyment. She smiled ... and the Faun of Praxiteles, indolent, as young as she, effeminate, sensual also, seemed to be smiling at her from one corner, from behind the branches of an oleander, athwart the thin smoke which rose from a bronze perfuming-pan upon an antique tripod. The beauty was alone. Enchanted by the sounds, the beauty, the glitter and perfume of the night, shaken to the very depths of my soul by the spectacle of that young, calm, brilliant happiness, I totally forgot my companion, forgot in what strange wise I had become a witness of that life which was so distant, so remote, so strange to me—and I wanted to step through the window; I wanted to enter into conversation. ...

My whole body quivered from a forcible blow—as though I had touched a Leyden jar. I glanced round. ... Ellis's face was gloomy and menacing, despite all its transparency; wrath glowed dully in her eyes, which had suddenly been opened to their full extent. …

"Away !"—she whispered furiously; and again there was the whirlwind and gloom and dizziness. … Only this time it was not the shout of the legions, but the voice of the songstress, broken short off on a high note, which lingered in my ears. …

We halted. A high note, that same high note, continued to ring out and did not cease to resound, although I felt an entirely different air, a different odour. … Invigorating freshness breathed upon me, as from a great river, and there was the scent of hay, of smoke, of hemp. The long-drawn note was followed by a second, then by a third, but with such an indubitable shading, such a familiar turn characteristic of my native land, that I immediately said to myself: "That is a Russian man singing a Russian song,"—and at that moment everything round about me grew clear.

XV

We found ourselves above a flat shore. On the left, stretched out, losing themselves in infinity, lay mowed meadows, dotted with huge haystacks; on the right, to an equally unlimited extent, spread out the level expanse of a vast river abounding in water. Not far from the shores huge, dark barges were rocking quietly at an anchor, slightly moving the tips of their masts like index-fingers. From one of these barges were wafted to me the sounds of a flowing voice, and on it burned lights, quivering and rocking in the water with their long, red reflections. Here and there both on the river and in the fields twinkled other light—the eye was unable to discern whether near at hand or far away; now they blinked, again they stood forth in large, radiant spots; numberless katydids shrilled ceaselessly—quite equal to the frogs on the Pontine Marshes; and beneath the cloudless, but low-hanging, dark sky invisible birds uttered their calls from time to time.

"Are we in Russia?"—I asked Ellis.

"This is the Volga," she replied.

We soared along the bank.—"Why hast thou torn me thence, from that beautiful land?"—I began.—"Wert thou envious, pray? Did not jealousy awake in thee?"

Ellis's lips quivered faintly, and a menace again flashed in her eyes. … But her whole face immediately grew rigid once more.

"I want to go home,"—I said.

"Wait, wait,"—replied Ellis.—"To-night is a great night. It will not soon return. Thou mayest be the spectator. … Wait."

And suddenly we flew across the Volga, in a slanting direction, close above the water, low and abruptly, like swallows before the storm. The broad waves gurgled heavily below us, the keen river wind beat us with its cold, strong wing. … the lofty right shore soon began to rise before us in the semi-darkness. Steep hills with great clefts made their appearance. We approached them.

"Shout, 'Tow-path men to the prow!'" Ellis whispered to me.

I remembered the dread which I had experienced at the appearance of the Roman spectres, I felt fatigue and certain strange anguish, as though my heart were melting within me—and I did not wish to utter the fateful words. I knew beforehand that in reply to them something monstrous would appear, like Freischütz, in the Volga Valley.—But my lips parted against my will, and I shouted in a weak, strained voice: "Tow-path men to the prow!"[2]

XVI

At first all remained dumb, as before the Roman ruin.—But suddenly close to my very ear, a coarse bark-hauler's[3] laugh rang out, and something fell with a bang into the water and began to choke. … I glanced round: no one was anywhere to be seen, but an echo rebounded from the shore, and instantly and from all quarters a deafening uproar arose. What was there not in that chaos of sounds! Shouts and whines; violent swearing and laughter, laughter most of all; strokes of oars and of axes; the crash as of breaking in doors and chests; the creaking of rigging and wheels, and the galloping of horses; the sound of alarm-bells and the clanking of chains; the rumble and roar of conflagrations, drunken songs and interchange of hurried speech; inconsolable, despairing weeping, and imperious exclamations; the death-rattle, and audacious whistling; the yelling and trampling of the dance. … "Beat! Hang! Drown! Cut his throat! That's fine! That's fine! So! Show no pity!"—were distinctly audible; even the broken breathing of panting men was audible;—and nevertheless, everywhere round about, as far as the eye could see, nothing came into sight, nothing underwent any change. The river flowed past mysteriously, almost morosely; the very shore seemed more deserted and wild than before—that was all.

I turned to Ellis, but she laid her finger on her lips. …

"Stepán Timoféitch! Stepán Timoféitch is coming!"—arose a rustling round about;—"our dear little father is coming, our atamán, our nourisher!"—As before, I saw no one, but it suddenly seemed to me as though a huge body were moving straight at me. … Frólka! Where art thou, dog?"—thundered a terrible voice.—"Set fire on all sides—and put them under the axe, my little White-hands!"[4]

---

2   According to tradition, this was the war-cry of the Volga brigands when they captured vessels.—TRANSLATOR.

3   Before the introduction of steamers on the Volga, all vessels were hauled up-stream from Ástrakhan to Nízhni-Nóvgorod—or even further—by men walking along the tow-paths on the shore.—TRANSLATOR.

4   The bandit chief, generally known in history as Sténka Rázin and Frol or Frólka, his younger brother and inseparable companion, captured and laid waste great stretches of the Volga. Their memory still lives in epic

The heat of a flame close at hand breathed upon me, and the bitter reek of smoke,—and at the same moment something warm, like blood, spattered upon my face and hands. ... Wild laughter roared round about. ...

I lost consciousness and when I recovered my senses, Ellis and I were slipping along the familiar verge of my forest, straight toward the old oak-tree. ...

"Seest thou yonder path?"—Ellis said to me.—"yonder where the moon is shining dimly and two small birch-trees are bending over? ... Dost thou wish to go thither?"

But I felt so shattered and exhausted, that in reply I could say only:—"Home ... home!"...

"Thou art at home,"—answered Ellis.

In fact, I was standing in front of the door of my house—alone. Ellis had vanished. The watch-dog was about to approach, glared suspiciously at me—and fled howling.

With difficulty I dragged myself to my bed, and fell asleep, without undressing.

XVII

On the following morning I had a headache, and could hardly move my feet; but I paid no attention to my bodily indisposition, I was gnawed by penitence, stifled with vexation.

I was extremely displeased with myself. "Pusillanimous!"—I kept repeating incessantly:—"Yes—Ellis is right. What did I fear? How could I fail to profit by the opportunity? ... I might have beheld Caesar himself—and I swooned with terror, I squealed, I turned away, like a child from the rod. Well, Rázin—that is quite a different matter. In my quality of nobleman and land-owner ... However, what was the actual cause of my fright in that case also? Pusillanimous, pusillanimous!"...

"But is it not in a dream that I am seeing all this?"—I asked myself at last. I called my housekeeper.

"Márfa, at what time did I go to bed last night?—dost thou remember?"

"Why, who knows, my benefactor. ... Late, I think, in the gloaming thou didst leave the house; and thou were clattering thy heels in thy bedroom after midnight. Just before dawn—yes. And this is the third day it has been like that. Evidently, something has happened to worry thee."

"Ehe-he!"—I thought.—"There can be no doubt as to the flying."—"Well, and how do I look to-day?"—I added aloud.

"How dost thou look? Let me look at thee. Thy cheeks are somewhat sunken. And thou art pale, my nourisher; there now, there isn't a drop of blood in thy face."

I winced slightly. ... I dismissed Márfa.

ballads and among the peasants.—TRANSLATOR.

"If thou goest on like this thou wilt surely die or lose thy mind,"—I reasoned, as I sat meditating by the window. "I must abandon all this. It is dangerous. And, here now, how strangely my heart is beating! And when I am flying, it constantly seems to me as though some one were sucking it, or as though something were seeping out of it—like the spring sap from a birch, if you thrust an axe into it. And yet I feel sorry. And there is Ellis. ... She is playing with me as a cat plays with a mouse ... but it is unlikely that she wishes any evil to me. I'll surrender myself to her for the last time—I'll gaze my fill—and then. ... But what if she is drinking my blood? This is terrible. Moreover, such swift motion cannot fail to be injurious; they say that on the railways in England it is forbidden to go more than one hundred and twenty versts an hour. ..."

Thus did I meditate—but at ten o'clock in the evening I was already standing before the aged oak.

XVIII

The night was cold, dim, and grey; there was a scent of rain in the air. To my surprise, I found no one under the oak; I made the circuit of it several times, walked as far as the verge of the forest, and returned, staring assiduously into the darkness. ... Everything was deserted. I waited a while, then uttered Ellis's name several times in succession, with ever-increasing loudness. ... but she did not show herself. I was seized with sadness, almost with anguish; my former apprehensions vanished; I could not reconcile myself to the thought that my companion would never return to me.

"Ellis! Ellis! Do come! Wilt thou not come?"—I shouted for the last time.

A crow which had been awakened by my voice suddenly began to fidget about in the crest of a neighbouring tree, and becoming entangled in the branches, set to flapping its wings. ... But Ellis did not appear.

With drooping head I wended my way homeward. Ahead of me the willows on the dam stood out in a black mass, and the light in the window of my room twinkled among the apple-trees of the garden,—twinkled and vanished, like the eye of a man watching me,—when suddenly the faint swish of swiftly-cloven air became audible behind me, and something with one swoop embraced and seized hold of me from below upward: that is the way a buzzard seizes, "smashes" a quail. ... It was Ellis who had flown upon me, I felt her cheek on my cheek, the girdle of her arms around my body—and like a keen chill the whisper of her mouth pierced my ear: "Here am I!" I was simultaneously alarmed and delighted. ... We floated off not far above the ground.

"Thou didst not mean to come to-day?"—I said.

"But thou didst languish for me! Thou lovest me? Oh, thou art mine!"

Ellis's last words disconcerted me. ... I did not know what to say.

"I was detained"—she went on;—"they set a guard over me."

"Who could detain thee?"

"Whither dost thou wish to go?"—queried Ellis, not replying to my question, as usual.

"Carry me to Italy, to that lake—dost thou remember?"

Ellis drew back a little and shook her head in negation. Then for the first time did I perceive that she had ceased to be transparent. And her face seemed to have grown rosy; a crimson flush spread over its cloudy whiteness. I looked into her eyes ... and dread came upon me: in those eyes something was moving—with the slow, unceasing and vicious motion of a serpent which has coiled itself and, congealed in that position, is beginning to grow warm in the sunshine.

"Ellis!"—I exclaimed:—"Who art thou? Tell me, who art thou?"

Ellis merely shrugged her shoulders.

I was vexed. ... I wanted to punish her;—and suddenly it occurred to me to order her to carry me to Paris. "That's where thou wilt have occasion for jealousy,"—I thought.—"Ellis!"—I said aloud;—"thou art not afraid of large cities, Paris, for example, art thou?"

"No."

"No? Not even of those places where it is bright, as on the boulevards?"

"That is not the light of day."

"Very good; then carry me immediately to the Boulevard des Italiens."

Ellis threw over my head the end of her long, flowing sleeve. I was immediately enveloped in a sort of white mist, with a soporific scent of poppies. Everything disappeared instantaneously; all light, all sound—and almost consciousness itself. The sensation of life alone remained—and it was not unpleasant. Suddenly the mist vanished; Ellis had removed her sleeve from my head, and I beheld before me a huge mass of buildings crowded together, brilliancy, movement, din. ... I beheld Paris.

XIX

I had been in Paris before, and therefore immediately recognised the spot to which Ellis had shaped her course. It was the garden of the Tuileries, with its aged chestnut-trees, iron fences, fortress-moat, and beast-like Zouaves on guard. Passing the palace, passing the Church of St. Roch, on whose steps the first Napoleon shed French blood for the first time, we halted high above the Boulevard des Italiens, where the third Napoleon did the same thing, and with equal success. Crowds of people—young and old dandies, workmen, women in sumptuous attire—were thronging the sidewalks; the glided restaurants and cafes were blazing with lights, carriages of all sorts and aspects were driving up and down the boulevard; everything was fairly seething and glittering. In every direction, where-ever the eye fell. ... But, strange to say, I did not feel like quitting my pure, dark, airy height; I did not wish to approach that human ant-hill. It seemed as though a hot, oppressive, copper-coloured exhalation rose up thence, not precisely fragrant, nor yet precisely stinking; a very great deal of life had been collected there in one heap. I wavered. … But now the voice of a street-courtesan, sharp as the screech of iron rails, suddenly was wafted to my ear; like a naked blade it thrust itself out upward, that voice; it stung me like the fangs of a viper. I immediately pictured to myself the stony, greedy, flat Parisian face, with high cheek-bones, the eyes of a usurer, rouge, powder, curled hair, and a bouquet of bright-hued artificial flowers on the high-peaked hat, the scraped nails in the shape of claws, the monstrous crinoline. … I pictured to myself also a steppe-dweller like myself pursuing the venal doll with detestable tripping gait. … I pictured to myself how, confused to the point of rudeness, and lisping with his efforts, he endeavours to imitate in his manners the waiters at Véfour's, squeals, keeps on the alert, wheedles—and a feeling of loathing took possession of me. … "No,"—I thought,—"Ellis will have no occasion to feel jealous here. …"

In the meantime, I noticed that we were beginning gradually to descend. … Paris rose to meet us with all its din and reek. …

"Halt!"—I turned to Ellis.—"Dost thou not find it stifling here, oppressive?"

"It was thou thyself who asked me to bring thee hither."

"I was wrong, I recall my word. Carry me away, Ellis, I entreat thee. Just as I thought: yonder goes Prince Kulmamétoff, hobbling along the boulevard; and his friend Baraksin is waving his hand at him and crying: Iván Stepánitch, *allons souper*, as quickly as possible, and engage Rigolbosch itself!' Carry me away from these Mabilles and Maisons Dorés, away from fops, both male and female, from the Jockey Club and Figaro, from the closely-clipped soldiers' heads and the polished barracks, from the *sergents de ville* with their goatees and the glasses of turbid absinthe, from the players of domino in the cafes and the gamblers on 'Change, from the bits of red ribbon in the buttonhole of the coat and the buttonhole of the overcoat, from Monsieur de Foi, the inventor of 'the speciality of weddings' and from the free consultations of Dr. Charles Albert, from liberal lectures and governmental pamphlets, from Parisian comedies and Parisian operas and Parisian Ignorance. … Away! Away! Away!"

"Look down,"—Ellis answered me:—"thou art no longer over Paris."

I lowered my eyes. … It was a fact. A dark plain, here and there intersected by whitish lines of roads, was running swiftly past beneath us, and only behind, on the horizon, like the glow of a huge conflagration, the reflection of the innumerable lights of the world's capital throbbed upward.

XX

Again a veil fell across my eyes…. Again I lost consciousness. It dispersed at last.

What was that yonder, below? What park was that with avenues of clipped lindens, isolated spruce-trees in the form of parasols, with porticoes and temples in the Pompadour taste, and statues of nymphs and satyrs of the Bernini school, and rococo

Tritons in the centre of curving ponds, rimmed by low balustrades of blackened marble? Is it not Versailles? No, it is not Versailles. A small palace, also in rococo style, peers forth from clumps of curly oak-trees. The moon shines dimly, enveloped in a haze, and an extremely delicate smoke seems to be spread over the earth. The eye cannot distinguish what it is: moonlight or fog. Yonder on one of the ponds a swan is sleeping; its long back gleams white, like the snow of the steppes gripped by the frost, and yonder the glow-worms are burning like diamonds in the bluish shadow at the foot of the statues.

"We are close to Mannheim,"—said Ellis.—"That is the Schwetzingen Park."

"So we are in Germany,"—I thought, and began to listen. Everything was dumb; only somewhere a slender stream of falling water was plashing and babbling, isolated and invisible. It seemed to be repeating the same words over and over again: "Yes, yes, yes," always "yes." And suddenly it seemed to me as though in the very middle of one of the avenues, between the walls of shorn greenery, affectedly offering his arm to a lady in powdered coiffure and a gay-coloured farthingale, there stepped forth on his red heels a cavalier in a golden coat and lace cuffs, with a light, steel sword on his hip. ... They were strange, pale figures. ... I wanted to get a look at them. ... But everything had vanished, and only the water babbled on as before.

"Those are dreams roaming abroad,"—whispered Ellis.—"Yesterday a great deal might have been seen—a great deal. To-day even dreams shun the eye of mortal man. On! On!"

We soared upward and flew further. So smooth and even was our flight that we did not seem to be moving, but everything, on the contrary, appeared to be coming toward us. Mountains made their appearance, dark, undulating, covered with forests; they augmented and floated toward us. ... Now they are already flowing past beneath us, with all their sinuosities, ravines, narrow meadows, with the fiery points in the slumbering villages along the swift rivers at the bottom of the valleys; and ahead of us again other mountains loom up and float past. ... We are in the heart of the Schwarzwald.

Mountains, nothing but mountains ... and forest, the splendid, old, mighty forest. The night sky is clear; I can recognise every variety of tree; especially magnificent are the firs with their straight, white trunks. Here and there on the borders of the forests chamois are to be seen; stately and alert they stand on their slender legs and listen, with their heads finely turned, and their large, trumpet-shaped ears pricked up. The ruin of a tower sadly and blindly displays on a peak of naked crag its half-demolished battlements; above the ancient, forgotten stones a golden star glows peacefully. From a small, almost black lake, the moaning croak of tiny frogs rises up like a wail. I seem to hear other sounds, long, languid, like the sounds of a golden harp. ... Here it is, the land of legend! That same delicate shimmer of moonlight which had impressed me at Schwetzingen is here disseminated everywhere, and the further the mountains stand apart the thicker does that smoke become. I distinguish five, six, ten, different tones of the different layers of shadow on the slopes of the mountains, and over the silent diversity pensively reigns the moon. The air ripples on softly and lightly. I feel at ease and in a mood of lofty composure and melancholy as it were.

"Ellis, thou must love this land!"

"I love nothing."

"How is that? And how about me?"

"Yes … thee!"—she replies indifferently.

It strikes me that her arm clasps my waist more closely than before.

"On! On!"—says Ellis, with a sort of cold enthusiasm.

"On!"—I repeat.

XXI

A mighty fluctuating, ringing cry suddenly resounded overhead and was immediately repeated a little way in advance.

"Those are belated cranes flying to your land, to the north,"—said Ellis:—"wouldst thou like to join them?"

"Yes, yes! raise me to them."

We soared upward and in the twinkling of an eye found ourselves alongside of the flock which had flown past.

The huge, handsome birds (there were thirty of them in all) were flying in a wedge form abruptly and rarely flapping their inflated wings. With head and legs intently ahead and breast thrust sternly forward, they were forging onward, and that so swiftly that the air whistled around them. It was wonderful to see such hot, strong life, such unflinching will, at such a height, at such a distance from all living things. Without ceasing triumphantly to plough their way through space the cranes exchanged calls, from time to time, with their comrades in the vanguard, with their leader; and there was something proud, dignified, something invincibly confident in those loud cries, in the conversation under the clouds. "We shall fly to our goal, never fear, however difficult it may be," they seemed to be saying, encouraging one another.

And at this point it occurred to me that there are very few people in Russia—why do I say in Russia?—in the whole world—like those birds.

"We are now flying to Russia,"—said Ellis. This was not the first time I had noticed that she almost always knew what I was thinking about.—"Dost thou wish to return?"

"Let us return … or, no! I have been in Paris; take me to Petersburg."

"Now?"

"This instant. … Only cover my head with thy veil or I shall become dizzy."

Ellis raised her arm … but before the mist enveloped me I felt on my lips the touch of that soft, dull sting. …

XXII

"At-te-e-e-ention!"—a prolonged cry resounded in my ears. "At-te-e-e-ention!" came the response, as though in despair, from the distance. "At-te-e-e-ention!" died away somewhere at the end of the world. I started. A lofty golden spire met my eye: I recognised the Peter-Paul Fortress.

A pale, northern night! Yes, but was it night? Was it not a pale, ailing day? I have never liked the Petersburg nights; but this time I was even terrified: Ellis's form disappeared entirely, melted like the mist of morning in the July sun, and I clearly descried her whole body as it hung heavily and alone on a level with the Alexander column. So this was Petersburg! Yes, it really was. Those broad, empty, grey streets; those greyish-white, yellowish-grey, greyish-lilac, stuccoed and peeling houses with their sunken windows, brilliant sign-boards, iron pavilions over their porches, and nasty little vegetable-shops; those facades; those inscriptions, sentry-boxes, watering-troughs; the golden cap of St. Isaac's Cathedral; the useless, motley Exchange; the granite walls of the fortress and the broken wooden pavement; those barks laden with hay and firewood; that odour of dust, cabbage, bast-matting and stables; those petrified yard-porters in sheepskin coats at the gates, those cab-drivers curled up in death-like sleep on their rickety carriages,—yes, it was she, our Northern Palmyra. Everything was visible round about; everything was clear, painfully clear and distinct; everything was sleeping mournfully, strangely heaped up and outlined in the dimly-transparent air. The glow of sunset—a consumptive glow—has not yet departed, and will not depart until morning from the white, starless sky. It lies on the silky surface of the Nevá, and the river barely murmurs and barely undulates as it hastens onward its cold, blue waters. …

"Let us fly away,"—pleaded Ellis.

And, without awaiting my answer, she bore me across the Nevá, across the Palace Square, to the Litéinaya. Footsteps and voices were audible below: along the street a cluster of young men were walking with drink-sodden faces and discussing dancing-classes. "Sub-lieutenant Stolpakóff the seventh!" suddenly cried out in his sleep a soldier, who was standing on guard at the pyramid of rusty cannon-balls,[5] and a little further on, at the open window of a tall house I caught sight of a young girl in a crumpled silk gown without sleeves with a pearl net on her hair and a cigarette in her mouth. She was devoutly perusing a book: it was the work of one of the most recent Juvenals.

"Let us fly on!"—I said to Ellis.

A minute more, and the little forests of decaying spruce-trees and mossy swamps which surround Petersburg were flitting past us. We directed our course straight for the south; sky and earth gradually grew darker and darker. The diseased night, the diseased day, the diseased city—all were left behind.

---

5   At the Artillery Barracks.—Translator.

XXIII

We flew more slowly than usual, and I was able to watch how the broad expanse of my native land unrolled before me like a series of interminable panoramas. Forests, bushes, fields, ravines, rivers—now and then villages and churches—and then again fields, and forests, and bushes, and ravines. ... I grew melancholy,—and melancholy in an indifferent sort of way, somehow. And I was not melancholy and bored because we were flying over Russia in particular. No! The land itself, that flat surface which spread out beneath me; the whole earthly globe with its inhabitants, transitory, impotent, crushed by want, by sorrow, by diseases, fettered to a clod of contemptible earth; that rough, brittle crust, that excrescence on the fiery grain of sand of our planet, on which has broken out a mould dignified by us with the appellation of the organic, vegetable kingdom; those men-flies, a thousand times more insignificant than flies; their huts stuck together out of mud, the tiny traces of their petty, monotonous pother, their amusing struggles with the unchangeable and the inevitable,—how loathsome all this suddenly became to me! My heart slowly grew nauseated, and I did not wish to gaze any longer at those insignificant pictures, at that stale exhibition. ... Yes, I felt bored—worse than bored. I did not even feel compassion for my fellowmen: all emotions within me were drowned in one which I hardly venture to name: in a feeling of aversion; and that aversion was strongest of all and most of all toward myself.

"Stop,"—whispered Ellis:—"Stop, or I will not carry thee. Thou art becoming heavy."

"Go home."—I replied in the same sort of a tone with which I was accustomed to utter those words to my coachman on emerging, at four o'clock in the morning, from the houses of my Moscow friends with whom I had been discussing the future of Russia and the significance of the commune ever since dinner.—"Go home,"—I repeated, and closed my eyes.

XXIV

But I speedily opened them again. Ellis was pressing against me in a strange sort of way; she was almost pushing me. I looked at her, and the blood curdled in my veins. Any one who has chanced to behold on the face of another a sudden expression of profound terror the cause of which he does not suspect, will understand me. Terror, harassing terror, contorted, distorted the pale, almost obliterated features of Ellis. I have never beheld anything like it even on a living human face. A lifeless, shadowy phantom, a shadow ... and that swooning terror. ...

"Ellis, what ails thee?"—I said at last.

"'T is she ... 't is she. ..." she replied with an effort;—"'tis she!"

"She? Who is she?"

"Do not name her, do not name her,"—hurriedly stammered Ellis.—"We must flee, or there will be an end to all—and forever. ... Look: yonder!"

I turned my head in the direction which she indicated to me with trembling hand,—and saw something ... something really frightful.

This something was all the more frightful because it had no definite form. Something heavy, gloomy, yellowish-black in hue, mottled like the belly of a lizard,—not a storm-cloud, and not smoke,—was moving over the earth with a slow, serpentine motion. A measured, wide-reaching undulation downward and upward,—an undulation which reminded one of the ominous sweep of the wings of a bird of prey, when it is in search of its booty; at times an inexpressibly revolting swooping down to the earth,—that is the way a spider swoops down to the captured fly. ... Who art thou, what art thou, threatening mass? Under its influence—I saw it, I felt it—everything was annihilated, everything grew dumb. ... A rotten, pestilential odour emanated from it—and a chill that caused the heart to grow sick, and made things grow dark before the eyes, and the hair to stand on end. It was a power which was advancing;—the power which cannot be resisted to which all are subjects which, without sight, without form, without thought, sees everything, knows everything, and like a bird of prey chooses out its victims, like a serpent crashes them and licks them with its chilly sting. ...

"Ellis! Ellis!"—I shrieked like a madman.—

"That is Death! Death itself!"

The wailing sound which I had already heard, burst from Ellis's mouth—this time it bore more resemblance to a despairing, human scream—and we dashed away. But our flight was strange and frightfully uneven; Ellis kept turning somersaults in the air; she fell downward, she threw herself from side to side, like a partridge which is mortally wounded, or which is desirous of luring the hound away from her brood. And yet, long, wavy offshoots, separating themselves from the inexpressibly dreadful mass, rolled after us, like outstretched arms, like claws. ... The huge form of a muffled figure on a pale horse rose up for one moment, and soared up to the very sky. ... Still more agitatedly, still more despairingly did Ellis throw herself about. "She has seen me! All is over! I am lost!" ... her broken whisper became audible. "Oh, unhappy one that I am! I might have enjoyed, I might have acquired life ... but now ... Annihilation, annihilation!"

This was too unbearable. ... I lost consciousness.

XXV

When I came to myself I was lying prone upon the grass, and felt a dull pain all through my body, as though from a severe injury. Dawn was breaking in the sky: I was able to distinguish objects clearly. Not far away, along the edge of a birch-coppice, ran a road fringed with willows; the surroundings seemed familiar to me. I began to recall what had happened, to me,—and I shuddered all over, as soon as the last, monstrous vision recurred to my mind. ...

"But of what was Ellis afraid?" I thought. "Can it be possible that she also is subject to *its* power? Can it be that she is not immortal? Can it be that she is doomed to annihilation, to destruction? How is that possible? "

A soft moan resounded close at hand. I turned my head. Two paces distant from me lay, outstretched and motionless, a young woman in a white gown, with dishevelled hair and bared shoulders. One arm was thrown up over her head, the other fell upon her breast. Her eyes were closed, and a light crimson foam had burst forth upon the closely-compressed lips. Could that be Ellis? But Ellis was a phantom, while I beheld before me a living woman, I approached her, bent over. ...

"Ellis? Is it them?"—I exclaimed. Suddenly, with a slow quiver, the broad eyelids were lifted; dark, piercing eyes bored into me—and at that same moment the lips also clung to me, warm, moist, with a scent of blood ... the soft arms wound themselves tightly round my neck, the full, burning bosom was pressed convulsively to mine.— "Farewell! Farewell forever!"—a dying voice articulated distinctly,—and everything vanished.

I rose to my feet staggering like one intoxicated, and passing my hands several times across my face, I gazed attentively about me. I was close to the *** highway, a couple of versts from my manor-house. The sun had already risen when I reached home.

All the following nights I waited—and not without terror, I admit—for the appearance of my phantom; but it did not visit me again. I even went one day, in the twilight, to the old oak-tree; but nothing unusual occurred there either, I did not grieve overmuch, however, at the cessation of the strange friendship. I pondered much and long over this incomprehensible almost inexplicable affair—and I became convinced that not only is science unable to elucidate it, but that even in the fairy-tales, the legends, there is nothing of the sort to be encountered. What was Ellis, as a matter of fact? A vision, a wandering soul, an evil spirit, a sylph, a vampire? Sometimes it seemed to me once more that Ellis was a woman whom I had formerly known, and I made strenuous efforts to recall where I had seen her. ... There now, there,—it sometimes seemed to me,—I shall recall it directly, in another moment. ... In vain! again everything deliquesced like a dream. Yes, I pondered a great deal, and as was to be expected, I arrived at no conclusion. I could not make up my mind to ask the advice or opinion of other people, for I was afraid of gaining the reputation of a madman. At last I have cast aside all my surmises: to tell the truths I am in no mood for them. On the one hand, the Emancipation has taken place, with its division of arable land, and so forth, and so on; on the other hand, my health has failed; my chest has begun to pain me, I am subject to insomnia, and have a cough. My whole body is withering away. My face is yellow as that of a corpse. The doctor declares that I have very little blood, and calls my malady by a Greek name—"anæmia"—and has ordered me to Gastein. But the Arbiter of the Peace[6] fears that he "will not be able to deal with" the peasants without me. ...

So you see how matters stand!

But what signify those keen, piercingly-clear sounds,—the sounds of a harmonica,—which I hear as soon as people begin to talk to me about any one's death? They grow ever louder and more piercing. ... And why do I shudder in such torturing anguish at the mere thought of annihilation?

---

6   An official who was appointed after the Emancipation to arbitrate differences of opinion as to the division of the land between the landed proprietors and the serfs.—TRANSLATOR.

When the Dead Rise
From the Grave

By Mikhail Bulgakov

> Miracles do not happen in these times
> *A common saying*

In Kislovodsk, however, something happened that would make your hair stand on end …
    But let's start at the beginning:

On the 17th of June, 1925, in the eight year of the revolution, citizen Korabchevsky—resident of one of the apartments and former marksman—stepped out on the porch of 46 Highway Street in the city of Kislovodsk, and moaned loudly.

Some kind people gathered and began to ask:

"Korabchevsky! Korabchevsky! Why are you crying, you, a former marksman?"

To which he replied:

"How can I, a former marksman, not cry when my boy, Vitaly, my beloved son, has died?"

A women cried and asked,

"How unexpected! What did he die from?"

"Pneumonia," said Korabchevsky, wiping tears from his face.

Everyone expressed sympathy to Korabchevsky and then dispersed, but the sad father set out to register the death of his son.

And the boy had truly died.

Official documents attest to this fact.

For example, in the papers for No. 391, stamped by the authorities of Kislovodsk on the 18th of June of this year, it states:

CERTIFICATE

The Kislovodsk branch of the Registry Office affirms that citizen Vitaly Korabchevsky, nine months old, died on the 17ᵗʰ of June of this year from pneumonia. The statement recorded by No. 163.

Signature: Head of the Registry Office branch
Lidovsky

Original is certified accurate
Accountant, Miniralvodsk Insurance Agency
(signature unclear)

This is too brief. He not only died, but was buried, as well. And this was apparent from the testimony of the Kislovodsk bureau of records of its citizenry, which state that a male child, Vitaly Korabchevsky, was buried in a common grave.

Period! Couldn't die better.

But then …

It was an evil moonlit night in Kislovodsk several days after the burial of Korabchevsky's son.

Along comes a neighbor of Korabchevsky in a most excellent mood, whistling, and completely sober, and he sees a strange-looking woman, dressed all in white, standing near

Korabchevsky's apartment, her face looking green from the light of the moon. In her hands was a rolled bundle, and in the bundle was something small. The neighbor walks up to her and asks,

"Who's there? Oh, is it you, Mrs. Korobchevsky?"

And the woman answers in a voice from the grave,

"Yes, it's me."

"So what do you have in your hands," asks the neighbor with surprise.

"This," answered the woman softly, "is my deceased little boy Vitaly."

"How is it Vitaly?" asked the neighbor, as he felt himself getting goose bumps. "W-w-wasn't your Vitaly was just b-b-buried?"

"Yes," said the woman, "but he just up and came back."

Just at that moment, a ray of moonlight fell on the diaper-wrapped package, and the neighbor sees that in the woman's hands really is Vitaly, and that in the greenish shadows his face was of deathly decay.

"Help!" shouted the neighbor, and he darted down Highway Street.

The moon peered from behind the cypress with the face of a dead man, and it seemed to the neighbor that cold hands were grabbing at his trousers.

After an hour, the bravest of the residents of Kislovodsk stood on the little porch of Korabchevsky's house. Korabchevsky himself came out and told the following story:

"Day before yesterday, my wife and I were sitting when we suddenly heard a knock on our window. We looked out and nearly died then and there. Vitaly is standing in the air, not touching the ground, and he says, 'I've come back!'"

"Christ be with us!" cried out one of the women-folk.

"And?!" exclaimed the men.

"And there's nothing more to tell," answered Korabchevsky. "We had to take him back."

The crowd began to panic. In the moonlight, everyone's face looked green. But then the moon went behind a cloud and hid in a deep gloom the end of this ghastly story.

* * *

There's a panic at the newspaper "The Whistle," as well.

Someone cries out, "A miracle!" Another exclaims, "I don't understand anything," while yet another says "We should investigate!" In general, no one's doing any work.

The story is, indeed, a deathly one. It would be easiest to suggest that Vitaly actually didn't die, but then, excuse me, on what basis did coroner Borisov, who lives at 11 Nikolaevsky Street, issue a death certificate, and on what basis did the insurance commission give 17 rubles 10 kopecks to bury a living person?!

Or maybe he didn't come back to life?

Maybe the neighbor lied, perhaps, a satirist composed a story about the moon and the deceased?

Excuse me, but how did he not come back to life when a worker at the Mineralvodsk insurance agency, Vladimir Ivanovich Nikolaev, writes,

"It turns out that no member of the family of the above-mentioned Korabchevsky, died; that the latter, have obtained the appropriate document, illegally received burial benefits."

No, terrible things go on in the city of Kislovodsk!

News From Yalta

By Mikhail Bulgakov

At the same time that disaster struck Nikanor Ivanovich, not far away from no. 302-bis, on the same Sadovaya Street, in the office of the financial director of the Variety Theatre, Rimsky, there sat two men: Rimsky himself, and the administrator of the Variety, Varenukha.[1]

The big office on the second floor of the theatre had two windows on Sadovaya and one, just behind the back of the findirector, who was sitting at his desk, facing the summer garden of the Variety, where there were refreshment stands, a shooting gallery and an open-air stage. The furnishings of the office, apart from the desk, consisted of a bunch of old posters hanging on the wall, a small table with a carafe of water on it, four armchairs and, in the corner, a stand on which stood a dust-covered scale model of some past review. Well, it goes without saying that, in addition, there was in the office a small, shabby, peeling fireproof safe, to Rimsky's left, next to the desk.

Rimsky, now sitting at his desk, had been in bad spirits since morning, while Varenukha, on the contrary, was very animated and somehow especially restlessly active. Yet there was no outlet for his energy.

Varenukha was presently hiding in the findirector's office to escape the seekers of free passes, who poisoned his life, especially on days when the programme changed. And today was precisely such a day. As soon as the telephone started to ring, Varenukha would pick up the receiver and lie into it:

'Who? Varenukha? He's not here. He stepped out.'

'Please call Likhodeev again,' Rimsky asked vexedly.

'He's not home. I even sent Karpov, there's no one in the apartment.'

'Devil knows what's going on!' Rimsky hissed, clacking on the adding machine.

The door opened and an usher dragged in a thick stack of freshly printed extra posters; in big red letters on a green background was printed:

Today and Every Day at the Variety Theatre
an Additional Programme
PROFESSOR WOLAND
Séances of Black Magic and its Full Exposure

Varenukha stepped back from the poster, which he had thrown on to the scale model, admired it, and told the usher to send all the posters out immediately to be pasted up.

'Good ... Loud!' Varenukha observed on the usher's departure.

'And I dislike this undertaking extremely,' Rimsky grumbled, glancing spitefully at the poster through his horn-rimmed glasses, 'and generally I'm surprised he's been allowed to present it.'

'No, Grigory Danilovich, don't say so! This is a very subtle step. The salt is all in the exposure.'

'I don't know, I don't know, there's no salt, in my opinion ... and he's always coming up with things like this! ... He might at least show us his magician! Have you seen him? Where he dug him up, devil knows!'

It turned out that Varenukha had not seen the magician any more than Rimsky had. Yesterday Styopa had come running ('like crazy', in Rimsky's expression) to the findirector with the already written draft of a contract, ordered it copied straight away and the money handed over to Woland. And this magician had cleared out, and no one had seen him except Styopa himself.

Rimsky took out his watch, saw that it read five minutes past two, and flew into a complete rage. Really! Likhodeev had called at around eleven, said he'd come in half an hour, and not only had not come, but had disappeared from his apartment.

'He's holding up my business!' Rimsky was roaring now, jabbing his finger at a pile of unsigned papers.

'Might he have fallen under a tram-car like Berlioz?' Varenukha said as he held his ear to the receiver, from which came low, prolonged and utterly hopeless signals.

'Wouldn't be a bad thing ...' Rimsky said barely audibly through his teeth.

At that same moment a woman in a uniform jacket, visored cap, black skirt and sneakers came into the office. From a small pouch at her belt the woman took a small white square and a notebook and asked:

'Who here is Variety? A super-lightning telegram.[2] Sign here.'

Varenukha scribbled some flourish in the woman's notebook, and as soon as the door slammed behind her, he opened the square. After reading the telegram, he blinked and handed the square to Rimsky.

The telegram contained the following: 'Yalta to Moscow Variety. Today eleven thirty brown-haired man came criminal investigation nightshirt trousers shoeless mental case gave name Likhodeev Director Variety Wire Yalta criminal investigation where Director Likhodeev.'

'Hello and how do you do!' Rimsky exclaimed, and added: 'Another surprise!'

'A false Dmitri!'[3] said Varenukha, and he spoke into the receiver. 'Telegraph office? Variety account. Take a super-lightning telegram. Are you listening? "Yalta criminal investigation. Director Likhodeev Moscow Findirector Rimsky."'

Irrespective of the news about the Yalta impostor, Varenukha again began searching all over for Styopa by telephone, and naturally did not find him anywhere.

Just as Varenukha, receiver in hand, was pondering where else he might call, the same woman who had brought the first telegram came in and handed Varenukha a new envelope. Opening it hurriedly, Varenukha read the message and whistled.

'What now?' Rimsky asked, twitching nervously.

Varenukha silently handed him the telegram, and the findirector saw there the words: 'Beg believe thrown Yalta Woland hypnosis wire criminal investigation confirm identity Likhodeev.'

Rimsky and Varenukha, their heads touching, reread the telegram, and after rereading it, silently stared at each other.

'Citizens!' the woman got angry. 'Sign, and then be silent as much as you like! I deliver lightnings!'

Varenukha, without taking his eyes off the telegram, made a crooked scrawl in the notebook, and the woman vanished.

'Didn't you talk with him on the phone at a little past eleven?' the administrator began in total bewilderment.

'No, it's ridiculous!' Rimsky cried shrilly. 'Talk or not, he can't be in Yalta now! It's ridiculous!'

'He's drunk ...' said Varenukha.

'Who's drunk?' asked Rimsky, and again the two stared at each other.

That some impostor or madman had sent telegrams from Yalta, there was no doubt. But the strange thing was this: how did the Yalta mystifier know Woland, who had come to Moscow just the day before? How did he know about the connection between Likhodeev and Woland?

'Hypnosis ...' Varenukha kept repeating the word from the telegram. 'How does he know about Woland?' He blinked his eyes and suddenly cried resolutely: 'Ah, no! Nonsense! ... Nonsense, nonsense!'

'Where's he staying, this Woland, devil take him?' asked Rimsky.

Varenukha immediately got connected with the foreign tourist bureau and, to Rimsky's utter astonishment, announced that Woland was staying in Likhodeev's apartment. Dialling the number of the Likhodeev apartment after that, Varenukha listened for a long time to the low buzzing in the receiver. Amidst the buzzing, from somewhere far away, came a heavy, gloomy voice singing: '... rocks, my refuge ...'[4] and Varenukha decided that the telephone lines had crossed with a voice from a radio show.

'The apartment doesn't answer,' Varenukha said, putting down the receiver, 'or maybe I should call ...'

He did not finish. The same woman appeared in the door, and both men, Rimsky and Varenukha, rose to meet her, while she took from her pouch not a white sheet this time, but some sort of dark one.

'This is beginning to get interesting,' Varenukha said through his teeth, his eyes following the hurriedly departing woman. Rimsky was the first to take hold of the sheet.

On a dark background of photographic paper, some black handwritten lines were barely discernible:

'Proof my handwriting my signature wire urgently confirmation place secret watch Woland Likhodeev.'

In his twenty years of work in the theatre, Varenukha had seen all kinds of sights, but here he felt his mind becoming obscured as with a veil, and he could find nothing to say but the at once mundane and utterly absurd phrase:

'This cannot be!'

Rimsky acted otherwise. He stood up, opened the door, barked out to the messenger girl sitting on a stool:

'Let no one in except postmen!'—and locked the door with a key.

Then he took a pile of papers out of the desk and began carefully to compare the bold, back-slanting letters of the photogram with the letters in Styopa's resolutions and signatures, furnished with a corkscrew flourish. Varenukha, leaning his weight on the table, breathed hotly on Rimsky's cheek.

'It's his handwriting,' the findirector finally said firmly, and Varenu-kha repeated like an echo:

'His.'

Peering into Rimsky's face, the administrator marvelled at the change that had come over this face. Thin to begin with, the findirector seemed to have grown still thinner and even older, his eyes in their horn rims had lost their customary prickliness, and there appeared in them not only alarm, but even sorrow.

Varenukha did everything that a man in a moment of great astonishment ought to do. He raced up and down the office, he raised his arms twice like one crucified, he drank a whole glass of yellowish water from the carafe and exclaimed:

'I don't understand! I don't understand! I don't un-der-stand!'

Rimsky meanwhile was looking out the window, thinking hard about something. The findirector's position was very difficult. It was necessary at once, right on the spot, to invent ordinary explanations for extraordinary phenomena.

Narrowing his eyes, the findirector pictured to himself Styopa, in a nightshirt and shoeless, getting into some unprecedented super-highspeed airplane at around half past eleven that morning, and then the same Styopa, also at half past eleven, standing in his stocking feet at the airport in Yalta … devil knew what to make of it!

Maybe it was not Styopa who talked with him this morning over the phone from his own apartment? No, it was Styopa speaking! Who if not he should know Styopa's voice? And even if it was not Styopa speaking today, it was no earlier than yesterday, towards evening, that Styopa had come from his office to this very office with this idiotic contract and annoyed the findirector with his light-mindedness. How could he have gone or flown away without leaving word at the theatre? But if he had flown away yesterday evening—he would not have arrived by noon today. Or would he?

'How many miles is it to Yalta?' asked Rimsky.

Varenukha stopped his running and yelled:

'I thought of that! I already thought of it! By train it's over nine hundred miles to Sebastopol, plus another fifty to Yalta! Well, but by air, of course, it's less.'

Hm ... Yes ... There could be no question of any trains. But what then? Some fighter plane? Who would let Styopa on any fighter plane without his shoes? What for? Maybe he took his shoes off when he got to Yalta? It's the same thing: what for? And even with his shoes on they wouldn't have let him on a fighter! And what has the fighter got to do with it? It's written that he came to the investigators at half past eleven in the morning, and he talked on the telephone in Moscow ... excuse me ... (the face of Rimsky's watch emerged before his eyes).

Rimsky tried to remember where the hands had been ... Terrible! It had been twenty minutes past eleven!

So what does it boil down to? If one supposes that after the conversation Styopa instantly rushed to the airport, and reached it in say, five minutes (which, incidentally, was also unthinkable), it means that the plane, taking off at once, covered nearly a thousand miles in five minutes. Consequently, it was flying at twelve thousand miles an hour!!! That cannot be, and that means he's not in Yalta!

What remains, then? Hypnosis? There's no hypnosis in the world that can fling a man a thousand miles away! So he's imagining that he's in Yalta? He may be imagining it, but are the Yalta investigators also imagining it? No, no, sorry, that can't be! ... Yet they did telegraph from there?

The findirector's face was literally dreadful. The door handle was all the while being turned and pulled from outside, and the messenger girl could be heard through the door crying desperately:

'Impossible! I won't let you! Cut me to pieces! It's a meeting!'

Rimsky regained control of himself as well as he could, took the receiver of the phone, and said into it:

'A super-urgent call to Yalta, please.'

'Clever!' Varenukha observed mentally.

But the conversation with Yalta did not take place. Rimsky hung up the receiver and said:

'As luck would have it, the line's broken.'

It could be seen that the broken line especially upset him for some reason, and even made him lapse into thought. Having thought a little, he again took the receiver in one hand, and with the other began writing down what he said into it:

'Take a super-lightning. Variety. Yes. Yalta criminal investigation. Yes. "Today around eleven thirty Likhodeev talked me phone Moscow stop After that did not come work unable locate by phone stop Confirm handwriting stop Taking measures watch said artiste Findirector Rimsky."'

'Very clever!' thought Varenukha, but before he had time to think well, the words rushed through his head: 'Stupid! He can't be in Yalta!'

Rimsky meanwhile did the following: he neatly stacked all the received telegrams, plus the copy of his own, put the stack into an envelope, sealed it, wrote a few words on it, and handed it to Varenukha, saying:

'Go right now, Ivan Savelyevich, take it there personally.[5] Let them sort it out.'

'Now that is really clever!' thought Varenukha, and he put the envelope into his briefcase. Then, just in case, he dialled Styopa's apartment number on the telephone, listened, and began winking and grimacing joyfully and mysteriously. Rimsky stretched his neck.

'May I speak with the artiste Woland?' Varenukha asked sweetly.

'Mister's busy,' the receiver answered in a rattling voice, 'who's calling?'

'The administrator of the Variety, Varenukha.'

'Ivan Savelyevich? the receiver cried out joyfully. 'Terribly glad to hear your voice! How're you doing?'

'Merci,' Varenukha replied in amazement, 'and with whom am I speaking?'

'His assistant, his assistant and interpreter, Koroviev!' crackled the receiver. 'I'm entirely at your service, my dearest Ivan Savelyevich! Order me around as you like. And so?'

'Excuse me, but ... what, is Stepan Bogdanovich Likhodeev not at home now?'

'Alas, no! No!' the receiver shouted. 'He left!'

'For where?'

'Out of town, for a drive in the car.'

'Wh ... what? A dr ... drive? And when will he be back?'

'He said, I'll get a breath of fresh air and come back,'

'So ...' said the puzzled Varenukha, 'merci ... kindly tell Monsieur Woland that his performance is tonight in the third part of the programme.'

'Right. Of course. Absolutely. Urgently. Without fail. I'll tell him,' the receiver rapped out abruptly.

'Goodbye,' Varenukha said in astonishment.

'Please accept,' said the receiver, 'my best, warmest greetings and wishes! For success! Luck! Complete happiness! Everything!'

'But of course! Didn't I say so!' the administrator cried agitatedly. 'It's not any Yalta, he just went to the country!'

'Well, if that's so,' the findirector began, turning pale with anger, 'it's real swinishness, there's even no name for it!'

Here the administrator jumped up and shouted so that Rimsky gave a start:

'I remember! I remember! They've opened a new Georgian tavern in Pushkino called "Yalta"! It's all clear! He went there, got drunk, and now he's sending telegrams from there!'

'Well, now that's too much!' Rimsky answered, his cheek twitching, and deep, genuine anger burned in his eyes. 'Well, then, he's going to pay dearly for this little excursion! ...' He suddenly faltered and added irresolutely: 'But what about the criminal investigation ...'

'It's nonsense! His own little jokes,' the expansive administrator interrupted, and asked: 'Shall I take the envelope?'

'Absolutely,' replied Rimsky.

And again the door opened and in came that same ... 'Her!' thought Rimsky, for some reason with anguish. And both men rose to meet the postwoman.

This time the telegram contained the words:

'Thank you confirmation send five hundred urgently criminal investigation my name tomorrow fly Moscow Likhodeev.'

'He's lost his mind ...' Varenukha said weakly.

Rimsky jingled his key, took money from the fireproof safe, counted out five hundred roubles, rang the bell, handed the messenger the money, and sent him to the telegraph office.

'Good heavens, Grigory Danilovich,' Varenukha said, not believing his eyes, 'in my opinion you oughtn't to send the money.'

'It'll come back,' Rimsky replied quietly, 'but he'll have a hard time explaining this little picnic.' And he added, indicating the briefcase to Varenukha: 'Go, Ivan Savelyevich, don't delay.'

And Varenukha ran out of the office with the briefcase.

He went down to the ground floor, saw the longest line at the box office, found out from the box-office girl that she expected to sell out within the hour, because the public was simply pouring in since the additional poster had been put up, told the girl to earmark and hold thirty of the best seats in the gallery and the stalls, popped out of the box office, shook off importunate pass-seekers as he ran, and dived into his little office to get his cap. At that moment the telephone rattled.

'Yes!' Varenukha shouted.

'Ivan Savelyevich?' the receiver inquired in a most repulsive nasal voice.

'He's not in the theatre!' Varenukha was shouting, but the receiver interrupted him at once:

'Don't play the fool, Ivan Savelyevich, just listen. Do not take those telegrams anywhere or show them to anyone.'

'Who is this?' Varenukha bellowed. 'Stop these jokes, citizen! You'll be found out at once! What's your number?'

'Varenukha,' the same nasty voice returned, 'do you understand Russian? Don't take the telegrams anywhere.'

'Ah, so you won't stop?' the administrator cried furiously. 'Look out, then! You're going to pay for it!' He shouted some other threat, but fell silent, because he sensed that no one was listening to him any longer in the receiver.

Here it somehow began to grow dark very quickly in his little office. Varenukha ran out, slammed the door behind him, and rushed through the side entrance into the summer garden.

The administrator was agitated and full of energy. After the insolent phone call he had no doubts that it was a band of hooligans playing nasty tricks, and that these tricks were connected with the disappearance of Likhodeev. The administrator was choking with the desire to expose the malefactors, and, strange as it was, the anticipation of something enjoyable was born in him. It happens that way when a man strives to become the centre of attention, to bring sensational news somewhere.

In the garden the wind blew in the administrator's face and flung sand in his eyes, as if blocking his way, as if cautioning him. A window on the second floor slammed so that the glass nearly broke, the tops of the maples and lindens rustled alarmingly. It became darker and colder. The administrator rubbed his eyes and saw that a yellow-bellied storm cloud was creeping low over Moscow. There came a dense, distant rumbling.

However great Varenukha's hurry, an irrepressible desire pulled at him to run over to the summer toilet for a second on his way, to check whether the repairman had put a wire screen over the light-bulb.

Running past the shooting gallery, Varenukha came to a thick growth of lilacs where the light-blue toilet building stood. The repairman turned out to be an efficient fellow, the bulb under the roof of the gentlemen's side was covered with a wire screen, but the administrator was upset that even in the pre-storm darkness one could make out that the walls were already written all over in charcoal and pencil.

'Well, what sort of …' the administrator began and suddenly heard a voice purring behind him:

'Is that you, Ivan Savelyevich?'

Varenukha started, turned around, and saw before him a short, fat man with what seemed to him a cat-like physiognomy.

'So, it's me,' Varenukha answered hostilely.'

'Very, very glad,' the cat-like fat man responded in a squeaky voice and, suddenly swinging his arm, gave Varenukha such a blow on the ear that the cap flew off the administrator's head and vanished without a trace down the hole in the seat.

At the fat man's blow, the whole toilet lit up momentarily with a tremulous light, and a roll of thunder echoed in the sky. Then came another flash and a second man emerged before the administrator—short, but with athletic shoulders, hair red as fire, albugo in one eye, a fang in his mouth … This second, one, evidently a lefty, socked the administrator on the other ear. In response there was another roll of thunder in the sky, and rain poured down on the wooden roof of the toilet.

'What is it, comr ...' the half-crazed administrator whispered, realized at once that the word 'comrades' hardly fitted bandits attacking a man in a public toilet, rasped out: 'citiz ...'—figured that they did not merit this appellation either, and received a third terrible blow from he did not know which of them, so that blood gushed from his nose on to his Tolstoy blouse.

'What you got in the briefcase, parasite?' the one resembling a cat cried shrilly. 'Telegrams? Weren't you warned over the phone not to take them anywhere? Weren't you warned, I'm asking you?'

'I was wor ... wer ... warned ...' the administrator answered, suffocating.

'And you skipped off anyway? Gimme the briefcase, vermin!' the second one cried in the same nasal voice that had come over the telephone, and he yanked the briefcase from Varenukha's trembling hands.

And the two picked the administrator up under the arms, dragged him out of the garden, and raced down Sadovaya with him. The storm raged at full force, water streamed with a noise and howling down the drains, waves bubbled and billowed everywhere, water gushed from the roofs past the drainpipes, foamy streams ran from gateways. Everything living got washed off Sadovaya, and there was no one to save Ivan Savelyevich. Leaping through muddy rivers, under flashes of lightning, the bandits dragged the half-alive administrator in a split second to no. 302-bis, flew with him through the gateway, where two barefoot women, holding their shoes and stockings in their hands, pressed themselves to the wall. Then they dashed into the sixth entrance, and Varenukha, nearly insane, was taken up to the fifth floor and thrown down in the semi-dark front hall, so well known to him, of Styopa Likhodeev's apartment.

Here the two robbers vanished, and in their place there appeared in the front hall a completely naked girl – red-haired, her eyes burning with a phosphorescent gleam.

Varenukha understood that this was the most terrible of all things that had ever happened to him and, moaning, recoiled against the wall. But the girl came right up to the administrator and placed the palms of her hands on his shoulders. Varenukha's hair stood on end, because even through the cold, water-soaked cloth of his Tolstoy blouse he could feel that those palms were still colder, that their cold was the cold of ice.

'Let me give you a kiss,' the girl said tenderly, and there were shining eyes right in front of his eyes. Then Varenukha fainted and never felt the kiss.

A Werewolf Problem in Central Russia

By Victor Pelevin

J ust for a moment Sasha thought that the battered Zil would stop for him: it was so old and rattled so loudly, and was so obviously ready for the scrap heap, that it should have stopped—if only the law by which old people who have been have rude and inconsiderate all their lives suddenly become helpful and obliging shortly before they die had applied to the world of automobiles—but it didn't. With a bucket clanking beside its gas tank with a drunken, senile insolence, the Zil rattled past him, struggled up a small hill, giving vent to a whoop of indecent triumph and a jet of gray smoke at the summit, and disappeared silently behind the asphalt rise. Sasha stepped off the road, dropped his small backpack on to the grass and sat down on it. Something in it bent and cracked and Sasha felt the spiteful satisfaction of a person in trouble who learns that someone or something else is also having a hard time. He was just beginning to realize how serious his own situation was.

There were only two courses of action open to him: either he could go on waiting for a lift or head back to the village—a three mile walk. As far as the lift was concerned, the question seemed as good as settled already There were obviously certain regions in the country, or at least certain roads, where all the drivers belonged to some secret brotherhood of black-hearted villains. Hitchhiking became impossible, and you had to take great care the passing cars didn't splash you with mud from the puddles as you walked along the side of the road. The road from Konkovo to the nearest oasis on the railway line—a straight stretch of 15 miles—was one such enchanted highway. Not one of the five cars that had passed him had stopped, and if not for one aging lady wearing purple lipstick and an "I still love you" hairstyle who stuck her long arm out of the window of a red Niva to give him the finger, Sasha could have believed he'd become invisible. He'd still been hoping for that mythical driver, the kind you encounter in newspaper stories and films, who would stare silently through the dusty windscreen of his truck at the road ahead for the entire journey and then refuse any payment with a curt shake of his head (at this point you suddenly notice the photograph hanging above the steering wheel, showing a group of young men in paratrooper uniforms against a backdrop of distant mountains)—but when the Zil rattled past, even this hope had died.

Sasha glanced at his watch—it was twenty minutes past nine. It would get dark soon. He looked around. Beyond a hundred yards or so of broken ground (tiny hillocks, scattered bushes, and grass that was too high and luscious for his liking, because it suggested it was growing on a bog) there was the edge of a forest, thin and unhealthy looking, like the sickly offspring of an alcoholic. All the vegetation in the neighborhood looked strange, as though anything bigger than flowers and grass had to strain and struggle to grow, and even when it eventually reached normal size, it still gave the impression of only having grown under the threat of violence—otherwise it would have flattened itself against the ground like lichen. It was an unpleasant sort of place, oppressive and deserted, as though it was ready for removal from the face of the earth—but then, Sasha thought, if the earth does have a face, it must be somewhere else, not here.

Of the three villages he had seen that day only one had appeared more or less convincing—the last one, Konkovo; the others had been deserted, with just a few little houses inhabited by people waiting to die. The abandoned huts had reminded him more of an ethnographic exhibition than human dwellings. Even Konkovo, distinguished by a plaster sentry standing beside the road and a sign which read "Michurin Collective Farm," only seemed like a human settlement in comparison with the desolation of the other nameless villages nearby. Konkovo had a shop, and there was a poster for the village club, with the title of an avant-garde French film traced in green watercolor, flapping in the wind, while a tractor whined somewhere behind the houses—but even there he hadn't felt comfortable. There was no one on the streets—only one woman dressed in black had passed him, crossing herself hurriedly at the sight of Sasha's Hawaiian shirt with its design of multicolored magical symbols, and a man in spectacles had ridden by on a bicycle with a string shopping bag dangling from the handlebars. The bicycle was too big for him, so he couldn't sit in the saddle and stood instead on the pedals, looking as though he was running in the air above the heavy rusty frame. All the other villagers, if there were any, must have been staying indoors.

He had imagined his trip would be quite different. He would get off the small flat-bottomed riverboat, walk to the village, and there on the *zavalinkas*—Sasha had no idea what a *zavalinka* was, but he imagined it as a comfortable wooden bench set along the log wall of a peasant hut—there would be half-crazy old women sitting peacefully among the sunflowers, and clean-shaven old men playing chess quietly beneath the broad yellow discs of the blossoms. In other words, Sasha had imagined Tverskoi Boulevard in Moscow overgrown with sunflowers—with a cow occasionally lowing in the distance. After that he would make his way to the edge of the village to find a forest basking in the sun, a river with a boat drifting by on it or some country road cutting through an open field, and whichever way he walked, everything would be simply wonderful: he could light a fire, he could remember his childhood and climb trees—if, that is, his memories told him that was what he used to do. In the evening he would hitch a lift to the train.

What had actually happened was very different. It had been a colored photograph in a thick, tattered book that was to blame for everything, an illustration with the title "The ancient Russian village of Konkovo, now the main center of a millionaire collective farm." Sasha had found the spot from which the photograph that caught his eye had been taken, roundly cursed the American word "millionaire" and marveled at how different the same view can appear in a photograph and in real life.

Having promised himself never again to set out on a senseless journey purely on impulse, Sasha decided that at least he would watch the film in the village club. After buying a ticket from an invisible woman—he had to conduct his conversation with the plump freckled hand in the window, which tore off the blue scrap of paper and counted out his change—he made his way into the half-empty hall, spent one and a half bored hours there, occasionally turning to look at an old man who sat in his chair straight as a ramrod and whistled at certain points in the action—his criteria for whistling were quite incomprehensible, but his whistle had a wild bandit ring to it, a lingering note from Russia's receding past.

Afterwards, when the film was over, he looked at the whistler's straight back as it retreated from the club, at the street lamp under its conical tin cap, at the identical fences surrounding the little houses, and he shook the dust of Konkovo from his feet, with a sideways glance at the eroded hand and raised foot of the plaster Lenin in the plaster hat, doomed to stride for all eternity towards his brother in oblivion who stood, as if waiting for him, by the highway. Sasha had waited so long for the truck which finally dispelled his illusions that he had almost forgotten what he was waiting for. Standing up, he slung the backpack over his shoulder and set off back the way he had come, wondering where and how he would spend the night. He didn't want to try knocking on some woman's door—most of the women who let people in to spend the night live in the same mythical places as nightingale-whistling bandits and walking skeletons, and this was the "Michurin Collective Farm" (which was actually no less magical an idea, if you thought about it, but one with a different kind of magic, not one that offered any hope of a night's lodging in a stranger's house). The only reasonable way out Sasha was able to think of was to buy a ticket for the last showing at the club and hide behind the heavy green curtain after the film and spend the night there. If it was to work, he would have to leave his seat before they switched on the lights, so that he wouldn't be noticed by the woman in the homemade black uniform who escorted the customers to the exit. He'd have to watch the same dark, depressing film again, but he'd just have to put up with that.

As he was thinking all this through, Sasha came to a fork in the road. Passing this way twenty minutes before, he had thought that the road he was walking along was joined by a smaller side road, but now as he stood at the junction he couldn't decide which was the road he had come along—they both looked exactly the same. Probably it was the one on the right—there was that big tree by the road. Yes, that must be it—he had to go right. And surely there was a gray telephone pole in front of the tree. Where was it now? There it was—but it was on the left, and there was a small tree beside it. It didn't make sense. Sasha looked at the telephone pole, which had once supported wires, but now looked like a huge rake threatening the sky. He went left.

After he'd walked twenty steps, he stopped and looked back. Clearly visible against the dark stripes of the sunset, a bird which he had previously taken for an insulator caked with the dirt of many years launched itself into the air. He walked on—he had to hurry to get to Konkovo in time, and his road lay through the forest.

It occurred to him how incredibly unobservant he was. On the way from Konkovo he hadn't noticed this wide cut opening on to a clearing. When you're absorbed in your own thoughts, the world around you disappears. He probably wouldn't have noticed it this time either, if someone hadn't called out to him.

"Hey," the drunken voice shouted, "who are you?"

Several other voices broke into coarse laughter. In among the trees on the edge of the forest, right beside the cut, Sasha caught a quick glimpse of people and bottles—he refused to turn his head and only saw the young locals out of the corner of his eye. He started walking more quickly, believing that they wouldn't pursue him, but still he was unpleasantly alarmed.

"Whoa, what a wolf!" someone shouted after him.

"Maybe I'm going the wrong way?" Sasha thought when the road took a zig-zag that he didn't remember. But no, it seemed right—there was a long crack in the road surface that looked like the letter "W"; he'd seen something like that the last time. It was gradually getting dark and he still had a long way to go. To occupy his mind, he began thinking of ways of getting into the club once the film had started—from explaining that he'd come back for a cap he'd left behind to climbing down the chimney (if there was one, that is).

Half an hour later it became clear that he had taken the wrong road—the air was already blue and the first stars had broken through the sky. What made it obvious was the appearance of a tall metal pylon supporting three thick cables at the side of the road and a quiet crackling of electricity: there definitely hadn't been any pylons like that on the road from Konkovo. Everything was quite clear now; but still Sasha went on walking automatically until he reached the pylon. He stared with fixed concentration at the metal plaque with the lovingly executed drawing of a skull and the threatening inscription, then looked around and was astonished to think that he had just walked through that dark, terrifying forest. Walking back to the fork would mean another encounter with the young guys sitting beside the road, and discovering what state they had got into under the influence of fortified wine and evening twilight. Going forward meant walking into the unknown—but then, a road has to lead somewhere, surely?

The humming of the power cables served as a reminder that there were normal people living somewhere in the world, producing electricity by day and watching television with its help by night. If it came to spending the night in the forest, Sasha thought, the best thing would be to sleep under the pylon—it would be something like sleeping in a front hallway, and that was a well-tried move, absolutely safe. In the distance he heard a roaring which seemed to be filled with some ancient anguish—he could hardly make it out at first, and not until it became incredibly loud did Sasha realize that it was an airplane. He lifted his gaze to the sky in relief, and soon he could see above his head the triangle defined by its three different colored lights: as long as he could see the airplane, Sasha actually felt comfortable standing there on the dark forest road. When it moved out of sight, he walked on, looking straight ahead down the road that was gradually becoming the brightest thing in his surroundings.

The road was illuminated by a weak light, and he could walk along without any fear of stumbling. For some reason, probably simply the habit of a city dweller, Sasha felt sure that the light came from widely spaced street lamps, but when he tried to spot one, the truth struck him—of course there were no street lamps, it was the moon shining, and when Sasha looked upwards he could see its crisp white crescent in the sky. After gazing upwards for a while, he noticed that the stars were different colors—he'd never noticed that before, or if he had, he'd forgotten it ages ago.

Eventually the darkness became complete—that is, it became clear that it wasn't going to get any darker. Sasha took his jacket out of the backpack, put it on and closed all the zips—that made him feel more prepared for any further surprises the night might have in store. He ate two crumpled wedge-shaped pieces of "Friendship" processed cheese—the foil wrapping with the word "Friendship" printed on it gleamed dully in the moonlight, vaguely reminding him of the pennants that the human race is constantly launching into space.

Several times he heard the roar of engines as cars or trucks passed by in the distance. At one point the road emerged from the forest and ran through an open field for about five hundred yards, then plunged into another forest where the trees were older and taller. At the same time it narrowed, as did the strip of sky above his head. He had the feeling that he was plunging deeper and deeper into some abyss which the road would never lead him out of—it would take him into some dark thicket and end there in a kingdom of evil, among huge oak trees waving their branches like arms—just like in those children's horror films, where the victory of the hero in the red shirt makes you feel sorry for the wicked witch and the walking skeleton who fall victim to his triumph.

He heard the sound of an engine up ahead once again, but this time it was closer, and Sasha thought that he might actually get a lift somewhere where he would be enclosed by walls, with an electric lightbulb above his head, where he could fall asleep without feeling afraid. The sound of the engine grew closer and closer, then suddenly died away—the car had stopped. He started walking more quickly, and soon he heard the engine again—but this time it was far away, as though the car had taken a silent leap a mile back and was heading back over the journey it had already made. He realized he was hearing another car that was also traveling in his direction. In the forest it's hard to tell just how far away a sound is, but when the second car stopped, Sasha thought that it must be about a hundred yards away: he couldn't see any headlights, but there was a bend ahead.

This was very strange indeed—two cars one after the other suddenly stopping in the forest in the middle of the night. Just to be on the safe side Sasha went over to the edge of the road, ready to dive into the forest if circumstances required it, and then walked on stealthily, staring hard into the darkness. His fear gradually evaporated and he felt sure that he would either soon be getting into a car or he would just keep on walking the way he was. Just before the bend in the road he saw faint gleams of red on the leaves and heard voices talking and laughing. Another car drove up and stopped somewhere close by, slamming its doors.

Since whoever it was ahead was laughing, there was probably nothing very frightening going on. Or perhaps just the opposite, he thought suddenly He turned into the forest and moved on, feeling his way through the darkness with his hands, until he reached a spot from which he could see what was going on around the bend. He hid behind a tree and waited for his eyes to adjust to the new level of darkness, then he took a cautious peep.

Ahead of him there was a large clearing: about six cars were parked haphazardly on one edge, and the whole area was illuminated by a small campfire, around which people of different ages were standing, dressed in various ways, some of them holding sandwiches and clutching bottles. They were talking to each other and generally conversing like any group gathered around a fire at night—the only thing lacking was the music of a tapedeck straining against the silence. As though he had heard what Sasha was thinking, a thickset man walked over to a car and stuck his hand in through its window, and suddenly loud music began playing—only it wasn't the right kind of music for a picnic: it was the howling of hoarse, dark-toned horns. The group made no gesture of complaint—in fact, when the man who had switched on the music came back to the others, he received several slaps of congratulation on the shoulders. Looking closer, Sasha began to notice other things that were strange.

Standing alone by the fire was a military figure—he looked like a colonel. Everybody kept their distance from him, and sometimes he raised his hand in the direction of the moon. Several other men were dressed in suits and ties, as though they had come to the office, not the forest. A man in a loose black jacket wearing a leather hairband around his forehead came over to the near edge of the clearing and Sasha pressed himself tightly against his tree. Someone else turned a face distorted by the dancing firelight in Sasha's direction. But no, no one had seen him. He thought how easily it could all be explained: they'd probably been at some formal reception and had headed off into the forest out of boredom. The Colonel was there to protect them, or maybe he was selling tanks. But then why that music?

"Hey!" said a quiet voice behind him. Sasha turned cold. Slowly turning around he saw a girl in a tracksuit with an Adidas lily on her breast. "What are you doing here?" she asked in the same low voice. He forced his mouth open to answer:

"I … just happened along."

"How did you happen along?"

"I was just walking along the road and I ended up here."

"Just ended up here?" said the girl in astonishment. "You mean you didn't come with us?"

"No."

She made a movement as though she was about to spring away from him, but stayed where she was.

"You mean you came on your own? You just walked here?"

"What's so strange about that?" Sasha asked.

He thought for a moment that she was teasing him, but the girl shook her head in such sincere astonishment that he abandoned the idea and began to feel that he really must have made an outlandish gaffe. She thought for a minute without saying anything, then asked:

"So now what are you going to do?"

Sasha decided she must be talking about his status as a solitary pedestrian stranded in the night, and he said:

"What am I going to do? Ask someone to drive me to some station or other. When are you going back?"

She didn't answer. He repeated his question and she twirled her hand in an indefinite gesture.

"Or I'll keep on walking," Sasha blurted out.

The girl looked at him pityingly.

"Listen to me: don't even try to run. I mean it. You'd better wait about five minutes and then walk over to the fire as if you belong here. And make wild eyes. They'll ask you who you are and what you're doing here. You tell them that you heard the call. And sound as though you mean it. All right?"

"What call?"

"Just the call. I'm the one giving the advice here."

The girl looked Sasha up and down one more time, walked around him and went towards the clearing. When she got close to the fire a man wearing running shoes patted her on the head and gave her a sandwich.

"She's making fun of me," Sasha thought. But then he looked closely at the man with the leather band on his forehead who was still standing at the edge of the clearing, and decided that the girl must be serious: there was something very strange in the way the man was peering into the night. And in the center of the clearing he suddenly noticed a skull on a wooden stake thrust into the earth—the skull was long and narrow, with powerful jaws. A dog maybe? No, more like a wolf.

He gathered himself together, stepped out from behind the tree, and walked towards the orange-red blur of the campfire. He swayed as he walked, without understanding why, and his eyes were glued to the flames. The voices in the clearing instantly fell silent.

"Stop," said a hoarse voice by the stake with the skull.

He didn't stop—they came running over to him and he was seized by large male hands.

"What are you doing here?" asked the voice that had ordered him to stop.

"I heard the call," Sasha replied in a dull, expressionless voice, staring down at the ground.

"Aha, the call …" several voices repeated. They released him, the others suddenly laughed and someone said. "A new boy."

They gave Sasha a sandwich and a glass of water, and he was immediately forgotten. He remembered the backpack he had left behind the tree. "Just too bad," he thought, and started eating the sandwich. The girl in the tracksuit walked past him.

"Hey!" he said, "what's going on here? A picnic?"

"Wait a while and you'll find out."

She crooked her little finger at him in a gesture that looked cryptically Chinese, and went back to the group standing by the stake. Someone tugged at Sasha's sleeve. He turned around and shuddered: it was the army officer.

"There you go, new boy," he said, "fill that in."

A sheet of paper with lines of print and a pen appeared in Sasha's hands. The fire lit up the officer's high cheekbones and the writing on the sheet of paper: it was a standard form. Sasha squatted down on his haunches and writing awkwardly on his knee, began filling in the answers—where he was born, when, why, and so on. It certainly felt strange to be filling in a form in the forest in the middle of the night, but the presence of a man in uniform towering over him somehow balanced things out. The officer waited, occasionally sniffing at the air and glancing over Sasha's shoulder. When the last line had been filled in, he grabbed the pen and the form, bared his teeth in a smile and set off towards the car with a strange springy run.

While Sasha was filling in the form there had been obvious changes over by the fire. The people were still talking, but now their voices seemed to bark, and their movements and gestures had become smooth and dexterous. A man in an evening suit was squirming agilely in the grass, moving his head in an attempt to free it from his dangling tie. Another had frozen motionless on one leg like a stork and was gazing prayerfully at the moon, and through the tongues of flame Sasha could see someone else standing on all fours. Sasha himself could hear a ringing in his ears and his throat was dry. It was all definitely caused in some strange way by the music: it was faster now, and the hoarse notes of the horns were more and more strident, increasingly resembling a car alarm. The horns suddenly broke off on a sharp note that was followed by the howling of a gong.

"The elixir!" the Colonel ordered.

Sasha saw a skinny old woman wearing a long jacket and red beads. She was carrying a jar covered with paper—the kind they sell mayonnaise in. Suddenly there was a slight commotion by the stake with the skull.

"Well, look at that!" someone said in admiration, "without any elixir …

Sasha glanced in that direction and saw the girl in the track-suit kneeling on the ground. She looked very odd—her legs seemed to have grown shorter, while her face had stretched out into an incredible, fearsome muzzle almost like a wolf's.

"Magnificent," said the Colonel, looking around and inviting everyone to admire the event. "No other word for it! Quite magnificent! And they say young people today are good for nothing!"

A tremor ran through the body of the terrifying creature, followed by another and another, until it was shuddering violently. After a minute a young female wolf was standing among the people in the clearing.

"That's Lena from Tambov," someone said in Sasha's ear, "she's really talented."

The conversation died away, and everyone lined up in a rough row. The woman and the Colonel walked along it, giving everyone in turn a sip from the jar. Sasha, totally stupefied by what he'd just seen, found himself in the middle of the line. For a few minutes he couldn't take anything in, and then he saw the woman with the beads standing in front of him and holding out the jar. Sasha smelled something familiar— like the way leaves smell if you rub them against your palm. He started back, but the woman's hand reached further and thrust the rim of the jar up to his lips. Sasha took a little sip, at the same moment feeling that he was being held from behind. The woman walked on. He opened his eyes. As long as he held the liquid in his mouth, the taste actually seemed quite pleasant, but when he swallowed it, it almost made him sick.

A pungent smell of vegetation welled up and filled Sasha's empty head as though someone had suddenly pumped a jet of gas into a balloon. The balloon grew and stretched, straining upwards with ever greater force until suddenly it broke the slim thread binding it to the earth and soared upwards—leaving the forest and the clearing with the fire and the people far below, and the scattered clouds came rushing towards him, followed by the stars. Soon he couldn't see anything below him. He began looking upwards and saw he was getting close to the sky, which turned out to be a sphere of stone with shiny metal spikes protruding from its inner surface. From down below the spikes looked like stars, and one of the gleaming points was hurtling directly towards Sasha, and there was nothing he could do to prevent the collision—he was soaring up faster and faster. Finally he hit the spike and burst with a loud bang. All that was left of him was the stretched skin, swaying in the air, which began slowly sinking back down to earth. He fell for a long, long time, for a thousand years, until he finally felt solid ground under his feet. It felt so good that

Sasha wagged his tail vigorously in pleasure and gratitude, got up from his belly on to his four paws and howled gently.

There were several wolves standing beside him. He immediately recognized Lena among them, although he couldn't understand exactly how. The human features which had struck him earlier had disappeared, of course, and now she had those of a wolf. He would never have imagined that the expression of a wolf's muzzle could be simultaneously so mocking and dreamy if he hadn't seen it with his own eyes. Lena noticed his gaze.

"Like what you see?" she asked.

She didn't speak in words. She whined gently, whimpering—it was nothing like human speech, but Sasha not only understood her question, he even caught the familiar tone she imparted to her howling. He wanted to answer "Great!" What came out was a brief barking sound, but it expressed exactly what he wanted to say. Lena lay down in the grass and lowered her muzzle between her paws.

"Rest," she whined, "we'll be running for a long time."

Sasha looked around. By the stake the Colonel was rolling about on the ground, with fur growing right over his greatcoat: a thick bushy tail was appearing out of his trousers as fast as a blade of grass in a school biology film.

The clearing was now full with the wolf pack, and only the woman with the beads who had handed out the elixir was still in human form. She walked rather apprehensively around two large male wolves and climbed into a car. Sasha turned to Lena and whined:

"Isn't she one of us?"

"She just helps us. She turns into a cobra."

"Is she going to do that now?"

"It's too cold for her now. She goes to Central Asia."

The wolves were prowling around the clearing, going up to each other and barking quietly. Sasha sat on his haunches and tried to appreciate every aspect of his new condition.

He could sense numerous smells impregnating the air, in a way which felt like a second gift of sight—for instance, he could immediately smell his own backpack behind a tree that was quite a long way off, as well as the woman sitting in the car, the scent of a ground squirrel that had recently run along the edge of the clearing, the reliable, brave smell of the older wolves and the gentle aura of Lena's smell—perhaps the freshest and purest note in the entire unimaginably wide gamut of scents.

He felt a similar change in his perception of sounds: they had become far more meaningful, and their variety had increased significantly. He could distinguish the creaking of a branch in the wind a hundred yards from the clearing and the chirping of a cricket coming from precisely the opposite direction. He could follow the fluctuations in both sounds simultaneously, without dividing his attention.

But the greatest transformation that Sasha sensed was in his own awareness of himself. This was something very difficult to express in human language, and he began barking, whining and howling to himself in the same way that he used to think in words. The change in his self-awareness had affected the meaning of life, and he realized that people could talk about it, but they couldn't feel the meaning of life in the same way as they felt the wind or the cold. But now Sasha was able to feel it, he felt the meaning of life continuously and clearly as an eternal quality of the world itself, and that was the greatest charm of his present condition. No sooner did he realize this than he also realized that he was not likely ever to return to his former existence of his own free will—life without this feeling seemed like a long, tormenting dream, dim and incomprehensible.

"Ready?" the Colonel barked from the direction of the stake.

"Ready!" a dozen throats howled in response.

"Hang on ..." someone wheezed behind him. "I can't finish changing ..."

Sasha tried to look around, but he couldn't manage it. It turned out that his neck didn't bend very well, and he had to turn his entire body Lena came over, stuck her cold nose in his side and whined softly:

"Stop trying to turn around, just move your eyes. Like this." When she swiveled her eye it flashed red. Sasha tried doing the same, and he found that by turning his eyes he could see his back, his tail and the dying camp fire.

"Where are we going to run to?" he asked.

"To Konkovo," Lena replied, "there are two cows in a field there."

"But aren't they locked away now?"

"It's all been arranged. Ivan Sergeievich arranged a call from the top"—Lena jerked her muzzle upwards—"to say they were studying the effect of night grazing on milk yields, or something like that."

"You mean we have people up there"—Sasha repeated her gesture—"as well?"

"What do you think?"

Ivan Sergeievich, who before had been the man in the black jacket with the leather band on his forehead—it had turned into a strip of dark fur—nodded his muzzle significantly. Sasha squinted around at Lena. Suddenly she seemed incredibly beautiful— her smooth, shiny fur, the delicate curve of her spine, her slim, powerful hind legs, fluffy young tail and shoulder blades moving so touchingly beneath her skin—in her he sensed at one and the same time strength, a slightly reticent thirst for blood, and that special charm peculiar to young she-wolves that is quite impossible to express in wolf howls.

Noticing his glance, Lena felt embarrassed and moved off to the side, lowering her tail so that it lay on the grass. Sasha also felt embarrassed and he pretended to be biting burrs out of the fur on his paw.

"One more time, is everybody ready?" barked the leader in a low voice that filled the entire clearing.

"Ready!" they all howled together.

"Then, forward!"

The leader trotted to the edge of the forest—he seemed deliberately to be moving slowly and loosely, like a sprinter warming up before settling on the starting blocks in order to emphasize even more the speed and concentration he would demonstrate after the starting shot. At the edge of the clearing the leader bent his muzzle down to the ground, sniffed, howled, and suddenly leapt forward into the darkness. The others hurtled after him, barking and whining. For the first few seconds of this wild pursuit through a night studded with sharp branches and thorns, Sasha felt as if he'd dived into water without knowing how deep it was—he was afraid of splitting his head open. But it turned out that he could sense approaching obstacles and avoid them quite easily. Having realized that, he relaxed, and running became easy and enjoyable—his body seemed to be hurtling along by itself, simply releasing the power concealed within it.

The pack stretched out and formed itself into a diamond shape. The powerful, full-grown wolves raced along at its edges, while the she-wolves and cubs stayed in the center. The cubs somehow managed to play as they ran along, grabbing each other by the tail and making all sorts of unimaginable leaps and bounds. Sashay's place was at the leading corner of the diamond, just behind the leader, somehow he knew this was a place of honor which he had been granted today as a newcomer. The forest came to an end and they moved on through a large deserted field and on to a road—the pack raced along the asphalt, picking up speed and stretching out into a ribbon of gray along the edge of the highway. Sasha recognized the road. On his way to the clearing it had seemed dark and empty, but now he could see life everywhere: field mice darted across the road and disappeared down their burrows as soon as the wolves appeared; on the shoulder a hedgehog curled up into a ball of prickles and bounced off into the grass when it was struck lightly by a wolf's paw, two hares swept by like a jet plane, leaving a thick trail of scent which made it clear that they were frightened to death and that one of them w'as also a total idiot. Lena was running alongside Sasha.

"Be careful," she howled, pointing upwards with her muzzle.

He looked up, allowing his body to find its own way along. There were several owls flying along above the road at exactly the same speed as the wolves. The owls hooted threateningly, and the wolves growled in reply. Sasha felt a strange connection between the owls and the pack. They were hostile to each other, but somehow alike.

"Who are they?" he asked Lena.

"Were-owls. They're tough customers—if they catch you alone."

Lena growled something else and looked up with hate in her eyes. The owls began moving away from the road and climbing higher—they flew without flapping their wings, simply stretching them out in the air. Circling once, they turned towards the rising moon.

"They're heading for the poultry farm," Lena growled, "during the day they're the sponsors there."

They had reached the fork in the road. There ahead was the familiar telephone pole and the tall tree. Sasha sensed the scent trail he had left when he was still human, and even an echo of the thoughts that had come into his head on the road several hours ago—the echo lingered in the smell. The pack flowed smoothly around the bend and raced on towards Konkovo. Lena had fallen back a little, and now the Colonel was running along beside Sasha—he was a large reddish wolf with a muzzle that looked as though it had been singed. There was something strange about the way he moved—when Sasha looked more closely he noticed that the Colonel sometimes fell into a canter.

"Comrade Colonel!" he howled. The actual sound was something like "Rrrr-uuu-vviii," but the Colonel understood perfectly and looked around in a friendly fashion.

"Are there many werewolves in the army?" Sasha asked, without really knowing why.

"Yes," answered the Colonel.

"Have they been there for long?"

They leapt high, flew over a long puddle and went racing on.

"From the very beginning," barked the Colonel, "how d'you think we drove the Whites all the way across Siberia?"

He gave a series of short growls rather like chuckles and moved ahead, his tail raised high like a flag on the stern of a ship. The plaster watchman hurtled past them, followed by the sign for the "Michurin Collective Farm," and there in the distance were the sparsely scattered lights of Konkovo. The village had prepared itself well for the encounter. It was like a ship consisting of several watertight compartments. When night came to the streets, of which there were only three, an impenetrable darkness descended, the houses' hatches were firmly battened down, each maintaining the yellow electric gleam of rational life in isolation from the others. Konkovo met the werewolves with a yellow glow behind curtained windows, silence, empty streets, and a series of entirely autonomous human dwellings: there was no village any longer—only a few spots of light in the midst of the darkness covering the world. The long gray shadows rushed along the main street and circled in front of the club as they abandoned the momentum of their run. Two wolves separated from the pack and disappeared among the houses, while the rest remained sitting in the square. Sasha stayed in their circle and stared at the club building where only recently he had intended to spend the night. He turned to Lena:

"Lena, where have they …"

"They'll be back in a minute," she interrupted. "Shut up."

The moon had gone behind a long tattered cloud, and now the square was only lit by a single lamp under a tin cone that swayed in the wind. Looking around, Sasha found the scene sinister and beautiful: the steel-gray bodies sat motionless around an empty space like an arena, the dust raised by the wolves was settling, their eyes and fangs were gleaming. The humans' little painted houses with the TV aerials and chicken houses stuck to them and the crooked parthenon of the club building seemed less like a stage set for the reality which had focused itself in the center of the square than a parody of a stage.

Several minutes passed in motionless silence, then something moved out of a side alley on to the main street and Sasha saw the silhouettes of three wolves trotting towards the square. He knew two of them—Ivan Sergeievich and the Colonel—but the third was unknown to him. Sasha sniffed his scent, full of putrid self-satisfaction and at the same time fear, and he wondered who it could be.

As the wolves approached, the Colonel dropped back a little, before running up and knocking the third wolf into the ring with his chest. Then he and Ivan Sergeievich took the places that had been left for them. The circle was completed and the stranger was left in the center. Sasha took a good sniff at him. The impression he received was like that of a man of about fifty with a body shaped like a broad-based cone and a fat, insolent face—but somehow at the same time very lightweight, as though filled with air. The newcomer peered at the wolf who had shoved him from behind and said with uncertain humor:

"So Colonel Lebedenko's pack is all present and accounted for. But what's all the drama about? Why this circle in the night?"

"We want to have a word with you, Nikolai," their Colonel answered.

"Glad to oblige," howled Nikolai. "Any time—for instance, we could talk about my latest invention. I call it the soap bubble game. You know I've always been fond of games, and just recently ..."

Sasha suddenly realized that he was not following what Nikolai said, but the way he said it—he spoke rapidly, so that his words tumbled over each other, and he seemed to be using the words to defend himself from something which he found extremely unpleasant—as if the thing was scrambling up the stairs and Nikolai (for some reason Sasha imagined him in his human form), standing on the landing, was throwing everything that came to hand at it.

"... to create a smooth and shiny model of what is happening."

"What's the point of the game?" asked the leader of the pack. "Tell us. We like games too."

"It's very simple. You take a thought and you blow it up into a soap bubble. Shall I show you?"

"Yes, show us."

"For instance ..." Nikolai thought for a moment. "For instance, let's take something close at hand: you and I."

"Us and you," echoed the leader.

"Right. You're sitting around me and I'm standing in the center. That's what I'm going to blow into a bubble. And so ..."

Nikolai lay down on his belly and assumed a relaxed pose.

"And so, now you're standing and I'm lying in the center. What does that mean? It means that certain aspects of the reality drifting past me can be interpreted in such a fashion that I, having been dragged from my home in a somewhat crude fashion, appear to have been brought here and set in the center of a circle of what are apparently

wolves. Perhaps I'm dreaming it, or perhaps you're dreaming it, but one thing is certain: something is going on. Now, we've skimmed the surface and the bubble has begun to inflate. Let us turn to the more subtle fractions of the current event and you will see what delightful colors start playing on its thinning walls. I can see from your muzzles that you've come with the usual collection of stinging reproaches. I don't have to listen to you, I know what you're going to say. That I'm not a wolf but a pig—I eat off the garbage dump, live with a mongrel bitch, and so on. You think that's debased. And you think your crazy obsessive activity is exalted. But now the walls of my bubble reflect gray bodies that are absolutely identical—any of yours and mine—and they reflect the sky—and honestly, looking down from there a wolf and a mongrel and everything they do look very much the same. You run in order to get somewhere and I lie among a pile of old newspapers on my dump—how trifling the difference is in essence! What's more, if we take your state of motion as the starting point—note this, now!—it turns out that in fact I am running and you are simply jumping up and down on the spot."
He licked his lips and continued:

"Now the bubble is half-ready. Next we come to your major complaint against me: I break your laws. Note that: your laws, not mine. But if I am bound by laws, they are of my own making, and I believe that is my right—to choose which authority to submit to and in what way. You are not strong enough to allow yourselves that, but in order not to seem like idiots in your own eyes, you convince yourselves that the existence of individuals like me can harm you."

"You've hit the nail on the head there," the leader observed.

"Well now, I don't deny that, hypothetically speaking, I could cause you a certain degree of inconvenience. But if that does happen, why should you not regard it as a kind of natural calamity? If a hailstorm starts, surely instead of remonstrating with it, you try to take shelter. And am not I—from the abstract point of view—a natural phenomenon? In fact, it turns out that in my piggishness, as you call it, I am stronger than you are, because I don't come to you, but you come to me. That's another given. See how the bubble is growing. We just have to give it a final puff of air. I'm fed up with these nocturnal visits. It wasn't so bad when you came one at a time, but this time the whole pack has turned up. But now that it's happened, let's get things clear between us once and for all. What can you actually do to stop me? Nothing. You can't kill me—you know why yourselves. As for changing my mind—you simply haven't got the brains to do it. So what's left is just your word and mine, and on the walls of the bubble they are equal. Only mine is more elegant—though, in the final analysis that's a matter of taste. In my view, my life is a magical dance and yours is a senseless dash through the darkness. So wouldn't it be best for us to go our separate ways as quickly as possible? There, the bubble has separated now, it's flying. How do you like it?"

While Nikolai was howling, gesticulating with his tail and his left forepaw, the leader listened to him without speaking, looking down into the dust and occasionally nodding. Having heard Nikolai out, he slowly raised his muzzle and at that very moment the moon came out from behind a cloud, and Sasha saw its light gleam on the leader's fangs.

"Nikolai, you obviously think you're performing for stray dogs at the dump. I personally have no intention of arguing about life with you. I don't know who has been to visit you,"—the leader glanced around at the other wolves—"that's news to me. We're here on business."

"On what business?"

The leader addressed the circle.

"Who has the letter?"

A young she-wolf came out of the circle and dropped a rolled piece of paper from her jaws. The leader straightened it out with a paw that just for a moment became a human hand and read:

"'Dear Editor …'"

Nikolai, who had been wagging his tail, now dropped it into the dust.

"'This letter comes to you from one of the women of Konkovo. Our village is not far from Moscow, and the full address is shown on this envelope. I don't mention my name for reasons which will be clear from what follows. Recently there has been a series of articles in the press about phenomena which science previously dismissed out of hand. I wish to inform you of a remarkable phenomenon which from the scientific point of view is much more interesting than the phenomena which have been attracting so much attention, such as x-ray vision or Assyrian massage. You might take what I have to tell you as a joke, so let me tell you straight off that it is not. You have probably come across the word "werewolf" more than once, in the sense of a human being who can turn into a wolf. The point is that there is a real natural phenomenon behind the word. You could call it one of the most ancient traditions of our homeland, one which has miraculously survived all of the trials of the years of oppression. Our village is the home of Nikolai Petrovich Vakhromeiev, a man of great modesty and kindheartedness, who possesses this ancient knowledge. Probably only he can tell you what the essential nature of the phenomenon is. I myself would never have believed such things were possible if I had not accidentally witnessed how Nikolai Petrovich turned into a wolf and saved a little girl from a pack of wild dogs. …'"

"Is this all lies, or have you been conspiring with your old buddies?" the leader asked, interrupting himself.

Nikolai said nothing, and the leader carried on reading:

"'I gave Nikolai Petrovich my word that I wouldn't tell anyone about what I had seen, but I am breaking my promise because I believe that this remarkable natural phenomenon should be studied. Because of the promise I cannot give you my name, and I ask you please not to tell anyone about my letter. Nikolai Petrovich himself has never told a lie in his life and I do not know how I shall ever look him in the face if he finds out. I confess that apart from a desire to assist the development of our science I do have another motive. Nikolai Petrovich lives in very poor circumstances, with no income but a meager pension, which he generously shares with all comers. Although Nikolai Petrovich himself regards this side of life as entirely unimportant, I make bold to assert that the value of his knowledge for all of humanity is so great that he should be provided with quite different conditions. Nikolai Petrovich is such a kind and considerate man that I am sure he would not refuse to cooperate with scientists and journalists. I can tell you the small amount of information that Nikolai Petrovich has given me in our conversations—in particular several historical facts. …'"

The leader turned the letter over.

"Now … nothing interesting here … rubbish … what's Stenka Razin got to do with it? … where is it now … ah, here it is: 'Incidentally, it is an insult that a foreign word is still used for a fundamentally Russian concept. I would prefer the word *werevolk*—the Russian root indicates the origin of the phenomenon and the romance prefix sets it in the general European cultural context.'

"That final phase," said the leader, "makes it perfectly clear that the kind and considerate Nikolai Petrovich and the anonymous inhabitant of Konkovo are one and the same."

For several seconds there was silence. The leader tossed the piece of paper aside and looked at Nikolai.

"They'll come here," he said sadly "They're quite stupid enough to do that. They might have been here already if Ivan hadn't seen the letter. But you sent it to other journals as well, didn't you?"

Nikolai slammed his paw down into the dust.

"Listen, what's the point of all this hot air? I do what I think is right, there's no point in trying to change my mind, and I must confess that I don't much care for your company. So let's leave it at that." He raised his belly from the earth, as if to stand.

"Wait! Don't be in such a hurry. It's sad, but it looks as though your magical dance on the dump is about to come to an end."

"What does that mean?" asked Nikolai, pricking up his ears.

"Just that soap bubbles have a habit of bursting. We can't kill you, it's true. But take a look at him."

"I don't know him," yelped Nikolai. He looked down at Sasha's shadow. Sasha also looked down and his head spun with the shock: all the others had the shadows of humans, but he had the shadow of a wolf.

"He's new. He can take your nominal place in the pack if he defeats you. What do you think off that?" The leader's final question was phrased in obvious mimicry of Nikolai's typical bark.

"It seems you're quite a specialist on the ancient laws," Nikolai replied, attempting an ironical growl.

"Like yourself. Aren't they the commodity you intend to trade in? But you're not so clever. Who's going to pay you? Most of what we know is of no use to anyone."

"That still leaves something," Nikolai muttered, probing the circle with his gaze. There was no way out—the circle was closed. Sasha finally understood the meaning of what was happening: he would have to fight with this fat old wolf.

"But I only ended up here by accident," he thought. "I didn't hear any call—I don't even know what it is!"

He looked around—all eyes were fixed on him. "Maybe I should tell them everything? They might let me go ..."

He remembered his transformation, and then the way they had raced through the dark forest and along the road: it was the most beautiful thing he had ever experienced. "You're nothing but an impostor. You haven't got a chance," said a familiar voice inside his head. But at the same moment a different voice—the leader's—said:

"Sasha, this is your chance."

He was about to confess everything, but his paws stepped forward of their own accord and he heard a voice hoarse with excitement bark:

"I'm ready."

He realized that he had said it and immediately felt calm.

The wolf in him had taken control of his actions—he no longer had any doubts. The pack growled in approval. Nikolai slowly raised his dull yellow eyes to look at Sasha.

"Remember, my young friend, that it's only a very small chance," he said. "Very small indeed. It looks as though this is going to be your last night."

Sasha didn't reply. The old wolf lay on the ground in the same position.

"We're waiting for you, Nikolai," the leader said quietly.

Nikolai yawned lazily—and suddenly leapt into the air. His legs, rapidly straightening, threw him upwards like a spring, and when he struck the ground again there was nothing left in him of the old tired dog—this was a real wolf, filled with calm ferocity: his neck was tensed and his eyes stared right through Sasha. Once again a growl of approval ran through the pack. The wolves discussed something rapidly: one of them ran over to the leader and put his muzzle close to his ear.

"Yes," said the leader, "definitely." He turned to Sasha. "Before the fight there should be an exchange of insults. The pack desires it."

Sasha yawned nervously and glanced at Nikolai, who set off around the circle without taking his eyes off some object located just beyond Sasha—then Sasha also set off along the living wall, following his foe. They walked around the circle several times and then stopped.

"Nikolai Petrovich, I find you repulsive," Sasha managed to squeeze out.

"You can tell that to your daddy," Nikolai replied readily. Sasha felt the tension slip away.

"Why not," he said, "at least I know who he is."

He thought that was a phrase from an old French novel—it would have been more appropriate if the moonlit bulk of Notre Dame had been towering up behind him, but he couldn't think of anything better.

"I must keep it more simple," he thought, and asked:

"What's that wet spot under your tail?"

"That's where I smashed out the brains of a kid called Sasha," Nikolai growled. They started off again, along a slowly narrowing spiral, facing each other all the while.

"I suppose all sorts of things probably happen at the dump," said Sasha. "Don't you find the smells there irritating?"

"I find your smell irritating."

"Be patient. It'll pass—soon you'll be dead."

Nikolai stopped. Sasha stopped too and screwed up his eyes against the painful glare of the street lamp.

"Your stuffed body," Nikolai said softly, "will stand in the local secondary school next to the globe and they'll use it for the ceremony when children join the Pioneers."

"Enough," said Sasha, "let's finish on a more intimate note. Do you like Yesenin, Nick?" Nikolai replied with an obscene variation of the deceased poet's name.

"That's wrong of you. I can remember a quite remarkable line: *You whine like a bitch in the moonlight*. Good isn't it, terse yet expressive ..."

Nikolai Petrovich pounced.

Sasha had not the slightest idea of what a werewolf fight was like, but everything became clear in the course of events. While he and his opponent were walking around the circle and insulting each other, he had realized that the idea was not just to amuse the pack, but to allow the opponents to take a good look at each other and choose the moment to attack. He had made a mistake in getting carried away by the exchange of insults and his opponent had jumped at him while he was blinded by the light of the street lamp.

As soon as Nikolai's front paws and gaping jaws rose into the air, Sasha instantly thought through several possible courses of action, and his racing thoughts were entirely calm. He jumped to one side, first giving his body the command, then flying up from the earth into the dense gray air, making way for the heavy gray carcass as it fell. Sasha realized he had the advantage of being lighter and more agile. But his opponent was more experienced and stronger and was sure to know some special tricks—that was what Sasha had to watch out for.

When he landed he saw that Nikolai was standing sideways next to him, half-squatting and turning his muzzle in Sasha's direction. Nikolai's flank seemed to be exposed, and Sasha leapt, reaching with his open jaws for the patch of light fur which he somehow knew was the most vulnerable spot. Nikolai leapt as well, but in a strange way, twisting in the air. Sasha couldn't understand what was happening—Nikolai's entire hindquarters were exposed, he seemed to be laying himself open to Sasha's fangs. When he realized, it was too late—a tail like a whip of iron lashed across his eyes and nose, blinding him and depriving him of his sense of smell. The pain was unbearable, but Sasha knew that nothing serious had happened to him. The danger was that the second's blindness might be enough for his enemy to make another, decisive leap.

As he fell onto his outstretched paws, feeling that he was already defeated, Sasha suddenly realized that his enemy must once again be standing side on to him, and instead of jumping aside as instinct and pain prompted, he darted forwards, still unable to see, with the same feeling of fear he'd had during his first leap as a wolf—that leap from the clearing into the darkness among the trees. For a moment he hung in the air, and then his numbed nose rammed into something warm and yielding, and he closed his jaws as hard as he could.

The next second they were standing facing each other as they had at the beginning of the fight. Time had accelerated once again to its normal speed. Sasha shook his head as he recovered from the terrible blow of Nikolai's tail. He was waiting for his enemy to make another leap, but suddenly he noticed that Nikolai's front paws were trembling and his tongue was hanging out. A few more seconds passed, then Nikolai slumped over on to his side and a dark stain began to spread over the ground beside his throat. Sasha took a quick step forward, but he caught the leader's eye and stopped.

He looked at the dying werewolf. Nikolai shuddered a few times, then lay still. His eyes closed. Then his body began to tremble, but in a different way this time—Sasha could sense very clearly that the body was already dead, and the sight was terrifying. The outline of the recumbent figure began to blur, the stain beside the throat disappeared, and a fat man in his underpants and vest appeared on the trampled surface of the earth. He was snoring loudly, lying on his belly. His snores suddenly broke off, he turned on his side and made a movement with his hand as though he was straightening his pillow. The hand closed on emptiness, and the surprise was enough to wake him. He opened his eyes, looked around, and closed them again. A second later he opened them again and instantly burst into a wail so piercing that Sasha thought you could tune the most ear-rending police siren to it. He leapt to his feet, jumped clumsily over the nearest wolf and ran off into the distance along the dark street, all the while howling on the same note. When he eventually disappeared around the bend his wailing finally ceased.

The pack laughed wildly. Sasha glanced at his shadow and instead of the long silhouette of a muzzle he saw the outline of a rounded head and two protruding ears—his own, human ears. When he looked up he saw the leader staring directly at him.

"Do you understand?" the leader asked.

"I think so," said Sasha. "Will he remember anything?"

"No. For the rest of his life—if, of course, you can call it a life—he will think that he had a terrible nightmare," the leader replied and turned to the others: "Let's go."

Sasha retained no memory of their journey back. They went a different way, straight through the forest—it was shorter, but it took just as long because they had to run more slowly than on the highway. In the clearing the final embers of the fire were fading. The woman with the beads was dozing behind the windshield of a car: when the wolves appeared she opened her eyes, waved, and smiled. But she didn't get out of the car.

Sasha was sad. He felt rather sorry for the old wolf whom his bite had turned back into a human being. When he remembered the exchange of insults, and especially the change that had come over Nikolai a minute before the fight began, he almost felt a liking for him. He tried not to think about what had happened, and after a while he managed to forget it. His nose was still stinging from the blow: He lay down on the grass to think.

For a while he lay there with his eyes closed. Then he sensed how heavy the silence was and raised his muzzle—on every side the wolves were staring at him without speaking. They seemed to be waiting for something. "Shall I tell them?" Sasha thought.

He decided he would. Rising on to his paws, he set off around the circle as he had in Konkovo, but this time there was no opponent walking ahead of him. The only thing moving with him was his shadow—a human shadow like that of every member of the pack.

"I want to confess everything," he howled softly. "I have deceived you." The pack said nothing.

"I didn't hear any call. I don't even know what it is. I ended up here entirely by accident."

He closed his eyes and waited for a response. There was a moment's silence, followed by an explosion of barking, howling laughter. He opened his eyes.

"What are you laughing at?"

The reply was another eruption of laughter. Eventually the wolves calmed down and the leader asked him:

"How did you get here?"

"I lost my way in the forest."

"That's not what I mean. Try to remember why you came to Konkovo."

"No special reason. I like trips to the country."

"But why here?"

"Why? Let me think—That's it.—I saw a photograph that I liked; it was a very beautiful view. And the caption said it was the village of Konkovo near Moscow. Only everything here turned out quite different ..."

"And where did you see the photograph?"

"In a children's encyclopedia."

This time they all laughed even longer.

"All right," said the leader, "and what were you looking for in there?"

"I ..." Sasha suddenly remembered, and it was like a blinding flash of light inside his skull. "I was looking for a photograph of a wolf! Yes, I'd just woken up and I wanted to see a photograph of a wolf! I searched through all my books. I wanted to check something—and then I forgot—so that was the call?"

"Precisely," replied the leader.

Sasha looked at Lena, who had hidden her muzzle in her paws and was shaking with laughter.

"Then why didn't you tell me right away?"

"What for?" asked the old wolf, maintaining a calm expression among the general merriment. "Hearing the call's not the most important thing. That doesn't make you a werewolf. Do you know when you really became one?"

"When?"

"When you agreed to fight with Nikolai, believing that you had no chance of winning. That was when your shadow changed."

"Yes. Yes. That's right," several voices barked in unison.

Sasha said nothing for a while. His thoughts were a confused turmoil. Then he raised his muzzle and asked:

"But what was that elixir we drank?"

The wolves laughed so loudly that the woman in the car wound down the window and stuck her head out. The leader could hardly control himself—his muzzle twisted into a crooked smile.

"He liked it," he said, "give him some more elixir!"

Then he began to laugh as well. A small bottle fell on the ground by Sasha's paws. Straining his eyes, he read: Forest Joy. Elixir for the Teeth. Price: 92 kopecks.

"That was just a joke," said the leader. "But if you could have seen the way you looked when you were drinking it—Remember, a werewolf changes into a human being and back again as he wishes, at any time and in any place."

"But what about the cows?" Sasha asked, this time ignoring the howls of laughter. "You said we were running over to Konkovo to …"

He didn't finish the sentence and simply waved his paw in the air. Laughing, the wolves scattered over the clearing and lay down in the tall grass. The old wolf stayed sitting opposite Sasha.

"There's another thing I have to tell you," he said. "You must always remember that only werewolves are real people. If you look at your shadow you'll see that it's human. But if you look at people's shadows with your wolf's eyes, you'll see the shadows of pigs, cocks, toads …"

"And spiders, flies, and bats, too," said Ivan Sergeievich, who had stopped beside them.

"That's right. And then there are the monkeys, the rabbits, and the goats. Not to mention …"

"Don't frighten the boy," growled Ivan Sergeievich. "You're just making it all up as you go along. Don't you listen to him, Sasha." The two old wolves looked at each other and laughed.

"I might be making it up as I go along," said the leader, "but it's still true."

He turned to go, but stopped when he saw Sasha's inquiring gaze.

"Did you want to ask something?"

"What are werewolves, really?"

The leader looked him in the eye and bared his teeth slightly.

"What are people, really?"

Left on his own, Sasha lay down in the grass to think again. Lena came across and settled down beside him.

"The moon's about to reach its zenith," she said.

Sasha looked up.

"Surely that's not the zenith?"

"This is a special zenith, you have to listen to the moon, not watch it. Try it."

He pricked up his ears. At first all he could hear was the wind stirring the leaves on the trees and the buzzing of nighttime insects, and then another sound appeared, something like the sound of singing or music in the distance, when you can't tell whether it's an instrument or a voice. Once he'd picked up the sound, Sasha separated it out from all the others and it began growing stronger, until after a while he could listen to it without any strain. The melody seemed to be coming straight from the moon and it sounded like the music that had been played in the clearing before their transformation. It had sounded dark and menacing then, but now it was soothing. It was beautiful, but there were annoying gaps in it, empty patches. Suddenly he realized that he could fill them in with his own voice, and he began howling, quietly at first, then louder, raising his muzzle to the sky and forgetting everything else—and just then the melody blended with his howling and became perfect. Other voices sprang up beside his. All of them were quite different, but they didn't clash at all.

Soon the entire pack was howling. Sasha could understand the feelings expressed in every voice and the meaning of the whole business. Every voice howled its own theme: Lena was howling about something light and gentle like a drop of rain falling on a ringing tin roof; the leader's deep bass was howling about the immeasurably deep abysses he had crossed in great soaring leaps; the descant howling of the cubs was about their joy at being alive, the fact that morning came in the morning and evening came in the evening, and about a strange sadness that is like a joy. And all together they were howling about the incomprehensible beauty of the world, the center of which lay in the grass of the clearing. The music became louder and louder, the moon swam towards Sasha's eyes, covering the entire sky, and then came tumbling down on him—or perhaps he floated up from the earth and fell on to its advancing surface.

When he came around, he could feel a gentle jolting and hear the sound of an engine. He opened his eyes and discovered that he was half-slumped on the back seat of a car. His backpack lay at his feet, Lena was sleeping beside him with her head on his shoulder, and the leader of the pack, Colonel Lebedenko, was sitting in the driver's seat.

Sasha was about to say something, but he saw the Colonel press his finger to his lips in the rearview mirror. Sasha turned toward the window A long line of cars was racing along the highway. It was early in the morning, the sun had only just appeared, and the surface of the road ahead looked like an endless pink ribbon. On the horizon he could see the tiny doll's houses of the approaching city.

Night Watch

By Sergei Lukyanenko

The night got off to a bad start.

It was barely even dark when I woke up. I just lay there, watching the final gleams of daylight fading away in the cracks of the blinds, thinking things over. This was the fifth night of the hunt—and there was still nothing to show for it. And I wasn't likely to get lucky tonight either.

It was cold in the apartment; the radiators gave off hardly any heat at all. The only thing I like about winter is that it gets dark quickly, so there aren't many people out on the streets. If not for that, I'd have dropped the whole business ages ago and left Moscow for someplace like Yalta or Sochi. It would have to be the Black Sea, not some faraway island in a warm foreign ocean: I like to hear the sound of my own native language around me …

Stupid dreams, of course.

It's still too soon for me to be thinking of retiring to somewhere a bit warmer.

I haven't earned it yet.

The telephone must have been waiting for me to wake up—it started trilling in that loathsome, nagging way it has. I fumbled for the receiver and held it to my ear—quietly, without saying a word.

"Anton, answer."

I didn't say anything. Larissa's voice was brisk and focused, but already tired. She obviously hadn't slept all day long,

"Anton, shall I put you through to the boss?"

"No, don't do that," I growled.

"That's more like it. Are you awake?"

"Yes."

"It's the same again for you today."

"Anything new happen?"

"No, not a thing. Have you got anything for breakfast?"

"I' ll fnd something."

"Okay. Good luck."

It sounded feeble and unconvincing. Larissa didn't have any faith in me. No doubt the boss didn't either.

"Thanks," I said to the dial tone. I got up and made the trip to the toilet and the bathroom. I was just about to spread toothpaste on the brush when I realized I was getting ahead of myself and put it back down on the edge of the sink.

It was completely dark in the kitchen, but of course I didn't bother turning on the light. I opened the door of the refrigerator—the small light bulb I'd screwed out of its socket lay there freezing with the food. I looked at the saucepan with the colander sitting on top of it. Lying in the colander was a lump of half-defrosted meat. I lifted out the colander, raised the saucepan to my lips, and took a gulp.

If anyone thinks pig's blood tastes good, then he's wrong.

I put the saucepan with the remains of the thawed-out blood back in the refrigerator and walked through to the bathroom. The dull blue lamp hardly lightened the darkness at all. I took a long time cleaning my teeth, brushing furiously, then I gave in, made another trip to the kitchen and took a gulp of icy vodka from the refrigerator. Now my stomach didn't just feel warm, it felt hot. A wonderful set of sensations: frost on my teeth and fire in my stomach.

"I hope you …" I started thinking, about the boss, but I caught myself just in time. He was quite capable of sensing even a half-formed curse. I went through into my room and started gathering together the clothing scattered all over the place. I discovered my pants under the bed, my socks on the win-dowsill, and for some reason my shirt was hanging on the mask of Chkhoen.

The ancient king of Korea eyed me disapprovingly.

"Why can't you just watch over me?" I growled, and then the phone started screeching again. I hopped around the room until I found the receiver.

"Anton, was there something you wanted to say to me?" the disembodied voice asked.

"Not a thing," I said sullenly.

"I see. Now add 'glad to serve, your honor' to that."

"I'm not glad. And there's nothing to be done about it … your honor."

The boss paused for a moment:

"Anton, I really would like you to take this situation we have on our hands a bit more seriously. All right? I expect you to report back in the morning, in any case. And … good luck."

I didn't exactly feel ashamed. But I wasn't feeling quite so irritated anymore. I put my cell phone in my jacket pocket, opened the cupboard in the hallway, and wondered for a while what else I ought to pack. I had a few novel items of equipment that some friends had given me the previous week. But I settled on the usual selection anyway—it's fairly compact and gives pretty good all-round coverage.

Plus the mini-disc Walkman. I don't need my sense of hearing for anything, and boredom is an implacable enemy.

Before I went out I took a long look at the staircase through the spy-hole. Nobody there.

And that was the beginning of one more night.

I rode the metro for about six hours, switching aimlessly from line to line without any plan, sometimes dozing, letting my conscious mind take a break and my senses roam free. There was nothing going down. Well, I did see a few interesting things, but they were all ordinary incidents, tame beginners' stuff. It wasn't until about eleven, when the metro got less crowded, that the situation changed.

I was sitting there with my eyes closed, listening to Manfre-dini's Fifth Symphony for the third time that evening. The mini-disc in the player was totally eccentric; my personal selection, medieval Italian composers and Bach alternating with the rock group Alisa, Richie Blackmore, and Picnic. It's always interesting to see which melody coincides with which event. Today it was Manfredini.

I felt this sudden cramp—it ran all the way up from my toes to the back of my head. I even hissed as I opened my eyes and scanned the subway car.

I picked the woman out right away.

Very pretty, young. In a stylish fur coat, with a little purse and a book in her hands. And with a black vortex spinning above her head like I hadn't seen for at least three years!

I imagine I looked crazy, staring at her like that. The girl sensed it, took one look at me, back at me, and immediately turned away.

Try looking over your head instead!

No, of course, she's not able to see the twister anyway. The most she could possibly feel is a slight prickling of alarm. And out of the corner of her eye she can't get any more than the vaguest glimpse of that flickering above her head … like a swarm of midges swirling round and round, like the shimmering above the asphalt on a hot day …

She can't see a thing. Not a thing. And she'll go on living for another day or two, until she misses her step on the black ice, falls, and bangs her head so hard it kills her. Or ends up under a car. Or runs into a thug's knife in the hallway … a thug who has no real idea why he's killing this girl. And everyone will say: "She was so young, with her whole life ahead of her; everybody loved her …"

Yes. Of course. I believe it, she's a very good person, kind. There's weariness there, but no bitterness or spite. When you're with a girl like that you feel like a different person. You try to be better, and that's a strain. Men prefer to be friends with her kind, flirt a bit, share confidences. They don't often fall in love with girls like that, but everybody loves them.

Apart from one certain person, someone who has hired a Dark Magician.

A black vortex is actually a fairly ordinary phenomenon. If I looked closely, I could make out another five or six of them hanging above other passengers' heads. But they were all blurred and pale, barely even spinning. The results of perfectly ordinary, non-professional curses. Someone yelling after someone else: "I hope you die, you bastard." Someone had put it more simply and forcefully: "Go to hell, will you!" And a little black whirlwind had moved across from the Dark Side, draining good fortune and sucking in energy.

But an ordinary, amateurish, formless curse lasts no more than an hour or two, twenty-four hours at most. And its consequences may be unpleasant, but they're not fatal. That black twister hanging over the girl was the genuine article, stabilized and set in motion by an experienced magician. The girl didn't know it yet, but she was already dead.

I automatically reached for my pocket, then remembered where I was and frowned. Why don't cell phones work in the subway? Don't the people who have them ride underground?

Now I was torn between my principal assignment, which I had to carry through, even without any hope of success, and the doomed girl. I didn't know if she could still be helped, but I had to track down whoever had created this vortex …

Just at that moment I got a second jolt. But this time it was different. There was no cramp or pain; my throat just went dry and my gums went numb, the blood started pounding in my temples, and my fingertips started itching.

This was it!

But the timing couldn't have been worse.

I got up—the train was already braking as it pulled into a station. I walked past the girl and felt her eyes on me, following me. She was afraid. There was no way she could see the black vortex, but it was obviously making her feel anxious, making her pay close attention to the people around her.

Maybe that was why she was still alive?

Trying not to look in her direction, I lowered my hand into my pocket and fingered the amulet—a smooth rod carved out of cool onyx. I hesitated for a moment, trying to come up with some other course of action.

No, there was no other way.

I squeezed the amulet tight in the palm of my hand, feeling a prickly sensation in my fingers as the stone started warming up, giving out its accumulated energy. The sensation was no illusion, but you can't measure this heat with any thermometer. It felt like I was squeezing a coal taken out of a fire … it was covered with cold ash, but still red hot at the center.

When I'd drained the amulet completely, I glanced at the girl. The black twister was shuddering, leaning over slightly in my direction. This vortex was so powerful that it even possessed a rudimentary intelligence.

I struck.

If there'd been any Others in the carriage, or even anywhere in the train, they'd have seen a blinding flash that could pierce metal or concrete with equal ease …

I'd never tried striking at a black vortex with such a complex structure before. And I'd never used an amulet with such a powerful charge.

The effect was totally unexpected. The feeble curses hanging over other people's heads were completely swept away. An elderly woman who'd been rubbing her forehead looked at her hand in amazement: Her vicious migraine had suddenly disappeared. A young guy who'd been gazing dully out the window shuddered. His face relaxed and the look of hopeless misery disappeared from his eyes.

The black vortex above the girl was tossed back five meters; it even slipped halfway out of the carriage. But it maintained its structure and came zigzagging back through the air to its victim.

This was real power!

With real perseverance!

They say, though I've never actually seen it myself, that if a vortex is pushed even two or three meters away from its victim, it gets disoriented and attaches itself to the nearest person it can find. That's a pretty lousy thing to happen to anyone, but at least a curse meant for someone else has a much weaker effect, and the new victim has a good chance of escaping.

But this vortex just came straight back, like a faithful dog running to its master in trouble.

The train was stopping. I threw one last glance at the vortex—it was back in place, hanging there above the young woman's head; it had even started spinning faster … and there was nothing, absolutely nothing I could do about it. The target I'd been hunting all over Moscow for a week was somewhere close, right here in the station. My boss would have eaten me alive … and maybe not just in the figurative sense …

When the doors parted with a hiss, I gave the woman a final glance, hastily memorizing her aura. There wasn't much chance of ever finding her again in this massive city. But even so, I would have to try.

Only not right now,

I jumped out of the carriage and looked around. It was true, I was a bit short of field-work experience; the boss is absolutely right about that. But I didn't like the method he'd chosen for training me at all.

How in hell's name was I supposed to find the target?

Not one of the people I could see with my normal vision looked even slightly suspicious. There were plenty of them still jostling each other here—it was the circle line, after all, the Kursk station; there were passengers who'd just arrived on the main line, street traders making their way home, people in a hurry to change trains and ride out to the suburbs … But if I closed my eyes I could observe a more fascinating picture. Pale auras, the way they usually are by evening, and in among them the bright scarlet blob of fury, the strident orange glow of a couple obviously in a rush to get to bed, the washed-out, brownish-gray stripes of the disintegrating auras of the drunks.

But there wasn't a single trace of the target, apart from the dry-ness in my throat, the itching in my gums, the insane pounding of my heart. The faint taste of blood on my lips. A mounting sense of excitement.

The signs were all circumstantial, but at the same time they were too obvious to be ignored.

Who was it? Who?

The train started moving behind me. The feeling that the target was near didn't get any weaker, so we had to be still close to each other. The train going in the opposite direction appeared. I felt the target tremble and start moving toward it.

Forward!

I crossed the platform, weaving between the new arrivals staring up at the indicator boards, then set off toward the back of the train—and my sense of the target began to get weaker. I ran toward the front of the train—there it was again ... closer ...

It was like that children's game: First I was "cold," then I was "hot."

The people were boarding the cars. I ran along the train, feeling the sticky saliva filling up my mouth, my teeth starting to ache, my fingers starting to cramp up ... The music was roaring in my earphones.

In the shadow of the moon
She danced in the starlight,
Whispering a haunting tune
To the night ...

How appropriate. The song was absolutely perfect.

But it was a bad omen.

I jumped in through the closing doors and froze, concentrating on what I could feel. Had I guessed right or wrong? I still couldn't get a visual fix on the target ...

I'd guessed right.

The train hurtled on around the circle line. My instincts were raging, shouting at me: "Right here! Beside you!"

Maybe I'd even got the right car?

I gave my fellow passengers a surreptitious looking-over and dropped the idea. There was no one there worth taking any interest in.

I'd just have to wait, then ...

Feel no sorrow, feel no pain,
Feel no hurt, there's nothing gained ...
Only love will then remain,
She would say.

At Marx Prospect I sensed my target moving away from me. I jumped from the car and set off toward the other line. Right here, somewhere right beside me …

At the radial line station the feeling of the target became almost unbearably strong. I'd already picked out a few likely prospects: two girls, a young guy, a boy. They were all potential targets, but which one of them was it?

My four candidates got into the same car. That was a stroke of luck at last. I followed them in and waited.

One girl got out at Rizhskaya station.

The feeling of the target didn't get any weaker.

The young guy got out at Alekseevskaya.

Great. Was it the girl or the boy? Which one of them?

I risked a stealthy glance at both. The girl was plump and pink-cheeked; she was absorbed in reading her *MK* newspaper, showing no signs of any kind of agitation. The boy, in contrast, was skinny and frail, standing by the door and tracing his finger across the glass.

In my opinion the girl was a lot more … tempting. Two to one it was her.

But then, in judgments like that the question of sex decides pretty much everything.

I'd already begun hearing the Call. Still not verbalized yet, just a slow, gentle melody. I immediately stopped hearing the sound from the earphones. The Call easily drowned out the music.

Neither the girl nor the boy showed any signs of alarm. The target either had a very high threshold of resistance or had simply succumbed right away.

The train stopped at Exhibition. The boy took his hand away from the glass, stepped out onto the platform, and strode off rapidly toward the old exit. The girl stayed.

Damn!

They were both still too close to me. I couldn't tell which one I was sensing!

And then the melody of the Call soared triumphantly and words began insinuating themselves into it.

A female voice!

I jumped out through the closing doors and hurried after the boy.

Great. The hunt was nearing its end at last.

But how was I going to handle things with no charge in my amulet? I didn't have a clue.

Only a few people had got off the train, and there were four of us riding the escalator up. The boy at the front, a woman with a small child behind him, then me, followed by an aging, seedy-looking army colonel. The colonel's aura was beautiful, a glittering mass of steel-gray and light-blue tones. I thought with weary humor that I could call on him to help. Even these days people like that still believe in the idea of "officer's honor."

Except that any help I could get from the colonel would be about as much use as a fly swatter in an elephant hunt.

I dropped the stupid idea and took another look at the boy, with my eyes closed, scanning his aura.

The result was disheartening.

He was surrounded by a shimmering, semi-transparent glow. Sometimes it was tinged with red, sometimes it was flooded with a dense green, and sometimes it flared up in dark blue tones.

It was a rare case. A destiny still undefined. Undifferentiated potential. This boy could grow up to be a great villain, he could become a good and just person, or he could turn out to be a nobody, an empty space, which is actually what most people in the world are anyway. It was all still ahead of him, as they say. Auras like that are normal for children up to the age of two or three, but they disappear almost completely as people get older.

Now I could see why he was the one the Call was addressed to. There was no denying it—he was a real delicacy.

I felt my mouth starting to fill up with saliva.

This had all been going on for too long, far too long … I looked at the boy, at the thin neck under his scarf, and I cursed my boss and the traditions, and the rituals—everything that went to make up my job. My gums itched; my throat was parched.

Blood has a bitter, salty taste, but this thirst can't be quenched by anything else.

Damn!

The boy hopped off the escalator, ran across the lobby, and out through the glass doors. Just for a moment I felt relieved, I slowed down as I followed him out, and just caught his movement out of the corner of my eye as he ducked down into an underpass. He was already running, physically pulled by the lure of the Call.

Faster!

I ran over to a kiosk and said, trying not to show my teeth:

"The stuff for six rubles, with the ring."

The young guy with a pimply face handed me the quarter-liter bottle with a slow, sluggish movement—like he'd been taking a drop to keep warm on the job. He warned me honestly.

"It's not great vodka. Not gut-rot, of course, it's Dorokhov, but, you know …"

"Got to look after my health, anyway," I rapped. The vodka was obviously fake, but right now that was okay by me. With one hand I tore off the cap with the wire ring attached to it, and with the other I took out my cell phone and switched it to repeat dial. The young salesman's eyes popped out of his head; not many people who can afford a cellular would buy a cheap surroage vodka. I took a swallow as I walked along—the vodka stank like kerosene and tasted even worse; it was obviously bootleg liquor, bottled in the back of someone's garage—and ran to the underpass.

"Hello."

Larissa wasn't there anymore. Pavel's usually on duty at night.

"This is Anton. It's somewhere near the Cosmos hotel, in the back alleys. I'm in pursuit."

"You want the team?" The voice was beginning to sound interested.

"Yes, I've already discharged the amulet."

"What happened?"

A street bum bedded down halfway along the underpass reached out a hand as if he were hoping I'd gave him the bottle I'd just started. I ran on past.

"Something else came up … Make it quick, Pavel."

"The guys are already on their way."

I suddenly felt as if a red-hot wire had been stuck through my jaws. Ah, hell and damnation …

"Pasha, I can't answer for myself," I said quickly and broke off contact. I pulled up short, facing a police patrol.

Isn't that always the way? Why do the human guardians of law and order always turn up at the most inappropriate moment?

"Sergeant Kampinsky," a young policeman announced briskly. "Your papers …"

I wondered what they were planning to pin on me. Being drunk in a public place? That was probably it.

I put my hand into my pocket and touched the amulet. Just barely warm. But this wouldn't take a lot.

"I'm not here," I said.

The four eyes that had been probing me in anticipation of easy pickings went blank as the last spark of reason in them died.

"You're not here," both of them echoed in chorus.

There was no time to program them. I blurted out the first thing that came into my head:

"Buy some vodka and take a break. Immediately. Quick march!"

The order clearly fell on fertile ground. The policemen linked arms like kids out looking for fun and dashed off along the underpass toward the vending kiosks. I felt vaguely uncomfortable, picturing the consequences of my instructions, but there was no time to put things right.

I bounded up out of the underpass, certain I was already too late. But oddly enough, the boy still hadn't got very far. He was just standing there, swaying slightly, about a hundred meters away. That was serious resistance. The Call was so loud now, it seemed strange to me that the occasional passersby walking down the street didn't launch into a dance, that the trolleys didn't swing off the main avenue, forcing their way down along the alley toward their sweet fate …

The boy glanced around. I thought he looked at me. Then he set off, walking quickly.

That was it, he'd broken.

I followed him, frantically trying to decide what I was going to do. I ought to wait for the team—it would take them only ten minutes to get here, at most.

But that might not turn out so good—for the boy.

Pity's a dangerous thing. I gave way to it twice that day. The first time in the metro, when I spent the charge of the amulet in a fruitless attempt to displace the black vortex. And now the second time, when I set out after the boy.

Many years ago someone told me something that I flatly refused to accept. And I still don't accept it now, despite all the times I've seen it proved right.

"The common good and the individual good rarely coincide …"

Sure, I know. It's true.

But some truths are probably worse than lies.

I started running toward the Call. What I heard was probably not what the boy did. For him the Call was an alluring, enchanting melody, sapping his will and his strength. For me it was just the opposite, an alarm call stirring my blood.

Stirring up my blood …

The body I'd been treating so badly all week was rebelling. I was thirsty, but not for water—I could quite safely slake my thirst with the dirty city snow without doing myself any harm. And not for strong drink either—I had that bottle of lousy vodka with me and even that wouldn't do me any damage. What I wanted was blood.

Not pig's blood, or cow's blood, but real human blood. Curse this hunt …

"You have to go through this," the boss had said. "Five years in the analytical department's a bit too long, don't you think?" I don't know, maybe it is a bit too long, but I like it. And after all, the boss himself hasn't worked out in the field for more than a hundred years now. I ran past the bright shop windows with their displays of fake Gzhel ceramics and stage-set heaps of food. There were cars rushing past me along the avenue, a few pedestrians. That was all fake too, an illusion, just one facet of the world, the only one accessible to human beings. I was glad I wasn't one of them.

Without breaking my rapid stride, I summoned the Twilight.

The world sighed as it opened up. It was as if airport searchlights had suddenly come on behind me, casting a long, thin, sharp shadow. The shadow swirled up, acquiring volume; the shadow was drawing me into itself—into a dimension where there are no shadows. The shadow detached itself from the dirty asphalt surface, swirling and swaying like a column of heavy smoke. The shadow was running ahead of me …

Quickening my stride, I broke through the gray silhouette into the Twilight. The colors of the world dimmed and the cars on the avenue slowed, as if they were suddenly bogged down.

I was getting close to my goal.

As I dodged into the alleyway, I thought I would just catch the final scene. The boy's motionless, ravaged body, drained dry, the vampires disappearing.

But I wasn't too late after all.

The boy was standing in front of a girl-vampire who had already extended her fangs, slowly taking off his scarf. He was probably not afraid now—the Call completely numbs the conscious mind. More likely he was longing to feel the touch of those sharp, gleaming fangs.

There was a young male vampire standing beside them. I sensed immediately that he was the leader of the pair: He was the one who was initiating her, he was introducing her to the scent of blood. And the most sickening thing about it was that he had a Moscow registration tag. What a bastard!

But then, that only improved my chances …

The vampires turned toward me in confusion, not understanding what was going on. The boy was in their Twilight, I shouldn't have been able to see him … or them either.

Then the male vampire's face began to relax, he even smiled—a calm, friendly smile.

"Hi there …"

He'd taken me for one of his own. And he could hardly be blamed for his mistake: I really was one of them now. Almost. The week of preparation had not been wasted: I had begun to sense them … but I'd almost gone over to the Dark Side myself.

"Night Watch," I said. I held my hand out, holding the amulet. It was discharged, but that's not so easy to sense at a distance. "Leave the Twilight!"

The young guy would probably have obeyed me, hoping that I didn't know about the trail of blood he'd left behind him, that the whole business could just be classified as "an attempt at unauthorized interaction with a human being." But the girl lacked his self-control; she didn't understand.

"A-a-a-agh!" She threw herself at me with a long, drawn-out howl. It was a good thing she still hadn't sunk her teeth into the boy; she was out of her mind now, like a desperate junkie who's just stuck a needle in his vein only to have it jerked back out again, like a nymphomaniac after her man pulled out just a moment before orgasm.

Her lunge would have been too fast for any human being; no one could have parried it.

But I was in the same dimension of reality as the girl-vampire. I threw up my arm and splashed the liquid out of the open bottle into the hideously transformed face.

Why do vampires tolerate alcohol so poorly?

The menacing scream changed to a shrill squeal. The girl-vampire began whirling around on the spot, beating her hands against her face as it shed layers of skin and grayish flesh. The male vampire swung round, all set to dart away.

This was going too easily altogether. A registered vampire isn't some casual visitor I have to fight on equal terms. I threw the bottle at the girl-vampire, reached out my hand and grabbed hold of the cord of his registration tag, which had unraveled on command. The vampire gave a hoarse croak and clutched at his throat.

"Leave the Twilight!" I shouted.

I think he realized things were looking really bad now. He flung himself toward me, trying to reduce the pressure from the cord, extending his fangs and transforming as he came.

If the amulet had been fully charged, I could have simply stunned him.

As it was, I had to kill him.

The tag—a seal on the vampire's chest that gave off a faint blue glow—made a crunching sound when I gave the silent order. The energy implanted in it by someone with far more skill than me flooded into the dead body. The vampire was still running. He was well-fed and strong; other people's lives were still nourishing his dead flesh. But he couldn't possibly resist such a powerful blow: His skin shriveled until it was stretched as taut as parchment over his bones; slime gushed out of his eye sockets. Then his spine shattered and the twitching remains collapsed at my feet.

I swung around—the girl-vampire could have regenerated already. But there was no danger. She was running away across the yard between the buildings, taking huge bounds. She still hadn't left the Twilight, so I was the only one who could see this astounding sight. Apart from the dogs, of course. Somewhere off to one side a small canine broke into hysterical barking, transfixed simultaneously by hatred and fear and all the other feelings that dogs have felt for the living dead since time immemorial.

I didn't have enough strength left to chase the vampire. I straightened up and captured a 3-D image of her aura—gray, desiccated, rotten. We'd find her. There was nowhere she could hide now.

But where was the boy?

After he emerged from the Twilight created by the vampires, he could have fainted or fallen into a trance. But he wasn't in the alley. He couldn't have run past me … I bounded out of the alley into the yard and saw him. He was bolting, moving almost as fast as the vampire. Well, good for him! That was wonderful. No help required. It was bad that he would remember everything that had happened, but then who would believe a young boy? And before morning all his memories would fade and assume the less menacing features of a fantastic nightmare.

Or should I really go after the little guy?

"Anton!"

It was Igor and Garik, our inseparable duo of operatives, running down the alley from the avenue.

"The girl got away!" I shouted.

Garik kicked out at the vampire's shriveled corpse as he ran, sending a cloud of rotten dust flying up into the frosty air. He shouted:

"The image!"

I sent him the image of the girl-vampire running away. Garik frowned and started moving faster. Both operatives dashed off in pursuit. Igor shouted as he ran:

"Clear up the trash!"

I nodded, as if they needed an answer, and emerged from my own Twilight. The world blossomed. The operatives' silhouettes melted away, and their invisible feet even stopped leaving tracks in the snow lying in the human dimension of reality.

I sighed and walked over to their gray Volvo parked at the curb. There were a few primitive implements lying on the backseat: a heavy-duty plastic bag, a shovel, and a small sweeping brush. It took me about five minutes to scrape up the vampire's feather-light remains and put the bag in the trunk. I took some dirty snow from a decaying heap left by a careless yard-keeper, scattered it in the alley, and trampled it a bit, working the final dusty, rotten remains into the slush. No human burial for you, you're not human …

That was all.

I went back to the car, got into the driver's seat, and unbuttoned my jacket. I felt good, very good, in fact. The senior vampire was dead, the guys would pick up his girlfriend, and the boy was alive.

I could just imagine how delighted the boss would be!

Vampire Slaying

Protection From Blood Drinkers

By Konstantinos

So far, we haven't concretely proven that immortal blood drinkers exist, right? Then why include this chapter? We haven't exactly proven that immortal vampires don't exist, either. But that's beside the point. The first part of this chapter will deal with the methods given in folklore for protecting against vampirism as well as destroying the offending creatures. Considering that very few, if any, who read these hints will ever come face to face with a true undead, the descriptions of the methods are kept brief and are mainly included to show what the past inhabitants of countries around the world believed. It is the possible occult significance of each belief that will make up the majority of each entry. After all, the possible esoteric truths behind the legends are what we are after.

Now that we've reiterated just how rare it is to run into a true undead, it's likely that some of you are relieved of fear, and probably quite a few are filled with disappointment. The next few lines are meant especially for those in the latter category. As the last chapter showed, some of those who would be upset at the thought of immortal blood drinkers not being real are the same individuals who might practice blood drinking themselves. If you've ever considered taking part in that dangerous practice, whether on the giving or receiving end, or both, please read the last section in this chapter carefully. Although the bits of folklore given in the next few pages might never come in handy, the factual information given in the last section could save your life.

THWARTING THE UNDEAD

Vampires are real.

Someone could have made that statement in almost any language, in any land and at any time in recorded history, without being ridiculed. In any of those instances, there could have been many who personally disagreed, but it is likely that at least some did not. Those who felt the same way, and who came from the same land, likely also agreed on what the powers of the vampire are, and most important of all, how to thwart or even destroy the creature.

It is those shared beliefs that we shall now examine, starting with the more common ways to kill an immortal blood drinker, followed by a couple of methods for simply preventing such a creature from rising. Also included are some ways of keeping vampires that are running about from getting too close to either you or your house.

Keep in mind that a great many vampire countermeasures from folklore have achieved their own immortality in fiction. Let's begin our look at ways of killing the undead with a few of those.

The Wooden Stake

The wooden stake is without a doubt the most popular way in fiction to kill a vampire (not counting the power of the sun, the rising of which can't be controlled). In reality, it was, and still is, the most popular way to accomplish the task in Europe, Few people are ignorant to the fact that a sharpened stake should be driven through a vampire's heart to kill it. But what many don't know is why that should work.

First of all, let's look at a vampire as a human who is reanimated into a supernatural existence. How does the body of the creature function—when it ingests blood, is that blood circulated? In other words, does its undead heart beat? If that were so, then driving a stake through the organ and leaving it there would obviously disrupt the heart's ability to beat. Certainly, that might be one of the reasons staking was first implemented; we'll examine other evidence to support that theory in the related entry, "Heart Removal."

Another theory, put forth by vampirologist and author Raymond T. McNally, attempts to explain in a different way the beliefs of those individuals who performed the staking of vampires. According to McNally, the hunters felt that the power in this method came not from the stake itself, but from the earth. By driving the wood through a body, the bottom of its coffin, and into the earth, a hunter could effectively link an evil, animated corpse to the earth again, resulting in the vampire's decomposition.

A simpler version of that explanation, which many folklorists and vampirologists agree upon, is that the stake was meant to do nothing more than hold the vampire in place so it could not rise. Again, that depends upon the stake being driven clear through the body, the coffin, and into the earth. If the people of the past accepted that the stake only held a vampire in place and didn't actually kill it, that might be why the next method was often used in conjunction with it.

Beheading

While Hollywood special effects seem to be responsible for popularizing this method of vampire killing to life in modern times, it was used quite often in the past. Those who performed the decapitations of vampires were prompted by the idea that the act somehow ensured a vampire would not return from the grave. Why did they think that?

It is easy to imagine that vampire hunters of old knew that consciousness resided in the head. That is the part of the body, after all, where we process the majority of our sensory stimulation. Therefore, even if beheading a vampire didn't kill it (what vampire hunter could claim to fully understand the mysteries of the grave?), the creature wouldn't be able to hunt a human without being able to see, hear, or smell its prey. For that reason, the head of the undead was often simply placed by its feet, making it impossible for the vampire to pick it up again.

Clearly, even though the folklore of many countries contains tales of vampire beheadings, not all hunters felt the act ensured the true death of the creature. Besides placing the head of a vampire at its feet, another common practice was to place the decapitated head backward on the undead's neck so that even if it did rise again, it would not be able to see where it was going (they never seemed to consider the possibility that it might decide to walk backward).

If we consider our initial argument—that consciousness resides in the head—why would the hunters believe that the vampire might not die after it was decapitated? It seems likely that they believed removing a head from a supernatural creature wouldn't necessarily terminate the head's consciousness, any more than the physical cause of death in the person who became a vampire guaranteed he or she wouldn't come back. Decapitation was considered mostly to be a hindrance to a vampire. To be on the safe side, many hunters thought it wise to take a further precaution.

Burning

Vampires were often considered to be corpses animated by evil power. Burning the body of an undead therefore seemed to be a logical step to take. By separating and burying the remains, or by sometimes immersing them in running water and letting them be carried away there would, of course, be no body left for the evil force to reanimate.

(A quick note before we move on: In many books, you will find the remains of vampire bodies burned on pyres referred to as "ashes." That is not accurate; the temperatures necessary to achieve the modern process of cremation could never be matched by a normal fire. However, we will not get into descriptions of the actual appearance of the resulting bone fragments and other unburned remains, which is too ghoulish a subject even for this book. Let's just say that the remains were not ashes, and could not be left for the winds to scatter.)

Besides the physical destruction that burning accomplishes, the process is thought by many to do much more. It is a common occult belief that burning something releases its mystical power, essence, or force. Certain plants and herbs are burned as incense to accomplish magical goals; candles are burned for the same reason. There are numerous other examples of rituals that use burning as a release of power, but it is beyond the scope of this book to go into them (if you are interested, see some of the books on magic and mysticism that are listed in the Bibliography). For our purposes, it is sufficient to state that burning the body of a vampire was probably considered a potent method of destroying the creature for more than one reason.

Heart Removal

This technique is not as widely used as the aforementioned methods, although it's sometimes used with them. Removing a vampire's heart represents a somewhat logical alternative to staking or beheading (depending on the beliefs of a particular culture). The heart keeps the living alive, and it pumps blood. Does it do the same for an undead? Cultures that remove the heart from their alleged undead might believe it does.

As we saw in Chapter Three, in the case of the vampire from the Greek town of Pyrgos, sometimes a culture's worst fears can be materialized. There, the *vrykolakas'* heart was seen to beat upon the opening of the creature's chest. Now we know that the people of the area believed the heart must be removed to kill a vampire. So, is it possible that they saw what they expected to see, or were they simply correct in their belief?

By now you might have recognized that the basis for the practice of heart removal is similar to the idea put forth in the first "staking" theory given earlier. I mentioned there was further evidence to support the idea that vampires were staked to keep their hearts from animating them. The similarity of staking and heart removal cannot be denied, and it is possible that both practices could have stemmed from the same source. As with the other related bits of vampire lore covered earlier, similarity between two or more beliefs lends credibility to the vampire myth as a whole.

Holy or Blessed Weapons

A few obscure references to the use of some kind of blessed object against the undead can be found in folklore. In Eastern Europe, for example, a "sacred" bullet could be fired into the coffin of a vampire to kill it. It is not made clear, however, exactly how such a bullet would be made "sacred." Perhaps it would have to be blessed by a priest in the Orthodox Church (the predominant religion of Eastern Europe), or simply sprinkled with holy water.

On an occult level, the use of any blessed object against a supernatural creature could have a powerful effect. Practitioners of almost every type of mysticism agree that when an item is "charged" or blessed, it is infused with a form of willpower, as well as with an essence that becomes present on other levels. A good example of that is found in the practice of shamanism. Shamans can bring the spiritual essence or counterpart of an object of power along with them on their inner journeys, and can use it to work on other planes. Success in any such undertaking depends upon the shaman's belief in both the power of the item and in his or her ability to travel.

A similar principle would be at work if an item were blessed in ways that agree with a vampire hunter's religious beliefs. The hunter's belief in the religious potency of the object would make that object an extension of the hunter's will. Also, because the object would have a mystical essence of its own, it should be able to damage a supernatural creature in more than just physical ways. That is why exorcism rituals using objects such as a crucifix or holy water succeed; the occult essence of those objects would do the actual work on unseen levels. Of course, it can be argued that even if no evil spirits are present, the religious beliefs of the exorcist and the "possessed" person would make the ritual work.

Some fiction writers have picked up on the previous ideas, either through occult research or intuition. Many vampire stories and movies contain the idea that you must believe in a crucifix for it to actually work against an undead. Some fiction also presents the concept that the religious object used must be of the vampire's religion from when it was a mortal man or woman. If that were true, then it would agree with the last comment brought up about the exorcist and the "possessed" individual because the latter would have to believe in the symbols working for his or her benefit.

* * *

Next, let's look at a couple of ways to thwart an immortal blood drinker without "killing" it. These methods were used mostly to keep a vampire from rising from the grave in the first place. Some methods involve occult beliefs that are not exactly universal, but which were still common to many areas of Europe and the rest of the world. You might have noticed that the majority of the material in this chapter comes from European folklore. There is a motive behind that. The following chapters present the occult phenomena of psychic vampirism. The basis for that examination was partially derived from some of the commonly accepted principles of Western occultism, making the Western ideas presented in this chapter on blood drinkers relevant when covering psychic vampires.

Placing Holy Objects in the Coffin

In Europe, particularly in the Orthodox Christian countries, it is a common practice to bury the dead with either an icon, a crucifix, or both. This custom was originally intended to sanctify the corpse, making it impossible for an evil spirit to enter it. Keep in mind that the Church was not certain if vampires were possessed corpses or just corpses that somehow became animated by their own corrupt souls. If the latter was true, then the holy object buried with the body would act as a boundary that would keep the undead from leaving the coffin.

Placing Unsanctified Objects in the Coffin

In those areas of the world where Christianity was not dominant, and in a few where the religion did thrive, it was just as common a practice to put seemingly everyday, unsanctified objects in the grave as it was to place holy items there. Researching these practices is important because of the insight that they grant us to the types of superstition found in the world. More importantly the customs are interesting because they show common beliefs about the afterlife.

Let's start with the location in the coffin where the majority of items were placed—near the head. Again, most cultures placed a great deal of importance on the head as the center of consciousness. That belief was so well accepted that, by association, the head and its orifices (the most important of which was the mouth) became known as the link to the soul—a gateway to the spirit world by which spirits could either enter or leave a body

As for spirits entering a body, we've covered the idea that a vampire could be a corpse that is animated by an evil entity. So how could that be prevented? In Europe, bodies were often buried with items stuffed into their mouths. Those objects, which ranged from garlic to eggs, were thought to ward off evil spirits.

Although it's hard to distinguish between the two motives, sometimes the items placed in the mouth of a corpse were put there to keep the soul of the dead from escaping. That might seem a little bizarre at a glance to anyone who believes the soul moves on to some type of afterlife. However, that is not the process that was supposed to be halted; if a soul were to move on from its earthly remains, it would do so at the moment of death. If the soul had other intentions, like staying around to torment the living, then the objects placed in the corpse's mouth were meant to keep it from leaving the grave after interment.

Naturally; the last idea ties in with the belief that even blood-drinking vampires are not physical creatures, and that they rest only in their former bodies. This idea was popular because it seemed to account for how vampires could leave their graves without disturbing the soil, and how they could appear in any bedroom at night. (They would apparently materialize to attack.) As for how those spirit vampires would carry the blood back to the grave with them, little has been speculated. Regardless, the existence of the non-physical vampire was a widely accepted and feared possibility and definitely accounted for a large number of bodies buried with wards against evil placed in their mouths.

* * *

As promised, we'll complete this section on thwarting the undead with a quick look at what was commonly done to keep immortal blood drinkers away after they had already risen. Who knows when these precautions could come in handy?

Sharp Objects

Like repels like in the world of folklore. Vampires have sharp nails and teeth, and therefore would be repelled by sharp objects like thorns and knives. The entrances to a house were the ideal spots to place such items.

Foul-Smelling Objects

Why was garlic supposed to repel a vampire? Once again, like repels like. Vampires were considered foul-smelling and therefore would naturally hate garlic, as well as other substances with terrible odors, such as sulphur.

Objects of Mystical Power

The power of a holy item shows up numerous times in folklore. If vampires really are evil spirits (either ones that possess foreign bodies or inhabit their own), then an object of power might prove effective as a ward. However, you can't always be sure how potent the ritual that charged the object was.

Distractions

As odd as it might sound, people have put nets in their windows or sprinkled seeds around their property to keep vampires from entering by distracting them. Those who performed these countermeasures believed that a vampire could not pass a net without untying each knot. The seeds served a similar purpose—a vampire would have to count each seed before passing. However, even if those methods worked (they don't quite fit in with any occult school of thought), they would only delay an inevitable attack.

Mirrors

The occult power of a mirror is recognized by many cultures; they are often used in magical rituals to reflect evil back to its source. It is commonly believed that vampires cast no reflection in mirrors (that idea most likely originated with the belief that a vampire is a solidified spirit, and has no real physical image to reflect). They could therefore be repelled by not seeing anything in a mirror. If vampires cast reflections, then they might just as easily be turned away by what they do see.

MORTAL BLOOD DRINKERS: DANGEROUS?

The true undead is not the only type of blood drinker to fear. If you read the letters in the last chapter, then you already know something of the other type. They might not seem deadly—that's because, for the most part, they don't mean to be. The mortal blood drinkers who wrote the letters in Chapter Five seem considerate enough to drink only from willing donors. Chances are they aren't violent people who would kill those from whom they drink, intentionally at least.

If you would ever consider letting another person drink your blood, or have thought of drinking from someone else, consider this: There might be something just as life-altering in the blood of a mortal as in the blood of an immortal. That something is AIDS.

Scientists still have not isolated all the ways the deadly disease can spread, but they are certain that it is in an afflicted person's blood. Exchanging blood with someone with AIDS would ensure that you would get it as well.

What can a mortal vampire or donor do to protect him or herself? If the vampire or donor does not have AIDS, and is in a monogamous relationship with another vampire or donor who does not have AIDS, then the risk of AIDS is eliminated. However, AIDS is not the only thing to worry about.

The human mouth is not exactly germ-free; bacteria are present. Allowing such bacteria access to another person's bloodstream is not a very good idea, To make the explanation simple, antibodies and certain organs in the body clean blood of impurities, but those impurities can still make us ill.

Also, just how safe is the wound made in a donor? If it's too deep, and an artery or vein is severed, uncontrollable bleeding and maybe death could result. People have died of excessive bleeding during controlled surgery. Just how would a mortal vampire prevent such a terrible thing from happening when even medical professionals have failed in the past?

Furthermore, even if a wound made during a blood-drinking session is not deadly, is it sterile? Were sterile instruments used? Keep in mind that even if the wound is perfectly sterile, oral contact could cause an infection, for the reasons discussed earlier. Of course, for the same reasons, biting will almost certainly cause an infection, not to mention severe tissue damage, and possible excessive bleeding.

Finally, let's examine a minor danger inherent to the would-be vampire. Blood is a natural emetic. That is, a substance that could induce vomiting. Drink too much of it, and you could end up ruining that lovely cape. Of course, the amount of blood that induces vomiting varies in each individual, but it's another reason to avoid the practice of blood drinking.

In conclusion, to all the mortal blood drinkers reading this, I have this to say: Please reconsider your actions. Chances are, if you are reading this, you are interested in learning at least some of the mystical truths in our universe. Do not be in a rush to learn them all in the afterlife. The act of vampirism might sound glamorous to a fan of the creatures, but it really has no place among the living who wish to keep living.

* * *

We are finished with blood. Were this a typical vampire book, that would be a pretty ridiculous claim to make at this time (notice, there are lots of pages left). Next we're going to explore the types of vampires that occultists have proven do exist—psychic vampires—and they have no need for the red liquid.

The Rational Slayer

By Bruce A. McClelland

The violent and unjust excesses of the Inquisition in Western Europe and of a later, but parallel, series of witch trials in Hungary in the second half of the seventeenth century led, ultimately, to many philosophical, theological, and legal inquiries attempting to explain the phenomena of witchcraft. Growing intolerance for the rather lopsided system of accusation and persecution evolved into a concerted and widespread attack on religious zealotry in mainstream European society. However, the attempt to eliminate zealous witch persecutors naturally also resulted in the elimination of visible witches once and for all. The "scientific" explanations of witchcraft and sorcery (and vampirism) succeeded in pulling the rug out from under the Inquisitors by denying the reality of the very object of their accusations. Thus, rationalism was a more effective tool for eradicating witches than were the witch trials themselves, since the residual pagan beliefs that were held by the worshipers of Diana, for example, were shown to be simply irrational and thus not of any further consequence. Vampires likewise represented an impossibility, since from the new, Cartesian perspective, a being could not logically be dead and alive at the same time.

I propose that the new inquirers—such as Gerard van Swieten—who were charged by the leading political figures of Enlightenment Europe with proving the irrationality of pagan beliefs were in fact completing the task set by the Inquisition. They accomplished this not by bringing heretics to trial and executing them (which had the unintended effect of reifying the subversive power of the persecuted groups) but by effectively debunking heretical and pagan beliefs as superstition. Those who held on to such beliefs were no longer to be persecuted by the now magnanimous state; rather, they were to be pitied. In their reports, the investigators into witchcraft and vampirism attempted to show the absurdity of any beliefs that were not in accord with what could be proved by the emerging scientific method, on the one hand, or confirmed by Judeo-Christian scripture on the other. While this shift in attitude resulted in a drastic decrease in persecution of those individuals formerly at risk of being labeled witches, it also trivialized their actual beliefs and practices by considering them misguided and irrelevant rather than politically dangerous. The Catholic Church was rapidly losing political power to the secular state.

This rationalizing impulse led to the incursion of vampire beliefs into Western Europe from the Balkans. Beginning around the end of the seventeenth century, at the boundary between the territories of the Ottoman and Habsburg empires, local vampire beliefs were suddenly amplified by the same sort of epidemic hysteria that rose up around witchcraft beliefs in the West. Stories about vampires quickly became newsworthy and intriguing to the literate classes. Because Slavic vampire tales had until then been little known outside lands controlled by the Ottoman Porte, they represented a new threat, a new form of strange magic and supernaturalism from the Orient that needed to be dealt with in the same way as witchcraft: they needed to be explained away, lest a whole new project of inquisitional proportions arise.

In the eventual translation of the vampire from the Eastern into the Western European worldview, certain things were lost. First, the Slavic/Orthodox conceptions of the otherworld and the natural path of the soul after death were never taken into consideration in the reports of vampire activity brought back from Serbia. In fact, there was little attempt on the part of the investigators to understand the cultural context of the folklore; rather, they simply tried to somehow explain the reported phenomena as though the narratives referred to real events. Second, in the east-west boundary regions, vampires were seen as being conspiratorial, like witches, although this attribute is never found elsewhere in South Slavic folklore. It was difficult for the new rationalists, now peering more deeply into the strange Orient of the Ottoman Balkans, to understand in the vampire a mechanism for handling village accusation and justice under certain well-defined circumstances. Instead, they could only perceive the vampire as a strange variant of the witch, who, as an actual living being, was susceptible to the full force of a complex prosecutorial system inherited from Roman law.

Still, the rationalists' purpose was to completely destroy the imaginary and the folkloric and to replace them with the materialistic and scientific, partly as a reaction against the sort of violent, elaborate fantasies that had tormented the Inquisitors as much as their victims and led to cycles of extreme persecution and excessive punishment. Once science had explained away the vampire as unreal, it was no longer possible for this sort of folklore to have any autonomy among the folk—especially in those areas where the vampire was not native. No longer would the imaginings of illiterate farmers or herders in the mountain villages command the attention that was now properly devoted to the project of science and technology. In the West, vampire folklore could therefore never take root, but following the reports that began to flow into Austria and beyond, the vampire soon became an object of fascination to artists and writers, who saw in these tales new metaphoric opportunities for expressing symbolic aspects of social power relationships. The Western authors, however, were unaware that the version of the vampire they had inherited from the journalists had been contaminated by projected notions about witches and, thanks to medical materialism, epidemic disease. Perhaps the one person most responsible for the link between the vampire and epidemic disease was the Dutch physician Gerard van Swieten.

THE LOWLANDS SLAYER

Van Swieten was first and foremost a physician, eventually named chief physician at the Court of Vienna by Maria Theresa (r. 1740–80), who came to trust him more than she trusted any of her other advisors. In his early years, he had been one of the most gifted pupils of the renowned Dutch medical scientist Herman Boerhaave, and he already possessed a significant reputation as a physician in his home city of Leiden when his erudition and relationships to many eminent scientists came to the attention of the Austrian empress. Frank Brechka considers Van Swieten worthy of biography not because he was "a founder, maker or incarnation of the age" but, rather, because he was "so intimately involved in the typical problems and attitudes of the time." In the domain of medical science, Van Swieten became certainly the most important and visible representative of the Enlightenment in Austria. But beyond that and more important for our purposes, he served, as noted by Brechka, as an "intermediary between the Lowlands and Vienna, between the advanced culture of western Europe and the backward condition of Austria."

Gerard van Swieten.

Among its other holdings, the Habsburg Empire controlled most of the area to the north of the Ottoman-controlled Slavic countries on the other side of the Danube, having finally pushed back the Turks from Hungary in the late seventeenth century. In the middle of the eighteenth century, Austria was facing a crisis in the form of military challenges from two technologically advanced modern European powers to the west and north, France and Prussia. Frederick the Great had invaded Silesia in the north, and the newly enthroned empress quickly understood both the nature of the threat posed by European modernity and the need to reform the underdeveloped regions of the Habsburg dominion and bring it into contention with other emerging Enlightenment centers. For political reasons having to do primarily with serious tensions, at that time, between Roman Catholics and Protestants, the empress sought out advisors for her reforms who were, like her and like Austria itself, Roman Catholic. The Dutch, meanwhile, were widely admired for their scholarship and progressiveness, qualities that were not in abundance in Vienna.

Since the Lowlands, or southern Netherlands, belonged to Austria in 1714, Van Swieten was already a de facto citizen of the Habsburg Empire. Furthermore, though a devout Roman Catholic, he was reportedly anti-Jesuit and tended to hold a number of heterodox secular opinions, in part the result of his broad exposure to the scientific thought of the day. He had, for example, encountered through his brief education at the University of Louvain the views of the seventeenth-century Belgian Jansenist Zeger Bernhard van Espen, who had penned several anti-Jesuit treatises against religious fanaticism and veneration of saints, as well as essays asserting "the true foundation, origin, and nature of the two powers, God and Caesar." Later, at the University of Leiden, having abandoned the study of law at Louvain, Van Swieten became immersed in the wake of the late seventeenth-century controversy over Cartesianism and mechanistic philosophy. Leiden, where Descartes himself had lived for many years, was a focal point of discourse surrounding skeptical philosophy and natural science and had been the site of a great deal of interest in practical medicine (including anatomical dissection) and scientific experiment. It was at Leiden, under the influence of Boerhaave, the most brilliant and influential physician of Europe, that Van Swieten acquired his philosophy of and approach to medicine and science and naturally became a major proponent of Enlightenment values.

By virtue of his citizenship as well as his scientific knowledge and religious views, then, Gerard van Swieten was the perfect choice for Maria Theresa to employ in reforming Austro-Hungary's position in regard to science and medicine. Van Swieten had acquired his medical education just as the science of medicine was undergoing great change in the West, and experimental results were beginning to undercut the predominant but archaic theories of Galen. Van Swieten's mentor had called for physicians to be thoroughly versed in all branches of science, including chemistry, pharmacy, and botany. Understanding of anatomy and of the circulatory system was a mandatory precursor to understanding theoretical and therapeutic medicine. Van Swieten adhered to these recommendations tenaciously.

After receiving his medical degree, Van Swieten spent the years from 1725 to 1745 practicing in Leiden and working as a scholar of medicine and its history. Perhaps because he held Catholic religious beliefs (while the Netherlands was a Protestant country), but more likely thanks to the professional jealousy of his less erudite colleagues, he was never allowed to teach at the University of Leiden, though he did conduct private lessons. He attended virtually all lectures of Boerhaave for twenty years, and from his verbatim notes, he compiled a collection of Boerhaave's aphorisms, which he ultimately published with his own commentaries in five volumes (1769). In this work, he discussed contemporary theories of disease and therapy, especially in regard to the causes and treatment of fevers. However, since the germ theory had not yet been advanced, his conclusions about the physical causation of corporeal diseases remained vague and incomplete, and his popular books were eventually rejected as being incorrect and out of date. Still, his reputation as an encyclopedist of medical knowledge preceded him to Vienna.

In late 1744, Maria's sister, Marianne, the Austrian archduchess, became very sick with a septic high fever following the stillborn delivery of a girl, who would have been princess. Count Kaunitz, who was aware of Van Swieten's reputation (although the physician's chapter on diagnosing and treating fever had not yet been published), summoned him to Brussels to care for the archduchess. Van Swieten arrived on November 11 but was too late to save Marianne. This was not merely a personal loss for the empress; Marianne had been married to Charles of Lorraine, and her death weakened the political connection between the Houses of Habsburg and Lorraine. Although Van Swieten could not save Maria's only sister, he cared for her to the utmost, which ingratiated him to Maria Theresa enormously. After Van Swieten had returned to Leiden, the Austrian empress entered into a very warm correspondence with him, in which she expressed both her grief and her gratitude. On the basis of the trust built up during this correspondence, Van Swieten eventually moved to Vienna to become the court physician.

Van Swieten's primary role in the now formal coalition between Austria and Hungary (the Hungarian and Austrian provinces had been declared inseparable in the Pragmatic Sanction of 1723) was, in a sense, to bring the Enlightenment to the Habsburg domain. Hungary in particular had suffered from almost two centuries of defensive wars, and Maria Theresa well understood the need to improve culture, education, and science across the board. The task, as Brechka puts it, was to do away with faculties that taught useless knowledge and resisted new ideas, with apothecaries that dispensed incorrect drugs and threatened the lives of citizens, with papal agents who interfered with necessary change. A self-sufficient, unified, and effective state could afford neither divisiveness nor stupidity. Moreover, the new knowledge of the West would have to be admitted.

Van Swieten used his scholastic training and gift for classification and organization and his capacity as both chief physician (*protomedicus*) and court librarian (*biblioth-ecarius*) to help modernize the University of Vienna. He also eventually became the president of Maria Theresa's Chastity Commission (*Keuscheitskommission*), which had been created in 1753 to save the public (Catholic) morals and, more important, to limit exposure of the literate populace to any dangerous ideas that might potentially subvert the goal of bringing Austria into the enlightened West. Curiously, while Van Swieten had been hired to look forward and help create a progressive society, he nevertheless found himself in the position of having to ban certain books. He even maintained a list, the *Supplementum librorum prohibitorum*, apparently annotated in a script that only he could decipher.

It might seem a contradiction that the same person who sought to expose to the light of reason the fallacies and illogic of vampire beliefs should also uphold the mandate to suppress books of "false science." Among the books he condemned were works suggesting that there was a scientific basis for palmistry and astrology. Alchemy, too, was regarded as charlatanism. While, from today's perspective, we might view censorship itself as opposite to the aims of Enlightenment politics, it was actually Maria Theresa who created the Chastity Commission, out of fear that she would not be able to prevent contamination of the new, emerging knowledge by the old. This fear must have arisen in part as a result of the rapid resettlement that occurred following the decline of Turkish occupation of Hungary, whereby Bohemian Slavs from the north, Serbs from the south, and Germans from the west began to move into the Hungarian plains. Mobile ethnic groups tend to bring with them their religious beliefs. Meanwhile, witch accusations had become epidemic in the 1720s in southern Hungary (Szeged). Clearly Maria Theresa was concerned lest some of these beliefs reemerge and interfere with the task of advancing science and education.

The concern was pragmatic: theoretical sciences developed during the Renaissance were now being harnessed to practical and utilitarian aims. Science, as such, was to be utilized for the material betterment of humankind, in the form of better technology and better medicine. Superstitious belief was no longer a matter of religious heresy but, rather, was evidence that believers in such things could not successfully participate in the movement toward social enlightenment. Indeed, Central European anti-Semitism is evident even in the opinions of Van Swieten, who claimed that "the superstitions of the Jews prevented them from becoming *useful members of society.*" (italics added)

What is important to see in the co-occurrence of the attempt to create a progressive and enlightened state with the establishment of the Chastity Commission or the preservation of anti-Semitic beliefs is that the very blind spot that formed the logic of the Inquisition had not really been eliminated by Enlightenment politics. Rather, as the old beliefs were equated with ignorance, pity was shown to those who had been labeled sorcerers, witches, and the like—the empress herself pardoned a Bohemian peasant who had been sentenced to death for sorcery—and this pity effectively became a new mode of marginalization. Social usefulness became the greater measure of worth, and as Austria and Hungary attempted to align themselves with the more urbane cultures of the north and west, agrarian beliefs naturally confounded usefulness in the sense of scientific progress.

In regard to this book's theme, a shift occurred around the mid-eighteenth century that not only redefined the vampire as a symbolic (eventually literary) creature rather than a folkloric one but also established the role of the vampire slayer as a rationalist, whose tools against the vampire were no longer physically destructive and no longer belonged to the same ritual system but instead relied on learning and scientific knowledge to destroy the demons of the unconscious past. The victory of the new rationalism became self-evident, and any resistance to it constituted nothing more serious than a form of pitiable self-delusion. Paradoxically, in the attempt to destroy the social injustices that were being perpetuated on the purveyors of false religion and, therefore, false reason, alternative beliefs were ignominiously swept away by the growth of the new state.

In order to understand the logic that was being mobilized to squelch, once and for all, belief in vampires and witches, it is worth taking a look in some detail at the arguments that Van Swieten raised in his report from 1755. We shall see there that Van Swieten himself made no important distinction between witchcraft and vampires, at least with regard to their treatment after death. Curiously, despite his grand attempt to rationalize folk beliefs, he could not seem to avoid bringing religious ideas about the sacred and evil into his reasoning.

GERARD VAN SWIETEN AND HIS CONSIDERATION OF THE CLAIM OF POSTHUMOUS MAGIC

In 1755, Maria Theresa dispatched Van Swieten to Hermersdorf, Moravia, to investigate the postmortem treatment of a certain "Rosina Polackin" (Van Swieten's spelling). His primary obligation was to defuse any possibility of a renewed epidemic of vampirism such as had occurred twenty years prior. He would accomplish this by writing up for the empress a report in which he explained, according to the medical and biophysical understanding of the day the phenomena usually associated with vampires, especially regarding the physical state of their exhumed corpses. This report would then serve as guidance and rationale for imperial policy with respect to such beliefs and provide Maria Theresa with the scientific authority to intervene in any future cases where a deceased body was mutilated as a result of belief in vampires.

Van Swieten's ostensible goal, then, was not so much to destroy vampires as to undercut the motive for retributive violence done to the body or the grave of the deceased. In that respect, we cannot legitimately call Van Swieten a vampire slayer. He directed his antagonism, at least in his treatise, not at those who were considered vampires (who were, after all, from a medical point of view, quite dead) but, rather, at the survivors whose beliefs led to sacrilegious defilement and propagated irrational ideas about the processes of death and decomposition. But with the issuance of Van Swieten's report, which proposed the clear superiority of a materialist explanation for supernatural events, any remaining folkloric or mythological function of belief in the animated dead crumbled immediately into dust. Perhaps equally important is the fact that the so-called demonic ceased to exist, having been replaced for the time being by a more abstract, Christian view of evil, which the Catholic Van Swieten offered as a real force but one subservient to God. With the death of the demonic in Western Europe, vampires and witches ceased to have any real interest that was not either nostalgic or romantic.

Van Swieten's *Consideration of the Claim of Posthumous Magic* first sets up the problem of supernatural occurrences within a Christian frame. He personifies abstract evil as an "Evil Spirit" (*lo Spirito maligno*) or "the Demon" (*IlDemonio*), but never refers to it—as others had done so often during the Reformation and Counter-Reformation—as "Satan." Perhaps bowing to Maria Theresa's distaste for Protestants, Van Swieten finds it important to cite right away the philosophical problem of whether there can be supernatural causes behind phenomena that are not otherwise easily understood.

> When people observe extraordinary effects whose causes are unknown, they always attribute them to some higher powers. The history of every century demonstrates this. Now it is a certainty known from the Holy Scriptures, whether through the holy angels, His prophets, apostles or other holy men, that by His omnipotence God created such marvelous effects. Ecclesiastical history can convince those who are more incredulous that on account of the beautiful principle of Christianity such marvelous effects did not ever cease. Scholarly persons and honest Protestants have not been able to deny that the Holy Apostle of the Indians has proved his mission by such clear miracles. It is equally true that the Evil Spirit must have permission from God to produce effects that surpass natural causes. That which occurred when our Savior was tempted in the desert suffices to prove this.
>
> No Christian can deny that there are persons possessed by the Evil Spirit, and that consequently this malignant spirit can act upon human bodies. It is likewise true that the Demon disturbs men with noises and frightening visions. The Protestants themselves confess that the idolaters of the abominable Indians prove the malice of the Master, whom they serve; but as soon as they have destroyed the bonds of their slavery to the Demon through the holy sacrament of the baptism, and become members of the Church, the diabolic illusions come to an end; this has served to convert many people.

Here, Van Swieten is quite careful to establish that there exist both true miracles, which are authored by God alone, and supernatural illusions that are produced through the agency of a deceptive, "diabolic" force. Enticement by illusions is tantamount to possession. But these two similar phenomena can ultimately be distinguished through a kind of exorcistic gnosis; that is, the grace that accompanies baptism apparently has the power to banish possessing demonic forces. Dr. Van Swieten opposes both miracles and demonic illusions against a third class of appearances, those things that appear to be miraculous or supernatural because a reasonable physical explanation is not available. If, by the way, we examine Van Swieten's remarks from the point of view of the history of medicine, clearly the dominant rational belief in mid-eighteenth-century Vienna was that physical maladies had definite physiological—and therefore treatable—etiologies (even though not all of them may yet have been understood), while psychiatric diseases were still bound to demonic influence. In one sense, Van Swieten is fobbing off onto the church the intractability of psychiatric disorders, but there is a hint, in his text, that he is aware that these diseases, too, are medical in nature and subject to treatment. Perhaps it is no accident that psychiatry becomes a separate discipline in Vienna a hundred years after Van Swieten (d. 1772).

Van Swieten later points out how in the absence of scientific explanation, technological and perceptual curiosities can be exploited by those seeking to gain personal power. He assumes that "posthumous magic"—namely, the inexplicable failure of the body to decompose completely after burial—is one such type of exploitative wizardry, whereby people may be convinced of a supernatural cause when none really exists. He attributes the origin of the belief in vampires to the "Schismatic Greeks," which is correct to the extent that the belief arises in the context of conversion of the Balkan peoples to Byzantine (Greek) Orthodoxy, though he is naturally unaware that the word *vampir* is Slavic. He bases this conclusion on the writing of the French botanist Joseph Pitton de Tournefort, who had traveled to the Levant and described vampire beliefs he encountered during his travels.

> Gunpowder, electrical phenomena, or optical illusions have the ability to astonish all that do not know about them; and charlatans use this to make the credulous public believe they are most powerful wizards. Therefore it is again certain that marvels diminish when measured by science. The posthumous magic treated here provides new proof, because all those tales come from countries where ignorance reigns; and it is very likely that the Schismatic Greeks are the main progenitors. Tournefort, a scholar and evidently a doctor, and the greatest botanist of his century, was sent by Louis XIV into Asia, primarily to examine some plants in Greece that had been imperfectly described by ancient Greek medicine. There he was able to see at very close range a corpse that had been accused of demonic magic, and also how all means were used to impede the Demon, so that more would not use dead bodies in order to torment the living.

Curiously, Van Swieten seems to take the various reports of vampirism (and anti-vampire behavior) at face value, even though his entire physician's argument that such things are nonsense derives both from a devotion to autopsy (whose Greek-derived name literally means "seeing with one's own eyes") and from the logical arrangement of demonstrated facts. It is as if he is in such a hurry to provide a scientific explanation for the phenomena on which he is reporting that he ignores the question of whether these things really happened in the first place and, if they did, the question of whether the testimony surrounding them might exhibit any discrepancy that would suggest something other than peasant ignorance at work.

Van Swieten takes Tournefort's mention of vampires in Hungary (not Greece) as primary data and as the first mention of vampires that he is aware of. By the time of Tournefort's journey in the late seventeenth century, the epidemic aspect of the vampire was already present. Van Swieten includes the actual passage from the third letter of Tournefort's *Travels*, but he annotates it thus:

> This story can reveal what ought to be thought about that which happened in 1732, in a small town in Hungary, in a region named in Latin *Oppictum Heidonum*, situated between the Thiess [*Tisza*] and Transylvania. Posthumous magic predominated in this letter about the little town. The dead men, who were completely godless, were called "vampires," and they were believed to suck the blood of persons and even beasts, and when they had eaten the meat of such beings, they joined the dead men and changed into vampires; and in this way one who had been a passive vampire during life then became an active vampire after death, unless one consumed the earth of the vampire's sepulcher or rubbed it with its blood.
>
> I have not told this story without reason. I also believe that the official record was sent to the Imperial Council of War in Vienna at the beginning of 1732. The ceremony that was practiced was dictated by a *haiduk*, that is, by the local judge, a man quite expert in vampirism. A sharp stake is passed through the chest of the hunted vampire; then the head is cut off; everything is incinerated and the ashes are thrown into the grave.
>
> Vampirism spreads quickly and is as contagious as mange. Some credence is given to the notion that a cadaverous vampire in a very short time can infect every other body buried in the same cemetery if the first one is not destroyed immediately.

The fact that an "official record" of vampire events in rural eastern Hungary was submitted to Vienna is proof enough for Van Swieten, especially since the ritual for disposing of a vampire had been "dictated by a *haiduk*, ... a man quite expert in vampirism." Since the *haiduk*'s report describes actions that are cited in much vampire folklore in the Balkans and surrounding areas, there is certainly no reason to mistrust it, except for the fact that the actions prescribed are somewhat excessive: first the stake is driven in, then the head is lopped off, and then the whole dead thing is burned and the ashes are thrown back into the grave. Van Swieten does not question whether this report from Hungary might in fact include an expedient and exaggerated synthesis of several different practices known folklorically to the townsfolk (including the local judge). Rather, the official's presumed expertise in such matters passes as sufficient evidence that vampires in this Hungarian town were rekilled by every possible means. It is advantageous for Van Swieten to accept this distant testimony literally, since the excessive violence done to the dead serves his purpose and justifies authoritarian intervention in such extreme practices.

Despite the case Van Swieten is attempting to build—namely, that the existence of supernatural vampires cannot be proved by the visual evidence available at exhumation and, therefore, that there is no reason to exhume and immolate suspicious corpses—he cannot avoid repeating that the dead men in this case were "completely godless." Van Swieten's skepticism is still informed by religion-centered moral judgments, according to which some impiety may be, if not an excuse, at least a legitimate explanation for the reactions of the townspeople. Vampires or no, it is understandable—if we may read between Van Swieten's interpretive lines—that people would consider godless people to be somehow connected to evil and would thus be inclined to take violent action to stop its spread.

As I pointed out earlier, the idea that vampires are like disease (in this case, they are likened to mange) is a belief that attaches itself to vampire notions late and generally outside the Balkans proper. Here, if we are to believe Tournefort, the notion is encountered in Hungary, where vampire beliefs had come into contact with Western European witchcraft beliefs. But Van Swieten amplifies the urgency of dealing with this epidemic aspect: Tournefort's letter does suggest that bloodsucking or eating flesh of humans and vampires turns those (living) victims into vampires, but Van Swieten links this capability to the rapid spread of vampirism among the dead within a cemetery. This notion, as we shall presently see, possesses immediacy for Van Swieten because of his personal experience in Moravia. On the one hand, Van Swieten is quite certain that epidemic vampirism is a false belief needing to be demystified, yet on the other, the flat assertion that vampirism "spreads quickly and is as contagious as mange" contradicts the intention to show that vampirism does not exist. We must suspect that Van Swieten thus accepts that popular notions about vampires constitute an authentic, but misguided, version of some physiological facts that he can refute beyond doubt with counterevidence from his own experience as a scientist as well as from other reports.

> It is true that our vampires of 1755 had not yet become bloodsuckers, but they were all predisposed to becoming such. Because the executioner, a person no doubt quite truthful concerning the matters of his trade, asserted that in cutting up the cadavers that had been condemned to the fire, some blood

flowed out with vehemence and in abundance. This in spite of the fact that it is generally agreed that after death there usually remains no more than a spoonful. This affects the story a great deal. The extraordinary facts that are believed to have been observed can be brought down to these two points:

1. that cadavers of posthumous magic, or vampires, do not decompose, but instead remain whole and pliable;
2. that these vampires bother the living with apparitions, noises, suffocation, etc.

I will succinctly consider whether these two points are possible.

A corpse is ordinarily inclined to rot, during which process virtually all parts of the body are dissipated, except the bones … Proof of this is that when a coffin was opened fifteen years after a woman had died, and it had not been struck with anything, the corpse seemed to remain whole. The lines of the face and clothes etc. were still discernible. But when the casket was moved even quite deftly, everything immediately turned into shapeless powder, and only the bones remained.

Since the dead must make a place for the burial of their successors, there is a fixed term of fifteen years in many countries after which gravediggers may move the corpse. I have assisted many times at such tomb openings, and with a little bribe of food I was at least able to get the gravediggers to open some of the caskets very carefully. From that experience I remain convinced that after we die we are not the pasture of worms, at least not always, because if that were true, this powder would not retain facial details. When the contents of the grave are removed, sometimes whole corpses are encountered rather than putrefied ones, but they are quite desiccated nevertheless, and of a brownish hue, and the flesh is very toasted without the cadavers being in an embalmed state. The gravediggers assured me that it was common for about one out of every thirty corpses to be desiccated without putrefaction. I therefore concluded that a corpse can remain incorrupt for several years, without there being some supernatural cause.

Van Swieten evidently considers vampire beliefs—and perhaps all folkloric beliefs—to be superstitions based in ignorance: he reduces the evidence from vampire reports down to two basic assertions: that vampires do not decompose in the grave and, therefore, that they are capable of walking around and interfering with the society of the living. By demonstrating that the first assertion is illusory—in fact, under certain quite demonstrable and natural conditions, corpses decay only very slowly and may even retain some detail in their features, so long as the coffin is not jarred—it becomes easy to assert the impossibility of the second. The belief that the corpse can be ambulatory is contingent on the lifelike appearance of the desiccated corpse.

In contrast to this sort of explanation, it is worth noting that in most South Slavic folklore about vampires, the condition of the corpse is not of particular interest. The identity of the vampire only needs to be confirmed either by ritual means or with the help of some sort of vampire seer. The villagers may or may not go so far as to dig up the corpse and perform some vampire-destroying ritual, but if they were to take action, it would be extremely rare for anyone to go to the extremes cited by the *haiduk* (since carrying out the ritual violence in one form or another is all that is important). In other words, in the Orthodox context, physical evidence of vampirism after the fact is irrelevant, since the vampire is originally identified (i.e., instantiated) to explain certain local phenomena. Imagine if this were not the case: for example, if a particular deceased person were labeled a vampire for any of the reasons discussed in earlier chapters and then the corpse was dug up in order to be transfixed, what would happen if it were then discovered that the body had indeed decomposed naturally? Would this result somehow disprove the accusation of vampirism?

In Moravia, Silesia, and other areas around and within Austro-Hungary, vampire beliefs had migrated from regions across the Danube, and thus came to survive outside the context of Orthodox Christianity and its views of the afterlife. (Indeed, in Orthodox belief, failure of the body to decompose may be a sign of saintliness, not evil.) Within their new Protestant cultural context, the emphasis of vampire narratives shifted away from the problem of burial infelicity and toward descriptions of the more literal encounter with the decomposing body. The vampire now posed a different sort of philosophical problem, having to do with the dangerous kind of directed magical power (notice how Van Swieten and Tournefort refer to "posthumous magic") that had been the subject of accusations against witches and sorcerers. The question of the reality of this supernatural power to reanimate the inanimate was still on the minds of the post-Reformation politicians: in Central Europe, the vampire represented an instrument of this power, capable of infecting (in the same way witches were capable of "spoiling") various village resources (especially human).

In his *Consideration*, Van Swieten brings other evidence that corpses do not decompose at the same rate: he points to a case in Devonshire, England, in 1751, where a man buried in a family grave site eighty years earlier was exhumed, revealing the "body of a completely intact man." Since the local parish registry confirmed that no one had been buried in that crypt after 1669, Van Swieten amusedly points out, "[H]ere is an English vampire who over the course of eighty years stayed tranquilly in his tomb without disturbing anyone." Having brought forth secondary evidence disproving the contention that vampire corpses unnaturally refuse to decompose, Van Swieten then reports his personal experience—namely, the case that brought him to Moravia.

We see at last the facts alleged as evidence of vampirism. Rosina Po-lackin, who died on December 22, 1754, was disinterred on January 19, 1755, and declared a vampire worthy of cremation, because she had not yet decomposed. The anatomists can keep corpses in the open air during winter for up to six weeks, even two months without putrefaction. It should also be noted that this particular winter was severe beyond the norm. In all the other corpses, decomposition had already consumed the greater part of the body. It sufficed that if not everything had putrefied, the body was suddenly to be worthy of the fire! What ignorance! In the writings of the Consistory the sure signs or countersigns on the corpses of vampires are described, but these are not specific to any part. Two bumbling surgeons, who had never seen a desiccated corpse and did not know the details of the structure of the human body as they themselves confessed to the Commissary, testified that they recommended a sentence of burning. It is quite true that the Commissary of Olmutz had not always brought surgeons to examine the facts, they had only sent a spiritual Commissary, who quite unwillingly made judgments about cases of vampirism; since it had resulted from a previous act, that in the year 1723 they burned the body of a man thirteen days after his death, and in the sentence alleged that the reason was that his grandmother had not lived in good repute in the community. In 1724 they burned the corpse of a man eighteen days after death, because he was a relative of the person mentioned previously. It was enough to be related to a supposed vampire, and the trial became good and final. Thus, they burned the body of a man two days after his death for this very reason, without other testimony, that the corpse retained a good complexion after death, and the joints were still flexible.

A good deal of impatience is evident in this section of Van Swieten's treatise. He seems barely able to conceal his contempt for so-called surgeons whose ignorance of postmortem processes allows them to side with the authorities recommending cremation of an exhumed corpse. He is even more annoyed at the reasoning behind the desecration of a man's corpse only eighteen days after his death. The last straw for Van Swieten is the illogic of a case on April 23, 1723, where the Consistory of Olmutz caused nine corpses to be burned, since it was believed they had been infected by a vampire buried before them in the same cemetery. Such a violent fate, however, did not await those who had been buried before the supposed vampire. On the contrary, they received mercy, even though, later, "Commissaries Wabst and Gesser showed that in these unsuspicious corpses are still found parts not yet corrupt and in one, even a little blood." Van Swieten insists (rightly) that these two conditions are not necessarily compatible: if lack of decomposition and the presence of venous blood are sure signs of vampirism, then they cannot be conveniently ignored in the case where vampirism is instead determined by some presumed sequence of infection.

Van Swieten thus insists that there should be an internal logic to folkloric beliefs, which, of course, there frequently is not. In fact, we might claim that lack of coherent logic becomes the primary accusation of this Enlightenment physician, as if rational thought and reality were inextricably linked. Like dreams, folkloric narratives frequently embody apparent contradictions, yet Van Swieten uses this fact as confirmation that the narratives cannot possibly describe real events. The superordination of the empirically real to the imaginal is so critical to Van Swieten that he cannot see any social value in systems where contradictions and anomalies are not resolved.

Van Swieten's motive, we must not forget, is to promote the cessation of mistreatment of both the dead and the living as a result of these irrational folk beliefs. This apparently noble purpose, however, is linked to an intolerance for ambiguity and anomaly and thus ends up destroying one of the very mechanisms available for expressing conflicts that cannot be expressed in more Cartesian terms.

Van Swieten exhibits a clear compassion for those who are persecuted for their misguided superstitious beliefs. In one passage, for example, he shows that a peasant woman's herbal folk remedies and claims to magic were in fact harmless, amounting to nothing more than common chicanery. But her eventual exhumation and incineration, in Van Swieten's view, are excessive and completely unwarranted—a sentence, he claims, that could have only been harsher if she had been alive. His report, meanwhile, confirms for us that witches and vampires were interchangeable, since poor Mrs. Sallingherin is accused not of being a vampire but of having been a witch during life.

> A certain Sallingherin, also known as Wenzel-Richelin, had been buried for eighteen months. It was claimed she was a witch, and was the cause of many evils. But where is the proof of such witchcraft? This woman dispensed remedies, and her son discovered all her mysterious tricks. There were eyes of lobsters dissolved in water; some grasses and roots without a shadow of superstition. In order to embellish her cures and lend credence to their mystery, to make someone ill she would send four escutcheons grouped in one of their cases and then she would send the remedy. It was claimed that the disease was bewitchment. The Commissary has looked into this case and found that it was a serious but natural disease called *Colica pictonum*, which makes those who become ill attracted to their members. We are currently employed to heal similar diseases at the City Hospital. Other magicians have foretold the day when a disease would be cured. Here is all the evidence of witchcraft: these practices should not have been considered efficacious during the life of that woman. Since she attended the Sacrament, she died in the bosom of the Church and was buried with a sacred ceremony. And eighteen months after her death she became a witch suited for incineration.
>
> Upon foundations of this sort have arisen this entire history, sacrileges were committed, the asylum of the tomb was violated. The reputation of the

ancestors and their families remained blackened, who might expect the same fate if such abusive ways were not eliminated. The dead bodies of innocent lads were placed in the hands of the executioner; men whose way of life was above reproach underwent the disgrace of being disinterred in the cemetery, after a supposed witch had been buried. They are declared to be witches, their bodies are consigned to the executioner to reduce them to ashes, but they receive this sentence which could only have been harsher if they had been alive; and they burned their bodies with infamy, serving as notice of an example to their accomplices.

Van Swieten's anger, which is barely restrained by the end of his treatise, seems justified: "This transfixes me and so much anger rouses me that I must come to a conclusion in order to not go beyond my limits."

It may be difficult for us to imagine the frustration Van Swieten experienced when asked to explain the goings on in Moravia. He was, after all, a reasonable man who was devoted to the power of science to explain much that had previously been in the domain of religious belief and faith. It was that devotion that earned him the trust of Maria Theresa, who needed men like him to bolster her attempts to turn Austria and Hungary into more modern European states. From the foregoing examination of his *Consideration*, we see also that his sense of compassion had been piqued by the mistreatment—at the hands of officious, but ignorant, civil authorities—of people who were persecuted even after death. Clearly, it made no sense to Van Swieten to punish the dead, for the corpse was in fact nothing more than decayed matter, regardless of its possibly lifelike appearance, and was therefore incapable of any sort of reanimation. But his compassion for the victimized and his ostensibly noble motive ought not obscure the fact that in dismissing belief in vampires as absurd, he also destroyed the ground on which this imported agrarian folklore was based. By subjecting folklore—even if it happened to fit uncomfortably in the post-Reformation Habsburg Empire—to the intense light of rationalism, he was pushing those beliefs further into the shadows. More than anyone else, Van Swieten helped to destroy the folkloric vampire in Western Europe.

There were certainly several others from the late seventeenth to the mid-eighteenth century who participated in the rationalist movement to explain the stories of the walking dead that had entered into Western European consciousness from the Balkans as political contact increased with the countries occupied by the Ottoman Turks. About twenty years prior to Van Swieten, for example, an Austrian regimental field surgeon named Johannes Flückinger was sent by Emperor Charles VI to Medvegia (Serbia), to report on vampire activity there. His minor report *Visum et repertum* became a source of popular knowledge about vampire beliefs and customs. Yet despite these broad attempts to repress the irrational by means of explanation rather than violence, there was something in the stories of vampires that was, as we know, irrepressible, and the vampire was destined to rise again—this time, however, as a literary figure, much harder to kill than before.

The Vampire in Russian Popular Music

My Funeral

By Vladimir Vysotsky

I have this dream; here it is!—There's a grave in the middle of my apartment.
Vampires have come to my funeral.
They all started making speeches, all about longevity,
They decided to hold off sucking blood; it's tasty for dessert.
They somehow jumped into the grave, but the strongest werewolf
Kept squeezing in and slipping in, and became entirely flat.
He breathed with difficulty, spitting and sucking a yellow fang.
A very bold little vampire struck me on the knee.
Chased me down and on the quiet bit me in the vein.
But the wizened bloodsucker stood up by my bedside
And very inspirationally gave a toast about full bloodedness.
And the honor guard burst out crying for decorum,
But I sense a series of looks at my sleepy artery.
And if someone pierces my artery, then I'm done for.
But hang on, where the hell do you think you're going?
After all, I hear what's going on, that means I'm not dead?!
They've poisoned the wine, but you went for it
They wanted to give me a wake, but … they screwed up!
But he who put poison on his lips was a real fool.
Well, on me the vomit was like a love potion.
Because my health was quite good,
And I ate a good bit of the poison.
So why, then, am I lying here playing the fool?
So why, for example, I don't laugh out loud, don't frighten them?
After all I long ago could have chased them off with a burst of bravery,
I could take them, slip away, but … I don't do stupid things.
Safely, like a worm I lie, while the werewolf,
Fussing over his glass,
Surely any second will attack.

 **Online Bonus**

To learn more about Vladimir Vysotsky visit
http://en.wikipedia.org/wiki/Vladimir_Vysotsky

Still another looks askance at my neck …
Well, you vermin, you'll have to find out from me!!!
With bloodthirsty wails, they pulled out pins,
And drops of my blood flowed into goblets …
But just you wait, I'll pour it myself, I know, I know, it's tasty!
Here! Drink my blood, you vile bloodsuckers!
But I didn't even tighten up my muscles,
And didn't try to make a fist,
Because he who doesn't strain
Will last a lot longer.
Lethal goose bumps hide along my back,
But didn't I have good reason—to wake up …
What to say? What am I afraid of?
But the dreams are drawn out …
Until I will awaken,
And they'll remain …

—Vladimir Vysotsky Moscow, 1971

The Lone Moon

By Lika

«Одинóкая лунá»

В. Постовапов
певица «Лика»

Снóва зовёт в дорóгу
Ночь, не смыкáя глаз.
Я, позабы́в тревóгу,
Мчусь, забывáя страх.
Ночь отменя́ет дýшу.
В дóме моём темнó.
Я ничегó не ви́жу.
Мне ужé всё равнó.
Припев:

> Ты ведь знáешь, я однá,
> Как одинóкая лунá.
> Я не могý забы́ть тебя́
> Я без тебя́ схожý с умá!
> crazy!

Скóро настýпит ýтро,
Скóро придёт рассвéт.
Дай мне однóй минýтой
Вновь позабы́ть весь свет.

"The Lone Moon"

V. Postovapov
"Lika"

Again the night calls to the road,
The night doesn't close (its) eyes.
I, having forgotten (my) anxiety,
Rush, forgetting (my) fear.
The night changes the soul.
It's dark in my house.
I don't see anything.
It's already all the same to me.
Refrain:

> You do know that I'm alone
> Like a lone moon.
> I can't forget you,
> Without you I'm going

Soon morning will get here,
Soon the dawn will arrive.
Give me a minute
Again to forget the whole world.

Перед моей дорогой,
    road],
Дай мне любви глоток.
Знаю, что этой ночью
Ты, как и я, одинок.

Припев (2 раза)

Телефонистка:
Абонемент не отвечает или
времено недоступен.
Попробуйте позвонить позднее.

Before my road [Before I hit the road]

Give me a taste of love.

I know that this night

You, like me, are alone.

Chorus (2 times)

Operator:
The number is not answering or
is temporarily unavailable.
Try to call later.

The Crow

By Linda

"Ворона" –Линда

Тикают так, как вулканы поют.
Реки стоят–воду больше не пьпют.
Ты, как они. Я же, как ворона.

Стекла не бьют, потому что их
нет.
Сказка о том, где был солнечный
свет.
Я же пою, где поет ворона.

Кто–то стрелял и хотел напугать.
Я же сижу и не буду стоять.
Я не они – я же ворона!

Птицы от них улетают совсем.
Город затих – повеинуется всем.
Я же лечу, как летит ворона.

Я ворона, я ворона на–на–на–на.
Я ворона, я ворона на–на–на–на.
Я ворона, я ворона на–на–на–на.
На–на–на–на–на, на–на–на–на–на.

"The Crow"–Linda

They tick, tick like volcanoes sing.
Rivers are still—they don't drink water
anymore.
You are like them. But I, I am like the crow.

They can't break the windows, because
they're gone.
A tale about where there was sunshine.
But I, I sing where the crow sings.

Someone fired a shot, and hoped to frighten.
Me, I will sit and will not stand.
I am not them—I, I am like the crow.

Birds are flying from them, flying away.
The city is quiet—everyone obeys.
But I am flying, flying like the crow.

I am a crow, a crow row-row-row-row.
I am a crow, a crow row-row-row-row.
I am a crow, a crow row-row-row-row.
Row-row-row-row-row, row-row-row-row.

Тикают так, как вулканы поют.
Реки стоят—воду больше не пьпют
Ты, как они. Я же, как ворона.

They tick, tick like volcanoes sing.
Rivers stand still—don't drink water anymore.
You are like them. But I, I am like the crow.

Girls with Sharp Teeth

By Linda

«Девочки с острыми зубками»
       -- Линда

"Girls with Sharp Teeth"
       —Linda

Они уходят ночью
не остановить!
они кусают плечи
это не забыть!

They go out at night
Don't stop them!
The bite shoulders
Don't forget this!

     Смотри они с острым клыком
     тебя зовут красивым ногтем

Careful! They have a sharp fang
They call you with a pretty fingernail

Они оставят после
на тебе следы
как оставляют кошки
от такой игры

Later they'll leave
Tracks on you
Like cats leave behind
From such a game

     Смотри! Они с острым клыком
     тебя зовут красивым ногтем

Careful! They have a sharp fang
They call you with a pretty fingernail

     Иди
     за мной
     и будешь спасён
     и ночь
     тебя
     умоет дождём

Walk
Behind me
And you'll be saved
And the night
Will wash you
With rain

Девочки с острыми зубками
Девочки с мягкими губками

Girls with sharp teeth
Girls with soft lips

Blood, My Blood

By Destsl

Blood, my blood
Three shots to my chest nearly nailed me,
Under the gunshots my heart didn't want
        to beat.
My body couldn't move, my head was pounded.

The picture's fuzzy, but I breathe everything

They kicked me so much, that I couldn't
        get up.
Who could breathe, I couldn't even groan.
One son of a bitch stabbed me in the leg,
It was just that it was nothing for him to see the
        blood on my knee.

I crawled like a snake, looking at their evil mugs.
One of the dying beasts dared to spit on me.

Curling up into a ball, losing my ability to think,

I flew from my body like a bullet, observing
        myself.

Memorizing the intonation, structure, words,
With my last divine strength, I came to my
        senses.
Only the loud laughter of these dirty jerks,
Stamped on my memory the beginning of a war

without words.

Three months later, my head cooled.
I walked out of the hospital, and it was already
        spring outside.
My friend helped me find their addresses.
Having studied them from beginning to end, and
        having found out their names,
I got down to it, even though my body still hurt.
A horrible vengeance ruled me.
It boiled in me on that dark evening,
When those four bulls wanted to cripple me.
One liked classy cars,
He was accidentally run over in his garage.
The second was hooked on LSD and heroine.
The doctors made the diagnosis: an overdose.
The third decided to go skydiving for the first
        time.
His chute didn't open. Like in a bad joke.
The fourth understood what was up and took

Left the city for years, and disappeared.

I didn't beat my breast, no, I got even.
I simply reminded them: fight one on one.
And never spit on a beaten face,
Even if it's magically four on one.

Кровь, моя кровь

Децл

Кровь, моя кровь
Три кирпича на грудь меня чуть прибило,
Под выстрелами пушки сердце биться не.
    хотело.
Тело двигать не могло,по голове веслом.

Размытая картина, но я дышу всем на зло.
    evil.
Меня били ногами так, чтоб я не мог.
    встать,
Какой там дышать, я даже не мог простонать.
Один сукин сын вколол в мою ногу шило,
Просто так, ему ништяк увидеть кровь по
    колено.

Я полз как змея, рассматривая злые рыла.
Убитая одна скотина плюнуть на меня
    посмела.
Сжимаясь в комок, теряя мысленный
    контроль,
Я вылетел из тела пулей, наблюдая
    за собой.

Запоминая интонацию, структуру, слова,.
Из последних сил небесных, вернулся в
    себя.
Только громкий смех этих грязных козлов.
В памяти запечаталел начало войны без
    слов.

Три месяца спустя, остыла голова,
Я вышел из больницы, на дворе была уже
    весна.
Мой друг мне помог найти адреса.
Изучив от начала и до конца, узнав их
    имена.

Я приступил к делу, хотя ещё болело тело.
Страшная месть мною владела.
Во мне кипело как в тот тёмный вечер,
Когда меня четыре быка хотели покалечить.
Один любил шикарные автомобили,
Его случайно в гараже придавило.

Второй сидел на LSD И героине,.
Врачи поставили диагноз -- передоз в теле.
Третий впервые решил пригнуть с
      парашюта,
Он не раскрылся как в злом анецдоте.
Четвёртый понял, в чём дело, И удрал,
      off,
Из города на долгие года, без вести пропал.

Я в грудь не бил, мол, я отомстил.
Я просто напомнил -- дерись один на один.
И никогда не плюй в разбитое лицо,
Даже если превосходство четыре против
      одного.

Wolves

by *The Leg Cramps*

Зом - зом, ночь за окном
Звездная ночь падает с крыш
Жертвами дня пахнет земля
А ты смотришь в небо, я знаю,
      что ты не спишь
Нет, нет, я не забыл
Сколько с тобой мы, любимая, вместе
Ведь так, как мы, никто не любил
Может лет сто, а может и двести

ПРИПЕВ:
Если уснешь ты, я тоже усну
Чтоб навсегда быть рядом с тобою
Если уйдешь ты, я тоже уйду
Вслед за тобой
Как ночь за звездо-о-о-ю...

Вся холодна, тень не видна
Ты дождалась волчьего часа
Мы близки, а наши клыки
Помнят тепло свежего мяса

    ПРИПЕВ 2 раза

Night is outside the window
The starry night falls from the roofs
The ground smells of the deaths of the day
But you look to the sky and I know
      that you're not sleeping
No, no I haven't forgotten
How long, my love, we've been together
After all, no one has loved like us
Maybe a hundred, maybe two hundred years

REFRAIN:
If you'll fall asleep, I'll fall asleep, too
So that I'll always be next to you
If you walk away, then I'll walk away
Right behind you
Like the night follows a sta-a-a-ar …

All cold, the shadow is invisible
You've waited to the wolfing hour
We're close, and our fangs
Remember the warmth of fresh meat

    REFRAIN 2 times

M. Pekrovsky from *The Leg Cramps*, "Wolves." Translated by Thomas J. Garza. Copyright © 2005 by Thomas J. Garza. Permission to reprint granted by the author.

Wolves

by *B-2*

Волки уходят в небеса,
горят холодные глаза,
приказа верить в чудеса
не поступало.

И каждый день другая цель:
то стены гор то горы стен
и ждёт отчаянных гостей
чужая стая.

Припев:
Спиной к ветру и всё же
вырваться может
чья-то душа
спасёт но не поможет.
Чувствую кожей,
пропащая. . .

Не видят снов, не помнят слов,
переросли своих отцов
и кажется рука бойцов
колоть устала.

The wolves leave to the heavens,
Their cold eyes blaze,
The order to believe in miracles
Didn't arrive.

And every day a new objective:
First walls of mountains, then mountains of walls.
And a foreign pack waits for desperate guests.

Refrain:
Our back to the wind and still
It can tear away
Someone's soul.
It will rescue but won't help.
I feel it in my skin
Hopeless…

They don't dream, don't remember words;
They've outgrown their fathers
And it seems that the hand has grown weary
Of stabbing fighters.

 Online Bonus

To see B-2's music video of this song visit
http://www.youtube.com/watch?v=o5hXegkXPy8
&feature=related

Позор и слава в их крови
хватает смерти и любви.
Но сколько волка не корми,
ему всё мало.

Припев

Волки уходят.
Волки уходят.
Волки уходят.

Shame and glory are in their blood
There's enough death and love.
But no matter how much you feed a
wolf
It's still too little.

Refrain

The wolves are leaving.
The wolves are leaving.
The wolves are leaving.

Night Watch

By *Uma2rman*

There once lived Anton Gorodetsky,
his wife left him and he grieved deeply.
He went to a sorceress: "Now then cast me a spell!"
"Easy, my dear, I'll just clap my hands, and your
wife will return, and will turn her back on the other, and
the little life inside of her will cease to be."
But suddenly the shadows of ghosts pounced
on the witch, saying: "There will be no crime."
And what's with you, that you lowered your gaze?
Surrender, witch—"Night Watch."
And the world cracked in half, a smoking fault line,
and blood flows, there is a war of good and evil.
And light fades, in the corners a spider weaves a design,
along the dark streets flies the "Night Watch."
And Anton understood that he had done wrong,
and that the sorceress had duped him, like a mark.
But the strength of the "other" is in Anton's gaze
and that means he'll work in the "watch."
Years passed, Gorodetsky doesn't grieve,
he forgets with vodka, makes friends with vampires.
(His) good boss—the most wise Gesser, was a deputy
minister in the USSR.
But they are calling, we must go faster,
the vampire-barber along with his little girlfriend
has lured the youngster into his lair,
they decided to dine crudely and simply.
Anton made it in time, a fight broke out,
and with great difficulty, he did kill the ghoul,
in the battle he was wounded with scissors,

 **Online Bonus**

To see Uma2rman's music video of this song visit
http://www.youtube.com/
watch?v=ZpsKqAxJKnM

you could say he was on the brink of death.
But the kind Gesser quickly healed him,
and how, like the kind they won't take in the ministries.
And the world cracked in half, a smoking fault line,
and blood flows, there's war between good and evil.
And light fades, in the corners a spider weaves a design,
along the dark streets flies the "Night Watch."
And then—trouble after trouble, as if by design:
a raven flew into the turbine of a plane,
at the heating station something exploded,
and the guilty Sveta was in it all.
But having met the handsome Anton, she fell
in love, and the destruction stopped.
But the evil Zavulon from the "Day Watch"
made the son of Anton into an "Other."
And how does our hero cope with this?
Everyone watch the sequel!
And the world cracked in two the split smokes,
and blood flows, there is a war of good and evil.
And light fades, in the corners a spider weaves a design,
along the dark streets flies the "Night Watch."
And the world cracked in half, a smoking fault line,
and blood flows, there's war between good and evil.
And light fades, in the corners a spider weaves a design,
along the dark streets flies the "Night Watch."

"Ночной дозор"
Ума2рман

Жил-был на свете Антон Городецкий,
бросила жена, он грустил не по-детски.
Пришёл к колдунье: "А ну-ка наколдуй мне!"
"Легко, мой хороший, только хлопну в ладоши,
и жена вернётся, от того отвернётся,
и маленькая жизнь внутри неё оборвётся."
Но вдруг налетели на ведьму тени
привидений, говорят: "Не бывать преступленью"
Ну что же ты, что ты потупила взор?
Сдавайся, ведьма – «Ночной Дозор».
И треснул мир напополам, дымит разлом,
и льётся кровь, идёт война добра со злом.
И меркнет свет, в углах паук плетёт узор,
по тёмным улицам летит «ночной дозор».
И понял Антоха, что поступил плохо,
и то, что развела его колдунья, как лоха.
Но сила «иного» в антоновом взоре,
а значит, он будет работать в «дозоре».
Годы прошли, Городецкий не тужит,
водочку глушит, с вампирами дружит.
Начальник хороший – мудрейший Гесер,
был зам. министром in USSR.
Но вот вызывают, нужно ехать скорее,
вампир-парикмахер с подружкой своею
в логово к себе заманили подростка,
решили поужинать подло и просто.
Антоха успел, завязалась драка,
с огромным трудом, но всё ж убил вурдалака,
ножницами был тяжело ранен в бою,
при смерти был, можно сказать на краю.
Но добрый Гесер его вылечил быстро,
еще бы, абы кого не берут в замминистры.
И треснул мир напополам, дымит разлом,
и льётся кровь, идёт война добра со злом.
И меркнет свет, в углах паук плетёт узор,
по тёмным улицам летит «ночной дозор».

А дальше - беда за бедой, как по нотам:
ворона залетела в турбину самолёта,
На теплоцентрали чего-то взорвалось,
а Света виновна во всём оказалась,

Но, встретив красавца Антона, влюбилась,
и разрушение остановилось.
Но злой Завулон из «дозора дневного»
сделал из сына Антона «иного».
И как с этим справится наш герой?
Все на просмотр картины второй!
И треснул мир напополам, дымит разлом,
и льётся кровь, идёт война добра со злом.
И меркнет свет, в углах паук плетёт узор,
по тёмным улицам летит «ночной дозор».
И треснул мир напополам, дымит разлом,
и льётся кровь, идёт война добра со злом.
И меркнет свет, в углах паук плетёт узор,
по тёмным улицам летит «ночной   дозор».

The Wolf Hunt

By *Night Snipers*

My aim turned out to be most accurate;
No matter what, I'll never understand one thing:
How I could have been around here so long;
A hero is not great when whole and unharmed.

But the moon came out, my heart sank,
And with snowy brows, beasts go in the blue snow.
And to our backs lanterns burn like flares,
They slip along our backs like a broken waltz.

The wolf hunt is on.

Don't hold your tongue, don't look for a smoke,
«Good luck» are just words, not worth saying.
Print them full face with a black mark on the forehead.
It's better just to be quiet

The wolf hunt is on.

We took a breath together, only one exhaled.
It's surprising that I'm still alive,
It's surprising how much blood is in me,
I give it to noone, my blood is not for sale.

I'll have to clench my teeth and be quiet,
My legs break into a run.

The wolf hunt is on.
The wolf hunt is on.
The hunt is on.

Мой прицел оказался точнее всего,
Пол-локтя до виска, не пойму одного -
Как по краю могла столько лет столько зим;
Не великий герой целый и невредим.

Но случилась луна, сердце кануло вниз,
И бровями в снега, в синий снег животом.
А по спинам ракетами жгут фонари,
Дробным вальсом по спинам скользят.

Идёт охота на волчат.

Не прикусывай рта, не ищи покурить,
К чёрту просто слова, ни к чему говорить.
Чёрной меткой по лбу по анфасу печать,
Лучше просто молчать.

Идёт охота на волчат.

Вместе сделали вдох, выдыхать одному.
Удивительно, что до сих пор я живу,
Удивительно, как много крови во мне,
Никому не отдать, кровь моя не в цене.

Остаётся сцепить зубы и замолчать,
Ноги выбросить в бег.

Идёт охота на волчат.

Идёт охота на волчат.

Идёт охота.

The Snowstorm

By Grigoriy Leps

Где то там, за окном, ходит зима
Сеет снег, белый снег, ночью и днём.
И меня тишиной сводит с ума.
И опять не уснуть в доме пустом.

ПРИПЕВ:
Тихо саваном белым
Вьюга, дом мой укрой.
Где-то ты засыпаешь
Где-то, но не со мной.

Где то там, в тишине, ходит февраль
И ему, как и мне; сон не найти.
Где то там, в далеке, ты не поймёшь.
Где-то там не со мной,
Так и не узнаешь ты.

ПРИПЕВ:
Кружит белая вьюга
Тихо ходит зима
Слышишь, как замерзало
Снова я без тебя..

Somewhere, outside the window, winter moves
Scattering snow, white snow, night and day.
And it drives me crazy with the silence.
And again I can't sleep in this empty house.

REFRAIN:
Quietly, with a white blanket,
Snowstorm, cover my house.
You are falling asleep somewhere
Somewhere, but not with me.

Somewhere, in silence, February moves
And it, like me, can't find sleep.
Somewhere, in the distance, you won't understand.
Somewhere there not with me,
And you'll never find out.

REFRAIN:
The white snowstorm swirls
Quietly winter moves
Do you hear how everything's frozen
Again I'm without you.

Grigoriy Leps, "The Snowstorm." Translated by Thomas J. Garza. Copyright © 2007 by Thomas J. Garza. Permission to reprint granted by the author.

Just for the Vampire in Love

By Picnic

Лишь влюблённому вампиру —Пикник— Сон чудесный снится миру, Бледных улиц не узнать. Лишь влюбленному вампиру Снова будет не до сна.	Just for the Vampire in Love —Picnic— The world is having a wondrous dream; The pale streets are unseen. Only the vampire in love Will again not be able to sleep.
Он идет походкой лунной В дальний сад, где ночь без дна, Где за оградою чугунной Бродит девушка одна, Бродит девушка одна.	He walks like the moon to a Distant garden, where the night is deep, Where behind the iron gate A girl strolls alone, A girl strolls alone.
Ее веки чуть открыты, Ветвь увядшая в руках. Лихорадочный румянец Водит танцы на щеках, Водит танцы на щеках.	Her lashes are barely open, A willow branch is in her hands. A feverish blush Dances on her cheeks, Dances on her cheeks.
Вот он близок миг блаженный, Тень любимого лица, И на миг лишь станет тихо В их тоскующих сердцах, В их тоскующих сердцах.	The sacred moment is near, The shadow of the loving face, And in a instant all goes quiet In their longing hearts, In their longing hearts.
Кто они и что им надо? Пить да пить бы сладкий яд. До утра обнявшись крепко Так они и простоят.	Who are they and what do they want? Just to drink and drink sweet poison. Until morning, having embraced tightly, They will just stand there.

 Online Bonus

To see Picnic's music video of this song visit
http://www.youtube.com/
watch?v=VDUhrv4xDPs

Transylvania

By Agata Kristi

ТРАНСИЛЬВАНИЯ
Агата Кристи

Открытая дверь
На свежей земле.
Под землёй кипит работа,
Бесы варят позолоту.
Там в пещере Алладин -
Всемогущ и нелюдим.
Там внизу твоя могила.
До свиданья, милый, милый.
Милый.
Бывай!

Отличная ночь
Для смерти и зла.
На тебя роняет слёзы небо,
А на небе звёзды
Улыбаются во сне
Человеку на Луне.
Глубоко тебя зарыли.
До свиданья, милый, милый.
Милый.
Бывай!

Открытая дверь
На свежей земле.
Мы вколачиваем гвозди,

TRANSYLVANIA
Agata Kristi

An open door
On the fresh earth.
Work goes on underground,
Demons are melting gilt.
There in the cave is Aladdin,
All-powerful and inhuman.
Down below is your grave.
Good-bye, my dear, dear.
My dear.
Be like that.

It's a perfect night
For death and evil.
The sky drops tears on you,
And in the sky the stars
Smile in their sleep
At the Man in the Moon.
They've dug you down deep.
Good-bye, my dear, dear.
My dear.
Be like that.

An open door
On the fresh earth.
We're hammering in nails,

 Online Bonus

To see Agata Kristi's music video of this song visit http://www.youtube.com/watch?v=FnZhmaOTsLw&translated=1

Чтоб в гробу лежали кости.
Чтоб из-под земли не лез
На тебе поставлю крест.
Трижды плюну на могилу.
До свиданья, милый, милый.
До свиданья, милый, милый.
До свиданья, милый, милый.
Милый.
Бывай.
Бывай!
Глеб ©1995

So that the bones will stay in the grave.
So you won't climb out from underground
I'll put a cross on you.
I spit on your grave three times.
Good-bye, my dear, dear.
Good-bye, my dear, dear.
Good-bye, my dear, dear.
My dear.
Be like that.
Be like that.
T.J. Garza ©2009

A Gentle Vampire

By Nautilus Pompilius

Нежный Вампир	A Gentle Vampire
—Наутилус Помпилиус—	—Nautilus Pompilius—
Холоден ветер в открытом окне.	A cold wind in the open window.
Длинные тени лежат на столе.	Long shadows lie on the table.
Я таинственный гость	I'm the secret guest
в серебристом плаще,	in the silvery coat,
И ты знаешь зачем я явился к тебе.	and you know why I appeared before you.
Дать тебе силу,	To give you strength,
Дать тебе власть.	To give you power.
Целовать тебя в шею,	To kiss you on the neck,
Целовать тебя всласть,	To kiss you to my heart's content,
нежный вампир.	a gentle vampire.
Нежный вампир,	A gentle vampire,
невинный ребенок.	an innocent child.
Как нежный вампир	Like a gentle vampire
Встань!	Rise!
Подруги твои нюхают клей.	Your girlfriends sniff glue.
С каждым днем они становятся	Every day they become
немного глупей.	a little more stupid.
В этой стране вязкой как грязь,	In this sticky country like dirt,
Ты можешь стать толстой	You can get fat,
Ты можешь пропасть.	You can disappear.
Но я разожгу	But I'll ignite
Огонь твоих глаз.	The fire of your eyes.

 **Online Bonus**

To see Nautilus Pompilius's music video of this song visit

http://www.youtube.com/watch?v=QwsFQNLFbgY&translated=1

Я даю тебе силу.
Я даю тебе власть.

Я делаю тебя
Не такою как все,
Как агнец на закланье.
Я явился к тебе
И ты знаешь зачем …

I give you strength.
I give you power.

I make you
Unlike all the others,
Like a lamb on the altar.
I appeared before you
 And you know why…

The Vampire

By Aria

ВАМПИР
—Ария—
Рухнул мир, сгорел дотла,
Соблазны рвут тебя на части.
Смертный страх и жажда зла
Держат пари.
В темноте рычит зверье
Не видно глаз, но все в их власти.
Стань таким, возьми свое,
Или умри.

Будь наготове, всюду рыщет стража.
Линия крови путь тебе укажет.

Прочь, ты был одним из нас,
Но ангел тебя не спас.

Бьет струей кипящий сок;
Забудет смерть испивший зелье
Шаг за грань - один глоток -
Словно пароль.
Танцы ведьм и крики сов
Фальшивый праздник, где нет веселья.
Бой часов, один безумный зов
Голод и боль.

The Vampire
—Aria—
The world's collapsed, burned to the ground,
Temptation is tearing you to pieces.
A deadly fear and the thirst for evil
Are making a bet.
In the darkness the beasts are howling;
Can't see their eyes, but all's in their power.
Become like that, take your own,
Or die.

Be on the alert, the guard roams everywhere.
A line of blood will show you the way.

Go, you were one of us,
But the angel didn't save you.

A bubbling brew spurts;
He'll forget death once he drinks the potion.
One step over the edge – one swallow --
Like a password.
The dances of witches and screams of owls,
A fake holiday, where there's no joy.
The clock strikes, one insane call,
Hunger and pain.

Днем лихорадка - ночью пир.
Ты теперь демон, ты вампир.
В поисках новой жертвы в снег и
зной,
Вечный изгой
Но ты был одним из нас
Жаль ангел тебя не спас

Холстинин/Елин ©2001

In day there's fever, in the night a feast.
You're now a demon, you're a vampire.
In search of new victims in the snow and heat,
An eternal hunt.

But you were one of us,
Too bad the angel didn't save you.

T.J. Garza ©2009

A Road Song

By S Brigade

Дорожная
—Бригада С—
Эй, ямщик, поворачивай к черту,
Новой дорогой поедем домой.
Эй, ямщик, поворачивай к черту,
Это не наш лес, а чей-то чужой.
Эх, и елок навалено!
Ох, не продерись!
Камней навалено!
Только держись!
Поворачивай к черту!

Эй, ямщик, поворачивай к черту,
Видишь, мигают мне наши огни.
Эй, братан! Поворачивай к черту!
Шапку сними, да по жене всплакни.
Ведь здесь же елок повалено!

Ох, не продерись!
Камней навалено!
Только держись!
Поворачивай к черту!

A Road Song
—S Brigade—
Hey, driver, turn toward the devil,
Let's drive home by a new road.
Hey, driver, turn toward the devil,
This isn't our forest, but someone else's.
Ah, it's loaded with downed pines!
Oh, you won't get through!
It's piled with rocks!
Just hang on!
Turn toward the devil!

Hey, driver, turn toward the devil,
Do you see our lights are flashing at me.
Hey, bro! Turn toward the devil!
Take off your hat, and weep for your wife.
'Cause it's loaded with downed pines
  here!
Oh, you won't get through!
It's piled with rocks!
Just hang on!
Turn toward the devil!

Online Bonus

To see S Brigade's music video of this song visit http://www.youtube.com/watch?v=I4sgF0JcME8 &translated=1

Все, брат, прорвались, прямая
    дорожка!
Вольное место, да в небе луна.
Ты попридержи-ка лошадку
    немножко,
Видишь, совсем заморилась она.
Эх, дай папироску, ух, я затянусь!
Выложи форсу, богом клянусь,
А прорвались все к черту!!!

Г. Сукачев ©1993

That's it, bro, we got thorough—a straight
    road!
An open space, and the moon in the sky.
Pull up on the horse a bit,

You see, she's completely worn out,
Hey, give me cig, oh, I'll take a drag!
Let's see you show off, I swear to God,
'Cause we've all gone to hell!!!

T.J. Garza © 2009

CPSIA information can be obtained
at www.ICGtesting.com
Printed in the USA
FSOW02n1840040915
10725FS